# THE
# HITTITE DICTIONARY

OF THE ORIENTAL INSTITUTE OF THE UNIVERSITY OF CHICAGO

VOLUME Š

Editorial Staff

Theo van den Hout, Executive Editor

Harry A. Hoffner†, Senior Editor

Hans G. Güterbock†, Senior Editor

Petra M. Goedegebuure, Senior Editor

Richard H. Beal and Oğuz Soysal, Junior Editors

Dennis R. M. Campbell, Billie Jean Collins, Alice Mouton, Ahmed Ünal, Assistants

Gary M. Beckman, H. Craig Melchert, Gernot Wilhelm, Consultants

# THE HITTITE DICTIONARY

## OF THE ORIENTAL INSTITUTE OF THE UNIVERSITY OF CHICAGO

Edited by

Hans G. Güterbock†, Harry A. Hoffner†,
Theo P. J. van den Hout, and Petra M. Goedegebuure

Š

Published by
THE ORIENTAL INSTITUTE OF THE UNIVERSITY OF CHICAGO
2019

ISBN 978-1-61491-047-3
(Set 0-918986-26-5)
Library of Congress Catalog Card Number 79-53554
*The Oriental Institute*



The preparation of this volume of the Chicago Hittite Dictionary was made possible in part by grants from the Program for Research Tools and Reference Works of the National Endowment for the Humanities, an independent Federal Agency, as well as gifts from the Salus Mundi Foundation, Tucson, AZ, Mr. Philip Elenko, New York, Mr. Howard Hallengren, Chicago, Drs. Audrius and Sigita Plioplys, Chicago, Dr. Walter and Mrs. Susan Güterbock, Anacortes, WA, and many other donors.

Text was entered into Macintosh computers by the staff of the Hittite Dictionary and formatted by the staff of the Publications Office of the Oriental Institute.

CuneiformOriental and HittiteDictionary by Ecological Linguistics.

Printed and bound in the United States of America by Lake County Press, Waukegan, IL.

Seal on cover and title page copyright Prof. Schaeffer-Forrer, *Ugaritica* III (1956) 89.
Used with permission.

In memory of Harry A. Hoffner, Jr., co-founder and Executive Editor 1975-2015

# PREFACE

With the completion of all words starting with the letter Š, we are pleased to present the Chicago Hittite Dictionary's (CHD) third full volume. The Š is the fifth and thus far largest letter of the Hittite lexicon. No major editorial changes have taken place *vis-à-vis* the P-volume. The current list of abbreviations supplants all "Additions" of the previous fascicles. There have been, however, important changes in the editorial board. In the period leading up to the publication of the first fascicle Š/1 in 2002 we sadly lost Hans Gustav Güterbock, one of the two founders of the CHD, who died on March 29, 2000. Almost exactly fifteen years later, on March 10, 2015, the other founder, Harry A. Hoffner, passed away very suddenly while working on the final installment of the Š. With them, we have lost the two *auctores intellectuales* of our project, but their names will always be associated with the CHD and we very much carry on in their spirit, as we dedicate this volume to the memory of Harry Hoffner.

In 2006, we were joined by senior editor Petra M. Goedegebuure, significantly strengthening our linguistic expertise. Another important change took place in 2007 when we moved all our file cabinets from the office of Harry Hoffner to the spacious and hallowed former premises of the Chicago Assyrian Dictionary on the third floor of the Oriental Institute.

Many institutions and people have been instrumental in the completion of the volume before you. We are deeply grateful to the University of Chicago and its previous president Don Randel and current president Robert Zimmer, and the directors of the Oriental Institute (OI) during the entire period that this volume was in preparation, Gene Gragg, Gil Stein, and current director Christopher Woods.

We are also indebted to the National Endowment for the Humanities for supporting and making possible our project from its very inception in 1976 all the way through 2007. Since then we have been fortunate to receive funding from several institutions and individual donors. We especially mention here the financial support from the Salus Mundi Foundation in Tucson, AZ, as well as the generous and loyal donations from Philip Elenko, Howard Hallengren, Audrius and Sigita Plioplys, and Walter and Susan Güterbock. Without their help and that of many Oriental Institute members the CHD would not be possible.

With deep gratitude we mention the collegial support we have received over the years from the project *Hethitische Forschungen* and the *Hethitologie-Portal* at the *Akademie der Wissenschaften und der Literatur* in Mainz under its directors Profs. Gernot Wilhelm and Daniel Schwemer. Especially their generosity in sharing with us the electronic card files of the KBo volumes 55–70 has made an enormous difference. Also, the field of Hittitology would not be the same without the various excellent tools offered on the *Hethitologie-Portal*.

We also express our thanks to previous and current curators and directors of the archaeological museums whose Hittite tablets we have been allowed to collate and photograph.

As always, we benefited greatly from the advice, criticism, and suggestions shared by our outside consultants Profs. Gary Beckman (Ann Arbor), H. Craig Melchert (Chapel Hill), and Gernot Wilhelm (Hochheitsveim).

Over the many years that the Š-volume was in preparation we enjoyed the assistance of Research Associates Ahmet Ünal (until 1988), Billie Jean Collins (until 1995), Hripsime Haroutunian (until 2002), and Alice Mouton (visiting 2003), as well as the following students (both undergraduate and graduate) in chronological order: Joe Baruffi, Scott Branting, Steve Thurston, Kathleen Mineck, Simrit Dhesi, Dennis Campbell, Carl Thunem, Natasha Bershadsky, Andrei Chatskov, Edward Stratford, Anna MacCourt, Seunghee Yie, Oya Topçuoğlu, Joanna Derman, Joshua Cannon, Sabrina Hsieh, Phoebe Allardice, Robert Marineau, Jane Gordon, Katherine McFarlin, Thalia Lysen, Ryan Schnell, and Antonio Cruz Uribe. We also gratefully mention the help we received from the following OI volunteers during that same period: Irv Diamond, Julia van den Hout, Kristen Fanning, Shirlee Hoffman, and Barbara Jillson.

We thank the Oriental Institute's Publications Office headed by Thomas Urban and now Charissa Johnson and their assistants for their careful work in bringing our Dictionary to press.

Without exception, the support and help of all the above institutions and individuals have been invaluable in completing the current Š-volume and it is with deeply-felt gratitude that we mention them here. As we embark on the next letter and start work on the T-volume, we express the hope that we will find the same support and goodwill to complete the next stage!

The Editors

# LIST OF ABBREVIATIONS

## 1. Texts, Authors, Literature

| | |
|---|---|
| #/a › #/z | Inventory numbers of Boğazköy tablets excavated 1931–1967 |
| A | lexical series á A = *nâqu* |
| A | tablets in the collections of the Oriental Institute, University of Chicago |
| A-tablet | lexical list, *see* MSL 13:10–12 |
| AA | Archäologischer Anzeiger — Berlin |
| AAA | Annals of Archaeology and Anthropology — Liverpool |
| AANL | Atti della Accademia Nazionale dei Lincei, Rendiconti della Classe di Scienze morali, storiche e filologiche, Serie 8 — Rome |
| AASF | Annales Academiae Scientiarum Fennicae — Helsinki |
| AASOR | Annual of the American Schools of Oriental Research — New Haven |
| ÄAT | Ägypten und Altes Testament — Wiesbaden |
| AAWLM | Akademie der Wissenschaften und der Literatur, Mainz. Abhandlungen der geistes- und sozialwissenschaftlichen Klasse — Wiesbaden |
| ABAW | Abhandlungen der Bayerischen Akademie der Wissenschaften, philosophisch-historische Abteilung — Munich |
| ABoT | Ankara Arkeoloji Müzesinde Bulunan Boğazköy Tabletleri — Istanbul 1948 |
| ACh | C. Virolleaud, L'Astrologie Chaldéenne — Paris 1908 |
| ACME | Annali della Facoltà di Filosofia e Lettere dell'Università Statale di Milano — Milan |
| AfK | Archiv für Keilschriftforschung — Berlin |
| AfO | Archiv für Orientforschung — Berlin, Graz, Horn, Vienna |
| AGI | Archivio Glottologico Italiano — Turin, Florence |
| AhhTxts | G. Beckman, T. Bryce, and E. Cline, The Ahhiyawa Texts (WAW 28) — Atlanta 2011 |
| AHw | W. von Soden, Akkadisches Handwörterbuch — Wiesbaden 1958–1981 |
| Ai | lexical series ki.KI.KAL.bi.šè = *ana ittišu* (MSL 1) |
| AION | Annali dell'Istituto Universitario Orientale di Napoli — Rome, Naples |
| AIΩN | Annali del Seminario di Studi del Mondo Classico, Istituto Universitario Orientale di Napoli — Naples |
| AIPHOS | Annuaire de l'Institut de Philologie et d'Histoire Orientales et Slaves — Brussels |
| AJA | American Journal of Archaeology — Norwood, Massachusetts, Concord, New Hampshire, New York, Boston |
| AJNES | Aramazd. Armenian Journal of Near Eastern Studies — Yerevan |
| AJPh | American Journal of Philology — Baltimore |
| AJSL | American Journal of Semitic Languages and Literatures — Chicago |
| Akal Oriente | Akal Oriente — Tres Cantos |
| —— 3 | A. Bernabé and J. A. Álvarez-Pedrosa, Historia y Leyes de los Hititas: Textos del Imperio Antiguo, El Códico — 2000 |
| —— 8 | A. Bernabé and J. A. Álvarez-Pedrosa, Historia y Leyes de los Hititas: Textos del Reino Medio y del Imperio Nuevo — 2004 |
| —— 13 | J. M. González Salazar, Rituales Hititas y el Culto — 2009 |
| Akdoğan | *see* DBH 32 |
| Akurgal | E. Akurgal, The Art of the Hittites — London 1962 |
| Alakš. | Treaty of Muwatalli II with Alakšandu, ed. SV 2:42–102 |
| ALASP | Abhandlungen zur Literatur Alt-Syrien-Palästinas und Mesopotamiens — Münster |
| AlHeth. | H. A. Hoffner, Jr., Alimenta Hethaeorum (AOS 55) — New Haven 1974 |
| Alp, Beamt. | S. Alp, Untersuchungen zu den Beamtennamen im hethitischen Festzeremoniell — Leipzig 1940 |
| —— Siegel | —— Zylinder- und Stempelsiegel aus Karahöyük bei Konya (TTKYayın 5/26) — Ankara 1968 |

| | |
|---|---|
| —— Song | —— Song, Music, and Dance of Hittites — Ankara 2000 |
| —— Tempel | —— Beiträge zur Erforschung des hethitischen Tempels, Kultanlagen im Lichte der Keilschrifttexte (TTKYayın 6/23) — Ankara 1983 |
| —— | *see also* HBM, HKM |
| AM | A. Götze, Die Annalen des Muršiliš (MVAeG 38) — Leipzig 1933 |
| AMAVY | Anadolu Medeniyetlerini Araştırma ve Tanıtma Vakfı Yayınları — Ankara |
| AMMY | Anadolu Medeniyetleri Müzesi Yıllığı — Ankara |
| Amurru Akk | S. Izre'el, Amurru Akkadian: A Linguistic Study (HSSt 40–41) — Atlanta 1991 |
| An | lexical series An = *Anum* |
| An. | Ankara Museum, inventory numbers of tablets |
| Anadolu | Anadolu. Revue des études d'archéologie et d'histoire en Turquie — Paris |
| Anadolu/Anatolia | Anadolu/Anatolia. Journal of the Institute for Research in Near Eastern and Mediterranean Civilizations of the Faculty of Letters of the University of Ankara — Ankara |
| AnAn | Anatolia Antiqua — Paris |
| Anat&Indog. | Anatolisch und Indogermanisch/Anatolico e indoeuropeo: Akten des Kolloquiums der Indogermanischen Gesellschaft, Pavia 22.–25. September 1998 (IBS 100) — Innsbruck 2001 |
| Anatolica | Anatolica. Annuaire international pour les civilisations de l'Asie antérieure — Leiden |
| Ancient Magic | M. Meyer and P. Mirecki, eds., Ancient Magic and Ritual Power — Leiden 1995 |
| AnDergi | Ankara Üniversitesi Dil ve Tarih-Coğrafya Fakültesi Dergisi — Ankara |
| ANEHST | M. Chavalas, ed., The Ancient Near East: Historical Sources in Translation — Oxford 2006 |
| ANEP | J. B. Pritchard, ed., Ancient Near Eastern Pictures Relating to the Old Testament, 2nd ed., with suppl. — Princeton 1969 |
| ANET | J. B. Pritchard, ed., Ancient Near Eastern Texts Relating to the Old Testament, 2nd ed., with suppl. — Princeton 1969 (Hittite texts tr. by A. Goetze) |
| Animal World | B. J. Collins, ed., A History of the Animal World in the Ancient Near East, (HbOr 1/64) — Leiden 2002 |
| AnOr | Analecta Orientalia — Rome |
| AnSt | Anatolian Studies (Journal of the British Institute of Archaeology at Ankara) — London |
| Antagal | lexical series antagal = *šaqû* |
| AnYayın | Ankara Üniversitesi Dil ve Tarih Coğrafya Fakültesi Yayınları — Ankara |
| AO | Der Alte Orient — Leipzig |
| Ao&S Onomastik | M. Streck and S. Weninger, eds., Altorientalische und semitische Onomastik, (AOAT 296) — Münster 2002 |
| AOAT | Alter Orient und Altes Testament — Neukirchen-Vluyn |
| AOATS | AOAT, Sonderreihe |
| AÖAW | Anzeiger der phil.-hist. Klasse der Österreichischen Akademie der Wissenschaften — Vienna |
| AoF | Altorientalische Forschungen — Berlin |
| AOS | American Oriental Series — New Haven |
| APAW | Abhandlungen der Preussischen Akademie der Wissenschaften, philosophisch-historische Klasse — Berlin |
| Approaching Second | A. Halpern and Z. Zwicky, Approaching Second: Second Position Clitics and Related Phenomena (CSLI Lectures Notes No. 61) — Stanford 1996 |
| ArAn | Archivum Anatolicum; Anadolu Arşivleri — Ankara |
| Ardzinba, Ritualy | V. G. Ardzinba, Ritualy i mify drevnej Anatolii — Moscow 1982 |
| Arnaud | *see* Emar |
| ArOr | Archiv Orientální — Prague |
| AS | Assyriological Studies — Chicago |
| —— 24 | H. G. Güterbock and Th. P. J. van den Hout, The Hittite Instruction for the Royal Bodyguard — 1991 |
| —— 25 | G. McMahon, The Hittite State Cult of the Tutelary Deities — 1991 |
| —— 26 | H. G. Güterbock, Perspectives on Hittite Civilization: Selected Writings — Chicago 1997 |

| | |
|---|---|
| Asan, Diss. | A. Asan, Der Mythos vom erzürnten Gott (diss., Julius-Maximilians-Universität, Würzburg — 1988) |
| —— | *see also* DBH 41 |
| AT | D. J. Wiseman, The Alalakh Tablets (unmarked number refers to text, p. indicates page in the volume) — London 1953 |
| Athenaeum | Athenaeum — Pavia |
| Atti II CIH | O. Carruba et al., eds., Atti del II Congresso Internazionale di Hittitologia. *see* StMed 9 |
| AttiAccTosc. | Atti dell'Accademia Toscana di Scienze e Lettere "La Colombaria" — Florence |
| AU | F. Sommer, Die Aḫḫijavā-Urkunden (ABAW, NF 6) — Munich 1932 |
| AÜDTCFY | Ankara Üniversitesi Dil ve Tarih-Coğrafya Fakültesi Yayınları — Ankara |
| AuOr | Aula Orientalis: Revista de estudios del Próximo Oriente Antiguo — Sabadell |
| Außenseiter | V. Haas, ed., Außenseiter und Randgruppen. Beiträge zu einer Sozialgeschichte des Alten Orients (Xenia 32) — Konstanz 1992 |
| BA | Biblical Archaeologist — New Haven, Cambridge, Massachusetts, Ann Arbor, Philadelphia, Baltimore, Atlanta, Boston |
| Bab | Babyloniaca — Paris |
| BAC | Bochumer Altertumswissenschaftliches Colloquium — Bochum |
| —— 2 | E. Neu, Der alte Orient: Mythen der Hethiter — 1990 |
| —— 23 | G. Binder and K. Ehlich, eds., Kommunikation durch Zeichen und Wort (Stätten und Formen der Kommunikation im Altertum 4) — Trier 1995 |
| Bachvarova, Diss. | M. Bachvarova, From Hittite to Homer: The Role of Anatolians in the Transmission of Epic and Prayer Motifs from the Near East to the Greeks (diss., University of Chicago — 2002) |
| Badalì | *see* THeth 14 |
| Badalì/Zinko, Scientia 20 | E. Badalì and Chr. Zinko, Der 16. Tag des AN.TAḪ.ŠUM-Festes, 2nd ed., Scientia: Schriftenreihe der Innsbrucker Gesellschaft zur Pflege der Einzelwissenschaften und interdisziplinären Forschung 20 — Graz 1994 |
| BagM | Baghdader Mitteilungen — Berlin |
| Balkan, İnandık | K. Balkan, İnandık'ta 1966 Yılında Bulunan Eski Hitit Çağına Ait Bir Bağış Belgesi (AMAVY No. 1) — Ankara 1973 |
| BASOR | Bulletin of the American Schools of Oriental Research — South Hadley, Massachusetts, Missoula, Ann Arbor, Philadelphia, Baltimore |
| Bawanypeck | *see* THeth 25 |
| BBVO | Berliner Beiträge zum Vorderen Orient — Berlin |
| BCILL | Bibliothèque des Cahiers de l'Institut de Linguistique de Louvain — Louvain-la-Neuve |
| BDB | F. Brown, S. R. Driver, and C. Briggs, A Hebrew and English Lexicon of the Old Testament — Oxford 1907 |
| Beal, Diss. | R. Beal, The Organization of the Hittite Military (diss., University of Chicago — 1986) |
| —— | *see also* THeth 20 |
| Bechtel, *-sk-* | G. Bechtel, Hittite Verbs in *-sk-* — Ann Arbor 1936 |
| —— | *see also* Chrest. |
| Beckman, Babilili | G. M. Beckman, The *babilili*-Ritual from Hattusa (CTH 718) (MC 19) — Winona Lake 2014 |
| —— Diss. | —— Hittite Birth Rituals (diss., Yale University — 1977) |
| —— | *see also* DiplTexts, HFAC, StBoT 29 |
| Bel Madg. | *BĒL MADGALTI* instr., ed. Dienstanw. and HittInstr |
| Belleten | Türk Tarih Kurumu Belleten — Ankara |
| BeO | Bibbia e Oriente — Bornato in Franciacorta |
| Berman, Diss. | H. Berman, The Stem Formation of Hittite Nouns and Adjectives (diss., University of Chicago — 1972) |
| Bernabé, TLH | A. Bernabé, Textos literarios hetitas — Madrid 1987 |
| BibGlHurr | Th. Richter, Bibliographisches Glossar des Hurritischen — Wiesbaden 2012 |
| Bildbeschr. | C.-G. von Brandenstein, Hethitische Götter nach Bildbeschreibungen in Keilschrifttexten (MVAeG 46.2) — Leipzig 1943 |
| Bilgiç, App. | E. Bilgiç, Die einheimischen Appellativa der kappadokischen Texte — Ankara 1954 |
| Bin-Nun | *see* THeth 5 |
| BiOr | Bibliotheca Orientalis — Leiden |
| Bittel, Boğazköy | K. Bittel et al., Boğazköy, I–V — Berlin 1935, 1938, 1957, 1969, 1975 |

| | |
|---|---|
| —— Hattusha | —— Hattusha: Capital of the Hittites — New York 1970 |
| —— Hethiter | —— Die Hethiter (Universum der Kunst) — Munich 1976 |
| —— Yaz | —— Yazılıkaya (WVDOG 61) — Leipzig 1941 (Osnabrück 1967) |
| —— $Yaz^2$ | —— Das hethitische Felsheiligtum Yazılıkaya (BoHa 9) — Berlin 1975 |
| BM | Bibliotheca Mesopotamica — Malibu |
| BM | Tablets in the collections of the British Museum |
| BMECCJ | Bulletin of the Middle Eastern Culture Center in Japan — Wiesbaden |
| Bo | Inventory numbers of Boğazköy tablets excavated 1906–1912 |
| Bo year/ ... | Inventory numbers of Boğazköy tablets excavated 1968ff. |
| Boaz | *see* THeth 31 |
| BoHa | Boğazköy-Ḫattuša, Ergebnisse der Ausgrabungen — Berlin, Mainz |
| —— 14 | R. M. Boehmer and H. G. Güterbock, Glyptik aus dem Stadtgebiet von Boğazköy — 1987 |
| —— 19 | S. Herbordt, Die Prinzen-und Beamtensiegal der hethitischen Grossreichszeit auf Tonbullen aus dem Nişantepe-Archiv in Hattuša — 2005 |
| —— 22 | A. Dinçol and B. Dinçol, Die Prinzen- und Beamtensiegel aus der Oberstadt von Boğazköy-Hattuša vom 16. Jahrhundert bis zum Ende der Grossreichszeit — 2008 |
| —— 23 | S. Herbordt et al., Die Siegel der Grosskönige und Grossköniginnen auf Tonbullen aus dem Nişantepe — 2011 |
| Boissier, Mant. | A. Boissier, Mantique Babylonienne et Mantique Hittite — Paris 1935 |
| Boley, Dynamics | J. Boley, Dynamics of Transformation in Hitttite: The Hittite Particles *-kan*, *-ašta* and *-šan* (IBS 97) — Innsbruck, 2000 |
| —— *ḫark-* | —— The Hittite *ḫark-* Construction (IBS 44) — Innsbruck 1984 |
| —— Part. | —— The Sentence Particles and the Place Words in Old and Middle Hittite (IBS 60) — Innsbruck 1989 |
| Borger, Zeichenliste | R. Borger, Assyrisch-babylonische Zeichenliste (unmarked numbers refer to sign number) (AOAT 33, 33A) — Neukirchen-Vluyn 1978, 1981 |
| —— | *see also* MZL |
| Bossert, Heth.Kön. | H. T. Bossert, Ein hethitisches Königssiegel — Berlin 1944 |
| BoSt | Boghazköi-Studien — Leipzig |
| BoTU | E. Forrer, Die Boghazköi-Texte in Umschrift (WVDOG 41/42) (unmarked numbers following BoTU refer to texts published in translit. in BoTU 2; pages in BoTU 1 or 2 will be indicated by p(p).) — Leipzig 1922, 1926 |
| Boysan-Dietrich | *see* THeth 12 |
| von Brandenstein | *see* Bildbeschr. |
| von Bredow, Altanat.Gotth., | I. von Bredow, Die altanatolischen Gottheiten nach den althethitischen Texten — Sofia 1995 |
| van Brock, Dér.Nom.L | N. van Brock, Dérivés Nominaux en L du hittite et du louvite (RHA XX/71:69–168) — Paris 1962 |
| Brosch, Diss. | C. Brosch, Zum Ausdruck von Räumlichkeit im Hethitischen aus vergleichender Sicht (diss., Freie Universität Berlin — 2011) |
| Bryce, KgHitt | T. Bryce, The Kingdom of the Hittites — Oxford 1998 |
| Bryce, MHT | R. Bryce, The Major Historical Texts of Early Hittite History (Asian Studies Monograph 1) — Queensland n.d. |
| BSIEL | Brill's Studies in Indo-European Languages & Linguistics — Leiden |
| BSL | Bulletin de la Société de Linguistique de Paris |
| Burde | *see* StBoT 19 |
| CAD | The Assyrian Dictionary of the Oriental Institute of the University of Chicago — Chicago 1956–2010 |
| CAH | The Cambridge Ancient History, 3rd ed. — Cambridge 1970, 1971, 1973, 1975 |
| Cambi, Tempo e Aspetto | V. Cambi, Tempo e Aspetto in ittito: con particolare riferimento al suffisso -ske/a- (Memorie del Laboratorio di Linguistica della Scuola Normale Superiore di Pisa 6) — Alessandria 2007 |
| Cammarosano | *see* Eothen 14, HLC |
| CANE | J. Sasson et al., Civilizations of the Ancient Near East — New York 1995 |
| Carruba, Pal. | O. Carruba, Beiträge zum Palaischen (PIHANS 31) — Leiden 1972 |

| | |
|---|---|
| —— Part. | —— Die satzeinleitenden Partikeln in den indogermanischen Sprachen Anatoliens — Rome 1969 |
| —— | *see also* StBoT 2, 10, StMed 11, 15, 18 |
| Carter, Diss. | C. Carter, Hittite Cult Inventories (diss., University of Chicago — 1962) |
| Catsanicos, Faute Vocab | J. Catsanicos, Recherches sur le Vocabulaire de la Faute (Cahiers de NABU 2) — Paris 1991 |
| CCT | Cuneiform Texts from Cappadocian Tablets in the British Museum — London |
| CH | Codex Hammurabi |
| CHANE | Culture and History of the Ancient Near East — Leiden |
| CHD | The Hittite Dictionary of the Oriental Institute of the University of Chicago — Chicago 1980ff. |
| CHDS | Chicago Hittite Dictionary Supplements — Chicago |
| —— 1 | *see* ABoT 2 |
| —— 2 | O. Soysal, Unpublished Bo-Fragments in Transliteration I (Bo 9536–Bo 9736) — Chicago 2015 |
| CHLI | Corpus of Hieroglyphic Luwian Inscriptions (Untersuchungen zur indogermanischen Sprach- und Kulturwissenschaft N.F. 8) — Berlin |
| —— 1 | J. D. Hawkins, Inscriptions of the Iron Age — 2000 |
| —— 2 | H. Çambel, Karatepe-Aslantaş — 1999 |
| CHM | Cahiers d'Histoire Mondiale — Paris |
| Chrest. | E. H. Sturtevant and G. Bechtel, A Hittite Chrestomathy — Philadelphia 1935 |
| Christiansen | *see* StBoT 48, 53 |
| ChS | Corpus der hurritischen Sprachdenkmäler — Rome |
| —— I/1 | V. Haas, Die Serien itkaḫi und itkalzi des AZU-Priesters, Rituale für Tašmišarri und Tatuḫepa sowie weitere Texte mit Bezug auf Tašmišarri — 1984 |
| —— I/2 | M. Salvini and I. Wegner, Die Rituale des AZU-Priesters — 1986 |
| —— I/3-1 | I. Wegner, Hurritische Opferlisten aus hethitischen Festbeschreibungen — Rome 1995 |
| —— I/3-2 | I. Wegner, Hurritische Opferlisten aus hethitischen Festbeschreibungen II: Texte für Teššub, Ḫebat und weitere Gottheiten — Rome 2002 |
| —— I/3-3 | I. Wegner, Hurritische Opferlisten aus hethitischen Festbeschreibungen III: Das Glossar — 2004 |
| —— I/4 | I. Wegner and M. Salvini, Die hethitisch-hurritischen Ritualtafeln des (*ḫ*)*išuwa*-Festes — 1991 |
| —— I/5 | V. Haas and I. Wegner, Die Rituale der Beschwörerinnen SALŠU.GI — 1988 |
| —— I/6 | M. Salvini, Die mythologischen Texte — 2004 |
| —— I/7 | S. de Martino, Die mantischen Texte — 1992 |
| —— I/8 | M.-C. Trémouille, Texte verschiedenen Inhalts — 2005 |
| —— I/9 | V. Haas, Die hurritischen Ritualtermini in hethitischem Kontext — 1998 |
| —— Erg. 1 | G. Wilhelm, Ein Ritual des AZU-Priesters — 1995 |
| CLL | H. C. Melchert, Cuneiform Luvian Lexicon (Lexica Anatolica 2) — Chapel Hill 1993 |
| Cohen, Wisdom | Y. Cohen, Wisdom from the Late Bronze Age (WAW 34) — Atlanta 2013 |
| —— | *see also* THeth 24 |
| Coll.Anat. | Colloquium Anatolicum — Istanbul |
| Collins, Diss. | B. J. Collins, The Representation of Wild Animals in Hittite Texts (diss., Yale University — 1989) |
| —— Virginity | —— "Virginity" in Hrozný and Hittite: The First Hundred Years: Prague 11–14, 2015 — forthcoming |
| —— | *see also* Animal World |
| Cor.Ling. | Corolla Linguistica (FsSommer) — Wiesbaden 1955 |
| CoS | W. W. Hallo and K. L. Younger, eds., The Context of Scripture — Leiden 1997, 2000, 2002, 2017 |
| Coşkun, Kap İsimleri | Y. Coşkun, Boğazköy Metinlerinde Geçen Bazı Seçme Kap İsimleri (AnYayın 285) — Ankara 1979 |
| Cotticelli-Kurras | *see* THeth 18 |
| Couvreur, Ḫ | W. C. Couvreur, De hettitische Ḫ — Louvain 1937 |

| | |
|---|---|
| CRAIBL | Comptes Rendus de la Académie des Inscriptions et Belles-Lettres — Paris |
| Crisis Years | W. A. Ward and M. S. Joukowski, eds., The Crisis Years: The 12th Century B.C. From Beyond the Danube to the Tigris — Dubuque 1992 |
| CRRAI | Compte(s) rendu(s) de la ... Recontre Assyriologique Internationale (cited by date of congress, not date of publication), *see* RAI |
| CT | Cuneiform Texts from Babylonian Tablets in the British Museum — London |
| CTH | E. Laroche, Catalogue des textes hittites, 2nd ed. — Paris 1971 |
| Cult Image | N. H. Walls, ed., Cult Image and Divine Representation in the Ancient Near East (ASOR Books Series 10) — Boston 2005 |
| DAB | R. Campbell Thompson, Dictionary of Assyrian Botany — London 1949 |
| DACG | —— Dictionary of Assyrian Chemistry and Geology — Oxford 1936 |
| D'Alfonso | *see* StMed 17 |
| Dardano, L'aneddoto | P. Dardano, L'aneddoto e il racconto in età antico-hittita: La cosiddetta "Cronaca di Palazzo" — Rome 1997 |
| —— | *see also* StBoT 47 |
| Darga, Kadın | A. M. Darga, Eski Anadolu'da Kadın — Istanbul 1976 |
| —— Karahna | —— Karahna Şehri Kült-Envanteri (Keilschrifturkunden aus Boghazköi XXXVIII 12) (İÜEFY 1825) — İstanbul 1973 |
| —— Mimarlığı | —— Hitit Mimarlığı, I - Yapı Sanatı (İÜEFY 3221) — Istanbul 1985 |
| Daues | *see* StBoT 63 |
| DBH | Dresdner Beiträge zur Hethitologie — Dresden, Wiesbaden |
| —— 1 | A. Hagenbuchner-Dresel, Massangaben bei hethitischen Backwaren — 2002 |
| —— 2 | D. Groddek, Hethitische Texte in Transkription KBo 30 — 2002 |
| —— 4 | —— Hethitische Texte in Transkription KUB 55 — 2002 |
| —— 6 | —— A. Hagenbuchner and I. Hoffmann, Hethitische Texte in Transkription VS NF 12 — 2002 |
| —— 7 | *reprint of* Oettinger, Stammbildung, *q.v.* |
| —— 8 | R. Plöchl, Einführung ins Hieroglyphen-Luwische — 2003 |
| —— 10 | *see* GsForrer |
| —— 11 | D. Groddek, Hethitische Texte in Transkription KBo 39 — 2004 |
| —— 12 | K. K. Riemschneider†, Die akkadischen und hethitischen Omentexte aus Boğazköy — 2004 |
| —— 13 | D. Groddek, Hethitische Texte in Transkription KUB 20 — 2004 |
| —— 14 | —— Hethitische Texte in Transkription KUB 59 — 2004 |
| —— 15 | —— Hethitische Texte in Transkription KUB 51 — 2004 |
| —— 16 | H. Roszkowska-Mutschler, Hethitische Texte in Transkription KBo 45 — 2005 |
| —— 18 | J. V. García Trabazo, Hethitische Texte in Transkription KUB 58 — 2005 |
| —— 19 | D. Groddek and A. Kloekhorst, Hethitische Texte in Transkription KBo 35 — 2006 |
| —— 20 | —— Hethitische Texte in Transkription KUB 60 — 2006 |
| —— 21 | G. Neumann, Glossar des Lykischen — 2007 |
| —— 24 | H. Roszkowska-Mutschler, Hethitische Texte in Transkription KBo 44 — 2007 |
| —— 25 | *see* FsKošak |
| —— 28 | D. Groddek, Hethitische Texte in Transkription KBo 50 — 2008 |
| —— 29 | Th. Zehnder, Die hethitischen Frauennamen: Katalog und Interpretation — 2010 |
| —— 30 | D. Groddek, Hethitische Texte in Transkription KUB 2 — 2009 |
| —— 31 | —— Hethitische Texte in Transkription KBo 54 — 2010 |
| —— 32 | R. Akdoğan, Hethitische Texte in Transkription ABoT 2 — 2010 |
| —— 33 | D. Groddek, Hethitische Texte in Transkription KBo 47 — 2011 |
| —— 34 | H. Marquardt, Hethitische Logogramme: Funktion und Verwendung — 2011 |
| —— 35 | R. Fischer et al., eds., Hethitologie in Dresden: Textbearbeitungen, Arbeiten zur Forschungs- und Schriftsgeschichte — 2011 |
| —— 36 | D. Groddek, Hethitische Texte in Transkription KBo 57 — 2011 |

| | |
|---|---|
| —— 38 | —— Hethitische Texte in Transkription KBo 48 — 2012 |
| —— 39 | —— Hethitische Texte in Transkription KBo 39 — 2012 |
| —— 40 | —— Hethitische Texte in Transkription KBo 49 — 2013 |
| —— 41 | A. N. Asan, Der Mythos vom erzürnten Gott: Ein philologischer Beitrag zum religionshistorischen Verständnis des Telipinu-Mythos und verwandter Texte — 2014 |
| —— 42 | M. Maier, Hethitisch °uant- und Verwan(d)tes: Untersuchungen zur Vertretung des indogermanischen Possessivsuffixes *-uent- in den anatolischen Sprachen — 2013 |
| —— 43 | İ. Taş, Hethitische Texte in Transkription: Bo 8264–8485 — 2014 |
| —— 44 | D. Groddek, Hethitische Texte in Transkription KBo 59 — 2014 |
| —— 45 | *see* FsNowicki |
| —— 46/1 | R. Akdoğan, Hethitische Texte Bo 4658-Bo 5000: vol. 1: Transkriptionen — 2016 |
| —— 46/2 | —— Hethitische Texte Bo 4658-Bo 5000: vol. 2: Autographien — 2016 |
| —— 47 | D. Groddek, Hethitische Texte in Transkription KBo 46 — 2015 |
| —— 48 | M. Pallavidini, Diplomazia e propaganda in epoca imperiale ittita: Forma e prassi — 2016 |
| —— 49 | J. Tischler, Hethitische Texte in Transkription KUB 56 & 57 — 2016 |
| —— 50 | G. Torri and Fr. G. Barsacchi, Hethitische Texte in Transkription KBo 12 — 2018 |
| —— 51 | —— Hethitische Texte in Transkription KBo 13 — 2018 |
| de Martino, La danza | S. de Martino, La danza nella cultura ittita (Eothen 2) — Florence 1989 |
| —— | *see also* ChS 1/7, Eothen 5, 9, 10, 18, 19, 21, 22 |
| de Roos | *alphabetized as* Roos |
| de Vos | *see* StBoT Beih 5 |
| Deimel | *see* ŠL |
| Del Monte, L'annalistica | G. del Monte, L'annalistica ittita (TVOa 4.2) — Brescia 1993 |
| —— Muršili-Niqmepa | —— Il trattato fra Muršili II di Ḫattuša e di Ugarit (OAC 18) — Rome 1986 |
| —— | *see also* GestaSupp, RGTC 6, RGTC 6–2 |
| Delaporte, Élements | L. Delaporte, Élements de la grammaire hittite — Paris 1929 |
| Delbrück y la sintaxis | E. Crespo and J. García Ramón, eds., Berthold Delbrück y la sintaxis indoeuropea hoy. Actas del Coloquio de la Indogermanische Gesellschaft. Madrid, 21–24 de septiembre de 1994 — Madrid, Wiesbaden 1997 |
| DEP | *see* Plants |
| Dergi | *see* AnDergi |
| DeuteroGesch | Die deuteronomistischen Geschichtswerke: Redaktions- und religionsgeschichtliche Perspektiven zur "Deuteronomismus"-Diskussion in Tora und Vorderen Propheten — Berlin 2006 |
| Devecchi | *see* StMed 16 |
| DeVries, Diss. | B. DeVries, The Style of Hittite Epic and Mythology (diss., Brandeis University — 1967) |
| Diakonoff, Hurr.u.Urart | I. M. Diakonoff, Hurrisch und Urartäisch — Munich 1971 |
| Die Sprache | Die Sprache: Zeitschrift für Sprachwissenschaft — Vienna, Wiesbaden |
| Dienstanw. | E. von Schuler, Hethitische Dienstanweisungen für höhere Hof- und Staatsbeamte (AfO Beiheft 10) — Graz 1957 |
| DiplTexts | G. Beckman, Hittite Diplomatic Texts (WAW 7) — Atlanta 1996 |
| DiplTexts$^2$ | —— Hittite Diplomatic Texts (WAW 7), 2nd ed. — Atlanta 1999 |
| Diri | lexical series diri DIR *siāku* = (w)*atru* |
| DLL | E. Laroche, Dictionnaire de la langue louvite — Paris 1959 |
| DMOA | Documenta et Monumenta Orientis Antiqui — Leiden |
| DÖAW | Österreichische Akademie der Wissenschaften, Philosophisch-Historische Klasse Denkschriften |
| Domestication au tabou | B. Lion and C. Michel, eds., De la domestication au tabou: le cas des suidés dans le Proche-Orient ancient — Paris 2006 |
| Dressler, Plur. | W. Dressler, Studien zur verbalen Pluralität (SÖAW 259, 1) — Vienna 1968 |
| Drohla, Kongruenz | W. Drohla, Die Kongruenz zwischen Nomen und Attribut sowie zwischen Subjekt und Prädikat im Hethitischen (diss., Philipps-Universität, Marburg — 1933; revised version, mimeographed — 1953) |

| | |
|---|---|
| DŠ | H. G. Güterbock, The Deeds of Suppiluliuma as Told by his Son, Mursili II (JCS 10 (1956) 41–68, 75–98, 107–30) |
| Dunkel, LIPP | G. Dunkel, Lexikon der indogermanischen Partikeln und Pronominalstämme— Heidelberg 2014 |
| Dupp. | Treaty of Muršili II and Duppi-Tešub, ed. SV 1:1–48 |
| Ea | lexical series ea A = *nâqu* |
| EA | Texts from El-Amarna, numbered according to ed. of J. A. Knudtzon, Die El-Amarna-Tafeln (VAB 2) — Leipzig 1915 and tr. of W. Moran, Les Lettres d'El Amarna (LAPO 13) — Paris 1987 = The Amarna Letters — Baltimore 1992 |
| Edel, ÄHK | E. Edel, Die ägyptisch-hethitische Korrespondenz aus Boghazköi in babylonischer und hethitischer Sprache (Abhandlungen der Rheinisch-Westfälischen Akademie der Wissenschaften 77) — Opladen 1994 |
| EDHIL | A. Kloekhorst, Etymological Dictionary of the Hittite Inherited Lexicon — Leiden 2007 |
| EHGl | H. A. Hoffner, Jr., An English-Hittite Glossary (RHA XXV/80:1–99) — Paris 1967 |
| Eichner, Diss. | H. Eichner, Untersuchungen zur hethitischen Deklination (diss., Friedrich- Alexander Universität, Erlangen-Nuremberg — 1974) |
| —— IE Numerals | —— "Anatolien," in Indo-European Numerals, ed. J. Gvozdanović (Trends in Linguistics, Studies & Monographs 57:29–96) — Berlin 1992 |
| Ekiz, Statuettes | H. H. Ekiz, M.Ö. 2. Bin Hitit Dönemi İnsan ve Tanrı Heykelcikleri: The God and Man Statuettes Dating to the Hittite Period (2000 BC) (Kubaba: Arkeoloji-Sanat Tarihi-Tarih Dergisi 20) — Izmir 2012 |
| Emar | Mission archéologique de Meskéné-Emar. Recherches au pays d'Aštata — Paris |
| Emar VI/1-3 | D. Arnaud, Textes sumériens et accadiens: textes et planches (Éditions Recherche sur les Civilisations, «Synthèse» 18) — 1985–1986 |
| Emar VI/4 | —— Textes de la bibliothèque: transcriptions et traductions (Éditions Recherche sur les Civilisations, «Synthèse» 28) — 1987 |
| Engelhard, Diss. | D. Engelhard, Hittite Magical Practices: An Analysis (diss., Brandeis University — 1970) |
| Eothen | Eothen — Florence |
| —— 1 | *see* FsPugliese Carratelli |
| —— 2 | *see* de Martino, La danza |
| —— 3 | *see* Polvani, Minerali |
| —— 4 | F. Imparati, ed., Quattro studi ittiti — 1991 |
| —— 5 | St. de Martino, L'Anatolia occidentale nel Medio Regno ittita |
| —— 6 | *see* Glocker, Kuliwišna |
| —— 7 | *see* Trémouille, Ḫebat |
| —— 9 | St. de Martino and F. Imparati, eds., Studi e Testi I — 1998 |
| —— 10 | St. de Martino and F. Imparati, eds., Studi e Testi II — 1999 |
| —— 11 | *see* Mem. Imparati |
| —— 12 | Imparati, Studi sulla società e sulla religione degli ittiti — 2004 |
| —— 13 | D. Prechel, Motivation und Mechanismen des Kulturkontaktes in der Späten Bronzezeit — 2005 |
| —— 14 | M. Cammarosano, Il decreto antico-ittita di Pimpira — 2006 |
| —— 15 | M. Marizza, Dignitari ittiti del Tempo di Tutḫaliya I/II, Arnuwanda I, Tutḫaliya III — 2007 |
| —— 16 | K. Strobel, New Perspectives on the Historical Geography and Topography of Anatolia in the II and I Millennium — 2008 |
| —— 17 | K. Strobel, Empires after the Empire: Anatolia, Syria and Assyria after Suppiluliuma II (ca. 1200–800/700 B.C.) — 2011 |
| —— 18 | St. de Martino, Hurrian Personal Names in the Kingdom of Ḫatti — 2011 |
| —— 19 | St. de Martino and J. Miller, New Results and New Questions on the Reign of Suppiluliuma I — 2013 |
| —— 21 | St. de Martino and A. Süel, The Third Tablet of the *itkalzi* Ritual: Essays on the Hurrian Šapinuwa Tablets I — 2015 |
| —— 22 | —— The "Great *itkalzi* Ritual": Essays on the Hurrian Šapinuwa Tablets II — 2017 |
| Erg. | Ergänzungsheft, *see* HW 1.Erg. |
| Erimḫuš | lexical series erimḫuš = *anantu* |
| Erimḫuš Bogh. | Boğazköy version of Erimḫuš |

| | |
|---|---|
| Erman-Grapow | A. Erman and H. Grapow, Wörterbuch der aegyptischen Sprache — Leipzig 1925–1931 (–1955) |
| Ertem, Coğrafya | H. Ertem, Boğazköy Metinlerine Geçen Coğrafya Adları Dizini — Ankara 1973 |
| —— Fauna | —— Boğazköy Metinlerine Göre Hititler Devri Anadolu'sunun Faunası — Ankara 1965 |
| —— Flora | —— Boğazköy Metinlerine Göre Hititler Devri Anadolu'sunun Florası — Ankara 1974 |
| EVO | Egitto e Vicino Oriente — Pisa |
| FHG | E. Laroche, Fragments hittites de Genève (RA 45 (1951) 131–38, 184–94; RA 46 (1952) 42–50, 214) |
| FHL | —— Fragments hittites du Louvre, in Mém. Atatürk 73–107 |
| Finkelstein Mem. | M. Ellis, ed., Essays on the Ancient Near East in Memory of Jacob Joel Finkelstein (Memoirs of the Connecticut Academy of Arts and Sciences 19) — Hamden, Connecticut 1977 |
| Forrer | *see* BoTU, Forsch. |
| Forsch. | E. Forrer, Forschungen — Berlin 1926–1929 |
| Foster, Gilg. | B. Foster, The Epic of Gilgamesh — New York, 2001 |
| Francia, Avverbiali | R. Francia, Le funzioni sintattiche degli elementi avverbiali di luogo ittiti *anda(n)*, *āppa(n)*, *katta(n)*, *katti-*, *peran*, *parā*, *šer*, *šarā* (Studia Asiana 1) — Rome 2002 |
| Freu/Mazoyer, Débuts | J. Freu and M. Mazoyer, Les Débuts du Nouvel Empire Hittite: Les Hittites et leur histoire 2, Collection Kubaba Series Antiquité 12 — Paris 2007 |
| Friedrich | *see* HE, HG, HKL, HW, HW 1., 2., 3.Erg., HW$^2$, SV |
| Friedrich/ Kammenhuber | *see* HW$^2$ |
| Frisk | H. Frisk, Griechisches etymologisches Wörterbuch I–III — Heidelberg 1960–1972 |
| FsAlp | Hittite and Other Anatolian and Near Eastern Studies in Honour of Sedat Alp (Anadolu Medeniyetlerini Araştırma ve Tanıtma Vakfı Yayınları 1) — Ankara 1992 |
| FsBeckman | Beyond Hatti. A Tribute to Gary Beckman — Atlanta 2013 |
| FsBiggs | Studies Presented to Robert D. Biggs (AS 27) — Chicago 2007 |
| FsBittel | Beiträge zur Altertumskunde Kleinasiens. Festschrift für Kurt Bittel — Mainz 1983 |
| FsÇambel | Anatolian Metal 8: Eliten—Handwerk-Prestigegüter (Der Anschnitt Beiheft 39) — Bochum 2018 |
| FsCarruba | Interferenze linguistichi e contatti culturali in Anatolia tra II e I millennio A. C.: Studi in onore di Onofrio Carruba in occasione del suo 80° compleanno (StMed 24) — Pavia 2012 |
| FsÇop | *see* Linguistica 33 |
| FsCumont | Mélanges Franz Cumont (AIPHOS 4) — Brussels 1936 |
| FsDeMeyer | Cinquante-Deux reflexions sur le Proche-Orient ancien: offertes en homage à Léon De Meyer (Mesopotamian History and Environment Occasional Publications 2) — Louvain 1994 |
| FsDeRoos | The Life and Times of Ḫattušili III and Tutḫaliya IV (PIHANS 103) — Istanbul 2006 |
| FsDiakonoff | Societies and Languages of the Ancient Near East: Studies in Honour of I. M. Diakonoff — Warminster, England 1982 |
| FsDinçol | VITA: Festschrift in Honor of Belkıs Dinçol and Ali Dinçol — Istanbul 2007 |
| FsDörner | Studien zur Religion und Kultur Kleinasiens: Festschrift für Friedrich Karl Dörner zum 65. Geburtstag am 28. Februar 1976 — Leiden 1978 |
| FsDYoung | Go to the Land I Will Show You. Studies in Honor of Dwight W. Young — Winona Lake 1995 |
| FsEVermeule | The Ages of Homer: A Tribute to Emily Townsend Vermeule — Austin 1995 |
| FsEWegner | *see* AoF 34 |
| FsFreu | De Hattuša à Memphis — Jacques Freu in honorem — Paris 2013 |
| FsFriedrich | Festschrift J. Friedrich zum 65. Geburtstag gewidmet — Heidelberg 1959 |
| FsFronzaroli | Semitic and Assyriological Studies Presented to Pelio Fronzaroli by Pupils and Colleagues — Wiesbaden 2003 |
| FsGordon | Orient and Occident: Essays Presented to Cyrus H. Gordon (AOAT 22) — Neukirchen-Vluyn 1973 |

| | |
|---|---|
| FsGünbattı | Cahit Günbattı'ya Armağan: Studies in Honor of Cahit Günbattı (AÜDTCFY 417) — Ankara 2015 |
| FsGüterbock | Anatolian Studies Presented to Hans Gustav Güterbock on the Occasion of his 65th Birthday (PIHANS 33) — Leiden 1974 |
| FsGüterbock² | Kaniššuwar: A Tribute to Hans G. Güterbock on His Seventy-fifth Birthday May 27, 1983 (AS 23) — Chicago 1986 |
| FsHaas | Kulturgeschichten: Altorientalische Studien für Volkert Haas zum 65. Geburtstag Saarbrücken — 2001 |
| FsHallo | The Tablet and the Scroll. Near Eastern Studies in Honor of William W. Hallo — Bethesda 1993 |
| FsHeger | Texte, Sätze, Wörter und Moneme. Festschrift für Klaus Heger zum 65. Geburtstag — Heidelberg 1992 |
| FsHerzenberg | Hṛdā́ Mánasā: Studies Presented to Professor Leonard G. Herzenberg on the Occasion of his 70-birthday — St. Petersburg 2005 |
| FsHoffner | Hittite Studies in Honor of Harry A. Hoffner, Jr. on the Occasion of his 65th Birthday — Winona Lake 2003 |
| FsHouwink ten Cate | Studio Historiae Ardens: Ancient Near Eastern Studies Presented to Philo H. J. Houwink ten Cate on the Occasion of his 65th Birthday (PIHANS 74) — Leiden 1995 |
| FsKantor | Essays in Ancient Civilization Presented to Helene J. Kantor (SAOC 47) — Chicago 1989 |
| FsKnobloch | Sprachwissenschaftliche Forschungen: Festschrift für Johann Knobloch (IBK 23) — Innsbruck 1985 |
| FsKošak | Tabularia Hethaeorum: Hethitologische Beiträge Silvin Košak zum 65. Geburtstag (DBH 25) — Wiesbaden 2007 |
| FsKraus | Zikir Šumim: Assyriological Studies Presented to F. R. Kraus on the Occasion of his Seventieth Birthday — Leiden 1982 |
| FsLacheman | Studies on the Civilization and Culture of Nuzi and the Hurrians in Honor of Ernest R. Lacheman — Winona Lake 1981 |
| FsLandsberger | Studies in Honor of Benno Landsberger on his Seventy-fifth Birthday April 21, 1965 (AS 16) — 1965 |
| FsLaroche | Florilegium Anatolicum: Mélanges offerts à Emmanuel Laroche — Paris 1979 |
| FsLebrun 1 | Antiquus Oriens: Mélanges offerts au Professeur René Lebrun (Collection Kubaba: Série Antiquité 5) — Paris 2004 |
| FsLebrun 2 | Studia Anatolica et Varia: Mélanges offerts au Professeur René Lebrun (Collection Kubaba: Série Antiquité 6) — Paris 2004 |
| FsLong | "A Wise and Discerning Mind," Essays in Honor of Burke O. Long — Providence 2000 |
| FsMeid | Indogermanica Europaea. Festschrift für Wolfgang Meid zum 60. Geburtstag am 12. 11. 1989 (Grazer Linguistische Monographien 4) — Graz 1989 |
| FsMeissner | Altorientalische Studien Bruno Meissner zum 60. Geburtstag gewidmet (MAOG 4) — Leipzig 1928–1929 (1972) |
| FsMelchert | Ex Anatolia Lux: Anatolian and Indo-European Studies in Honor of H. Craig Melchert — Ann Arbor 2010 |
| FsMeriggi | Studi in onore di Piero Meriggi (Athenaeum NS 47, fasc. 1–4) — Pavia 1969 |
| FsMeriggi² | Studia Mediterranea Piero Meriggi dicata (StMed 1–2) — Pavia 1979 |
| FsMorpurgoDavies | Indo-European Perspectives: Studies in honour of Anna Morpurgo Davies — Oxford 2004 |
| FsNeumann | Serta Indogermanica: Festschrift für Günter Neumann zum 60. Geburtstag — Innsbruck 1982 |
| FsNeumann² | Novalis Indogermanica: Festschrift für Günther Neumann zum 80. Geburtstag (Grazer Vergleichende Arbeiten 17) — Graz 2002 |
| FsNeve | IM 43 — 1993 |
| FsNowicki | Na-wa/i-VIR.ZI/A MAGNUS.SCRIBA: Festschrift für Helmut Nowicki zum 70. Geburtstag (DBH 45) — Wiesbaden 2014 |
| FsNÖzgüç | Aspects of Art and Iconography: Anatolia and its Neighbors. Studies in Honor of Nimet Özgüç — Ankara 1993 |
| FsOberhuber | Im Bannkreis des Alten Orients: Studien zur Sprach- und Kulturgeschichte des Alten Orients und seines Ausstrahlungsraumes Karl Oberhuber zum 70. Geburtstag gewidmet (IBK 24) — Innsbruck 1986 |
| FsOtten | Festschrift Heinrich Otten — Wiesbaden 1973 |

| | |
|---|---|
| FsOtten[2] | Documentum Asiae Minoris Antiquae: Festschrift für Heinrich Otten zum 75. Geburtstag — Wiesbaden 1988 |
| FsPagliaro | Studia classica et orientalia Antonio Pagliaro oblata — Rome 1969 |
| FsPalmer | Studies in Greek, Italic and Indo-European Linguistics Offered to L. R. Palmer — Innsbruck 1976 |
| FsPedersen | Mélanges Linguistiques offerts à M. Holger Pedersen a l'occasion de son soixantedixième anniversaire, 7 avril 1937 (Acta Jutlandica 9/1) — Aarhus 1937 |
| FsPope | *see* Love & Death |
| FsPopko | Silva Anatolica — Warsaw 2002 |
| FsPugliese Carratelli | Studi di storia e di filologia anatolica dedicati a Giovanni Pugliese Carratelli (Eothen 1) — Florence 1988 |
| FsPuhvel | Studies in Ancient Languages and Philology in Honor of Jaan Puhvel — (JIES Monograph Series 18) — Washington, D.C. 1997 |
| FsRamer | The Linguist's Linguist: A Collection of Papers in Honour of Alexis Manaster Ramer — Munich 2002 |
| FsRanoszek | Anniversary Volume Dedicated to Rudolf Ranoszek on his Eighty-Fifth Birthday (= RO 41 fasc. 2) — Warsaw 1980 |
| FsReiner | Language, Literature and History: Philological and Historical Studies Presented to Erica Reiner (AOS 67) — New Haven 1987 |
| FsRisch | o-o-pe-ro-si: Festschrift für Ernst Risch zum 75. Geburtstag — Berlin 1986 |
| FsRix | Indogermanica et Italica: Festschrift für Helmut Rix zum 65. Geburtstag (IBS 72) — Innsbruck 1993 |
| FsSalonen | StOr 46 — 1975 |
| FsSiegelová | Audias fabulas veteres: Anatolian Studies in Honor of Jana Součková-Siegelová (CHANE 79) — 2016 |
| FsSinger | Pax Hethitica: Studies on the Hittites and their Neighbours in Honour of Itamar Singer (StBoT 51) — 2010 |
| FsSommer | *see* Cor.Ling. |
| FsStreiberg | Streitberg-Festgabe — Leipzig 1924 |
| FsSzemerényi | Studies in Diachronic, Synchronic, and Typological Linguistics: Festschrift for Oswald Szemerényi on the Occasion of his 65th Birthday — Amsterdam 1979 |
| FsTischler | Anatolica et Indogermanica: Studia linguistica in honorem Johannis Tischler septuagenarii dedicatae (IBS 155) — Innsbruck 2016 |
| FsTÖzgüç | Anatolia and the Ancient Near East: Studies in Honor of Tahsin Özgüç — Ankara 1989 |
| FsWatkins | Mír Curad: Studies in Honor of Calvert Watkins (IBS 92) — Innsbruck 1998 |
| FsWilhelm | Festschrift für Gernot Wilhelm anläßlich seines 65. Geburtstages am 28. Januar 2010 — Dresden 2010 |
| FuF | Forschungen und Fortschritte — Berlin |
| FWgesch. | Fischer Weltgeschichte: Die Altorientalischen Reiche — Frankfurt am Main 1965ff. |
| Furniture | G. Herrmann, ed., The Furniture of Western Asia: Ancient and Traditional — Mainz 1996 |
| GAG | W. von Soden, Grundriss der akkadischen Grammatik, with suppl. (AnOr 33/47) — Rome 1969 |
| Gamkrelidze, Laryngale | T. V. Gamkrelidze, Hittite et la théorie laryngale — Tiflis 1960 |
| Garelli, AC | P. Garelli, Les Assyriens en Cappadoce — Paris 1963 |
| García Trabazo, TextosRel. | J. V. García Trabazo, Textos religiosos hititas (Biblioteca de ciencias bíblicas y orientales 6) — Madrid 2002 |
| —— | *see also* DBH 18 |
| Garstang/Gurney | *see* Geogr |
| Gelb, Alishar | I. J. Gelb, Inscriptions from Alishar and Vicinity (OIP 27) — Chicago 1935 |
| —— HH | —— Hittite Hieroglyphs 1–3 (SAOC 2, 14, 21) — Chicago 1931–1942 |
| —— HHM | —— Hittite Hieroglyphic Monuments (OIP 45) — Chicago 1939 |
| Geogr | J. Garstang and O. R. Gurney, The Geography of the Hittite Empire — London 1959 |
| George, GilgTr | A. R. George, The Epic of Gilgamesh — Harmondsworth 1999 |
| Gertz, Diss. | J. E. Gertz, The Nominative-accusative Neuter Plural in Anatolian (diss., Yale University — 1982) |
| van Gessel | *see* OHP |
| GestaSupp | G. Del Monte, Le Gesta di Suppiluliuma — Pisa 2009 |
| Gilan | *see* THeth 29 |

| | |
|---|---|
| Gilg. | Gilgameš epic |
| GLH | E. Laroche, Glossaire de la langue hourrite (RHA XXXIV–XXXV) — Paris 1976–1977, pub. 1978–1979 |
| Gl.Hourrite | *see* GLH |
| Glocker, Kuliwišna | J. Glocker, Das Ritual für den Wettergott von Kuliwišna (Eothen 6) — Florence 1997 |
| Glotta | Glotta — Göttingen |
| Goedegebuure | *see* StBoT 55 |
| Goetze, Kl | A. Goetze, Kleinasien, 2nd ed. — Munich 1957 |
| —— | *see also* AM, Ḫatt., Kizz., Madd., MSpr, NBr, Pestgeb., Tunn. |
| Gordin | *see* StBoT 59 |
| Gordon, UT | C. Gordon, Ugaritic Textbook (AnOr 38) Rome 1965 |
| Görke, Aštu | S. Görke, Das Ritual der Aštu (CTH 490). Rekonstruktion und Tradition eines hurritisch-hethitischen Rituals aus Boğazköy/Ḫattuša (CHANE 40) — Leiden 2010 |
| Grazer Beiträge | Grazer Beiträge — Amsterdam |
| GrHL | H. A. Hoffner, Jr. and H. C. Melchert, A Grammar of the Hittite Language — Winona Lake 2008 |
| Groddek, KI.LAM | D. Groddek, Eine althethitische Tafel des KI.LAM-Festes (IJDL Supp. 1) — Munich 2004 |
| —— | *see also* DBH *passim* |
| Gröndahl | F. Gröndahl, Die Personennamen der Texte aus Ugarit (Stud. Pohl 1) — Rome 1967 |
| Grotiana | Grotiana — Assen, Leiden |
| GsAmmann | Sprachwissenschaft in Innsbruck (IBKS 50) — Innsbruck 1982 |
| GsBökönyi | Man and the Animal World: Studies in Archaeozoology, Archaeology, Anthropology and Palaeolinguistics in memoriam Sándo Bökönyi — Berlin 1998 |
| GsBossert | Anadolu Araştırmaları (JKF) vol. II 1–2 — Istanbul 1965 |
| GsForrer | *Šarnikzel* — Hethitologische Studien zum Gedenken an Emil Orgetorix Forrer — Dresden 2004 |
| GsGüntert | Antiquitates Indogermanicae: Gedenkschrift für Hermann Güntert zur 25. Wiederkehr seines Todestages — Innsbruck 1974 |
| GsKretschmer | ΜΝΗΜΗΣ ΧΑΡΙΝ: Gedenkschrift Paul Kretschmer — Vienna 1956 |
| GsKronasser | Investigationes Philologicae et Comparativae: Gedenkschrift für Heinz Kronasser — Wiesbaden 1982 |
| GsNeu | Investigationes Anatolicae: Gedenkschrift für Erich Neu (StBoT 52) — 2010 |
| GsOtten | Saeculum: Gedenkschrift für Heinrich Otten anlässlich seines 100. Geburtstags (StBoT 58) — Wiesbaden 2015 |
| GsPedersen | In Honorem Holger Pedersen. Kolloquium der Indogermanischen Gesellschaft vom 26. bis 28. März 1993 in Kopenhagen — Wiesbaden 1994 |
| GsPintore | Studi Orientalistici in ricordo di Franco Pintore (StMed 4) — Pavia 1983 |
| Gurney, AAA 27 | O. R. Gurney, Hittite Prayers of Muršili II (AAA 27) — Liverpool 1941 |
| —— Schweich | —— Some Aspects of Hittite Religion (The Schweich Lectures 1976) — Oxford 1977 |
| —— | *see also* Geogr |
| Gusmani, Lessico | R. Gusmani, Il lessico ittito — Naples 1968 |
| —— Lyd.Wb. | —— Lydisches Wörterbuch — Heidelberg 1964 |
| Güterbock, Frontiers | H. G. Güterbock, "Some Aspects of Hittite Prayers" in Frontiers of Human Knowledge (Skrifter rörande Uppsala universitet C:38: Acta Universitatis Upsaliensis) — Uppsala 1978, pp. 125–39 |
| —— | *see also* AS, BoHa, CHD, DŠ, Kum., SBo, Ullik. |
| Haas, Berggötter | V. Haas, Hethitische Berggötter und hurritische Steindämonen. Riten, Kulte, und Mythen — Mainz 1982 |
| —— Gesch.Relig. | —— Geschichte der hethitischen Religion (HdOr 1/15) — Leiden 1994 |
| —— KN | —— Der Kult von Nerik (Stud. Pohl 4) — Rome 1970 |
| —— Literatur | —— Die hethitische Literatur: Texte, Stilistik, Motive — Berlin 2006 |
| —— Materia | —— Materia Magica et Medica Hethitica — Berlin 2003 |
| —— Orakel | —— Hethitische Orakel, Vorzeichen und Abwehrstrategien: ein Beitrag zur hethitischen Kulturgeschichte — Berlin 2008 |
| —— | *see also* ChS I/9 |

| | |
|---|---|
| Haas/Thiel, AOAT 31 | V. Haas and H. Thiel, Die Beschwörungsrituale der Allaiturah(h)i und verwandte Texte (AOAT 31) — Neukirchen-Vluyn 1978 |
| Haas/Wilhelm, AOATS 3 | V. Haas and G. Wilhelm, Hurritische und luwische Riten aus Kizzuwatna (AOATS 3) — Neukirchen-Vluyn 1974 |
| Haase, Beobachtungen | R. Haase, Beobachtungen zur hethitischen Rechtssatzung — Leonberg 1995 |
| —— THR | —— Texte zum hethitischen Recht: Eine Auswahl — Wiesbaden 1984 |
| HAB | F. Sommer und A. Falkenstein, Die hethitisch-akkadische Bilingue des Ḫattušili I. (Labarna II.) (ABAW, NF 16) — Munich 1938 |
| Hagenbuchner | *see* DBH 1, 6, THeth 15–16 |
| Hahn, Naming | E. A. Hahn, Naming Constructions in Some Indo-European Languages (Philological Monographs of the American Philological Association 27) — Cleveland 1969 |
| Ḫatt | A. Götze, Ḫattušiliš. Der Bericht über seine Thronbesteigung nebst den Paralleltexten (MVAG 29.3) — Leipzig 1925; Ḫatt. also abbreviates Apology of Ḫattušili III, cited by col. and line in Ḫatt., NBr, Chrest., or StBoT 24 (Ḫatt. also abbreviates the royal name Ḫattušili, always followed by I, II, or III) |
| Hawkins | *see* HHL, StBoT Beih. 3 |
| Hazenbos, Habil. | "Wir stellten eine Orakelfrage": Untersuchungen zu den hethitischen Orakeltexten — Leipzig 2003 |
| —— Organization | —— The Organization of the Anatolian Local Cults during the Thirteenth Century B.C.: An Appraisal of Hittite Cult Inventories. Cuneiform Monographs 21 — Leiden 2003 |
| HBM | S. Alp, Hethitische Briefe aus Maşat-Höyük (Atatürk Kültür, Dil ve Tarih Yüksek Kurumu, TTKYayın VI/35) — Ankara 1991 |
| HbOr | Handbuch der Orientalistik — Leiden |
| HE | J. Friedrich, Hethitisches Elementarbuch, 2nd ed. — Heidelberg, HE 1 1960, HE 2 1967 |
| HED | J. Puhvel, Hittite Etymological Dictionary — Berlin 1984ff. |
| HEG | J. Tischler, Hethitisches etymologisches Glossar (IBS 20) — Innsbruck 1977–2016 |
| Heinhold-Krahmer | *see* THeth 8, 9 |
| Held, Rel. Sent. | W. H. Held, Jr., The Hittite Relative Sentence (Lg. Diss. no. 55; Lg. 33.4 part 2 suppl.) — Baltimore 1957 |
| Heth.u.Idg. | E. Neu and W. Meid, eds., Hethitisch und Indogermanisch: Vergleichende Studien zur historischen Grammatik und zur dialektgeographischen Stellung der indogermanischen Sprachgruppe Altkleinasiens (IBS 25) — Innsbruck 1979 |
| Hethitica | Hethitica: vol. I (Travaux de la Faculté de Philosophie et Lettres de l'Université Catholique de Louvain); subsequent vols. are a subseries of BCILL — Louvain-la-Neuve |
| HethLit | M. Hutter and S. Hutter-Braunsar, eds., Hethitische Literatur: Überlieferungsprozesse, Textstrukturen, Ausdrucksformen und Nachwirken (AOAT 391) — Münster 2011 |
| hetkonk | http://www.orient.uni.wuerzburg.de/hetkonk/hetkonk_abfrage.html |
| Heubeck, Lyd | A. Heubeck, Lydisch (in Altkleinasiatische Sprachen, (HbOr 1.2.1/2.2, pp. 397–427) — Leiden 1969 |
| Heubeck, Lydiaka | —— Lydiaka. Untersuchungen zu Schrift, Sprache und Götternamen der Lyder — Erlangen 1959 |
| HFAC | G. Beckman and H. A. Hoffner, Jr., Hittite Fragments in American Collections (JCS 37/1) — Philadelphia 1985 |
| HG | J. Friedrich, Die hethitischen Gesetze (DMOA 7) — Leiden 1959, 2nd ed. 1971 |
| Ḫg. | lexical series ḪAR.gud = *imrû* = *ballu* (MSL 5–11) |
| Ḫh. | lexical series ḪAR.ra = *ḫubullu* (MSL 5–10) |
| HHB | H.-S. Schuster, Die hattisch-hethitischen Bilinguen I/1 (DMOA 17/1), I/2–3 (DMOA 17/2) — Leiden 1974, 2002 |
| HHL | J. D. Hawkins, A. Morpurgo-Davies, and G. Neumann, Hittite Hieroglyphs and Luwian: New Evidence for the Connection (NAWG 1973 No. 6) — Göttingen 1974 |
| HHT | K. Riemschneider, Hurritische und hethitische Texte — Munich 1974 (mimeographed) |
| Hidden Futures | J.M. Bremer, Th. van den Hout, R. Peters, eds., Hidden Futures —Amsterdam 1994 |

| | |
|---|---|
| Hipp.heth. | A. Kammenhuber, Hippologia hethitica — Wiesbaden 1961 |
| Hit.Kongr | Papers of International Hittitological Congresses, *see also* ICH |
| —— 1 | Uluslararası 1. Hititoloji Kongresi Bildirileri (19–21 Temmuz 1990), Çorum |
| —— 2 | (Pavia 1993) *see* StMed 9 |
| —— 3 | III. Uluslararası Hititoloji Kongresi Bildirileri, Çorum 16–22 Eylül 1996 — Ankara 1998 |
| —— 4 | (Würzburg 1999) *see* StBoT 45 |
| HittInstr | J. Miller, Royal Hittite Instructions and Related Administrative Texts (WAW 31) — Atlanta 2013 |
| Hittite Myths | H. A. Hoffner, Jr., Hittite Myths (WAW 2) — Atlanta 1990 |
| Hittite Myths$^2$ | H. A. Hoffner, Jr., Hittite Myths (WAW 2), 2nd edition — Atlanta 1998 |
| HittitePrayers | I. Singer, Hittite Prayers (WAW 11) — Atlanta 2002 |
| HKL | J. Friedrich, Hethitisches Keilschrift-Lesebuch 1, 2 — Heidelberg 1960 |
| HKM | S. Alp, Hethitische Keilschrifttafeln aus Maşat-Höyük (Atatürk Kültür, Dil ve Tarih Yüksek Kurumu, TTKYayın VI/34) — Ankara 1991 |
| HLC | M. Cammarosano, Hittite Local Cults (WAW 40) — Atlanta 2018 |
| Hoffmann | *see* THeth 11 |
| Hoffner, Diss. | H. A. Hoffner, Jr., The Laws of the Hittites (diss., Brandeis University — 1963) |
| —— | *see also* AlHeth, CHD, EHGl, FsGordon, FsGüterbock$^2$, GrHL, HFAC, Hittite Myths$^2$, LawColl, Letters, LH |
| Holland, Diss. | G. B. Holland, Problems of Word Order Change in Selected Indo-European Languages (diss., University of California at Berkeley — 1980) |
| Holland/Zorman | *see* StMed 19. |
| van den Hout, Diss. | Th. P. J. van den Hout, Studien zum Spätjunghethitischen: Texte der Zeit Tudhalijas IV. KBo IV 10 + (CTH 106) (diss., Universiteit van Amsterdam — 1989) |
| —— Purity | Th. van den Hout, The Purity of Kingship: An Edition of CTH 569 and Related Hittite Oracle Inquiries of Tutḫaliya IV (DMOA 25) — Leiden 1998 |
| —— | *see also* AS 24, StBoT 38 |
| Houwink ten Cate, Mursilis II... Karakterschets | Ph. H. J. Houwink ten Cate, Muršiliš II, de bronnen voor een Karakterschets — Leiden 1966 |
| —— | *see also* Records |
| How Purity Is Made | P. Rösch and U. Simon, eds., How Purity is Made — Wiesbaden 2012 |
| HPMM | Hethitologie Portal Mainz — Materialien — Wiesbaden |
| —— 6 | F. Fuscagni, Hethitische unveröffentlichte Texte aus den Jahren 1906–1912 in der Sekundärliteratur — Wiesbaden 2007 |
| HR | History of Religions — Chicago |
| Hrozný, CH | B. Hrozný, Code Hittite provenant de l'Asie Mineure, I. — Paris 1922 |
| —— HKT | —— Hethitische Keilschrifttexte aus Boghazköi in Umschrift, Übersetzung und Kommentar (BoSt 3) — Leipzig 1919 |
| —— IHH | —— Les Inscriptions Hittites Hiéroglyphiques 1–3 — Prague 1933–1937 |
| —— SH | —— Die Sprache der Hethiter (BoSt 12) — Leipzig 1917 |
| —— VSpr | —— Über die Völker und Sprachen des alten Chatti-Landes (BoSt 5) — Leipzig 1920 |
| HS | Historische Sprachforschung, *see* KZ |
| HSM | Harvard Semitic Museum, inventory number |
| HSSt | Harvard Semitic Studies — Atlanta |
| HT | Hittite Texts in the Cuneiform Character in the British Museum — London 1920 |
| HTR | H. Otten, Hethitische Totenrituale (VIO 37) — Berlin 1958 |
| HUCA | Hebrew Union College Annual — Cincinnati |
| Ḫuqq. | The Treaty of Šuppiluliuma I with Ḫuqqana, ed. SV 2:103–63 |
| Hutter, Behexung | M. Hutter, Behexung, Entsühnung und Heilung: Das Ritual der Tunnawiya für ein Königspaar aus mittelhethitischer Zeit (KBo XXI 1 — KUB IX 34 — KBo XXI 6) (OBO 82) — Göttingen 1988 |
| HW | J. Friedrich, Hethitisches Wörterbuch — Heidelberg 1952(–1954) |
| HW 1., 2., 3. Erg. | J. Friedrich, Hethitisches Wörterbuch 1.–3. Ergänzungsheft — Heidelberg 1957, 1961, 1966 |

| | |
|---|---|
| HW² | J. Friedrich and A. Kammenhuber, Hethitisches Wörterbuch, 2nd ed. — Heidelberg 1975ff. |
| HWHT | O. Soysal, Hattischer Wortschatz in hethitischer Textüberlieferung (HbOr I/74) — Leiden 2004 |
| HZL | Chr. Rüster and E. Neu, Hethitisches Zeichenlexikon: Inventar und Interpretation der Keilschriftzeichen aus den Boğazköy-Texten (StBoT Beih. 2) — 1989 |
| IAK | E. Ebeling, B. Meissner, and E. F. Weidner, eds., Die Inschriften der altassyrischen Könige — Leipzig 1926 |
| IBK(S) | Innsbrucker Beiträge zur Kulturwissenschaft (Sonderheft) — Innsbruck |
| IBoT | İstanbul Arkeoloji Müzelerinde Bulunan Boğazköy Tabletleri(nden Seçme Metinler) — Istanbul 1944, 1947, 1954; Ankara 1988 |
| IBS | Innsbrucker Beiträge zur Sprachwissenschaft — Innsbruck |
| IBS-VKS | Innsbrucker Beiträge zur Sprachwissenschaft - Vorträge und Kleinere Schriften — Innsbruck |
| ICH | International Congress of Hittitology |
| —— 1 | Uluslararası 1. Hititoloji Kongresi Bildirileri (19–21 Temmuz 1990) — Çorum |
| —— 2 | (Pavia 1993) *see* StMed 9 |
| —— 3 | III. Uluslararası Hititoloji Kongresi Bildirileri, Çorum 16–22 Eylül 1996 — Ankara 1998 |
| —— 4 | (Würzburg 1999) *see* StBoT 45 — 2001 |
| —— 5 | V. Uluslararası Hititoloji Kongresi Bildirileri Çorum 02–08 Eylül 2002 — Ankara 2005 |
| —— 6 | (Rome 2005) *see* SMEA 49–50 (2007) |
| —— 7 | VII. Uluslararası Hititoloji Kongresi Bildirileri Çorum 25–31 Ağustos 2008 — Ankara 2010 |
| —— 8 | Proceedings of the Eighth International Congress of Hittitology, Warsaw 4–9 September 2011 — Warsaw 2014 |
| —— 9 | (Çorum 2014) *forthcoming* |
| —— 10 | (Chicago 2017) *forthcoming* |
| Idg.Bibl. | Indogermanische Bibliothek — Heidelberg |
| Idg.Gr. | Indogermanische Grammatik — Heidelberg 1968ff. |
| IdgNomen | Indogermanisches Nomen: Derivation, Flexion und Ablaut: Akten der Arbeitstagung der Indogermanischen Gesellschaft: Freiburg, 19. bis 22. September 2001 — Bremen 2003 |
| Idu | lexical series Á = *idu* |
| IEJ | Israel Exploration Journal — Jerusalem |
| IESt | Indo-European Studies, Dept. of Linguistics, Harvard University — Cambridge, Massachusetts |
| IF | Indogermanische Forschungen — Strasbourg, Berlin |
| Igituḫ | lexical series igituḫ = *tāmartu*; Igituḫ short version (ed. Landsberger/Gurney, AfO 18:81ff.) |
| IJDL | International Journal of Diachronic Linguistics and Linguistic Reconstruction — Munich |
| IJDL Supp. 1 | *see* Groddek, KI.LAM |
| Illuy. | Illuyanka myth |
| IM | Istanbuler Mitteilungen — Berlin |
| Imparati, Leggi | F. Imparati, Le leggi ittite — Rome 1964 |
| —— | *see also* Eothen 4, 9, 10, 11, 12 |
| IncLing | Incontri Linguistici — Pisa |
| Inglese, Subordination | G. Inglese, Subordination and Sentence Connectives in Old Hittite: A Corpus-Based Study of Clause Linkage Strategies in Hittite (LINCOM Studies in Indo-European Linguistics 49) — Munich 2016 |
| IstF | Istanbuler Forschungen — Bamberg, Berlin, and Tübingen |
| İÜEFY | İstanbul Üniversitesi Edebiyat Fakültesi Yayınları — İstanbul |
| IYKPh | Indojevropejskoje jazykoznanije i klassicheskaja filologija — St. Petersburg |
| Izi | lexical series izi = *išātu* (MSL 13:154–226) |
| Izi Bogh. | Boğazköy version of Izi (MSL 13:132–47) |
| JA | Journal asiatique — Paris |
| Jakob-Rost, Familienzwist | L. Jakob-Rost, Ein hethitisches Ritual gegen Familienzwist (MIO 1:345–79) — Berlin 1953 |
| —— | *see also* Mašt., THeth 2 |
| JANES | Journal of the Ancient Near Eastern Society — New York |
| JAOS | Journal of the American Oriental Society — New Haven, Ann Arbor |

| | |
|---|---|
| JBL | Journal of Biblical Literature — New Haven, Philadelphia, Missoula, Richmond, Atlanta, Decatur |
| JCS | Journal of Cuneiform Studies — New Haven, Cambridge, Massachusetts, Philadelphia, Baltimore, Boston |
| JEOL | Jaarbericht van het Vooraziatisch-Egyptisch Genootschap (earlier Gezelschap) "Ex Oriente Lux" — Leiden |
| JESHO | Journal of the Economic and Social History of the Orient — Leiden |
| JIES | Journal of Indo-European Studies — Hattiesburg, Washington, DC |
| Jin Jie, RetrGlos | A Complete Retrograde Glossary of the Hittite Language (PIHANS 71) — Leiden 1994 |
| JKF | Jahrbuch für kleinasiatische Forschungen (= Anadolu Araştırmaları) — Heidelberg, Istanbul |
| JLR | Journal of Language Relationship— Moscow |
| JNES | Journal of Near Eastern Studies — Chicago |
| Josephson, Part. | F. Josephson, The Function of Sentence Particles in Old and Middle Hittite (Acta Universitatis Upsaliensis. Studia Indoeuropea Upsaliensia 2) — Uppsala 1972 |
| JRAS | Journal of the Royal Asiatic Society of Great Britain and Ireland — London |
| JSOR | Journal of the Society of Oriental Research — Chicago |
| Kagal | lexical series kagal = *abullu* (MSL 13) |
| Kammenhuber, HbOr | A. Kammenhuber, Hethitisch, Palaisch, Luwisch, und Hieroglyphenluwisch (in Altkleinasiatische Sprachen, HbOr I.2.1/2.2, pp. 119–357, 428–546) — Leiden 1969 |
| —— | *see also* Hipp.heth., HW$^2$, Materialien, THeth 7, 19 |
| Kaškäer | E. von Schuler, Die Kaškäer (UAVA 3) — Berlin 1965 |
| Kaskal | Kaskal—Rivista di storia, ambienti e culture del Vicino Oriente Antico — Pavia, Florence |
| Kassian, Zip. | A. Kassian, Two Middle Hittite Rituals mentioning [f]Ziplantawija, sister of Hittite King Tuthalija II/I — Moscow 2000 |
| Kassian et al., Funerary | A. Kassian, A. Korolëv, A. Sidel'tsev, Hittite Funerary Ritual *šalliš waštaiš* (AOAT 288) — Münster 2002 |
| KBo | Keilschrifttexte aus Boghazköi (vols. 1–22 are a subseries of WVDOG) — Leipzig, Berlin |
| Kellerman, Diss. | G. Kellerman, Recherche sur les rituels de fondation hittites (diss., University of Paris — 1980) |
| Kempinski, ÄAT 4 | A. Kempinski, Syrien und Palästina (Kanaan) in der letzten Phase der Mittelbronze IIB-Zeit (ÄAT 4) — Wiesbaden 1983 |
| Kerns Mem. | Bono Homini Donum: Essays in Historical Linguistics in Memory of J. Alexander Kerns (Amsterdam Studies in the Theory and History of Linguistic Science 4. Current Issues in Linguistic Theory 16) — Amsterdam 1981 |
| Kestemont, Diplomatique | G. Kestemont, Diplomatique et droit international en Asie occidentale (1600–1200 av. J.C.) (Publications de l'Institut Orientaliste de Louvain 9) — Louvain-la-Neuve 1974 |
| Kikk. | Kikkuli text, ed. Kammenhuber, Hipp. heth., pp. 54–147 |
| King | *see* HT, STC |
| Kizz. | A. Goetze, Kizzuwatna and the Problem of Hittite Geography (YOSR 22) — New Haven 1940 |
| Klengel, Gesch.Syr | H. Klengel, Die Geschichte Syriens im 2. Jahrtausend — Berlin 1965, 1969, 1970 |
| KlF | F. Sommer and H. Ehelolf, eds., Kleinasiatische Forschungen, vol. 1 — Weimar (1927–)1930 |
| Klinger | *see* StBoT 37 |
| Kloekhorst, | *see* EDHIL, StBoT 56. |
| KlPauly | Der kleine Pauly: Lexikon der Antike — Stuttgart 1964ff. |
| Knudtzon, Arz. | J. A. Knudtzon, Die zwei Arzawa-Briefe: Die ältesten Urkunden in indogermanischer Sprache — Leipzig 1902 |
| —— | *see also* EA |
| König | F. W. König, Handbuch der chaldischen Inschriften (AfO Beiheft 8) — Graz 1955–1957 |
| Košak | *see* StBoT 34, 39, THeth 10 |
| Kronasser, EHS | H. Kronasser, Etymologie der hethitischen Sprache — Wiesbaden 1963–1966, 1987 |
| —— VLFH | —— Vergleichende Laut- und Formenlehre des Hethitischen — Heidelberg 1955 |
| —— | *see also* Schw.Gotth. |

| | |
|---|---|
| Ktèma | Ktèma: Civilisations de l'Orient, de la Grèce et de Rome Antiques — Strasbourg |
| KUB | Keilschrifturkunden aus Boghazköi — Berlin |
| Kühne | *see* StBoT 16 |
| Kum. | H. G. Güterbock, Kumarbi. Mythen vom churritischen Kronos (Istanbuler Schriften 16) — Zürich, New York 1946 |
| Kümmel | *see* StBoT 3 |
| Kup. | Treaty of Muršili II with Kupanta-$^{d}$LAMMA, ed. SV 1:95–181 |
| Kupper, Nomades | J.-R. Kupper, Les nomades en Mésopotamie au temps des rois de Mari — Paris 1957 |
| KuSa | Kuşaklı-Sarissa—Rahden/Westf. |
| KuSa I/1 | G. Wilhelm, Keilschrifttexte aus Gebäude A (KuSa I/1) — 1997 |
| KuT | texts from Kuşaklı-Sarissa, published by Wilhelm, KuSa I/1 and MDOG 130 (1998) 175–187 |
| KZ | Historische Sprachforschung = Zeitschrift für Vergleichende Sprachforschung ("Kuhns Zeitschrift") — Berlin, Gütersloh, Wiesbaden |
| LÄ | Lexikon der Agyptologie — Wiesbaden 1975ff. |
| Labat | R. Labat, Manuel d'Épigraphie Akkadienne (numbers refer to sign number, not page) — Paris 1976 |
| —— AkkBo | —— L'Akkadien de Boghaz-Köi — Bordeaux 1932 |
| Landsberger, Fauna | B. Landsberger, Die Fauna des alten Mesopotamien nach der 14. Tafel der ḪAR.RA = *ḫubullu* — Leipzig 1934 |
| Lanu | lexical series alam = *lānu* |
| LAPO | Littératures Anciennes du Proche-Orient — Paris |
| Laroche, HH | E. Laroche, Les hiéroglyphes hittites I (unmarked number following "Laroche" refers to sign) — Paris 1960 |
| —— Myth. | —— Textes mythologiques hittites en transcription (RHA XXIII/77, XXVI/ 82) — Paris 1965, 1968 |
| —— Onom. | —— Recueil d'onomastique hittite — Paris 1951 |

| | |
|---|---|
| —— prière hittite | —— La prière hittite: vocabulaire et typologie (École pratique des Hautes Études, V$^{e}$ section, Sciences Religieuses; Annuaire, tome 72) — Paris 1964/1965 |
| —— Rech. | —— Recherches sur les noms des dieux hittites (RHA VII/46) — Paris 1947 |
| —— | *see also* CTH, DLL, GLH, NH |
| LawColl | M. Roth, Law Collections from Mesopotamia and Asia Minor (WAW 6) with a contribution [Hittite Laws] by H. A. Hoffner, Jr. — Atlanta 1995 |
| Lebrun, Hymnes | R. Lebrun, Hymnes et Prières Hittites (Homo Religiosus 4) — Louvain-la-Neuve 1980 |
| —— Samuha | —— Samuha, foyer religieux de l'empire hittite (Publications de l'institut orientaliste de Louvain 11) — Louvain-la-Neuve 1976 |
| Lehrman, Diss. | A. Lehrman, Simple Thematic Imperfectives in Anatolian and in Indo-European (diss., Yale University — 1985) |
| Leichty, Izbu | E. Leichty, The Omen Series Šumma Izbu (TCS 4) — Locust Valley 1970 |
| Lettere | M. Marizza, Lettere ittite di re e dignitari: la corrispondenza interna del Medio Regno e dell'Età imperiale, TVOa 4/4 — Brescia 2009 |
| Letters | H. A. Hoffner, Letters from the Hittite Kingdom, WAW 15 — Atlanta 2009 |
| Levitikus | Levitikus als Buch (Bonner biblische Beiträge 119) — Bodenheim 1999 |
| Lg | Language. Journal of the Linguistic Society of America — Baltimore |
| Lg.Diss. | Language Dissertations — Baltimore |
| LH | H. A. Hoffner, Jr., The Laws of the Hittites (DMOA 23) — Leiden 1997 |
| Liddell/Scott | H. Liddell and R. Scott, A Greek-English Lexicon, revised by H. S. Jones — Oxford 1925–1940 (–1968) |
| LingBalk | Linguistique Balkanique/Balkansko Ezikoznanie — Sofia |
| Linguistica | Linguistica — Ljubljana |
| LMI | F. Pecchioli Daddi, and A. M. Polvani, La mitologia ittita (TVOa 4.1) — Brescia 1990 |
| Love & Death | Love and Death in the Ancient Near East: Essays in Honor of Marvin H. Pope — Guilford, Connecticut 1987 |
| Löw, Flora | I. Löw, Die Flora der Juden — Vienna, Leipzig 1926–1934 |

| | |
|---|---|
| LS | K. Riemschneider, Die hethitischen Landschenkungsurkunden (MIO 6:321–81) — Berlin 1958 |
| LSS | Leipziger Semitische Studien — Leipzig |
| LTU | H. Otten, Luvische Texte in Umschrift (VIO 17) — Berlin 1953 |
| Lu | lexical series lú = *ša* (MSL 12:87–147) |
| Luraghi, Old Hittite | S. Luraghi, Old Hittite Sentence Structure — London 1990 |
| Macqueen, The Hittites | J. G. Macqueen, The Hittites and their Contemporaries in Asia Minor, 2nd ed. — London 1986 |
| Madd. | A. Götze, Madduwattaš (MVAeG 32.1) — Leipzig 1928 |
| Magic and Ritual | P. Mirecki and M. Meyer, eds., Magic and Ritual in the Ancient World (Religions in the Graeco-Roman World 141) — Leiden 2002 |
| Magic and Ritual Power | M. Meyer and P. Mirecki, eds., Ancient Magic and Ritual Power (Religions in the Graeco-Roman World 129) — Leiden 1995 |
| Man. | Treaty of Muršili II with Manapa-[d]U, ed. SV 2:1–41 |
| MAOG | Mitteilungen der Altorientalischen Gesellschaft — Leipzig |
| Marazzi, AkkBoğaz | M. Marazzi, Beiträge zu den akkadischen Texten aus Boğazköy in althethitischer Zeit (Biblioteca di ricerche linguistiche e filologiche 18) — Rome 1986 |
| —— Il geroglifico | —— Il geroglifico anatolico: problemi di analisi e prospettive di ricerca (Biblioteca di ricerche linguistiche e filologiche 24) — Rome 1990 |
| —— | *see also* Lettere *and* Eothen 15 |
| Masson, Douze Dieux | E. Masson, Les douze dieux de l'immortalité — Paris 1989 |
| Mašt. | Ritual of Maštigga against family quarrels (CTH 404); 2Mašt. previously cited according to the edition of L. Rost, MIO 1 (1953) 348–367, see now StBoT 46:52–124 (1.I.A) |
| Materialien | A. Kammenhuber, Materialien zu einem hethitischen Thesaurus — Heidelberg 1973ff. |
| MAW | S. Kramer, ed., Mythologies of the Ancient World — Garden City 1961 |
| Mazoyer, Télipinu | M. Mazoyer, Télipinu, le dieu au marécage (Kubaba Série Antiquité 2) — Paris 2003 |
| MC | Mesopotamian Civilizations — Winona Lake |
| McMahon, Diss. | J. G. McMahon, The Hittite State Cult of the Tutelary Deities (diss., University of Chicago — 1988) |
| —— | *see also* AS 25 |
| MDOG | Mitteilungen der Deutschen Orient-Gesellschaft zu Berlin — Berlin |
| MEE | Materiali Epigrafici di Ebla — Naples and Rome |
| Melchert, AHP | H. C. Melchert, Anatolian Historical Phonology (Leiden Studies in Indo-European 3) — Amsterdam, Atlanta 1994 |
| —— Diss. | —— Ablative and Instrumental in Hittite (diss., Harvard University — 1977) |
| —— Phon. | —— Studies in Hittite Historical Phonology (KZ Erg. 32) — Göttingen 1984 |
| —— | *see also* CLL |
| Mém.Atatürk | Mémorial Atatürk: Études d'archéologie et de philologie anatoliennes. Institut Français d'études Anatoliennes (Éditions recherche sur les civilisations: Synthèse 10) — Paris 1982 |
| Mem.Black | Your Praise is Sweet: A Memorial Volume for Jeremy Black from Students, Colleagues and Friends — London 2010 |
| Mem.Carter | The Asia Minor Connexion: Studies on the Pre-Greek Languages in Memory of Charles Carter (Orbis Supplementa 13) — Leuven 2000 |
| Mem.Diakonoff | Memoriae Igor Diakonoff (Orientalia et Classica 8, Babel und Bibel 2) — Winona Lake 2005 |
| Mem.Güterbock | Recent Developments in Hittite Archaeology and History: Papers in Memory of Hans G. Güterbock — Winona Lake 2002 |
| Mem.Hurowitz | Marbah Ḫokmah: Studies in the Bible and the Ancient Near East in Loving Memory of Victor Avigdor Hurowitz — Winona Lake 2015 |
| Mem.Imparati | Anatolia Antica, Studi in Memoria di Fiorella Imparati (Eothen 11) — Florence 2002 |
| Mem.Quattordio-Moreschini | do-ra-qe pe-re: Studi in memoria di Adriana Quattordio Moreschini — Pisa 1998 |

| | |
|---|---|
| Mem.R.Young | From Athens to Gordion: The Papers of a Memorial Symposium for Rodney S. Young, University Museum Papers 1—Philadelphia 1980 |
| Mem.Schindler | Compositiones Indogermanicae in Memoriam Jochem Schindler — Prague 1999 |
| Meriggi, HhGl | P. Meriggi, Hieroglyphisch-hethitisches Glossar, 2nd ed. — Wiesbaden 1962 |
| —— Manuale | —— Manuale di eteo geroglifico I, II — Rome 1966–1975 |
| —— Schizzo | —— Schizzo grammaticale dell'Anatolico (Atti dell'Accademia Nazionale dei Lincei, Memorie, anno 377, series 8 vol. 24 fasc. 3) — Rome 1980 |
| Mes. | Mesopotamia: Rivista di archeologia, epigrafia e storia orientale antica — Turin |
| Meskéné-Emar | D. Beyer, ed., Meskéné-Emar: Dix ans de travaux, 1972–1982 — Paris 1982 |
| Mestieri | F. Pecchioli Daddi, Mestieri, professioni e dignità nell'Anatolia ittita (Incunabula Graeca 79) — Rome 1982 |
| Miller | *see* HittInstr, StBoT 46 |
| MIO | Mitteilungen des Instituts für Orientforschung — Berlin |
| Moore, Thesis | G. C. Moore, The Disappearing Deity Motif in Hittite Texts: A Study in Religious History (BLitt. Thesis, Oxford University — 1975) |
| Mora | *see* StMed 6 |
| Moran, Amarna Letters | W. Moran, The Amarna Letters — Baltimore 1992 |
| —— | *see also* EA |
| Mouton, Naissance | A. Mouton, Les rituels de naissance kizzuwatniens: un exemple de rite de passage en Anatolie hittite — Paris 2008 |
| —— Rêves | —— Rêves hittites: Contribution à une histoire et une anthropologie du rêve en Anatolie ancienne, (CHANE 28) — Leiden 2007 |
| —— | *see also* RMPH |
| Moyer, Diss. | J. Moyer, The Concept of Ritual Purity among the Hittites (diss., Brandeis University — 1969) |
| MRS | Mission de Ras Shamra — Paris |
| Msk | Siglum of texts from Meskene-Emar |
| MSL | B. Landsberger et al., Materialien zum sumerischen Lexikon —Rome |
| MSpr. | A. Götze and H. Pedersen, Muršilis Sprachlähmung (Det Kgl. Danske Videnskabernes Selskab, Historisk-filologiske Meddelelser 21/1) — Copenhagen 1934 |
| MSS | Münchener Studien zur Sprachwissenschaft — Munich |
| Mşt | Maşat text, cited by inventory number |
| Müller | *see* StBoT 60 |
| Muséon | Le Muséon — Louvain |
| MVAeG | Mitteilungen der Vorderasiatisch-ägyptischen Gesellschaft Leipzig |
| MVAG | Mitteilungen der Vorderasiatischen Gesellschaft — Leipzig |
| Myth. | *see* Laroche, Myth. |
| MZL$^2$ | R. Borger, — Mesopotamisches Zeichenlexikon, 2nd ed. (AOAT 305) — Münster 2010 |
| Nabnitu | lexical series SIG$_7$+ALAM = *nabnītu* |
| NABU | N.A.B.U. Nouvelles Assyriologiques Brèves et Utilitaires — Paris (cited as year:pages or year/article no.) |
| Nakamura, Diss. | M. Nakamura — Das hethitische nuntarrijašḫa-Fest (diss. Julius-Maximilians-Universität, Würzburg — 1993) |
| —— *Nuntarriyašḫa* | —— Das hethitische *nuntarriyašḫa*-Fest (PIHANS 94) — Leiden 2002 |
| Natural Phenomena | D. J. W. Meijer, ed., Natural Phenomena: Their Meaning, Depiction and Description in the Ancient Near East — Amsterdam 1992 |
| NAWG | Nachrichten der Akademie der Wissenschaften in Göttingen, philologisch-historische Klasse — Göttingen |
| NBC | Nies Babylonian Collection, Yale University |
| NBr | A. Götze, Neue Bruchstücke zum großen Text des Ḫattušiliš und den Paralleltexten (MVAeG 34.2) — Leipzig 1930 |
| NERT | W. Beyerlin, ed., Near Eastern Religious Texts relating to the Old Testament — Philadelphia 1978 (= tr. of RTAT) |
| Neu, Hurritische | E. Neu, Das Hurritische: Eine altorientalische Sprache in neuem Licht (AAWLM 1988 no. 3) — Mainz 1988 |
| —— Lok. | —— Studien zum endungslosen "Lokativ" des Hethitischen (IBS-VKS 23) — Innsbruck 1980 |

| | |
|---|---|
| —— | *see also* Heth.u.Idg., StBoT 5, 6, 12, 18, 21, 25, 26, 32, 35, 40, StBoT Beih. 2 |
| Neufeld, HL | E. Neufeld, The Hittite Laws — London 1951 |
| Neumann, Weiterleben | G. Neumann, Untersuchungen zum Weiterleben hethitischen und luwischen Sprachgutes in hellenistischer und römischer Zeit — Wiesbaden 1961 |
| Neve, Ḫattuša | P. Neve, Ḫattuša — Stadt der Götter und Tempel. Neue Ausgrabungen in der Hauptstadt der Hethiter (Antike Welt. Zeitschrift für Archäologie und Kulturgeschichte. 23. Jahrgang. Sondernummer 1992) — Mainz 1992 |
| New Horizons... Syria | M. Chavalas and J. Hayes, eds., New Horizons in the Study of Ancient Syria (BM 25) — Malibu 1992 |
| NF | Neue Folge |
| NH | E. Laroche, Les noms des Hittites — Paris 1966 |
| NH Suppl. | —— Les noms des Hittites: supplément, (Hethitica 4:3–58) — Louvain-la-Neuve 1981 |
| NHF | G. Walser, ed., Neuere Hethiterforschung (Historia Einzelschriften 7) — Wiesbaden 1964 |
| NHL | Neues Handbuch der Literaturwissenschaft |
| Nigga | lexical series nigga = *makkūru* (MSL 13:91–124) |
| NPN | I. J. Gelb, P. A. Purves, A. A. MacRae, Nuzi Personal Names (OIP 57) — Chicago 1943 |
| NS | Nova Series, New Series |
| NTS | Norsk Tidskrift for Sprogvidenskap — Oslo |
| OA | Oriens Antiquus — Rome |
| OAC | Orientis antiqui collectio — Rome |
| OAM | Orientis Antiqui Miscellanea — Rome |
| OBO | Orbis Biblicus et Orientalis — Göttingen |
| —— 129 | B. Janowski, K. Koch, G. Wilhelm, eds., Religionsgeschichtliche Beziehungen zwischen Kleinasien, Nordsyrien und dem Alten Testament (OBO 129) — Freibourg/Göttingen 1993 |
| OED | The Oxford English Dictionary — Oxford 1933 |
| Oettinger, "Indo-Hittite" -Hypothese | N. Oettinger, "Indo-Hittite"-Hypothese und Wortbildung (IBS-VKS 37) — Innsbruck 1986 |
| —— Stammbildung | —— Die Stammbildung des hethitischen Verbums (Erlanger Beiträge zur Sprach- und Kunstwissenschaft 64) — Nuremberg 1979 (reprinted as DBH 7) |
| —— | *see also* StBoT 22 |
| Offizielle Religion | M. Hutter and S. Hutter-Braunsar, eds., Offizielle Religion, lokale Kulte und individuelle Religiosität (AOAT 318) — Münster 2004 |
| OHP | B. H. L. van Gessel, The Onomasticon of the Hittite Pantheon (HbOr I/33) — Leiden 1998–2001 |
| OIP | Oriental Institute Publications — Chicago |
| OLA | Orientalia Lovaniensia Analecta — Louvain |
| OLP | Orientalia Lovaniensia Periodica — Louvain |
| OLZ | Orientalistische Literaturzeitung — Leipzig, Berlin |
| Oppenheim, Dreams | A. L. Oppenheim, The Interpretation of Dreams in the Ancient Near East (TAPS, NS 46.3) — Philadelphia 1956 |
| Or | Orientalia — Rome |
| Or. | Siglum of texts from Ortaköy-Šapinuwa |
| Oracles and Divination | M. Loewe and C. Blacker, eds., Oracles and Divination — Boulder 1981 |
| Oriens | Oriens. Journal of the International Society for Oriental Research — Leiden |
| OrS | Orientalia Suecana — Uppsala |
| Ose, Sup. | F. Ose, Supinum and Infinitiv im Hethitischen (MVAeG 47.1) — Leipzig 1944 |
| OT | Old Testament |
| Otten, Bronzetafel | H. Otten, Die 1986 in Boğazköy gefundene Bronzetafel. Zwei Vorträge (1. Ein hethitischer Staatsvertrag des 13. Jh. v. Chr.; 2. Zu den rechtlichen und religiösen Grundlagen des hethitischen Königtums) (IBS-VKS 42) — Innsbruck 1989 |
| —— Königshaus | —— Das hethitische Königshaus im 15. Jahrhundert v. Chr.: Zum Neufund einiger Landschenkungsurkunden in Boğazköy (AÖAW 123) — Vienna 1987 |
| —— Luv. | —— Zur grammatikalischen und lexikalischen Bestimmung des Luvischen (VIO 19) — Berlin 1953 |
| —— MGK | —— Mythen vom Gotte Kumarbi (VIO 3) — Berlin 1950 |

| | |
|---|---|
| —— Puduḫepa | —— Puduḫepa: Eine hethitische Königin in ihren Textzeugnissen (AAWLM 1975:1) — Mainz 1975 |
| —— Tel. | —— Die Überlieferungen des Telipinu-Mythus (MVAeG 46.1) — Leipzig 1942 |
| —— | *see also* HTR, LTU, StBoT 1, 7, 8, 11, 13, 15, 16, 17, 24, StBoT Beih. 1 |
| Özgüç, İnandıktepe | T. Özgüç, İnandıktepe, An important Cult Center in the Old Hittite Period (TTKYayın 5/43) — Ankara 1988 |
| Pap. | F. Sommer and H. Ehelolf, Das hethitische Ritual des Pāpanikri von Komana (BoSt 10) — Leipzig 1924 |
| Patri | *see* StBoT 49 |
| PD | E. Weidner, Politische Dokumente aus Kleinasien (BoSt 8–9) — Leipzig 1923 (1968) |
| PdP | Parola del Passato |
| Pecchioli Daddi | *see* LMI, Mestieri, StMed 14 |
| Pedersen, Hitt. | H. Pedersen, Hittitisch und die anderen indoeuropäischen Sprachen (Det Kongelige Danske Videnskabernes Selskab, Historisk-filologiske Meddelelser 25/2) — Copenhagen 1938 |
| —— Tocharisch | H. Pedersen, Tocharisch vom Gesichtspunkt der indoeuropäischen Sprachvergleichung (Det Danske Videnskabernes Selskab: Historisk-filologiske Meddelelser 28/1) — Copenhagen 1941 |
| Pestgeb. | A. Götze, Die Pestgebete des Muršiliš (KlF 1:161–251) — Weimar 1930 |
| PIHANS | Publications de l'Institut historique et archéologique néerlandais de Stamboul = Uitgaven van het Nederlands Historisch-Archaeologisch Instituut te Istanbul — Leiden |
| Plants | J. C. Th. Uphoff, Dictionary of Economic Plants — Lehre 1968 |
| Pluralismus | M. Hutter and S. Hutter-Braunsar, eds., Pluralismus und Wandel in den Religionen im vorhellenistischen Anatolien (AOAT 337) — Münster 2006 |
| Poetto | *see* StMed 3, 8 |
| Pokorny | J. Pokorny, Indogermanisches etymologisches Wörterbuch — Bern/Munich 1959, 1965–1969 |
| Polvani, Minerali | A. M. Polvani, La terminologia dei minerali nei testi ittiti. Parte prima (Eothen 3) — Florence 1988 |
| Popko, CTH 447 | M. Popko, Das hethitische Ritual CTH 447 — Warsaw 2003 |
| —— Kultobjekte | —— Kultobjekte in der hethitischen Religion (nach keilschriftlichen Quellen) — Warsaw 1978 |
| —— Religions | —— Religions of Asia Minor — Warsaw 1995 |
| —— | *see also* StBoT 50, THeth 21 |
| POT | D. J. Wiseman, ed., Peoples of Old Testament Times — Oxford 1973 |
| Potratz | H. A. Potratz, Das Pferd in der Frühzeit — Rostock 1938 |
| POTW | A. J. Hoerth, ed., Peoples of the Old Testament World — Grand Rapids 1994 |
| Pouvoirs locaux | A. Finet, ed., Les pouvoirs locaux en Mésopotamie et dans les régions adjacents (Colloquium Jan. 28–29, 1980) — Brussels 1982 |
| PP 1, 2, 3, 4 | 1st, 2nd, 3rd, 4th Plague Prayers of Muršili II, ed. Pestgeb. |
| Practical Vocabulary Assur | lexical text (Landsberger/Gurney, AfO 18:328–41) |
| Pragmatische Kategorien | Pragmatische Kategorien: Form, Funktion und Diachronie. Akten der Arbeitstagung der Indogermanischen Gesellschaft vom 24. bis 26 September 2007 im Marburg — Wiesbaden 2009 |
| Prechel, Išḫara | D. Prechel, Die Göttin Išḫara (ALASP 11) — Münster 1996 |
| Prins, Neut.Sg. | A. Prins, Hittite Neuter Singular—Neuter Plural: Some Evidence for a Connection — Leiden 1997 |
| Proto-Diri | *see* Diri |
| Proto-Ea | *see* Ea (MSL 2:35–94) |
| Proto-Izi | lexical series (MSL 13:7–59) |
| Proto-Kagal | lexical series (MSL 13:63–88) |
| Proto-Lu | lexical series (MSL 12:25–84) |
| PRU | Le palais royal d'Ugarit (subseries of MRS) — Paris 1955ff. |
| PSD | The Sumerian Dictionary of the University Museum of the University of Pennsylvania — Philadelphia 1984ff. |
| Quattro studi ittiti | Quattro studi ittiti (Eothen 4) — Florence 1991 |
| RA | Revue d'Assyriologie et d'Archéologie orientale — Paris |

| | |
|---|---|
| RAI | Rencontre Assyriologique Internationale (when a date is given it is the date of the conference, not the date of publication), *also* CRRAI |
| —— 1 | (1950, Paris) Comptes rendus de la première Rencontre Assyriologique Internationale — Leiden 1951 |
| —— 2 | (1951, Paris) Compte rendu de la seconde Recontre Assyriologique Internationale — Paris 1951 |
| —— 3 | (1952, Leiden) Compte rendu de la troisième Recontre Assyriologique Internationale, Leiden (Nederlands Instituut voor het Nabije Oosten) 1954. |
| —— 4 | (1953, Paris) Le problème des Habiru à la 4e Recontre Assyriologique Internationale (Cahiers de la Société Asiatique 13) — Paris 1954 |
| —— 5 | (1955, Paris) (no volume published) |
| —— 6 | (1956, Paris) (no volume published) |
| —— 7 | (1958, Paris) Gilgamesh et sa légende – Études recueillies par Paul Garelli à l'occasion de la VIIe Rencontre Assyriologique Internationale (Paris – 1958) (Cahiers du Groupe François-Thureau-Dangin) — Paris 1960 |
| —— 8 | (1959, Heidelberg) (no volume published) |
| —— 9 | (1960, Geneva) Aspects du contact suméro-akkadien, Geneva, N.S. 8 (1960) 241–314. |
| —— 10 | (1961, Paris) (no volume published) |
| —— 11 | (1962, Leiden) Compte rendu de l'onzième Recontre Assyriologique Internationale (Publications de l'Institut Néerlandais pour le Proche-Orient à Leiden 2) — 1964 |
| —— 12 | (1963, London) Warfare in the Ancient Near East, see Iraq 25 (1963) 110–93. |
| —— 13 | (1964, Paris) Vox populi, see RA 58 (1964) 149–84 |
| —— 14 | (1965, Strasbourg) La divination en Mésopotamie ancienne et dans les régions voisines — Paris 1966 |
| —— 15 | (1966, Liège) La civilisation de Mari, (Bibliothèque de la Faculté de Philosophie et Lettres de l'Université de Liège 182) — Paris 1967 |
| —— 16 | (1967, Chicago), see JNES 27 (1968) 161–261 |
| —— 17 | (1969, Brussels) Actes de la XVIIe Rencontre Assyriologique Internationale — Ham-sur-Heure 1970 |
| —— 18 | (1970, Munich) Gesellschaftsklassen im Alten Zweistromland und in den angrenzenden Gebieten (ABAW NF 75) — Munich 1972 |
| —— 19 | (1971, Paris) Le Palais et la Royauté (Archéologie et Civilisation) — Paris 1974 |
| —— 20 | (1972, Leiden) Le Temple et le Culte (PIHANS 37) — Leiden 1975 |
| —— 21 | (1974, Rome) Études sur le Panthéon systématique et les Panthéons locaux, see Or NS 45 (1976) 1–226 |
| —— 22 | (1975, Göttingen) (no volume published) |
| —— 23 | (1976, Birmingham) Trade in the Ancient Near East, see Iraq 29 (1977) 1–231 |
| —— 24 | (1977, Paris) Actes de la XXIVe Rencontre Assyriologique Internationale, Paris 1977 – Les Hourrites, see RHA XXXVI (1978) |
| —— 25 | (1978, Berlin) Mesopotamien und seine Nachbarn. Politische und kulturelle Wechselbeziehungen im Alten Vorderasien vom 4. bis 1. Jahrtausend v. Chr. (BBVO 1) — Berlin 1982 |
| —— 26 | (1979, Copenhagen) Death in Mesopotamia, XXVIe Rencontre assyriologique internationale (Mesopotamia 8) — Copenhagen 1980 |
| —— 27 | (1980, Paris) La Syrie au Bronze Récent, Cinquantenaire d'Ougarit – Ras Shamra (Extraits de la XXVIIe R.A.I., Paris 1980) (Editions Recherche sur les civilisations, Mémoire no. 15) — Paris 1982 |
| —— 28 | (1981, Vienna) Vorträge gehalten auf der 28. Rencontre Assyriologique Internationale in Wien 6.–10. Juli 1981 (AfO Beiheft 19) — Horn 1982 |
| —— 29 | (1982, London) XXIX Rencontre Assyriologique Internationale, London, 5th–9th July 1982, see Iraq 45 (1983) 1–164 |
| —— 30 | (1983, Leiden) Cuneiform Archives and Libraries. Papers read at the 30e Rencontre Assyriologique Internationale Leiden, 4–8 July 1983 — (PIHANS 57) — Leiden 1986 |
| —— 31 | (1984, Leningrad) (no volume published) |

—— 32 (1985, Münster) Keilschriftliche Literaturen. Ausgewählte Vorträge der XXXII. Rencontre Assyriologique Internationale (BBVO 6) — Berlin 1986

—— 33 (1986, Paris) La Femme dans le Proche-Orient antique. XXXIIIe Rencontre Assyriologique Internationale (Paris, 7–10 juillet 1986) (Editions Recherche sur les Civilisations) — Paris 1987

—— 34 (1987, Istanbul) XXXIVème Rencontre Assyriologique Internationale – XXXIV. Uluslararası Assiriyoloji Kongresi (TTK-Yayın 26 Dizi Sa. 3) — Ankara 1998

—— 35 (1988, Philadelphia) Nippur at the Centennial. Papers Read at the 35e Rencontre Assyriologique Internationale, Philadelphia, 1988 (Occasional Publications of the Samuel Noah Kramer Fund 14) — Philadelphia 1992

—— 36 (1989, Ghent) Mésopotamie et Elam. Actes de la XXXVIème Rencontre Assyriologique Internationale, Gand, 10–14 juillet 1989 (Mesopotamian History and Environment, Occasional Publications 1) — Ghent 1991

—— 38 (1991, Paris) La circulation des biens, des personnes et des idées dans le Proche-Orient ancien. Actes de la XXXVIIIe Rencontre Assyriologique Internationale (Paris, 8–10 juillet 1991) (Editions Recherche sur les Civilisations) — Paris 1992

—— 39 (1992, Heidelberg) Assyrien im Wandel der Zeiten. XXXIXe Rencontre Assyriologique Internationale, Heidelberg, 6.–10. Juli 1992 (Heidelberger Studien zum Alten Orient 6) — Heidelberg 1997

—— 40 (1993, Leiden) Houses and Households in Ancient Mesopotamia. Papers read at the 40th Rencontre Assyriologique Internationale, Leiden, July 5–8, 1993 (PIHANS 78) — Leiden 1996

—— 41 (1994, Berlin) Landwirtschaft im Alten Orient. Ausgewählte Vorträge der XLI. Rencontre Assyriologique Internationale, Berlin, 4.–8.7.1994 (BBVO 18) — 1999

—— 42 (1995, Louvain) Languages and Cultures in Contact. At the Crossroads of Civilizations in the Syro-Mesopotamian Realm. Proceedings of the 42th RAI (OLA 96) — Louvain 2001

—— 43 (1996, Prague) Intellectual Life of the Ancient Near East. Papers Presented at the 43rd Rencontre Assyriologique Internationale, Prague, July 1–5, 1996 — Prague 1998

—— 44 (1997, Venice) Landscapes, Territories, Frontiers and Horizons in the Ancient Near East. Papers Presented to the XLIV Rencontre Assyriologique Internationale Venezia, 7–11 July, 1997 (History of the Ancient Near East / Monographs 3/1–3) — Padua 1999

—— 45 (1998, Cambridge & New Haven) Proceedings of the XLVe Rencontre Assyriologique Internationale — Bethesda 2001

—— 46 (2000, Paris) Nomades et sédentaires dans le Proche-Orient ancien. Compte rendu de la XLVIe Rencontre Assyriologique Internationale, Paris, 10–13 juillet 2000 (Amurru 3, Editions Recherche sur les Civilisations) — Paris, 2004

—— 47 (2001, Helsinki & Tartu) Sex and Gender in the Ancient Near East. Proceedings of the 47th Rencontre Assyriologique Internationale, Helsinki, July 2-6, 2001 — Helsinki 2002

—— 48 (2002, Leiden) Ethnicity in Ancient Mesopotamia. Papers read at the 48th Rencontre Assyriologique Internationale, Leiden, July 1–4, 2002 (PIHANS 102) — Leiden 2005

—— 49 (2003, London) Nineveh: Papers of the XLIXe Rencontre Assyriologique Internationale, London, 7–11 July 2003 see Iraq 66 (2004) and 67/1 (2005)

—— 50 (2004, Skukuza) RAI 50 Skukuza, South Africa 1–6 August 2004 (Tydskrif vir Semitistiek 16/3) — Pretoria 2007

—— 51 (2005, Chicago) Proceedings of the 51st Rencontre Assyriologique Internationale, Held at the Oriental Institute of the University of Chicago, July 18–22, 2005 (SAOC 62) — Chicago 2008

—— 52 (2006, Münster) Krieg und Frieden (AOAT 401) — Münster 2014

—— 53 (2007, Moscow & St. Petersburg) Proceedings of the 53e Rencontre Assyriologique Internationale vol. 1: Language in the Ancient Near East (Babel und Bibel 4); vol. 2: City Administration in the Ancient Near East (Babel und Bibel 5) — Winona Lake 2010

| | |
|---|---|
| —— 54 | (2008, Würzburg) Organization, Representation and Symbols of Power in the Ancient Near East — Winona Lake 2012 |
| —— 55 | (2009, Paris) La famille dans le Proche-Orient ancien: réalités, symbolismes et images — Winona Lake 2014 |
| —— 56 | (2010, Barcelona) Time and History in the Ancient Near East — Winona Lake 2013 |
| —— 57 | (2011, Rome) Tradition and Innovation in the Ancient Near East — Winona Lake 2014 |
| —— 58 | (2012, Leiden) Private and State in the Ancient Near East — Winona Lake 2017 |
| —— 59 | (2013, Ghent) (forthcoming) |
| —— 60 | (2014, Warsaw) Fortune and Misfortune in the Ancient Near East — Winona Lake 2017 |
| —— 61 | (2015, Geneva & Bern) Text and Image: Proceedings of the 61e Rencontre Assyriologique Internationale, Geneva and Bern, 22–26 June 2015 (OBO Series Archaeologica 40) — Louvain 2018. |
| —— 62 | (2016, Philadelphia) (forthcoming) |
| —— 63 | (2017, Marburg) (forthcoming) |
| —— 64 | (2018, Innsbruck) (forthcoming) |
| RANT | Res Antiquae — Brussels |
| RAW | S. I. Johnston, ed., Religions of the Ancient World: A Guide — Cambridge, Massachusetts 2004 |
| Records | Ph. H. J. Houwink ten Cate, The Records of the Early Hittite Empire (c. 1450–1380 B.C.) (PIHANS 26) — Leiden 1970 |
| Relig.Bez. | B. Janowski et al., eds., Religionsgeschichtliche Beziehungen zwischen Kleinasien, Nordsyrien und dem Alten Testament am 2. und 1. vorchristlichen Jahrtausend: Akten des Internationalen Symposions. Hamburg 17–21 März 1990 (OBO 129) — Fribourg & Göttingen 1993 |
| Religions of Antiquity | Religions of Antiquity (Religion, History, and Culture. Selections from The Encyclopedia of Religion) — New York 1989 |
| RGTC | Répertoire Géographique des Textes Cunéiformes (Tübinger Atlas des Vorderen Orients Beihefte Reihe B7) — Wiesbaden |
| —— 6 | G. F. del Monte and J. Tischler, Die Orts- und Gewässernamen der hethitischen Texte — 1978 |
| —— 6/2 | G. F. del Monte, Die Orts- und Gewässernamen der hethitischen Texte Supplement — 1992 |
| RHA | Revue hittite et asianique — Paris |
| RHR | Revue de l'histoire des religions — Paris |
| Richter | *see* BibGlHurr |
| RIDA | Revue internationale des droits de l'antiquité, 3rd series — Brussels |
| Riedel | W. Riedel, Bemerkungen zu den hethitischen Keilschrifttafeln aus Boghazköi — Stockholm 1949 (mimeographed) |
| Rieken | E. Rieken, Einführung in die hethitische Sprache und Schrift (Lehrbücher orientalischer Sprache 1: Cuneiform Languages 2) — Münster 2011 |
| —— | *see also* StBoT 44, 63 |
| Riemschneider, Omentexte | K. Riemschneider, Die hethitischen und akkadischen Omentexte aus Boğazköy (unpub. ms. in Oriental Institute), now rearranged and published as DBH 12 |
| —— | *see also* DBH 12, HHT, LS, StBoT 9 |
| RIL | Rendiconti: Istituto Lombardo Accademia di Scienze e Lettere, Classe di Lettere e Scienze Morali e Storiche — Milan |
| RlA | Reallexikon der Assyriologie und Vorderasiatischen Archäologie — Berlin |
| RMPH | A. Mouton, Rituels/Rites, Mythes et Prières Hittites (LAPO 21) — Paris 2016 |
| RO | Rocznik Orientalistyczny — Warsaw |
| de Roos, Diss. | J. de Roos, Hettitische Geloften: Een teksteditie van Hettitische geloften met inleiding, vertaling en critische noten (diss., Universiteit van Amsterdam — 1984) |
| —— Votive | —— Hittite Votive Texts (PIHANS 109) — Istanbul 2007 |
| Rosenkranz, Luv. | B. Rosenkranz, Beiträge zur Erforschung des Luvischen — Wiesbaden 1952 |
| Rost | *see* Jakob-Rost |
| Roszkowska-Mutschler | *see* DBH 16, 24 |
| Roth | *see* LawColl |
| RPO | R. Labat, ed., Les religions du Proche-Orient asiatique: Textes babyloniens, ougaritiques, hittites — Paris 1970 (Hittite texts tr. M. Vieyra) |
| RS | Ras Shamra text, cited by inventory number |

| | |
|---|---|
| RSO | Rivista degli Studi Orientali — Rome |
| RTAT | W. Beyerlin, ed., Grundrisse zum Alten Testament 1: Religionsgeschichtliches Textbuch zum Alten Testament — Göttingen 1975 (Hittite texts tr. C. Kühne) |
| Rüster | *see* HZL, StBoT 20, 21, 35, 40, StBoT Beih. 4 |
| S[a] | lexical series Syllabary A (MSL 3:3–45) |
| S[a] Voc. | lexical series Syllabary A Vocabulary (MSL 3:51–87) |
| Sachs Mem. | A Scientific Humanist: Studies in Memory of Abraham Sachs — Philadelphia 1988 |
| SAG 1 instr. | instructions for LÚ.MEŠ.SAG = CTH 255.2, ed. Dienstanw. 8–21 |
| SAG 2 instr. | instructions for princes, lords and LÚ.MEŠ. SAG CTH 255.1, ed. Dienstanw. 22–34 |
| Sakuma, Diss. | Hethitische Vogelorakeltexte (diss. Julius-Maximilians-Universität, Würzburg — 2009) |
| Salisbury, Diss. | D. Salisbury, Local Adverbs in Hittite (diss., University of North Carolina at Chapel Hill — 2005) |
| Salonen, Agric. | A Salonen, Agricultura Mesopotamica nach sumerisch-akkadischen Quellen (AASF B 149) — Helsinki 1968 |
| Salvatori | *see* StMed 3 |
| Salvini | *see* ChS I/2 |
| SAOC | Studies in Ancient Oriental Civilization — Chicago |
| Savaş, Madencilik | S. Ö. Savaş, Çivi Yazılı Belgeler Işığında Anadolu'da (İ.Ö.2.Bin Yılında) Madencilik ve Maden Kullanımı — Ankara 2006 |
| S[b] | lexical series Syllabary B (MSL 3:96–128, 132–153) |
| SBo | H. G. Güterbock, Siegel aus Boğazköy I, II (AfO Beiheft 5, 7) — Berlin 1940, 1942 (1967) |
| SCCNH | Studies in the Culture and Civilization of Nuzi and the Hurrians — Winona Lake |
| Scheucher, Diss. | The Transmissional and Functional Context of the Lexical Lists from Ḫattuša and from the Contemporaneous Traditions in Late-Bronze-Age Syria (diss., Universiteit Leiden — 2012) |
| Schimmel | Ancient Art: The Norbert Schimmel Collection — Mainz 1974 |
| Schrijvend Verleden | K. R. Veenhof, ed., Schrijvend verleden: Documenten uit het oude Nabije Oosten vertaald en toegelicht — Leiden 1983 |
| von Schuler | *see* Dienstanw., Kaškäer |
| Schuster | *see* HHB |
| Schw.Gotth. | H. Kronasser, Die Umsiedelung der schwarzen Gottheit: Das hethitische Ritual KUB XXIX 4 (des Ulippi) (SÖAW 241.3) — Vienna 1963 |
| Schwartz Mem. | A Linguistic Happening in Memory of Ben Schwartz — Louvain-la-Neuve 1988 |
| Schwemer | *see* THeth 23 |
| SCO | Studi Classici e Orientali — Pisa |
| SEL | Studi Epigrafici e Linguistici — Verona |
| SEV | Studi Egei e Vicinorientali — Paris |
| Siegelová, Eisen | J. Siegelová, "Gewinnung und Verarbeitung von Eisen im hethitischen Reich im 2. Jahrtausend v. u. Z." (Annals of the Náprstek Museum 12, pp. 71–168) — Prague 1984 |
| —— Verw. | —— Hethitische Verwaltungspraxis im Lichte der Wirtschafts- und Inventardokumente — Prague 1986 |
| —— | *see also* StBoT 14 |
| Sign. lyr. | The trilingual composition entitled Signalement lyrique, ed. Nougayrol, Ugar. 5 (= MRS 16) pp. 444–45, 310–19, and Laroche, Ugar. 5 pp. 773–79 — Paris 1968 |
| Silbenvokabular | lexical series |
| Singer, Diss. | I. Singer, The Hittite KI.LAM Festival (diss., University of Tel Aviv — 1978) |
| —— Muw.Pr. | —— Muwatalli's Prayer to the Assembly of Gods through the Storm-God of Lightning (CTH 381) — Atlanta 1996 |
| —— | *see also* Hittite Prayers, StBoT 27, 28 |
| SkSw | Sprachkontakt und Sprachwandel: Akten der XI. Fachtagung der Indogermanischen Gesellschaft, 17.–23. September 2000 — Wiesbaden 2005 |
| ŠL | A. Deimel, Šumerisches Lexikon — Rome 1925–1950 |
| SMEA | Studi micenei ed egeo-anatolici — Rome |
| SMSR | Studi e materiali di storia delle religioni — Rome |
| SÖAW | Sitzungsberichte der österreichischen Akademie der Wissenschaft, philosophisch-historische Klasse — Vienna |

| | |
|---|---|
| von Soden | *see* AHw, GAG, StBoT 7 |
| von Soden/ Röllig, Syll. | W. von Soden and W. Röllig, Das akkadische Syllabar, 2nd ed. with suppl. (AnOr 42/42a) — Rome 1967, 1976 |
| Sommer, AS | F. Sommer, Aḫḫijavāfrage und Sprachwissenschaft (ABAW, NF 9) — Munich 1934 |
| —— Heth. | —— Hethitisches 1, 2 (BoSt 4, 7) — Leipzig 1920, 1922 |
| —— HuH | —— Hethiter und Hethitisch — Stuttgart 1947 |
| —— | *see also* AU |
| Sommer/Ehelolf | *see* Pap. |
| Sommer/Falkenstein | *see* HAB |
| Souček | *see* StBoT 1, 8 |
| Soysal, Diss. | O. Soysal, Muršili I. Eine historische Studie (diss., Julius-Maximilians-Universität, Würzburg — 1989) |
| —— | *see also* HWHT |
| SPAW | Sitzungsberichte der Preussischen Akademie der Wissenschaften, philosophisch-historische Klasse — Berlin |
| Speiser, Intr. | E. A. Speiser, Introduction to Hurrian (AASOR 20) — New Haven 1941 |
| Sprache | *see* Die Sprache |
| Sprache&Kultur | Sprache und Kultur der Indogermanen: Akten der X. Fachtagung der Indogermanischen Gesellschaft: Innsbruck, 22.–28. September 1996 (IBS 93) — Innsbruck 1998 |
| Sprachkontakt& Sprachwandel | Sprachkontakt und Sprachwandel: Akten der XI. Fachtagung der Indogermanischen Gesellschaft, 17.–23. September 2000, Halle an der Saale — Wiesbaden 2005 |
| SR | Studi e Ricerche — Florence |
| Starke | *see* StBoT 23, 30, 31, 41 |
| StAs | Studia Asiana — Rome, Florence |
| —— 2 | *see* Torri, Magia |
| —— 3 | F. Pecchioli Daddi and M. C. Guidotti, eds., Narrare gli eventi: Atti del convegno degli egittologi e degli orientalisti italiani in margine all mostra "La Battaglia di Qadesh" — Rome 2005 |
| —— 5 | F. Pecchioli Daddi, et al., eds., Central-North Anatolia in the Hittite Period: New Perspectives in Light of Recent Research: Acts of the International Conference Held at the University of Florence (7–9 February 2007) — Rome 2009 |
| —— 9 | Sacred Landscapes of the Hittites and Luwians: Proceedings of the International Conference in Honour of Franca Pecchioli Daddi — Florence 2015 |
| —— 12 | F. Barsacchi, Le feste ittite del tuono: Edizione critica di CTH 631 — Florence 2017 |
| Stato, economia lavoro | S. Allam et al., eds., Stato, economia e lavoro nel Vicino Oriente Antico — Milan 1988 |
| StBoT | Studien zu den Boğazköy Texten — Wiesbaden |
| —— 1 | H. Otten and V. Souček, Das Gelübde der Königin Puduḫepa an die Göttin Lelwani — 1965 |
| —— 2 | O. Carruba, Das Beschwörungsritual für die Göttin Wišurijanza — 1966 |
| —— 3 | H. M. Kümmel, Ersatzrituale für den hethitischen König — 1967 |
| —— 4 | R. Werner, Hethitische Gerichtsprotokolle — 1967 |
| —— 5 | E. Neu, Interpretation der hethitischen mediopassiven Verbalformen — 1968 |
| —— 6 | E. Neu, Das hethitische Mediopassiv und seine indogermanischen Grundlagen — 1968 |
| —— 7 | H. Otten and W. von Soden, Das akkadisch-hethitische Vokabular KBo I 44 + KBo XIII 1 — 1968 |
| —— 8 | H. Otten and V. Souček, Ein althethitisches Ritual für das Königspaar — 1969 |
| —— 9 | K. K. Riemschneider, Babylonische Geburtsomina in hethitischer Übersetzung — 1970 |
| —— 10 | O. Carruba, Das Palaische: Texte, Grammatik, Lexikon — 1970 |
| —— 11 | H. Otten, Sprachliche Stellung und Datierung des Madduwatta-Textes — 1969 |
| —— 12 | E. Neu, Ein althethitisches Gewitterritual — 1970 |
| —— 13 | H. Otten, Ein hethitisches Festritual (KBo XIX 128) — 1971 |
| —— 14 | J. Siegelová, Appu-Märchen und Ḫedammu-Mythus — 1971 |
| —— 15 | H. Otten, Materialien zum hethitischen Lexikon — 1971 |
| —— 16 | C. Kühne and H. Otten, Der Šaušgamuwa-Vertrag — 1971 |

| | |
|---|---|
| — 17 | H. Otten, Eine althethitische Erzählung um die Stadt Zalpa — 1973 |
| — 18 | E. Neu, Der Anitta-Text — 1974 |
| — 19 | C. Burde, Hethitische medizinische Texte — 1974 |
| — 20 | C. Rüster, Hethitische Keilschrift-Paläographie — 1972 |
| — 21 | E. Neu and C. Rüster, Hethitische Keilschrift-Paläographie II — 1975 |
| — 22 | N. Oettinger, Die militärischen Eide der Hethiter — 1976 |
| — 23 | F. Starke, Die Funktionen der dimensionalen Kasus und Adverbien im Althethitischen — 1977 |
| — 24 | H. Otten, Die Apologie Hattusilis III. Das Bild der Überlieferung — 1981 |
| — 25 | E. Neu, Althethitische Ritualtexte in Umschrift — 1980 |
| — 26 | E. Neu, Glossar zu den althethitischen Ritualtexten — 1983 |
| — 27 | I. Singer, The Hittite KI.LAM Festival. Part One — 1983 |
| — 28 | I. Singer, The Hittite KI.LAM Festival. Part Two — 1984 |
| — 29 | G. M. Beckman, Hittite Birth Rituals, 2nd revised ed. — 1983 |
| — 30 | F. Starke, Die keilschrift-luwischen Texte in Umschrift — 1985 |
| — 31 | F. Starke, Untersuchung zur Stammbildung des keilschriftluwischen Nomens — 1990 |
| — 32 | E. Neu, Das hurritische Epos der Freilassung I: Untersuchungen zu einem hurritisch-hethitischen Textensemble aus Ḫattuša — 1996 |
| — 34 | S. Košak, Konkordanz der Keilschrifttafeln I. Die Texte der Grabung 1931 — 1992 |
| — 35 | Chr. Rüster and E. Neu, Deutsch-Sumerographisches Wörterverzeichnis — 1991 |
| — 36 | G. Wilhelm, Medizinische Omina aus Ḫattuša in akkadischer Sprache — 1994 |
| — 37 | J. Klinger, Untersuchungen zur Rekonstruktion der hattischen Kultschicht — 1996 |
| — 38 | Th. van den Hout, Der Ulmitešub-Vertrag: Eine prosopographische Untersuchung — 1995 |
| — 39 | S. Košak, Konkordanz der Keilschrifttafeln II. Die Texte der Grabung 1932 — 1995 |
| — 40 | Chr. Rüster and E. Neu, Konträr-Index der hethitischen Keilschriftzeichen — 1993 |
| — 41 | F. Starke, Ausbildung und Training von Streitwagenpferden: Eine hippologisch orientierte Interpretation des Kikkuli-Textes — 1995 |
| — 44 | E. Rieken, Untersuchungen zur nominalen Stammbildung des Hethitischen — 1999 |
| — 45 | Akten des IV. Internationalen Kongresses für Hethitologie — 2001 |
| — 46 | J. Miller, Studies in the Origins, Development and Interpretation of the Kizzuwatna Rituals — 2004 |
| — 47 | P. Dardano, Die hethitischen Tontafelkataloge aus Ḫattuša (CTH 276–282) — 2006 |
| — 48 | B. Christiansen, Die Ritualtradition der Ambazzi — 2006 |
| — 49 | S. Patri, L'alignement syntaxique dans les langues indo-européennes d'Anatolie — 2007 |
| — 50 | M. Popko, Arinna, Eine heilige Stadt der Hethiter — 2009 |
| — 51 | *see* FsSinger |
| — 52 | *see* GsNeu |
| — 53 | B. Christiansen, Schicksalsbestimmende Kommunikation: Sprachliche, gesellschaftliche und religiöse Aspekte hethitischer Fluch-, Segens- und Eidesformeln |
| — 54 | M. Weeden, Hittite Logograms and Hittite Scholarship — 2011 |
| — 55 | P. Goedegebuure, The Hittite Demonstratives: Studies in Deixis, Topics and Focus — 2014 |
| — 56 | A. Kloekhorst, Accent in Hittite: A Study in Plene Spelling, Consonant Gradation, Clitics and Metrics — 2014 |
| — 57 | W. Waal, Hittite Diplomatics: Studies in Ancient Document Format and Record Management — 2015 |
| — 58 | *see* GsOtten |
| — 59 | Sh. Gordin, Hittite Scribal Circles: Scholarly Tradition and Writing Habits — 2015 |
| — 60 | G. Müller, Liturgie oder Literatur? Die Kultrituale der Hethiter im transkulturellen Vergleich — 2016 |

| | |
|---|---|
| —— 61 | P. Taracha, Two Festivals Celebrated by a Hittite Prince (CTH 647 I & II–III): New Light on the Local Cults of North-Central Anatolia in the Second Millennium B.C. — 2017 |
| —— 62 | Ch. Steitler, The Solar Deities of Bronze Age Anatolia: Studies in Texts of the Early Hittite Kingdom — 2017 |
| —— 63 | A. Daues and E. Rieken, Das persönliche Gebet bei den Hethitern: Eine textlinguistische Untersuchung — 2018 |
| —— 64 | G. Wilhelm, Kleine Beiträge zum Hurritischen — 2018 |
| StBoT Beih. | Studien zu den Boğazköy-Texten. Beiheft — Wiesbaden |
| —— 1 | H. Otten, Die Bronzetafel aus Boğazköy: Ein Staatsvertrag Tutḫalijas IV. — 1988 |
| —— 2 | *see* HZL |
| —— 3 | J. D. Hawkins, The Hieroglyphic Inscription of the Sacred Pool Complex at Hattusa (SÜDBURG) — 1995 |
| —— 4 | Chr. Rüster and G. Wilhelm, Landschenkungsurkunden hethitischer Könige — 2012 |
| —— 5 | A. de Vos, Die Lebermodelle aus Boğazköy — 2013 |
| STC | L. W. King, The Seven Tablets of Creation — London 1902 |
| Stefanini, Pud. | R. Stefanini, Una lettera della regina Puduhepa al re di Alasija (KUB XXI 38) (AttiAccTosc. 29:3–69) — Florence 1964–1965 |
| Steitler | *see* StBoT 62 |
| StMed | Studia Mediterranea — Pavia |
| ——1–2 | Studia Mediterranea Piero Meriggi dicata — 1979 |
| —— 3 | M. Poetto and S. Salvatori, La collezione anatolica di E. Borowski — 1981 |
| —— 4 | Studi orientalistici in ricordo di Franco Pintore — 1983 |
| —— 5 | D. Sürenhagen, Paritätische Staatsverträge aus hethitischer Sicht — 1985 |
| —— 6 | C. Mora, La glittica anatolica del II millennio A. C. Classificazione tipologica — 1987 |
| —— 7 | Per una grammatica ittita. Towards a Hittite Grammar — 1992 |
| —— 8 | M. Poetto, L'iscrizione Luvio-Geroglifica di *Yalburt* — 1993 |
| —— 9 | Atti del II Congresso Internazionale di Hittitologia — 1995 |
| —— 11 | O. Carruba, Analecta Linguistica Anatolica — 1997 |
| —— 12 | St. de Martino, Annali e Res Gestae Antico Ittiti — 2003 |
| —— 13 | O. Carruba, Anittae Res Gestae — 2003 |
| —— 14 | F. Pecchioli Daddi, Il vincolo per i governatori di provincia — 2003 |
| —— 15 | O. Carruba, Analecta Philologica Anatolica — 2005 |
| —— 16 | E. Devecchi, Gli Annali di Ḫattušili I nella versione accadica — 2005 |
| —— 17 | L. D'Alfonso, Le procedure giudiziarie ittite in Siria (XII sec. a. C.) — 2005 |
| —— 18 | O. Carruba, Annali etei del Medio Regno — 2008 |
| —— 19 | G. Holland/M. Zorman, The Tale of Zalpa: Myth, Morality and Coherence in a Hittite Myth — 2007 |
| —— 20 | A. Rizza, I pronomi enclitici nei testi etei di traduzione dal hattico — 2007 |
| —— 23 | M.E. Balza et al., eds., Archivi, depositi, magazzini presso gli ittiti — 2012 |
| —— 24 | *see* FsCarruba |
| Stol, On Trees | M. Stol, On Trees, Mountains and Millstones in the Ancient Near East, (Mededelingen en verhandelingen van het Vooraziatisch-Egyptisch Genootschap "Ex Oriente Lux" 21) — Leiden 1979 |
| StOr | Studia Orientalia (Societas Orientalis Fennica) — Helsinki |
| Strauß, Reinigung | R. Strauß, Reinigungsrituale aus Kizzuwatna — Berlin 2006 |
| Studia Troica | Studia Troica — Mainz |
| Stud.Pohl | Studia Pohl — Rome |
| Sturtevant, CGr | E. H. Sturtevant, A Comparative Grammar of the Hittite Language — Philadelphia 1933; 2nd ed., vol. 1 — New Haven 1951 |
| —— Gl. | —— A Hittite Glossary, 2nd ed. — Philadelphia 1936 |
| —— Suppl. | —— Supplement to A Hittite Glossary — Philadelphia 1939 |
| —— | *see also* Chrest. |

| | |
|---|---|
| Süel, Direktif Metni | A. Süel, Hitit Kaynaklarında Tapınak Görevlileri İle İlgili Bir Direktif Metni (AnYayın 350) — Ankara 1985 |
| —— | *see also* Eothen 21, 22 |
| Sürenhagen, Staatsv. | *see* StMed 5 |
| SV | J. Friedrich, Staatsverträge des Ḫatti-Reiches in hethitischer Sprache (MVAeG 31.1, 34.1) — Leipzig 1926, 1930 |
| Symb.Böhl | Symbolae biblicae et Mesopotamicae Francisco Mario Theodoro de Liagre Böhl dedicatae — Leiden 1973 |
| Symb.Hrozný | Symbolae Hrozný. Symbolae ad studia Orientis pertinentes Fr. Hrozný dedicatae (ArOr 17–18) — Prague 1941–1950 |
| Symb.Koschaker | Symbolae Koschaker, Symbolae ad iura Orientis Antiqui pertinentes P. Koschaker dedicatae — Leiden 1939 |
| Szabó | *see* THeth 1 |
| SZM | inventory number of the Szépmüveszeti Múzeum, Budapest |
| TAD | Türk Arkeoloji Dergisi — Ankara |
| Taggar-Cohen | *see* THeth 26 |
| TAM | Tituli Asiae Minoris — Vienna |
| TAM Erg. 14 | G. Dobesch and G. Rehrenböck, Die epigraphische und altertumskundliche Erforschung Kleinasiens (DÖAW 236) — Vienna 1993 |
| TAPA | Transactions of the American Philological Association |
| TAPS | Transactions of the American Philosophical Society — Philadelphia |
| Taracha, Ersetzen | P. Taracha, Ersetzen und Entsühnen: Das mittelhethitische Ersatzritual für den Großkönig Tutḫalija (CTH *448.4) und verwandte Texte (CHANE 5) — Leiden 2000 |
| —— | *see also* StBoT 61 |
| Targ. | Treaty of Muršili II with Targašnalli, ed. SV 1:51–94 |
| Taş | *see* DBH 43 |
| Taw. | Tawagalawa letter, ed. AU |
| TCL | Musée du Louvre, Département des Antiquités Orientales; Textes Cunéiformes — Paris |
| TCS | Texts from Cuneiform Sources — Locust Valley, New York |
| Tel Aviv | Tel Aviv. Journal of the Tel Aviv University Institute of Archaeology — Tel Aviv |
| Tel.myth | Telipinu myth |
| Tel.pr | Telipinu proclamation |
| Temple Building | M. J. Boda and J. Novotny, eds., From the Foundations to the Crenellations: Essays on Temple Building in the Ancient Near East and the Hebrew Bible, AOAT 366 — Münster 2010 |
| THeth | Texte der Hethiter — Heidelberg |
| —— 1 | G. Szabó, Ein hethitisches Entsühnungsritual für das Königspaar Tutḫaliya und Nikalmati — 1971 |
| —— 2 | L. Jakob-Rost, Das Ritual der Malli aus Arzawa gegen Behexung (KUB 24.9 +) — 1972 |
| —— 3–4 | A. Ünal, Ḫattušili III., Part 1: Ḫattušili bis zu seiner Thronbesteigung; vol. I: Historischer Abriss (THeth 3); vol. II: Quellen (THeth 4) — 1974 |
| —— 5 | S. Bin-Nun, The Tawananna in the Hittite Kingdom — 1975 |
| —— 6 | A. Ünal, Ein Orakeltext über die Intrigen am hethitischen Hof (KUB XXII 70 = Bo 2011) — 1978 |
| —— 7 | A. Kammenhuber, Orakelpraxis, Träume und Vorzeichenschau bei den Hethitern — 1976 |
| —— 8 | S. Heinhold-Krahmer, Arzawa: Untersuchungen zu seiner Geschichte nach den hethitischen Quellen — 1977 |
| —— 9 | S. Heinhold-Krahmer, I. Hoffmann, A. Kammenhuber, and G. Mauer, Probleme der Textdatierung in der Hethitologie — 1979 |
| —— 10 | S. Košak, Hittite inventory texts (CTH 241–250) — 1982 |
| —— 11 | I. Hoffmann, Der Erlaß Telipinus — 1984 |
| —— 12 | N. Boysan-Dietrich, Das hethitische Lehmhaus aus der Sicht der Keilschriftquellen — 1987 |
| —— 13 | D. Yoshida, Die Syntax des althethitischen substantivischen Genitivs — 1987 |
| —— 14 | E. Badalì, Strumenti musicali, musici e musica nella celebrazione delle feste ittite — 1991 |
| —— 15–16 | A. Hagenbuchner, Die Korrespondenz der Hethiter — 1989 |

| | |
|---|---|
| —— 18 | P. Cotticelli-Kurras, Das hethitische Verbum 'sein' — 1991 |
| —— 19 | A. Kammenhuber, Kleine Schriften — 1993 |
| —— 20 | R. H. Beal, The Organisation of the Hittite Military — 1992 |
| —— 21 | M. Popko, Zippalanda: Ein Kultzentrum im hethitischen Kleinasien — 1994 |
| —— 22 | D. Yoshida, Untersuchungen zu den Sonnengottheiten bei den Hethitern — 1996 |
| —— 23 | D. Schwemer, Akkadische Rituale aus Hattusa: Die Sammeltafel KBo XXXVI 29 und verwandte Fragmente — 1998 |
| —— 24 | Y. Cohen, Taboos and Prohibitions in Hittite Society: A Study of the Hittite Expression *natta āra* ("not permitted") — 2002 |
| —— 25 | D. Bawanypeck, Die Rituale der Auguren — 2005 |
| —— 26 | A. Taggar-Cohen, Hittite Priesthood — 2006 |
| —— 27 | M. Gander, Die geographischen Beziehungen der Lukka-Länder — 2010 |
| —— 28 | F. Giusfredi, Sources for a Socio-Economic History of the Neo-Hittite States — 2010 |
| —— 29 | A. Gilan, Formen und Inhalte althethitischer historischer Literatur — 2015 |
| —— 31 | St. Boaz, The Reign of Tudhaliya II and Šuppiluliuma I: The Contribution of the Hittite Documentation to a Reconstruction of the Amarna Age — 2015 |
| TIES | Tocharian and Indo-European Studies — Reykjavik and Copenhagen |
| Tischler, Gass. | J. Tischler, Das hethitische Gebet der Gassulijawija (IBS 37) — Innsbruck 1981 |
| —— HdW | —— Hethitisch-deutsches Wörterverzeichnis (IBS 39) — Innsbruck 1982 |
| —— HHwb | —— Hethitisches Handwörterbuch (IBS 102) — Innsbruck 2001 |
| —— | *see also* DBH 49, HED |
| Tjerkstra, Principles | F. Tjerkstra, Principles of the Relation between Local Adverb, Verb, and Sentence Particle in Hittite (Cuneiform Monographs 15) — Groningen 1999 |
| Toch&IESt | Tocharian and Indo European Studies — Copenhagen |
| Torri, Lelwani | G. Torri, Lelwani: il culto di una dea ittita (Vicino Oriente Quaderno 2) — Rome 1999 |
| —— Magia | —— La similitudine nella magia analogica ittita (StAs 2) — Rome 2003 |
| —— | *see also* DBH 50, 51 |
| TPS | Transactions of the Philological Society (London) |
| Trabazo | *see* García Trabazo |
| Trémouille, Ḫebat | M.-Cl. Trémouille, $^{d}$Ḫebat: Une divinité syro-anatolienne (Eothen 7) — Florence 1997 |
| —— | *see also* ChS 1/8 |
| TrLawCov | K. A. Kitchen and Paul J. N. Lawrence, Treaty, Law and Covenant in the Ancient Near East — Wiesbaden 2012 |
| Troy & the Trojan War | M. Mellink, ed., Troy and the Trojan War: A Symposium on the Trojan War held at Bryn Mawr College October 1984 — Bryn Mawr 1986 |
| TTAED | Türk Tarih, Arkeologya ve Etnografya Dergisi — Istanbul |
| TTK | Türk Tarih Kurumu — Ankara |
| TTKYayın | Türk Tarih Kurumu Yayınları — Ankara |
| TUAT | Texte aus der Umwelt des Alten Testaments — Gütersloh |
| —— 1.1 | Rechtsbücher (Hittite texts tr. E. von Schuler) — 1982 |
| —— 1.2 | Staatsverträge (Hittite texts tr. E. von Schuler) — 1983 |
| —— 1.3 | Dokumente zum Rechts- und Wirtschaftsleben (Hittite text tr. E. von Schuler) — 1983 |
| —— 1.5 | Historisch-chronologische Texte II (Hittite texts tr. H. M. Kümmel) — 1985 |
| —— 2.2 | Rituale und Beschwörungen I (Hittite texts tr. H. M. Kümmel) — 1987 |
| —— 3.4 | Weisheitstexte, Mythen und Epen (Hittite texts tr. A. ünal) — 1994 |
| —— Erg. | Ergänzungslieferung (Hittite texts tr. J. Klinger) — 2001 |
| Tunn. | A. Goetze, The Hittite Ritual of Tunnawi (AOS 14) — New Haven 1938 |
| TVOa | Testi del Vicino Oriente antico — Brescia |
| —— 4.1 | *see* LMI |
| —— 4.2 | *see* del Monte, L'annalistica |
| —— 4.4 | *see* Lettere |
| UAVA | Untersuchungen zur Assyriologie und Vorderasiatischen Archäologie. Ergänzungsbände zur ZA — Berlin |

| | |
|---|---|
| UF | Ugarit-Forschungen — Neukirchen-Vluyn |
| Ugar. | Ugaritica — Paris |
| Ugumu | lexical series (MSL 9:51–65) |
| Ugumu Bil | lexical series (MSL 9:67–73) |
| Ullik. | Ullikummi myth, cited according to H. G. Güterbock, "The Song of Ullikummi. Revised Text of the Hittite Version of a Hurrian Myth," JCS 5:135–161; 6:8–42 |
| Ünal, Entrikalar | A. Ünal, Hitit Sarayındaki Entrikalar Hakkında Bir Fal Metni (KUB XXII 70 = Bo 2011) — Ankara 1983 |
| —— Ḫantitaššu | —— The Hittite Ritual of Ḫantitaššu from the City of Ḫurma against Troublesome Years (TTKYayın VI/46) — Ankara 1996 |
| —— Ortaköy | —— Hittite and Hurrian Cuneiform Tablets from Ortaköy (Çorum), Central Turkey — Istanbul 1998 |
| —— | *see also* THeth 3, 4, 6 |
| Unity & Diversity | H. Goedicke and J. J. M. Roberts, eds., Unity & Diversity: Essays in the History, Literature, and Religion of the Ancient Near East — Baltimore 1975 |
| Uruanna | lexical series uruanna = *maštakal* |
| VAB | Vorderasiatische Bibliothek — Leipzig |
| van Brock | *alphabetized as* Brock |
| van den Hout | *alphabetized as* Hout |
| van Gessel | *see* OHP |
| VAT | Inventory numbers of tablets in the Staatliche Museen in Berlin |
| VBoT | A. Götze, Verstreute Boghazköi-Texte — Marburg 1930 |
| VDI | Vestnik Drevnei Istorii — Moscow |
| VIO | Veröffentlichungen des Instituts für Orientforschung der Deutschen Akademie der Wissenschaften — Berlin |
| VO | Vicino Oriente — Rome |
| von Brandenstein | *alphabetized as* Brandenstein |
| von Bredow | *alphabetized as* Bredow |
| von Schuler | *alphabetized as* Schuler |
| von Soden | *alphabetized as* Soden |
| VS | Vorderasiatische Schriftdenkmäler der Staatlichen Museen zu Berlin |
| Waal, Diss. | W. Waal, The Source as Object. Studies in Hittite Diplomatics (diss., Universiteit Leiden — 2010) |
| —— | *see also* StBoT 57 |
| Walther, HC | A. Walther, The Hittite Code (in J. M. Powis Smith, The Origin and History of Hebrew Law, App. IV) — Chicago 1931 |
| Watkins, Dragon | C. Watkins, How to Kill a Dragon: Aspects of Indo-European Poetics — Oxford 1995 |
| —— Idg.Gr | —— Idg. Gr 3. I Formenlehre. Geschichte der indogermanischen Verbalflexion — Heidelberg 1969 |
| —— IESt | —— Indo-European Studies, Special Report to NSF, Report HARV-LING-01-72, Dept. of Linguistics, Harvard University — Cambridge, Massachusetts 1972 |
| —— IESt II | —— Indo-European Studies II, Report HARV-LING-02-75, Dept. of Linguistics, Harvard University — Cambridge, Massachusetts 1975 |
| WAW | Writings from the Ancient World — Atlanta |
| Wb.Myth | H. W. Haussig, ed., Wörterbuch der Mythologie — Stuttgart (1962–)1965 |
| Webster | Webster's New International Dictionary of the English Language, 2nd ed. unabridged — Springfield, Massachusetts 1934 |
| Weeden | *see* StBoT 54 |
| Wegner, AOAT 36 | I. Wegner, Gestalt und Kult der Ištar-Šawuška in Kleinasien (AOAT 36) — Neukirchen-Vluyn 1981 |
| —— Hurritisch | —— Hurritisch: Einführung in die hurritische Sprache — Wiesbaden 2000 |
| —— Hurritisch$^2$ | —— Hurritisch: Einführung in die hurritische Sprache, 2. überarbeitete Auflage — Wiesbaden 2007 |
| —— | *see also* ChS |
| Weidner, Studien | E. Weidner, Studien zur hethitischen Sprachwissenschaft (LSS 7:1/2) — Leipzig 1917 |
| —— | *see also* PD |
| Weitenberg, U-Stämme | J. J. S. Weitenberg, Die hethitischen U-Stämme — Amsterdam 1984 |
| Werner | *see* StBoT 4 |
| Wilhelm | *see* ChS Erg. 1, KuSa I/1, StBoT 64, StBoT Beih. 4. |
| Witzel, HKU | M. Witzel, Hethitische Keilschrifturkunden in Transcription und Übersetzung mit Kommentar (Keilinschriftliche Studien 4) — Fulda 1924 |
| WO | Die Welt des Orients — Göttingen |

| | |
|---|---|
| Wolf, Diss. | H. M. Wolf, The Apology of Ḫattušiliš Compared with Other Political Self-justifications of the Ancient Near East (diss., Brandeis University — 1967) |
| Women in Antiquity | St. Budin and J. Turfa, eds., Women in Antiquity: Real Women across the Ancient World — London/New York 2016 |
| Wright, Disposal | D. P. Wright, The Disposal of Impurity: Elimination Rites in the Bible and in Hittite and Mesopotamian Literature (Society of Biblical Literature Dissertation Series 101) — Atlanta 1987 |
| WVDOG | Wissenschaftliche Veröffentlichungen der Deutschen Orient-Gesellschaft — Leipzig, Berlin |
| WZKM | Wiener Zeitschrift für die Kunde des Morgenlandes — Vienna |
| Xenia | Xenia: Konstanzer althistorische Vorträge und Forschungen — Konstanz |
| Yakubovich, Sociolinguistics | I. Yakubovich, Sociolinguistics of the Luvian Language, (BSIEL 2) — Leiden 2010 |
| Yaz$^2$ | Das hethitische Felsheiligtum Yazılıkaya (BoHa 9) — Berlin 1975 |
| YBC | tablets in the Yale Babylonian Collection |
| YOS | Yale Oriental Series, Babylonian Texts — New Haven |
| Yoshida, D. | *see* THeth 13 |
| Yoshida, K., Mediopassive | K. Yoshida, The Hittite Mediopassive Endings in *-ri* (Untersuchungen zur indogermanischen Sprach- und Kulturwissenschaft NF 5) — Berlin 1990 |
| YOSR | Yale Oriental Series, Researches — New Haven |
| ZA | Zeitschrift für Assyriologie und verwandte Gebiete — Leipzig, Weimar, Strassburg, Berlin |
| ZDMG | Zeitschrift der Deutschen Morgenländischen Gesellschaft — Leipzig, Wiesbaden, Stuttgart |
| Zehnder | *see* DBH 29 |
| Zimmern/Friedrich, HGes | H. Zimmern and J. Friedrich, Hethitische Gesetze aus dem Staatsarchiv von Boghazköi (AO 23.2) — Leipzig 1922 |
| Zuntz, Ortsadv. | L. Zuntz, Die hethitischen Ortsadverbien *arḫa, parā, piran* als selbständige Adverbien und in ihrer Verbindung mit Nomina und Verba (diss., Ludwig-Maximilians-Universität, Munich — 1936) |
| —— Scongiuri | —— Un testo ittita di scongiuri (Atti del Reale Istituto Veneto di Scienze Lettere ed Arti 96) — Venice 1937 |

## 2. General

| | |
|---|---|
| abbr. | abbreviation |
| abl. | ablative |
| abs. | absolute, absolutive |
| acc. | accusative |
| act. | active |
| adj. | adjective |
| adv. | adverb |
| Akk. | Akkadian |
| all. | allative |
| ann. | annals |
| apod. | apodosis |
| app. | appendix |
| Arn. | Arnuwanda |
| Ašm. | Ašmunikal |
| astron. | astronomical |
| biblio. | bibliography |
| bil. | bilingual |
| bk. | book |
| Bogh. | Boghazköy, Boğazköy, Boğazkale |
| C | any consonant |
| cat. | catalogue |
| caus. | causative |
| cf. | compare |
| chap. | chapter |
| chron. | chronicle |
| cm | centimeter(s) |
| CLuw. | cuneiform Luwian |
| col. | column |
| coll. | collated, collation |
| coll. ph. | collated from photo |
| coll. W. | collation of Arnold Walther entered in his personal copies of KBo, KUB, etc. |
| collec. | collective |
| com. | common (gender) |

| | |
|---|---|
| comm. | comment, commentary |
| comp. | compound |
| compl. | complement(ed) |
| conj. | conjunction |
| corr. | correspond(s), corresponding, correspondence |
| cun. | cuneiform |
| dat. | dative |
| dem. | demonstrative |
| denom. | denominative |
| dep(os). | deposition (in court) |
| depon. | deponent |
| descr. | description |
| det. | determinative |
| det. annals | detailed annals |
| disc. | discussion |
| diss. | dissertation |
| dittogr. | dittography |
| d.-l. | dative-locative |
| DN | divine name |
| dupl(s). | duplicate(s) |
| dur. | durative |
| eadem | the same (author, fem.) |
| ed. | edition, edited (by) |
| e.g. | for example |
| Engl. | English |
| ENS | Early New Hittite Script |
| eras. | erasure |
| erg. | ergative |
| Erg. | Ergänzungsheft (supplement) |
| esp. | especially |
| ess. | essive |
| etc. | et cetera |
| ex(x). | example(s) |
| ext. | extispicy |
| f(f). | following |
| fasc. | fascicle |
| fem. | feminine |
| fest. | festival |
| frag. | fragment |
| Fs | Festschrift |
| gen. | genitive |
| Ger. | German |
| gloss. | glossary |
| GN | geographical name |
| Gr. | Greek |
| gram. | grammatical |
| Gs | Gedenkschrift (memorial vol.) |
| HAH | H. A. Hoffner |
| hapax | hapax legomenon |
| Ḫatt. | Ḫattušili |
| HGG | H. G. Güterbock |
| hierogl. | hieroglyph(ic) |
| hipp. | hippological |
| hist. | historical |
| Hitt. | Hittite |
| HLuw. | hieroglyphic Luwian |
| Hurr. | Hurrian |
| ibid. | in the same place |
| idem | the same (author, masc.) |
| i.e. | that is |
| IE | Indo-European |
| imp. | imperative |
| imperf. | imperfective |
| impers. | impersonal |
| incant. | incantation |
| incl. | including |
| indef. | indefinite |
| indir. | indirect |
| inf. | infinitive |
| inscr. | inscription |
| inst. | instrumental |
| instr. | instruction(s) |
| interj. | interjection |
| interrog. | interrogative |
| intrans. | intransitive |
| inv. | inventory |
| invoc. | invocation |

| | |
|---|---|
| iter. | iterative |
| Kizz. | Kizzuwatna |
| km | kilometer(s) |
| l(l). | line(s) |
| l.e. | left edge |
| lex. | lexical |
| lit. | literary, literally |
| LNS | Late New Hittite Script |
| loc. | locative |
| loc. cit. | in the place cited |
| log. | logogram, logographic |
| Luw. | Luwian |
| lw. | loan word |
| m | meter(s) |
| masc. | masculine |
| med. | medical |
| MH | Middle Hittite |
| mid. | middle (voice) |
| misc. | miscellaneous |
| mng. | meaning |
| MS | Middle Hittite Script |
| ms(s) | manuscript(s) |
| Msk | inventory numbers of Meskene tablets |
| Murš. | Muršili |
| Muw. | Muwatalli |
| myth. | mythological |
| n(n). | (foot)note(s), noun |
| n.d. | no date |
| neut. | neuter |
| NH | New Hittite |
| no. | number |
| nom. | nominative |
| NS | New Hittite Script |
| obj. | object |
| obl. | oblique |
| obv. | obverse |
| OH | Old Hittite |
| op. cit. | in the work cited |
| opp. | opposite |
| OS | Old Hittite Script |
| p(p). | page(s) |
| Pal. | Palaic |
| par(s). | parallel(s) |
| part. | participle |
| pass. | passive |
| perf. | perfect |
| pers. | person(al) |
| PIE | Proto-Indo-European |
| pl. | plural |
| pl. tantum | plurale tantum (plural only) |
| PN | personal name |
| poss. | possessive |
| postpos. | postposition |
| pr. | proclamation |
| pres. | present |
| pret. | preterite |
| prev. | preverb(s) |
| prob. | probably |
| pron. | pronoun |
| publ. | published |
| Pud. | Puduḫepa |
| purif. | purification |
| q.v. | which see |
| ref(s). | reference(s) |
| rel. | relative |
| resp. | respectively |
| rest. | restored, restoration |
| rev. | reverse |
| rit. | ritual |
| RN | royal name |
| rt. | right |
| sc(il). | namely |
| sec. | section |
| sg. | singular |
| sim. | similar |
| subst. | substantive, substitution |
| Sum. | Sumerian |
| sup. | supine |

| | |
|---|---|
| Šupp. | Šuppiluliuma, Šuppiluliyama |
| suppl. | supplement(ary) |
| s.v. | under the word |
| syll. | syllable, syllabic, syllabically |
| synt. | syntax |
| Tel. | Telipinu |
| TOS | Typical Old Script |
| tr. | translation, translated (by) |
| trans. | transitive |
| translit. | transliteration, transliterated (by) |
| Tudḫ. | Tudḫaliya |
| uncert. | uncertain |
| undecl. | undeclined |
| unkn. | unknown |
| unpubl. | unpublished |
| v. | verb |
| V | any vowel |
| var(s). | variant(s) |
| ver(s). | version(s) |
| viz. | namely |
| voc. | vocative |
| vocab. | vocabulary |
| vol. | volume |
| vs. | versus |
| w. | with |
| wr. | written |
| yr. | year |
| × | (in transliteration) indicates an inscribed sign or ligature<br>(preceded by a number) times |
| o | space within a lacuna for a sign |
| x | illegible sign |
| = | equivalences in duplicates, lexical texts and bilinguals |
| § | new paragraph |
| □ | introduces comment in semantic section |
| ø | lacking |
| › | goes to |
| * | unattested form |
| # | any number |

| | |
|---|---|
| ( ) | in lemma encloses omissible part of the stem |
| ( ) | in morphology encloses the line number of a partially broken example |
| ( ) | in translation encloses words not in the Hittite but needed to make sense in English |
| [ ] | encloses material lost in break |
| [( )] | encloses material restored from a duplicate |
| ⸢ ⸣ | encloses partly broken sign(s) |
| ‹ › | omitted by scribal error |
| ‹( )› | omitted by scribal error and restored from a duplicate |
| « » | to be omitted |
| … / … | end of line |
| …/… | alternation or possibilities |
| † | all known occurrences are cited |
| ⸗ | marking clitic boundaries; also used only in CHD L-N for division of transcribed Hittite or Akkadian word at the end of a printed line |
| ~ | for division of transcribed Hittite or Akkadian word or Sumerogram at the end of a printed line, used in CHD P and Š |
| : | single- or double-wedge marker ("Glossenkeil"), see OrNS 25:113ff., used in CHD L-P/2 |
| 𒀹 | single-wedge marker ("Glossenkeil") used in CHD P/3 and Š |
| 𒑱 | double-wedge marker ("Glossenkeil") used in CHD P/3 and Š |

Hittite abbreviations are written, e.g., $^{f}$*Zi.* or *ke.-eš.*

## -šma/i- A, -ša/e/ima/i- A, -šum(m)a/i- A

enclitic poss. pron.; your (pl.); from OS; wr. syll. and akkadographically *-KUNU*.

For the various spellings of the cluster *-šm-* after vowels and consonants including *š* and *z* see the enclitic personal pronoun *-š(a)maš* "(to/for) you" (pl. both dir. and indir. object) and "to/for them." In contrast to *-š(a)maš*, however, both poss. prons. "your" (pl.) and "their" (s.v. *-šma/i-* B) show frequent epenthesis of the vowels *e, i,* and *u* (*-šem*V-/*-šim*V-/*-šum*V-) in addition to *a*. Whereas epenthesis with *a* and *e* is well attested for OS already, the earliest evidence for *u* is MS (HKM 57:21, see below *-šma/i-* B "their" under sg. dat.-loc.); epenthesis with *i* is rare, attested only in NS and for *-šma/i-* B "their" (see under sg. nom.-acc. neut.). On the spelling of both *šuppa*=*š-mi-it* and =*š-me-et* in the same OS text (KBo 20.16 iv! 3 and 5, respectively), the latter possibly with *me* written over an earlier *mi*, see Berman, BiOr 38:654.

For the use and chronology of poss. prons. in Hittite see *-mi-/-ma-* "my, mine" and *-ši-* B, *-ša-* "his, her, its" as well as GrHL Ch. 6. Indications of the unfamiliarity with these prons. in NH are their rare and often incorrect use in that period, compare, for instance, *zaḫḫiya*(d.-l.)=*(a)š-mi-iš* (sg. nom. com.) KBo 22.6 i 24, for which see Güterbock, MDOG 101:24, Rieken, StBoT 45:581, or LUGAL-*u(š)*(com.)=*š-me-e[t]*(neut.) KBo 3.38 rev. 31 (OH/NS) vs. the dupl. correctly LUGAL-*uš-mi-iš* KBo 22.2 rev. 15 (OS).

**sg. nom. com.** *-šmiš*: -V*š-mi-iš* KBo 22.2 rev. 15 (OS), KBo 17.3 ii 13 (OS), KUB 60.156 obv. 7 (OH/NS), -V*š-mi-š(a)* KBo 23.52 iii 6 (MS), here or pl. 3? KUB 7.58 i 7 (2×) (NS).

**sg. acc. com.** *-šman*: here? *-(a)š-ma-n(a-za-pa)* KBo 39.18 left col. 9 (MS).

**nom.-acc. neut.** -V*š-me-e[t]* KBo 3.38 rev. 31 (OH/NS) (wrongly used with a sg. nom. com., dupl. KBo 22.2 rev. 15 (OS) correctly has *-šmiš*), here or pl. 3? -V*š-mi-it* KUB 7.58 i 11 (NS), *-še-me-et* KBo 8.35 ii 21 (MH/MS), KBo 50.3:7 (NS), *-ša-mi-it* KUB 60.156 obv. 9 (OH/NS), here? *-šum-mi-it* KUB 24.3 ii 18 (Murš. II; or under *-šum(m)a/i-* A "our"?).

**dat.-loc.** *-šmi*: -(V)*š-mi* KBo 17.1 i 12, 13 (OS), KUB 23.77 rev. 72 (MH/MS), KUB 31.104 i 11 (MH/MS), here? KUB 31.74 ii 8 (NS).

**all.** *-šma*: -V*š-ma* KBo 22.1:22 (OS).

**pl. nom. com.** *-šmeš*: -V*š-me-eš* KBo 6.3 iii 22 (OH/NS), here? -V*š-mi-eš* KBo 31.143 rev.? 14 (MS).

**acc. com.** *-šmuš*: -(V)*š-mu-uš* KBo 39.18 left col. 8 (MS), here? KBo 17.1 iv (40) (but see Neu, StBoT 26:169 n. 504).

**frag.** *-šum*[-...] KBo 13.110 rev.? 2 (NS).

**a.** sg. nom. com. *-šmiš*: *ūk*=*wa* LUGAL-*u(š)*=*š-mi-iš kišḫa* "I will become your king!" KBo 22.2 rev. 15 (Zalpa Tale, OS), ed. StBoT 17:12f., StMed 19:32, 40 ☐ note that the NS dupl. KBo 3.38 rev. 31 has the grammatical monstrum LUGAL-*uš-me-e[t]*.

**b.** sg. acc. com.: see below pl. acc. com.

**c.** nom.-acc. neut. *-šme/it*: ("If you come to attack Ḫatti-Land, ...") *nu šumenzan*=*pat ker*=*še-me-et iškarrannian[(du)]* "may they (i.e., your arrows) pierce your own heart!" KBo 8.35 ii 21 (treaty w. Kaška, MH/MS), w. dupl. KUB 26.6:19 (MH/MS), ed. StBoT 53:180f., tr. Kaškäer 111.

**d.** gen.: not attested.

**e.** dat.-loc. *-šmi*: ("and I speak to the king and queen as follows": §) *[(k)]āšata*=*šmaš*=*kan utniyandan lāluš dāḫḫu[n (irm)]a(n)*=*šmaš*=*kan dāḫḫun kardi*=*(i)š-mi*=*(ya?*=*)at*=*kan dāḫḫu[n (ḫarš)]ni*=*(i)š-mi*=*(ya?*=*)at*=*kan dāḫḫun* "Hereby I have taken from you the (evil) tongues of the people, I have taken from you illness, I have taken (both?) what is in your heart (and?) in your head" KBo 17.1 i 11-13 (rit. for the royal couple, OS), w. dupl. KBo 17.3 i 6-8 (OS), ed. StBoT 8:18f., translit. StBoT 25:5.

**f.** all. *-šma*: *mān*=*š(a)maš ABI parna*=*(a)š-ma tarnai nu*=*šmaš mānḫanda ḫatreškezzi natta*=*š(a)maš* LÚ.MEŠ.DUGUD-*aš ḫazzian ḫarzi* "When my father lets you go home (lit. to your house/home), has he not engraved a tablet for you, dignitaries, just as he always writes to you?" KBo 22.1:21-23 (OS), ed. Archi, FsLaroche 45, 47, HittInstr 74f.

**g.–h.** abl. and inst.: not attested.

**i.** pl. nom. com. *-šmeš*: ("He (i.e., the father of the king) had them recorded on an official sealed document (saying):") *ītten māḫḫanda are(š)*=*š-me-eš šu[(mešš*=*a)] apēniššan īšten* "Go, do just as your peers" KBo 6.3 iii 22-23 (OH/NS), w. dupl. KBo 6.2 iii 19-20 (OS), ed. LH 67f., HW[2] E 94 (w. *īšten* as imp. 2 pl. of *eš-/aš-* "to be").

**j.** acc. com. *-šmuš*: *[...ekute]n? azzikiten [...p]ūriuš*=*(š)-mu-uš [...]lala(n)*=*(a)š-ma-n*=*a*=*apa* [...] *ḫarten* "[...you must (?) ea]t (and) you must drink! [...] your [l]ips [...] while you must hold [...] your tongue" KBo 39.18 left col. 7-8 (MS), ed. Fuscagni, hethiter.net/: CTH 458.18 ☐ for *-šman* here as the sg. acc. com. poss. pron. and the analysis of the sequence as *lala(n)*=*šman*=*a*=*z*=*apa* see Groddek, HS 130:26;

the surrounding pl. 2nd person forms make the interpretation of the two *-šma/i-* attestations as likewise pl. 2nd persons likely.

**k.-l.** nom.-acc. neut. and oblique cases: not attested.

Starke, StBoT 31 (1990) 79-82; Hoffner/Melchert, GrHL (2008) 137-141 w. previous bibliography; Groddek, HS 126 (2013) 118-122; Groddek, HS 130 (2017) 17-41.

## -šma/i- B, -ša/e/ima/i- B, -šum(m)a/i- B

enclitic poss. pron.; their; from OS; wr. syll. and Akkadographically *-ŠUNU*.

For spellings and use see *-šma/i-* A, *-ša/e/ima/i-* A, *-šum(m)a/i-* A. The spelling *šīna(š)≠š-ma-an* KUB 17.18 ii 13 (thus recte vs. *šīnaš≠ma≠šma*!⟨*š*⟩ CHD s.v. (NINDA)*šīna-*, *šēna/i-* A 1 a 1' c') is probably scribal error for *-aš-ma-aš* containing *-šmaš* "for them" q.v.

**sg. nom. com.** -(V)*š-mi-iš* KBo 3.22 rev. 47 (OS), KBo 17.22 ii 14 (OS), KUB 56.46 ii 8 (OH/NS), here? KBo 8.42 rev. 7 (OS), here or pl. 2? KUB 7.58 i 7 (2×, NS), *-(a)z-mi-iš-š(a)* (< *-z≠šmiš*) KUB 41.23 ii 19 (OH/NS), KUB 57.86:5, 7 (OH/NS), *-(a)z-za-mi-iš-š(a)* (< *-z≠šmiš*) KUB 41.23 ii 21 (OH/NS), *-še-me-iš* KUB 56.46 ii 16 (OH/NS), *-še-mi-iš* KBo 10.31 iii 16 (NS).

**acc. com.** *-šman*: -(V)*š-ma-an* KUB 29.36:4 (OS), KBo 6.26 iii 33, 44 (OH/NS), *-ša-ma-an* KBo 3.34 ii 23 (OH/NS).

**nom.-acc. neut.** -V*š-me-et* KBo 36.110 rev. 10 (OS), KUB 36.104 rev. 7 (OS), KBo 20.16 iv! 5 (OS), KUB 17.10 iv 15 (OH/MS), KUB 57.60 ii? 21 (OH/NS), KUB 57.63 ii 31 (OH/NS), KBo 22.6 iv 24 (pre-NH/NS), -V*š-mi-it* KBo 17.33:5 (OS), KBo 20.22 i 11 (OS), KBo 20.16 iv! 3 (OS), KBo 3.67 iii 9 (OH/NS), KBo 12.126 i 8 (MH/NS), KUB 53.15 ii! 20 (NS), KBo 20.32 iii 14 (OH/LNS)(wrongly used with a sg. d.-l.), KUB 20.38 obv. 15 (NS), KUB 41.23 ii 21 (OH/NS) (wrongly used w. sg. nom. com.), here or pl. 2? KUB 7.58 i 11 (NS), *-ša-me-et* KBo 17.1 ii 16 (OS), KBo 17.4 ii 6 (OS), KBo 17.3 iii 11, iv 17 (OS), KBo 30.71 iii 19 (NS), VS 28.34 rev.? 3 (NS), *-ša-mi-it* KUB 36.55 ii 41, 42 (MH?/MS), KBo 25.190 obv. 27 (MS), KBo 26.100 i 6 (MS), *-še-mi-it* KBo 3.23 obv. 9 (OH/MS), KBo 25.18 rev. 11 (OH/NS), *-še-me-et* KUB 36.104 obv. 18 (OS)//KBo 3.34 i 20 (OH/NS), KBo 17.6 ii 14 (OS), KUB 31.64 ii 38 (OH?/NS), *-ši-me-et* KBo 46.138 rev. 6 (NS), *-še-me-t(a)* KBo 17.1 i 31 (OS), *-ši-mi-it* KUB 31.115:12 (OH/NS), *-šum-mi-it* KBo 3.1 i 22 (Tel./NS), *-šum-me-et* KUB 57.63 ii 35 (OH/NS), KUB 57.60 ii? 24 (OH/NS) (both wrongly used with a sg. d.-l.), uncertain if pl. 3rd pers. KUB 57.26:8 (OH/NS), -⟨*š*⟩*-mi-it* KBo 10.45 iv 46 (MH/NS), *-(a)z-mi-it* KBo 17.4 iii 13 (OS).

**gen.** *-šmaš*: -V*š-ma-aš* KUB 33.66 iii 15 (OH/MS).

**d.-l.** *-šmi*: *-(i)š-mi* KBo 22.2 obv. 13, rev. 15(?) (OS), KBo 17.3 iv 28 (OS), KBo 8.35 ii 21 (MH/MS), KBo 17.105 ii 30 (MS), IBoT 1.36 ii 3, 7, 50, 54, 58 (MH/MS; all w. *katti-*), *-(a)š-mi* KBo 17.105 ii 33 (MS), *-(e)š-mi* KBo 11.51 iv 10 (NS), *-šu-mi* HKM 57:21 (MH/MS), *-šum-mi* KUB 31.66 ii 11 (NS), KBo 14.12 iv 31, 32, 36, 39 (Murš. II), *-šu-um-me* KBo 22.58:9 (Tudḫ. IV), KUB 26.81 i 7, iv 9 (NS; both w. *ištarni-*), ⟨*-iš*⟩*-mi* KBo 3.23 obv. 4, rev. 6 (OH/MS).

**all.** *-šma*: -V*š-ma* KBo 17.2 i 6, 8 (OS), KBo 3.41:8 (OH/NS), KBo 42.74:6 (NS), here? KBo 3.34 i 18 (OH/NS; or pl. d.-l. *-aš-ma*⟨*-aš*⟩?), KUB 24.8 i 5 (pre-NH/NS), *-šum-m[a(?)]* KBo 22.7 obv.? 5 (OH/NS).

**abl.** *-(a)z-mi-it* KBo 17.1 i 18 (OS), KBo 17.3 i 13 (OS), KBo 17.7 iv? 6-7 (4×) (OS), KBo 16.80 iii 3 (MS?), *-(a)z-me-et* KBo 25.138:4 (OH/NS), *-(a)z-aš-mi-it* KBo 25.54 i 14 (OS).

**inst.** *-(i)z-me-et* KBo 17.1 iv 34 (OS), *-(i)z-mi-it* KBo 17.4 iv 30 (OS), *-(i)z-mi-d(a-)* KBo 17.3 i 14, iv (OS), *-(i)š-mi-t(a-)* KBo 17.1 i 19 (OS).

**pl. nom. com.** *-šmeš*: -(V)*š-me-eš* KBo 6.2 iii 14 (OS), KBo 6.6 i 22 (OH/NS), KBo 29.15 obv. (11) (OH/NS), *-(e)š-mi-eš* KBo 31.143 rev.? 14 (MS), -V*š-mi-š(≠a)* KBo 30.20 iii 6, 12 (MS), here? *-šum-mi-iš* KBo 22.6 iv 18 (pre-NH/NS).

**acc. com.** *-šmuš*: -(V)*š-mu-uš* KBo 22.2 obv. 18 (OS), KBo 17.1 iv 31 (OS), KBo 17.3 iv 23, 27 (OS), KBo 17.15 obv.! 5 (OS), KBo 20.20 i 10 (OS), KBo 20.22 i 7 (OS), KBo 30.18 iv 4 (MS?), Bo 3542 ii 7 (⟨*-uš*⟩?), 13 (MS? apud Akdoğan, FsÜnal 2-6), KBo 3.34 ii 28 (OH/NS), KBo 10.31 iii 33, iv 31 (NS), KUB 43.75 obv. 17 (OH/NS), *-šu-mu-uš* KUB 31.38 iii 14 (OH/NS).

**nom.-acc. neut.** -V*š-me-et* KBo 17.1 i 24 (OS), KBo 20.16 obv.? 5 (OS), KBo 3.34 i 21 (OH/NS), -V*š-mi-it* KBo 20.16 obv.? 3 (OS), KBo 10.31 iii 31 (NS), *-šum-mi-it* KBo 3.45 obv. 5 (OH/NS).

**gen.** *-šman*: -(V)*š-ma-an* KUB 54.75 obv. 3 (OH/NS), KUB 56.46 ii (27) (OH/NS).

**dat.-loc.** -V*š-ma-aš* KBo 3.1 i 21 (OH/NS), KUB 31.115:8 (OH/NS), KUB 36.91 i 9 (OH/NS), here? KBo 3.34 i 18 (OH/NS; see above under all.), *-ša-ma-aš* KUB 11.1 i 21 (OH/MS?), *-ma-aš* (in DUMU.MEŠ*-ma-aš-š≠a*?) KBo 17.1 iii 10 (OS), *-(a)š-ma-š(a-pa)* KUB 41.32 obv. 6 (NS).

**a.** in OH — **1′** sg. nom. com. *-šmiš*: *mān≠aš appezziyan≠a kištanziattat š≠an* d*Ḫalmaš[uiz]* d*Šīuš≠(š)-mi-iš parā paiš* "But when it (i.e., the town) later on suffered a famine, Ḫalmaš[uit], their god, handed it over" KBo 3.22 rev. 45-47 (Anitta text, OS), ed. StBoT 18:12f., Singer, ICH 2:348, tr. Hoffner, CoS 1:183; [dUT]U*-i* MUNUS.LUGAL MUNUS. LUGAL*-aš ḫuišš[u?- ... /* DINGIR.ME]Š*-naš āššuš≠(š)-mi-iš* [...] KBo 17.22 ii 13-14 (bil. prayer, OS), translit. StBoT 25:207.

**2′** acc. com. *-šman* (only in NS): m!*Išpudašinaran* LUGAL*-uš dāš* m*Šuppiuman* m*Maraššann≠a* UGULA 1! *LI* LÚ.MEŠKUŠ$_7$ *ešer* *apūn=a* ^LÚ^*uralla(n)=š-ša-ma-an iēt* "The king took Išpudašinara – Šuppiuman and Marašša (text has Maraššan in acc.) were the chiefs of thousand chariot fighters – and made him their overseer" KBo 3.34 ii 21-23 (anecdotes, OH/NS), ed. THeth 20:535f., Dardano, L'aneddoto 50f; *takku* LÚ *ELLUM* (erased: *arauwanniuš*) *annanekuš anna(n)=(a)š-ma-ann=a uenzi* "If a free man has intercourse with (erased: free) sisters of the same mother and with their mother" KBo 6.26 iii 32-33 (Laws, OH/NS), ed. LH 150f. (§191, see also §194).

**3′** nom.-acc. neut. *-šme/it, -šumme/it* (in OS, MS, NS): *nu=z=apa utniyanza ḫūmanza iškiš=(š)-me-et anda* ^URU^*Ḫattuša lagan ḫard[u]* "and may the entire population hold their back(s) toward Ḫattuša" KUB 36.110 iii 9-10 (benedictions for the labarna, OS), ed. Hoffner, FsHawkins 131f. ☐ see the sg. nom.-acc. neut. of the pl. 1st pers. poss. pron. *šaḫeššar=šum-me-e[t]* "our fortress" ibid. iii 8; compare similarly [...] *iški(š)=šum-me-et aššuli* [Ø?] *andan lagan ēš*[-...] IBoT 3.113 rev.? 3-4 (frag. of prayer to Sungoddess of Arinna, OH/NS); LÚ.MEŠ DUGUD LÚ.MEŠ ŠUKUR ZABAR *pera(n)=š-mi-it ašanzi* "The officials (and) the bronze spearmen are seated in front of them" KBo 36.104 rev. 7 (anecdotes, OS), ed. Dardano, L'aneddoto 60f., THeth 20 500f. w. n. 1848; ("Do not let the king's servants d[ie] in oppression") *zig=a* SAG.GÉME.ÌR.MEŠ *ēšḫar=še-mi-it* (par. *išḫar=ši-mi-it*) *šanḫa* "You, avenge the male and female servants' blood (lit. the... servants, their blood)!" KBo 3.23 obv. 9 (OH/MS), ed. Eothen 14:19, 26, w. par. KUB 31.115:12 (OH/NS); [...(^URU^K)]Á.DINGIR.RA-*aš kue=šum-mi-it* (dupl. *kuit=*) *dā[uen]* "What of Babylon, of theirs (i.e., the gods), [we] took, ..." KBo 3.45 obv. 5 (Murš. against Babylon, OH/MS), w. dupl. KBo 22.7:2 (OH/NS), ed. Soysal, Diss. 54f., 101 (reading *ku-e-az-mi-it*), Hoffner, Unity&Diversity 56f., tr. Soysal, AoF 25:30; (The princes' servants became corrupt) *išḫa[š](=a?)=š-ma-aš=ššan* (dupl. *-ša-ma-aš-*) *[(t)]aštašeškeuwan dāer nu ēšḫar=šum-mi-it ēššuwan tīēr* "They started to conspire against their masters and they began to shed their blood" KBo 3.1 i 21-22 (Tel.pr., OH/NS), w. dupl. KUB 11.1 i 21-22 (OH/MS?), ed. THeth. 11:16f., tr. Goedegebuure, ANEHST 230 ☐ for the problems with the analysis of *išḫašašmaššan* see Groddek, HS 130:27f. Starke, WO 16:107, considers *-šummit* here as pl. 1st pers., which is formally acceptable because of the *-u-* vocalism, but the passage requires pl. 3rd person "their" (see also GrHL 139 n. 23). *-šummit* is either corrupt or shows an anaptyctic *-u-* to break up the three-consonant cluster *-ršm-* (cf. Rieken HS 113:172 and *š(u)-*). Compare similarly *aruš=šu-mu-uš* "their colleagues" KBo 3.34 iii 14 (anecdotes, OS), ed. Dardano, L'aneddoto 56f. or *katti=šu-mi* (*parā neḫḫūn*) "to you (I dispatched)" HKM 57:21 (letter, MH/MS), ed. HBM 228f. ("zu euch"), Letters 205 ("to you"), see also GrHL 139 n. 16; *kuīšš=a=aš labarnaš ḫantezziš=šiš āššuwanteš* LÚ.MEŠ GAL.GAL=*ŠU* ÉRIN.MEŠ=*ŠU* ANŠE.KUR.RA.MEŠ=*ŠU antū=š-me-et-t=a apūšš=a* ^d^UTU-*uš=pat š[(uw)]āru mayanza [(lab)]arnaš* ^MUNUS^*tawannannaš [(kiš)]šari=šum-me-et* TI-*an ḫarak* "And whoever is the Labarna's chief, his valued grandees, his troops, his chariots, may only you, fully grown Sun God, keep both their possessions and those themselves (i.e., grandees, troops and chariots) alive in the Labarna's and Tawannanna's (lit. their) hand" KUB 57.63 ii 29-36 (OH/NS), w. dupls. KUB 57.60 ii? 19-24 (OH/NS), KBo 54.243 ii 1-6, ed. Rieken et al., hethiter.net/: CTH 385.10 (TX 2016-11-24, TRde 2016-11-24), Archi, FsOtten² 20f.; see also KBo 3.67 iii 8-9, w. dupls. in *šai-* 1 b.

**4′** gen.: not attested.

**5′** d.-l. *-šmi*: *nu=zza* DUMU.⌈NITA⌉.MEŠ *karti=(i)š-mi peran mēmer* "The sons said to themselves (lit. to their heart)" KBo 22.2 obv. 13-14 (tale of Zalpa, OS), ed. StBoT 17:6f.; KBo 17.3 iv 28, for which see below 10′ pl. acc. com.; *nu=š[(m)]aš=kan NĪŠ* DINGIR.MEŠ DUMU.ḪI.A=*KUNU andan kardi=(i)š-mi=pa[(t a)]zzikkandu* "May the Oath Deities eat your sons' very hearts out! (lit. eat for you your sons right in their heart)" KBo 8.35 ii 23-24 (treaty w. Kaškaeans, MH/MS), w. dupl. KBo 16.29 (+) KUB 31.104 i 11, tr. Kaškäer 111; for erroneous NS use of *-šummet* as dat.-loc. in KUB 57.63 ii 35, see a 3′, above.

**6′** all. *-šma, -šumma* (only in NS): *[(ta=za)] utnē ḫarnikmi kīdanda natīda t=an karda=(a)š-ma* (var. ŠÀ) *šal[(ikti)]* "I will destroy the country with this arrow and you (O arrow) will plunge into their heart" KUB 31.4:9 + KBo 3.41:8 (OH/NS), w. dupl. KBo 13.78 obv. 9-10 (OH/NS), ed. *šalik(i)-* 3 a;

*š=an* ᵐ*Šarmāššūi* ᵐ*Nunnūi=ya šakuwa=(a)š-ma ḫuēkta* "and he (i.e., the man of the gold spear) slaughtered him (i.e., an in-law of Nunnu) before Šarmaššu's and Nunnu's eyes (lit. before Šarmaššu and Nunnu their eyes)" KBo 3.34 i 17-18 (anecdotes, OH/NS), ed. Dardano, L'aneddoto 32f. (emending to *-šma‹š›*), *šakui-* 1 a 6', Groddek, HS 130:28; for *tarna=šma* "on their head" in the Appu Tale see likewise Groddek, HS 130:32; *ta kuera=šumm*[*a*(?)] / [*š*(*ālikuwaštati*)] "Thei[r] field we entered (unlawfully(?))" KBo 22.7 obv.? 5 (Murš. I and Babylon, OH/NS), w. dupl. KBo 3.45 obv. 8-9 (OH/NS), ed. Soysal, Diss. 54f., 100f., Hoffner, Unity & Diversity 56f.

**7′–8′** abl. and inst. *-šme/it* (only in OS): *gāpinan kalulupi*(*t*)*=z-mi-it ḫaḫḫallit mārkaḫḫi* "With the *ḫaḫḫal* I separate the thread from their fingers" KBo 17.4 iv 30 (rit. for the royal couple, OS), ed. StBoT 8:38f., *mark-* 1, translit. StBoT 25:18; [D]UMU.É.GAL LUGAL-*waš* MUNUS.LUGAL-*š=a iššaz=*(*š*)*-mi-it lālan* AN.BA[(R-*aš*) *d*]*āi* "The palace attendant takes the iron tongue from the king's and queen's (lit. their) mouths" KBo 17.3 i 13-14 (rit. for the royal couple, OS), w. dupl. KBo 17.1 i 18-19 (OS), ed. StBoT 8:20f., translit. StBoT 25:12.

**9′** pl. nom. com. *-šmeš, -šummiš*(?): *karū* ÉRIN.MEŠ *MANDA* ... ᴸᵁ́.ᴹᴱŠKUŠ$_7$ ᴸᵁ́.ᴹᴱŠ*karuḫaleš=*(*š*)*-me-eš-š=a luzzi natta karpe*[*r*] "Formerly, the *MANDA* troops, (other troops), chariot fighters and their *karuḫala*-men did not render corvée-services" KBo 6.2 iii 12, 14-15 (Laws, OS), w. dupls. KBo 6.3 iii 17 (OH/NS), KBo 6.6 i 22 (OH/NS), KBo 29.15 obv. (11) (OH/NS), ed. LH 65f.; for KBo 31.143 rev.? 14 see *šuku?ant-*; for *-šummiš* in KBo 22.6 iv 18 see *-šum*(*m*)*a-* C, *-šum*(*m*)*i-* C.

**10′** acc. com. *-šmuš* (in OS and NS): *ta šīni tēmi dā* LUGAL-*aš* MUNUS.LUGAL-*š=a aīn wāīn pittuliuš=*(*š*)*-mu-uš-š=a ta ḫāḫḫallit gāpinan dāḫḫe kalulupi=*(*i*)*š-mi ḫulalian kuit=a anda ḫalkiyaš=a* ZÍZ.ḪI.A-*š=a ḫaršārr=a nu apātt=a* GÌR*=ŠUNU kitta* "and I tell the figurine: take the king and queen's pain, woe, and their fears. With the *ḫaḫḫal* I take the thread that is wound around their finger. As to the heads of both the grain and wheat, those, too, lie at their feet" KBo 17.3 iv 26-29 (rit. for the royal couple, OS), ed. StBoT 8:38f., Goedegebuure, forthcoming, translit. StBoT 25:17; *kuid=a* ᴸᵁ́.ᴹᴱŠKUŠ$_7$ (erasure) *āmmiyantuš=*(*š*)*-mu-uš n=uš* ᵐ*Išpudašinaraš maniyaḫḫeškezzi* "as far as their junior chariot fighters were concerned, Išpudašinara instructed ("hist." pres.) them" KBo 3.34 ii 27-28 (anecdotes, OH/NS), ed. Goedegebuure, forthcoming, Dardano, L'aneddoto 52f., THeth 20:535f. (differently) □ for the recognition that *kuid=a* introduces contrasting topics, see Goedegebuure, forthcoming.

**11′** nom.-acc. neut. *-šme/it* (only in OS): *šā*⌈*ku*⌉*wa=š-me-et išḫaškanta* "Their (i.e., of the Ḫantašepa deities) eyes are blood-red" KBo 17.1 i 24 (rit. for the royal couple, OS), ed. StBoT 8:20f., translit. StBoT 25:6.

**12′** gen. *-šman*: [(10+)]5 ᴺᴵᴺᴰᴬ*šarāma* LÚ.MEŠ ᴳᴵŠBANŠUR *udanzi* ᴸᵁ́.ᴹ[(ᴱŠ*ḫāpiaš*) *p*(*ataš=*(*š*)*-ma-a*)*n* (*kattan*)] *išparanzi* "The table-men bring fifteen *šarāma*-breads (and) spread (them) next to the *ḫapi*-men's feet (lit. the *ḫapi*-men, their feet)" KBo 25.31 iii 9-10 (OS), w. dupls. KUB 56.46 ii 26-28 (OH/NS), KUB 54.75 obv. 1-4 (OH/NS), KBo 20.32 ii 1-3 (OH/NS), ed. Groddek, HS 126:118-122.

**13′** d.-l. *-šmaš* (only in MS and NS): [(*n*)]*u=šmaš* NINDA-*an* ŠU.MEŠ-*aš-ma-aš anda dāi* "put bread in their hands" (lit. "for them ... in their hands") KUB 31.115:8 (edict of Pimpira, OH/NS), ed. Eothen 14:22, 28 □ compare par. *nu=šmaš=kan* NINDA-*an kiššari=mi* (lit. "for them ... in my hand") *an*[*da dāi*] KBo 3.23 obv. 4 (OH/MS), emended to *kiššari=‹-iš›-mi* "in their hand"; [*...=m*]*u=ššan idālu ai*!*š=šmit* DINGIR.M[EŠ ...]ᵈUTU-*i* ᵈU-*ni=ya pūriya*(*š*)*=š-ma-aš pidānz*[*i*] "[Whoever(?) use] their evil mouths against [m]e [before] the gods [and] bring [...] to the Sun Deity and the Stormgod on their lips, ..." KUB 43.68 i 14-15 + KUB 36.91 i 9 + KUB 43.71 i 5 (OH/NS), ed. Rieken et al., hethiter.net/: CTH 389.2, tr. Singer, Prayers 24 (without KUB 43.71); for KBo 3.1 i 21 (Tel.pr., OH/NS) see above a 3′ □ for the possible non-writing of the initial *š* of the poss. pron. in DUMU.MEŠ-*ma-aš-ša* = DUMU.MEŠ*=*(*š*)*mašš=a* KBo 17.1 iii 10 (OS) "and of their children" see Groddek, HS 130:27.

**b.** in MH — **1′** nom.-acc. neut. *-šme/it* (only in NS): [(*nu*) ... ]x-*aš* KI-*paš laga*(*n*)*=š-mi-it* (var + *arḫa*) *ēp* "O dark earth, restrain their (i.e., the evil deities) inclination!" KUB 41.8 iv 1 (rit. for netherworld deities, MH/NS), w. dupl. KBo 10.45 iv 1-2, ed. Otten, ZA 54:134f., *lagan*.

**2′** d.-l. *-šmi* (only in MS): (Kaštanda had bought a woman but two men had stolen her from him. §) *kinun=a=kan kāš[a]* m*Kaštandan* ÌR LÚ DUMU.SANGA *katti=šu-mi parā neḫḫun* "But now I have sent here Kaštanda, the male servant of the Junior Priest (or: of the Priest's son) along with them. (You must judge his lawsuit and settle it for him)" HKM 57:18-22 (MS/MH), ed. HBM 228f. ("zu euch"), Letters 205 ("to you"), *šankun(n)i-* 1 a 6′; (Spear men are marching) GAL LÚ.MEŠ.ŠUKUR=*ya=šmaš* NIMGIR.ÉRIN.MEŠ=*ya katti=(i)š-mi iyanta* "Both their chief of the spear men and the army bailiff march with them" IBoT 1.36 ii 50 (instr. for the royal bodyguard, MH/MS), ed. AS 24:20f.; [(*ta=ššan ši*)]*uni=(i)š-mi ḫukanzi* LUGAL-*i* UZUNÍG.GIG [(*u*)]*dan*[(*zi*)] "They slaughter (a kid) for their god. They bring the liver to the king" KBo 16.68 i! 6 + KBo 35.179 rev.? 2 and passim (KI.LAM *MELQITU*, MS but older composition?), translit. StBoT 28:108 (rest. after par. passages in same text).

**3′** pl. nom. com. *-šmiš* (only in MS): 15 *ŠA* UR.MAḪ.ḪI.A [ o o -]x-*da ḫulpazenieš=(š)-mi-š(=a)* ⸢KÙ.GI *U*⸣ *ŠA* KÙ.BABBAR "fifteen lion [...- ]x-s, their *ḫulpazena*'s of gold and silver" KBo 30.20 iii 11-12 (OH?/MS), translit. StBoT 28:116, Groddek, DBH 2:25.

**c.** in NH, d.-l. *-šummi*: ("'The king that will [...] emerge will not say [to the c]ountries the (following) word: "I have made this treaty with you!"'") GIM-*an=ma=nnaš=kan* ḪUL-*uwa AWATE*MEŠ *ištarni=šum!-mi ueḫtat* "But when bad words went back and forth among them against us (I feared those words)" KUB 31.66 ii 10-11 (dep., Murš. III), ed. Houwink ten Cate, FsGüterbock[1] 130, 132 ("in your/their midst"), Rieken, hethiter.net/: CTH 387.1 (24.08.2015) ("unter ihnen"); (My father (i.e., Šuppiluliuma I) asked for the tablet that said ... ) *nu=kan* dU-*aš* [*ANA*] KUR URU*Mizri U ANA* KUR URU*Ḫatti maḫḫan* [*išḫ*]*iūl ištarni=šum-mi išḫiyat uktūri=at=kan* [*m*]*aḫḫan ištarni=šum-mi āššiyanteš* "how the Stormgod imposed a [tre]aty [on] Egypt and on Ḫatti between them (and) [h]ow they were for ever friendly between them" KBo 14.12 iv 29-32 (DŠ, Murš. II), ed. DŠ 98 □ see similarly ibid. iv 39 but note that the same combination *ištarni=šu[mmi]* in iv 37 is the pl. 1 poss. pron. because of the enclitic *=nnaš* "us"; [*k*]*arūiliyaza=wa* URU*Ḫattušaš* [URU]U*Mizrašš=a ištarni=šum-mi āššiyanteš* [*e*]*šer kinun=a=wa=nnaš=kan kī=ya ištarni=šu*[*m-mi*] / [*kiš*]*at nu=wa=kan* KUR URU*Ḫatti* KUR URU*Mizr*[*i=ya*] / [*ukt*]*ūri namma ištarni=šum-mi āššiy*[*anteš*] "In the past Ḫattuša and Egypt were on good terms with each other. But now this, too, has happened between us! The land of Hatti [and] the land of Egypt [will] again be on lasting good terms with each other" KBo 14.12 iv 35-39 (DŠ, Murš. II), ed. DŠ 98, Francia, SMEA 35:95f., GestaSupp 95, 125 □ in this NH composition, when enclitic possessives were no longer part of speakers' own grammar, the correct sense of *ištarni=šummi* (surely taken from the earlier MH treaty) was misunderstood to mean simply 'mutually' (Francia, SMEA 35:96: 'tra noi, voi, loro'), applicable to all plural persons.

Starke, StBoT 31 (1990) 79-82; Hoffner/Melchert, GrHL (2008) 137-141 w. previous bibliography; Groddek, HS 126 (2013) 118-122; Groddek, HS 130 (2017) 17-41.

**-šmaš A, -šamaš A** enclitic personal pron.; you (pl.) (dat. and acc.); from OS.

From OS onwards *-š.* is as a rule spelled -V*š-ma-aš* after vowels and -VC-*ša-ma-aš* after consonants, logograms and some plene writings. Writing -V*š-ma-aš* after *-a* mostly concerns the clitics *-a/-ya, -a/-ma, -wa* and the connective *ta* but also words ending in *-a*, e.g. *menaḫḫanda=šmaš* KUB 23.79 rev. 9 (myth, MS). Exx. for *-iš-ma-aš* are rare, cf. *ke-e-da-ni-iš-ma-aš* KUB 41.8 iii 7 (rit. for netherworld deities, MH/NS), for KUB 22.70 rev. 60 see below. Examples of *-uš-ma-aš* occur very frequently after the connective *nu* (*nu=šmaš*). After *-ma* the sequence *-ma-aš-ma-aš* = *-ma=šmaš* could haplographically be shortened to *-ma-aš*: ("They tend to them (i.e., the horses)") *wātar-ma-aš UL pāi* "but he doesn't give them water" KUB 1.11 i 11 (Kikk., MH/MS), ed. Hipp. heth. 106f., cf. also ibid. ii 47, iv 27; LÚ.MEŠŠU!.GI LÚ.MEŠ*UBĀRU šarā tianzi t=at UŠKÊNNU* LÚZABAR.DAB-*ma-aš* GEŠTIN *akuwanna pāi* "The ŠU.GI-priests (and) the foreigners stand up and they bow. The ZABAR.DAB-man gives them wine to drink" KUB 20.78 iii 21-25 (fest. of the month, NS), ed. StBoT 37:488f. (emending to LÚZABAR.DAB‹-*aš*›-*ma-aš*); (One sender to two addressees:) DINGIR.MEŠ-*ma-aš* TI-*an ḫarkandu* "May the gods keep you alive" VS 28.129 obv. 5 (letter, NS), ed.

Hagenbuchner, ZA 89:51f.; for a discussion see Cammarosano, ICH 8:144-148.

The spelling -VC-*ša-ma-aš* after consonants (e.g. *ku-it-ša-ma-aš* KBo 3.56 obv. 11 (hist. frag., OH/NS)) is found after *n, r,* and *t* (for *š* see below): *[k]inun≠* IBoT 2.131 obv. 7 (cult inv., NH), *maḫḫan≠* HKM 15:4, HKM 16:5, and HKM passim (letters, MH/MS), *mān≠* KBo 22.1 obv. 21 (instr., OS), KUB 23.68 obv. 21 (treaty w. Išmerikka, MH/NS), KUB 31.1 ii 10 (Naramsin in Asia Minor, NS), *n≠an≠* KBo 8.35 ii 7 (treaty w. Kaškaeans, MS), *n≠at≠* KBo 41.6 rev. 6 (rit. of Mallidunna, MH/NS), cf. also dupl. *na-at-ša-ma-ša-at* = *n≠at≠šmaš≠at*) KBo 31.113:5 (MH/MS?), *uttar≠* Bo 4171 i? 6 (rit. for Sungoddess of the Earth, NS), translit. Otten/Rüster, ZA 68:271 and HPMM 6:67, *wātar≠* KUB 1.13 iv 10 et passim (Kikk., MH/NS). For logograms see ŠÀ.GAL≠ KUB 1.13 iii 61 (Kikk., MH/NS), ⌈*UNŪTUM*⌉*≠* KUB 13.35 + KBo 16.62 iv 16 (dep., NS).

After *š* one sibilant could serve as both the final -*š* of the preceding word and the initial sibilant of the pron. -*š*.: e.g. *šu-um-me-eš-ma-aš* = *šummeš≠(š)maš* KUB 26.1 i 6 (instr. for eunuchs, Tudḫ. IV), cf. similarly KUB 26.1 iii 45; see further $^{\text{NINDA}}$*wagatāš≠(š)maš* KBo 20.50:1, 7 (rit. frag., OS), *kiššaraš≠(š)maš* KBo 32.176 obv. 18 (Walkui's rit., MH/MS), ANŠE.KUR.RA-*eš-ma-aš* KBo 31.47 ii 2 (dep., NH/NS), $^{\text{LÚ.MEŠ}}$*ḫal-li-ia-re-e-eš-ma-aš* KUB 11.13 ii 6 (*ANDAḪŠUM*-fest., NS). Sometimes, however, the final -*š* of a word could be treated as a consonant and thus followed by -*ša-ma-aš* as seen above: *nu≠uš≠* KBo 16.45 rev. 4 (frag., OS); for the order of clitics see GrHL §30.19 and see below; *kuiš≠* KUB 31.103:12 (treaty frag.?, MS), $^{\text{d}}$*Enkiduš≠* KUB 17.2:8 (Gilg., NS), $^{\text{d}}$U-*aš≠* KBo 10.45 iii 45 (rit. for netherworld deities, MH/NS), *kūš≠* KBo 22.260 obv. 4 (oracle question, NH), *parunkuš≠* KUB 44.60 iii 1 (Hattian bil., NS), correct CHD s.v. *parunka-* where -*ša-* was mistakenly left out. Although the same situation applies to *z* (= /ts/) (see spellings like ⌈*ki-iš-ša*⌉*-r[a-az-(me-et)]* = *kiššaraz≠(š)met* KBo 17.3 ii 24, w. dupl. KBo 17.6 ii 19, for the poss. pron. -*šmi/a-*), such cases do not seem to be attested for -*š*. Note that in combinations of -*š*. with a preceding consonant, regular assimilatory developments (-*nš-* > -*šš-*) or simplified writings (/ts/ expressed through -*z-* in combinations of /t/ or /n/ + /s/) seem to be generally avoided. Spellings like *d[a]-a-aḫ-ḫu-uš-ma[(-aš-ta)]* = *daḫḫu(n)≠šmaš≠(š)ta* FHG 6 iv 13 (= KBo 17.1 iv 39), w. dupl. KBo 17.3 iv 35 (rit. for the royal couple, OS) and *pé-ra-aš-ma-a[š]* = *pera(n)≠šmaš* KUB 12.63 obv. 5 (Zuwi's rit., MH/MS) are rare.

The following spellings of -*ša-ma-aš/š*V- after a plene-written vowel are attested: *pa-ra-a-ša-ma-aš-ša-an* = *parā≠šmaš≠šan* KUB 10.93 iv 7 (fest. for tutelary deity, NS), *ki-i-ša-ma-aš-kán* = *kī≠šmaš≠kan* KUB 22.70 rev. 60 (oracle question, NH), *[k]a-ru-ú-ša-ma-ša-at* = *karū≠šmaš≠at* KUB 45.49 iv 13 (frag. of Hitt.-Hurr. rit., NS). The only counter ex. is *ša-ra-a-aš-ma-aš* HT 10:5 (Gilg., NS) where the par. KBo 10.47c iv 21 has *ša-ra-a-aš* = *šarā≠aš* with the acc. pl. 3rd pers. clitic. The sequence *ka-a-aš-ma-aš* KUB 41.8 iii 34 (rit. for netherworld deities, MH/NS) is to be read as *kāšma≠šmaš* (see below for haplography of -*ma-aš* for -*ma-aš-ma-aš*).

The three instances of -*ša-ma-aš* after the negation *natta* (*na-at-ta-ša-ma-aš* KBo 22.1 obv. 23 (instr., OS), *Ú-UL-aš-ša-ma-aš-kán* KBo 10.45 iii 44 (rit., MH/NS), w. dupl. *Ú-UL-aš-ma-aš-ša-an* KUB 41.8 iii 34 (MH/NS)), could reflect *nat≠šmaš* with the shorter variant of *natta* as considered possible s.v. *natta* a 1′ e′ (and see also *natt≠(u)wa≠z* ibid. a 1′ a′). Note that a writing like LÚ.MEŠ $^{\text{URU}}$*Ḫa-at-ti-ša-ma-aš* (GÙB-*tar*) "(the unfavorableness) of the men of Ḫatti" can represent a spoken **Ḫattušumm/naš≠šmaš*.

If -*š*. is followed by another clitic starting in a vowel or *š*, -V*š-ma-š*V- is written, e.g. *nu-uš-ma-ši-kán* for *nu≠šmaš≠(š)i≠kan* KBo 20.34 rev. 7 (Ḫantitaššu's rit., MS); see further *nu-uš-ma-ša-at* = *nu≠šmaš≠at* KBo 38.234:8 (rit, frag., NS), KBo 41.208 obv. 16 (vow, LNS), *ut-ni-ia-aš-ma-ša-pa* = *utniya≠šmaš≠apa*, KUB 41.32 ii 6 (rit. frag., NS), *nu-uš-ma-ša-an* = *nu≠šmaš≠(š)an*) KUB 30.34 iii 7 (Iriya's rit., NS).

There is no good evidence for a spelling -*šu-ma-aš*: the sequence *ta-a-aš-šu-ma-aš* KUB 2.5 iii 42 (*ANDAḪŠUM*-fest. 16th day, NS) is probably to be taken as d.-l. pl. from *t/daššu-* "strong, sturdy, important, hard" (differently Badalì/Zinko, Scientia 20:84f., 173). Anomalous is EN.SISKUR-*ia-ša-ma-aš-za* KUB 46.40 obv. 10 (rit., LNS) assuming it stands for EN.SISKUR≠*ya≠šmaš≠za*. The sequence ⌈*ka*⌉?*-a-ša-aš-ša-ma-aš-kán* could be parsed *kāša≠aš≠šmaš≠kan* KUB 41.22 iii 3 (rit. frag., NS) with an irregular sequence of clitic elements (instead of an expected **ka-a-ša-aš-ma-ša-aš-kán* = **kāša≠šmaš≠aš≠kan*) but -*aš-ša-* shows traces of erasure.

Position in the clause. In the chain of clitic particles -*š*. comes in second place after the quotative particle -*wa(r-)* and before the clitic pron. of the third pers. sg. and pl., and of the first, second, and third pers. sg.; a second clitic pron. in the same function is excluded; see GrHL 410f. (§30.15 and 19).

**a.** (dat.) to/for/from you (pl.) — **1′** in OH — **a′** in OS: *[(k)]āša≠ta≠(a)š-ma-aš≠kan utniyandan lāluš dāḫḫun [(erm)]a(n)≠š-ma-aš≠kan dāḫḫun kardi≠šmi≠at≠kan dāḫḫu[n] / [(ḫarš)]ani≠šmi≠at≠kan dāḫḫun ta≠aš-ma-aš ḫurtiya[llan / (par)]ā ēpmi* "Right now I have taken from you the slander of the people, I have taken from you illness, I have taken it from your heart, I have taken it from your head and I hold out to you a *ḫurtiya[lla]*-vessel(?)" KBo 17.1 i 11-14 (rit. for the royal couple, OS), ed. StBoT 8:18f., Montuori, hethiter.net/: CTH 416, translit. StBoT 25:5 □ for the -*ta-* in *kāša≠ta* see Neu, StBoT 26:4 n. 11, Rieken, Pragmatische Kategorien 270f.; see also KBo 22.1 rev. 21-23 below b 1′ a′.

**b′** in OH/MS: (not attested).

**c′** in OH/NS: [*ug*]*=a=*(*a*)*š-ma-aš* $^{GIŠ}$*intaluzzit šunnaḫḫi* "I, however, will fill/pour for you (pl.) using a shovel" KBo 3.38 rev. 16-17 (in broken context in Zalpa story, OH/NS), ed. StMed 19:34, 42, StBoT 17:10f., Soysal, Diss. 48, 99, *šunna-* d; ("If someone commits evil ...") *nu=*(*u*)*š-ma-š*(*a*)*=an* $^{UZU}$KA×UD-*it* [(*ka*)]*ripten* "you must devour him with (your) teeth!" KUB 11.2:12 + IBoT 3.84:12 (+) KBo 19.97:4 (Tel. pr., OH/NS), w. dupls. KBo 3.1 ii 73 (OH/NS), KBo 12.6:3 (OH/NS), ed. THeth. 11:38f. □ for *-š* here as poss. dat. see *-še, -ši* A c 4′.

**2′** in MH — **a′** in MH/MS: (The priestess says:) *aiš* EME-*aš gagāš qāša=*(*a*)*š-ma-aš=kan parkuin mišriwantan ḫarkin* $^{GIŠ}$GIDRU *UL walḫantan* UDU-*un šipantaḫḫun* "O mouth, tongue (and) tooth, I have offered to you here a pure, bright, white sheep untouched by a stick" KBo 15.10 ii 8-10 (rit. for Tudḫ. I and Nikalmadi, MH/MS), ed. Kassian, Zip. 36f., Görke, hethiter.net/: CTH 443.1; *kāšma=*(*a*)*š-ma-aš tuppi* $^{m}$*Piše*[*niyaš*] *uppaḫḫun=pat nu=*(*u*)*š-ma-š*(*a*)*=at=kan* [*p*]*eran ḫalzi*[*andu*] "I have hereby sent you the tablet of Mr. Piše[ni] and [let them] read it out to you" HKM 25:22-25 (letter, MH/MS), ed. HBM 164f., Letters 141; *katta=*(*a*)*š-ma-aš ḫūman* SIG$_5$-*in ēštu* "May all be well with you!" HKM 57:6-7 (letter, MH/MS), ed. HBM 226f., Letters 205.

**b′** in MH/NS: (In instruction to guards of a temple:) *nu=*(*u*)*š-ma-aš tešḫaš lē ēšzi namma=*(*a*)*š-ma-aš ḫāli arḫa šarran ēšdu* "There shall be no sleep for you! Furthermore, let the watch be divided among you" KUB 13.4 iii 17-18 (instr. for temple personnel, MH/NS), ed. THeth. 26:56, 78; *mān=ša-ma*[-*aš*]*=kan idalu=ma uttar kuiški peran* [*t*]*ezzi* "But if someone says an evil word in your presence" KUB 23.68 obv. 21 (treaty w. people of Išmeriga, Arn. I/NS), ed. Kempinski/Košak, WO 5:194f., tr. DiplTexts² 15; (If you and another person do not support His Majesty) *nu=*(*u*)*š-ma-aš kī uttar NĪŠ* DINGIR.MEŠ EGIR-*an lē tarnanzi nu=*(*u*)*š-ma-ša*!-*at*! (tablet: *-at-ša*) *lē āra ienzi nu=*(*u*)*š-ma-aš takšan ḫarninkandu* "may the Oath Gods not condone this behavior for you, may they not make it right for you and let them destroy you both" KBo 5.3 ii 7-9 (Huqq., Šupp. I), ed. SV 114f., tr. DiplTexts² 29.

**3′** in NH: *našma=kan mān* [*amm*]*uk=ma kuitki šarnikzel ḫanti išḫiyattēni* [*n=a*]*t=mu tešḫaz memišten nu=*(*u*)*š-ma-š*(*a*)*=at peḫḫi* "Or if you separately impose on [m]e some compensation, tell it to me in a dream and I will give it to you" KUB 14.8 rev. 34-36 (PP2, Murš. II), ed. Pestgeb. 216f., tr. Prayers 60; *nu=*(*u*)*š-ma-aš apāš mem*[(*ya*)]*š* GAM *NĪŠ* DINGIR-*LIM* GAR-*ru* "That matter must be subject to divine oath for you" KUB 26.12 i 10 (instr. for princes, commanders, and eunuchs, Tudḫ. IV), w. dupl. KUB 26.13 i (10-)11, ed. HittInstr. 284f., Dienstanw. 23.

**b.** (acc.) you — **1′** in OH — **a′** in OS: *mān=ša-ma-aš ABI parna=šma tarnai nu=*(*u*)*š-ma-aš mānḫanda ḫatreškezzi natta=ša-ma-aš* $^{LÚ.MEŠ}$DUGUD *tuppi ḫazzian ḫarzi* "When my father lets you go home (lit. to your house/home), has he not engraved a tablet for you, dignitaries, just as he always writes to you?" KBo 22.1 rev. 21-23 (instr., OS), ed. Archi, FsLaroche 46f., HittInstr. 74f., THeth. 29:109 □ the second and third *-š*. are both d.-l.

**b′** in OH/MS: (not attested).

**c′** in OH/NS: [*n*]*u=*(*u*)*š-ma-aš arḫa paraḫḫandu* "May they chase you away!" KBo 12.109:13 (rit. frag., OH/NS), ed. *parḫ-* 2 a 1′.

**2′** in MH — **a′** in MH/MS: ("When this letter reaches you, drive quickly to My Majesty and bring Marruwa, the man from Gagadduwa") *mān UL=ma nu=*(*u*)*š-ma-aš=šan uwanzi apiya pēdi tašuwaḫḫanzi* "If not they will blind you over there (i.e., where you are) on the spot" HKM 14:10-14 (letter, MH/MS), ed. HBM 140f., Letters 120 □ for *apiya* as a second person dem., see Goedegebuure, StBoT 55:237; *nu=wa=*(*a*)*š-ma-aš* $^{d}$*SÎN walḫannau* "May the Moongod strike you!" KUB 43.38 rev. 21 (military oath, MH/MS), ed. StBoT 22:20f., Görke, hethiter.net/: CTH 493.

**b′** in MH/NS: (in an oath ceremony: "Just as they stain this (animal) skin blood-red and its blood-red color doesn't go away") *šumāš=a linkiyanteš anda QĀTAMMA appandu nu=*(*u*)*š-ma-š=at=kan arḫa lē paizzi* "may the Oath Deities likewise seize you and may it not go away from you" KBo 6.34 iv 1-3 (MH/NS), ed. StBoT 22:14f.

□ the sg. 3rd pers. *paizzi* probably refers to the "blood-red color" of the animal skin, which is what the oath takers will look like after they have transgressed the oath and angered the oath deities.

**3′** in NH: DINGIR.MEŠ-*ma-aš* (= *=ma=šmaš*) TI-*an ḫarkandu* "May the gods keep you alive!" VS 28.129 obv. 5 (letter, NH), ed. Hagenbuchner, ZA 89:51f.

**c.** standing for the particle *-za* (see GrHL §28.32 ) — **1′** in nominal sentences w. pl. subject (only NH): *šummeš=(š)-ma-aš kuiēš* LÚ.MEŠ SAG "You who are eunuchs" KUB 26.1 i 6 (instr. for eunuchs, Tudḫ. IV), ed. HittInstr 296f., Dienstanw. 8 *šumeš=wa=(a)š-ma-aš* ÌR.MEŠ *AB*[*I=YA* (*ēšten*)] "You were subjects of [my] fat[her]" KUB 14.16 iii 26 (Extensive ann. of Murš. II), w. dupl. KUB 14.15 iii 56, ed. AM 58f.

**2′** w. verbs or constructions normally requiring *-za*: *nu=(u)š-ma-aš* $GU_5$-*zi* NAG-*zi* "They eat (and) drink" KUB 17.35 i 27 (cult inv., NH), ed. HLC 168f.; *nu=(u)š-ma-aš takšan šarran* LÚ.MEŠ URU*Ḫatti ḫalzeššanzi takšan šarra(n)=ma=(a)š-ma-aš* LÚ.MEŠ URU*Māša ḫalzišanzi* "They call half (of them) 'Men of Ḫatti' while they call the other half 'Men of Māša'" KUB 17.35 iii 10-11 (cult inv., NH), ed. *šarra-* B, *šarran-* 2, HLC 172f.

Friedrich, HE 1 (1960) 63; Tischler, HEG S/2 (2006) 1106-1109; Hoffner/Melchert, GrHL (2008) 135f.; Kloekhorst, EDHIL (2008) 115f., 770.

**-šmaš B, -šamaš B** enclitic personal pron.; to/for/from them (dat.); from OS.

For spellings of *-š.* see *-šmaš* A, *-šamaš* A.

**a.** (dat.) to/for/from them — **1′** in OH — **a′** in OS: 3-*kiš=a=(a)š-ma-aš šī*[*n*]*an* [*pa*]*rā ēpzi* GUD-*n=a=(a)š-ma-aš* 3-*iš parā ēpzi* "Three times she holds out to them (i.e., the king and queen) the figurine while three times she holds out to them the ox" KBo 17.1 (= FHG 6 i 2-3 + IBoT 1.26:3-4) i 3-5 (rit. for royal couple, OS), ed. StBoT 8:18f., translit. StBoT 25:5; *nu=(u)š-ma-aš akuanna pianzi* "and they give them to drink" KUB 34.115 iii 12 + KBo 30.28:13 (fest. celebrated by the prince, OS), translit. StBoT 26:372, tr. von Bredow, Altanat.Gotth. 70 (mistakenly translates sg. "ihm").

**b′** in OH/MS: ("O male deities of the Storm-god of Kuliwišna, eat and satisfy your hunger. Drink and satisfy your thirst") [*n*]*u=(u)š-ma-aš* ŠÀ=*KUNU šaknuan ēštu* ZI=*KUNU=ma=(a)š-ma-aš* [*li*?]*mmuanza ēštu* "Let your stomach be filled with fat/oil and your soul be filled with [*li*]*mma*-beer" KUB 33.62 iii 12-13 (rit., OH?/MS), ed. *šaknuwant-* B a, Glocker, Eothen 6:40f. (differently [*kart*]*immuanza*).

**c′** in OH/NS: GIŠTUKUL.ḪI.A-*uš=šuš=(š)ta* ZAG.UDU-*za daḫḫun nu=(u)š-ma-aš* GIŠŠÙ[DUN?] *peḫḫun* "I took their weapons from (their) shoulders and gave them a y[oke(?)]" KBo 3.1 ii 30 (Tel.pr., OH/NS), ed. THeth. 11:30f., tr. Goedegebuure, ANEHST 232.

**2′** in MH — **a′** in MH/MS: ("The question of your opponents in court that you wrote me about, right now I have (it, i.e., your tablet(?) or the affair under control(?))") *n=at INA* É.GAL-*LIM memaḫḫi nu=(u)š-ma-aš antuḫšaš paizzi n=aš MAḪAR* dUTU-*ŠI uwatezzi* "I will report it to the palace and a person will go to them and bring them before His Majesty" HKM 10 rev. 49-52 (letter, MH/MS), ed. HBM 136f., tr. Letters 116 □ for the tr. of *andatiyattalla*- "opponent in court" see Hoffner, Letters 116f.; Alp, HBM 137 mistakenly takes *-š.* here as 2 pl. ("zu euch").

**b′** in MH/NS: *uktūri=ma=(a)š-ma-aš tiyauwa*[*r*]*=pat* [É]*arkiwi tapušza* (Wherever the guards are,) "the aforementioned standing next to the canopy is the unchanging rule for them" IBoT 1.36 i 71-72 (instr. for the royal bodyguard, MH/NS), ed. AS 24:12f.; ("Furthermore, this sister of mine whom I have given to you as a wife has many sisters from her own family (and) from her extended family") [(*ŠA* NU)MUN=*K*]*A=at=ta*«-*at*» *apē=ya zig=a=(a)š-ma-aš=za* $NIN_9$=[(*SU ku*)]*it ḫarši* "they belong to your extended family as well, because you have their (lit. for them her) sister" KBo 5.3 iii 27 (Ḫuqq., Šupp. I), w. dupl. KBo 19.44 iv 16, ed. SV 124f., tr. DiplTexts[2] 31.

**3′** in NH: *nu* dUTU-*ŠI ANA* LÚ.MEŠ URU*Māša antuḫšan uiyanun nu=(u)š-ma-aš kiššan AŠPUR* "I, My Majesty, sent a man to the people of Māša and wrote to them as follows" KUB 6.41 i 45-46 (Kup.,

Murš. II), ed. SV 1:112f., tr. DiplTexts[2] 75; *nu=(u)š-ma-aš šaḫḫan luzzi lē ēšzi AWAT NĀRĀRI=(a)š-ma-aš lē ēšzi kuit=at imma kuit šaḫḫan luzzi nu=(u)š-ma-aš peran* EGIR-*pa lē kuiški paizzi* "There shall be no *šaḫḫan* (and) corvée for them; there shall be no request for help from them. Whatever *šaḫḫan* (and) corvée there is, nobody shall go back before them" Bronze Tablet iii 53-55 (treaty w. Kuruntiya, Tudḫ. IV), ed. StBoT Beih. 1:22f., tr. DiplTexts[2] 120; ("They take from your [mouth], O god, ox (and) [sheep] meat") *nu=(u)š-ma-aš parkunuanzi* "Shall they cleanse themselves (and compensate an ox with [an ox and a sheep with a sh]eep?)" KUB 16.39 ii 15 (oracle question, NH), ed. HTR 108f., *parkunu-* 1 a 2′ a′.

Friedrich, HE 1 (1960) 63; Tischler, HEG S/2 (2006) 1109-1113; Hoffner/Melchert, GrHL (2008) 135f.; Kloekhorst, EDHIL (2008) 115f., 770.

## -šmi- see *-šma/i-* A and B.

## š(u)-, conj.; so, for this reason, as a result, and, so that, and thus, yet; from OS.†

**a.** distribution and use of *š.*
- **1′** distribution w. respect to tense
- **2′** function as marker of cause and effect
- **3′** distribution w. respect to clitics and subordination
- **4′** alternation w. *nu*
- **5′** loss of *š.* and its replacement w. *nu*

**b.** *š.* connecting main clauses
- **1′** w. additive meaning
  - **a′** introducing a result clause
    - **1″** in OS
    - **2″** in OH/NS
  - **b′** introducing an intended result or fulfilled purpose clause
    - **1″** in OS
    - **2″** in OH/MS
    - **3″** in OH/NS
  - **c′** introducing an unintended ("and so") or intended result ("so that")
    - **1″** in OS
    - **2″** in OH/NS
  - **d′** expressing a temporal sequence, in OH/NS
- **2′** w. concessive meaning ("yet"), in OH/NS
- **3′** meaning unclear
  - **a′** because of ambiguous or unclear context
    - **1″** in OS
    - **2″** in OH/MS
  - **b′** because of fragmentary context
    - **1″** in OS
    - **2″** in OH/NS

**c.** connecting a main clause with its preceding subordinate clause:
- **1′** the events described in the subordinate clause provide the cause or motivation for the state of affairs of the main clause
  - **a′** following a temporal clause with *mān* "when"
    - **1″** in OS
    - **2″** in OH/NS
  - **b′** following a relative clause, in OH/NS
  - **c′** following an extra-clausal constituent (i.e., a *casus pendens*) introduced by *kuit*, in OH/NS
- **2′** expressing temporal consecution, following a relative clause, in OH/NS
- **3′** expressing concurrent action, following a relative clause, in OH/NS
- **4′** meaning unclear, often in fragmentary context
  - **a′** following a relative clause
    - **1″** in OS
    - **2″** in OH/NS
  - **b′** following *mān* "just as, like"

**followed by encl. pron. sg. nom. com. *-aš*:** *ša-aš* KBo 8.42 rev.? 9 (OS), KBo 22.2 rev. 2, 7, 14 (OS), KUB 36.99 rev. (3)? (OS), KBo 55.8 ii 13 (OH/MS), KUB 17.10 i 34 (OH/MS), KUB 33.2 i 19 (OH/MS), KBo 3.34 ii 7, 19, iii 9 (OH/NS), KBo 3.35:15 (OH/NS), KBo 3.36:8?, 15 (OH/NS), KBo 3.38 rev. (18), 22, 31 (OH/NS), KBo 3.46 obv. 35 (OH/NS), KBo 3.53 obv. 6, 7 (OH/NS), KBo 3.54:11 (OH/NS), KBo 12.14 obv. 5 (OH/NS), KBo 19.90:12 (OH/NS), KUB 23.28:12 (OH/NS), KUB 26.71 i 15 (OH/NS), KUB 40.5 ii 4 (OH/NS), KUB 48.79 rev. 4, 9, 18 (OH/NS), KUB 48.81:1, 3 (OH/NS), KUB 48.89 obv. 7 (OH/NS), *ša⟨-aš⟩* KBo 3.56:6 (OH/NS), *ša-aš(-kán)* KBo 3.56:5 (OH/NS), KUB 36.103:11 (OH/NS).

**followed by encl. pron. sg. acc. com. *-an*:** *ša-an* KBo 3.22 rev. 45, 46, 47, 54 (OS), KBo 8.42 obv.? 3, rev.? 7 (OS), KBo 8.67:12 (OS), KBo 17.23 obv. 7 (OS), KBo 22.2 obv. 14, rev. 8, 9 (OS), KUB 36.99 rev. 5 (OS), KUB 36.104 obv. (11), 15 (OS), KUB 36.100 obv. 16 (OS?), KBo 25.151:4 (OH/MS), KBo 26.136 obv. 8 (OH/MS), KBo 31.77 iv! 4, 6, 11 (OH/MS), KBo 43.4 iii 6 (OH/MS), KBo 55.8 ii 13 (OH/MS), KBo 3.16 iii (2), (3), 4 (OH/NS), KBo 3.17 obv. 7(?) (OH/NS), KBo 3.18 iii 5, 6 (OH/NS), KBo 3.28 ii 19 (OH/NS), KBo 3.34 i 4 (2×), 13 (2×), 17, 25, ii 7, 10 (2×), 11, 15, 16, 17 (OH/NS), KBo 3.36:9, 10, 17 (2×), 21, 23 (OH/NS), KBo 3.38 obv. 5, rev. 24, (26) (OH/NS), KBo 3.44:8 (OH/NS), KBo 3.46 obv. (25) (?), 46 (OH/NS), KBo 3.60 ii 13, 21 (OH/NS), KBo 3.67 ii 2 (OH/NS), KBo 10.2 i 4 (OH/NS), KBo 12.3 iv 14 (OH/NS), KBo 12.8 i 8 (OH/NS), KBo 12.10:2 (OH/NS), KBo 13.44 i 4 (OH/NS), KBo 27.18:9 (OH/NS), KBo 50.8 rt. col. 2 (OH/NS), KUB 1.17 iii 38 (OH/NS), KUB 26.71 i (3) (OH/NS), KUB 31.110:11 (OH/NS, not *ša-ap*, *pace* Kammenhuber, Materialien 1/2:3), KUB 33.52 ii 7 (OH/NS), KUB 33.55 ii 14 (OH/NS), KUB 33.56 rev. (1) (OH/NS), KUB 48.81:4 (OH/NS), VBoT 33:7, 8, Bo 2896 ii 13 (OH/NS), KBo 40.18 obv.? 4(?) (NS), *ša-n(a-ap)* KBo 3.60 ii 3, 5, 18, iii 9 (OH/NS), *ša-n(a-aš-ta)* KUB 36.104 obv. 6 (OS), KBo 3.24 + KBo 53.275 obv. 15 (OH/NS), KBo 3.34 i 8, ii 9, 19 (OH/NS), KBo 3.36:14, (17), (24) (OH/NS), KBo 3.41 obv. 17 (OH/NS), KBo 13.44 i 8 (OH/NS), *ša-na-aš-ta*! (photo has *-ša*) KBo 3.34 ii 6 (OH/NS), *ša-n(a[-aš-ta])* KBo 3.38 obv. 18 (OH/NS), *ša-an(-kán)* KBo 31.77 iv! (14) (OH/MS), KBo 3.60 iii 9 (OH/NS), *ša-an(-za-pa)* KBo 12.18 obv. 6 (OH/NS), KBo 12.63 ii 3 (OH/NS), KUB 43.60 i 30 (OH/NS).

**followed by encl. pron. sg. nom.-acc. neut. *-at***: *ša-at* KBo 14.98 i 15 (OH/MS?), KBo 24.51 obv. 2 (OH/MS?), KBo 47.309:6 (MS?), VBoT 58 iv 4 (OH/NS).

**followed by encl. pron. pl. nom. com. *-e***: *še* KBo 22.2 rev. 13 (OS), KBo 3.16 ii 14 (OH/NS), KBo 3.34 i 2, 3 (OH/NS), KBo 3.60 iii 4 (OH/NS), KBo 3.67 ii 7 (OH/NS), KBo 13.44 i 2, 3 (OH/NS), KUB 31.64 ii 38 (OH/NS, not KUR, *pace* StMed 12:172), KUB 36.103:2 (OH/NS), *še(-a)* KBo 3.38 rev. 29 (OH/NS).

**followed by encl. pron. pl. nom.-acc. neut. *-e***: *še-(kán)* KBo 38.188 left col. 3 (?) (OH/MS).

**followed by encl. pron. pl. acc. com. *-uš***: *šu-uš* KBo 3.22 obv. 37 (OS), KBo 17.1 iv 22 (OS), KBo 17.3 iv 18 (OS), KBo 22.2 obv. (3), 5, 7, rev. 12 (OS), KUB 36.99 obv. 4 (OS), KBo 3.28 ii 17 (OH/NS), KBo 3.34 ii 32 (OH/NS), KBo 3.38 obv. 16 (?) (OH/NS), KBo 3.46 obv. 17, 40 (OH/NS), KBo 3.53 obv. 10 (OH/NS), KBo 3.60 iii 6 (OH/NS), KBo 12.3 iii 22 (OH/NS), KBo 16.86 i 6 (OH/NS), KBo 22.3:6 (OH/NS), KBo 26.126:1 (OH/NS), KUB 31.5:10 (OH/NS), KUB 31.110:7 (OH/NS), KUB 36.98a:(7) (OH/NS), KUB 36.101 ii 3 (OH/NS), KUB 36.102 rt. col. 4 (OH/NS), KUB 37.148 obv. 8 (OH/NS), *šu-š(a-ap)* KBo 3.60 iii 3 (OH/NS), *šu-uš(-kán)* KBo 50.9 obv.? 10 (OS?), KBo 3.45:2, KUB 31.64 ii 39 (OH/NS). Prob. not *šu-uš* but a poss. clitic: KBo 12.4 iii 9.

**followed by encl. pron. pl. acc. com. *-aš***: *ša-aš* KBo 3.13 obv. 16 (OH/NS).

**followed by encl. pron. sg. dat. *-mu***: *šu-mu* KBo 3.22 rev. 75 (OS), KBo 3.28 ii 6 (OH/NS), KBo 3.43 rev. 2 (OH/NS), KBo 12.81 obv.? ii 5 (OH/NS), *šu-mu-u(z)* KBo 3.43 rev. 3 (OH/NS).

**followed by quotative particle *-wa(r)-***: *šu-wa* KBo 22.2 rev. 5, 6 (OS), KBo 14.98 i 8, (9), ii 4, 5, 9, 15 (OH/MS?), KBo 3.38 rev. 21 (OH/NS), KUB 33.61 iv 3 (OH/NS), KUB 34.60:11 (OH/NS), Bo 2896 (Popko, AoF 33:155) ii 4, 6 (2×), 8, 9, iii 9, 11 (OH/NS), Bo 6660:3, 5, 8 (OH/NS), *šu-wa*! KBo 3.38 rev. 21 (OH/NS), *šu-wa-r(a-aš)* KUB 33.58:8 (OH/NS), *šu-wa-r(a-aš-ta)* KUB 33.63 rev. 6 (OH/NS), *šu-wa-r(u-uš)* Bo 2896 ii 3 (Popko, AoF 33:155) (OH/NS).

**unclear due to broken context:** *še* KUB 31.5:11 (OH/NS), *še-(pa)* KUB 36.27:2 (OH/NS), *še-e(-pa)* KUB 43.36:2, 6 (NS).

Several instances of *š.* are based on errors in the hand copy: ("Let the bee bring it") ⌈*na*⌉(coll. ph.)*-an pēdi≠šši dāu* "and put it in its place" KUB 43.60 i 6 (myth, OH/NS), ed. Watkins, Dragon 285f., Polvani ICH 5:615f., Archi, JANER 7:172f., Fuscagni (ed.), hethiter.net/: CTH 457.7.1 (TX 13.10.2014, TRde 20.12.2012) (all reading *ša-an*); *ta*(coll. ph.)*-aš INA* É [d]*Zinduḫiya* [*paizzi*] KBo 41.94 i 5 (cult of Arinna, NS), ed. Popko, StBoT 50:58 (reading *ta*[!]*-aš*); *ta*(coll. ph.) *appā*[*i*] KBo 17.101 iii 10 (fest. frag., NS); *ta*(coll. ph.)*-an parkunu*[(*zzi*)] KBo 19.3 i 12 (Laws, OH/NS), w. dupl. KBo 6.2 iii 35 (OS), ed. LH 73 n. 236 ("Güterbock field transliteration: *ta*, photo ambiguous"). Other real cases of *š.* could be errors for *ta*, so for example *ša namma* UDU*-un arḫa palzaḫā*[(*iz*)]*zi*, KUB 24.14 iv 9, dupl. KUB 28.78 iv 1. Because of the minimal difference in the sign forms of ŠA and TA, there is no guarantee that any particular instance of *š.* followed by *-aš*, *-an* or *-at* indeed belongs with *š.* A candidate for emendation is GAL *MEŠEDI peran ḫūwāi t≠aš ḫaššī tapušza tiyazi ta≠kkan wal(a)ḫḫiyaš* [DUG]KAB.KA.DÙ*-an anda udanzi ša-an ANA* GIŠ.[d]INANNA.ḪI.A *tapušza tianzi* "The head of the body guards marches in front and steps next to the hearth. They bring in a *PĪḪU* vessel of *walḫi*-drink in order to place it next to the GIŠ.[d]INANNA-instruments" KUB 1.17 iii 32-39 (festival of months, OH/NS), ed. StBoT 37:430f. While placing the drink next to the musical instruments is the ultimate purpose of bringing the drinks inside (compare section b), *ša-an* could simply be an error for *ta-an*.

Unlike *nu* and *ta*, *š.* is not attested as an independent connective but is always followed by clitics. The possible exception *šu-u*, suggested to Weitenberg (StMed 7:338 n. 9) by Houwink ten Cate, occurs in a broken context (KBo 12.14 rev. 4 (OH/NS)) and is perhaps better interpreted as *šūu* "full" (s.v., b). *š.* is most often found with forms of the third person com. enclitic pronoun *-a-*, but four times (see above) with a neuter, invalidating the claims of Carruba, Part. 61, Weitenberg, StMed 7:316, and Boley ICH 5:152 that *š.* only occurs with com. gender clitics.

Since *š.* does not occur independently as **šu*, and is never followed immediately by clitics that start with a consonant other than *m* and *w*, its phonological shape must be different from *nu*, which does occur as *nu, nu≠šše, nu≠šmaš, nu≠z, nu≠kan* etc. The vowel *-u* in *šu-wa* and *šu-mu* is conditioned by the *w* and *m*. In all other cases the initial vowel of the clitic immediately follows (*ša-aš, ša-an, ša-at, še*, and *šu-uš*). Clitics starting in a consonant can only occur after a clitic starting in a vowel: *ša-an-za* and *šu-uš-kán* are possible, but not **šu-uz* and **šu-kán*. The combination *ša-az*[?] in KUB 40.5 ii 4 (so Kammenhuber, Materialien 1/2:3; HEG S/2:1123) has to be read as *ša-aš*, providing the clause with an intransitive encl. subj.: *ša-aš āppa* KASKAL*-az wēḫta* "and (so?) he turned back from the campaign" (ed. StBoT 17:60), cf. dupl. [*ša-*]*aš* EGIR*-pa* KASKAL*-azza*[ ...] KBo 12.13:5.

(Akk.) *INA* [URU]*Šaḫuitta allik≠ma UL uḫalliq* "I went against Šaḫuitta but did not destroy (it)" KBo 10.1 obv. 2, ed. StMed 16:34f. = (Hitt.) [(*IN*)*A* [URU]*Š*]*anaurītta pait ša-an natta* [(*ḫarni*)*kt*]*a* "He went to [the city of Š]anawitta, yet he did not destr[oy] it" KBo 10.2 i 4-5 (OH/NS), w. dupl. KBo 10.3 i 2-3 (OH/NS), ed. StMed 12:30f., cf. b 2′.

**a.** distribution and use of *š.* — **1′** distribution with respect to tense: The connectives *š.* and *ta* (q.v.), both mainly attested in OH, are overwhelmingly in complementary distribution with respect to tense: Weitenberg (StMed 7), working with a corpus consisting of OH originals only, observed that, as a rule, *š.* is used with the preterite and *ta* with the present-future. There are only four assured examples of *š* (KBo 3.60 ii 3, 5; KBo 17.1 iv 22; KUB 33.61 iv 3) that occur with a present-future among the more than 110 examples of *š.* where the tense of the verb can be established (GrHL 390 n. 7).

**2′** function as marker of cause and effect: The main function of *š.* is to indicate a logical connection between the contents of two conjoined clauses (so Pedersen, Tocharisch (1941) 4f., Boley, IF 109:141, the latter with ref. to *šu≠wa* and *šu≠mu* only). In the majority of cases this connection is one of cause and effect situated in the past. The clause introduced by *š.* is almost always the realized result, either volitional or non-volitional, of the event or situation described in the preceding clause (cf. b 1′ and 2′, c 1′). In the few cases that *š.* occurs in a clause with a non-past verb form, it is certain that the event will be realized, irrespective of the circumstances ("I throw a cloth over them so that (*šu-uš*) no man shall see them" KBo 17.1 iv 22, cf. b 1′ b′ 1″. "Whatever person among them d[ies], (*ša-n≠ap*) they devour him. When they see a fa[t] person, they will kill him in order to (*ša-n≠ap*) devour him" KBo 3.60 ii 2-5, see c 1′ b′).

**3′** distribution w. respect to clitics and subordination: In addition to the syntactic environments described in *nu* A h (q.v.), *š.* never introduces a subordinate clause. *š.* does not occur without clitics, and cannot occur with clitics that start with a consonant (see the morphological section). In order to express a cause-effect relation in the past in these environments, *nu* is used. After preposed subordinate clauses *nu* is also by far the most frequent connective, more so than expected based on the relative frequencies of *nu, š.* and *ta* (Inglese, Subordination 55f.). *š.* never appears after a conditional clause. The commitment to the realization of an event explains why *š.* is the only connective that cannot introduce the apodosis of a conditional clause: conditional sentences describe hypothetical situations that may never be realized.

**4′** alternation w. *nu*: The conjunction *nu* expresses cause-effect in the environments where resultative *š.* is prohibited, but it also expresses mere temporal consecution and concurrent action. In the Anitta text (KBo 3.22), for example, *nu* is used to express non-causality in environments where *š.* would formally be allowed: [*nu*? ᵐ*Pi*]*tḫānaš attaš≠maš āppan šaniya uitti* [*ḫ*]*ullanzan ḫullanun* ᵈUTU-*az utnē* [*kuit k*]*uit≠pat araiš nu-uš* (not *šu-uš*) *ḫūmanduš≠pat ḫullanun* "After my father [Pi]tḫāna's death), in the same year, I suppressed a revolt. Whatever country rebelled ..., I defeated them all" KBo 3.22 i 10-12 (also see KBo 3.22 i 3). Otherwise, in resultative past tense clauses and when a clitic starting with a vowel is warranted, *š.* is used (for the rare use of *ta* in past tense environments, see *ta*):

| | Resultative | Non-resultative |
|---|---|---|
| past, followed by clitic w. vowel | *š.* | *nu* |
| past, other | *nu* | *nu* |

**5′** loss of *š.* and its replacement w. *nu*: Given that *nu* occurred in more syntactic environments than *š.*, while sharing the meaning of *š.* in environments where *š.* was prohibited, *nu* was already far more productive than *š.* in the earliest texts. Its higher frequency and greater semantic flexibility led to the obsolescence and ultimately the loss of *š.* (Inglese, Subordination 182f.). As a result, *š.* is sometimes replaced by or alternates with *nu* in NS copies: compare *šu-uš* KBo 22.2 rev. 12 (OS) and *nu-uš* KBo 3.38 rev. 29 (OH/NS); *šu-wa-r*(*a-aš-ta*) KUB 33.63 rev. 7 (OH/NS) and *nu-wa-r*(*a-aš-ta*) KUB 36.51 rev. 8 (OH/NS). Later copies of OH texts are therefore unreliable for determining the function of *š.*

**b.** *š.* connecting main clauses — **1′** w. additive meaning — **a′** introducing a result clause: "so, for this/that reason, as a result." The immediately preceding clause provides the cause or reason for the events described in the *š.*-clause (compare *nu* A a 1′ c′). The *š.*-clause in almost all cases expresses the unintended effect. The preceding clause answers the question why the event of the *š.*-clause has taken place: "why did the event of the *š.*-clause happen? Because of the event in the preceding clause" — **1″** in OS: ("But [the]reafter I, Great King Anitta, carried our deity back from Zalpuwa to Neša. I brought Ḫuzziya, king of Zalpuwa, to Neša [alive]") URU*Ḫattuša*⌈*š*⸗*a*⌉ LU[GAL-*uš* (or: B[ÀD-*eššar*(?))] ⌈*tak*⌉*kišta ša-an tālaḫḫun* "but the ki[ng] of Ḫattuša had put up [a fortification (?)] (or: but Ḫattuša had [bu]ilt a fo[rtification (?)]), so I left it alone" KBo 3.22 rev. 44-45 (Anitta text, OS), ed. StBoT 18:12f. (w. comm. on 27f., "der? Kön[ig] von Ḫattuša aber (-*a*)[/[fü]gte? zu"), StMed 13:36f. ("Später paktierte der König der Stadt Hattusa. Ich (ver)ließ sie."), tr. Haas, Literatur 30 ("[ ] Später aber [paktierte] der König von Hattusa. Da ließ ich sie (die Stadt noch) in Ruhe"), differently Hoffner, CoS 1:183 ("P[iyusti] had [f]ortified Ḫattuša. So I left it alone"), Klinger, TUAT NF 2:140 ("Die Stadt Ḫattuša aber hatte P[ijušti b]efestigt. Und ich ließ sie (zurück)"), Beckman, ANEHST 218 ("(The city) of Ḫattuša inflicted [evil on me], and I released it") □ Neu, StBoT 18:28, suggests LU[GAL- …], followed by Carruba, StMed 13:36, and Haas (Literatur 30), but the sign is also consistent with *P*[*í*-, so Hoffner (CoS 1:183) and Klinger (TUAT NF 2:140); URU*Ḫattuša*⌈*š*⸗*a*⌉ should then be read as acc. sg. com. URU*Ḫattuša*⌈*n*⸗*a*⌉, but that would leave the personal name without a person marker. This is otherwise not attested in this text, so we prefer either URU*Ḫattuša*⌈*š*⸗*a*⌉ L[UGAL-*uš*] "the king of Ḫattuša" or even URU*Ḫattuša*⌈*š*⸗*a*⌉ B[ÀD-*eššar* (?) …] "Ḫattuša (had put up) a fortification"; ("I turned my face toward Šalatiwara") ⌈URU*Ša*⌉*latiwaraš*⸗*a mēnaḫḫanda* GIŠ*tūr*[*iu*(*š*? *udāš*)] [(*u*)*tnia*]⌈*z*⌉ ÉRIN.MEŠ⸗*ŠU ḫuettiyati ša-an* URU*Nēš*[(*a pēḫut*)*enun*] "but Šalatiwara brought (its) spears before (me). Its army withdrew from (its) c[ountry (?)], so [I] carr[ied] it (i.e., the population of Šalatiwara) off to Neša" KBo 3.22 rev. 53-54 (Anitta text, OS), w. dupl. KBo 50.1:5-7 (NS), KUB 26.71 i 2-3 (NS), KUB 36.98b obv. 1-2 (NS), ed. Soysal, ZA 95:124f. (editing the dupl. KBo 50.1 (= Bo 69/911)), translit. DBH 28:1, differently StBoT 18:12f., StMed 13:38f., tr. Hoffner, CoS 1:183, Beckman, ANEHST 218, Haas, Literatur 30, Klinger, TUAT NF 2:141 (all without the duplicate KBo 50.1); […(URU*Kummanni* EGIR-*pa paizzi*)] [(URU*Zalpašš*⸗*a*)] *IKKIR ša-aš* (dupl. *ta-aš*) ⌈URU⌉[(*K*)*ummanniaz arḫ*(*a pait* m*Ḫappišš*⸗)] *a* URU*Alḫi*⌈*uta*⌉ [*pait*(?)] "[…] went (lit. goes) back to Kummanni. But Zalpa became hostile, so he departed [from] the city of K[ummanni], while Ḫappi [went (?)] to the city of Alḫiuta" KBo 22.2 rev. 1-3 (Zalpa tale, OS), w. dupl. KBo 3.38 rev. 17-19 (NS), KUB 48.79 rev. 5 (NS), ed. StBoT 17:10f., StMed 19:31, 39, 42, THeth 29:187, tr. Hoffner, CoS 1:182, Haas, Literatur 26; ("Ḫappi said to the men of Zalpa":) ⌈*ūk*⸗*wa a*⌉[(*tti*)]⸗*m*[(*i*)] [*natt*]*a* (var. *UL*) *āššuš šu-wa* URU*Ḫattuša ḫengani pāun U* DUMU.MEŠ URU*Zalpa katti*⸗*mmi* 1 *ME* ÉRIN.MEŠ-*za ea natta šu-wa kuit natta aker* "I am not in good standing with my father, so I went to Ḫattuša to die (lit. to death), and the sons of Zalpa (were) with me. (Were there) not a hundred troops there? So why didn't (anyone) die?" KBo 22.2 rev. 4-6 (Zalpa tale, OS), w. dupl. KBo 3.38 rev. 20-22 (NS), KUB 48.79 rev. 7-8 (NS), ed. StMed 19:31, 39, StBoT 17:10f. (differently, "und die Einwohner von Zalpa bei mir, (sind) das nicht einhundert Mann, die doch nicht umgekommen sind?!"), Haas, Literatur 26 (idem), THeth 29:187, tr. Hoffner, CoS 1:182 (differently) □ the last two clauses of this passage contain several grammatical difficulties. The major problem is the sequence 1 *ME* ÉRIN.MEŠ-*za*(-)*e-a*. Not understanding this sequence, the scribe of the NS dupl. KBo 3.38 omitted -*za*(-)*e-a natta*, creating a slightly different sentence 1 ME ÉRIN.MEŠ *šu*⸗*wa*! *kuit natta aker* (StMed 19:35 w. n. 39) while maintaining the sense of the passage "(There were) one hundred troops, so why didn't (anyone) die?" We may at least resolve some of the difficulties if we take *ea* as the as-yet-unattested place adverb "there" of the distal demonstrative *aši*, formally matching *kā* "here" and *apiya* "there" (Melchert *apud* Goedegebuure, StBoT 55:109, 128f.). The other difficulty resides in the nature of the combination of *š.* and *kuit*. We prefer a resultative translation "so why" (so also Boley, IF 109:141) over the contrastive interpretation otherwise attributed to *kuit* ("doch," StBoT 17:11, "yet," Hoffner, CoS 1:182), which is not attested for this conjunction; compare frag. *šu-mu kuit natta ḫuš*⌈*gi*⌉[*t*] "so why [did] he not wait for me?" KBo 12.81 ii 5 (mythological frag., NS), cf. *nu* A e; LUGAL-*š*⸗*a IŠME ša-aš yanniš* URU*Ḫaraḫšua*⸗*aš āršа U* ÉRIN.MEŠ URU*Zalpa menaḫḫanda uit ša-an* LUGAL-*uš ḫullit* "But the king heard (about it), so he set out (for Zalpa). He arrived at the city of Ḫaraḫšu. The troops from Zalpa came against (him), and so the king fought them" KBo 22.2 rev. 7-8 (Zalpa tale, OS), w. dupl. KBo 3.38 rev. 22-24 (NS), KUB 48.79 rev. 9-10 (NS), ed. StMed 19:31, 40, StBoT 17:12f., THeth 29:188, tr. Hoffner, CoS 1:182, Haas, Literatur 26; *INA* MU.3.KAM LUGAL-*uš pait* URU*Zalpan a*⌈*r*⌉*aḫzanda wetet* MU.2.KAM *kattan ēšta* m*Tabarnan* m*Ḫappinn=a katta wekta U* LÚ.MEŠ URU-*LIM natta pianzi šu-uš* (dupl. *nu-uš*) *tamešš̌er še* (*š=e*) *aker* (dupl. *še-a eker*) "In (his) third year the king went (and) besieged the city of Zalpa. He stayed down there for two years. He asked for Tabarna and Ḫappi. The inhabitants of the city, however, would not surrender (them), so they (the Hittites) besieged them, and as a result they died" KBo 22.2 rev. 10-13 (Zalpa text, OS), w. dupl. KBo 3.38 rev. 27-29 + Bo 9511:2 (NS), KUB 48.79 rev. 13-16 (NS), ed. StBoT 17:12f., StMed 19:31, 40, THeth 29:188, tr. Hoffner, CoS 1:182 □ the scribe of KBo 3.38 either modified the text or used a different *Vorlage*, leading him to [*IN*]*A* MU.3.KAM LUGAL-*uš INA* URU*Zalpa pait* ⌈*I*⌉[*N*]*A* URU*Zalpa* MU.3.KAM *katta* [*ēšt*]*a Tabarnaš* m*Ḫappin* URU-*a*[*z*] *katta wekta* [*U* LÚ.]MEŠ URU-*LIM UL pianzi n=uš damm*[*i*]*ššar še-a eker* "In (his) third year the king went to Zalpa. He stayed down at Zalpa for three years. Tabarna requested Ḫappi from the city. The inhabitants of the city however would not surrender (him), and they besieged them, so they died." The sequence *še-a e-ke-er* is probably the result of erroneous parsing of the sign KIR/KER (HZL nr. 244). The beginning of the sign KER in the original sequence *še a-ker* resembles the sign E, thus leading to a sequence ŠE A E. The second half of the sign KER might have triggered the sign KI, leading to the unusual spelling of *eker* as *e-ke-er* instead of *e-ker*; ("Nunnu, the representative of the city of Ḫurma, stayed in Arzawa, but he does not bring the silver (and) gold") *kuit wemizz*[(*i ap*)]*āš=a pa*[*r*(*na=šša pittaizzi*)] / [(*š*)]*a-an* LÚ URU*Ḫundarā išiaḫḫiš* [(*ABI* LUGAL *I*)*ŠP*(*UR š=an šarā*)] / [(*u*)]*water* "What(ever) he finds he carries off to his house, so the representative of the city of Ḫundara denounced him. The father of the king sent (for him), so that they could bring him up (to the palace)" KUB 36.104 obv. 10-12 (anecdotes, OS), w. dupl. KBo 3.34 i 12-14 (NS), KBo 12.10:2-3 (+) KBo 13.44a i 4-5 (NS), ed. Soysal, Diss. 11, 83, Dardano, L'aneddoto 32f., THeth 29:117f., tr. Klinger, TUAT Erg. 62 □ *š.* in *š=an šarā uwater* introduces an intended result clause, cf. b 1′ b′ 3″ below.

**2″** in OH/NS: ("Thus (said) the Great King":) URU*Kuššari ABI* LUGAL [NINDA*tu*]*ninki paššilan IṢBAT še* (*š=e*) *pāer* "In the city of Kuššar the father of the king caught a pebble in [(his) *tu*]*nink*-[bread], so they went ((and) they fanned a fire on a mountain, in an em[pt]y (place) (?))" KBo 3.34 i 1-2 (anecdotes, OH/NS), w. dupl. KBo 13.44 i 1-2 (NS), ed. Soysal, Diss. 10, 83, Dardano, L'aneddoto 28f., THeth 29:116, tr. Klinger, TUAT Erg. 62 □ *še* contains the plural subject clitic pronoun *-e*, which means that the verb needs to be intransitive (GrHL 280). Consequently, *pāer* is an independent verb and not phraseologically used (van den Hout, Heth. 16:199, *pace* Dardano, L'aneddoto 72); (Zidi the cup-bearer has provided two members of the royal family with other wine than that approved by the king. Both complain:) *apāšš=a uit* LUGAL-*i tet natta apūn* GEŠTIN-*an piyer* LUGAL-*uš kuin aušta apāšš=a uit QĀTAMMA IQBI ša-na-aš-ta*! (*š=an=ašta*) *arḫa pēḫuter š=an ēšši*‹*š*›*ker ša-aš* BA.ÚŠ "One came (and) said to the king: "They did not give (us) that wine, which you, the king, have seen." The other one came too (and) said likewise, so they led him (i.e., Zidi) off so that they could work him over, and as a result (or: so that) he died" KBo 3.34 ii 4-7 (anecdotes, OH/NS), w. dupl. KBo 3.36:13-15 (NS), ed. Soysal, Diss. 12, 85, Dardano, L'aneddoto 44f., Beal, JCS 35:123f., THeth 29:121, tr. Klinger, TUAT Erg. 63 □ *š.* in *š=an ēšši*‹*š*›*ker* expresses the intended result of the preceding clause, cf. b 1′ b′ 3″ below; *man=an=kan* m*Āškaliyaš kuienzi ša-an ANA* ÉEN.NU.UN *daiš* "Āskaliya wanted to kill him (i.e., Išpudaš-Inara), so he put him in jail" KBo 3.34 ii 17 (anecdotes, OH/NS), w. dupl. KBo 3.36:22-23 (NS), ed. Soysal, Diss. 13, 84, Dardano, L'aneddoto 48f., THeth 29:122, tr. Klinger, TUAT Erg. 63, cf. s.v. *pe*(*i*)*ye*- c and *man* a 2′ a′ □ note that whereas *nu* in *man* ... *nu* ... appears to have an adversative nuance (*man* b 1′), in this case, at least *š.* in *man* ... *š.* ... does not; also cf. *ša-an arnut* KBo 3.34 ii 10 (anecdotes, OH/NS), w. dupl. KBo 3.36:17 (NS) (cf. b 2′); *kēda=mmu apāš iezzi šu-mu* DINGIR.DIDLI DUMU URU*Pur*[*ušḫandumnan*] *kišri=mi daier* "He treats me thus, so the gods put the Pur[ušḫandean] (lit. the son of P.) in my hand(s)" KBo 3.28 ii 6-7 (anecdotes, OH/NS), ed. Laroche, FsOtten[1], 186f. ("C'est ainsi qu'il agit envers moi. Or, le fils, le Puru[shandien], (...)"), Soysal, Diss. 31f., 91, Dardano, OrNS 71:377 ("et de cette façon celui-ci agit à mon égard;

alors les dieux posèrent (...)"), Marazzi (ed.), hethiter.net/: CTH 9.6 (TX 16.07.2012, TRde 02.10.2011), THeth 29:111; ("The men of Zalpa heard (about it)") *ša-n≈a[šta* ......]x-*pinaz katta tarner* "so they released him [...] from [...]...-pina" KBo 3.38 obv. 18 (Zalpa tale, OH/NS), ed. StBoT 17:8f., StMed 19:33, 42, THeth 29:184, tr. Hoffner, CoS 1:181, Eichner, Die Sprache 20:185 (differently, see discussion s.v. NINDA*šaraman*); [...] *š≈uš≈ap eter* m*Z[ūppaš≈a QADU* AMA≈*ŠU* (?)] *išparzašta še* (*š≈e*) *ḫušuē*[*r*] DUMU.MEŠ *ŠIPRI≈ŠU ŠA* LUGAL URU*Ḫala*[*p*] *ēppuen šu-uš āppa* URU*Ḫalpa*KI *tarnuen* AMA≈*ŠU ŠA* m*Zūppa INA* URU*Tinišipa ēpper ša-an≈kan kuener š≈an≈ap eter* "They devoured them. Zū[ppa, however(?)], escaped [together with his mother(?)], and so they stayed alive. We captured the messengers of the king of Ḫalpa, and (so?) we let them go back to Ḫalpa. They (i.e., the messengers?) captured Zūppa's mother in Tinišipa, and so they killed her so that they could eat her" KBo 3.60 iii 3-9 (Cannibal text, OH/NS), ed. Güterbock ZA 44:106f., THeth 29:265, cf. KBo 3.60 ii 2-5, see c 1′ b′ □ *š.* in *šu-uš* ... *tarnuen* could also simply express temporal "and then," cf. b 1′ d′. *š≈an≈ap eter* expresses the intended result, cf. b 1′ b′; MUNUS.LUGAL URU*Šukziya≈wa aku ša-an ē*[*pper š≈an≈kan* (?) *QADU* DUMU.MEŠ≈*ŠU kue*(*nner*)] "'The queen of Šukziya must die!' So [they] ar[rested] her [and kil]led [her with her children]" KBo 3.67 ii 2 (Tel.pr, OH/NS), w. dupl. KBo 3.1 i 56, ed. THeth 11:22f. i 57, cf. Soysal, OrNS 59:275 □ for the readings and restorations followed here, cf. the Akk. version [...] *ṣabta* (?) MUNUS.LUGAL *iqbi≈m*[*i* ...] / [...]x *iṣbatu≈šu qadu* DUMU.MEŠ≈*šu* [*iduku≈šu* (?)] "[...] 'Arrest the queen,' he said. [...] They arrested her (and) [killed her] with her children" KBo 1.27 obv. 3-4, ed. Soysal, OrNS 59:273f.; ("The soul is great, the soul is great. Whose soul is great? The mortal soul is great") *nu kuin* KASKAL-*an ḫarzi uran* KASKAL-*an ḫarzi marnuwalan* KASKAL-*an ḫarzi ša-an≈z≈apa* KASKAL-*ši* LÚKASKAL-*laš ḫandāit* "And what road should it take? It should take the great road, it should take the invisible(?) road. And so the guide has prepared it for the journey" KUB 43.60 i 28-30 (myth, OH/NS), ed. Watkins, Dragon 285f., Polvani ICH 5:615f., Archi, JANER 7:172f., tr. Hittite Myths² 34; differently HEG U 87 ("Und der sich auf den Weg macht bereitet sie für sich auf den Weg vor") □ if *marnuwala-* indeed means 'invisible' (s.v. *marnuwala-*), the soul would require guidance, and *š.* can be understood as expressing a cause-effect relationship; perhaps here *ša-an naḫta* "so he became afraid" KUB 33.52 ii 7 (myth of Inara, OH/NS), w. dupl. KUB 33.55 ii 14, KUB 33.56 rev. 1; [o o o-*š*]*alit aḫḫa*⌈*ti*⌉ *ša-at UL daḫḫun* ZAG-*nit≈a* [*UL*(?)] *aḫḫati n≈apa d*[*aḫ*]*ḫun* DINGIR.MEŠ-*an uddār n≈e≈zz≈a*[*n*] [... *and*]*a*(?) *šuḫḫaḫḫun aīš≈mit ḫalaš≈miš ḫattal*[*u* Ø? ] [...]x≈*ma išgarakkaš n≈a*(*t*)≈*ššan šer teḫḫun* UZU*ḫarš*[*ani≈mi*] "I became warm on the [l]eft side [...], so I could not take them. But I [did not(?)] become warm on the right side, so I s[ei]zed the words of the gods. I poured them [i]n(?) my [...]. My mouth (and) my skull (are) locks, while [...] (is) an *išgarakka*-stone. I placed them (i.e., the words) on [my] he[ad.] (I did not let the words of the gods perish at all)" VBoT 58 iv 4-7 (missing Sungod myth, OH/NS), ed. Rieken et al., hethiter.net/: CTH 323.1 (TX 2009-08-26, TRde 2009-08-26) (with partial tr.), translit. Myth. 25, tr. Moore, Thesis 169 (differs), partial tr. Hittite Myths² 28 □ Moore's, Thesis 169 n. 22, reading of *a/u/ iḫ-ḫa-ti* as *uḫḫati*, contraction of *uwaḫḫati*, 1st pers. sg. mid. of *auš-* "I showed myself, was visible" is not assured. Neu, StBoT 5:3 read UḪ-*ḫati* (with UḪ for regular $UḪ_7$), middle of *alwanzaḫḫ-* 'to bewitch', followed by LMI 68 w. n. 26, and Haas, Literatur 119. As an alternative we assume that *aḫḫati* is the 1st pers. sg. mid. of *ā-* 'to be warm, hot'.

**b′** introducing an intended result or fulfilled purpose clause: "and, so that, so, and so, and thus, so ... could, so ... be able to, so ... would." The action in the preceding clause is planned to achieve the action in the *š.* clause. Especially verbs of transitive motion (taking, fetching, sending) tend to be followed by clauses indicating the fulfilled purpose of the action. The *š.*-clause answers the question of why the event of the preceding clause has taken place: "why did the event in the immediately preceding clause happen? Because of the event in the *š.*-clause" — **1″** in OS: *šēr≈a≈ššan* GAD-*an peššiemi šu-uš* [(LÚ-*aš*)] *natta aušzi* "I throw a cloth over them so that no man shall see them" KBo 17.1 iv 22 (rit., OS), w. dupl. KBo 17.3 iv 18-19 (OS), ed. StBoT 8:38f.; *tuppuš šaganda šunnaš nu* DUMU.MEŠ≈*ŠU andan zikēt* [*š*]*u-uš* ÍD-*a tarnaš* ÍD-*š≈a ANA* A.AB.BA KUR

URU*Zalpuwa pēdaš* [DING]IR.DIDLI-*š*=*a* DUMU.MEŠ-*uš* A.AB.BA-*az šarā dāer šu-uš šallanušker* "She (i.e., the queen of Neša) filled baskets with grease and then placed her sons inside, so that she could launch them into the river. The river carried (them) to the sea, to the country of Zalpuwa. The gods took the boys up from the sea and raised them" KBo 22.2 obv. 2-5 (Zalpa tale, OS), w. dupl. KBo 26.126:1 (NS), ed. StBoT 17:6f., StMed 19:30, 39, THeth 29:118, tr. Hoffner, CoS 1:181; ("And the boys spoke to themselves":) *kuin*=*wa šanḫiškiweni UMM*[*A*]=*NI ša-an wemiyawen* "Whom have we been seeking? Our mother! And thus/so we have found her!" KBo 22.2 obv. 14 (Zalpa tale, OS), ed. StMed 19:30, 39 w. comm. 51f., Starke ZA 69:51 n. 8, THeth 29:182f., translit. DBH 24:9; tr. differently: Hoffner, CoS 1:181, Haas, Literatur 23, Watkins, FsMorpurgo Davies 70, cf. s.v. *šanḫ-* 1 a 1′ (tr. *kui-* as a relative adnominal); reading the sentence particle *-šan* instead of *š*=*an*: StBoT 17:6f. (*UM-MA-NI-ša-an*), StBoT 54:634 □ following StMed 19: 51f., analyzing the *kui-* clause as a relative clause is ungrammatical: relative noun phrases with specific and identifiable referents (i.e., definite noun phrases) are never fronted. The sentence *kuin*=*wa šanḫiškeweni* is therefore a question (so also StBoT 17:6f., Haas, Literatur 23, Watkins, FsMorpurgo Davies 70). The seeking is performed in order to achieve the finding, hence *š.* expresses fulfilled purpose; ("But the king heard (about it), so he set out (for Zalpa). He arrived at the city of Ḫaraḫšu. The troops from Zalpa came against (him), and so the king fought them") m*Ḫāppiš*=*a išparzašta* m*Tamnaššun*=*a ḫušuwantan IṢBATŪ ša-an* URU*Ḫattuša uwatet* "Ḫappi escaped. Tamnaššu, however, they caught alive, so that he (i.e., the king) was able to bring him to Ḫattuša" KBo 22.2 rev. 8-9 (Zalpa tale, OS), w. dupl. KBo 3.38 rev. 24-26 (NS), KUB 48.79 rev. 10-12 (NS), ed. StMed 19:31, 40, StBoT 17:12f., THeth 29:188, tr. Hoffner, CoS 1:182, Haas, Literatur 26 □ we take *š.* in *ša-an* URU*Ḫattuša uwatet* as introducing an intended result clause. The phrase *ēpp-* + acc. "seize someone" is otherwise not attested with *ḫušuwant-* "alive." Since people are usually caught alive, the addition of the adjective means that they did not only catch Tamnaššu alive but also decided to keep him alive. Rather than paraphrasing "Why did he bring him to Ḫattuša? — Because they caught him alive," the paraphrase "why did they catch Tamnaššu alive? — In order to bring him to Ḫattuša" allows for emphasis on the intentionality of catching and keeping Tamnaššu alive, with the reason expressed in the *š.*-clause; ("The king returned to Ḫattuša to worship the gods") *U* LUGAL ŠU.GI *apiya tāliš ša-aš šarā* URU-⌈*y*⌉*a pait* "but he left the old king there (in Zalpa) so that he could go up to the city ((with the words): '*I* will become your king')" KBo 22.2 rev. 14 (Zalpa tale, OS), w. dupls. KBo 3.38 rev. 30-31 (NS), KUB 48.79 rev. 18 (NS), ed. StBoT 17:12f., StMed 19:31, 40, THeth 29:118f., tr. Hoffner, CoS 1:182; the dupl. reads *U* LÚ.MEŠ GAL [*apiya*] *dāliš ša-aš ANA* LÚ.MEŠ URU-*LIM te*[*t*] "while he left the dignitaries [there]. He said to the inhabitants of the city" KBo 3.38 rev. 30-31 (NS) □ the replacement of *ša-aš šarā* URU-⌈*y*⌉*a pait*, with correct use of the nominative clitic *-aš*, by means of *ša-aš ANA* LÚ.MEŠ URU-*LIM te*[*t*] led to the incorrect use of *-aš* in a transitive clause; (as punishment for embezzling *marnuan*-beer) [*AN*]⌈*A*⌉ GAL *m*[*arnua*(*ndaš*)] [(M)]UN-*an šuḫḫaer ša-na-aš-ta* (i.e., *š*=*an*=*ašta*) *eukta diššum*⌈*mi*⌉*n*=*a* [(*ANA* SAG.DU=*ŠU*)] *tuwarner* "They poured salt into a cup of *marnuwan*-beer so that he drank it. The cup they smashed on his head" KUB 36.104 obv. 5-7 (anecdotes, OS), w. dupl. KBo 3.34 i 7-9 (NS), KBo 13.44 i 8 (NS), KUB 48.77:4 (NS), ed. Soysal, Diss. 17, Dardano, L'aneddoto 30f., THeth 29:117, tr. Klinger, TUAT Erg. 62; ("The father of the king sent a Gold-Spear man") [(m*Šarmāššun* m*Nunnunn*=*a*)] ḪUR.SAG*Taḫayai peḫuter n*=*uš* [(GUD-*li turer* m*Nunnušš*=*a*)] LÚ*gaina*(*n*)=*ššan ēpper ša-an* m[(*Šarmāššuwi* m*Nunnuwi*=*ya šakuwa*=*šma*)] [(*ḫ*)]*uēkta* "They brought Šarmāššu and Nunnu to Mt. Taḫaya. They yoked them like oxen and also seized a kinsman of Nunnu, and slaughtered him before the eyes of Šarmaššu and Nunnu" KUB 36.104 obv. 13-16 (anecdotes, OS), w. dupl. KBo 3.34 i 15-18 (NS), KBo 12.10:5-7 (+) KBo 13.44a i 8 (NS), ed. Soysal, Diss. 18, 83f., Dardano, L'aneddoto 32f., THeth 29:118, tr. Klinger, TUAT Erg. 62, cf. s.v. *šakui-* 1 a 6′ □ the *š.* clause provides the motivation, and thus the intended result, for the two preceding and probably concurrent actions: "Why did they (1) yoke them and also (2) seize the kinsman?" — "in order to (2) slaughter him, (1) in front of their eyes after they were immobilized (and humiliated)."

**2″** in OH/MS: (in a therapeutic ritual where a puppy licks the afflicted areas:) [...] ⌈*u*⌉*watet šu-wa mēna*=*ššet* [*lipta š*]*u-wa ēšḫar*=*šet lipta* *[li]pta=wa šākuwa⟨š?⟩ ištarkiyauwar* "she brought [a puppy(?)] so that it [lick]ed his face, licked his blood, [lick]ed the disease of(?) the eyes" KBo 14.98 i 8-10 (frag. Zuwi rit., OH/MS?), ed. s.v. *meni-* A 1, Haas, Materia 527; [...]x*=at karpun ša-at pargaš peššiyanun* "I lifted it [...] so that I was able to throw it at the *parga*-s" KBo 24.51 obv. 2 + KBo 38.168 obv. 7 (Zuwi's rit., OH/MS?), translit. Groddek, AoF 28:110.

**3″** in OH/NS: ("[Behin]d them he turned into a bull, and its horns (were) a little bit crack[ed]. [So] I ask [him:] 'why (are) its horns cracked?' He says":) *[aruna]n mān laḫḫeškinun nu=nnaš* ḪUR.SAG-*aš nakkiēt kāš=a* GUD.M[AḪ] *[daššu]š ēšta mān=aš uēt nu uni* ḪUR.SAG-*an karpta ša-n=ašta [edi nā]eš arunan=a tarḫuen nu kara*⌜*wa*⌝*r=šet apēda lipšan* "Always when I made war on the [se]a, the mountain was an obstacle to us. But this bu[ll] was [stron]g. When it came, it lifted that mountain so that it could [tur]n it [aside], and we conquered the sea. So that is why its horns (are) cracked" KBo 3.41 + KUB 31.4 obv.! 16-18 (Puḫanu chronicle, OH/NS), ed. Otten, ZA 55:160f., Soysal, Hethitica 7:175, 180, Steiner, GsImparati 812, 814, THeth 29:300, tr. Hoffner, CoS 1:184f.; ("In the city of Kuššar the father of the king seized a pebble in [(his) *tu*]*nink*-[bread], so they went (and)") ḪUR.SAG-*i ša[nnapil]i paḫḫur parer še (š=e)* ᴸᵁNINDA.DÙ.DÙ *ḫūpper* "they fanned a fire on a mountain, in an em[pt]y (place), so they could inflict harm against the breadbaker" KBo 3.34 i 2-3 (anecdotes, OH/NS), w. dupl. KBo 13.44 i 2-3 (NS), ed. Soysal, Diss. 10, 83, Dardano, L'aneddoto 28f., THeth 29:116f., tr. Klinger, TUAT Erg. 62, cf. s.v. *šamenu-* A e □ for lighting a fire in an empty place, see KUB 39.48:8. For intransitive *ḫuwapp-* "to do evil against" with a dat. of the maltreated person, see the discussion under *šamenu-* A e and Melchert, FsKošak 513f. We follow Neu's restoration of *ša[nnapil]i* (FsHouwink ten Cate 242). Dardano (L'aneddoto 72, 112) has shown that not the adjective *šannapili* but *danatt(a/i)-* modifies localities. Thus we classify *šannapili* here as the substantive *šannapili* B "empty (place)" (s.v.); *ABI* LUGAL *I[ŠP]UR ša-an šarā uwater* "The father of the king sent (for him), and so they brought him up" KBo 3.34 i 13-14 (anecdotes, OH/NS); ("Šanda, a palace-attendant (and) a man from Ḫurma, stayed in Ḫaššu") *ḫurlašš=a [na]ḫta nu ešḫe penniš ABI* L[UGAL *I*]*ŠPUR ša-an kukkureškei* "He, however, was afraid of the Hurrians, so he drove to (his) master. The father of the k[ing] sent (for him) so that they would mutilate him" KBo 3.34 i 24-25 (anecdotes, OH/NS), w. dupl. KBo 3.35:1 (NS), ed. Dardano, L'aneddoto 36f., THeth 29:119, tr. Klinger, TUAT Erg. 63; *ša-an ēšši⟨š⟩ker* KBo 3.34 ii 7 (anecdotes, OH/NS), cf. b 1′ a′ 2″ above; *ša-an* ᵁᴿᵁ*Ankui IRDI ša-an* ᵁᴿᵁ*Ankui=pat* ᴸᵁAGRIG-*an iēt* KBo 3.34 ii 10-11 (anecdotes, OH/NS), w. dupl. KBo 3.36:17-18 (NS), cf. b 2′ below for the context □ the first *š.* could also be merely sequential (cf. b 1′ d′); ("Išpudaš-Inara was a potter, yet Āškaliya, ruler of Ḫurma, took him") *ša-an INA* ᵁᴿᵁ*Ul*ˡ*lam*ˡ*mi* (var. *Ullamma*) ᴸᵁ*maniaḫḫatallan iēt* "and made him (his) administrator in Ullamma" KBo 3.34 ii 16 (anecdotes, OH/NS), w. dupl. KBo 3.36:21-22 (NS), also see b 2′ below; ("Āskaliya wanted to kill him (i.e., Išpudaš-Inara), so he put him in jail") ᵐ*Āškali=ma uddā*⌜*r*⌝ *arāiš* ᵐ*Išputašinari=ma pīer ša-na-aš-ta* (i.e., *š=an=ašta*) *IŠTU* ᴱEN.NU.UN *tarner š=aš* ᵐ*Āškili=pat tiēt maršanza=wa zik* "But affairs arose against Aškaliya. They sent for Išpudaš-Inara, and so he was released (lit. and so they released him) from jail. He stepped up to that same Aškaliya (saying): 'It is *you* who are deceitful(, not me)!'" KBo 3.34 ii 18-20 (anecdotes, OH/NS), w. dupl. KBo 3.36:23-24 (NS), ed. Soysal, Diss. 13, 84, Dardano, L'aneddoto 48f., THeth 29:122, tr. Klinger, TUAT Erg. 63, cf. s.v. *pe(i)ye-* c □ perhaps *š.* in *š=aš* ᵐ*Āškili=pat tiēt* also marks the intended result of the preceding clause: they released Išpudaš-Inara so that he could provide testimony against Aškaliya. If it is merely temporal this instance belongs under b 1′ d′; *kūn apāš annanut kūšš=a ABI* LUGAL *ANA Nakkilit* GAL ⁽ᴸᵁ⁾ᴹᴱŠSAGI *paiš kūš* ᵐ*Ḫuzzī* GAL ᴸᵁ.ᴹᴱŠNIMGIR *kūš* ᵐ*Kizzui* GAL ᴸᵁ.ᴹᴱŠ*MEŠEDI paiš šu-uš ulkeššaraḫḫer* "One (of the apprentice chariot fighters) he (i.e., Išpudaš-Inara) trained, and others the king gave to Nakkili, the chief of the cupbearers. (Still) others he gave to Ḫuzzi, chief of the heralds, the rest to Kizzu, chief of the guards, so that they made them skilled" KBo 3.34 ii 30-32 (anecdotes, OH/NS), ed. Soysal, Diss. 14, 85, Dardano, L'aneddoto 52f., THeth 29:123, THeth 20:535f., tr. Klinger, TUAT Erg. 64; *[n=ašta(?)* ᵁ]ᴿᵁ*Ḫurmaz* ᵐ*Laḫḫuerin š*⌜*ū*⌝[*(er* ᵐ*Āšk)aliyan=a*] / [*šar*]*ā? uwater ša-an pedi=šš*[*i dai(ēr)*] "They expelled Laḫḫueri from the [c]ity of Ḫurma. They brought Ašk[aliya u]p(?) (to the city) so that they could [pu]t him in hi[s] place" VBoT 33:6-7 (anecdotes, OH/NS), w. dupl. KUB 31.38 obv.? 33, KUB 36.105 rev. 4-5 (MS), ed. Dardano, L'aneddoto 66f. ☐ for the restoration *šarā uwate-* in VBoT 33:7, see KBo 3.34 i 13-14; (Kaniu, a local Syrian king, wants to test whether a captive member of a cannibalistic society is human or divine by giving him pork to eat. If the visitor guesses correctly that it is not human meat, he is divine, if he guesses incorrectly, he is human) ᵐ*Kaniūš* UZU.ŠAḪ *zēandan dāš ša-an* ᵐDUMU.EN!.LÍL*-aš peran dā*⌜*iš*⌝ "Kaniu took cooked pork and placed it before DUMU.EN!.LÍL" KBo 3.60 ii 12-13 (Cannibal text, OH/NS), ed. Güterbock, ZA 44:106f., Collins, JANER 6:167 w. n. 43, THeth 29:264f.; ᵐDUMU.EN!.LÍL UZU.ŠAḪ [*dāš*] *ša-na-ap* (i.e., *š=an=ap*) *ēzta* "DUMU.EN!.LÍL [took] the pork and devoured it" KBo 3.60 ii 17-18 (Cannibal text, OH/NS), ed. Güterbock, ZA 44:106f., Collins, JANER 6:167 w. n. 43, THeth 29:264f.

**c′** introducing an unintended ("and so") or intended result ("so that") — **1″** in OS: ("But when it (i.e., Ḫattuša) afterwards became beset with famine") *š=*⌜*an* ᵈ⌝*Ḫalmaš*[*uiz*] ᵈ*šīuš=*(*š*)*miš parā paiš ša-an išpandi nakkit dāḫḫun* "their deity Ḫalmaš[uit] gave it up, and so I took it at night by assault (or: so that I was able to take it at night by assault)" KBo 3.22 rev. 47-48 (Anitta text, OS), ed. StBoT 18:12f., StBoT 23:141, StMed 13:36f., tr. Singer, StMed 9:348, Hoffner, CoS 1:183, Beckman, ANEHST 218, Haas, Literatur 30, Klinger, TUAT NF 2:140 ☐ the intended result reading "so that" follows if the surrender of Ḫattuša to the enemy, i.e., Anitta, by Ḫalmaššuit is seen as divine retribution. For the first *ša-an*, see c 1′ a′ 1″ below.

**2″** in OH/NS: ("When Ḫantili inquired about the queen of Šu[kziya and her sons] (asking): 'Who kill[e]d them?', the chief of the palace attendants delivered the (following) message. They had gathered her [fa]mily and [brought] them to Taga[laḫa]") *n=uš=šan ḫaḫḫallaš parḫer še* (i.e., *š=e*) ⌜*a*⌝[*ker*] "And they chased them into the bushes, so that (or: and so) they di[ed]" KBo 3.67 ii 7 (Tel. pr, OH/NS), ed. THeth 11:22f. i 62, Soysal, OrNS 59/2:276.

**d′** expressing a temporal sequence (compare *nu* A 1′ b′), in OH/NS: *apašš=a* (var. *apaš=a*) *ḫuittitti ša-aš iyanneš* "But (then) he withdrew and marched off" KUB 26.71 i 15 (Anitta text, OH/NS), w. dupl. KBo 3.22 rev. 72 (OS), ed. StBoT 18:14f., StMed 13:50f., tr. Hoffner, CoS 1:184 ("[...] he drew up and marched off"), Beckman, ANEHST 218 ("he gathered up [his treasure] and departed"); *ša-aš* ᵐ*Āškili=pat tiēt* KBo 3.34 ii 19 (anecdotes, OH/NS), w. dupl. KBo 3.36:24 (NS), see b 1′ a′ 2″ above for context; [... ᵁᴿᵁ*Ḫu*]*rmaz kattan arḫa ḫuittiyat* (var. *dāš*) *š=aš* ᵁᴿᵁ*Šukz*[(*iya*)] [*pāit* (?) *š=aš*(?) *IN*]*A* ᵁᴿᵁ*Šukziya gimaniēt ša-aš akkiškiē*[*t*] "[...] withdrew (var. took) [...] from [the city of Ḫu]rma, and [went (?)] to the city of Šukziya. [So (?) he] wintered [i]n Šukziya, and [was] dying" KBo 19.90 + KBo 3.53 (= BoTU 2, 17B*α*) obv. 6-7 (Muršili's Hurrian campaigns, OH/NS), w. dupl. KBo 3.46 obv. 35-36 (NS), ed. Kempinski/Košak, Tel Aviv 9:90, 93, De Martino, StMed 12:136f., Soysal, Diss. 44, 97; (Naramsin wants to know whether his opponents are human or divine by checking whether they bleed after being stabbed: no bleeding means divine, bleeding means human. "But when the servants went, one of his servants stabbed (one) with a spit (and) cut (him) with a dagger") [*t*]*a=šši=šta ēšḫar šiyati še* (*š=e*) EGIR*-pa ANA* ᵐ*Naram-*ᵈ*SÎN-na* [E]N*-a=šši ḫalukan pēter* (var. *āppa memier*) "and blood spurted from him. They brought the message back (var. they replied) to Naramsin, their(!) lord" KBo 3.16 ii 14-15 (Narām Sîn epic, OH/NS), w. dupl. KBo 3.18 iii 1, ed. Güterbock, ZA 44:52f., Boley, RANT 1:85 ("and they went back to N. and brought him the news") ☐ the occurrence of the encl. subj. pron. *-e* in this transitive clause is highly problematic, since subject clitics only occur in intransitive clauses (GrHL 280). Boley's translation suggests an emendation of the text to the intransitive clause *še* EGIR*-pa ANA* ᵐ*Naram-*ᵈ*SÎN-na* ⟨*paēr*⟩, followed by [*t*]*a=šši ḫalukan pēter*. While this would also solve the other grammatical problems (namely, the incorrect use of the allative case for persons, and of the poss. clitic *=ši* "his" instead of *=šmi* "their" (Starke, StBoT 23:44)), there does not seem to be enough space to restore [*t*]*a* at the beginning of ii 15. We therefore prefer the original restoration [E]N and accept the many grammatical errors in this passage; [*ḫa*]*ntezziya* (var. [*ḫantez*]*zi*) *palši* 18 (var. 19) $SIG_7$ ÉRIN.MEŠ [(*p*)]*ēḫutenun ša-an ḫullēr* [(*tān* 12 $SIG_7$ ÉRIN.MEŠ *p*)]*ēḫutenun ša-*

*an namma ḫul*[(*lēr*) *teri*]*yanna* (var. 3-*na*) 6 $SIG_7$ ÉRIN.MEŠ *pēḫutenun* [(*ša-a*)]*n namma ḫuller* "The [fir]st time I led 180,000 troops and they defeated them. The second time I led 120,000 troops and they defeated them again. The third time I led 60,000 troops and they defeated them again" KBo 3.18 iii 4-8 (Narām Sîn epic, OH/NS), w. dupl. KBo 3.16 iii 1-4, ed. Güterbock, ZA 44:54f., cf. *palša-* 7 a; *araīš apāš=a šu=w*[*a*...*dāš*] *šu=wa* GA.KIN.AG *dāš šu=*[*wa*] *marnuan dāš walḫi d*[*āš*] (var. adds *šākan dāš*) *šu=wa* TÚG!*kureššar dā*[*š*] *šu=wa* TÚG!*galuppan* ⌜*dā*⌝[*š*] "S/he got up, and [took...], and took cheese, and took *marnu*-drink, took *walḫi*-drink, (var. adds: took oil,) and took a scarf, and took a *galuppa*-garment" Bo 2896 ii 5-9 (myth frag., OH/NS), w. dupl. Bo 6660:4-8, ed. Rieken et al., hethiter.net/: CTH 370.I.46 (2009sqq.), translit. Popko, AoF 33:155, w. tr. and comm. 157f.

**2′** concessive "yet" (compare *nu* A a 2′), in OH/NS: ("[Great King Tabar]na, — Ḫattušili, Great King, [King of the Land of Ḫa]tti, man of Kuššar— exercised [kingship] over the land of Ḫatti, (being) the son of the brother of the Tawananna") [(*IN*)*A* URU*Š*]*anauitta pait ša-an natta* [(*ḫarn*)*ikt*]*a nu udnē=ššet ḫarnikta* "He went to [the city of Š]anawitta, yet he did not destr[oy] it. He destroyed its countryside (instead)" KBo 10.2 i 4-5 (Annals of Ḫattušili I, OH/NS), w. dupl. KBo 10.3 i 2-3 (NS), ed. StMed 12:30f., tr. Beckman, ANEHST 219; m*Āšgaliyaš* URU*Ḫurmi* EN-*aš ēšta apāšš=a kuwatta kuwatta* LÚ-*eš ēšta ša-na-aš-ta* (i.e., *š=an=ašta*) *atti=mi paknuer š=an arnut š=an* URU*Ankui IRDI š=an* URU*Ankui=pat* LÚAGRIG-*an iēt* "Ašgaliya was a lord in Ḫurma. He was a man in every respect, yet they defamed him to my father. So he (i.e., my father) had him transferred and brought to Ankuwa, and made him an administrator in Ankuwa only" KBo 3.34 ii 8-11 (anecdotes, OH/NS), w. dupl. KBo 3.36:16-18 (NS), ed. Soysal, Diss. 13, 84, Dardano, L'anedotto 46f., THeth 29:121, tr. Klinger, TUAT Erg. 63, cf. Puhvel, AJNES IV/2:81 (on *paknu-* 'arraign (?) > nab, nail, bust'), Puhvel, StBoT 52:212, see s.v. *paknu-* □ *š.* in *š=an arnut* is resultative ('why did he transfer him? — because he was defamed'), the other two are introducing intended result clauses (a 1′ b′ 3″), although *š.* in *š=an* URU*Ankui IRDI* could also be sequential (a 1′ d′ 2″); m*Išpudašinaraš* LÚ*ḫupralaš ēšta ša-an* m*Āškaliyaš* LÚ URU*Ḫurma dāš š=an INA* URU*Ul*!*lam*!*mi* (var. *Ullamma*) LÚ*maniaḫḫatallan iēt* "Išpudaš-Inara was a potter, yet Āškaliya, ruler of Ḫurma, took him and made him (his) administrator in Ullamma" KBo 3.34 ii 15-16 (anecdotes, OH/NS), w. dupl. KBo 3.36:21-22 (NS), ed. Dardano, L'aneddoto 48f., THeth 29:122, tr. Klinger, TUAT Erg. 63; ("Presently, if a prince offends the person of the king in any way, he shall [su]mmon the Ri[ver God] and he must go (to the river). If he becomes pure, he [shall] see your eyes. B[ut] if the River God rejects (him), he shall just remain in his house. (...) Do not take him to prison. Do not harm him: do not seek death for him, do not sel[l him (as a slave)]. (...)" §) *attaš=maš ḫaršanī* dÍD-*ya mekkeš paprešker šu-uš ABI* LUGAL *natta ḫuišnuškēt* m*Kizzuwaš=pat ANA* SAG *ABI=*⌜*YA*⌝ dÍD-*ya papritta ša-an attaš=*⌜*miš*⌝ m*Kizzuwan nat*⟨*ta*⟩ *ḫu*⌜*e*⌝⟨*š*⟩*nūt* "In (the matter of offending) the person of my father many were proven guilty in the River (ordeal), yet didn't the king's father let them live? Especially Kizzuwa was proven guilty in the River (ordeal) in (the matter of offending) the person of my father, yet didn't my father let him, Kizzuwa, live?" KBo 3.28 ii 17-19 (anecdotes, OH/NS), ed. Watkins, TPS 70:79, Laroche, FsOtten[1] 187, Dardano, Or NS 71:365, THeth 29:112, hethiter.net/: CTH 9.6 (TX 16.07.2012, TRde 02.10.2011), cf. s.v. *papre-* 1 (all differently) □ the plene writings of the final syllables of *ḫuišnuškēt* and *ḫu*⌜*e*⌝⟨*š*⟩*nūt* are neither scribal errors nor archaisms (*pace* Kloekhorst, StBoT 56:67, 496) but indicators of interrogative intonation (for this phenomenon see GrHL 348, § 27.2). By using negative rhetorical questions the author emphasizes that the father of the king indeed let live those pronounced guilty in a river ordeal, thus reinforcing the rules of conduct stated in the preceding paragraph. For the alternative reading of ḪAR-*šanī* as a borrowing of Akk. *ḫuršānu* "ordeal (by water)" (cf. CAD, s.v. *ḫuršānu* B), see Riemschneider, JESHO 20:121f. n. 32, followed by Marazzi, FsKošak 494.

**3′** Meaning temporal, resultative, or concessive — **a′** because of ambiguous or unclear context — **1″** in OS: *mān* MU.ḪI.A *ištarna pāer nu* M[UNUS.LU]GAL *nam*⌜*ma*⌝ 30 MUNUS.DUMU *ḫāšta šu-uš apašila šallanušket* "As the years went by, the q[ueen] again gave birth, to thirty daughters (this time) (var. thirty children), and (or: so, yet) she raised them herself (having earlier abandoned her thirty sons)" KBo 22.2 obv. 6-7 (Zalpa tale, OS), w. dupl. KBo 26.126:2 (NS), ed. StBoT 17:6f., StMed 19:30, 39, THeth 29:181f., tr. Hoffner, CoS 1:181, Haas, Literatur 23, Watkins, FsMorpurgo Davies 70 □ *š.* could also be resultative if the queen decided to keep the children because they were female. Alternatively, if raising the daughters was considered unexpected given that the queen abandoned her thirty sons before, then *š.* might even be understood as concessive "yet."

**2″** in OH/MS: ("The[reup]on the Stormgod began to search for Telipinu. He [come]s (to) the main gate in his city, but does not manage to open (it). He broke his mallet (and) his wedge, the [mighty(?)] Stormgod") *nu=za=kan anda karīēt ša-aš ešati* $^{d}$NIN.TU-*aš* [NIM.LÀL-*an IŠP*]*UR īt=wa* $^{d}$*Telipinun zik šanḫa* "He paused among (the remains), and sat down (or: to sit down). Ḫannaḫanna [sen]t [a bee]: "*You* go search for Telipinu!" KUB 17.10 i 34-35 (Tel.myth, OH/MS), w. dupl. KUB 33.2 i 19-20 (OH/MS), ed. García Trabazo, TextosRel. 116f., Puhvel, HED K 82, LMI 80, differently ed. Rieken et al. (ed.), hethiter.net/: CTH 324.1 (TX 2012-06-08, TRde 2012-06-08 ("er hüllte sich (in sein Gewand) ein und setzte sich hin"), Mazoyer, Télipinu 45, 74 ("il séjourna à l'intérieur, il s'installa (dans la ville)"), tr. Hittite Myths$^{2}$ 15 ("he wrapped himself up (in his garment) and sat down"), Beckman, CoS 1:152, Haas, Literatur 107 □ for *kariya-* "to stop, pause, rest," see HED K 82f. It is also possible that the Stormgod paused in order to sit down, and thus that *š.* introduces an intended result clause, cf. a 1′ b′; DUMU.MUNUS $^{d}$UTU *kukk*[*u*]⸢*i*⸣*nāit ša-an* $^{d}$[UTU-*uš*] *nēpiši i*[*št*]*amašta* "The daughter of the Sungod *kukkuinai*-ed, and (so?) the [Sun]god heard her in the sky" KBo 31.78 + KBo 43.3 iii 5-7 (MH/MS), ed. StBoT 62:356f.

**b′** fragmentary context — **1″** in OS: *mān* ⸢*ANA* (?)⸣ [... (*laḫḫa pāun*)] *nu* LÚ $^{URU}$⸢*Purušḫan*⸣ [(*da katti=mi ḫenkum*)*uš* ...] *šu-mu* 1 $^{GIŠ}$ŠÚ.A AN.BAR 1 PA.GAM AN.BAR [(*ḫengur udaš*)] "When I went on campaign t[o ...], the ruler (lit. man) of Purušḫanda [sent (?)] gift-bearer[s] along to me, in order to bring to me, as a gift, one iron throne and one iron scepter" KBo 3.22 rev. 73-75 (Anitta text, OS), w. dupl. KUB 26.71 obv. 16-17 (NS), KUB 36.98b rev. 3-4 (NS), ed. StBoT 18:14f., HW$^{2}$ Ḫ 568, tr. Haas, Literatur 31, Hoffner, CoS 1:184, Beckman, ANEHST 218 ("... [brought] ... gifts"), Klinger, TUAT NF 2:141 ("brachte ... Abgaben"), differently StMed 13:50f. (restoring *ḫenkuni* instead of *ḫenkumuš*), HED Ḫ 291 (idem), EDHIL 268 (idem), Inglese, Subordination 31 (restoring *ḫenku*[*nit uet*] "came with gifts") □ deriving the acc. pl. com. *ḫenkum*[*uš*] from *ḫengur* "gift" is problematic. Formally *ḫenkumuš* < **ḫenkuwuš* should be built to either an *u-* or *wa-*stem (Neu, StBoT 18:116, Weitenberg, U-Stämme 270, Rieken, StBoT 44:336). Such a stem is attested in $^{(LÚ)}$*ḫenkuwa-* "gift-bearer" (q.v.).

**2″** in OH/NS: $^{m}$*Ḫakipuilin=a ḫikanni ḫuiš*⸢*nut*⸣ *ša-an* ⸢*A*⸣[*BI*(?) LUGAL *dāš*(?)] *š=an* $^{LÚ}$AGRIG-*ḫiš* "But he saved Ḫakipuili from death, and (or: so) the fa[ther(?) of the king took(?)] him and appointed him as a $^{LÚ}$AGRIG" KBo 3.36:9-10 (anecdotes, OH/NS), ed. Soysal, Diss. 22f., 88, Dardano, L'anedotto 42f., THeth 29:120f.; [*m*]*ān* $^{d}$UTU-*waš=*⸢*a*⸣ [*per*(*an paiši*) *nu* ...] *namma lē iy*[(*aši ḫūman*) ...] *šu-wa paiši karš*[*i kišš*(⸢*ū*⸣*wan*)] *tēši kuwāpi* [*paimi nu kuit*] $^{d}$UTU-*uš tezzi z*[(*ig=a iya*)] "But when you go [be]fore the Sungod, you may no longer do [...]. Everything [...], and (or: so) you shall go (and) speak forthr[ight in this kind of] way: "Where [must I go?]" [Whatever] the Sungod says, *you* will do!" KUB 33.61 iv 1-5 (myth of Inara, OH/NS), w. dupl. KUB 33.60 rev. 2-5 (NS), KUB 43.25:1-5 (OS), ed. Tischler, HEG S/2:1123 (differently), translit. Myth. 153; perhaps here if *še-kán* is indeed *š=e=kan* and not the measure of length *šekan* s.v.: *še-kán* EGIR-*an uit* "and (so?) they came behind (it/him/her)" KBo 38.188 left col. 3 (myth frag., OH/MS), ed. Fuscagni, hethiter.net/: CTH 458.25 (TX 13.10.2014, TRde 03.09.2013) (reads *šekan* "Spanne").

**c.** connecting a main clause with its preceding subordinate clause — **1′** the events described in the subordinate clause provide the cause or motivation for the state of affairs of the main clause — **a′** following a temporal clause with *mān* "when" — **1″** in OS: ⸢*m*⸣*ān=aš* ⸢*ap*⸣*pizziyan=a kištanziattat ša-*⸢*an* $^{d}$⸣*Ḫalmaš*[*uiz*] $^{d}$*šīu*(*š*)*=šmiš parā paiš š=an išpandi nakkit dāḫḫun* "But when it (i.e., Ḫattuša) afterwards became beset with famine, as a result their deity Ḫalmaš[uit] gave it up, and so I took it at night by storm(?)/by force(?)" KBo 3.22 rev. 45-48

(Anitta text, OS), ed. StBoT 23:141 (restoring $^{d}$*Ḫalmaš[uīz]* and analyzing $^{d}$*šīuš=miš* as "meine Gottheit")), Inglese, Subordination 88 (following Singer, StMed 9:348), tr. Singer, StMed 9:348 (restoring $^{d}$*Ḫalmaš[uiz]* and analyzing $^{d}$*šīuš=(š)miš* as "their god"), Hoffner, CoS 1:183 (following Singer), Beckman, ANEHST 218 (idem), s.v. *šiu-* 1 d, differently ed. StBoT 18:12f. (restoring *Ḫalmaš[uitti]* and tr. "lieferte sie mein Gott Šiu der Throngöttin Ḫalmašuit aus"), similarly StMed 13:36f., w. comm. 119f., Haas, Literatur 30 (idem), Klinger, TUAT NF 2:140 ("und der Ḫalmašš[uit] lieferte ihre Gottheit sie aus") ☐ although *š.* could also denote mere temporal sequentiality, it is conceivable that the deity of Ḫattuša abandoned the city because she no longer received her cultic provisions. For *š=an išpandi nakkit dāḫḫun* see b 1′ c′ 1″ above.

**2″** in OH/NS: [*mān par*]⌜*ā*⌝ *šiyati ša-aš* $^{URU}$⌜*A*⌝[(*rzawiyaš utniya iyanniš*)] "[When] (nature) sprouted forth (i.e., it became spring), he marched to the land of Arzawiya" KBo 19.90:12 (Hurrian campaigns, Murš. I/NS), w. dupl. KBo 3.46 obv. 42 (NS), ed. StMed 12:138f. (reading *ta-aš*), translit. THeth 8:280, cf. s.v. *šāi-* B 8, Kempinski/Košak, Tel Aviv 9:90, 93; probably here [*mān parā ši*]*yati ša-aš* $^{URU}$*Ḫattuša*⌜*š*⌝ [...] KBo 3.54:11 (Hurrian campaigns, Murš. I/NS), ed. StMed 12:142f.

**b′** following a relative clause, in OH/NS: *kuiš ištarni=šmi antu*⌜*waḫḫiš*⌝ *a*[*ki*] *ša-na-ap* (i.e., *š=an=ap*) *azzikanzi mān uwarka*[*ntan*] *antuḫšan uwanzi n=an=kan kunanzi š=an=ap atānz*[*i*] "Whatever a person among them d[ies], they devour him. When they see a fa[t] person, they will kill him and devour him" KBo 3.60 ii 2-5 (Cannibal text, OH/NS), ed. Güterbock, ZA 44:104f., THeth 29:264, Kempinski, ÄAT 4:42, Bayun, JAC 10:22, 24, Dardano, GsForrer 244 ☐ the second clause with *š.* expresses the motivation for the action of the preceding clause, cf. b 1′ b′ above; LUGAL-*i kuiēš* [(URU.DIDLI)...(x *appišker*)] *šu-uš* LUGAL-*uš ḫarnikta* [($^{URU}$*Ḫat*)*tuš*(*aš karūil*)]*iyadda* ⌜*ki*⌝*ša* "Those who kept taking the cities [...] from the king, the king destroyed them. Ḫattuša will become as before. (Ḫattuša will again take [its] place. The king [will begin] to conduct campaigns as of old)" KUB 37.148 obv. 7-9 (benedictions for Labarna, OH/NS?), w. dupl. KBo 16.86 i 5-7, s.v. *la*(*ḫ*)*ḫiyai-* d ☐ the obverse of KUB 37.148 has not yet been published in hand copy, but a photo is available on hethiter.net/: PhotArch Phb11571.

**c′** following an extra-clausal constituent (i.e., a *casus pendens*) introduced by *kuit*, in OH/NS: ("The king found a pebble in his bread, so they went (and) fanned a fire on a mountain, in an em[pt]y (place), so they could inflict harm on the baker") *kuid=a* [*anda*(?) *pašši*]*lan šallin ša-an ḫattanner š=an šami*[*nuer*] "But as for the [pebb]le [in (the bread) (?)], being large, they crushed it (lit. repeatedly hit it), and [made] it disappear" KBo 3.34 i 3-4 (anecdotes, OH/NS), w. dupl. KBo 13.44 i 3-4 (NS), KUB 36.104 obv. 2 (OS), ed. Dardano, L'anedotto 28f., 74f., Soysal, Diss. 10, 83, THeth 29:116f., HW$^{2}$ 486 (s.v. *ḫatta*(*i*)-), Inglese, Subordination 112, tr. Klinger, TUAT Erg. 62, cf. s.v. *šamenu-* A e (all differently) ☐ instead of restoring *IṢBAT* in KBo 3.34 i 3 (so, e.g., Dardano, L'aneddoto 28 w. disc. 74f., and s.v. *šamenu-* A e), we prefer to restore an extraposed constituent which only consists of *kuid=a* followed by the noun phrase [*pašši*]*lan šallin* and perhaps *anda*. This noun phrase already appears in the grammatical case in which it will be resumed in the following main clause. The function of such a construction is to (re)introduce a contrastive topic for further discussion (see Goedegebuure, StBoT 55:442 n. 476). Thus, instead of impaling or drilling holes in the baker (so Dardano, L'aneddoto 29, s.v. *šamenu-* A e), the large stone is destroyed by crushing it. By breaking it into small pieces, the stone can be made to disappear, a proper act for ritually unclean objects. The punishment of the baker, on the other hand, involves the fire. *š.* in *š=an šami*[*nuer*] marks its clause as the intended result of the preceding action.

**2′** expressing temporal consecution, following a relative clause, in OH/NS: [ŠU.NIGI]N 17 LUGAL.MEŠ *ANA* MÈ.KALAG[.GA=*YA*? *k*]*uiēš tīēr ša-aš ḫulla*[*nun*] "[The totalit]y of seventeen kings who entered [my?] intense battle, [I] defeat[ed] them" KBo 3.13 obv. 16 (Narām Sîn epic, OH/NS), ed. Güterbock, ZA 44:70f., Soysal, FsGünbattı 258f. ☐ the scribe replaced the correct OH acc. pl. com. *-uš* with the NH acc. pl. com. *-aš*, thus showing that he understood *ša-aš* as the conjunction *š.* followed by the enclitic pronoun *-a-*.

**3′** expressing concurrent action, following a relative clause, in OH/NS: § *kuwāpit* UD-*at* L[(UGAL-*iz*)*nait*?] *ša-an-za-pa* (i.e., *š=an=z=apa*) *āššu šuw*[(*at*)*ten* (*nunn=a=p*)*a*] *āššu šuwatte*[*n*] "On any day that [he held(?)] the throne, you look[ed] at him favorably. Now, too, look at (him) favorably" KBo 12.18 i 5-7 (Zalpa frag., OH/NS), w. dupl. KBo 50.3:10-12, KBo 12.63 obv. rt. col. 1-6 (OH/NS), ed. Corti, Mem.Imparati 172-174 ("Dove un/di giorno la re[(gali)tà (?) ] e proprio lui guar[date] bene [(e lui poi) guar[date] bene [...]"), HW[2] Ḫ 473 ("ha[bt] ihr Gutes auf ihn zugetrieben"), Soysal, Diss. 77, 109 (without dupls., "trei[bt] ihn gut! ... treib(t) gut") □ the translation assumes that *nunna=* is *kinunn=a*. Hoffmann (THeth 11:135) suggests to emend to ‹*ki*›*nunn=a*, but perhaps we see used the bare *nun* "now," which is subsequently combined with *ki*. Alternatively understanding *nunna* as *nu*+*an* > *nu=n* rather than expected *n=an* would supply the missing object of the second clause, but the gemination of the *n* would be hard to explain. *Nun* is the attested acc. of *nu*(*t*)- "contentment" (q.v.), but this word is always written plene and does not make sense in the context.

**4′** meaning unclear, often in fragmentary context — **a′** following a relative clause — **1″** in OS: ("For a second time Piyūšti, king of Ḫatti, came") *šardia*(*n*)*=šann=a kuin uwatet šu-uš* [URU]*Šal*[(*ampi*)...] "and the auxiliary troops of his which he had brought, [...] them in Šalampa" KBo 3.22 obv. 37 (Anitta, OS), w. dupl. KUB 36.98a:6-7 (NS), ed. StBoT 18:12f., StMed 13:32f., tr. Hoffner, CoS 1:183, Beckman, ANEHST 217, cf. s.v. [(LÚ)]*šardiya-* A a.

**2″** in OH/NS: [URU]*Lakkurišši=ma* 3 *LIM* ÉRIN.MEŠ LÚ.MEŠ *ḫapi*[(*riš*)] [(LÚ-*ann=a* ARAD.M)]EŠ *ḫarpanteš* LUGAL-*uš kui*[*u*]*š taru*⌈*ppun*⌉ *šu-uš* [(*ašandulaš*)] [...] *nu=ššan ḫaraptati ta kū*[(*ttar=šet kišati*)] "But the 3,000 troops, a combination of *ḫapiri*-men and servants of freemen, that I, the king, had assembled in the city of Lakkurišša, [I made(?)...] them [into] the garrison [troops (?)]. They banded together, and thus (?) became its (i.e., the garrison's) backbone" KBo 19.90 + KBo 3.53 (= BoTU 2, 17B*α*) obv. 9-11 (Hurrian campaigns, Murš I/NS), w. dupl. KBo 3.46 obv. 39-41 (NS), ed. Kempinski/Košak, Tel Aviv 9:90, 93, StMed 12:136-39, Melchert, FsNeu, 180f., THeth 29:243f., translit. THeth 8:279f.; frag. (here?) [... *kui*]⌈*ē*⌉*š ešer šu-uš ēpper* KBo 3.46 obv. 17 (Hurrian campaigns, Murš I/NS).

**b′** following *mān* "just as, like": [...]x.MEŠ *mān aker še-e=pa* EGIR-*pa*[...] KUB 43.36:2, [...] *mān ḫarker še-e=pa* EGIR[-*pa* ...] ibid. 6.

Hrozný, SH (1917) 137 (demonstrative *ša-* < PIE **so-*); Götze, Madd. (1928) 137 (pronoun *ša-* with forms *šaš, šan, šēl, šēz, šuš, še, šietani*); Delaporte, Éléments (1929) 39f. (idem); Petersen, AJPh 53 (1932) 194f. n. 4; Sturtevant, CGr (1933) 29, 200 (pronoun *sas* 'is', "to be identified with IE *so, sā*"); Petersen, AJPh 58 (1937) 307, 311, 312, 316 (demonstrative *sas* derived from PIE **so*); Sommer, HAB (1938) 78 (pronoun *šaš, šan* etc. does not exist; instead, "altheth. Satzeinleitungspartikel *šu*"); Pedersen, Hitt. (1938) 63-67, 196 (separation of conjunction *šu* "deshalb, und so" + *-a-* and pronoun *šiya-* < PIE **si*(*j*)*o-*); Pedersen, Tocharisch (1941) 4f. (conjunction "deshalb, und so"); Sturtevant, CGr[2] (1951) 108 (connective particle *šu*); Kronasser, VLFH (1955) 153 (conjunction *su*, from pronominal stem **so-*); Friedrich, HE (1960) 36 (§38b), 64 (§105b), 161 (§317) ("und"); Sturtevant, Language 38/2 (1962) 108 (*ta* < **to* "then, next"; *šu* < **so* "and" (used when there was no change of subject)); Watkins, Celtica 6 (1963) 14, 17 (part. *šu* corresponds with Old Irish preverb *se*); Kronasser, EHS 1 (1966) 29, 46 ("und"); Sternemann, MIO 11 (1966) 396f. (conjunction); Kammenhuber, KZ 83 (1969) 281, 282 (on *š.* as dating criterion); eadem, HbOr (1969) 137 (sentence connecting particle); Carruba, Part. (1969) 57-63 (conjunction *su* does not exist; pronoun *sa-* < PIE demonstrative **so* is nonenclitic third person pronoun with forms *sas, san, sat?/tat, siel, sietani, sīēz, se, sus/sas, ta*, with enclitic counterpart *-a-* (forms *-as, -an, -at, edani, edi, ediz/edaza, -e/-at, -us/-as, -e/-at*)); Eichner, MSS 29 (1971) 36; Werner, BiOr 29 (1972) 50; Kammenhuber, Materialien 1 (1973): *šu*, 2-16 (Old Hittite clause introducing conjunction "dann, (und) dann"; rejects < PIE **so, *sā, *tod*); Otten, StBoT 17 (1973) 45 n. 8, 76 (conjunction); Neu, StBoT 18 (1974) 101f. (*šu* is a paratactic conjunction expressing close connection ("engere gedankliche Verbindung")); Carruba, Grammatische Kategorien (1983) 81f. (conjunction *su* does not exist; pronoun *sa-* derived from PIE **so*); Luraghi, Old Hittite (1990) 50, 62-70, 121 (*š.* expresses weak addition; source is IE demonstrative); Weitenberg, StMed 7 (1992) 305-353 (*šu* correlates with past tense verbs); Neu, FsHouwink ten Cate (1995) 240; Rieken, 125 Jahre Indogermanistik in Graz (2000) 411f. (on dating texts containing conjunction *šu*); Boley, IF 108 (2003) 140f. (pronoun *sas* derived from PIE **so*); eadem, RANT 1 (2004) 77-82, 98f., 109 (suggests to distinguish between rare sentence connective *su* and more common pronoun *sas, san, se* and *sus* as reflex of animate PIE **só-*); eadem, IF 109 (2004) 141 (on conjunction *su*, distinct from *sas*, expressing "causal, or perhaps resultative, bond between clauses"); eadem, GsForrer (2004) 193-199 (*šaš* < PIE pronoun **só*); eadem, ICH 5 (2005) 152; Tischler, HEG S/2 (2006) 1120-1125 (paratactic conjunction *šu*); Hoffner & Melchert, GrHL (2008) 389-395 (clause-linking conjunction, in complementary distribution with *ta*); Kloekhorst, EDHIL (2008) 772, 801 (clause conjunctive particle); Brosch, HS 124 (2011) 60; Rieken, Einführung (2011) 67 (conjunction); Dunkel, LIPP (2014) 229 (*š.* < affirmative particle ***$h_1$*su*); Kloekhorst, StBoT 56 (2014) 601-604 (*nu, ta*, and *šu* as proclitic conjunctions); Inglese, Subordination (2016) passim.

Cf. *nu, ta.*

**šū- A** adj.; full, see *šūu-*.

**šū- B, šūwa-,** v.; **1.** to fill, **2.** to swell up (mid.), **3.** to close, satisfy, be done with; from OS.

**pres. pl. 3** *šu-u-wa-an-zi* KBo 14.88 ii 16 (MH/MS), KBo 21.13 iv (2) (MH?/NS), KBo 57.113:10 + Bo 4615:(4) (Tudḫ. IV), KUB 13.32 obv. (4) (Tudḫ. IV), KUB 25.22 ii 6, iii 10 (Tudḫ. IV), KUB 25.23 i 6, 20, 21, 30, 46, ii (3), left edge b (2) (Tudḫ. IV), KBo 26.199:(3) (NH), KBo 26.227 iii 16 (NH), KUB 17.37 i 6, iv 6 (NH), KUB 38.25 i? 23 (NH), KUB 38.32 obv. (16) (NH), KUB 42.91 ii (19) (NH), KUB 44.20:5 (NH), KUB 51.33 i 7 (NH), KUB 57.102 iv (3), 13, (20) (NH), VBoT 122:7 (NH), *šu-wa-an-zi* KBo 26.211:(2) (NH), KUB 17.37 i 11 (NH), KUB 44.1 rev. 11 (NH), KUB 60.140 rev. 13 (Tudḫ. IV), *šu-u-an-zi* KUB 36.89 obv. 8 (NH).

**mid. pres. sg. 3** *šu-wa-at-ta-ri* KUB 13.2 iii 24 (MH/NS).

**pret. sg. 3** *šu-u-wa-at-ta-at* KUB 30.39 rev. 10 (OH/NS), *šu-wa-at-ta-at* KBo 10.20 iv (27) (OH/NS), KBo 48.30:(8) (OH/NS), *šu-ut-ta-ti* KBo 6.34 iii 17 (MH/NS).

**imp. sg. 3** *šu-ut-ta-ru* KBo 6.34 iii 21 (MH/NS).

**part. sg. nom. com.** *šu-u-an-za* KBo 15.33 ii 15 (MH/MS), KUB 58.37 rt. col. 5, 6 (MS), KUB 30.26 i 9, 10 (NS), *šu-wa-an-za* KUB 55.57 i 9 (pre-NH/NS), Bo 2810 ii 7 (NH) (Klengel, AoF 1:171-73), *šu-u-wa-an-za* HT 38 iii 3 (OH/NS), KBo 25.190 + KBo 40.38 obv. 20 (MH/MS), KUB 15.34 i 17 (MH/MS), KBo 23.18 obv. 6 (MS), KBo 5.2 i 29, iv 37, 40 (MH/NS), KBo 10.34 i 25 (MH/NS), KBo 12.96 i 10 (2×) (MH/NS), KUB 13.2 iii 40 (MH/NS), RS 25.421 obv. (29), 37, 40, rev. (53), KBo 25.184 iii 69 (pre-NH/NS), KUB 41.13 ii 23, 24 (pre-NH/NS), HFAC 8 obv.? rt. col. 3, 4 (NH), KUB 31.71 iii! 31 (NH), KBo 13.101 rev. 28 (NS), KBo 18.194:2 (NS), KBo 47.120 obv. 8 (NS), KBo 27.45:4, KBo 41.119:4, KUB 59.67 ii (14). [For [*š*]*u*?-*u-an-za* KBo 48.272 i 19, so DBH 38:165, perhaps read [Š]U.U-*an*=*za*.]

**acc. com.** *šu-u-un-ta-an* IBoT 1.36 ii 41 (MH/MS), *šu-u-an-da-an* KUB 11.34 i 8 (MS), KUB 58.37 rt. col. (3) (MS), KBo 29.211 iv? 20 (NS), *šu-u-an-da*‹*-an*› KUB 10.13 iv 14 (OH?/NS), *šu-u-wa-an-da-an* KBo 29.140 rev. 3 (MS?), KUB 20.59 i 8 (OH or MH/NS), KBo 23.15 iv (15) (MH/NS), KBo 29.211 iv? 16 (NS), KBo 39.188 rt. col. 11 (NS), KUB 39.71 ii 16 (NS), KUB 11.9 iv 23 (NH), KUB 15.5 iii 23 (Murš. III), KBo 11.22 iv 19 (NS), KBo 24.41 iv 10 (NS), KUB 41.13 ii 20 (pre-NH/NS), KUB 41.31 obv. 19 (NS), KUB 46.18 obv.? 20, KUB 51.62 obv. 17 (pre-NH/NS), KUB 54.10 ii 8 (NS), KUB 58.83 iii 7 (NS), *šu-wa-an-da-an* KBo 42.145 i 8 (NH).

**nom.-acc. neut.** *šu-u-an* KUB 12.8 ii 3 (OH/NS), KUB 15.34 i 15 (MH/MS), KUB 58.37 rt. col.12 (MS), *šu-wa-an* KUB 30.15 obv. 3 (MH/NS), KUB 26.1 i 11 (Tudḫ. IV), KBo 44.97 ii 9 (NS), *šu-u-wa-an* KBo 21.72 ii 8 (OH/NS), KBo 15.31 i 9 (MH/MS), KBo 24.26 iii 31 (MH/MS), KBo 20.107 i 8 (MH/MS?), KBo 5.1 ii 39, 40, 42, 43 (MH?/NS), KBo 5.2 ii 37, 38 (MH/NS), KBo 9.126:6 (pre-NH/NS), KBo 10.34 i 29, KBo 25.184 iii 60 (pre-NH/NS), KUB 6.45 + KBo 57.18 i 7, 8 (Muw. II), KBo 18.172 obv. 4 (NH), KUB 27.1 iv 48 (NH), KUB 41.13 ii 16 (pre-NH/NS), KUB 27.57 ii 16 (NS), KUB 44.44:(3) (NS), *šu-u-wa-a-an* KBo 5.1 ii 37 (MH?/NS).

**pl. nom. com.** *šu-u-wa-an-te-eš* KBo 25.190 rev. 6 (MH/MS), KBo 29.94 iv 9 (MS), KUB 9.28 iii 18 (MH/NS), KBo 38.34 obv.? 6 (NS), KUB 54.65 ii! 5 (NH), KUB 30.26 i 9 (NS), KUB 55.38 ii 10 (NS), *šu-wa-an-te-eš* KBo 55.94:10 (NS).

**acc. com.** *šu-u-wa-du-uš* KUB 29.1 ii 7 (OH/NS), *šu-u-wa-an-du-uš* KBo 21.34 i 25, 52, ii 5 (MH/NS), KBo 21.78 iii 7 (NS), KUB 54.10 ii 20 (NS), *šu-u-wa-an-du*‹*-uš*› KBo 21.34 i 41 (MH/NS), *šu-u-wa-an-te-eš* KBo 4.9 i 17 (OH?/NS), KUB 10.95 iii? 6 (pre-NH/NS), KUB 15.11 iii 17 (Ḫatt. III).

**nom.-acc. neut.** *šu-u-an-ta* KBo 21.47 iii! 15 (MH/MS), *šu-u-an-da* KBo 10.34 i 27 (MH/NS), *šu-u-wa-an-da* KUB 58.34 iii 13 (NS), *šu-u-wa-an-ta* KUB 54.35 rev.? 14 (NS), *šu-wa-an-da* KBo 21.20 i 22 (NH).

**imperf. act. pres. sg. 2** *šu-uš-ke-ši* KUB 31.143 ii 22 (2×) (OS).

**pres. pl. 3** *šu-uš-kán-zi* KBo 15.33 ii (6), (10) (MH/MS).

**mid. pres. pl. 3** *šu-u-wa-*⸢*e*?⸣*-*[*eš-kán-ta-ri*?] KUB 34.14 + KBo 34.122 iii 5-6 (NS).

The mid. *šu-ut-ta-ti* and *šu-ut-ta-ru* and the imperf. *šu-uš-k°* show that *šū-* was the original stem and *šuwa-* a secondary *-a-* stem. When written plene, *š.* "to fill" consistently shows *-u-* (hence with o-vocalism), whereas *šuwaye-* "to look (at)" and *šuwe-* "to push" almost always show *ú* (u-vocalism). Confusion, however, between all these stems is possible in the absence of plene writing.

Kronasser, EHS 1:479, Oettinger, Stammbildung 295, Kloekhorst, EDHIL 797, and Tischler, HEG S/2:1217 cite *šu-wa-u-e-ni* (pres.pl.1) in KUB 12.63 obv. 29 (*UMMA ŠU*=*MA UL*=*za šuwaueni*) among the occurrences of *š.* 'to fill'. Due to context and the reflexive particle *-za* this form rather belongs with *šuwe-* "to push, shove" q.v., and the sentence there is to be translated with Friedrich, Or NS 13:209 w. n. 5 as "He (said) thus: 'We do not push ourselves (to do it).'" Hoffmann, THeth 11:136, similarly interprets: "Wir wollen uns nicht in Bewegung setzen."

For *šu-wa-a-id-du* as imp. sg. 3 of *šuwe-* "to push" instead of "to fill," see Kloekhorst, EDHIL 797. With the removal of this form there is no longer evidence of a stem *šuwai-* "to fill."

In a lyric description of a mother: (Sum.) ("My mother is an alabaster statuette") [dìm-ma-zú-til-la ḫi-li šu-gìr gùr-ru-a] = (Akk.) ⸢*ma*⸣*-ku-ut šinni qú-ut-tù-tù* [*š*]*a ul-ṣa ma-la-at* "a finished pillar(?) of ivory (lit. tooth) that is full of delight" = (Hitt.) *laḫpaš*=*ma*=*aš kurakkiš mā*⸢*n z*⸣*innanza n*=*aš* ME.LÁM-⸢*az*⸣ *šu-*⸢*u*⸣*-*[*w*]*a-an-za* "she is like a finished pillar of ivory(?); she is filled with radiance" RS 25.421 obv. 28-29 (signalement lyrique), ed. Laroche, Ugar. 5:773, 775, 777 (Hitt.), Nougayrol, Ugar. 5:313, 315 (Sum. and Akk.).

(Sum.) [kiri$_6$ la-la(-me) asilal-lá s]a$_5$! = (Sum. pronunciation) ki-ri la-li-me a-ši-l[a š]a-a = (Akk.) $^{GIŠ}$*kirû la-le-e ša* ˹*ri*˺-*ša-ti ma-lu-u* = "(She is) a garden of desire, full of joy" = (Hitt.) $^{GIŠ}$KIRI$_6$-*aš*=*ma*=*aš* GIM-*an ilaliyan*[*za*] *dammetarwantit šu-u-wa-an-za* "She is like a desir[ed] garden, filled with luxuriant growth" RS 25.421 obv. 36-37, ed. Laroche, Ugar. 5:774, 775 (Hitt.), Nougayrol, Ugar. 5:313, 315 (Sum. and Akk.).

(Sum.) [$^{giš}$ù-suḫ$_5$ a-dé-a $^{giš}$še-ù-suḫ$_5$ šu-tag-ga] = (Sum. pronunciation) a-šu-uḫ ši-da-a še-nu-a-šu-uḫ ši-táq-qa = (Akk.) $^{GIŠ}$Ù.SUḪ$_5$ (= $^{GIŠ}$*ašūḫ*) *ši-iq-qa-ti ša te-re-en-na-a-ti zu-ʾu-na-at* "(She (i.e., the mother) is) a fir tree from an irrigated plot (Sum.: an irrigated fir tree), adorned with fir cones" = (Hitt.) $^{GIŠ}$*šuinilaš*=*ma*=*aš* GIM-*an šeššuraš n*=*aš āššuīt š*[*arā*?] *šu-u-wa-an-za* "She is like a *šuinila*-tree from an irrigated field; she is filled u[p](?) with good things" RS 25.421 obv. 38-40, ed. Nougayrol, Ugar. 5:313, 315 (Sum. and Akk.), Laroche, Ugar. 5:774, 775 (Hitt.), Cohen, Wisdom 70, ed. CAD Š s.v. *šiqītu*.

(Sum.) [ama-mu ezen siskur-re asilal-lá s]a$_5$ (for restorations see Civil, JNES 23:4) = (Sum. pronunciation) am-ma-an-ku i-ši-en d[á-aš-gu]r-ra a-ši-la [š]a-a "My mother is an offering-festival full with joy" = (Akk.) AMA-*mi* ˹x x x x x x˺ ˹*ša ri-ša*˺-*ti* ˹*ma-lu*˺-*u* "My mother [...] full of joy = (Hitt.) ˹*anna*˺*š*=˹*miš*=*a* x x x˺ *n*=*aš* [...]˹x-x-*anza*˺ *š*[*u-u*]-*w*[*a-an-za*] RS 25.421 rev. 52-53, ed. Laroche, Ugar. 5:774f. (Hitt.), Nougayrol, Ugar. 5:314, 315 (Akk.).

(Sum.) [lú-šà-ta-ḫ]a-la = (Sum. pronunciation) lu-ša-da-ḫa-la = (Akk.) *em-ru* "one suffering from colic" = (Hitt.) ⸗*šu-u-wa-an*[*-za*...] KBo 1.39 obv. ii 3 (Proto-lú vocab., NS), ed. MSL 12:216f., Scheucher, Diss. 608f. The gloss is used in this vocab. consistently as a marker indicating that the word in question had run over its appropriate column (cf. MSL 12:217 n. 1), and *š.* consequently should not be taken as a "Glossenkeil" word. Possible restorations for the rest of the column are: *šu-u-wa-an-za ku-iš* or *šu-u-wa-an-za* UN-*aš*. For discussion on the Akk. counterpart *emru* "suffering from colic" and *emēru* "to have intestinal distress (colic or the like)" see s.v. *paparriy*[*a*(-)] "to suffer from colic(?), be flatulent(?)," which is translated in this vocabulary with the same Akk. word.

**1.** to fill — **a.** as a finite verb or predicative participle, generally "to fill (containers)," with filling materials often mentioned in preceding lines (cf. *šun*(*n*)*a*- c) — **1′** without particle: [... GA]L *šu-uš-ki-ši* ˹*pal*˺*ḫaea*$^{HI.A}$ GAL *šu*-˹*uš-ke-ši*˺ "(O god Telipinu), you always fill [the lar]ge [...], you always fill the large storage jars" KUB 31.143 ii 22 (invoc., OS), ed. Gertz, Diss. 17-19, Hoffmann, THeth 11:136 (differently: "die gro]ßen bewegst du immer wieder. Die breiten Wasser, die großen, bewegst du immer wieder"), translit. StBoT 25:186, cf. StBoT 26:134 w. n. 420a, and s.v. discussion $^{(DUG)}$*palḫi*- B b 2′; *nu kuit*[*man šu-u*]*š-kán-zi* "Whi[le] they are [fi]lling (several containers)" KBo 15.33 ii 6 (rit. of Kuliwišna, MH/MS), ed. Glocker, Eothen 6:64f., sim. ii 10; *n*=*ašta ANA* ˹DUG-*ya*˺ *šiḫelliyaš wātar kuit anda nu*=*za apēz ā*˹*rri*˺ $^{DUG}$GAL=*ma kuiš šu-u-wa-an-za n*=*at AN*[*A*] *wašši*$^{HI.A}$ *dāi nu wašši*$^{HI.A}$ *kuškuššanzi* "As for the water of purification that is (still) in the jug, with that (water) he washes himself. As for the (earthen) cup filled (with the water of purification from the jug), he takes it for the ingredients. They crush the ingredients" (and he drinks the solution) KBo 5.2 iv 38-41 (Ammiḫatna's rit., MH/NS), ed. Strauß, Reinigung 231f., 244; cf. KBo 5.2 iv 36-38, see d 1′ p′; with $^{DUG}$DÍLIM.GAL "bowl" KUB 41.13 ii 23 (fest. frag., pre-NH/NS), w. par. KUB 58.37 rt. col. (5) (MS); $^{DUG}$*KUKŪB* "pitcher" KBo 9.126:6; [*takku*] ˹ITU˺ZÍZ.˹A˺ [A]N.TA.LÙ $^{d}$UTU-*aš kīšar*[*i*] ˹*ḫe*˺*yauēš kīšantari* ÍD.MEŠ *šu-u-wa*-˹*iz*˺[*-zi*] "[If] a solar eclipse occur[s] in the [e]leventh month, rains will occur, [it] will fill the rivers" KUB 34.14 + KBo 34.122 iii 5-6 (solar omen, NS), ed. Riemschneider, DBH 12:121f. ☐ Riemschneider, DBH 12:122, translates ÍD.MEŠ *šu-u-wa*-x-[...] as "die Flüsse [werden] anschwellen," and ibid., 262, lists this occurrence s.v. *šuwai*- "füllen, anschwellen." He compares this sentence with an Akkadian parallel *zunnu u mīlu* [TÚ]G-*u* "rain and flood will occur" in KUB 4.63 iii 23. The identification of the last broken sign in *šu-u-wa*-x-[...] is problematic. According to Riemscheider and confirmed by collation (photo), it is either *-e-* or *-iz-*. He prefers the reading *-e-* and expects a *šk*-formation of *š.* here. However, *šūwaēške*-, with the vowel sequence *-aē-*, would be a highly unusual *-ške-* formation. For that reason but also because the attested iter. is *šuške*-, we reject *šu-u-wa*-˹*e*?˺-[*eš-k*°].

**2′** with particle (mainly in the expression *BIBRI*$^{HI.A}$=*kan š.* in NH): [...] *ŠA* GA.KIN.AG ḪÁD.DU.A *tarnaš* 1 *wakšur* LÀL [...] Ì *pittalwan n*=*ašta* $^{DUG}$*kullita šu-u-an-da* [1? $^{DUG}$*gu*]*lliša ŠA* LÀL 1 $^{DUG}$*gulliša ŠA* Ì "[...] of dried cheese of (a) *tarna*-measure, one *wakšur* of honey, [... *wakšur*(?) of] plain oil. And the *kulli*-vessels are filled: [one(?) *gu*]*lli*-vessel of honey, one *gulli*-vessel of oil" KBo 10.34 i 26-28 (enthronement rit. in the cult of Teššub and Ḫebat, MH/NS) ☐ for the Luwianism

$^{DUG}$*kulli*-, with Luwian neuter particle -*ša* and neuter plural *kullita*, see HED K, 239; ("The administrator of the city Takuppaša gives three cups for *walḫi*- (and) three cups for *marnuwa*-. The cupbearers give three cups for wine") *šuppa zeyandaza ḫuešawaza tianzi* NINDA.GUR$_4$.RA *paršiyanzi BIBRI*$^{ḪI.A}$*=kan šu-u-an-zi* "they place meat, (some) cooked, (some) raw. They break thick bread. They fill the rhyta" KUB 36.89 obv. 7-8 (ritual and prayer, NH), ed. Haas, KN 142f.; *BIBRI*$^{ḪI.A}$*=kan š.* also in KUB 25.23 i 20, 30, 46 + Bo 7337:4, KBo 26.227 iii (4), KBo 57.113:10 + Bo 4615:(4), KUB 25.22 iii 10, KUB 38.25 i? 23, and passim; 1 NINDA *tarna*[*š parš*]*iyanzi* (eras.) $^{DUG}$*talaimiuš=kan šu-u-wa-an-*[*zi*] "They [brea]k one bread of (a) *tarna*-measure. They fil[l] the *talaimi*-vessels" KUB 42.91 ii 18-19 (cult inv., NH), ed. Hazenbos, Organization 112, 114. Cf. similarly with *šunna*- "to fill" (see HW 200): NINDA. GUR$_4$.RA.MEŠ *tarnaš=(š)maš paršiyanzi* $^{DUG}$*talaimiuš=kan šunna⟨n⟩zi* "They break the thick breads of (a) *tarna*-measure for them, (and) they(!) fill the *talaimi*-vessels" KBo 2.13 obv. 20 (cult inv., NH); cf. also with $^{DUG}$*tala*(*i*)*mi*- "*t*.-vessel" KUB 17.37 i 6 (cult. inv., NH); and with ZA.ḪUM KÙ.BABBAR "silver pitcher" KUB 51.33 i 7 (cult. inv., NH).

**b.** as finite verb or predicative participle, generally with mention of both the filled container and the substance (inst. or abl.), usually no particle, (cf. *šun*(*n*)*a*- d) — **1′** in MH: [...]*n=aš IŠTU* $^{GI}$KAK.Ú.TAG.GA *šu-u-wa-an-za* "It is filled with arrows" KBo 23.18 obv. 6 (MS); 16 $^{DUG}$*ḫupuwāi=ma IŠTU* LÀL Ì $^{GIŠ}$*SERTUM* $^{GIŠ}$PÈŠ $^{GIŠ}$GEŠTIN ḪÁD. DU.A $^{GIŠ}$*SERTUM šu-u-wa-an* "sixteen pots(?) are filled with the honey, olive oil, fig(s), raisin(s), olive(s)" KBo 5.2 ii 37-38 (Ammiḫatna's rit., MH/NS), ed. Strauß, Reinigung 225, 238; 14 $^{DUG}$*purpuriš* ŠÀ.BA 7 $^{DUG}$*purpuriš IŠTU* Ì.DÙG.GA *šu-u-wa-an* 7 $^{DUG}$*purpuriš=ma IŠTU* Ì.GIŠ *šu-u-wa-an* "There are fourteen *purpuriš* vessels. Among them seven *purpuriš* vessels are filled with refined oil, seven *purpuriš* vessels are filled with vegetable oil" KBo 5.1 ii 41-43 (Papanikri's rit., MH?/NS), ed. Strauß, Reinigung 290, 299, Pap. 8*f.; 7 $^{GIŠ}$*GANNUM* AD.KID *šer=ma=ššan* 7 $^{GIŠ}$MA.SÁ.AB *kitta nu=ššan* $^{GIŠ}$*INBI*$^{ḪI.A}$ *išḫūwan* 7 $^{GIŠ}$*ariyala* AD.KID*=ya n=at IŠTU* $^{GIŠ}$*INBI* ⸓*šu-u-wa-a-an* "There are seven stands of wickerwork. Seven baskets are placed on them, and fruits are poured onto them. There are also seven baskets/trays(?) of wickerwork, and they are filled with fruit" KBo 5.1 ii 34-37 (Papanikri's rit., MH?/NS), ed. Strauß, Reinigung 290, 299, Pap. 6*f.; 7 ANŠE. KUR.RA GIR$_4$ 7 GUD GIR$_4$ 7 MUŠEN GIR$_4$ 7 $^{DUG}$*pulluri*(*=*)*ya n=at IŠTU* LÀL *šu-u-wa-an šer=ma=at=kan IŠTU* $^{GIŠ}$PÈŠ *ištappan* "There are seven terracotta horses, seven terracotta oxen, seven terracotta birds, seven *pulluri*(*ya*)-containers. They are filled with honey and covered with fig(s) on top" KBo 5.1 ii 38-40 (Papanikri's rit., MH?/NS), ed. Strauß, Reinigung 290, 299, Pap. 8*f.; also cf. KUB 55.57 i 7-9 (e 1′ e′); for an example with -*kan*, see d 4′.

**2′** in NH: ("He lead me then in some other palace(room)s. And there, where one makes offerings to the gods, and where one arranges the table of the god, the storage-pits were ... ") *nu=wa=*⸢*kan A*⸣*NA* 1 ÉSAG $^{DUG}$*aganniš* ⸢*m*⸣*ān anda nu=war=aš* $^{SÍG}$*iyatnaza* ⸢*šu-u*⸣*-wa-an-za* "and in one storage-pit there was something like an *aganni*-container, and it was filled with a wealth of wool" KUB 31.71 iii! 29-31 (queen's dream, NH), ed. van den Hout, AoF 21:311, 313, Mouton, Rêves 273, 278.

**c.** as attributive participle modifying a container or location, often accompanied by the materials (inst. or abl.) that fill the containers or locations: EGIR-*anda=ma kalti* KÙ.G[(I)] *udanzi nu=ššan* GEŠTIN KU$_7$ *ḫandān ta=ššan* $^{GIŠ}$DAG-*ti tia*[*nzi*] § $^{DUG}$GUR$_4$.GUR$_4$ KÙ.GI*=ya IŠTU* GEŠTIN *šu-u-an-da⟨-an⟩ u*[(*danzi*)] (var. [$^{DUG}$GU]R$_4$.GUR$_4$ KÙ.GI *udanzi IŠTU* GE[ŠTIN ...]) *n=an kaltiya kattan* [*tianzi*] "Thereafter they bring a golden *kalti*. Sweet wine is readied in it, and they place (the *kalti*) on the throne dais. § They bring a golden pitcher fille⟨d⟩ with wine (var. "They bring a golden pitcher. [It is filled] with win[e]"), and they place it next to the *kalti*-vessel" KUB 10.13 iv 9-14 (KI.LAM fest., OH?/NS), w. dupl. KBo 25.176 rev. 26-29 (NS), translit. dupl. StBoT 28:94; *namma=kan ANA PĀNI* $^{d}$IM 2 GAL.ḪI.A *IŠTU* GEŠTIN *šu-u-wa-an-du-uš lāḫūwanzi* "then they pour in front of the Stormgod the two cups filled with wine" KBo 21.34 i 24-25 (fest. for Teššub and Ḫebat of Lawazantiya, MH/NS); DUMU*=YA=ma=mu kuin* INIM

$^{GIŠ}$MÁ *TAŠPUR ḫalkiyaza≈wa* 1 *ME* $^{GIŠ}$MÁ *šu-wa-an-za uit* "Regarding the matter of the ship(s), about which you, my son, wrote to me: 'One hundred ships loaded (lit. filled) with grain have come (to me)!' Bo 2810 ii 6-7 (letter, NH), ed. Klengel, AoF 1:172f., Letters 363.

**d.** types of containers — **1′** cups, and other vessels — **a′** *aganni*-cup or bowl: *nu≈wa≈*⌜*kan A*⌝*NA* 1 ÉSAG $^{DUG}$*aganniš* ⌜*m*⌝*ān anda nu≈war≈aš* $^{SÍG}$*iyatnaza* ⌜*šu-u*⌝*-wa-an-za* "and in one storage-pit there was something like an *aganni*-container, and it was filled with a wealth of wool" KUB 31.71 iii! 29-31 (queen's dream, NH), ed. van den Hout, AoF 21:311, 313, Mouton, Rêves 273, 278.

**b′** $^{GIŠ}$*ariyala-* "basket, tray": see KBo 5.1 ii 34-37, in b 1', above.

**c′** $^{DUG}$*ḫariulli-*: [...]x *marnuan* 1 $^{DUG}$*ḫariulli* [*ḫa*]*palzilit šu-u-an tianzi* "They place [...] *marnuan*-drink, one *ḫ*.-vessel filled with *ḫapalzil*-meal" KUB 12.8 ii 2-3 (Tuḫumiyara fest., OH/NS).

**d′** *ḫuppar* "bowl": 2 *ḫuppar* KÙ.BABBAR *išpantuzziaš* GEŠTIN-*it šu-u-wa-an-te-eš šuppaš* ZAG-*naz* GÙB-*lazz≈iya tianzi* "They place two silver bowls filled with wine from a libation vessel to the right and to the left of the meat" KBo 4.9 i 16-19 (*ANDAḪŠUM* fest., OH?/NS), tr. Klinger, TUAT NF 4:198; filled with Ì.DÙG.GA "refined oil" KUB 30.15 obv. 3 (royal funerary rit., MH/LNS).

**e′** $^{DUG}$*ḫupuwai-* "pot(?)": filled with KAŠ. GEŠTIN KBo 5.2 ii 36-37 (Ammiḫatna's rit., MH/NS); with oil, honey, fruits KBo 5.2 ii 37-38 (see e 2′ b′).

**f′** *ḫutanni-*: 1 *ḫuta*'*nnin* KÙ.BABBAR 1 *ḫūtannin* K[Ù.GI] *IŠTU* Ì.DÙG.GA *šu-u-wa-an-te-eš* "one silver and one gol[den] *ḫutanni*-vessel filled with fine oil" KUB 15.11 iii 16-17 (vow, Ḫatt. III).

**g′** *išpanduwa-* "libation vessel": *išpanduwan* KÙ.BABBAR GEŠTIN-*it šu-u-an-da-a*[*n*] "silver libation vessel filled with wine" KBo 29.211 iv? 20 (NS).

**h′** *kantašuwalliš*: 4 $^{URUDU}$*kantašuw*[*a*]*lliš IŠTU* GEŠTIN KAŠ *marnuit walaḫ*[*ḫ*]*it šu-u-wa-an-te-eš ANA PĀNI* DINGIR-*LIM tianzi* "They place four *kantašuw*[*a*]*lli*-vessels filled with wine, beer, *marnuwa-* (and) *walḫi-* in front of the god" KUB 55.38 ii 9-11 (Ištanuwian fest., NS), ed. Polvani, Hethitica 9:174, translit. StBoT 31:601, DBH 4:63.

**i′** *kulli*-vessel: KBo 10.34 i 27-28 (enthronement rit. in the cult of Teššub and Ḫebat, MH/NS), see 1 a 2′.

**j′** *kurtalla/i-* "crate": ⌜$^{GI}$⌝[*kurtall*]*aš≈šan kuiš* ZÍD.DA-*it šu-u-an-za ŠAPAL* $^{GIŠ}$BÚGIN *kittat n≈an* $^{DUG}$*išnūraš awan katta tianzi* "As for the crate filled with flour that had been placed under the box, they place it next to the dough bowls" KBo 15.33 ii 14-16 (rit. of Kuliwisna, MH/MS), ed. Glocker, Eothen 6:64-67; *nu* 1 $^{GI}$*kurtalli*(!) *šu-u-wa-an udanz*[*i*] *šēr≈a≈ššan* 1 NINDA *LABKU kitta* [ Ø ] *n≈at ištanāni peran tian*[*zi*] "They brin[g] the filled crate. A moist/soft(?) bread is placed on it. They pu[t] it in front of the altar" KBo 24.26 iii 31-33 (cult of Ḫuwaššanna, MH/MS).

**k′** *palḫi* "storage jar": KUB 31.143 ii 22 (invoc., OS), see 1 a 1′.

**l′** $^{DUG}$*purpuriš*, a globular vessel: 14 $^{DUG}$*purpuriš* ŠÀ.BA 7 $^{DUG}$*purpuriš IŠTU* Ì.DÙG.GA *šu-u-wa-an* 7 $^{DUG}$*purpuriš≈ma IŠTU* Ì.GIŠ *šu-u-wa-an* "There are fourteen *purpuriš* vessels. Of those, seven *purpuriš* vessels are filled with refined oil, seven *purpuriš* vessels are filled with vegetable oil" KBo 5.1 ii 41-43 (Papanikri's rit., MH?/NS), ed. Strauß, Reinigung 290, 299, Pap. 8*f.

**m′** $^{DUG}$*tala*(*i*)*mi-* "*t.*-vessel": KUB 42.91 ii 18-19 (cult. inv., NH), KUB 17.37 i 6 (cult. inv., NH).

**n′** *tapišana/i-* vessel: UGULA $^{LÚ}$MUḪALDIM *tapišanin* GEŠTIN-*it šu-u-wa-an-da-an dāi* LUGAL-*i pāi* "the chief cook takes a *tapišana*-vessel filled with wine, (and) gives (it) to the king" KBo 11.22 iv 17-20 (mixed festivals, NS), w. dupl. KUB 10.16 iv 5-8 (NS); GAL $^{LÚ.MEŠ}$MUḪALDIM *tapišanan* GIR$_4$ *marnuwantet šu-u-wa-an dāi* "The chief of the cooks takes a ceramic *tapišana-* filled with *marnuwan* (he presents it to the prince and the prince places a hand toward it") KBo 21.72 ii 7-8 + KBo 39.82 ii 14-15 (fest. celebrated by the prince, NS).

**o′** GIŠDÍLIM.GAL "bowl": *nu* GIŠDÍLIM.GAL *šu-u-an-za* (var. *šu-u-wa-an-za*) 1 *NAMMANTA*=*ya* [(A-*it*)] *šu-u-an-za* (var. *šu-u-wa-an-za*) "there is a filled bowl, and also a *NAMMANTU*-vessel filled with water" KUB 58.37 rt. col. 5-6 (rit. frag., MS), w. par. KUB 41.13 ii 23-24 (NS), translit. DBH 18:97, ed. dupl. ChS I/3-1:118f.; *memal*=*ma* DUGDÍLIM.GAL *šu-u-wa-an* "bowl filled (with) coarsely ground meal" KUB 6.45 + KBo 57.18 i 7-8 (prayer, Muw. II); filled (with) porridge KBo 5.2 i 29 (Ammiḫatna's rit., MH/NS), see e 3′ a′.

**p′** DUG "jar": ⌈*nu*=*za*⌉ GIŠ*GANNUM-it kuiš* DUG-*iš* ⌈*šiḫilliyaš witenit*⌉ *šu-u-wa-an-za artari nu*=*kan* LÚAZU *apēz* ⌈*šer arḫa*⌉ *lāḫui nu* DUGGAL.GIR$_4$ *šunnai* "as for the jar filled with the water of purification that stands with a stand, the exorcist pours out (the purifying water) from the top of that (jar), and fills an earthen cup (with it)" KBo 5.2 iv 36-38 (Ammiḫatna's rit., MH/NS), ed. Strauß, Reinigung 231, 244; DUG.KAŠ "beer vessel" KUB 27.57 ii 16 (NH).

**q′** GAL "cup": *namma*=*kan ANA PĀNI* dIM 2 GAL.ḪI.A *IŠTU* GEŠTIN *šu-u-wa-an-du-uš lāḫūwanzi* "then they pour in front of the Storm-god the two cups filled with wine" KBo 21.34 i 24-25 (fest. for Teššub and Ḫebat of Lawazantiya, MH/NS), cf. ibid. i 40-41, 52-53, ii 4-5; 2 GAL *IŠTU* ZÍD.DA ZÍZ *šu-u-wa-*⌈*an-d*⌉*u-uš* "two cups filled with wheat flour" KUB 54.10 ii 20 (witaššiyaš-fest., NS); with DUḪ.LÀL "wax" KUB 10.95 iii ? 5 (fest. frag., pre-NH/NS), see e 3′ c′; see also GAL KÙ.BABBAR "silver cup" filled with *tawal*-wine KUB 11.34 i 7-8 (fest. of haste, pre-NH/MS), see e 1′ e′; GAL.GIR$_4$ "earthen cup" KUB 47.39 obv.? 9 (offerings on the throne of Ḫebat, NS); filled with wine KUB 11.9 iv 23, with Ì.DÙG.GA "refined oil" KUB 41.13 ii 20 (pre-NH/NS); with KAŠ.GEŠTIN KBo 9.126:8 (Ḫuwarlu's rit, NS).

**r′** DUGGUR$_4$.GUR$_4$ "pitcher": filled with wine KUB 10.13 iv 13-14 (KI.LAM fest., OH?/NS), see c above, KBo 23.15 iv 15.

**s′** GIŠMA.SÁ.AB "basket": 2 GIŠMA.SÁ.AB *ḫalk*[*iyaz*(?)] *šu-u-wa-an-te-eš* ŠÀ.BA 1 GIŠMA.SÁ.AB ZÍZ *šu-u-an-za* [1 GIŠMA.SÁ.AB] ŠE *šu-u-an-za* "There are two baskets filled [with] grai[n(?)]. Among them there is one basket filled (with) wheat, [(and) one basket] filled (with) barley" KUB 30.26 i 8-10 (Zelliya's rit., NS), ed. Otten, HTR 102f.; see also [GIŠM]A.SÁ.AB *IŠTU* ZÍZ *šu-wa-an* KBo 44.97 ii 9 (Ḫamrišḫara's rit., NS).

**t′** DUGÚTUL "bowl": NINDA.Ì.E.DÉ.A DUGÚTUL *šu-u-wa-an* "pot full of NINDA.Ì.E.DÉ.A oil cake" KUB 6.45 + KBo 57.18 i 7 (prayer, Muw. II), KUB 15.34 i 17 (MH/MS).

**u′** ZA.ḪUM "pitcher": ZA.ḪUM KÙ.BABBAR *ŠA* KAŠ *šu-u-wa-an-da-an* KUB 39.71 ii 16 (NH), KUB 51.33 i 7 (cult. inv., NH).

**v′** *BIBRU* "animal shaped vessel": *BIBRI*ḪI.A=*kan šu-u-an-zi* KUB 36.89 obv. 7-8 (ritual and prayer, NH), see 1 a 2′, and passim; *BIBRA* KÙ.GI KUB 54.10 ii 8 (frag. *witaššiya*-fest., NS), see e 1′ c′.

**w′** DUG*KUKŪBU* "pitcher": DUG*KUKŪB* KBo 5.1 ii 40 (NS), DUG*KUKŪB* KÙ.GI "golden pitcher" KUB 27.1 iv 47-48 (NH), both filled with wine; ⌈x⌉ DUG*KUKŪBI*ḪI.A *IŠTU* KAŠ.GEŠTIN *dawal walḫi šu-w*[*a-an-*...] "x pitchers fil[led] with 'wine-beer,' *tawal*-wine (and) *walḫi*-beer" KUB 55.57 i 6 (rit. frag., NS); *nu* 2 DUG*KUKŪB Š*[*A*...] ⌈x-x-x⌉ *kantit šu-u-an-*[...] "two pitchers o[f ... ] filled with *kant*-grain" KUB 58.37 rt. col.15 (fest. frag., MS).

**x′** *NAMMANTU*: *nu* GIŠDÍLIM.GAL *šu-u-an-za* (var. *šu-u-wa-an-za*) 1 *NAMMANTA*=*ya* [(A-*it*)] *šu-u-an-za* (var. *šu-u-wa-an-za*) "there is a filled bowl, and also a *NAMMANTU*-vessel filled with water" KUB 58.37 rt. col. 5-6 (rit. frag., MS), w. dupl. KUB 41.13 ii 23-24 (NS), translit. DBH 18:97, ed. dupl. ChS I/3-1:118f.; 1 DUG*NAMMANTU*[*M I*]*ŠTU* GEŠTIN LÀL Ì.DÙG.GA *anda īmmiyantit šu-u-an* "one *NAMMANTU*-vessel filled with wine, honey and fine oil (that are) mixed together" KUB 15.34 i 14-15 (evocation rit., MH/MS), ed. Haas/Wilhelm, AOATS 3:184f.

**2′** the land of Ḫatti is filled with royal progeny: (His Majesty has many brothers. There are also many brothers of his father) KUR URU*Ḫ*⌈*a*⌉[*tti*=*kan*? *IŠT*]*U* NUMUN LUGAL-*UTTI šu-wa-an* "The land of Ḫa[tti] is filled [wi]th royal progeny." (In Ḫatti the descendants of Šuppiluliuma, of Muršili, of Muwatalli and of Ḫattušili are many) KUB 26.1 i 10-11 (instr. for eunuchs, Tudḫ. IV), ed. Dienstanw. 9, HittInstr 296f.

**3′** the hunting-bag: [(KUŠ*kurš*)]*an* ⌜*šu*⌝-*u*-*wa-an-za Labarnaš* dLA[MMA-*aš*] "Labarna's tut[elary] deity who fills the hunting-bag" KUB 2.1 ii 32 (fest. for all dLAMMAs, Tudḫ. IV), w. dupl. KUB 44.16 iii? 11, ed. McMahon, AS 25:102f. w. n. 89 (w. discussion of the syntax) □ this is a rare example of the participle of a transitive verb with an active interpretation, and exceptionally a dependent acc. For the generic interpretation of such participles, see GrHL 339 (§ 25.39).

**4′** mouth and throat: *aiš*=*za*=*kan* Ì-*it* ⌜*šu*⌝-*u*-*wa-an-za ēš* UZU*ḫurḫurta*=*ma*=*za*=*kan ḫalwamnaz šu-u-wa-an-za ēš* "O mouth, be filled with fat, O throat, be filled with laughter" KBo 12.96 i 9-11 (rit. for dLAMMA of the hunting-bag, MH/NS), ed. Badalì, Or NS 59:133, Rosenkranz, Or NS 33:239, 241, THeth 11:138 (paraphrasing, "sei einer, dessen Mund voller Öl ist"), THeth 25:73f. □ Dardano, ICH 8:254 and HW² Ḫ 644 treat *aiš* and *ḫurḫurta* as acc. of respect ("with respect to the mouth be filled with fat, with respect to the throat be filled with laughter"). This requires the emendation of UZU*ḫurḫurta* to UZU*ḫurḫurta*⟨*n*⟩. Since the vocative of *a*-stems has an ending in zero (GrHL 75), we reject the emendation and take UZU*ḫurḫurta* and thus also neuter *aiš* as vocatives.

**5′** quiver full of arrows: (One palace attendant steps forward) *nu*=*šši* LÚŠÀ.TAM GIŠ⌜BAN *ḫui*⌝*ttian an*[*d*]*a*=⌜*ma*=*at*⌝=*kan* (coll.) KUŠ*parduganni tarnan* 1 KUŠÉ.MÁ.URU$_5$.URU=*ši*!? *ŠA* LÚ GIŠŠUK[UR o?] *IŠTU* ⌜GI⌝.KAK.Ú.TAG.GA *šu-u-un-ta-an pāi* "and the quartermaster gives him a strung bow, kept in a bowcase, and a spearman's quiver, filled with arrow(s)" IBoT 1.36 ii 39-41 (instr. for the *MEŠEDI*-guards, MH/MS), ed. AS 24:18f. (w. collations), Jakob-Rost, MIO 11:184-187 □ against Laroche's misquotation of *šunnan* in RHA XXXI 92, the reading *šūntan* is certain. The form is acc. com., contra AS 24:83. It is a contraction of the regular participle *šuwant*-. Also note that in the same text ii 48 a similar participle formation (*peran*) *tint*- "advanced" (beside usual *tiyant*- ibid. ii 53) is attested, see Kloekhorst, EDHIL 797; cf. also [KUŠÉ.M]Á.URU$_5$ *IŠTU* GIŠKAK.Ú.TAG.GA *šu-u-wa-an-da-an* KUB 15.5 iii 23 (NH); *n*=*aš IŠTU* GIKAK.Ú.TAG.GA *šu-u-wa-an-za* KBo 23.18 obv. 6 (MS).

**6′** ship filled (i.e., loaded) with grain: DUMU=*YA*=*ma*=*mu kuin* INIM GIŠMÁ *TAŠPUR ḫalkiyaza*=*wa* 1 *ME* GIŠMÁ *šu-wa-an-za uit nu*=*mu* DUMU=*YA kuwat iyat apeneššuwan INA* UD.1.KAM=*pat*=*aš*=*ta kuwat* GAM-*an ēšta* "Regarding the matter of the ship(s), about which you, my son, wrote to me: 'One hundred ships loaded (lit. filled) with grain have come (to me)!' My son, why have you acted this way towards me? Why did it (i.e., the grain) remain with you even one single day? (My son, don't you realize that there has been a famine in the midst of my lands? But now, my son, send it)" Bo 2810 ii 6-10 (letter, NH), ed. Klengel, AoF 1:172-174, Hoffner, Letters 363 □ for a brief discussion of the extremely high number of ships see Klengel, ibid. 173 nn. 39, 41.

**7′** spindles: (The eagle replies to Ḫalmašuit what deities are doing:) GIŠ*ḫūlali ḫarzi* GIŠ*ḫūšuš šu-u wa du uš ḫarkanzi* § *nu* LUGAL-*waš* MU.KAM.ḪI.A-*uš malkiyanzi* "(One god) holds a distaff, (others) hold full spindles. § They are spinning the years of the king" KUB 29.1 ii 6-8 (myth in rit., OH/NS), ed. Carini, Athenaeum NS 60:492f., Kellerman, Diss. 13, 27, Görke (ed.), hethiter.net/: CTH 414.1 (TX 11.06.2015, TRde 13.03.2015); cf. also Güterbock & Hamp, RHA XIV/58:23.

**8′** filled (i.e., stuffed) *danna*(*š*)-breads(?): *šu-u-wa-an-te-eš dannaza* (var. [*dann*]*anza*) *kitta* "filled *danna*-breads (are) placed" KUB 9.28 iii 18 (rit. for the Heptad, MH/NS), w. dupl. KBo 19.132 rev.? 7 (MH/NS) □ for discussions of the form *dannaza* (it occurs in the same text in i 23 and iv 22 with determinative NINDA) and whether it is sg. or pl., and belongs with NINDA*dannaš*, NINDA*danna* (KBo 64.155:1) or with *dannatt*(*a*/*i*)- "empty," see Goetze, FsPedersen 494 n.2, Kronasser, EHS 1:327f., Tischler HEG T/D 1:100.

**9′** [*š*]*ammaizzili*- "?": [*ša*]*nḫunta kuitta parā tepu* [*ḫarš*]*aniliš euwan parḫūenaš* GÚ.GAL.GAL [GÚ.TUR G]IŠ*šamama duwarnanda* GIŠKÍN.ḪI.A *duwarnanda* [...*š*]*ammaizziliš šu-u-wa-an-za* "[Ro]asted (items), of each one a little bit: [*harš*]*anili*-, *ewan*-grain, *parḫuena*-grain, broad beans, [lentils], shelled (lit. broken) *šamama*-nuts, shelled KÍN-nuts, and [...] a filled/stuffed [*š*]*ammaizzili*-" KBo 10.34 i 22-25 (enthronement rit. in the cult of Teššub and Ḫebat, MH/NS), cf. Güterbock, JAOS 88:69 w. n.14, 70, see *šammaizzili*-.

**e**. substances and objects used to fill — **1′** liquids — **a′** *watar*/A "water": *nu* $^{GIŠ}$DÍLIM.GAL *šu-u-an-za* (var. *šu-u-wa-an-za*) 1 *NAMMANTA*=*ya* [(A-*it*)] *šu-u-an-za* (var. *šu-u-wa-an-za*) "there is a filled bowl, and also a *NAMMANTU*-vessel filled with water" KUB 58.37 rt. col. 5-6 (rit. frag., MS), w. dupl. KUB 41.13 ii 23-24 (NS), translit. DBH 18:97, ed. dupl. ChS I/3-1:118f.; DINGIR-*LAM*=*ma*=*kan* ⌈*ku*⌉*ēzza witenaz* GÌR.MEŠ=*ŠU* ⌈*arri*⌉*škanzi nu* 1 *kiššaraš* x[...]x ⌈*we*⌉*tenit* [*š*]*u-u-wa-an n*=*an* ⌈*A*⌉*NA* DINGIR-[*L*]*IM* ⌈GÙB⌉-*laz ti*[*anzi*] "but the water with which they wash the deity's feet, one [...] of the hand [f]illed with water, they pla[ce] it to the left of the deity" KUB 41.13 ii 13-16 (rit. frag., pre-NH/NS), ed. ChS I/3-1:118f.; ⌈*nu*=*za*⌉ $^{GIŠ}$*GANNUM-it kuiš* DUG-*iš* ⌈*šiḫilliyaš witenit*⌉ *šu-u-wa-an-za artari* "as for the jar filled with the water of purification that stands with a stand, (the exorcist pours out (the purifying water) from the top of that (jar), and fills an earthen cup (with it))" KBo 5.2 iv 36-37 (Ammiḫatna's rit., MH/NS), ed. Strauß, Reinigung 231, 244, and see d 1′ p′.

**b′** GEŠTIN "wine": [...]x GEŠTIN-*it šu-u-wa-an*-⌈*zi*⌉ KBo 14.88 ii 16 (fest. frag., MH/MS); UGULA $^{LÚ}$MUḪALDIM *tapišanin* GEŠTIN-*it šu-u-wa-an-da-an dāi* LUGAL-*i pāi* "The chief cook takes a *tapišana*-vessel filled with wine, gives (it) to the king" KBo 11.22 iv 17-20 (mixed festivals, NS), see c 1′ n′; *namma*=*kan ANA PĀNI* $^{d}$IM 2 GAL.ḪI.A *IŠTU* GEŠTIN *šu-u-wa-an-du-uš lāḫūwanzi* "Then they pour in front of the Stormgod the two cups filled with wine" KBo 21.34 i 24-25 (fest. for Teššub and Ḫebat of Lawazantiya, MH/NS); cf. ibid. i 40-41, 52-53, ii 4-5; other containers filled with wine: *ḫuppar* KÙ.BABBAR "silver bowl" KBo 4.9 i 16-19 (see d 1′ d′); *išpanduwa*-KÙ.BABBAR "silver libation vessel" KBo 29.211 iv? 20 (NS); GAL (see d 1′ q′); GAL.GIR$_4$ "earthen cup" KUB 11.9 iv 23 (NS); $^{DUG}$GUR$_4$.GUR$_4$ "pitcher" KBo 23.15 iv 15 (NS); $^{DUG}$GUR$_4$.GUR$_4$ KÙ.GI "golden pitcher" KUB 10.13 iv 9-14 (NS); $^{DUG}$*KUKŪB* "pitcher" KBo 5.1 ii 40 (NS); $^{DUG}$*KUKŪB* KÙ.GI "golden pitcher" KUB 27.1 iv 47-48 (NS); $^{NINDA}$*takarmuwaš*=*ma*=*ššan anda* $^{DUG}$*zalḫāit* GEŠTIN-*it šu-u-wa-an-da dāi* "he places the (containers) filled with wine by means of the *zalḫai*-vessel on the *takarmu*-loaves" KUB 58.34 iii 12-13 (fest. frag., NS).

**c′** KAŠ "beer": *BIBRA* KÙ.GI=*ya*=*šmaš auwauwaš* KAŠ-*it šu-u-wa-an-da-an peran pē ḫarkanzi* "beforehand they hold ready for them a golden rhyton in the shape of an *a*.-animal filled with beer" KUB 54.10 ii 8-9 (*witaššiya*-fest. frag., NS); cf. also KBo 29.140 rev. 3 (MS), KBo 39.62 v 16 (MS), KUB 32.125:3 (NS), KUB 39.71 ii 16 (NS).

**d′** oils and honey: $^{DUG}$*purpuriš* filled with Ì.DÙG.GA "refined oil" KBo 5.1 ii 41-43 (Papanikri's rit., MH?/NS), see d 1′ l′; $^{DUG}$*purpuriš* filled with Ì.GIŠ "vegetable oil" KBo 5.1 ii 41-43 (Papanikri's rit., MH?/NS), see d 1′ l′; cf. also other containers filled with Ì.DÙG.GA "refined oil": *ḫuppar* KÙ.BABBAR "silver bowl" KUB 30.15 obv. 3 (NS); GAL.GIR$_4$ "earthen cup" KUB 41.13 ii 20 (pre-NH/NS); silver and gol[den] *ḫutanni*-vessels KUB 15.11 iii 16-17 (Ḫatt. III) (see d 1′ f′); $^{DUG}$*ḫupuwāi*- "pot(?)" filled with LÀL Ì $^{GIŠ}$*SERTUM* etc. "honey, olive oil (etc.)" KBo 5.2 ii 37-38 (see e 2′ b′).

**e′** other beverages or mixtures: GAL KÙ.BABBAR=*ya tāuwalit šu-u-an-da-an ḫarzi* "he also holds a silver cup filled with *tawal*-wine" KUB 11.34 i 7-8 (fest. of haste, pre-NH/MS), w. dupl. KBo 45.8 rev. vi 10-11, ed. Nakamura, Nuntarriyašḫaš 224, 226; cf. also containers filled with KAŠ.GEŠTIN: $^{DUG}$*ḫupuwāi*- "pot(?)" KBo 5.2 ii 36-37 (Ammiḫatna's rit, MH/NS); GAL.GIR$_4$ "earthen cup" KBo 9.126:8 (Ḫuwarlu's rit. NS); 4 $^{URUDU}$*kantašuw*[*a*]*lliš IŠTU* GEŠTIN KAŠ *marnuit walaḫ*[*ḫ*]*it šu-u-wa-an-te-eš* "four *kantašuw*[*a*]*lli*-vessels filled with wine, beer, *marnuwa*-beer (and) *walḫi*-beer" KUB 55.38 ii 9-10 (Ištanuwian fest., NS), see d 1′ h′; ⌈x⌉ $^{DUG}$*KUKŪBI*$^{ḪI.A}$ *IŠTU* KAŠ.GEŠTIN *dawal walḫi šu-w*[*a-an-*... ] "x pitchers fil[led] with "wine-beer," *tawal*-wine (and) *walḫi*-beer" KUB 55.57 i 6 (rit. frag., NS); 1 $^{DUG}$*NAMMANTU*[*M I*]*ŠTU* GEŠTIN LÀL Ì.DÙG.GA *anda īmmiyantit šu-u-an* "one *NAMMANTU*-vessel filled with wine, honey and fine oil (that are) mixed together" KUB 15.34 i 14-15 (evocation rit.,

MH/MS), ed. Haas/Wilhelm, AOATS 3:184f.; a ceramic *tapišana-* filled with *marnuwan*-beer KBo 21.72 ii 7-8 + KBo 39.82 ii 14-15 (fest. celebrated by the prince), see d 1′ n′.

**f′** *šeḫur* "urine": [*š*]*ēḫunit šu-u-wa-a*[*n-*...] / [DU]GÚTUL *dannarantan* [...] / [...*āp*?*p*]*an ḫarkanzi* "[a...?] fill[ed] with [u]rine [...], an empty pot, [...] they hold behind [...]" KBo 12.111:7-9 (rit. frag., NS).

**2′** solids — **a′** grains, seeds and their flours: crate filled with ZÍD.DA "flour" KBo 15.33 ii 14-16 (see d 1′ j′); DUG*ḫariulli* filled with *ḫapalzil*-meal KUB 12.8 ii 2-3 (see d 1′ c′); DUGDÍLIM.GAL "bowl" full of *memal* "coarsely ground meal" KUB 6.45 + KBo 57.18 i 7-8 (prayer, Muw. II); GAL "cup" filled with ZÍD.DA ZÍZ "wheat flour" KUB 54.10 ii 20 (NS); DUG*KUKŪB* filled with *kant*-grain KUB 58.37 rt. col.15 (fest. frag., MS), see d 1′ w′; GIŠMA.SÁ.AB "basket" filled with ZÍZ "wheat," ŠE "barley" KUB 30.26 i 8-10 (Zelliya's rit., NS), see d 1′ s′, KBo 44.97 ii 9 (NS).

**b′** fruits: 16 DUG*ḫupuwāi≈ma IŠTU* LÀL Ì GIŠ*SERTUM* GIŠPÈŠ GIŠGEŠTIN ḪÁD.DU.A GIŠ*SERTUM šu-u-wa-an* "sixteen pots(?) are filled with the honey, olive oil, fig(s), raisin(s), olive(s)" KBo 5.2 ii 37-38 (Ammiḫatna's rit., MH/NS); cf. KBo 5.1 ii 34-37 (see d 1′ b′), KUB 58.37 rt. col. 12.

**c′** MUN "salt": [ ... *I*]*ŠTU* MUN *šu-u-wa-an* KBo 10.34 i 29.

**d′** breads and cakes: NINDA.Ì.E.DÉ.A DUGÚTUL *šu-u-wa-an* "pot" full of NINDA.Ì.E.DÉ.A "oil cake" KUB 6.45 + KBo 57.18 i 7 (prayer, Muw. II), KUB 15.34 i 17 (MH/MS).

**e′** a mix of grains and herbs: 1 DUG KA.GAG TUR *ŠA* 1 ⸢*UP*⸣*NI iyanza n≈aš IŠTU* GÚ.[ŠEŠ ...] ⸢*tar*⸣*šandaza kantit dammelaza paššuilaza* [...*a*]*nda immiyantet šu-wa-an-za* "one small vessel for KA.GAG beer of 1 *UPNU* capacity is prepared (lit. made), and it is filled with [bitter] vetch [...], dried/roasted *kant*-grain, fresh *paššuil*, [and ... ], (all) mixed [t]ogether" (and three drinking tubes are inserted into it) KUB 55.57 i 7-9 (rit. frag. pre-NH/NS), ed. *paḫšuil* b, translit. DBH 4:103.

**f′** wool: *nu≈war≈aš* SÍG*iyatnaza* ⸢*šu-u*⸣*-wa-an-za* "it was filled with a wealth of wool" KUB 31.71 iii! 30-31 (queen's dream, NH), see d 1′ a′.

**g′** arrows: IBoT 1.36 ii 40 (MH/MS), KUB 15.5 iii 23 (NS), KBo 23.18 obv. 6 (MS), see d 5′.

**3′** semi-solids — **a′** TU7BA.BA.ZA "porridge": 14 GIŠ⸢DÍLIM⸣.GAL SIG TU7BA.BA.ZA *šu-u-wa-an-za* "fourteen flat bowls filled (with) porridge" KBo 5.2 i 29 (Ammiḫatna's rit., MH/NS).

**b′** Ì "fat": *aiš≈za≈kan* Ì*-it* ⸢*šu*⸣*-u-wa-an-za ēš* "O mouth, be filled with fat" KBo 12.96 i 9-10 (rit. for dLAMMA of the hunting-bag, MH/NS), see d 4′.

**c′** DUḪ.LÀL "wax": SAG.DU.MEŠ GÌR.MEŠ*≈ma kuedaš ANA* GUNNI.MEŠ *warāni nu≈kan* DUGGAL.ḪI.A DUḪ.LÀL*-ant*[*et*?] GEŠTIN*-nit šu-u-wa-an-te-eš tian*[*zi*?] "[they] place the cups filled wit[h] wax (honeycomb?) and wine at the hearths where the heads and feet are burning" KUB 10.95 iii? 3-6 (fest. frag., pre-NH/NS).

**4′** intangibles — **a′** laughter: ("O mouth, be filled with fat") UZU*ḫurḫurta≈ma≈za≈kan ḫalwamnaz šu-u-wa-an-za ēš* "O throat, be filled with laughter" KBo 12.96 i 9-11 (rit. for dLAMMA of the hunting-bag, MH/NS) □ for discussion see d 4′.

**b′** radiance, luxuriant growth, and good things: a mother RS 25.421 obv. 28-29, obv. 38-40, see lexicographic section above.

**5′** people: NUMUN "seed" in the sense of offspring KUB 26.1 i 10-11, see d 2′.

**6′** *alpa-* "cloud": [ ... *-i*]*tta alpit šu-u-wa-an*(-)[...] KBo 61.11 left.col.3, cf. Otten, ZA 66:99.

**7′** unclear: *aḫḫuwatra*(?)-: 4 *malwīš* ⸢x⸣ [...] *aḫḫuwatanaza šu-u-wa-an-za* 1*-E*[*N*...] *šu-u-wa-an-za* "Four *malwiš*, [...] filled with *aḫḫuwatra*-(?). One [...] filled [with...]" HFAC 8 obv.? rt. col. 2-4 (inventory, NH) □ for uncertain *aḫḫuwatra-* and its stem see Košak, THeth 10:46, 206, Siegelová, Verw. 1:54 n.3.

**f.** w. associated preverb EGIR-*pa* ("refill"): [...]-*za* LÚ-*LUM* $^{GIŠ}$*intaluzzi* KÙ.BABBAR [... *šu*]*nniezzi nu kiššan* [...] EGIR-*pa šu-u-wa-an ēšdu* "[...] a man [takes(?)] a silver shovel for himself, [and f]ills [...], and [says] thus: ['...] may be filled again'" KBo 25.184 iii 58-60 (funerary rit., pre-NH/NS).

**2.** (mid.) be(come) filled > to swell up: ("He places a male figurine —its inside full of water— in their hands, and he says thus:)" [*k*]⌈*ā*⌉*š*=*wa kuiš U*[*L*=*ma*(?) *l*]*inkiškit* [*nu*] DINGIR.MEŠ-*aš pera*[*n link*]*atta* [*n*]*amma*=*kan NĪŠ* DINGIR-*L*[*IM šarr*]*adda n*=*an linkianteš ēpper n*=*aš*=*ša*[*n*] ŠÀ=*ŠU šu-ut-ta-ti nu*=*za šarḫuwandan QĀTI*=*ŠÚ peran* UGU-*a karpan ḫarzi n*=*ašta kuiš kūš NĪŠ* DINGIR-*LIM šarrizzi* ⌈*n*⌉=*an kē NĪŠ* DINGIR.MEŠ *appandu n*=[*a*]*š*=*šan* ŠÀ=*ŠU šu-ut-ta-ru* "Who is [t]his? Did he n[ot s]wear an oath? He [sw]ore an oath befo[re] the gods, [and t]hen he [transg]ressed the oat[h]. The oath gods seized him, and his inside has swollen up, his hand has lifted (his) belly up in front. Whoever transgresses these oaths, may these oath gods seize him, and may his inside swell up" KBo 6.34 iii 14-21 (soldiers' oath, MH/NS), ed. StBoT 22:12f. ☐ a person whose belly has swollen up suffers from dropsy, see the discussion s.v. *šūu-* "full" a 1′ a′.

**3.** to close, satisfy, be done with (syn. w. *aššanu-*) — **a.** be done with cups: NINDA.GUR$_4$.⌈RA⌉ *paršiyanzi BIBRI*$^{ḪI.A}$=*kan šu-u-wa-an-zi adanzi akuwanzi* GAL.ḪI.A=*kan šu-u-wa-an-zi PĀNI* DINGIR-*LIM* GEŠPÚ *ḫulḫuli*!*ya tieškanzi duškiškanzi* "They break thick bread. They fill the rhyta. They eat (and) drink. They are done with the cups. In the presence of the god they begin boxing (and) wrestling. They entertain (the deity)" KUB 25.23 i 20-22 (cult inv., Tudḫ. IV), ed. Carter, Diss. 155, 165, Hazenbos, Organization 31f., 36 ☐ *š.* is used instead of the regular expression with *aššanu-*, see for example GAL.ḪI.A *aššanuwanzi* KUB 25.23 i 31, 47, *et passim*.

**b.** peasant is filled (i.e., satisfied) with fields: ("Whoever remains in place of a resettled person who leaves your province") *nu*=*šši* ⌈NUMUN⌉.ḪI.A *aniya*=*pat namma*=*aš*=*kan* A.ŠÀ.ḪI.A-*it šu-u-wa-an-za ēšt*⌈*u*⌉ "You yourself must sow seed for him. Furthermore, he must be satisfied with regard to fields," (so they shall promptly assign him a plot) KUB 13.2 iii 40 (*BĒL MADGALTI*, MH/NS), ed. von Schuler, Dienstanw. 48, Miller, HittInstr 230f.

**c.** (said of a a legal case, affair, matter): (When someone brings a legal case) *nu auriyaš* EN-*aš DĪNAM* SIG$_5$-*in ḫannau n*=*at*=*kan aššanuddu* (var. *ašnuandu*) *mān*=*kan DĪNU*=*ma šu-wa-at-ta-ri n*=*at MAḪAR* $^{d}$UTU-*ŠI uppau* "the governor of the border province shall judge the case properly and bring (var. they will bring) it to conclusion. When the case has been closed, he shall send it to My Majesty" KUB 13.2 iii 22-24 (*BĒL MADGALTI*, MH/NS), w. dupl. KUB 31.86 iv 6-10, KBo 48.238:4-6, ed. Dienstanw. 47f., HittInstr 228f. ("becomes (too) onerous"), StBoT 5:159 ("sich aber weitet"), HEG S/2:1217 ("zu umfangreich wird") ☐ the expression *mān*=*kan DĪNU*=*ma š.* is usually understood as "but when the law case becomes (too) onerous/extensive." Such situations are indeed described in other texts, but in those cases it is always explicitly mentioned that the king will take care of the law case: *mān DĪNU*=*ma kuitki šallešzi n*=*at arḫa ēppuwanzi UL taruḫteni n*=*at*=*kan duwān MAḪAR* $^{d}$UTU-⌈*ŠI parā naišten n*=*at* $^{d}$UTU⌉-*ŠI arḫa ēpzi* "But if some judicial matter becomes (too) big, and you are not able to handle it, then send it subsequently into the presence of My Majesty, and My Majesty will handle it" KBo 3.3 iii 29-33 (join count iii 53-59) ☐ for *duwān* "later, subsequently" see Melchert, FsKoch 203f.; *kuit*=*ma* DI-*šar šumel UL taruḫḫūwaš n*=*at* LUGAL-*i*! *ANA*! *BĒLI*=*KUNU menaḫḫanda udatten n*=*at* LUGAL-*uš apāšila punušzi* "A law case that you cannot manage yourselves, though, you must bring before the king, your lord, and the king himself will investigate it" KUB 13.20 i 36-37. For the use of *š.* "to fill" in the sense of "to complete, finish" compare Engl. to fulfill; ŠÀ-*ta šiyanna*⟨*š*⟩ $^{d}$*Zitḫariyaš ANA* EZEN$_4$ *ANDAHŠUM*$^{SAR}$ *INA* É=*ŠU* $^{URU}$*Ḫattuši apēl INA* $^{É}$*karimmi paiškitta ariyan*=*ma*=*at* DINGIR-*LIM-it uttar*=*kan šu-u-wa-at-ta-at* (var. *kuit uttar šu-wa-a*[*t-ta-at*]) "To remember: for the *ANDAHŠUM* festival of Zitḫariya one goes to his temple in Ḫattuša, (that is) to his own temple. It was (thus) determined by the god: the matter has been closed (var. that the matter has been closed)" KUB 30.39 rev. 7-10 (*ANDAHŠUM-* fest. outline, OH/NS), w. dupl. KBo 10.20 iv 24-27 (NS), KBo 48.30:4-8 (OH/NS), ed. Güterbock

JNES 19:84f., 87 ("the wording was too long"), StBoT 5:159 ("Der Text war angeschwollen").

The verb *š.* (mng. 1) partially overlaps in meaning with *šun(n)a-* "to fill, pour" (mng. c and d) (see HW 200, HEG S/2:1217). *š.* only occurs with containers as grammatical object, never with stuff that fills a container as the object. *š.* and *šun(n)a-* therefore only alternate in the following type of context: compare NINDA.GUR$_4$.RA.MEŠ *tarnaš=(š)maš paršiyanzi* $^{DUG}$*talaimiuš=kan šunna⟨n⟩zi* "They break the thick breads of (a) *tarna*-measure for them, (and) they(!) fill the *talaimi*-vessels" KBo 2.13 obv. 20 (cult inv., NH) with 1 NINDA *tarna[š parš]iyanzi* (eras.) $^{DUG}$*talaimiuš=kan šu-u-wa-an-[zi]* "They [brea]k one bread of (a) *tarna*-measure. They fil[l] the *talaimi*-vessels" KUB 42.91 ii 18-19 (cult inv., NH), ed. Hazenbos, Organization 112, 114. *š.* as finite verb occurs mostly in the expression *BIBRI*$^{HI.A}$*=kan š.* "they fill the rhytons" and with a few other vessels, otherwise *šun(n)a-* is used. However, as the participle, *šunnant-*, is rare: we mostly find *šuwant-*, often occurring in the same text w. *šunna-*; see for example ⌈*nu=za*⌉ $^{GIŠ}$*GANNUM-it kuiš* DUG-*iš* ⌈*šiḫilliyaš witenit*⌉ *šu-u-wa-an-za artari ... nu* $^{DUG}$GAL.GIR$_4$ *šunnai* "as for the jar filled with the water of purification that stands with a stand, ..., and fills an earthen cup (with it)" KBo 5.2 iv 36-38 (Ammiḫatna's rit., MH/NS) (see d 1′ p′). For finite *š.* and the imperf. of *šun(n)a-* in the same text, see for example *BIBRI*$^{HI.A}$*=kan šu-u-wa-an-zi ... nu=kan* UD.KAM-*li BIBRI*$^{HI.A}$ *šunneškanzi* KUB 25.22 iii 10-11 (cult of Nerik, Tudḫ. IV).

Hrozný, SH (1917) 139 n. 12 (on part. "gefüllt," and perhaps "füllend"); Friedrich, ZA 35 (1924) 184 (suggests connection between mid. and *šuwaye-* "to look (at)"); Sommer/Ehelolf Pap. (1924) 55; Laroche, JCS 1 (1947) 206 (on the iter. form *šušk-*); Friedrich, HW (1952) 200 (distinguishes between stem *šuwai-* "füllen" and *šuwa-* mid. "anschwellen(?); zu umfangreich werden(?)," 201; Goetze, Lg. 30 (1954) 403f. (on mid. belonging with *šuwa-* "to fill"); Güterbock/Hamp, RHA XIV/58 (1956) 23, 25 n. 6 (on part. *šunt-*); Kammenhuber, RHA XIV/58 (1956) 2f.; von Schuler, Dienstanw. (1957) 57 (on mid.); Kronasser, EHS 1 (1962) 479 (denominative on *-aye-*); Neumann, Die Sprache 8 (1962) 206 (mid. belongs with *šū-, šuwa-*); Neu, StBoT 5 (1968) 159 (mid. "sich füllen, sich weiten, anschwellen, voll werden"); Oettinger, StBoT 22 (1976) 114 (on mid.; takes stem as *šuwi-* "schwellen"); Oettinger, Stammbildung (1979) 295f. (*šuwae-* "füllen"), 294 (mid. belongs with *šuwe-* "verstoßen"), 297; Hoffmann, THeth 11 (1984) 133, 138-140 (stem *šuwai-*. Merges *š.* and *šuwe-*); Tischler, HEG S/2 (2006) 1216-18 (*šuwai-* "füllen, voll machen"; mid. "anschwellen, voll werden, zu umfangreich werden"), 1219f. (part. *šuwant-*); Kloekhorst, EDHIL (2008) 797f., 798 (mid. belongs with *šuwe-* "to push").

Cf. *šunt-*, *šun(n)a-*, *šūu*.

**šuwai- A** n. com.; abandonment, rejection.†

**sg. nom. com.** *šu-wa-iš* KBo 26.34 i 15 (NS).

(Sum.) [ḪU] = (Akk.) [*ezēbu*] "to abandon, desert, leave behind" = (Hitt.) *šu-wa-iš* "abandonment, rejection" KBo 26.34 i 15 (Boğazköy S$^a$ vocabulary), ed. Cohen, Mem.Black 38.

This word is commonly taken as equivalent to MUŠEN-*eš* "bird" of the parallel lexical list HT 42 obv. 4 (MSL 3:55) (see Otten and von Soden, StBoT 7:40). However, the ḪU sections of the S$^a$ vocabularies KBo 26.34 i 12-15 and HT 42 obv. 1-5 represent divergent traditions, only sharing the entry [ḪU] = [*naprušu*] = *watku(w)ar* "flying, fleeing" KBo 26.34 i 13, HT 42 obv. 3. Therefore, the meaning of *š.* cannot be assumed to be "bird" based on this single occurrence, cf. Cohen, Mem.Black 36, Rößle, GsForrer 545f. Instead, *š.* is best understood as the action noun "abandonment, rejection" of *šuwe-* "to shove off, push off," q.v.

Otten/von Soden, StBoT 7 (1968) 40 w. n. 2; Rieken, StBoT 44 (1999) 24f. ("Vogel"); Rößle, GsForrer (2004) 545ff. ("Wort unbekannter Herkunft"); Tischler, HEG S/2 (2006) 1215f. ("Vogel" (?)); Kloekhorst, EDHIL (2008) 795 ("rejection," quoting Cohen, forthcoming = Mem.Black); Cohen, Mem. Black (2010) 35f. ("abandonment, rejection").

Cf. *šuwe-*.

**šuwai- B** v., see *šuwaye-*.

**šuwai- C** v., see *šuwe-*.

**šuwaye-, šuwaya-, šuwai- B** v.; **1.** (intrans.) to look (at), to look for compensation (in OH legal idioms), **2.** (trans.) to regard (favorably); from OS.†

**pres. sg. 2** *šu-wa-i-e-ši* VBoT 124 iii! (5) (OS), KUB 60.20 rev.? 5, 6 (OH/NS).

**sg. 3.** *šu-wa-i-ez-zi* KBo 6.2 i 2, 3, 10, 12, (21), 41, 44, 59, iii 26, 32, 37, (52), (57), iv 9, 17, 18, 20, 43, 50 (OS), KUB 29.16 iii (6), (11) (OS), *šu-wa-a-i-ez-zi* KBo 6.3 i 30, 32, 36, 38, iii 34, 62, iv 2, 12, 14, 23, 25 (OH/NS), *šu-wa-a-i-e-ez-zi* KBo 3.1 ii 51 (OH/NS), KBo 6.3 i 34 (OH/NS), KBo 6.4 i 34 (OH/NS), *šu-wa-ya-az-zi* KUB 29.28 i 9 (OS), *šu-wa-ya-az-z[i?]* KBo 47.217:6 (MS), *šu-wa-iz-zi* KBo 6.5 i 13, 15, 17 (OH/NS), KBo 31.64:4 (OH/NS), *šu-wa-a-iz-zi* KBo 19.3 i (11) (OH/NS), KBo 6.3 i 3, 5, 7, 9, 11, (18), (20), iii 29, 36, 39, 42, 45, 47, 59, 68, iv 30 (OH/NS), KBo 6.5 i 22 (OH/NS), KBo 6.6 i 38, (46) (OH/NS), KBo 6.10 ii 19, (32), iii (31) (OH/NS), KBo 6.11 i (3), 10, 14 (OH/NS), KBo 6.12 i 16 (OH/NS), KBo 6.20 ii 8 (OH/NS), KBo 12.48:4 (OH/NS), KUB 29.22 i 2, (6) (OH/NS), KBo 6.14 i 14 (OH/NS), KBo 12.49 ii (6) (OH/NS), *šu-w[a-...?-iz-zi]* KUB 13.31:3 (OH/NS), *šu-ú-wa-a-iz-z[i]* KUB 13.13 obv. 7 (OH/NS), *[šu]-ú-wa-a-iz-[zi]* KBo 19.3 iv 11 (OH/ENS), *[šu]-⸢ú⸣-wa-a-iz-[zi]* KBo 19.9:8 (OH/NS), *šu-ú-wa-⸢a⸣-[iz-zi]* KBo 19.3 i 18 (OH/ENS).

**pl. 3.** *šu-ú-wa-i-ya-a[n-zi]* KBo 31.117:7 (NS).

**pret. sg. 1.** *šu-wa-ya-nu!-un* KUB 29.1 ii 1 (OH/NS).

**sg. 3.** *šu-wa-i-et* KUB 17.6 i 24 (OH/NS), *šu-wa-ya-at* KBo 13.94:9 (NS).

**pl. 2** *šu-w[a-at-te-en]* KBo 12.18 i (6) (OH/NS), *šu-u-wa-at-[te-en]* KBo 12.63 obv. rt. col. 4 (OH/NS).

**imp. sg. 2.** *šu-ú-wa-ya* KUB 29.1 i 52 (OH/NS), *šu-ú-wa-i* KUB 41.23 ii 10 (OH/NS), here? *šu-wa-ya* (uncertain if a Hittite or Hattic word) KUB 48.13 obv. 16 (NS).

**pl. 2.** *šu-wa-a-at-te-en* KBo 59.183 iii (3) (OH/NS), *šu-wa-at-te-[en]* KBo 12.18 i 7 (OH/NS), *šu-u-wa-at-[te-en]* KBo 12.63 obv. rt. col. 6 (OH/NS).

**infin.** here? *[š]u?-wa-u-wa-an-zi* KUB 24.7 i 16 (hymn to Ištar, NH), so Güterbock, JAOS 103:160 i 16 following Archi, OA 16 305-311, against expected **šuwayawanzi*. However, the trace of the sign in both photo (hethiter.net/: PhotArch N05650) and hand copy appears to end in a broken vertical.

*š.* originally had an alternating stem in *e/a*. Although the verb had become obsolete by MH, NH copyists treated *š.* like other verbs in *e/a* that shifted to *-āi-* stems in NH. Hence we find forms like *šu-wa-a-iz-zi*, *šu-ú-wa-i* (*-āi-* class) besides original *šu-wa-i-ez-zi*, *šu-ú-wa-ya* (*-e/a-* class). Because *šuwe-* 'to push' (s.v.) also shifted from the *-e/a-* class to the *-āi-* class in NH, and both verbs can be spelled with plene *ú* or occasionally *u*, it is not always possible to formally distinguish *š.* from *šuwe-*.

**1.** to look, w. all., dat.-loc. ("at" or "to") or abl. ("from" or "through") (compare *šakuwai-* C 2) — **a.** in OH legal idiom w. all. *parna=šše=a* "to look to the (offender's) house (to search) for it (i.e., compensation)." The agent of the act is the offended party, or, in the case of homicide, the legal representative of the deceased victim: *[ta]kku* ^LÚ^DAM.GÀR (var. adds ^URU^*Ḫatti*) *kuiški kuēnzi* 1 *ME* MA.NA KÙ.BABBAR *pāi parna=ššē=a šu-wa-i-ez-zi* (var. *šu-wa-a-ez-zi*) "If anyone kills a (Hittite) merchant, he shall pay one hundred minas of silver, and he (i.e., victim's representative) shall look to (his) house for it" KBo 6.2 i 3 (Laws §5, OS), w. dupl. KBo 6.3 i 10-11 (OH/NS), ed. LH 19; *[(takku* ^URU^*)]Ḫatt⸢u⸣ši=pat* LÚ ^URU^*Ḫatti* LÚ ^URU^*Luīn kuiški tāīzzi [n]=an ANA* KUR *Luwiya peḫutezzi karū* 12 SAG.DU *pišker [k]inun=a* 6 SAG.DU *pāi parna=ššē=a šu-wa-i-ez-zi* (var. *[...]-e-ez-zi*) "If a Hittite abducts a Luwian in the city of Ḫattuša itself, [and] leads him away to the land of Luwiya, formerly they used to give twenty persons (lit. heads), but [n]ow he shall give six persons, and he shall look to (his) house for it" KBo 6.2 i 39-41 (Laws §19b, OS), w. dupl. KBo 6.3 i 47-49 (OH/NS), ed. LH 30; *takku* ŠAḪ *ḫi⸢lan⸣naš kuiški taīzzi* 6 GÍN KÙ.BABBAR *pāi parna=še=a šu-wa-i-ez-zi* (var. *šu-wa-a-i-ez-[z]i*) "If anyone steals a pig of the courtyard, he shall pay six shekels of silver, and he shall look to (his) house for it" KBo 6.2 iv 18 (Laws §82, OS), w. dupl. KBo 6.3 iv 13-14 (OH/NS), ed. LH 86. The offences in the Hittite Laws which result in the verdict of *parna=šše=a š.*: homicide (§§1-5, see above), assault and injury of a person (§§7-8, 11-15, 17), abduction (§19b, see above, 20), burglary (§§94-97), killing or theft of domesticated animals (§82, above, §§57-65, 67-70, 72, 77, 81, 83, 84, §87-88, 91, 119), theft of or damage to crops (§§104-105, 107-108), theft (§§121-124, 127, 129-130, 143), failure to deliver (§149), defiling a pond or cistern (§25).

**b.** in non-legal texts, w. all. or dat.-loc.: ("When the king enters the house, the Throne calls the eagle:") *eḫu=ta aruna pēimi mān pāiši=ma nu uliliya* ^GIŠ⸢^TIR⸣*-na šu-ú-wa-ya kuiēš ašanzi* § *apāšš=a* EGIR-*pa tez⸢zi⸣ šu-wa-ya-nu!-un=wa* (var. C: *šu-⸢ú?⸣[-...]*) *nu=wa* ^d^*Išduštayaš* ^d^*Papayaš katterre[š] karūeliēš* DINGIR.MEŠ *kūšeš ḫālianteš ašanzi* "'Come, I am sending you to the sea. When you go, look into the greenery (and) forest. Who are present (there)?' § (The eagle) replies: 'I looked. Išduštaya (and) Papaya, the infernal, primordial female gods, are (there), kneeling'" KUB 29.1 i 51-ii 4 (rit. for a new palace, OH/NS), w. dupl. Bo 7388:1-5 (C), Bo 6124:4-7, ed. Kellerman,

Diss. 12f., 27, Carini, Athenaeum NS 60:490f., Marazzi, VO 5:152f., Güterbock, RHA XIV/58:22f. w. n. 5, García Trabazo, TextosRel. 490f., RMPH 98f. (“scrute la forêt dans la *verdure*! Qui sont ceux (qui s’y trouvent)?”), Görke, hethiter.net/: CTH 414.1 (TX 11.06.2015, TRde 13.03.2015), tr. Beckman, Temple Building 73 (“When you go, spy out the grove in the steppe. Who is present (there)?”); *kuiš* ŠEŠ.MEŠ-*na* NIN.MEŠ-*na ištarna idālu iyazi nu* LUGAL-*waš ḫaraššanā* (coll. photo) *šu-wa-a-i-e-ez-zi nu tuliyan ḫalzišten mān≈apa uttar≈⸢šet⸣ paizzi nu* SAG.DU-*naz šarnikdu* “Whoever commits evil among (his or her royal) brothers and sisters and sets his sight on (lit. look at) the person (lit. head) of the king, convoke the assembly. If his case goes (against him), he shall make compensation with (his) person” KBo 3.1 ii 50-52 (Tel.pr., OH/NS), ed. THeth 11:34f. w. disc. 123f., HW$^{2}$ Ḫ 352b (“und gegen des Königs [...] Person verstößt”), tr. van den Hout, CoS 1:197 w. nn. 54-5 (“and lays eyes on the king’s head”), for this passage see also Beckman, JAOS 102:439f., Hoffner, JAOS 102:507f., Marazzi, FsNeumann 152, Melchert, Diss. 223f., *pai-* 5 h (“He who does harm among his (royal) brothers and sisters, let him look to the head of the king. Call an assembly”) □ comparing *ḫaraššanā š.* with *parna*(*≈šše≈a*) *š.* “have recourse to the offender’s house,” Hoffner (JAOS 102:507f.) argues that the offender is the king, and that the offended party, i.e., one of the siblings of the king, is the subject of *š.*: “Whatever (king) ‘does evil’ among (his) brothers and sisters, he (the one who claims redress) shall ‘look to’ (= have recourse to) the person (lit. ‘head’) of the king (i.e., the offender in this case).” However, it is unlikely that the king is referred to as a full lexical noun phrase in the clause with *š.* instead of an expected clitic poss. *-ša* “his (all.)” while he is not overtly expressed in the preceding relative clause. It is therefore preferable to take the king as the target of the evil plans of the prince or princess. For offenses committed by the king, see KBo 3.1 ii 46-49, ed. Hoffmann, THeth 11:124; (“The singer recites thus”) [*tandukišni* $^{d}$UT(U(?)-*uš zi*)*k* DINGIR.MEŠ-]*nan≈a ištarna* [...M(UNUS. LUGAL-*aš*)] $^{URU}$*Ḫaškaḫaškiwa*-x[...] / [...*an*$^{?}$]*da lē šu-wa-i-e-ši taknaš≈ta* $^{d}$UTU-*uš* ⸢*aušzi*⸣ § [...$^{URU}$(*Šuppa*)]*l*⸢*ē*⸣[(*š*)*n*]*i lē šu-wa-i-e-ši* [$^{d}$... *au*(*šzi* $^{UR}$)]$^{U}$*Taḫāpini pēdan≈tet* “[To mankind] yo[u] are the S[ungoddess(?)]. But among [the god]s [you are ...], [q]ueen. [At(?)] the town of Ḫaškaḫaškiwa(-)[...] do not look in[to ... ], the Sungoddess of the Earth will see you § [...] Do not look at/into [the town of ]Šuppalešna (or: the cattle pen?). [The ...-deity (will) see you.] Your place is in the town of Taḫāpina” KUB 60.20 rev.? 3-7 (invoc. to Hattic deities, OH/NS), w. dupl. VBoT 124 iii! 3-7 (OS), ed. StBoT 62:276f. w. n. 877 (differently: “the solar deity is looking *to the earth*”), translit. StBoT 25:189, DBH 20:18, cf. Hoffmann, THeth 11:135 (“treibe nicht hinein”), HEG S/2:1179 (“treibe [...] nicht in den Viehpferch!” ) □ cf. StBoT 26:358 w. n. 5 for the reading $^{URU}$Šuppalešni, but see RGTC 6/2:148 (“Fraglich ob ON”).

**c.** w. abl. and *arḫa*: (“The goddess Inara instructed Ḫupašiya: ‘When I go out to the open country, do not look out (*arḫa auš-*) the window. If you do look out (*arḫa auš-*), you will see (*auš-*) your wife and your children’”) *mān* UD.20.KAM *pait apāš≈*⸢*a* $^{GIŠ}$*lut*⸣[*tanza*] *arḫa šu-wa-i-et nu* DAM≈*SU*! (text has *KA*) DUMU.MEŠ≈[*ŠU aušta*] “When twenty days had passed, he peered out of the win[dow] and [saw] his wife (and) [his] children” KUB 17.6 i 23-24 (Illuyanka Myth, OH/NS), ed. Beckman, JANES 14:14, 19, Rieken et al., hethiter.net/: CTH 321 (TX 2012-06-08, TRde 2012-06-08), tr. Hittite Myths$^{2}$ 12.

**2.** to regard (favorably), w. acc. (compare *šakuwai-* C 3): $^{LÚ}$AZU *malti āššū šakuwa≈t*$^{!}$[*tet lāk*] *nu labarnan āššu šu-ú-wa-i ē*[*šri≈ššet newāḫ*] *n≈an* EGIR-*pa mayantaḫ* “The exorcist recites: ‘[Incline your] kind ey[es] and watch the Labarna favorably: [Renew his frame] and make him young again’” KUB 41.23 ii 9-11 (incant., OH/NS), ed. [*šakuwap*[(-)...]], differently: Fuscagni, hethiter.net/: CTH 458.10.1 (TX 13.10.2014, TRde 05.02.2013) (“Fülle Labarna *mit Wohl*!”), Archi, FsMeriggi$^{2}$ 43 (“riempi” = *šu-, šuwa-*) □ with CHD [*šakuwap*[(-)...] (against *šakuwai-* C 2 b), restore *šakuwa≈t*$^{!}$[*tet lāk*] instead of *šakuwaya*$^{!}$, compare the phrase “incline your eyes” in the indirect join KUB 43.63 obv. 7 ([...] IGI.ḪI.A≈*KA lāk*), 12 ([...≈*t*]*et lāk*), and KUB 43.61 i 5 ([...]*ṷan≈*[*t*]*et lāk*, dupl. of KUB 43.63 obv. 18); [...*nu lab*]*arnan āššu šu-wa-a-at-t*[*e-en*] KBo 59.183 (+ KUB 41.23) iii 3 (incant., OH/NS), ed. Fuscagni, hethiter.net/: CTH 458.10.1 (Expl. A, 13.10.2014); cf. [...*nu lab*]*arnan āššu šu-wa*[*-i*(*a*) *ēšri≈ššet*] / [*newā*]*ḫ n≈an* EGIR-*pa* GURUŠ-*aḫ* Bo 3995 ii 14-15, ed. Fuscagni, hethiter.net/: CTH 458.10.3 (TX 05.02.2013, TRde 05.02.2013); § *kuwāpit* UD-*at* L[(UGAL-*iz*)*nait*$^{?}$] *š≈an≈z≈apa āššu šu-w*[(*a-at*)*-te-en* (var. *šu-u-wa-at*[*-te-en*)] [(*nunn⸗a⸗p)a*] *āššu šu-wa-at-te-*[*en*] (var. *šu-u-wa-at*[*-te-en*]) "On any day that [he held(?)] the throne, you regarded him favorably. Now, too, regard (him) favorably" KBo 12.18 i 5-7 (Zalpa frag., OH/NS), w. dupl. KBo 50.3:10-12, KBo 12.63 obv. rt. col. 1-6 (OH/NS), ed. Corti, Mem.Imparati 172-174 ("Dove un/di giorno la re[(gali)tà (?) ] e proprio lui guar[date] bene [(e lui poi) guar[date] bene [...]"), HW² Ḫ 473 ("ha[bt] ihr Gutes auf ihn zugetrieben"), Soysal, Diss. 77, 109 (without dupls., "trei[bt] ihn gut! ... treib(t) gut"); see *š*(*u*)- c 3′ for discussion □ the expression *āššu š.* means 'regard favorably', not 'fill with favor' or 'push favor (to) someone'. *š.* was replaced in MH by *šakuwai-* C 'to see' (s.v.), cf. *āššū* IGI.ḪI.A*⸗KA lāk LIM laplippuš karp n⸗a*[*pa*] / [L]UGAL*-un anda āššu šakuwaya* KBo 7.28 + KBo 8.92 obv. 11-12; uncertain [...*-i*]*t laplipit* / [...]x *šu-wa-ya* "wi[th ... ], with eyelashes [...] look (at) [ ... !]" KUB 48.13 obv.15-16 (fest. for Stormgod of Nerik, NS) □ Hoffmann, THeth 11:144, restores and interprets lines 15-16 as [*inniri*]*t laplipit* / [x] *šuwaya* "[mit der Augenbrau]e, mit der Wimper / [x] halte Ausschau!" One must use caution in considering all these words Hittite, since the preceding (13-14) and following lines (17) are in Hattic, and the whole paragraph seems to belong to the same recitation.

*š.* was only productive in OH (Starke, StBoT 23:37). *š.* is never used to express mere sight. Intransitive *š.* (mng. 1) is used if the subject is intentionally looking to find or see something, without necessarily seeing the object (compare *šakuwai-* C 2). Transitive *š.* only occurs in the expression *āššu š.* 'to observe, regard favorably' and was replaced by *āššū anda šakuwai-* (in MH) and $SIG_5$*-it/takšulit šakuit anda auš-/ušk-* 'regard with benevolent eyes' (e.g., KBo 11.1 obv. 11).

Güterbock apud Friedrich, HW (1952) 200; Güterbock/Hamp, RHA XIV/58 (1956) 22-25 ("to look"); Friedrich, HW 1. Erg. (1957) 19 ("spähen, ausschauen"); Haase, BiOr 19 (1962) 121-122 (*parnaššea š.* par. to Akk. *bītam dagālu*); Starke, StBoT 23 (1977) 36-37 ("spähen, ausschauen"); Oettinger, Stammbildung (1979) 295f.; Josephson, Heth.u.Idg. (1979) 96-98; Szemerényi, FsMeriggi² (1979) 628-630; Haase, WO 11 (1980) 93-98 ("spähen"); Hoffner, JAOS 102 (1982) 507-509 (on the legal idiom *š.* with the allative); Marazzi, FsNeumann (1982) 151-152; Güterbock, Or NS 52 (1983) 73-80 ("blicken"); Hoffmann, THeth 11 (1984) 123-144 (*š.* in *parnaššea š.* "und das zu seinem Haus gehörige (als Ersatz) zur Verfügung stellen" belongs with *šuwai-* "in Bewegung setzen, ins Werk setzen" (= *šuwe-* 'to push', s.v.)), 143-144 ("spähen, Ausschau halten"), 176; Hoffner, LH (1997) 168-169 (w. further bibl.); Tischler, HEG S (2006) 1223-1226; Kloekhorst, EDHIL (2008) 795-796.

[*šuwayazkilanza*(-)] KBo 17.90 ii 12 see ⁽ᴳᴵŠ⁾*šušiyaz*(*za*)*kel*.

**⁽ᴳᴵŠ⁾šuwaitar** n. neut.; (a fruit or other plant product); OH/NS.†

**sg. nom.-acc.** ᴳᴵŠ*šu-wa-i-tar* KUB 29.1 iv 7 (OH/NS).

("They take the following from the palace: one *wakšur*-measure of lard, one *wakšur*-measure of honey, one cheese, one rennet, white wool, black wool, one *SŪTU*-measure of beer-bread, one *SŪTU*-measure of malt") ᴳᴵŠ*šamama* ᴳᴵŠGEŠTIN.ḪÁD.DU.A ᴳᴵŠ*lēti* ᴳᴵŠ*šu-wa-i-tar* KUŠ GUD MUN *mašiwan⸗šan ḫaššī anda ḫandaittari* "*šamama*-(fruit or nut), raisin(s), *lēti*-(plant or nut), *š.*, 'cow-hide' (i.e., fruit leather = Turk. pestil?), salt, as much as can be arranged on the hearth" KUB 29.1 iv 6-8 (rit. for the founding of a temple, OH/NS), ed. Marazzi, VO 5:160f., Kellerman, Diss. 18, 31, Haas, Materia 227.

Schwartz, Or NS 16 (1947) 45, 53 (a kind of fruit); Kronasser, EHS 1 (1966) 284 ("eine Obstpflanze"); Ertem, Flora (1974) 74 (a fruit and its tree); Kellerman, Diss. (1980) 70 ("un fruit ou une noix"); Tischler, HDW (1982) 80 ("ein Baum"); idem HHW (2001) 157; idem, HEG S/2 (2006) 1226 ("ein Baum bzw. sein Holz oder seine Frucht; vielleicht Benennung einer Art Nüsse").

[*šuwala*] Hurrian deity sometimes written without divine det. appearing along with or following the goddess ⁽ᵈ⁾Nabarbi; for attestations see van Gessel, OHP 418f.; cf. BibGlHurr 416. With Schwemer, Coll.Anat. 10:251, not related to the deity Šuwaliyatt or *šuwali-* q.v.

**šuwali-** n.; (mng. unkn.); NS.†

**sg.? nom.** *šu-wa-li-i*[*š*?] KBo 38.18 iii 39 (NS), *šu-u-wa-li-iš* KBo 31.175:7 (NS).

§ EGIR*-ŠU⸗ma* x[...]x x [...] *šipanti* [...] *šu-wa-li-i*[*š*? ...] *namma* GAL*-i*[*š*?...] *nu* LUGAL*-uš* x[...] *memāi* [...] "Then [...] he offers/sacrifices/libates [...] *š.* [...] then a big [...] and the king [...] he says [...] KBo 38.18 iii 37-42 (*hišuwa*-fest., NS); [ ... ᴰᵁᴳ*KUK*]*UB* GEŠTIN 1*-ŠU šipan*[*ti*...] / [... *me*]*mai šu-u-wa-li-iš kilu*[*štea*...] "[a pit]cher of wine he liba[tes] once [?] / [...sa]ys '*š. kilu[štea* ...]'" KBo 31.175:6-7 (*ḫišuwa*-fest., NS).

Haas/Wegner, OLZ 96 (2001) 702; Richter, BibGlHurr (2012) 416.

**šūwan[(-)...]**; part. of *šū-* B, *šūwa-*, s.v.

[*šuwanalli-*] *šu-wa-na-al-li*(-) KBo 6.18 iv 3 (OH/NS), see *išuwanalli-*.

**šūwanaššari-** n. or adj.; mng. unkn.; MS.†

**sg. acc. com.** *šu-u-wa-na-aš-ša-a-ri-i[n]* KBo 32.163:4 (MS), [*šu-u-wa-n*]*a-aš-ša-ri-in* KBo 32.157 left col. 3 (MS), KBo 32.181a:(1) (MS).

**broken, here?** ⌜*šu*⌝-*u*[-...] KBo 32.158 i 9 (MS).

[...*ka*]*t*?*tan arḫa t*[*ittanu-*(?)...] / [...]x *šu-u-wa-na-aš-ša-a-ri-i*[*n*...] / [...*m*]*ān*⸗*aš aki*⸗*ma nu*⸗*šš*[*an* ...] "[...]... *š*. [...] but [i]f (s)he dies, ...[...]" KBo 32.163:3-5 (frag. of unkn. nature, MS) □ the tentative restoration to *tittanu-* in line 3 is based on line 2 and the related frag. KBo 32.157 left col. 6.

**šuwanti(ya)-** n. com.; (mng. unkn.); from MS.†

**sg. acc.** *šu-ú-wa-*⌜*an-ti*⌝-*i*[*n*] KBo 24.110 iv 4 (MS), *šu-wa-an-ti-ia-an* KBo 19.145 iii 44 (NH).

**broken, here?** *šu-wa*[- ... ] KUB 54.67 obv. 9 (LNS).

(Hurr.) [...-*š*]*a*? *pí-tar-ri-wa*$_a$-*ap bi-tar-ri-wa-ap ḫa-a-i* = ? (Hitt.) *nu* GUD-*aš šu-wa-an-ti-ia-an datten* "(When you go, go to the courtyard,) and take the *š*. of an ox" KBo 19.145 iv 43-45, iii 43-45 (Šalašu's rit., NH), see below.

(In a ritual against sorcery the practitioner says: "Inside the door I freed a bewitched woman from a spell, inside the door I freed a bewitched man from a spell") [*m*]*ān iyadduma n*⸗*ašta ḫī*[*l*]*i ītten nu* GUD-*aš šu-wa-an-ti-ia-an dātten ki*[*tp*]*andalaz išḫiyandan* ⌜*l*⌝*ātten* $^{LÚ}$GIŠ-[*ruwa*]*ndan*⸗*ma*⸗*kan* GIŠ-*ruwaz* [*par*]⌜*ā*⌝ (?) *tarna*[*tten*] "[W]hen you (pl.) go, go to the court[ya]rd, and take the *š*. of an ox. He[nce]forth free him who was bound, relea[se] the pe[gg]ed one from the peg" KBo 19.145 iii 43-47 (NH), ed. Haas/Thiel, AOAT 31:304f., Laroche, RHA XXVIII 60f., Wegner, FsHaas, 445, translit. ChS 1/5:215; *ANA* ⌜É⌝ GUD *šu-ú-wa-*⌜*an-ti*⌝-*i*[*n*...] *nu*⸗*wa maškiddu* "[He...-s] a *š*. to the cattle barn [..., saying (thus):] 'Let it disappear(?)'" KBo 24.110 iv 4-5 (rit. frag., MS), ed. Bawanypeck/Görke, FsHaas 42, 48, cf. s.v. *ma-*; perhaps this word: 4 GUD-*ma*⸗*šši* 30 UZ$_6$ *šu-wa-*[...] KUB 54.67 obv. 9 (cult inv., LNS).

Laroche, RHA XXVIII (1970) 63; Haas/Thiel, AOAT 31 (1978) 357 ("Teil eines Rindes"); Bawanypeck/Görke, FsHaas (2001) 42 n. 72 ("Pflock?"); Tischler, HEG S/2 (2006) 1231 ("Nomen u.B. in Zusammenhang mit Kuh bzw. Kuhstall").

**šuwari-** adj., Hurr.; (mng. unkn.); NH.†

**Hurr. pl. abs. or pl. gen.** (w. anaphoric suffix *-na*): *šu-wa-ra-še-na* KUB 27.1 iii 1 (NH), [*šu-w*]*a-ra-a-ši-na* KUB 27.3 iv 10.

Among bread offerings to Hurrian deities: 1 NINDA.⌜SIG⌝ DINGIR.MEŠ-*na*«*šina*» *šu-wa-ra-še-na* (var. [*šu-w*]*a-ra-a-ši-na*) *turaḫišena* (var. *turu*[*ḫ*]*ḫena*) ⌜*t*⌝*erra* TUŠ-*aš* KI.MIN (= *paršiya*) "Seated, ditto (= he breaks) one flat bread (for) the *š*.-gods, male (gods), and *teri*(-gods) (or: (and) the *teri*)" KUB 27.1 iii 1-2 (fest. of Šauška of Šamuḫa, NH), w. dupl. KUB 27.3 left col. 10-11 (NH), ed. Lebrun, Samuha 81, 91, Wegner, ChS I/3-1:45, 48 □ the Hurrian of this passage is problematic. The form DINGIR.MEŠ-*našina* is pl. gen. with pl. abs. Suffixaufnahme. Expected is the pl. abs. DINGIR.MEŠ-*na* (cf. i 71, 72, ii 71, 72, iii 4, 5) as the recipient of the bread offering. The "gods" are modified by pl. abs. (see DINGIR.MEŠ-*na kulubadi*⸗*na* "the unnamed ... gods" iii 5, see Wegner, SMEA 36:97f.) or by gen. w. pl. abs. Suffixaufnahme (see DINGIR.MEŠ-*na omini*⸗*ve*⸗*na* $^{URU}$*Ḫatte*⸗*ne*⸗*ve*⸗*na aštoḫi*⸗*na* "the female gods of the land, of Ḫatti" ii 72-73). *š*. is therefore either pl. abs. w. derivational morpheme ⸗*a*⸗*š*(*š*)*e* (*šuwar*(*i*)⸗*a*⸗*že*⸗*na*) or pl. gen. w. pl. abs. Suffixaufnahme (*šuwar*(*i*)⸗*r*(< *na*)⸗*až*⸗*e*⸗*na*).

Lebrun, Samuha (1976) 103; Laroche, GLH (1979) 246 ("pl. gén.dét."); Wegner, ChS I/3-1 (1995) 45, 48; Wegner, ChS I/3-3 (2004) 62 ("Bd. unbk."); Richter, BibGlHurr (2012) 416.

***Úšuwarit-** n. neut.; (a plant); NS.†

**sg. nom.-acc.** $^{Ú}$*šu-*⌜*wa-ri*⌝ KBo 21.19 i 7 (NS).

**here? broken** $^{Ú}$*šu-wa-*⌜*a*⌝[-...] KUB 44.1 rev. 14 (Tudḫ. IV).

**Luw. gen. adj. nom. pl. com.** $^{Ú}$*šu*(over eras.)-*wa-ri-ta-aš-š*[*i-iš*?] KBo 21.19 i 9 (NS).

A-*ni*⸗*kan kuit* $^{Ú}$*šu-*⌜*wa-ri*⌝ *anda* [...] *nu*⸗*šši parašduš* ⌜x-x⌝-[...]-⌜x⌝-*ni takk*[*i* ...] *nu* $^{Ú}$*šu*(eras.)-*wa-ri-ta-aš-š*[*i-iš*?] ⌜*paraš*⌝*duš*⸗(*š*)*mi*[*š* ...] $^{Ú}$*ārnitašši*[*š*? *p*]⌜*araš*⌝*duš* [...] "The *š*.-plant which [...-s] in water, its leaf/foliage corresponds to [...]. The leaf/foliage of the *šuwarit*-plant(s) [...] the leaf/foliage of the *ārnit*-plant [...]" KBo 21.19 i 7-10 (medical frag,., NS), translit. Burde, StBoT 19:36, $^{\text{(GIŠ)}}$*paršdu-* b; [... *ḫame*]*šḫanza* DÙ-*ri nu⸗kan* É.DINGIR-*LIM šanḫanzi nu⸗kan* $^{\text{Ú}}$*šu-wa-*⸢*a*⸣-[...] / [...-*y*]*ali*$^{\text{ḪI.A}}$ *šuppiyaḫanzi* "[When sprin]gtime comes they sweep the temple, and they purify the [...-]s [with(?)] *š*.-plants" KUB 44.1 rev.14-15 (fest., Tudḫ. IV) □ *š*. at the end of line 14 is tentatively listed here, and not under *šuwaru-* B (a plant or plant product, q.v.); although the latter is attested as a purifier in the cult, it is not otherwise attested with the Ú determinative.

A connection to *šuwaru-* B (a plant or plant product) and/or $^{\text{GIŠ}}$*šuwarti-* cannot be ruled out.

Carruba, StBoT 2 (1966) 14 ($^{\text{Ú}}$*šuwaritašši-*); Burde, StBoT 19 (1974) 73 ($^{\text{Ú}}$*šuwarita-* c. "ein Heilkraut"); Ertem, Flora (1974) 143; Starke, StBoT 31 (1990) 209 (*šuwarit-** n. "eine Pflanze"); Melchert, CLL (1993) 198 ("a plant"); Trémouille, RANT 1 (2004) 214f. ("piante"); Soysal, FsNeumann$^{2}$ (2002) 473f. n. 20; Tischler, HEG S/2 (2006) 231f.

Cf. $^{\text{GIŠ}}$*šuwarti-, šuwaru-* B.

[$^{\text{Ú}}$*šuwaritašši-*] KBo 21.19 i 9. The stem is *$^{\text{Ú}}$*šuwarit-* q.v., according to Starke, StBoT 31:209 (contra Carruba, StBoT 2:14 and Ertem, Flora 143).

**$^{\text{GIŠ}}$šuwarti** n.; (a wooden object); OH/NS.†

**sg./pl. nom.-acc. neut.** $^{\text{GIŠ}}$*šu-wa-ar-ti* KUB 33.55 i 4 (OH/NS).

[...-*š*]*a?⸗šmaš* 3 ⸢x x x⸣ TUR 2 $^{\text{GIŠ}}$*šu-wa-ar-ti* [...S]A$_{5}$? *kēz⸗ma⸗at IŠTU* SÍG ZA.GÌN [...] *išdanani dāi* "[...] for them [...] three small ... (and?) two *š*. [On one side with r]ed(?), on the other with blue wool [...] he/she places it/them on the altar" KUB 33.55 i 5-7 (OH/NS), translit. Moore, Thesis 151 (reading $^{\text{GIŠ}}$TÚG-*wa-ar-ti*), Rieken et al., hethiter.net/:CTH 336.1 (INTR 2009-08-12).

Tischler, HEG S/2 (2006) 1231 (same word as $^{\text{Ú}}$*šuwaritašši-*).

Cf. $^{\text{Ú}}$*šuwarit-, šuwaru-* A.

**šuwaru A** adj./adv.; full(y); from OS.†

**sg. or pl. nom.-acc. neut.** *šu-wa-a-ru* KBo 17.11 iv 7, 15 (OS), KBo 17.74 iv 33, 41 (OH/MS), KUB 30.10 rev. 7 (OH/MS), KUB 57.60 ii 22 (OH or MH/NS), KUB 57.63 ii (33) (NS), IBoT 4.282 obv. (6), [𒑱?*š*]*u-wa-ru* KUB 23.85 rev.? 8 (preceded by gloss wedges? see below; NH), KUB 21.38 i 3, (5) (NH), KUB 31.127 i 10 (OH/NS), KUB 57.107:16 (NS), (𒑱?)*šu-u-wa-ru* KUB 36.2b ii 22 (NS).

[LUGAL (*U* MUNUS.LUGAL *ešanda*)] *šu-wa-a-ru kue* GAL.ḪI.A *ak*⸢*kušk*⸣[(*anzi*)] / [*ta* (*apūš⸗pat akuan*)]*zi tuḫ*⸢*ḫuš*⸣[(*ta*)] "[The king] and the queen sit down. They only drink those(!) cups they usually drink fully. (Festival) finished" KBo 17.11 iv 15-16 (storm & thunder fest., OS), w. dupl. KBo 17.74 + ABoT 1.9 iv 41-42 (OH/MS), ed. StBoT 12:34f., translit. StBoT 25:69, cf. [(LUG)]AL-*uš eša šu-wa-a-ru kue* GAL.ḪI.A *akkuškez*⸢*zi*⸣ [(*ta apē⸗pat*)] *ekuzi* KBo 17.11 iv 7-8 (storm & thunder fest., OS), w. dupl. KBo 17.74 iv 33-34 □ in the dupl. KBo 17.74 + ABoT 1.9 iv 41-42 the com. gender dem. pron. *apūš* does not agree w. the neut. rel. pron. *kue*. The par. passage ibid. iv 33-34 has the expected *apē* referring back to the cups. An interpretation as adj. ("the full cups that ...") cannot be excluded; $^{\text{d}}$UTU-*uš šu-wa-ru mayanza* DUMU $^{\text{d}}$N[I]N.GAL *zamakur⸗tet ŠA* $^{\text{NA}_4}$ZA.GÌN-*aš* "O Sun God, fully grown-up son of N[i]ngal! Your beard is of lapis lazuli" KUB 31.127 i 10-11 (prayer to Sungod, OH/NS), ed. Güterbock, JAOS 78:239 ("fully grown-up"), Lebrun, Hymnes 94, 101, tr. Hittite Prayers 36 ("most vigorous"); [$^{\text{d}}$UTU-*u*]*š šu-wa-a-ru mayanza* [DUMU $^{\text{d}}$EN.Z]U *U* $^{\text{d}}$NIN.GA[L...⸗*Š*]*UNU zik* "O Sun God, fully grown-up [son of the Moon Go]d and Ninga[l!] You are their [...]" KUB 30.10 rev. 7-8 (Kantuzili's prayer, OH/MS), ed. Lebrun, Hymnes 114, 117, tr. Hittite Prayers 32f., cf. also Güterbock, Oriens 10:358; *antu⸗šmett⸗a a*[(*pūšš⸗a*)] $^{\text{d}}$UTU-*uš⸗pat šu-wa-a-*⸢*ru*⸣ *mayan*[(*za*)] *labarnaš* $^{\text{MUNUS}}$*tawan*[(*nannaš*)] ⸢*kiš*⸣[(*a*)]*ri⸗šumm*[(*e*)]*t* TI-*an ḫ*[(*arak*)] "May only you, fully grown-up Sun God, keep both their possessions and those themselves (i.e., all people belonging to the Labarna) alive in the hand of Labarna and Tawannanna" KUB 57.60 ii 21-24 (rit. frag., OH or MH/NS), w. dupls. KUB 57.63 ii 32-36 (NS), KBo 54.243 ii 3-6, ed. Rieken et al., hethiter.net/: CTH 385.10 (TX 2016-11-24, TRde 2016-11-24), Archi, FsOtten$^{2}$ 20f.; ("You, Tattamaru, had taken the daughter of my sister in marriage. Then Fate dealt you a grievous blow (so that) she died on you. Why do people say thus:) *akkantaš⸗wa* $^{\text{LÚ}}$*ḪADĀNU* [𒑱(?)*š*]*u-wa-ru-pát* $^{\text{LÚ}}$*ḪADĀNU zik⸗ma⸗mu⸗za* $^{\text{LÚ}}$*ḪADĀNU ēšta* "'An in-law of a deceased one is nevertheless fully an in-law!' You were my in-law" (reproaches and perhaps admonitions/requests follow) KUB 23.85

rev.? 7-8 (letter of queen to Tattamaru, NH), ed. Letters 365 ("A male in-law remains nevertheless fully an inlaw even if his wife dies"), Stefanini, Athenaeum NS 40:4-5, Güterbock, Oriens 10:358 □ the double gloss wedge is usually restored in order to fill the narrow space that seems left compared to the immediately preceding lines; for a possible attestation of *š.* with a preceding gloss wedge, which was subsequently erased, compare in broken context *n≠aš* x (=⸌?) *šu-u-wa-ru≠pat* KUB 36.2 b ii 22, cf. Güterbock, Oriens 10:358; [*ANA* DA]M *ŠA* ŠEŠ≠*KA* TI-*tar šu-wa-ru* "[For] your brother's [wi]fe, life is full" KUB 21.38 obv. 3 (letter of Pud. to Ramses II), ed. Letters 282 ("full"), Starke apud Edel, ÄHK 1:216f. ("[(Mir), der Gemah]lin deines Bruders ist Leben (und) Unversehrtheit eigen"), Stefanini, Pud. 5 ("vita fiorente"), cf. 18 (phrase is equivalent to Akk. *šulmu*), Helck, JCS 17:87 ("besonders"), tr. DiplTexts² 132 ("enjoys full life"); *namma≠mu≠kan* [Š]À KUR.KUR.[MEŠ ...] / [TI-*tar šu-w*]*a-ru* "Furthermore, [life] is full within my lands, [my ... and my ...]" KUB 21.38 obv. 4-5, ed. Starke apud Edel, ÄHK 1:216f. ("(und in deinen Ländern) ‹sei› (ebenfalls Leben und) [Unverseh]rtheit !"); possibly here, but more likely *šuwaru-* B is KBo 32.7 rev. 10-11 (missing deity myth, NS) see *šuwaru-* B d.

Güterbock, Oriens 10 (1957) 357-358 ("true, truly"); Laroche, DLL (1959) 88 ("pleinement?"); Stefanini, Athenaeum NS 40 (1962) 3-10; idem, Pud. (1964-1965) 5 ("fiorente"), 18 (TI-*tar šuwaru* = Akk. *šulmu*); Carruba, StBoT 2 (1966) 14 ("voll, vollständig"); Neu, StBoT 12 (1970) 34f., 91 (adverbiell "voll" (?)); Puhvel, JAOS 101 (1981) 213-214 ("weighty, hefty, mighty; heavily, mightily, greatly"); Neu, StBoT 26 (1983) 177 w. n. 535; Weitenberg, U-Stämme (1984) 191-194; Archi, FsOtten² (1988) 9, 30 (*šuwaru mayant-* "vollkräftig; in voller Blüte stehend"); de Martino, Eothen 1 (1988) 60f.; Starke apud Edel, ÄHK (1994) 1:216f., 2:326-328 ("Unversehrtheit"); Soysal, FsNeumann² (2002) 471f. (discussion of *š. šaḫ-* as either "stuff fully" or "stuff *š.*-plant"); Tischler, HEG S/2 (2006) 1232-34 ("voll, ganz," adv. "vollständig, zur Gänze, für immer"); Kloekhorst, EDHIL (2008) 796 (does not distinguish between *šuwaru* A and B, only mng. "full, complete").

**šuwaru- B** n. neut.; (a plant or plant product used for purification); from MS.†

**sg. nom.-acc.** ⸢*šu*⸣*-wa-ru* KBo 27.40 obv.? 8 (NS), KBo 49.160:4 (NS), KBo 49.160:4 (NS), *šu-wa-a-ru* KUB 54.85 obv. 12 (MS), KBo 47.17 obv. 2 (MS), KBo 32.7 obv. 11 (NS), *šu-u-wa-ru* KUB 10.27 i 31 (MH/NS), KUB 35.55 iii? (12) (NS), ⸢*šu*⸣*-ú!-wa-ru* KBo 19.144 i 12 (NH), *šu-ú-wa-ru-ú* KUB 12.29 i? 3.

**abl.** *šu-wa-ru-az* KBo 19.144 i 15 (NH), *šu-wa-ru-wa-*[*az*?] KBo 27.40 obv.? 8 (NS), *šu-wa-ru-wa-*⸢*az*?⸣ KUB 58.60 vi 12 (NS).

**inst.** [*š*]*u-wa-ru-ú-it* KBo 15.25 obv.7 (MH/NS), ⸌(erased) *šu-u-wa-ru-it* KUB 44.50 i? 10 (LNS).

**a.** inserted or situated in cups, vessels etc.: *nu šiḫelliyaš kuit wātar n≠at IŠTU* $^{DUG}$*KUKUBI udanzi anda≠ma≠kan šu-u-wa-ru tarnai namma* $^{DUG}$*KUKUB I*[*ŠT*]*U* GADA *anda k*⸢*āriy*⸣[*a*]*nzi* "As for the water that is for purification, they bring it with a pitcher. (S)he inserts *š.* (in that pitcher). Then they cov[e]r the pitcher w[it]h linen" KUB 10.27 i 28-33 (fest. of Ištar of Nineveh, MH/NS), ed. Beckman, MemHurowitz 52, 58, translit. ChS 1/3-1:161; [EGIR-*and*]*a≠ma≠za* GAL.GIR$_4$ *wit*[*enaš*...] / [...]x *anda≠ma≠kan šu-u-w*[*a*?*-ru*?...] / [*kittar*]*i*(?)/ [*tarnattar*]*i*(?) ⸢MUN≠*ya≠kan*⸣ [*anda išḫuwān*(?)] "[Thereaft]er, an earthenware cup of wa[ter...] Therein *š.* [is lyi]ng/[is insert]ed, and salt [is poured in(?)]" KUB 35.55 iii? 11-13 (Puriyanni's rit., NS), translit. StBoT 30:71, Otten, LTU 62.

**b.** used to sprinkle (consecrated) liquids: 1 DUMU.É.GAL≠*ma IŠTU* GAL *parā watkunumaš wātar pāi* ⸢*šu*⸣*-wa-ru≠ya≠kan anda nu wātar šu-wa-ru-wa-*[*az*?] ⸢1⸣*-ŠU parā išparnuzi* "One palace attendant gives water in a cup for splashing (or: water for splashing in a cup), and there is also *š.* in (it). He sprinkles the water [with] (a?) *š.* once" KBo 27.40 obv.? 6-9 (fest. for deities of the netherworld, NS); *nu≠za* $^{MUNUS}$ŠU.GI (over erasure) $^{GIŠ}$⸢x⸣[...] ⸢*nu≠š*⸣*šan* $^{MUNUS}$ŠU.GI *ANA* $^{DUG}$*NAMMA*[*NTIM*...] *kuit≠ma≠at wātar nu UL kuitki* [...] / [*a*]*nda≠ma≠kan* ⸢*šu*⸣*-ú!-wa-ru ki*[*ttari*?] § [*n≠*]*aš paḫḫuenaš e*⸢*d*⸣*ez pera*[*n*...] / [*m*]*aḫḫan≠ma≠kan* EN.SÍSKUR *paḫḫur* x[...] / [*nu*]*≠šši≠kan* $^{MUNUS}$ŠU.GI *šu-wa-ru-az w*[*ātar*...] "The Old Woman [...-s] a wooden(?) [...] and the Old Woman [...-s] into a *NAMMA*[*NTU*]-vessel. But since it is (just?) water (and?) nothin[g...,] in it li[es] *š.* § She [...-s] in front of the fires on the other side [...] When the ritual patron [...-s] the fire(s), the Old Woman [sprinkles?] w[ater] with (a?) *š.* on him" KBo 19.144 i 9-15 (Hurrian rit., NH), ed. Görke, Ašdu 123f., 129; [... LÚ] $^{d}$U *šu-ú-wa-ru-ú dāi* [...L]Ú $^{d}$U *wātar ANA* EN.SISKUR [...*i*]*šparnuškezzi* "[The man] of the

Stormgod takes *š*. [... the m]an of the Stormgod [s]prinkles water on the ritual patron [...]" KUB 12.29 i 3-5 (rit. frag., NS); [ ... Ì.DÙ]G.GA (˹erased) *šu-u-wa-ru-it peran papparaške*˹*z*˺[*zi*] "(S)he sprinkles the fine oil with (a?) *š*. before [him (i.e, the ritual patron?)]" KUB 44.50 i? 10 (rit. frag., LNS).

**c.** used as purifier for divine images: *nu=ššan* ᵈ*Wišuriyandan katta* Í[D-*i pēdaḫḫi*] *nu=ššan paimi ANA PĀNI* ÍD ᴳᴵˢZA.LAM.G[AR *tarnaḫḫ*]*i nu* ᵈ*Wišuriyandan wappuwaš* [IM-*it*? *š*]*u-wa-ru-ú-it-t=a warapmi* "[I carry] the (image of) the goddess Wišuriyanza down [to the] r[iver]. I go (and) [pitc]h a ten[t] in front of the river. I wash the (image of) the goddess Wišuriyanza [with clay(?)] of the riverbank and with (a?) *š*." KBo 15.25 obv. 5-8 (rit. for Wišuriyanza, MH/NS), ed. Carruba, StBoT 2:2f.; ᴸᵁ́SANGA ᵈU *U* ᴸᵁ́SANGA ᵈUTU [D]INGIR.MEŠ *šu-wa-ru-wa-*˹*az*?˺ *tuḫḫūešnaz=*˹*iya*˺ [KÙ-*a*]˹*nzi*˺ "The priest of the Stormgod and the priest of the Sungoddess [puri]fy the gods(' image) with (a?) *š*. and *tuḫḫueššar*" KUB 58.60 vi 11-13 (fest., NS), translit. DBH 18:158f.

**d.** used to fill or stuff containers: 1 ᴰᵁᴳ!*KUKU*‹*B*› (var. ᴰᵁᴳGUR₄.GUR₄) GEŠTIN 1 ˹*N*˺*ARKABU* MUN 1 ᴰᵁᴳ[...] *šu-wa-a-ru šaḫān PĀNI* DINGIR-*LIM dāi* "one pitcher of wine, one upper grindstone, salt, one [...] vessel [...] (in there) *š*. is stuffed (or "fully (*šuwaru* A) stuffed"). (S)he places (them) in front of the god" KBo 32.7 rev.10-11 (missing deity myth., NS), w. dupl. KUB 54.85 obv. 11-12 (MS), ed. *šaḫ-* A b 2′, translit. Rüster, FsAlp 476; ˹*šu*˺-*wa-ru* / [...] *šāḫi* KBo 49.160:4-5, cf. StBoT 2:14 (as 249/t); and [...]=*kan ANA* ᴰᵁᴳ*ḪABANNA*˹*TUM*˺ [...] / [...] *šu-wa-a-ru šāḫi n=at* ᴹᵁᴺᵁˢSUḪUR.[LAL ...] KBo 47.17 obv.1-2 (MS), ed. StBoT 2:13f. (as 1262/v).

Götze, NBr 64 w. n. 3, pointed out the concrete nature of *š*. and took it as the phonetic equivalent of ᴳᴵˢŠINIG "tamarisk," based upon a textual parallelism (KUB 10.27 i 31 and KBo 5.2 iii 43). Güterbock, Oriens 10:357, rejected this identification due to insufficient evidence. He proposed distinguishing two words *š*.: one a noun, denoting a substance, and the second an adj. or adv. (see *šuwaru* A). Carruba, StBoT 2:13-15, convincingly explains the concrete *š*. as a plant substance. Despite this, Puhvel, JAOS 101:213f., tried to unify all of *š*. occurrences under *šuwaru* A. Stefanini, Athenaeum NS 40:3-10, connected both mngs. of *š*. as adj. "blooming" and nominalized "shoot, bud." Soysal, FsNeumann² 473, tentatively upholds Goetze's identification with ᴳᴵˢŠINIG. The concrete nature of *š*. is certain since it is "taken" by a priest KUB 12.29 i 3 (above under b).

Although the uses of *š*. resemble those of the "tamarisk" (written log. ᴳᴵˢŠINIG, and syll. ᴳᴵˢ*paini-* q.v.), as laid out by Soysal, a direct identification of the two is unlikely. Note that *š*. never has the GIŠ det. A connection of *š*. with **šuwaruil*(*i*)- KUB 9.28 iii 20 (MH/NS), ᵁ́*šuwarit*(*ašši*)- KBo 21.19 i 9 (NS), ᴳᴵˢ*šuwarti* KUB 33.55 i 4 (OH/NS), *šuwāruša* KUB 32.18 obv.? i 5 (Palaic) is possible but unsubstantiated.

For **šuwaruk* (thus Haas, SMEA 14:138, Haas/Wegner, ChS I/5:301) as an incorrect reading of the abl. *šuwaruaz* see Görke, Ašdu 133.

Götze, NBr (1930) 64 w. n. 3, 86 ("Tamariske(?)"); Güterbock apud Friedrich, HW (1952) 201 (not "Tamariske"); Vieyra, RA 51 (1957) 98 ("une substance"); Friedrich, 1. Erg. (1957) 19 ("eine Substanz"); Güterbock, Oriens 10 (1957) 357 (a substance); Friedrich, 2. Erg. (1961) 23; Stefanini, Athenaeum NS 40 (1962) 9-10 ("germoglio, gemma," "viticcio?, tralcio?"); Friedrich, 3. Erg. (1966) 30 ("Knospe, Sproß, Sprößling"); Carruba, StBoT 2 (1966) 13-15 ("eine holz- oder grasartige (oder aus einer Pflanze hergestellte) Substanz"), 62 ("eine seifenartige Substanz"); Stefanini, AGI 54 (1969) 157-160; Weitenberg, Anatolica 4 (1971-72) 167-169; Ertem, Flora (1974) 165; Puhvel, JAOS 101 (1981) 213-214; Weitenberg, U-Stämme (1984) 191-194; de Martino, Eothen 1 (1988) 60-61; Soysal, FsNeumann² (2002) 465-74; Tischler, HEG S/2 (2006) 1234-1236; Kloekhorst, EDHIL (2008) 796 (does not distinguish between *šuwaru* A and B; only mng. "full, complete"); Görke, Ašdu (2010) 133.

Cf. *šuwaru* A, *šuwaruili-*, ᵁ́*šuwarit-*, ᴳᴵˢ*šuwarti*.

**šuwaruil(a/i?)-** n.; (mng. unkn.); MH/NS.†

**inst.** *šu-wa-ru-i-li-it* KUB 9.28 iii 20 (MH/NS).

*šūwanteš dannaza kitta perann=a* KASKAL-*ši* GI-*aš* KÁ.GAL-*TIM šer anda šu-wa-ru-i-li-it išḫiyanza n=aš arḫa kitta* "Filled *danna*(*š*)-breads (are) placed also in front, on the road, a gate of reed is tied together on top with *š.*, and it is placed away (i.e., turned away, to the side?)" KUB 9.28 iii 18-21 (rit. for the Heptad, MH/NS), w. dupl. KBo 19.132 rev.? 7-9 (MH/NS), ed. Kloekhorst, EDHIL 796f. (differs), see Stefanini, Athenaeum NS 40:10, *nata-* 1 b.

According to the context *š.* serves to bind or tie the reed(s) to make a gate-like structure. Since *šuwaru-* B q.v. is a plant or plant product *š.* could denote some plant fiber, or a cord made of plant fiber.

Stefanini, Athenaeum NS 40 (1962) 10; Friedrich, HW 3. Erg. (1966) 30 ("Binse(?)"); Carruba, StBoT 2 (1966) 13 ("ein Bindemittel aus Vegetabilien"); Stefanini, AGI 54 (1969) 157 ("a un legame, a fibre di natura vegetale"); Weitenberg, Anatolica 4 (1971-72) 168 w. n. 31-32 (word formation); Puhvel, JAOS 101 (1981) 213, 214 n.14 (translates *šuwaruilit* adverbially "heavily"); Weitenberg, U-Stämme (1984) 192 ("Binse(?)"); de Martino, FsCarratelli (1988) 61 n.12; Soysal, FsNeumann$^{2}$ (2002) 473f. n. 20; Tischler, HEG S/2 (2006) 1236f.; Kloekhorst, EDHIL (2008) 796f.

Cf. *šuwaru-* B.

[**šuwaruk*] Haas, SMEA 14:138, Haas/Wegner, ChS I/5:301, read *šuwaruaz*, see *šuwaru-* B.

**šuwarzapa** (name of a town), **šuwarziya** (Hurrian name of a holy mountain); see under *šurzi-* B.

**LÚšuwaššali-** n. com.; groom(?), stable man(?); NH.†

**sg. nom. com.** LÚ*šu-u-wa-aš-ša-liš* KBo 4.14 iii 42 (NH).

*[m]⌜ā⌝nn=a* LUGAL-*i QĀTAMMA* ⁝*kuwatai* LÚ*šu-u-wa-aš-ša-liš=ma⌜n⌝=kán* EG[IR-*an*(?)] ⌜*U*⌝*L ašzi* ANŠE.KUR.RA.MEŠ=*man kuiš tūriyazi man=aš* ⌜*UL ē*⌝*šzi* É=*man UL ēšzi anda=man=aš=kan* ⌜*ku*⌝*wapi paizzi tuk=ma apedani meḫuni ANA* ZI LUGAL UGU *parā namma* ⁝*kuwayatadu* "And [i]f it worries the king thus: (What) if there remained no groom(?)/stable man(?), there would be no one there who would harness the horses. (What) if there were no house, where one could go in? Then, at that time, there should be even more concern to you for the life of the king" KBo 4.14 iii 42-46 (treaty, Tudḫ. IV or Šupp. II), ed. Stefanini, AANL 20:46 ("un impiegato di palazzo"), van den Hout, Diss. 294f. (no tr.).

Although *š.* is a hapax, the context indicates that this functionary has to do with horses either as a stable man or groom. Note also a similar situation is foreseen in the following paragraph where a charioteer (LÚ*KARTAPPU*) abandons his chariot which would likewise mean trouble for the king (iii 47-48). *š.* probably contains the *-al(l)a-* (professional) suffix that often shows *i*-stem variants under Luw. influence, cf. Rieken, HS 107:49f.

Friedrich, HW (1952) 201 ("Palastangestellter"); Kronasser, EHS 1 (1966) 214; Pecchioli Daddi, Mestieri (1982) 117; Tischler, GsAmmann (1982) 222 ("ein Würdenträger"); idem, HEG S/2 (2006) 1237 ("ein Palastangestellter").

**šu(?)wa-x-a(šši?)-** (mng. and function unkn.); NS.†

*panzi ANA* DINGIR-*LIM* x[...] *nu=šši ḫazziw[i* ...] *šu?-wa-*⌜x⌝*-aš-ši-kán* x[...] *nu* KIN SIG$_5$-*ru* "Shall they go (and) to the god [...] and for him a rit[e ... ]. *š.* ..[...], then the oracle should be favorable" KUB 52.87 iv 2-5 (oracle question, NS).

**DUGšuwattar** n. neut.; Luw. LW; (a storage jar); from MS.†

**Luw. pl. nom.-acc.** DUG*šu-ú-wa-at-ra* KBo 29.65 i 25 (MS?), KUB 27.59 i 9 (NS), [DU]G*šu-ú-wa-at-ra*ḪI.A KBo 29.65 i 3 (MS?) DUG*šu-wa-at-ra* KUB 46.51 rev.? 11 (NS), KUB 54.24 i (5) (NS), DUG*šu-*⌜*wa-at*⌝*-ra*ḪI.A KUB 27.59 i 19 (NS).
**Hitt. pl. nom.-acc.** [DUG*šu-ú-w*]*a*(?)*-at-ri*ḪI.A KUB 54.15:5.
**pl. dat.-loc.** DUG*šu-ú-wa-at-na-aš* KBo 29.65 i 16, 19, (20), 22, (23) (MS?), KBo 29.77:11 (MS).
**abl.** DUG*šu-ú-wa-at-na-az* KBo 29.65 i 10 (MS?).
**broken:** DUG*šu-ú-wa-at-*x(-)[...] KBo 29.77:10 (MS).

**a.** broken open and contents utilized: *n=ašta* 3 DUG*šu-ú-wa-at-ra kinuanz[i* ...] MUN=*y[a ḫ]*⌜*ūm*⌝*an šarā dāi* "They brea[k] open three *š.*-vessels [...] an[d] he takes out [a]ll of the salt" KBo 29.65 i 25-26 (cult of Ḫuwaššanna, MS?), HEG S/2:1237 (mistakenly adds ḪI.A to DUG*šuwatra*); *ma*⌜*ḫ*⌝*ḫan=ma=za ḫandāuanzi zinnizi n=ašt[a* ...] *kīnuzi n=ašta* ZÍD.DA DUG*šu-ú-wa-at-na-az kuēzz[=iya* ...] *tepu šer arḫa dāi n=uš* 3 NINDA.GUR$_4$.RA.ḪI.A *ŞEḪḪERŪT[IM iēzzi* ?] *n=uš šarā ANA* d*Ḫuwaššanna* É*karēm[i*...] "As soon as he finishes preparing, th[en] he breaks open [three *šuwatra*-vessels(?).] He takes out a little flour from on top of each *š.*-vessel [...]. He [makes(?)] three small thick bread loaves from them. He [carries] them up to Ḫuwaššana's temp[le]" KBo 29.65 i 9-12 (cult of Ḫuwaššanna, MS?); cf. also [... $^{d}$*Ḫuwašš]anna kāša=tta* [... $^{DUG}$*šu-ú-w]a(?)-at-ri*$^{HI.A}$ *kinummi* "[O Ḫuwašš]anna! I break open [... *šuw]atra*-[vessels] for you now" KUB 54.15:4-5 (cult of Ḫuwaššanna) □ if the restoration is correct, according to Starke, StBoT 31:465, $^{DUG}$*šūwatri*$^{HI.A}$ should be Hittite while the forms $^{DUG}$*šūwatra*$^{HI.A}$ are Luwian.

**b.** foodstuffs in the *š.*-vessel: ("If the *alḫuitra*-priestess' house is outside [...], she carries three small bread loaves out on the road, and br[eaks] them. She speaks thus":) $^{d}$*Ḫuwaššanna [B]ĒLI=YA tiwali[ya Ø?] kāša=tta* $^{DUG}$*šu-ú-wa-at-na-aš ši*⸢*e*⸣[*ššar* N]INDA.GUR$_4$.RA *n=aš=ka[n Ø?] menaḫḫanda au* "O Ḫuwaššanna, my [l]ord, migh[ty one(?)!] Here in the *š.*-vessels there are for you be[er and thick b]read, examine them carefully" KBo 29.65 i 15-17 (cult of Ḫuwaššanna., MS?); cf. $^{DUG}$*šu-ú-wa-at-na-aš* NINDA.GUR$_4$.RA in KBo 29.77:11 (MS).

**c.** "of the *witašša*-festival": ("The man of the temple offers beer and says thus":) *kā*⸢*š*⸣*a ŠA* EZ[EN$_4$] ⸢*u*⸣*itaš*[(*ša*)] $^{DUG}$*šu-*⸢*wa-at*⸣*-ra*$^{HI.A}$ (var. omits ḪI.A ?) *d*[(*aḫḫ*)]*un nu=mu=ššan ti[wal]iy[aš]* $^{d}$*Ḫuwaššannaš* ⸢*anda*⸣ *aššuli arḫut* "Here now I have taken the *š.*-vessels of the *witašša*-fest[ival.] O mi[gh]t[y (?)] Ḫuwaššanna, stand in benevolence with me" KUB 27.59 + KBo 29.66 i 18-20 (*witašš(iy)aš*-fest., NS), w. dupl. KUB 54.24 i 5-7 (NS); *nu BĒL* SÍSKUR *PĀNI* DINGIR-*LIM* [... $^{d}$*Ḫuwaššanna*] *tiwaliya kāša=tt[a ŠA* EZEN$_4$ *witašša*] $^{DUG}$*šu-wa-at-ra titt*⸢*an*⸣[*unun*] "And the sacrificer [speaks] before the god[: 'O Ḫuwaššanna], mighty one(?), [I have] set up here for yo[u] *š.*-vessels [of the *witašša*-festival]'" KUB 46.51 rev.? 9-11 (*witašš(iy)aš*-fest., NS.), ed. THeth 26:301; cf. KUB 27.59 i 18 (*witašš(iy)aš*-fest., NS); cf. also KUB 54.15:4-5.

**d.** location used in slaughtering: *nu=kan* 1 UDU $^{DUG}$*šu-ú-wa-at-na-aš peran AN[A ...] šipanti n=an=šan* $^{DUG}$*šu-ú-wa-at-na-a[š šer(?)] ḫūkanzi nu šuppa ḫuišu* $^{UZU}$GABA UZ[U ...] $^{DUG}$*šu-*⸢*ú-wa*⸣*-at-na-aš peran tianzi* [...] *n=at=šan* EGIR-*pa* $^{DUG}$*šu-ú-wa-at-n[a-aš šer ...] n=aš UŠKÊN* "He sacrifices one sheep t[o (DN)?] in front of *š.*-vessels, and they slaughter it [over(?)] the *š.*-vessels. They place the raw meat, the breast meat, the [... meat] in front of the *š.*-vessels. [...] And [...] them again [over(?) the] *š.*-vessels. And he bows." KBo 29.65 i 19-24 (cult of Ḫuwaššanna, MS).

$^{DUG}$*š.* belongs to the Luwian cult, especially that of Ḫuwaššanna. This explains the Luw. forms and the retention of the *-tn*-sequence (cf. GrHL 42 §1.112). The (partly restored) pl. nom.-acc. neut. [$^{DUG}$*šu-ú-w]a(?)-at-ri*$^{HI.A}$ shows the Hitt. pl. neut. ending *-i* characteristic of heteroclitic *r/n*-stems.

Laroche, DLL (1959) 88, 177; Tischler, HDW (1982) 80 ("ein Gefäß"); Starke, StBoT 31 (1990) 465 (*šuu̯atta/šuu̯attu-*: "Fülle, Füllung, Vorratsgefäß"); Melchert, CLL (1993) 198 ("fullness; storage jar"); Tischler, HHwb (2001) 157 ("ein Gefäß, 'Fülle'"); idem, HEG S/2 (2006) 1237f. ("Fülle").

**šuḫḫa- A, šūḫ-** n. com. and neut.; roof; from OS.

**sg. nom.-acc, neut.** *šu-uḫ-ḫa-an* KUB 56.14 iv 4 (NS).

**acc. com.** *šu-uḫ-ḫa-an* KBo 38.184 iv 6 (MS), KUB 41.8 iv 36 (pre-NH/NS), KUB 53.4 rev. 28 (NS).

**sg. gen.?** *šu-uḫ-ḫa-aš* KBo 18.170a rev. 5 (NH).

**sg. loc.** *šu-u-uḫ-ḫi* KBo 20.8 obv.? 8 (OS), KBo 44.142 obv. 5 (OS), KBo 27.165 obv. 13 (MS), *šu-uḫ-ḫi* KBo 8.91 rev.! 17 (MH/MS), KBo 21.37 obv.! 10, rev.! 23 (MH/MS), KBo 11.34 i 9 (OH/NS), KUB 29.4 ii 46, 55, iv 12 (NH), KBo 11.34 i 9 (OH/NS), KBo 54.123 iii 16 (NS).

**all.** *šu-uḫ-ḫa* KUB 60.121 rev. 21 (MS), KBo 30.61 obv.? 8 (MH/MS), KUB 55.39 i 18, 19, iv 29 (OH/NS), KUB 7.1 ii 19 (pre-NH/NS), KUB 25.27 i 13 (NH).

**abl.** *šu-u-uḫ-za* KBo 44.142 obv. 4 (OS), KUB 43.30 iii 18 (OS), *šu-u-uḫ-ḫa-az* KBo 12.123:7 (pre-NH/NS), *šu-uḫ-ḫa-az* KUB 55.39 i 11 (OH/NS), KUB 31.86 iii 4 (MH/NS), KUB 41.8 i 12 (MH/LNS), KUB 33.106 ii 8 (NH), *šu-uḫ-ḫa*‹*-az*› KUB 7.1 ii 31 (pre-NH/NS), *šu-uḫ-ḫa-za* KBo 11.32 obv. 16 (OH/NS), KUB 57.110 ii 9 (NS), *šu-uḫ-ḫa-z(=iya)* KUB 51.64:10 (NS) (here or pres. 3 pl. of *šuḫḫa-* C).

**pl. acc. com.** *šu-uḫ-ḫu-uš* KUB 9.15 iii 8, 13 (NH).

**(collec.?) nom.-acc. neut.** *šu-uḫ-ḫa* KBo 10.45 iv 38 (pre-NH/NS; but see below c), ⸢*šu*⸣*-uḫ-ḫa* KUB 31.89 ii 7 (MH/NS).

**dat.-loc.** *šu-uḫ-ḫa-aš* KBo 20.82 iii 7 (OH?/NS?).

**a.** in general: *nu maḫḫan* $^{d}$*Ḫepadduš* $^{d}$*Tašmišun aušta nu=kan* $^{d}$*Ḫepaduš šu-uḫ-ḫa-az* *katta maušš̄uwanzi waqqareš* "When Ḫebat saw Tašmisu, Ḫebat almost fell down from the roof" KUB 33.106 ii 7-8 (Ullik., NH), ed. Güterbock, JCS 6:20f., Arıkan, ArAn. 6:54f.; *mān⸗šan* TI$_8$$^{MUŠEN}$ É.MEŠ-*naš šu-uḫ-ḫi* [*ešari*] "If an eagle [alights] on the roof of a house complex" KBo 10.6 i 12 (cat., NH), ed. StBoT 47:82f.; *n⸗aš⸗za naššu* $^{É}$*ḫalinduwaš šu-uḫ-ḫi ēštat našma⸗zz⸗(š)an INA* É.DINGIR.MEŠ *šu-uḫ-ḫi ēštat* "It (i.e., a bird) alighted either on the roof of the palace complex or it alighted on the roof of the temple buildings" KUB 30.34 iv 2-4 (rit. for purification of a town, MH/NS), ed. Arıkan, ArAn. 6:42.

**b.** construction or maintenance: ("At the gate, the prince, four priests of the town of Kašḫa, the *ammama*-woman, (and) the Lord of Ḫanḫana keep heaping up the mud into their(!) (w. var. his) *šeknu*-garment(s) with a silver inlaid spade (and) hoe") [(*n⸗aš⸗šan*)] *INA* É.DINGIR-*LIM šu-uḫ-ḫi* (var. B: Ø) *š*[(*arā* 9-*ŠU*!)] (var. C: UGU 7-*ŠU*) *pēdanzi ŠA* $^{d}$*T*[(*elipinuaš*)] *šu-uḫ-ḫa-an pūru*[(*ddanzi*)] "They carry it (i.e., the mud) nine (var. seven) times to the temple, up to the roof, (and) they plaster the roof of Telipinu's (temple) with (that) mud" KUB 53.3 v 6-8 (fest. for Telipinu, NS), w. dupls. KUB 53.4 rev. 27-28 (B) (NS), KBo 54.123 iv 12-15 (C) (NS), ed. *purut* c 2′.

**c.** exposed to the weather: *karizza⸗kan* GIM-*an* URU-*az šēḫur* (var. *ŠĒTUM*) IM-*an ārri šu-uḫ-ḫa⸗ma⸗kan* (var. *šu-uḫ-ḫa-an⸗kan*) A-*az ārri n⸗at⸗kan* GAM $^{GIŠ}$ŠEN-*az ār*⟨(*š*)⟩*zi kell⸗a* URU-*aš parnaš* HUL-*lun* EME-*an kāš aniyawaranza QĀTAMMA parkunuddu* "As a flood washes away the urine (and) the dirt from the city, and the water washes the roofs (var. roof) and flows down the drain, let this ritual likewise cleanse the evil tongue of the houses of this city too" KBo 10.45 iv 37-41 (ritual, pre-NH/NS), w. dupl. KUB 41.8 iv 36-39 + Bo 8139, ed. THeth 12:100, Otten, ZA 54:138f. □ in light of the var. *šuḫḫan* KUB 41.8 iv 36 it is also possible to take *šuḫḫa* as sg. acc. com. w. assimilation of the -*n*, for which see GrHL 43 (§1.118) □ We take *ŠE-E-TUM* of the variant's join-piece Bo 8139:2 as Akk. *šittu* (CAD *šittu* C) "excrement," add to CHD *šeḫur* 1 c; *nu* É.DINGIR-*LIM andurza araḫza ḫurniyanzi šu-uḫ-ḫu-uš zappiyaz paḫšanuwanzi* "They sprinkle the temple inside (and) outside and keep the roofs from leaking" KUB 9.15 iii 7-8 (purification rit., NH), ed. THeth 26:18f., tr. Collins CoS 1:171, Miller, TUAT NF 4:217.

**d.** *šuḫḫa warḫui* "rough roof" perhaps with weeds growing up through the mud, or needing to be rolled: BÀD⸗*ma puruttiyauwanzi* (or *purut tiyauwanzi*) ⌜2?-*an*?⌝ *allā*[(*n ēšdu*)] *namma⸗at ištalgan ēšdu n⸗ašta šu-u*[(*ḫ-ḫa lē*)] *war*[(*ḫ*)]*ui zappiyattari lē* "Let the fortification wall be two(?)... in order to apply mud plaster. Then let it be smoothed over. Let the roofs not be rough. Do not let (them) leak" KBo 57.10 rt. col. 5-7 + KUB 31.86 ii 16-18 (instr.for border-governors, MH/NS), w. dupl. KUB 31.89 ii 5-7, ed. Miller, HittInstr 222f., StMed 14:114-17 ("il tetto ruvido non faccia acqua"), translit. Miller, ZA 98:125, tr. McMahon, CoS 1:223 ("a thatched roof may become leaky. Let it not (happen)"), cf. Hoffner, JCS 29:151f. and CHD s.v. *lē* ("a roof (which is) weedgrown will leak. Let it not be (so)"), *puruttai-* ("a roof (which) is rough (i.e., full of cracks?) will leak. (It) should not be!"), differently HED L 75 ("a thatched roof is leakproof," w. dupl. "an unthatched roof is leakprone"), THeth 12:93, Carruba, SMEA 22:363 ("il tetto di sterpi non (deve) affatto perde(re)"), StBoT 5:206 ("das Gestrüpp(?)dach darf nicht undicht sein"), von Schuler, Dienstanw. 43, Kammenhuber, HuI 126 (taking *š.* as all.), Arıkan, ArAn 6:20; *kī⸗wa* GIM-*an šu-uḫ-ḫa-an ḫameshandaza warḫui* ⸓*ḫištaran⸗ya⸗war⸗at* "As this roof is "rough" because of the spring and it is *ḫištara*" KUB 56.14 iv 4-5 (dream/vow, NH), ed. de Roos, Votive 238, 240, HW² Ḫ 615 ("Dach ... bewachsen(?) (wörtlich "rauh") (ist)") □ both the dem. *kī* and the following -*at* show *š.* to be neut.

**e.** used in religious rituals/festivals — **1′** the roof of a temple: *nu šeḫell*[*iya*]*š* A.A.ḪI.A-*ar karūili ANA* É.DINGIR-*LIM ped*[*a*]*nzi n⸗at⸗šan šu-uḫ-ḫi tianzi* "They carry the waters for purification to the old temple and place them on the roof" KUB 29.4 ii 44-46 (dividing the Goddess of the Night rit., NH), ed. StBoT 46:283, 285; ... 1 $^{DUG}$*ḫūppar* KAŠ 1 $^{DUG}$GUR$_4$.GUR$_4$ GEŠTIN *kī ANA* $^{d}$*Pirinkir keldiya šu-uḫ-ḫi⸗ššan šer danzi* "..., one vessel of beer (and) one vessel of wine; they take this up to the roof, for the (offering of) wellbeing for Pirinkir" KUB 29.4 ii 54-56 (dividing the Goddess of the Night ritual, NH), ed. StBoT 46:284f.; ("When on the fourth day the star appears, the ritual patron comes to the temple and takes a stand behind Pirinkir. They make a wellbeing-offering to Pirinkir. When they finish it") *n=ašta* DINGIR-*LAM šu-uḫ-ḫa-az katta udanzi* "they bring the goddess down from the roof (... and carry her into the temple)" KUB 29.4 iii 5 (dividing the Goddess of the Night rit., NH), ed. StBoT 46:287; *nu šeḫel«el»liya‹š›* A.A.ḪI.A-*ar INA* É.DINGIR-*LIM* GIBIL *pēdanzi n=at=šan šu-uḫ-ḫi tianzi n=at ŠAPAL* MUL.ḪI.A *šešzi* "They bring the waters of purification to the new temple. They place them on the roof and they (i.e., the waters) spend the night beneath the stars" KUB 29.4 iv 11-13 (dividing the Goddess of the Night rit., NH), ed. StBoT 46:294f.; LUGAL-*uš UŠKÊN n=aš=kan šu-uḫ-ḫa-az* GAM *uizzi n=aš dunnakkišna paizzi* "The king bows. He comes down from the roof. He goes into the inner chamber" KUB 55.39 i 11-12 (fest., OH/NS), ed. Alp, Tempel 228f., translit. StBoT 26:366; *nu=ššan* $^{\text{LÚ}}$*purapšiš unuwanza šu-uḫ-ḫi artari nu* $^{\text{GIŠ}}$TUKUL *kuin ḫarzi n=an=kan peran katta tarnai nu=ššan* $^{\text{UZU}}$*karši* GUD *peran ḫamankanzi n=an=šan šu-uḫ-ḫi šarā ḫūittianzi n=an=za=an apāš dāi* "The adorned *purapši*-priest stands on the roof. He lets down in front the mace that he holds. They bind *karši*-meat of an ox in front and they pull it (i.e., the mace and attached meat) up onto the roof. He takes it for himself" KUB 30.40 i 20-25 (*ḫišuwaš*-fest., NS), ed. Arıkan, ArAn 6:31; 1 $^{\text{LÚ}}$*purapšiš=ma=kan kuiš šu-uḫ-ḫi šer artari* "The one *purapši*-priest who stands atop the roof (speaks the following *kuwarayalla* (words?) before the king: 'O king do not fear')" KBo 15.52 + KUB 34.116 v 11-12 (fest., MH/NS), ed. Groddek, RANT 7:371, 378.

**2′** the roof of other or unspecified buildings connected with religious/magical ceremonies: LUGAL-*uš=kan* É.ŠÀ-*az uizzi t=aš* $^{\text{É}}$*ḫalintui tiyazi* DUMU.MEŠ É.GAL*=ma=kan šuḫḫaz katta* $^{\text{GIŠ}}$*ueran* 1 $^{\text{DUG}}$*KUKUB* GEŠTIN*=ya udanzi* "The king comes from the inner chamber and steps into the palace complex; the palace attendants bring down from the roof a wooden plate(?) and a vessel of wine" KUB 55.39 i 13-15 (festival, NS), ed. Alp, Tempel 228f. (as Bo 2372); *šu-uḫ-ḫi=kan šer* $^{\text{d}}$UTU-*i menaḫḫanda* 2 $^{\text{GIŠ}}$BANŠUR AD.KID [*k*]*āriyanda dāi ... nu=kan* LUGAL-*uš šu-uḫ-ḫi šarā paizzi* "He places two covered wicker tables on the roof facing the Sungod ... The king goes up onto the roof (and bows before the Sungod of Heaven)" KUB 6.45 + KBo 57.18 i 4-5, 9 (Prayer to the Stormgod of Lightning, Muw. II), ed. Singer, Muw.Pr. 7, 31; *nu* $^{\text{GIŠ}}$IG *kuiš ḫašzi nu* (coll.) *šu-uḫ-ḫa parkiyanzi n=an šarā* SUD-*anzi* "As for the one who opens the door—they go up to the roof and pull him up" IBoT 3.148 iii 13-14 (evocation rit., MH?/NS), ed. s.v. *park-* 2 a (w. biblio.), ChS 1/9:118f.; ("He goes into the *šinapši*-building...") *nu=kan šu-uḫ-*[*ḫa*]*-az kattanda* 6-*ŠU memai* "and he speaks down from the roof six times" KUB 30.28 rev. 8-9 (rit., NS), ed. Otten, HTR 96f., tr. van den Hout, Hidden Futures 42; $^{\text{URU}}$*Tammelḫa=ma* $^{\text{LÚ}}$*išpunnala*[*š*] *parna pānzi ta=z=kan* SAG.DU.MEŠ *šu-uḫ-ḫi warpanzi* "In Tammelḫa they go to the house of the *išpunnala*-man and wash their heads on the roof" KBo 11.34 i 7-9 (rit., OH/NS), ed. THeth 12:87f.; [...]x UDU.ḪI.A*=ya šu-u-uḫ-ḫa-az peššianzi* "They throw [...] and the sheep from the roof" KBo 12.123:7 (rit., NS), Arıkan, ArAn. 6:14; *n=aš=kan šu-uḫ-ḫi šer* $^{\text{GIŠ}}$ZA.LAM.GAR-*aš kattan* [...] "And up on the roof beneath the tents he/she [...-s] (or: he/she [...-s] them)" KBo 8.91 obv. 17 (Kizzuwatnan rit., MH/MS), ed. Trémouille, Eothen 4:91f. ("essi sul tetto la tenda giù [...]"), translit. eadem, Eothen 11:847; [...] *šu-uḫ-ḫi šer* $^{\text{GIŠ}}$BANŠUR *daninuzzi* "He sets up a table on top the roof. (They place meat [on it]. Half a *SUTU* of flour and 1 *ḫuppar* vessel of beer t[hey pour out])" KUB 25.22 lower edge 4 (cult of Nerik), ed. KN 238f.; cf. [...] *mākkizziyaš šu-u-uḫ-ḫ*[*i* ...] KBo 20.8 i 8 (fest., OS), ed. $^{\text{É}}$*makzi*(*ya*)-, translit. StBoT 25:69.

Ehelolf apud Götze, KlF 1 (1930) 199f. n. 3; Friedrich, SV 2 (1930) 171; Krause, IF 11 (1940) 51; von Schuler, Dienstanw. (1957) 54; Kronasser EHS 1 (1966) 548; Naumann, Architektur Kleinasiens (1971) 153-160, 379; Boysan-Dietrich, THeth 12 (1987) 85-105; Archi, FsOtten (1988) 31; Rieken, StBoT 44 (1999) 65f.; Melchert, Toch&IESt 9 (2000) 64 (pl. neut. as collect.); Arıkan, ArAn. 6 (2003) 11-57; Tischler, HEG S (2006) 1129-1130; Kloekhorst, EDHIL (2008) 772-773.

$^{\text{NINDA?}}$**šuḫḫa(?) B** n.; (a bread or pastry?).†

⌜$^{\text{NINDA?}}$*šu-uḫ-ḫa*⌝ KBo 26.196 obv. 12 (NS).

The reading of this very fragmentary and abraded piece of a cult inv. is very uncertain. Hazenbos, Organization 72, reads 4? *šu-uḫ-ḫ*[*a*]. A $^{NINDA}$*š*. is not otherwise attested (see AlHeth., DBH 1); a roof-shaped pastry or bread (see *šuḫḫa-* A) is conceivable though.

**šuḫ(ḫ)a- C** v.; to pour; from OH/OS.

**pres. sg. 1** *šu-uḫ-ḫa-aḫ-ḫi* KBo 17.25 rev.? (5) (OS), KBo 12.96 i (3) (MH/NS), KUB 51.48:7 (NS), Bo 3911:7, 8 (apud Neu, StBoT 26:172 n. 520), *šu-uḫ-ḫa-a-mi* KUB 44.15 i 5 (NS).

**sg. 3** *šu-uḫ-ḫa-i* KBo 25.29 ii? (1)? (OS), KUB 53.10 rev. 8 (OH?), KUB 32.135 iv 4 (OH/MS), KBo 10.37 iii 17, 21 (OH/NS), KBo 11.32 obv. 13, lower edge 41 (OH/NS), KUB 2.13 iii 11 (OH/NS), KBo 20.89 rev.? (11) (MS?), KBo 5.2 ii 41 (MH/NS), KUB 9.31 ii 8 (MH/NS), VBoT 24 ii 8 (MH/NS), KUB 46.25 ii 9 (pre-NH/NS), KUB 12.58 i 11 (NS), KUB 6.45 iv 7, 12, 16, 21, 27, (32), 54, 58 (Muw. II), KUB 6.46 i 43, 48, 51, 56, 60, 64 (Muw. II), KUB 12.26 ii 22 (NH), KUB 17.25 i 17 (NH), KUB 44.15 i 10 (NS), *šu-uḫ-ḫa-a-i* KBo 7.38 left col. 2, 5 (OS), KBo 21.80 i 12 (OH/MS), KUB 32.135 iv 4, 6 (OH/MS), KBo 20.71:5 (OH/MS?), KBo 34.15 rev. 4, (9) + KBo 23.91 iv 7, 12, (15) (OH/MS?), KBo 16.82 rev.! 5, 9 (OH/MS?), KUB 2.4 iv 8 (OH/NS), KUB 2.13 i 26, 42, ii 60 (OH/NS), KUB 29.1 ii 14 (OH/NS), KBo 39.8 ii (57), iii 24 (MH/MS), KUB 32.95 rev. 2 (MS), KBo 5.2 ii 20 (MH/NS), KUB 27.67 ii 62, iii 7, 13, (47), 63, iv (36) (MH/NS), KUB 33.70 ii 11 (MH/NS), KUB 10.11 iv 9, 24 (NH), KUB 11.31 i 23 (NH), KUB 44.15 i 7 (NS), *šu-ḫa-a-i* KBo 25.149 obv. 7 (OS), .

**pl. 1** *šu-uḫ-ḫa-u-e-*[*ni*] KBo 10.37 iii 25 (OH/NS).

**pl. 3** *šu-uḫ-ḫa-an-zi* KUB 43.30 iii (16), 17, (18) (OS), KBo 17.46:26, 27 + KBo 34.2:50, 51 (OH/MS?), KBo 27.165 rev. 16 (MS), KBo 47.35 rev. 9 (MS), KUB 56.40 iii 17 (NS), KUB 57.97 i 7 (NS), KUB 58.58 obv. 22 (NS), KUB 17.35 ii 9, 10 (NH), KUB 38.26 obv. 40, rev. 16 (NH), IBoT 2.103 iv 6, 9 (NH), *šu-ḫa-an-zi* KBo 26.182 i 14 (NH), VBoT 49:4 (NS), *šu-uḫ-ḫa-a-an-zi* KBo 2.7 obv. 6, 20 (NH).

**pret. sg. 1** *šu-uḫ-ḫa-aḫ-ḫu-un* VBoT 58 iv 6 (OH/NS).

**sg. 3** *šu-uḫ-ḫa-aš* ABoT 1.44 i 53 (OH/NS), KBo 3.38 obv. (4) (OH/NS), KUB 7.23:6 (NS), KUB 59.54 obv. 6 (LNS).

**pl. 3** *šu-uḫ-ḫa-er* KUB 36.104 obv. 6 (OS), KUB 29.1 iii 9 (OH/NS), KBo 15.10 ii 12 (MH/MS), *šu-uḫ-ḫa-a-er* KBo 3.34 i 8 (OH/NS), KBo 15.10 iii 55 (MH/MS), KUB 57.39 obv.? (4) (MH).

**imp. sg. 3** here? *šu-uḫ-du* KBo 49.194:5 (NS).

**mid. pret. sg. 3** *šu-uḫ-ḫa-ti* Bo 6172:4 (NS; Soysal, NABU 2017:81).

**imp. sg. 3** [*š*]*u*?-*uḫ-ḫa-a-ru* KUB 45.20 i 12 (NS) (very doubtful whether *šuḫḫa-*).

**verbal subst. gen.** *šu-ḫa-wa-aš* KBo 26.182 i 4 (NH), *šu-uḫ-ḫa-wa-aš* KUB 38.32 obv. 6 (NH), KUB 54.45 obv.? 10 (NH), *šu-uḫ-ḫa-u-wa-aš* KUB 25.23 iv 50 (NH), KUB 42.105 iii 8 (NH), VBoT 26:8 (NH), KBo 26.151 iii (17) (LNS), *šu-uḫ-ḫa-ú-wa-aš* KUB 25.23 i 37 (NH), *šu-uḫ-ḫu-wa-aš* KUB 17.35 ii 2, iv 1 (NH).

**part. sg. nom. com.** *šu-uḫ-ḫa-*⌜*an*⌝*-za* KUB 9.28 ii 11 (MH/NS); **nom.-acc. neut.** *šu-uḫ-ḫa-an* KBo 25.102 rev.? (3) (OS), KBo 39.8 iv 23 (MH/MS), KBo 2.3 iv 3 (MH/NS), KBo 11.14 i 7, 18 (MH/NS), KUB 9.28 i 24 (MH/NS), KUB 43.57 i 7, 19 (MH/NS), *šu-uḫ-ḫa-a-an* KUB 9.6 i 12, (15) (MH/NS); **pl. nom. com.** *šu-uḫ-ḫa-an-te-eš* Bo 3081 obv.? 11 (MH/MS, courtesy Soysal), KUB 58.1 i 8 (NS), KUB 58.4 v 18 (NS), KUB 17.30 iii 13 (NS), ⌜*šu*⌝*-uḫ-ḫa-an-te-eš*$_{17}$ KUB 43.60 iv 9 (OH/NS).

**broken:** *šu-uḫ-ḫa-a-*[...] IBoT 4.160 rev. 3 (NS), *šu-uḫ-ḫa-u-*⌜x⌝-[...] KBo 10.37 iii 25 (OH/NS).

The existence of a 3. sg. pret. [*šu-uḫ-ḫ*]*a-iš*, as read by Güterbock, JKF 10:207, is uncertain according to the sign traces in the copy, l. 17, but looks possible on the tablet photograph on the cover of T. Özgüç, Maşat Höyük II.

**a.** to pour something w. acc. obj. (usually non-liquids but see a 3′) — **1′** obj. dry goods (in contrast to *lāḫ-*, *laḫ*(*ḫ*)*u-*/*laḫ*(*ḫ*)*uwai-, lilḫuwai-* "to pour (out) (liquids, intangibles)" q.vv.) — **a′** foodstuffs — **1″** cheese: $^{NINDA}$*purpūruš* 4 GA.KIN.A[G ...] *šu-uḫ-ḫa-*[*a-i*] "He pours out ball breads (and) four cheeses [...]" Bo 5005 rev. 6-7, translit. StBoT 28:31, cf. KBo 19.128 iii 22-23 (OH?/NS).

**2″** fruits: *INBU*, $^{GIŠ}$*INBI*$^{ḪI.A}$ "fruit(s)" KBo 5.2 ii 41 (MH/NS), KBo 13.177 i 9 (NH?), KUB 9.28 i 24 (MH/NS); also specific fruits: $^{GIŠ}$*ḫašikka-* "?" KUB 29.1 ii 16 (OH/NS), KUB 29.2 ii 8 (OH/NS); $^{GIŠ}$*šamama-* (a kind of nut) KUB 43.60 iv 8-9 (OH/NS); *šanḫuwa-* "?" KUB 43.60 iv 8-9 (OH/NS); $^{GIŠ}$⌜x⌝*-iša-* KUB 43.60 iv 8-9 (OH/NS); $^{GIŠ}$GEŠTIN ḪÁD.DU.A "raisin" KUB 29.1 ii 16 (OH/NS), KUB 43.60 iv 8-9 (OH/NS); $^{GIŠ}$PÈŠ "fig" KUB 29.1 ii 14 (OH/NS), KUB 29.2 ii 6 (OH/NS, writes erroneously $^{GIŠ}$ZU).

**3″** grains, seeds, and their products: *ewa-* KBo 11.14 i 6-7 (MH/NS), KUB 29.1 iii 9 (OH/NS); *ḫalki-* "grain, barley" KUB 27.67 iii 13 (MH/NS), ABoT 1.44 i 53 (OH/NS); *ḫattar* "lentils" KBo 11.14 i 6-7 (MH/NS) □ for *ḫattar* see Watkins, FsKnoblock 494f.; *kappani-* GE$_6$ "(roasted) black caraway seed" KBo 39.8 ii 56-57 (MH/MS); *karaš* (a wheat variety) KBo 39.8 iii 24 (MH/MS), KBo 11.14 i 6-7 (MH/NS), KUB 27.67 iii 13 (MH/NS) (roasted) KBo 12.96 i 2-3 (MH/NS); cf. also *karaš=kan anda šu-uḫ-ḫa-a-i* (par. *karšann=a=kan anda išḫui*)

"She pours the *karaš*-grain in (there)" KBo 39.8 iii 24 (2Mašt., MH/MS), w. par. KBo 2.3 ii 32 (1Mašt., MH/NS), ed. StBoT 46:86; *kutiya-* KBo 11.14 i 7 (MH/NS); *memal* "coarsely ground meal" KUB 6.46 i 43, 47-48, 51, 55-56, 59-60, 63-64 (Muw. II), KBo 11.32 lower edge 41 (OH/NS), IBoT 3.1 obv. 23-25 (OH/NS) (meal of chick peas); cf. also EGIR-*ŠU*=*ma* NINDA.Ì.E.DÉ.A *mem(m)al* *ANA* NINDA.GUR$_4$.RA.ḪI.A *šer šu-uḫ-ḫa-i* "Afterwards, he pours the oil cake (and) the coarsely ground meal on top of the thick-breads" KUB 6.46 i 43, 47-48, 51, 55-56, 59-60, 63-64 (prayer to the Stormgod of Lightning, Muw. II); *pakkuššuwant-* "cracked-wheat/bulgur(?)" KUB 9.6 i 2-4, 10-12, 14-15 (MH/NS); *parḫuena-* (a kind of grain) KBo 11.14 i 6-7 (MH/NS); NINDA*purpura-* (ball-shaped bread/cake) KUB 58.1 i 10-12 (NS), w. dupls. KUB 58.4 v 21-22 (NS), IBoT 4.343 obv. 6 (NS); *šemeḫuna-* (a grain product) KUB 43.30 iii 16-17 (OS); *šeppit-* (a grain) KBo 11.14 i 6-7 (MH/NS), KUB 29.1 iii 9 (OH/NS), KUB 38.32 rev. 22 (NH), KUB 43.57 i (5)-7 (MH/NS), KUB 58.58 obv. 18 (LNS); *zinail-* (mng. unkn.) KBo 11.14 i 7 (MH/NS), KUB 43.57 i 6-7 (MH/NS); NINDA.GUR$_4$.RA "thick-bread" KUB 9.31 ii 7-8 (MH/NS), KBo 11.32 lower edge 41 (OH/NS); NINDA.Ì.E.DÉ.A "oil cake" KUB 6.46 i 43, 47-48, 51, 55-56, 59-60, 63-64 (Muw. II); NUMUN "seed" KBo 11.14 i 4-5, 7; ŠE.LÚSAR "coriander" VBoT 24 ii 8 (cf. i 4, roasted) (MH/NS); ZÍD.DA "meal" KBo 25.182:2-3 (OH/MS); also specific flours: ZÍD.DA ŠE "barley flour" KUB 41.4 ii 11 (NH), KUB 44.15 i 5 (NS); ZÍD.DA ZÍZ "wheat flour" KBo 11.14 i 20 (MH/NS); ZÍZ(*-tar*) "(emmer) wheat" KBo 11.14 i 6-7 (MH/NS), KUB 38.32 rev. 22 (NH), KUB 38.35 i 6 (Tudḫ. IV), KUB 43.57 i 5-7 (MH/NS), KUB 58.58 obv. 18 (LNS).

**4″** meat: UZUNÍG.GIG [...] / [*ANA* UGULA] LÚ.MEŠÚ.ḪÚB *ḫuppi*=*šši šu-uḫ-ḫa-an-z*[*i*] "They pour out (pieces of?) liver [ ... for the overseer of] the deaf men in his *ḫuppa/i*-container" KUB 43.30 iii 16-17 (OS), ed. HW² Ḫ 728b, translit. StBoT 25:78; ("(S)he takes one thick-bread and places cedar oil and [...] on (it)") *ANA* GEŠTU UDU *tepu* [*k*]*uerzi* UZU*šarnum*⟨*ma*⟩*š*=*a* [(SÍG BABBAR *t*)]*epu kuerzi nu*=*kan IŠTU* NINDA.GUR$_4$.RA *ḫaššī šu-uḫ-ḫa-i* "(S)he cuts a bit from the sheep's ear, (s)he cuts a bit of white wool of the *šarnum*⟨*ma*⟩*r* and along with the thick bread pours them onto the hearth" KUB 44.15 i 9-10 (fest. for *IŠTAR* of Nineveh, NS), w. dupl. Bo 3727 (see Otten/Rüster, ZA 64:48), ed. UZU*šarnum*(*m*)*ar* □ for the preceding context with a different spelling of *š*. (*šu-uḫ-ḫa-a-i* KUB 44.15 i 7) see below a 1′ b′ 2″ (embers).

**b′** non-foodstuffs — **1″** balls (*purpura-*): [*nu*=*z*(*a purpu*)]*raš šu-uḫ-ḫa-a-i* "He pours balls" KUB 33.70 ii 11 (missing god rit., OH/MS?), w. dupl. KUB 33.71 iv 3 (OH/NS), ed. *purpura-* e, Görke, hethiter.net/: CTH 403.3.1 (INTR 2015-04-15); LÚ.MEŠ AN.BAR 20 [*pur*]*puruš* AN.BAR *šu-uḫ-ḫa-an-z*[*i*] LÚ.MEŠ KÙ.BABBAR 20 [*pur*]*puruš* KÙ.BABBAR *šu-uḫ-ḫa-a*[*n-zi*] "The iron-men pour out 20 [b]alls of iron; the silver-men pour out 20 [b]alls of silver" KBo 17.46:26-27 + KBo 34.2:50-51 (KI.LAM fest., OH/MS?), translit. StBoT 28:91 (= lines 50-51).

**2″** embers, burning coals: (Fire complains to his mother Kamrušepa: "'The embers in (my) *ginupi*-vessel have vanished.' Kamrušepa answers: 'Let's [therefore] take (some) from someone!' They led him se[cretly?] to the river. They, the embers [...] on/in [...]. They stuck [the *ginupi*-vessel(?)] in front on a shepherd's staff. They held it [...], and the river glowed. They [held] it out [to] ...[...], and [the...] glowed") § [*n*=*a*]*t*=*kan uellu pē ḫarkanzi nu* Ú.SAL *warā*[*ni*] / [*n*]=*at*=*kan* ḪUR.SAG.MEŠ *pē ḫarkanzi nu* ḪUR.SAG.MEŠ *wara*[*ndari*] *nu*=*kan* DUMU.LÚ.U$_{19}$.LU *ištarna arḫa ḫāndāit n*=*aš*=*ši*[=*ššan*] *šu-uḫ-ḫa-ti išḫarwanza lappiyaš n*=*aš*=*ši*=*šša*[*n* ...] *lappiyaš nu iyauwaniškezzi* "They present [i]t (to) the meadow, and the meadow bur[ns]. They present it (to) the mountains, and the mountains bu[rn]. A mortal had settled in the middle. They had been poured (out) over him, the blood-red embers (text sg.); they had been [...] over him, the [...] embers. He is crying" KUB 17.8 iv 27-31 + Bo 6172:1-5 (myth, NS), ed. Soysal, NABU 2017:80-82 (differently); § [...]x *dāi nu*=*ššan paḫḫur šu-uḫ-ḫa-a-i* "(S)he takes/puts [...] and pours embers on it" KUB 44.15 i 7 (fest., NS); cf. KUB 7.18:5 (NS); ("On the ground down in front of the table a baked clay cup is placed") *nu*=*ššan* IZI *šu-uḫ-ḫa-an* "Embers are poured onto (it)" KBo 11.14 i 18 (Ḫantitaššu's rit., MH/NS), ed. Ünal, Ḫantitaššu 18, 28, Chrzanowska, hethiter.net/: CTH 395.1 (INTR 2016-03-23); cf. KBo 41.16 obv. 28 (NS), see StBoT 5:150 (as 110/e).

**3″** metals: KÙ.BABBAR "silver" KUB 27.67 ii 59-62, iii 61-63, iv 34-36 (MH/NS); KÙ.GI "gold" KUB 27.67 ii 59-62, iii 61-63, iv 34-36 (MH/NS); AN.BAR "iron" KUB 27.67 ii 61-62, iii 62, iv 35-36 (MH/NS); NAGGA "tin" KUB 27.67 ii 61-62, iii 62-63, iv 35-36 (MH/NS); URUDU "copper" KUB 27.67 ii 61-62, iii 62, iv 35-36 (MH/NS); ZABAR "bronze" KUB 27.67 ii 61-62, iii 63, iv 35-36 (MH/NS).

**4″** (clay) models of tongues: [*nu QAD*]*U kurdāli idālamuš* EME.ḪI.A *arḫa šu-uḫ-ḫa-er* "They poured out the evil tongues [wit]h the *kurdali*-container" KBo 15.10 ii 12 (rit., MH/MS), ed. THeth 1:22f., Görke, hethiter.net/: CTH 443.1 (INTR 2013-12-19); cf. ibid. iii 54; *k*[*āša* ḪUL-*la*]*muš* EME.MEŠ [A.ŠÀ]*mariyanī šu-uḫ-ḫ*[*a*]*-i* ... *kinuna* x[ o o -] x ⌈ḪUL⌉-*luš* EME.MEŠ-*uš INA* [A.ŠÀ]*mari*[*ya*]*nī šu-uḫ-ḫa-u-*⌈*e*⌉-[*ni*] "(S)He now pours the evil tongues on the *mariyana*-field ... now we will pour [...] (and) the evil tongues on the *mariyana*-field" KBo 10.37 iii 21, 24-25 (rit., OH?/NS), ed. StBoT 48:200f., van den Hout, FsHawkins 238.

**5″** natron, salt: (Pappa, the *urianni*-functionary, was fraudulent in distributing loaves and beverages) [(*I*)*N*(*A*? GAL *m*)*arnuw*]*andaš* MUN-*an šu-uḫ-ḫa-a-er* (var.: *šu-uḫ-ḫa-er*) *š*=*an*=*ašta* [(*eukta*)] "I[n]to a cup of *m*[*arnuw*]*ant*-beer they poured salt, and he drank it" KBo 3.34 i 7-8 (anecdotes, OH/NS), w. dupls. KUB 36.104 obv. 5-6 (OS), ed. Dardano, L'aneddoto 31, Soysal, Diss. 10, 83, StBoT 23:143; ("The Old Woman takes water from a cup or bowl and presents it to the two ritual patrons") [NA4]*nitri*=*ya*=*kan anda šu-uḫ-ḫa-an* (3Mašt.: [(*a*)]*nda išḫūwānzi*) "and natron is also poured in (3Mašt.: "they pour the natron in")" KBo 2.3 iv 3 (1Mašt. rit., MH/NS), w. par. KBo 9.106 iii 37 (3Mašt. MH/NS), ed. StBoT 46:104 □ note that 3Mašt. uses the (near) synonym *išḫuwa-* instead of *š*.; on this phenomenon in ritual texts see Marcuson/van den Hout, JANER 15:151 and passim; *šerr*=*a*=*ššan* ZÍD.DA ZÍZ MUN=*ya šu-uḫ-ḫa-i* "And he (i.e., the ritual practitioner) pours on top (of a brazier) flour of emmer wheat and salt" KBo 11.14 i 20 (Ḫantitaššu's rit., NS), ed. Ünal, Ḫantitaššu 18, 28, Chrzanowska, hethiter.net/: CTH 395.1 (INTR 2016-03-23).

**6″** sacrifice remainders(?) (*kuptar*): ("'O Tarpatašša ... take this (i.e., mouse as a carrier) while we give you another one to eat'") *nu kuptar arḫa šu-uḫ-ḫ*[*a-a-*]*i* "And (s)he pours out the remainders of the ritual" KUB 27.67 iii 47 (MH/NS), ed. StBoT 48:52f.

**7″** samples (*anaḫita-*): *namma* [LÚ]SANGA *anaḫita dāi* [...] *ḫuprušḫi parā šu-uḫ-ḫa-i* "Next, the priest takes samples [...and] he pours [them(?)] out on the incense burner(?)" KUB 11.31 i 22-23 (MS).

**8″** stones: [NA4]GUG "carnelian" KUB 27.67 ii 60-62, iii 61-63, iv 34-36 (MH/NS); [NA4]KÁ.DINGIR.RA "Babylon-stone" KUB 27.67 ii 60-62, iii 61-63, iv 34-36 (MH/NS); [NA4]TI "life-stone" KUB 27.67 ii 60 (MH/NS); [NA4]ZA.GÌN "lapis lazuli" KUB 27.67 iii 61-63, iv 34-36 (MH/NS); [NA4]*parašḫi* (a semi-precious stone) KUB 27.67 iii 62-63, iv 35 (MH/NS); [NA4]*lulluri-* (a mineral) KUB 27.67 ii 60-62, iii 62-63, iv 35-36 (MH/NS); [NA4]*nitri-* "natron" KBo 39.8 iv 22-23 (MH/MS), KBo 44.17 iv 5-6 (MH/MS), KBo 2.3 iv 3 (MH/NS); [NA4]*paššila-* "pebble" KUB 7.23:5 (NS); *šamana-* "foundation stone": *mān*=*za* LUGAL-*uš* É.ḪI.A GIBIL-*TIM kuwapikki* [o? ]x? *uetezzi mān*=*ašta šāmānuš šu-uḫ-ḫa-an-zi* ... § [d]UTU-*uš*=*wa*=*z* [URU]*Liḫzini uetet* [*nu*]=*war*=*uš*=*za*=*kan išḫuwaš šamānuš* "When the king builds himself a new palace (lit. houses/house complex) somewhere, (and) when they pour the foundations, (a water carrier performs the ritual and speaks the following words:) § 'The Sungoddess built herself (a house) in Liḫzina and she poured them, that is, the foundations'" KBo 37.1 i-ii 1-2, ii 3b-4b (Hattian-Hittite foundation bil., NS), ed. Rizza, StMed 20:111f., Kammenhuber, RHA XX/70:2-3 (as 2121/c+), StBoT 37:638f., *ša*(*m*)*mana-* 1 d-e, Torri, hethiter.net/: CTH 726.1 (INTR 2017-01-12) □ the use of =(*a*)*šta* with *š*. is very rare; note that the Hitt. version uses *išḫuwaš* (ii 4b) "poured" instead of *š*. in the incipit for Hattian *āštaḫḫil* (i 4a), see Klinger, StBoT 37:652, Soysal, HWHT 388f.

**9″** tree/reed parts: [GIŠ]*alanza*(*na*)- "*alanza*(*na*)-wood" KUB 59.54 obv. (6) (NS), HKM 116 ii? 20-24 (NS); *ḫašduir* "brushwood" KBo 13.199:7-8(?) (NS); [GIŠ]*ḫattalkišna-* "hawthorn wood" KUB 59.54 obv. 5-6 (NS), HKM 116 ii? (21)-24 (NS); *ḫulliš-* "pine cone" KUB 27.67 iii 7 (MH/NS); *laḫḫuwarnuzzi-* "greenery"

HKM 116 ii? (22)-24 (NS); *kalwišna*-(plant) HKM 116 ii? (23)-24 (NS); GIŠ*maršikka*- "*maršikka*-wood" KUB 59.54 obv. 5-6 (NS); GIŠ*šamaliya*- "*šamaliya*-wood" KUB 59.54 obv. (5)-6 (NS), HKM 116 ii? 21-24 (NS); *šumanza(n)*- "rush" HKM 116 ii? 23-24 (NS); *tuḫḫueššar* "resin?" HKM 116 ii? 23-24 (NS); GIŠERIN "cedar" KUB 41.4 ii 11-12 (NH).

**2′** intangibles: *n*=*apa d*[*aḫ*]*ḫun* DINGIR.MEŠ-*an uddār n*=*e*=*zz*=*an* [...] / [...*and*]*a*(?) *šu-uḫ-ḫa-aḫ-ḫu-un* "I s[ei]zed the words of the gods. I poured them [i]n (?) my [...]" VBoT 58 iv 5-6 (missing Sungod rit., OH/NS), ed. Rieken et al., hethiter.net/: CTH 323.1 (TX 2009-08-26, TRde 2009-08-26), translit. Myth. 25, tr. Hittite Myths² 28; see also the pouring of "evil tongues" KBo 10.37 iii 21, 24-25 cited a 1′ b′ 4″.

**3′** liquids (syn. *lāḫ*-, *laḫ*(*ḫ*)*u*-/*laḫ*(*ḫ*)*uwai*-, *lilḫuwai*-): KAŠ GEŠTIN LÀL-*it wātar anda* GEŠTIN-*aš šu-uḫ-ḫa*-⌈*an*⌉-*za nu šipanti* "(There is) wine, beer, honey, (and) water, wine is poured in and he performs a libation" KUB 9.28 ii 10-11 (rit. for the Heptad, MH/NS); cf. [...]x (or: x [ o ]) LÀL *šu-uḫ-ḫa*-⌈*a-i*⌉ x[...]/ ⌈*PĀ*⌉*NI* d*Ḫebat dāi* "[...] (s)he pours honey [...] and places [it/them?] before Hebat" KUB 32.95 rev. 1-3 (rit., MS); note also the mixed grammatical obj. Ì=*kan memal* IZI-*i šu-uḫ-ḫa-i* "(S)he pours out oil (and) coarsely-ground meal onto the fire" KBo 11.32 obv. 13 (OH/NS).

**b.** elliptical "to pour (the contents of) a container": 1 DU[GGA]L *dāi n*=*an ḫappina šu-uḫ-ḫa-i U* [D]UGGAL-*AM duwarn*«*an*»*azzi* "He takes one c[u]p, pours it(s contents) into the open flame and breaks the cup" KUB 9.28 ii 7-8 (rit. for the Heptad, MH/NS); GIŠ*paddur*=*ma*=*kan apiy*[*a*] / [*AN*]*A* A.[Š]À*mar*[*iyan*]*ī šu-uḫ-ḫa-i* "(S)he pours (the contents of) the mortar(?) ther[e ont]o the *mar*[*iyan*]*i*-fi[el]d" KBo 10.37 iii 16-17 (rit. against curse, OH/NS), ed. StBoT 48:198f., GIŠ*paddur*.

**c.** to pour w. something (abl.-inst.) into something (rare): GIM-*an*=*kan* ⌈*A*⌉*NA* dU URU*Guršamašša* DUG*ḫarši šu-uḫ-ḫa-an-z*[*i*] *ANA* dUTU *MĒ*=*ya*=*kan* DUG*ḫarši* TA NINDA.GUR$_4$.RA *šu-uḫ-ḫa-an-z*[*i*] "When they pour into the pithos for the Stormgod of Guršamašša, they pour with thick-bread into the pithos for the Sun-deity of the Water as well" KUB 17.35 ii 9-10 (cult inv., Tudḫ. IV), ed. Carter, Diss. 126, 140 □ while *š*. is almost always construed w. dir. obj. of the substance poured, this is a rare occurrence of "pouring into something with a substance" in the abl. or inst. (TA NINDA.GUR$_4$.RA).

**d.** locations or objects (all. or dat.-loc.) where pouring is done — **1′** body parts: *aiš*- "mouth": dUTU-*uš memal išša*=*šša šu-uḫ-ḫ*[*a-aš*...]x x[...] *š*=*an ištaḫta* "The Sun-deity po[ured] the coarsely ground meal into her (i.e., the Earth, her daughter's) mouth [...] ... [...] and she savored it" KBo 3.38 obv. 4-5 (Zalpa text, OH/NS), ed. StMed 19:32, 40, StBoT 17.8f., *memal* c 2′; (UZU)ÚR "lap"(?): [...UZU?]⌈ÚR=*ši* *šu-uḫ-ḫa-i*⌉ EN.SISKUR *UŠ*[*KĒN*] "He/she pours [...] onto his lap. The ritual patron bo[ws]" KUB 58.80 obv. 3 (Allaituraḫi's rit., NS), translit. Popko, AoF 16:88.

**2′** vessels — **a′** DUG*ḫarši*- — **1″** in general: [GIM-*a*]*n*=*ma zeni* DÙ-*ri ANA* dU ḪUR.SAG*Arnuwanda ANA* DINGIR.MEŠ *dapiaš* DUG*ḫarši kišan šu-uḫ-ḫa-a*[*n-zi*] / [3 BÁN(?)] ZÍZ DUG*ḫarši* dU 3 BÁN ZÍZ DUG*ḫarši* ḪUR.SAG*Ar*⌈*nuanda*⌉ "[Whe]n it becomes fall, they pour into the pithos for the Stormgod, for the Mountain Arnuwanda (and) for all the deities in the following way: [3 BÁN(?) measure] of wheat into the pithos (for) the Stormgod, 3 BÁN measures of wheat into the pithos (for) the Mountain Arnuanda" KBo 2.13 obv. 25-26 (cult inv., NH), ed. HLC 222f., Carter, Diss. 107, 112f.; [...] *zēni* 1 *PA*. ZÍZ 1 *PA*. *šeppitaš* DUG*ḫaršiyaš šu-uḫ-ḫa*-[*an-zi*] "[...] in the fall they pour one *PARĪSU*-measure of wheat (and) one *PARĪSU*-measure of *šeppit*-grain into the pithoi" KUB 38.32 rev. 22 (cult inv., NS) □ as Güterbock, Oriens 15:349 n. 1, pointed out, the act DUG*ḫarši šuḫḫa*-, which is made in the fall, is contrasted with "opening the jars" performed in the springtime.

**2″** in the expression DUG*ḫarši šuḫ*(*ḫ*)*a*(*u*)*waš*/*šuḫḫuwaš*: 1 EZEN$_4$ *zeni* DUG*ḫarši šu-uḫ-ḫu-wa-aš* "One fall festival of pouring into the pithos" KUB 17.35 iv 1 (Tudḫ. IV), ed. HLC 176f., Carter, Diss. 132, 145; cf. ibid. ii 2; 2 EZEN$_4$=*ši* DUG*ḫarši šu-uḫ-ḫa-wa-aš* *ḫēšu*[*waš*] *katta ḫamankatta* "For him/her (i.e., the deity) he mandated two feasts—of pouring into (and) of opening the pithos" KUB 38.32 obv. 6 (NH); cf. KBo 26.151 iii (17) (NH), KBo 26.182 i 4 (NH), KUB 25.23 i 37, iv 50 (Tudḫ. IV), KUB 42.105 iii 7-8 (Tudḫ. IV), KUB 54.45 obv.? 10 (Tudḫ. IV), VBoT 26:8 (Tudḫ. IV); cf. Carter, Diss. 181, 183

**b′** other vessels: GAL.GIR$_4$ "earthen cup": see KBo 11.14 i 17-18 (Ḫantitaššu's rit., MH/NS); GAL *marnuwandaš* "cup of *marnuan*-beer" KBo 3.34 i 7-8 (OH/NS), w. dupl. KUB 36.104 obv. 5-6 (OS), see a 1′ b′ 5″; *ḫuprušḫi*-vessel" KUB 11.31 i 23 (Tudḫ. IV's enthronement) see a 1′ b′ 7″; $^{DUG}$*ḫupuwai* (of clay) KBo 39.8 ii 55; $^{(DUG)}$*išnura/i*- "kneeding trough of clay" KBo 39.8 iii 24 (2Mašt., MH/MS), w. par. KBo 2.3 ii 32 (1Mašt., MH/NS), see a 1′ a′ 3″.

**3′** basket ($^{GI}$*pattar*): [*nu*]*=ššan ḫalkin karaš* $^{GI}$*paddanī šu-uḫ-ḫa-a-i* "(S)he pours grain (and) *karaš*-grain in the basket" KUB 27.67 iii 13 (MH/NS), ed. StBoT 48:50f.; cf. KBo 12.96 i 2-3 (rit., MH/NS), translit. $^{(GIŠ/GI)}$*pattar* B a; also w. $^{GI}$*pattar* as "sieve" KUB 9.6 i 3, 11-12, 14-15 (rit., NS), ed. $^{(GIŠ/GI)}$*pattar* B b, Popko, JCS 26:181.

**4′** foodstuffs: $^{NINDA}$*mulati*-: *memall=a šarāmnaz arḫa išḫuwāi šarāmnaz=ma=kan ANA* $^{NINDA}$*mulāti šer šu-uḫ-ḫa-a-i* "(The exorcist) pours out meal from above, he pours (it) from above on top of the *mulati*-bread" KBo 5.2 ii 18-20 (Ammiḫatna's rit., MH/NS), w. dupl. KUB 45.12 ii 4-6 (MH/NS), ed. *šarāmnaz*; $^{NINDA}$*ḫarši*-/NINDA.GUR$_4$.RA "thick bread" KBo 25.149 obv. 7 (OS), KUB 6.45 iv 11-12, 16, 26-27, 31+KBo 57.18:31, 54, 57-58 (Muw. II), KUB 6.46 i 43, 48, 51, 56, 60, 64 (Muw. II); NINDA.ÉRIN.MEŠ "soldier-bread" KBo 11.14 i 4-5 (MH/NS); NINDA.SIG "thin/flat bread" KBo 5.2 ii 41 (MH/NS); GA.KIN.AG "(crumbled) cheese" KBo 19.128 iii 21-23 (OH?/NS).

**5′** furniture/emplacements: *ištanana*- "altar" KUB 53.11 ii 17 (MS); $^{GIŠ}$BANŠUR "table" KUB 9.28 i 21-24 (with other foodstuffs on it, 21-23) (MH/NS); $^{GIŠ}$BANŠUR AD.KID "wicker table" KUB 58.1 i 5-8 (NS), w. dupl. KUB 58.4 v 15-18 (NS), translit. DBH 18:1, 12f.; $^{GIŠ}$*laḫḫura*- "offering table/stand" KUB 9.31 ii 8 (NH); $^{GIŠ}$*tipa*- (kitchen implement) KUB 43.60 iv 9 (OH/NS).

**6′** parts of a sanctuary: *nu=kan* $^{GIŠ}$*ērḫuy*[*a*]*z memal ḫaššungāizzi nu=ššan iš*⌈*ta*⌉*nā*⌈*ni*⌉ 3-*ŠU šu-uḫ-ḫa-a-i* $^{d}$*Kappariyamūi* 1-*ŠU ḫaššī ištarna pēdi* 1-*ŠU* $^{GIŠ}$*ḫalmaššuitti* 1-*ŠU* ⌈$^{GIŠ}$⌉*luttiya* 1-*ŠU* $^{GIŠ}$*ḫattaluwaš* GIŠ-*rui* 1-*ŠU namma ḫaššī tapušza* 1-*ŠU šu-uḫ-ḫa-a-i* "He sifts the coarsely ground meal through a basket and pours (it) on the altar three times. He (also) pours once on (an image of the god) Kappariyamu, once into the center of the hearth, once at the throne, once at the window, once on the door bolt, finally once to the side of the hearth" KUB 53.11 ii 16-21 (fest. for $^{d}$LAMMA, MS), ed. McMahon, AS 25:240f.; *ḫalmaššuit*(*ta*)/$^{GIŠ}$DAG "throne" KUB 10.11 iv 14-24 (NH), KUB 11.35 ii 23-25 (OH/NS), KUB 32.135 iv 4-6 (OH/MS); *ḫašša*-/GUNNI "hearth, brazier" KBo 13.213 i 8-11 (NS), KBo 30.59 ii 3-7 (NS), KBo 39.90 iv? 7-9 (NS), KUB 2.4 iv (5)-8, KUB 11.35 ii 23-25 (OH/NS); the interior of the hearth KUB 10.11 iv 13-14 (NS); to the side of the hearth KUB 32.135 iv 5-6 (OH/MS), KBo 13.213 i 10-11 (NS), KUB 11.35 ii 25 (OH/NS); $^{(GIŠ)}$*ḫat*(*t*)*alwaš* GIŠ(-*ru*) "door bolt" KBo 7.38 left col. 4-5 (OS), KBo 13.213 i 9-11 (NS), KBo 25.30:7-8 (NS), KBo 30.59 ii (5)-7 (NS), KBo 39.90 iv? (8-9) (NS), KUB 11.35 ii 24-25 (OH/NS), KUB 32.135 iv 5-6 (OH/MS); *ištanana*-/ZAG.GAR.RA "offering table, altar" KBo 13.213 i 7-11 (NS), KUB 11.35 ii 22-23 (OH/NS); *luttai*-/$^{GIŠ}$AB "window" KBo 21.80 i 11-12 (OH/MS), KBo 39.90 iv? 5-(9) (NS), KUB 10.11 iv 15-25 (NH), KUB 11.35 ii 24-25 (OH/NS), KUB 32.135 iv 5-6 (OH/MS); *taršanzipa*- KUB 2.4 iv 7-8 (OH/NS).

**7′** images of deities, deified objects, and (deceased) kings: [*AN*]*A* ALAM $^{m.GIŠ}$GIDRU.DINGIR-*LIM* 1-*ŠU* [*AN*]*A* ALAM $^{m}$*Dutḫaliya* 1-*ŠU* ⌈*A*⌉*NA* ALAM $^{m}$*Šuppiluliuma* 1-*ŠU šu-uḫ-ḫa-a-i* "He pours (the coarsely ground meal) once [o]n the image of Ḫattušili, once [o]n the image of Dutḫaliya, once on the image of Šuppiluliuma" KUB 10.11 iv 21-24 (offerings to royal images, NH); $^{d}$Ḫu[rtali(ya)] KBo 30.59 ii 2-7 (NS) (restoration follows KBo 20.100 rev.? 3, KBo 21.49 i 3, iii 11); $^{d}$Kappariyamu see previous section; $^{d}$*Kataḫzipuri* $^{GIŠ}$GIDRU.ḪI.A-*aš peran* 1-*ŠU šu-uḫ-ḫa-a-i* "He pours out once for Kataḫzipuri before the staffs" KUB 58.44 iii ? 4-6 (NS), Bo 4998 iv 9-11 (StBoT 26:367); $^{KUŠ}$*kurša*- "hunting bag" KUB 32.135 iv 4 (OH/NS); (image of)

ḪUR.SAG.MEŠ "mountains" KBo 39.90 iv? 9 (NS); [...M]U.ḪI.A-*aš peran* 1-*ŠU šu-uḫ-ḫa-i* "(S)he pours [...] once before the 'years'" KBo 25.30:8 (NS).

**8′** other things: *ḫappina-* "open flame" KUB 9.28 ii 7 (MH/NS); IZI "fire" KBo 11.32:13, 41 (OH/NS); NA4*paššila-/paššuela-* "pebble" KUB 59.54 obv. 6 (LNS), HKM 116 ii? 24 (NS); GIŠ*eya(n)*-(branches?) KUB 7.18:(5) (pre-NH/NS), w. dupl. KBo 17.54 iv 17 (pre-NH/MS); A.ŠÀ*mariyanī* "*m.*-field" KBo 10.37 iii (17), 21, 24-25 (OH/NS); TÚL "pond, spring" KBo 26.182 i 14 (NH); *ḫuppa/i-* "?": [...] x *U* GAL DUMU.MEŠ É.GAL *ANA* UGULA LÚ.MEŠ⌈Ú.ḪÚB⌉ *ḫū[ppi=šši]* / [*šu-uḫ-ḫa-a*]*n-zi memal šemeḫunan* UZUNÍG.GI[G ...] / [*ANA* UGULA L]Ú.MEŠÚ.ḪÚB *ḫūppi=šši šu-uḫ-ḫa-an-z*[*i*] "[The ...-man ?] and the chief of the palace attendants [pour...] into/onto the chief of the deaf men['s] *ḫ.* [Th]ey pour coarsely ground meal, *šemeḫuna*-food (and) live[r...into/onto the chief] of the deaf men's *ḫ.*" KUB 43.30 iii 15-17 (rit., OS), translit. Neu, StBoT 25:78 □ Starke, StBoT 23:78-80, and Neu, StBoT 26:72 with n. 298, suggest *ḫuppi-* is the same word as DUG*ḫuppi-*. Neu calls it "ein Gefäß." However, *ḫ.* has no DUG determinative in the passage above, making this identification uncertain.

**e.** associated preverbs, postpositions, or adverbs — **1′** *anda*: KUB 9.28 ii 10-11 (MH/NS) (a 3′), KBo 31.216:(6) (NS?); (with *-kan*): KBo 2.3 iv 3 (a 1′ b′ 5″), KBo 39.8 ii 56-57 (2Mašt.), iii 24 (a 1′ a′ 3″), iv 22-23 (a 1′ b′ 8″), KBo 47.35 rev. 9 (MS).

**2′** *āppa*: [...-*t*]*a šūḫza āppa* DINGIR.LÚ.MEŠ *šu-u*[*ḫ*-...] KUB 43.30 iii 18 (fest., OS), translit. StBoT 25:78.

**3′** *arḫa*: KBo 11.14 i 7, KBo 13.199:8 (NS), KBo 15.10 ii 12, iii 54-55 (a 1′ b′ 4″), KUB 27.67 iii 47 (a 1′ b′ 6″), KUB 58.106 ii! 11 (NS), VBoT 24 ii 8 (a 1′ a′ 3″).

**4′** *katta* (with *-šan*): KUB 9.6 i 2-3 (a 1′ a′ 3″).

**5′** *kattan*: IBoT 3.1 obv. 25 (OH/NS) (a 1′ a′ 3″), KBo 10.24 iv 27-28 (OH/NS), KBo 30.6:6 (MS?).

**6′** GAM-*anda*: KBo 26.182 i 14 (d 8′).

**7′** *parā*: KUB 11.31 i 23 (a 1′ b′ 7″).

**8′** *peran*: KBo 25.30:8 (d 7′), KBo 30.59 ii 4-7 (d 7′), KUB 10.11 iv 8-9 (d 7′), KUB 53.10 rev. 8, KUB 58.44 iii? 5-6 (d 7′), Bo 4998 iv 10-11 (StBoT 26:367) (d 7′).

**9′** *peran katta*: IBoT 4.343:(7-8) (a 1′ a′ 3″), KUB 58.1 i 11-12 (a 1′ a′ 3″), KUB 58.4 v 21-22 (a 1′ a′ 3″).

**10′** *šer*: KUB 6.45 iv 16, 21, 26-27, 54, 57-58 (d 4′), KUB 6.46 i 43, 48, 51, 56, 60, 64 (a 1′ a′ 3″); (w. *-kan*): KBo 64.164:9-10 (NS), KBo 5.2 ii 19-20 (d 4′), KUB 6.45 iv 11-12 (d 4′); (w. *-šan*): KBo 11.14 i 20 (a 1′ a′ 3″), KBo 19.128 iii 22-23 (a 1′ a′ 1″), KUB 2.13 i 26, 42, ii 60 (OH/NS), KUB 32.135 iv 3-4 (OH/MS), KUB 58.4 v 17-18 (d 5′); (w. *ANA*): KBo 5.2 ii 41 (a 1′ a′ 2″); (w. *INA*): KBo 11.14 i 4-5 (a 1′ a′ 3″), KUB 7.18:5 (a 1′ b′ 2″), KUB 9.6 i 14-15 (d 3′), KUB 59.54 obv. 6 (a 1′ b′ 9″).

**11′** *tapušza*: KBo 13.213 i (10)-11 (d 6′), KUB 11.35 ii 25 (d 6′), KUB 32.135 iv 5-6 (d 6′), KUB 34.117:4 (NS), KUB 53.11 ii 21 (d 6′).

The verb appears frequently without any particle or with *-kan*, or *-šan*, but very rarely with *-ašta* (KBo 37.1 obv.1-2, see a 1′ a′ 8″).

Friedrich, HW (1952) 196 ("schütten"); Güterbock, Oriens 15 (1962) 349 n. 1; Oettinger, Stammbildung (1979) 60f., 503 w. n. 18; Boysan-Dietrich, THeth 12 (1987) 41; Melchert, AHP (1994) 58, 169, 170 (specifies the meaning as "pour"); Tischler, HEG S (2006) 1130-1135; Kloekhorst, EDHIL (2008) 773-774 ("scatter").

Cf. *išḫuwa-*, *šuḫḫuwai-*.

**šuḫḫešḫu[...]** (mng. unkn.); OS.†

*šu-uḫ-ḫe-eš-ḫu-*[...] KBo 25.102 rev.? 4 (OS).

In a broken context dealing with religious matters: [*š*]*u*(?)*ḫḫan* x[...] / [...]x *šu-uḫ-ḫe-eš-ḫu-*[...] KBo 25.102 rev.? 3-4. Neu, StBoT 25:177 n. 594, proposes a restoration of *šuḫḫešḫu*[*n*] or *šuḫḫešḫw*[*eni*].

**šuḫmili-** adj.; firm, rigid; from OH/MS.

**sg. nom. com.** *šu-uḫ-mi-li-iš* KUB 43.23 rev. 13, 17 (MS), KBo 10.37 iii 1 (OH/NS), KUB 9.28 iii (24) (MH/NS), KBo 38.58 rev.? (6) (NS), KBo 61.17:9 (NS), *šu-u-uḫ-mi-li-iš* KBo 19.132 rev.? 11 (MH/NS), *šu-uḫ-mi-li*!⟨-*iš*⟩ or *šu-uḫ-mi*-⟨*li*-⟩*iš*! KBo 13.156 obv. 11 (OH/NS).

**acc. com.** ? *šu-uḫ-mi-li-*˹*in*˺ (sic) KBo 10.37 ii 33 (OH/NS).

**dat.-loc.** *šu-uḫ-mi-li* KUB 43.23 rev. 57 (MS), KBo 10.37 iii 7 (OH/NS), KBo 13.121:(4) (OH/NS), KBo 13.156 obv. (8) (OH/NS).

**a.** referring to the earth or a deified "genius" of the earth: *šu-uḫ-mi-li-iš dankuiš daganzip*[*aš taknāšš=a*(?)] ˹$^{d}$˺[UTU-*uš*(?)] *uwatten* $^{d}$IM-*naš* ˹EZEN$_4$˺-*ni nu=za ēz*[*zatten*] *ekutten nu šer katt*[*a*] *nēpišza* $^{d}$˹IM˺(?)-*aš* LUGAL-*i* [*āššu*] *ḫuišwatar miyatar tar*˹*ḫ*˺*uili* $^{GIŠ}$*tūri piški*[*ddu*] *katta šarā=ma taknāz šu-uḫ-mi-li-iš ta*˺*ganzi*˹*p*˺*aš taknāšš=a* $^{d}$UTU-*uš ANA* LUGAL *āššu ḫuišwatar tarḫuili* $^{GIŠ}$*tūri piškiddu* "(You), firm (and) dark geniu[s] of the earth [and Sungoddess of the Earth(?)] come to the festival of the Stormgod. Eat, drink! Dow[n] from the sky above [let] the Stormgod(?) give to the king [goodness,] life, growth, (and) a victorious spear. Up from the earth below let the firm genius of the earth and the Sungoddess of the Earth give to the king goodness, life, (and) a victorious spear" KUB 43.23 rev. 13-22 (blessings on Labarna, MS), ed. Archi, FsMeriggi$^2$ 34, Haas, FsOtten$^2$ 134f.; cf. also [*šu-u*]*ḫ-mi-li-iš* in KBo 38.58 rev.? 6 (NS; dupl. or par. to KUB 43.23 rev. 17) which is listed in KBo 38 Indices, p. xv, under "Götternamen"; 1 NINDA.GUR$_4$.RA [*gullanten*] *šu-uḫ-mi-li* GE$_6$-*i* KI-*pi paršiya* "He breaks one [*gullanti*]-thick bread for the firm (and) dark earth" KBo 10.37 iii 6-7 (rit. against curse, OH/NS), w. dupl. KBo 13.121:3-4 and par. KBo 13.156 obv. 8 (both OH/NS), ed. Catsanicos, BSL 81/1:128 ("bien fixée"); ˹3˺ NINDA.GUR$_4$.RA ˹*gul.*˺ 1 GAL GEŠTIN 1 ŠAḪ.TUR *ANA* KI *šu-uḫ-mi-li taknaš* $^{d}$UTU-*i pera(n)=ššitt=a kuiēš ueḫan*˹*ta*˺ "three crumbled(?) thick-breads, one cup of wine, one piglet for the firm earth (and for) the Sungoddess of the Earth and (for those) who are circling in front of her" KUB 43.23 rev. 56-61 (blessings on Labarna, MS) □ given the adj. *gullanti-* appearing with NINDA.GUR$_4$.RA in KBo 13.156 obv. 7, 8 we provisionally take the sign GUL here as an abbreviation for *gullanti-* (cf. $^{NINDA}$*wa* for $^{NINDA}$*wageššar*); reading Sumerographically GUL ("broken, crumbled" for *walḫant-*?) or GIR$_4$ w. Kloekhorst, EDHIL 775, seems less attractive.

**b.** referring to the knee: (The gods are asked to bestow on a child virile abilities:) *nu=šš*[*i*] ˹*ḫa*˺*š*˹*taliy*˺[*atar*] *pešten nu=šši išḫunauwa*˹*r*˺ *šiyauwa*˹*r*˺ *pešten nu=šši šu-uḫ-mi-li-*˹*in*˺(sic) *gēnu pešten* "Give hi[m] val[or], give him shooting power (lit. power (and) shooting"), give him a firm knee" KBo 10.37 ii 31-33 (rit. against curse, OH/NS), ed. StBoT 48:194f. ("gutgefügtes/festes"), Kloekhorst, EDHIL 775 ("knee (and/with) *šuḫmili-*"), Haroutunian, FsHoffner 154, 160 ("fir[m]"), Güterbock, FsAlp 239 ("firm"), Catsanicos, BSL 81/1:147f. ("bien fixé (> ferme)," Oettinger, MSS 35:93 ("Pfeil") □ there seems to be a lack of gender concord between neut. noun *genu-* and com. adj. *šuḫmilin* (acc.); this might have been caused by indecision on the part of the scribe since *genu-* in Hittite occurs in both com. and neut. genders (compare Kloekhorst, EDHIL 467); for another explanation see Catsanicos, BSL 81/1:147 n. 154 (*šuḫmilin* < **šuḫmiliyan* sg. nom.-acc. neut. of **šuḫmiliyant-*), followed by Christiansen, StBoT 48:242.

**c.** referring to a drinking straw/tube: 2 $^{DUG}$*KUKUB* ŠÀ.BA *INA* 1 $^{DUG}$GUR$_4$.GUR$_4$-*BI* (var. [*IN*]*A* 1 $^{DUG}$*KUKUBI*) *akuwannaš paršuil šūš* 1 GI [(*š*)]*u-uḫ-mi-li-iš* (var. *šu-u-uḫ-mi-li-iš*) *tarnanza* "(There are) two pitchers: among these, in one pitcher for drinking, full (of) *paršuil*, a firm (or: rigid) drinking straw is inserted" KUB 9.28 iii 22-24 (rit. for Heptad, MH/NS), w. dupl. KBo 19.132 rev.? 10-11 (MH/NS), ed. *šūu-* b, differently BSL 81/1:153, *paršuil* □ for the reading $^{DUG}$GUR$_4$.GUR$_4$-*BI* instead of $^{DUG}$ḪAB.ḪAB KAŠ, see Weeden, StBoT 54:242. Contra the interpretation of *š.* as "arrow" by Laroche, OLZ 57:30f., and Oettinger, Stammbildung 155 n. 42 (cf. also Oettinger, MSS 35:93), the word is not a noun but, following Hoffner, apud Güterbock, FsAlp 239f. n. 18, modifies the preceding GI "reed," which, according to the context, means "drinking straw/tube." Not one of the occurrences of *šuḫmili-* mentioned above fits a meaning "arrow."

Laroche, OLZ 57 (1962) 30f. ("une des lectures possibles du sumérogramme GI 'roseau, flèche'"); Kronasser, EHS 1 (1962) 213 (= GI "Rohr, Pfeil"); Friedrich, HW 3.Erg. (1966) 29 ("Rohr"); Oettinger, MSS 35 (1976) 93; idem, Stammbildung (1979) 155 n. 42, 550 ("Pfeil"); Archi, FsMeriggi$^2$ (1979) 27 n. 4 ("freccia"), 34 ("vigoroso"); Tischler, HDW (1982) 77 ("Rohr; Pfeil"); Weitenberg, U-Stämme (1984) 38 ("Pfeil"); Melchert, Anatolian Phonology (1984) 98 ("firmly planted"); Catsanicos, BSL 81/1 (1986) 121-180 ("bien fixé"); Eichner, Sprache 32 (1986) 456; Haas, FsOtten$^2$ (1988) 135 n. 56; Hoffner apud Güterbock, FsAlp (1992) 239; Tischler, HEG S/2 (2006) 1135-36 (adj. "'fest' (Erde), 'stark' (Knie), 'kräftig' (Trinkrohr)"); Kloekhorst, EDHIL (2008) 774-777.

**LÚšuḫpili-** n. com.; (mng. unkn., a cult functionary?).†

**sg. acc.** [...]*šu-uḫ-pí-li-in* KUB 51.63 rev. 6 (NS).
**pl.** LÚ.MEŠ*šu-uḫ-*⸢*pí*⸣-[...] KUB 51.63 rev. 8 (NS).

[...]*šu-uḫ-pí-li-in* x-x[...] / [... *e*]*kuzi* 3 NINDA.GUR$_4$.RA *par*[*ši-*...] / [...] LÚ.MEŠ*šu-uḫ-*⸢*pí*⸣-[...] KUB 51.63 rev. 6-8 (NS), translit. DBH 15:101. Because of lacking word space LÚ.MEŠ seems to function as a det.; differently, Kloekhorst, EDHIL 777, who reads G[E$_6$(?) in line 6 and connects *š.* with *šuḫmili-* q.v. because of the combination *šuḫmili- dankui-*/GE$_6$*-i- daganzipa-* "the dark earth."

Cf. *šuḫmili-*.

**[*šuḫruḫḫuwatra-*]** KUB 12.1 iv 9 (NH), thus read by Košak, Linguistica 18:101, 105, and Siegelová, Verw. 446f., is to be analyzed as Akk. *ŠU-UḪ-RU* (cf. CAD Š Part III 368, Siegelová, Verw. 318f.) and Luw. *aḫ-ḫu-u-wa-at-ra*, for which see Starke, StBoT 31:509 w. n. 1875, CLL 5, building on a suggestion by Košak, THeth 10:46.

**šuḫda** (mng. unkn.); NS.†

**unclear** *šu-uḫ-da* KUB 43.36:7 (OH/NS).

[...]x KI.MIN *šu-uḫ-da maḫḫan wa-*[...] KUB 43.36:7 (myth. frag.?, OH/NS), translit. Rieken et al., hethiter.net/:CTH370.I.76 (TX 2009-08-26). Since *š.* follows KI.MIN "ditto," there is a good chance that *š.* is the first word of a new sentence and probably a noun. In this case, *maḫḫan* could be a postposition "like."

**šuḫḫuwai-** v.; to pour; NS.†

**pres. sg. 3** *šu-uḫ-ḫu-wa-i* KBo 30.115 ii! 5 (NS).

§ [...*ḫašš*]⸢*ī*⸣ 3-*ŠU šu-uḫ-ḫu-wa-i* "Three times s/he pours [...] at/on the [hearth]" KBo 30.115 ii! 5 (fest., NS), translit. DBH 2:161.

With Kloekhorst, EDHIL 773, *š.* could be a hybrid form of the near-synonymous verbal forms *šu-uḫ-ḫa-i* and *iš-ḫu-wa-i* "he/she pours"; one could also consider influence from *la*(*ḫ*)*ḫuwai-*, q.v.

Kloekhorst, EDHIL 773.

Cf. *šuḫḫa-* C, *išḫuwai-*.

**šuḫulzina(i)-** v.; (to have a particular symptom); NH.†

**pres. sg. 3** *šu-ḫu-ul-zi-na-a-i* KUB 8.36 iii 5 (NH).

In a medicinal text mentioned in a tablet catalog *š.* is specified among sicknesses and physical anomalies of human beings: *mān antuḫšaš šu-ḫu-ul-zi-na-a-i* [...?] *našma⸗an SU'ĀLU ēpzi* "If a person *š.*-s, or a cough sizes him" KUB 8.36 iii 5-6 (shelf list, NH), ed. StBoT 47:226f. ("Schluckauf?"), StBoT 19:38f. ("Schluckauf?"), CTH pp. 189f. ("hoquet(?)" = "hiccup").

Because of its appearance along with Akk. *SU'ĀLU* "cough," *š.* should describe a similar action such as "to sneeze," "to have the hiccups" or "to snore." The final element *-zina*(*i*) is reminiscent of the verb **ḫulpanzina*(*i*)- "to emboss(?)," attested in the Luwian part. *ḫulpanzinaim/i-*, cf. Melchert, CLL 72, Puhvel, HED 3:425. The first element *šuḫul-* could be onomatopoetic.

Laroche, CTH (1971) 189f. ("hoquet(?)"); Burde, StBoT 19 (1974) 38f. ("Schluckauf?"); Haas, OLZ 97 (2002) 509 ("Schluckauf haben"; "Abgeleitet scheint das Verbum von akkadisch *su'ālu* 'Verschleimung, Husten' zu sein"), idem, Materia (2003) 61; Tischler, HEG S (2006) 1138 (*suhulzina-* "an einer bestimmten Krankheit leiden, 'Schluckauf haben'?"); Dardano, StBoT 47 (2006) 230.

**šuḫunniešš[a?... ]** n., Hurr; (mng. unkn.); NS.†

**unclear** *šu-ḫu-un-ni-eš-š*[*a*?] KUB 27.7:6 (rit. frag., NS); here? *šu-ḫ*[*u-*...] KUB 27.34 iii 11 (rit. frag., NS).

Mentioned among bread offerings: [... 1? NINDA.GUR$_4$.RA⸗*y*]*a paršiya* EGIR-*ŠU⸗ma* x[...] / [...]x ⸢EGIR⸣-*ŠU⸗ma šu-ḫu-un-ni-eš-š*[*a*? ...] / [... *š*]*ipanti* 1 NINDA.GUR$_4$.RA⸗*ya paršiy*[*a*] KUB 27.7:5-7 (frag. of Kizzuwatna rit., NS); cf. also 1 NINDA.SIG⸗*ma šu-ḫ*[*u-*...] KUB 27.34 iii 11 (NS).

Laroche, GLH 240, lists *š.* under *šuḫunni-* along w. *šu-ḫu-un-na* VBoT 50:4 (NS) and *šu-u-ḫu-un-na-ši* KBo 12.80 iv 4 (LNS) which occur in pure Hurrian contexts, for which see Wegner, ChS I/3-3:61 ("*šuḫni/šuḫuni* 'Wand, Mauer'"). For *šuḫunni-* attested at Nuzi and Elam, see also CAD Š/3:210 and BibGlHurr 405.

Laroche, GLH (1979) 240.

**šuḫurribi** Hurr. gen.; "of life"; (used adjectivally as an epithet of the Stormgod (Teššub) in Hitt. religious contexts); written syll., Sum. TI(-*bi*); NH.†

**Hurr. sg. gen.** *šu-ḫur-ri-bi* KUB 6.45 i 39 (Muw. II), KUB 6.46 ii (5) (Muw. II), *šu-u-ḫu-ur-ri-wi$_i$* KBo 30.183:6 (NS), TI-*bi* KBo 14.142 i 3 (NS), Bo 6030 iii 8 (apud Haas, Or NS 68:138), TI KBo 7.27:2 (NS).

**here? in Hurr. context:** *šu-ku-úr-ri-wi$_i$* KBo 20.119 vi 7 (MS?).

(Sum.) BE = (Akk.) *balāṭu* = (Hurr.) *šuḫ*[*uri*] = (Ugar.) *ḥiyyūma* RS Quad. 137 i 20, ed. Ugaritica 5:240f., 456f.; (Hurr.) *šuḫurni* = (Ugar.) *ḥiyyūma* RS Quad. 131:6, cf. GLH 240 s.v. *šuḫur*.

dUTU *ŠAMĒ* dUTU URUTÚL-*na* dU URUTÚL-*na* d*Mizzullaš* d*Ḫullaš* DINGIR.MUNUS *Zindu*⌈*ḫi*⌉*yaš* DINGIR.LÚ.MEŠ DINGIR.MUNUS.MEŠ ḪUR.SAG.ME.EŠ ÍD.MEŠ *ŠA* URU*Arinna* dU *eḫellipi* dU *šu-ḫur-ri-bi* "Sungod of Heaven, Sungoddess of Arinna, Stormgod of Arinna, Mizzulla, Ḫulla, Goddess Zinduḫiya, male gods, female gods, mountains (and) rivers of Arinna, Stormgod of Salvation, Stormgod of Life" KUB 6.45 i 37-39 (prayer, Muw. II), w. dupl. KUB 6.46 ii 2-5, ed. Singer, MuwPr 10, 33; cf. also: [... d?]⌈IM?⌉-*an šu-u-ḫu-ur-ri-wi$_i$ irḫāizz*[*i*] / [... LÚ.MEŠBAL]AG SÌR-*RU* "He/she makes the rounds of [... Stormgo]d(?) of Life. [... The players of the BAL]AG-instrument make music" KBo 30.183:6-7 (Hurr.-Hitt. rit., NS); note the divine name d*Šu-ḫu-ri-bi* "(the God) of Life" IBoT 2.58:5 (NS); cf. possibly in unilingual Hurr. context: dU-*ub šu-ku-úr-ri-wi$_i$* KBo 20.119 vi 7 (MS?), translit. Wegner, ChS I/3-2:220 □ Trémouille, AOAT 337:200 n. 23 takes -*ku*- as scribal error for -*ḫu*-.

Laroche, GLH (1979) 240 s.v. *šuḫuri* "vie"; Bawanypeck, BoHa 23 (2011) 74; Richter, BibGlHurr (2012) 402-403 s.v. *šuḫ*- 1.

Cf. *šubri-, šuburribi.*

**šu-ú-⌈e⌉[(-)** KBo 3.7 ii 11 see *šu-ú-*⌈*ga/e*⌉[(-)...].

**šuwe-, šuwai- C, šuwiye-** v.; **1.** to shove off, push off (physically), **2.** to shove off, push off (figuratively), divorce, disown, drive out, banish, forfeit, expel, **3.** to push oneself, to especially exert oneself; from OS.†

[**pres. sg. 1** *šu-e-*[*mi*] KUB 26.77 i 11 (OH/NS), restore instead *šu-e-*[*et*], for the rejection of the restoration *šu-e-*[*mi*] see 2 e 1′].

**pres. sg. 3** *šu-ú-ez-zi* KBo 6.2 iv 48 (OS), KBo 6.3 ii (52), iv 58 (OH/NS), KBo 16.25 iv 5 (MH/MS), *šu-ú-*[*ez-zi*] KUB 26.56 ii 4 (OH/MS), *šu-ú-e-ez-*[*zi*] KBo 19.4 iv 6 (OH/NS), *šu-ú-i-e-ez-zi* KUB 8.81 iii 7 (MH/MS), *šu-ú-i-ez-zi* KBo 6.26 ii 4 (OH/NS), *šu-wa-a-iz-zi* KBo 6.5 ii (2), iv (13) (OH/NS), KBo 6.13 i 14 (OH/NS), KBo 12.49 ii (11) (OH/NS), KUB 29.19:7 (OH/NS), *šu-ú-wa-iz-*[*zi*] KBo 9.69 + KBo 69.80:6 (OH/NS?), *šu-wa-ya-zi* KBo 6.5 iv 15 (OH/NS) (formally this form is similar to the pres.sg.3 of *šuwaye-* "to look").

**pl. 1** *šu-wa-u-e-ni* KUB 12.63 obv. 29 (OH/MS).

**pl. 3** *šu-wa-an-zi* KUB 13.7 i 7 (MH/NS), KBo 13.92:13 (NS), *šu-ú-i-ya-an-zi* KUB 23.52:9 (NS).

**pret. sg. 1** *šu-wa-nu-un* KUB 24.14 i 20 (NH).

**sg. 3** *šu-ú-e-et* KBo 32.14 ii 2 (MH/MS), *šu-e-*[*et*] KUB 26.77 i 11 (OH/NS), *šu-ú-et* KBo 16.25 i 68 (MH/MS), *šu-u-wa-it* KUB 18.3 left col. 19 (NH).

**pl. 2** *šu-wa-at-te-en* KUB 4.1 ii 13, 18 (MH/NS).

**pl. 3** *šu-ú-er* KUB 36.105:4 (OH/MS), VBoT 33:(6) (OH/NS), *šu-wa-a-er* KBo 22.103:2 (NS?).

**imp. sg. 3** *šu-wa-a-id-du* KUB 24.10 iii (12) (MH/NS), KBo 52.26 iii 22 (also published as KUB 24.11 iii 10) (MH/NS).

**pl. 2** [*š*]*u-wa-at-tén* KUB 41.8 iv 27 (MH/NS), *šu-wa-a-at-tén* KBo 10.45 iv 28 (MH/NS), *šu-u-wa-at-tén* KBo 4.2 i 15 (pre-NH/NS).

**pl. 3** *šu-u-wa-an-du* KBo 4.2 i 68, 70 (pre-NH/NS), *šu-wa-an-du* KBo 10.45 iv 1 (MH/NS), *šu-ú-wa-an-d*[*u*?] KBo 22.107 i 17 (NH).

**mid. pret. sg. 3** *šu-ú-wa-at-ta* KBo 42.6:3 (pre-NH/NS).

[**imp. pl. 2** *šu-wa-an-du-ma-at* KBo 10.45 iv 1 (MH/NS), analyze as *šu-wa-an-du*=*ma*=*at*].

*š.* originally had an alternating stem in *e/a* but shifted to an -*āi*- stem in NH. Hence we find forms like *šu-wa-a-iz-zi, šu-u-wa-it* (-*āi*- class) besides original *šu-ú-ez-zi, šu-ú-e-et* (-*e/a*- class). The pres. sg. 3 *šu-wa-ya-zi* (KBo 6.5 iv 15) is probably a hypercorrection due to the collapse of *šuwaye-* "to look" (s.v.) and *š.* into *šuwai-/šuwā-*.

(Hurr.) *na-a-li i-te-*[*e*]*-*⌈*i*⌉*-ni-eš pa-pa-an-ni-iš me-la-aḫ-ḫu-un* KBo 32.14 i 1-2 = (Hitt.) *ali*⌈*ya*⌉*n*[*an*]=*za apēl tuēgga*[*z*=*šet*] ḪUR.SAG-*aš awan arḫa šu-ú-e-et* "A mountain expelled a deer from its body" KBo 32.14 ii 1-2 (Hurro-Hitt. bil. wisdom and myth, MH/MS), ed. Neu, StBoT 32:74f.

**1.** "to shove, push off (physically)" — **a.** without prev./adv.: *takku* LÚ-*aš* GUD.ḪI.A ÍD-*an zēnuškizzi tamāiš=a=an šu-wa-*[*a*]*-iz-zi* (var. B: *šu-*⸢*ú*-⸣[...]) *nu* KUN GUD *ēpzi ta* ÍD-*an zāi nu* EN GUD ÍD-*aš pēdāi šu-wa-ya-zi=ma=an kuiš* (vars. A, B Ø) *nu=za apūn=pat dāi* (var. A&B: *nu=zza apūn=pat dan*[(*zi*)]) "If a man is bringing his oxen across a river, and another man pushes him off, grasps the tail of the ox, and crosses the river, but the river carries off the owner of the ox, (the dead man's heir) shall take that (man) who pushes(!) him off (var. A&B: They (i.e., the heirs) shall take that (man))" KBo 6.5 iv 12-15 (Laws §43, OH/NS), w. dupls. KBo 6.2 ii 30-32 (OS) (var. A), KBo 6.3 ii 52-53 (OH/NS) (var. B), ed. LH 51f. □ *šuwayazi*(*=ma=an kuiš*) in KBo 6.5 iv 15 is only present in the new Hittite copy and is similar to the pres. sg. 3 of the verb *šuwaye-* "to look" (s.v. *šuwaye-*). It is probably a hypercorrection due to the collapse of both verbs into *šuwai-/šuwā-*. The correct form *šuwāizzi* appears earlier in the same passage, in iv 13.

**b.** w. *āppanda* "to push from behind," opp. of *parā ḫuittiya-* "to pull forth": (addressing the gods of the Underworld: "a beer-vessel(?) for drinking is emptied out for you") *n=an*(var. *=aš*)*=šan* ḪUL-⸢*ui*⸣ *papranni li*[(*nkiy*)]*a wašduli išḫan*⸢*ī*⸣ *ḫ*⸢*u*⸣*rtiya ḫa*⸢*pput*⸣*ri ḫameinkaddu* (var. *ḫaminkandu*) *n=at ap*⸢*iya*⸣ *parā ḫūittiyaddu šumeš=ma=at* ⸢EGIR-*ant*⸣*a šu-wa-a-at-tén* (var. EGIR-*and*[*a š*]*u-wa-at-tén*) "Let them tie it as a(n ox-)harness on to evil, impurity, perjury, sin, bloodshed, curse. Let it pull them (i.e., the evils) forth to there (where you are). And you, (gods), may you push them from behind" KBo 10.45 iv 25-28 (rit. for the Underworld, MH/NS), w. dupl. KUB 41.8 iv 24-27 (MH/NS), ed. Otten, ZA 54:136f. ("ihr aber, stoßt es hinter euch"), tr. Miller, TUAT NF 4:216 ("Ihr aber sollt sie hinten anschieben"), Collins, CoS 1:171 ("and may you push them from behind"); [*n=a*]*t*? DINGIR.MEŠ URU-*LIM* x[...] ⸢EGI⸣R-*an šu-wa-an-du=ma=at nu* $GE_6$-*iš* KI-*aš l*[(*aga*(*n*)*=šmit*)] *arḫa* (dupl. Ø) *ēp* "[Let] the gods of the city [take?] them (i.e., the evils), and let them push them from behind. O dark earth, seize their inclination(?) (and swallow up the murder, sin etc. of the house (and) city)" KBo 10.45 iii 69-iv 2 (rit. for the underworld, MH/NS), w. dupl. KUB 41.8 iv 1 (MH/NS), ed. Otten, ZA 54:134f. (*šu-wa-an-du-ma-at* as a mid. imp. pl. 2 "stoßt von euch!"), Neu, StBoT 5:160 ("Fälschliche Nasalierung"; w. Otten), Tischler, HEG S/2:1222, tr. Collins CoS 1:171 ("push yourselves back!") □ *šu-wa-an-du-ma-at* is usually analyzed as a middle, with nasal anticipation instead of *šu-wa-ad-du-ma-at*, see Melchert, AHP 172. Kronasser, EHS 1:474 w. n. 3 parsed *šuwandu=ma=at*, under the assumption that the mid. of *šuwe-* "to push" was not attested, but see now *šu-ú-wa-at-ta* in KBo 42.6:3. This would lead to "O gods of the city, hold yourselves behind [...]." However, the *-at* in KBo 10.45 iii 69 points at an enclitic object, which is incompatible with the middle. Despite the odd placement of the clitics, ⸢EGIR⸣-*an šu-wa-an-du=ma=at* needs to be understood as a complete sentence; ("Then the statues say: 'Bring (the sorcery). We will carry (it) away.' Let the man dress (them?) and let him put it on their feet. Let him guard it. Let him carry it away"§) [(*ḫaḫḫar*)]*it* (var. adds *=at*) EGIR-*anda ḫaḫḫariyaddu* [$^{GIŠ}$(*intalu*)]*zzit* EGIR-*anda šu-wa-a-id-du* [*mar*]*iḫšiwalit=ma=at* SÍG-*nit* UGU ⸢*ā*⸣*nšan ēšdu* "Let him rake it with the rake from behind. Let him shove (it) with the shovel(?) from behind. Let it be wiped up with uncarded(?) wool" KBo 52.26 iii 21-24 (Alli's rit., MH/NS), w. dupls. KBo 12.127 + KUB 24.9 iii 18-19, KBo 21.8 iii 1-2, KUB 24.10 iii 11-13 (all MH/NS), ed. THeth 2:44f. (differently: "mit der Schaufel füllen"), Mouton, FsBeckman 215, 227 ("qu'il remplisse"), cf. HEG S/2:1220 ("mit der Schaufel soll er füllen") □ for *šu-wa-a-id-du* as imp. sg. 3 of "to push" instead of "to fill," see Kloekhorst, EDHIL 797. This passage describes the different ways in which the sorcery is to be collected and removed (i.e., carrying away, *š.*, raking, wiping up). Treating the sorcery as a container and filling it with an unknown substance does not contribute to the sorcery's removal. For *šūwa-* "to fill" with an *intaluzzi* "shovel," see KBo 25.184 iii 58-60 (s.v. *šū-* B, *šūwa-* e). Cf. s.v. *šarā* B 4 for the improved reading UGU *anš-* "to wipe up."

**2.** "to push off (figuratively), divorce, disown, forfeit, expel, drive out, banish — **a.** with *-za* "shove, push off from one's own family" — **1′** without prev./adv. "to divorce (a spouse)": [(*takku=za* MUNUS-*za* LÚ)]-⸢*an*⸣ *šu-wa-a-*[*iz-zi* (var. *m*[*immai*]) *nu=šši* LÚ-*aš*...(*pāi*)] [(*U ŠA* NUMUN.ḪI.A-*aš k*)]*uššan* [MUNUS-*za dāi*] [... (DUMU)].MEŠ*=ya=za* LÚ-*aš d*[*āi*] "If a woman divorces (var. re[fuses]) a man, the man shall give to her [...], and [the woman shall take] a wage for her offspring. [...] But the man shall take the [child]ren for himself" KBo 12.49 ii 11-13 (Laws §26a, OH/NS), w. dupl. KUB 26.56 ii 1-3 (MS), ed. LH 35; *takk*[*u*⸗ *za* LÚ-*š*⸗*a* MUNUS-*an*] *šu-wa-*⌈*a*⌉-[*iz-z*(*i*) (par. *šu-ú-*[*ez-zi*])] "I[f, on the other hand, a man] divorc[es a woman]" KBo 6.5 ii 2 (Laws §26c, OH/NS), w. dupl. KBo 6.3 i 71, w. restorations from par. KUB 26.56 ii 4 (§26b, MS), ed. LH 35.

**2′** w. *parā* and *-kan* "to disown (a child)": *takku annaš* DUMU.NITA-*i*⸗*šši* TÚG⸗*SU edi nāi nu*⸗*za*⸗*kan* DUMU⸗*ŠU parā šu-wa-a-iz-zi* (var. *šu-ú-i-ez-zi*) "If a mother removes her son's garment, she disowns her son. (If her son comes back into her house, (s)he takes her door leaf and removes it, (s)he takes her ... and ... and removes them, and places them back, she makes her son her son again)" KBo 6.13 i 13-14 (Laws §171, OH/NS), w. dupl. KBo 6.26 ii 3-4 (OH/NS), ed. LH 137 and s.v. *nai-* 9 c.

**b.** without *-za* "to expel from one's ownership > to forfeit (a slave)" — **1′** without prev./adv. (OH): ("If a slave burglarizes a house, he shall give back precisely in full value. He shall pay six shekels of silver for the theft. He shall cut (off) the slave's nose and ears, and they will give him back to his owner (...)") [*takku B*(*ĒL*⸗*Š*)]⌈*U te*⌉*zzi šēr*⸗ *šit*⸗*wa* ⌈*šarnik*⌉*mi nu šarnikz*[*i takku mi*(*mmai*⸗*ma nu*)] ⌈ÌR-*an*⸗*pat*⌉ *šu-ú-ez-zi* (var. P: *šu-wa-a-iz-*⌈*zi*⌉, Y: *šu-ú-wa-iz-*[*zi*]) "[If h]is [o]wner says 'I will make compensation for him' then he shall make compensation. [But if he r]efuses, he shall forfeit that aforementioned slave" KBo 6.2 iv 47-48 (Laws §95, OS), w. dupls. KBo 6.3 iv 46-47 (NS), KUB 29.19:6-7 (var. P), KBo 9.69 + KBo 69.80:5-6 (var. Y, NS), ed. LH 93f.; ("If a slave sets fire to a house, his owner shall make compensation for him, and they shall cut (off) the slave's nose and ears and return him to his owner") *takku U*⌈*L*⌉⸗*ma šarnikzi* ⌈*nu ap*⌉*ūn*⸗*pat* ⌈*šu-ú-ez*⌉*-zi* (var. *šu-ú-e-ez-*[*zi*]) "But if (the owner) does not make compensation, he shall forfeit that aforementioned slave" KBo 6.3 iv 57-58 (Laws §99, OH/NS), w. dupls. KBo 19.4 iv 5-6 (NS), KBo 6.2 iv 58 (OS), KBo 19.5:3 (NS), ed. LH 96f.

**2′** w. *parā* (MH): ("If a slave conceals a fugitive, and his owner does not give compensation for him, then he will not give twelve persons §") *mān*⸗*ši*⸗*kan BĒL*⸗*ŠU*! *šer UL šarnikzi nu* ÌR⸗*pat parā šu-ú-i-e-ez-zi* "If his owner does not give compensation for him, he shall forfeit that aforementioned slave" KUB 8.81 iii 6-7 (Šunaššura treaty, MH/MS), ed. Götze, ZA 36:12f., Petschow, ZA 55:243, Del Monte, OA 20:217f., tr. DiplTexts² 25f.

**c.** w. *awan arḫa* "to expel from a body" (synonymous w. *parḫ-* 2 b, q.v.) — **1′** w. *-za*, w. abl. and without sentence particle, "expel from one's own body": *ali*⌈*ya*⌉*n*[*an*]⸗*za apēl tuēgga*[*z*⸗*šet*] ḪUR.SAG-*aš awan arḫa šu-ú-e-et* "A mountain expelled a deer from [its] own body" KBo 32.14 ii 1-2 (Hurro-Hitt. bil. wisdom and myth, MH/MS), ed. Neu, StBoT 32:75, cf. bil. sec. above.

**2′** without *-za*, w. abl. and w. *-ašta/-kan*, "expel from someone else's body or body part": ᵈ*Agalmatin*⸗*ta awan arḫa tittanunun* ᵈ*Ānnamilulin*⸗ *ma*⸗*ta*⸗*kkan* SAG.DU-*az awan arḫa šu-wa-nu-un* "I have completely removed the deity Agalmati from you. I have completely expelled the deity Ānnamiluli from your head. (I have extinguished the fire on your head and ignited it on the head of the sorcerer)" KUB 24.14 i 18-20 (Ḫepattarakki's rit., NH), w. dupl. KUB 24.15 obv. 17-18, ed. Engelhard, Diss. 64f., Collins, JCS 42:216 w. n. 26; frag., without prev./adv. preserved: [*n*]⸗*ašta pa*[*ḫḫur*...] [*tu*]⌈*ē*⌉*ggaz šu-ú-wa-an-d*[*u*] "Le[t] them expel the fi[re] from [the patient's(?) b]ody" KBo 22.107 + KBo 40.164 i 16-17 (rit. frag., NS), ed. Fuscagni (ed.), hethiter.net/: CTH 458.73 (TX 13.10.2014, TRde 08.08.2014) (differently), translit. DBH 24:100, Ünal, FsAlp 500 (KBo 22.107), for the join see Soysal, FsPopko 322 n. 19.

**d.** w. *parā*, *-kan* and optional abl., "to expel from within a building" (synonymous w. *parḫ-* 2 a 2′, q.v.): ("The augur and the Old Woman speak thus":) *kāša*⸗*wa*⸗*nnaš* ⌈*p*⌉*īēr* DINGIR.MEŠ *nepišaz* LÚ.MEŠ ᴳᴵŠGIDRU *itten*⸗*wa*⸗*kan IŠTU* É.GAL-*LIM kallar* INIM-*tar parā šu-u-wa-at-tén* "The gods have just sent us the scepter-bearers from heaven (saying): 'Go, and drive the ominous things out of the palace'" KBo 4.2 i 14-15

(Ḫuwarlu's rit., pre-NH/NS), ed. Kronasser, Die Sprache 8:90, 95, Bawanypeck, THeth 25:22f., eadem, hethiter.net/: CTH 398 (TX 03.11.2010, TRde 10.11.2014); *kāša=wa ŠA* ᵈIM LÚ.MEŠ ᴳᴵŠGIDRU *uwanteš nu=wa=kan kuit kuit kallar idālu uttar kēdani* É*-ri anda nu=war=at=kan parā šu-u-wa-an-du nu=wa=kan idālu uddār parā pēdandu nu=wa=z* ᴳᴵŠ*tūrin kuwannanaš dandu nu=wa=kan kallar uttar parā šu-u-wa-an-du* "The scepterbearers of the Stormgod have just arrived. Whatever ominous, evil thing is present in this house, let them (i.e., the scepterbearers) drive it out. Let them carry out the evil things. Let them take a spear of copper and drive out the ominous thing" ibid. i 66-70, ed. Kronasser, Die Sprache 8:92, 97, Bawanypeck, THeth 25:28f.

**e.** w. *arḫa* "to banish, exile (from a location other than a building)" (synonymous w. *parḫ-* 2 a 1′, q.v.) — **1′** without sent. part. or location in the abl.: [*kui*ˀ]*t=a šumaš=a* ᵐ*Alluwamna* ᶠ*Ḫara*[*pšeki=ya*] / [*nu=šm*]*aš QADU* DUMU.MEŠ*=KUNU arḫa šu-e-*[*et*?] [*nu=šma*]*š ANA* ᵁᴿᵁ*Mallitaškuri* [*maniya*]*ḫḫiš pāntu=war=e apiya aš*[*antu*] "But [as for(?)] you (pl.), Alluwamna [and] Ḫar[apšeki, he] banish[ed] you along with your children. He [allo]cated you to the city of Mallitaškuri (saying) 'Let them go (and) li[ve] there'" KUB 26.77 i 10-13 (frag. naming Alluwamna, OH/NS), ed. Bin-Nun, JCS 26:116-118 (restores *šu-e-*[*nu-un*]), THeth 5:223f. (idem), THeth 11:141f., cf. also Soysal, Hethitica 14:140 n. 75, cf. HEG S/2:1221, EDHIL 797, who both restore *šu-e-*[*mi*], following Oettinger Stammbildung 294 and Carruba FsGüterbock 80 □ with Hoffman, THeth 11:141f., we prefer to restore a pret. sg. 3 instead of a sg. 1 in view of the following pret. sg. 3 [*maniya*]*ḫḫiš* (or [*parara*]*ḫḫiš* "he chased," so Soysal), for the restoration of [*kui*ˀ]*t=a* and the observation that *kuit=a* introduces contrasting topics, see Goedegebuure, forthcoming

**2′** with *-ašta* (and perhaps *-kan*) and location in the abl.: *šumeš=a* DINGIR.MEŠ *ŠA* KUR ᵁᴿᵁ*Gašga šulletten n=ašta ŠA* KUR ᵁᴿᵁ*Ḫatti* DINGIR.MEŠ KUR*-az arḫa šu-wa-at-te-en šumeš=a=za* KUR*=SUNU datten* § ᴸᵁ́.ᴹᴱŠ*Gašga=ya šuller n=ašta ANA* LÚ.MEŠ ᵁᴿᵁ*Ḫatti* URU.DIDLI.ḪI.A*=ŠUNU arḫa dātten* ᴬ.ŠÀ*kuerazzi=ya=aš*[*=kan*] *IŠTU* ᴳᴵŠKIRI$_6$.GEŠTIN.ḪI.A*=ŠUNU arḫa šu-wa-at-te-e*[*n*] "But you, the gods of the land of Kaška, have become rebellious. You have expelled the gods of Ḫatti from (their) land, while you have taken their land for yourselves. § The Kaškaeans have also become rebellious. You have taken away from the people of Ḫatti their towns, and you have also expelle[d] them from (their) fields (and) their vineyards" KUB 4.1 ii 11-18 (rit. before a campaign, MH/NS), ed. Kaškäer 170f., García Trabazo, TextosRel. 516f., Melchert, FsHerzenberg 92f., tr. van den Hout, Grotiana NS 12-13:24; cf. also [...]x*-an* KUR*-yaz arḫa šu-ú-et* "He drove [...] away from the land. (But now you must protect [...])" KBo 16.25 i 68 (instr., MH/MS), ed. Rizzi Mellini, FsMeriggi² 526f.; *nu* ᴸᵁ́MÁŠDA *l*[*ē*] [... *n=an=kan*(?) KUR*-yaz a*]*rḫa lē šu-ú-ez-zi* "Let him no[t mistreat(?)] the poor (man), [and] let him not drive [him a]way [from the land]" ibid. iv 4-5, ed. Rizzi Mellini, FsMeriggi² 534f.; [... ᵁ(ᴿᵁ*Ḫurmaz* ᵐ*Laḫḫuerin*)] ⌈*šu*⌉*-ú-er* ᵐ*Āšk*[*aliyan šar*(*ā*)] [(*uwater š=an pedi=šš*)*i pei*]*ēr apāšš=a and*[*uwašalliš*?] / [(*ēšta*)] "They banished Laḫḫueri from the city of Ḫurma. They brought up Āškaliya and installed him in his place. He too was ..." KUB 36.105:4-5 (anecdotes, OH/MS), w. dupl. VBoT 33:6-8 (NS), KUB 31.38 obv. 33, ed. Soysal, Diss. 29, 90, Dardano, L'aneddoto 63f.; [*n=an=kan*? *IŠ*]*TU* LÚ.MEŠ [...] *arḫa šu-wa-an-zi* KUB 13.7 i 4-7 (decree of Tudḫ., MH/NS), ed. HittInstr 140f. n. 46, 350 (discussion of readings in break); *weš=a=kan kuwapi* ÉRIN.MEŠ! ᵁᴿᵁ*Ḫarranašši IŠTU* URU.DIDLI.ḪI.A*=NI arḫa* ⌈*šu*⌉*-wa-ú-e-ni* "When will we expel the troops of Ḫarranašši from our cities?" KUB 31.42 iii 9-11 (MH/NS), ed. Boley, Dynamics 160.

**3′** w. *arḫa* and w. location expressed as *-za peran* "in the subject's presence": (regarding the interrogation of *dammarā*-women) [...*=wa=nn*]*aš=za peran ar*⌈*ḫa*⌉ *šu-u-wa-it* "He banished [u]s from his presence" KUB 18.3 iv 19 (in testimony in oracle question, NH), ed. van den Hout, Purity 23 (differs: "he chased away in front of us") □ there is no evidence for the use of oracle birds in this text, so there is no support for *š.* denoting the motion of an oracle bird (contra THeth 11:136 and HEG S/2:1220 ("und (der Orakelvogel) stieß sich vorne ab (= 'flog weg')")).

**3.** "to push oneself/to especially exert oneself", w. *-za*: [...] LÚ.MEŠ *āppa iyanner UMMA*

*ŠU⟨NU⟩=MA UL=za šu-wa-u-e-ni* "The men came back [...]. ⟨T⟩he⟨y⟩ (said) thus: 'We will not push ourselves (to perform the tasks)!' (So they did not shorten the long ways, they did not lengthen the short ways; they did not lower the high mountains, they did not raise the low mountains)" KUB 12.63 obv. 29 (Zuwi's rit., OH/MS), ed. Friedrich, Or NS 13:209 □ the interpretation of *šuwaueni* follows Hoffmann, THeth 11:136 ("Wir wollen uns nicht in Bewegung setzen") and partly Friedrich, Or NS 13:209 w. n. 5, contra Oettinger, Stammbildung 295 and HEG S/2:1220 ("Wir können (die Aufgaben) nicht erfüllen"), who both cite it among the occurrences of *šuwai-* "to fill"; for the passage see also [*parganula-*].

Due to similar spellings in later Hittite, attribution of forms to *šuwaye-* "to see," *šu*(*wa*)- "to fill" or *šuwe-* "to push" is sometimes problematic. In NH *šuwe-* "to push" was fully transferred to the *ḫatrai-* class. NS copies of the OH verb *šuwaye-* "to see" (s.v.) also sometimes show the transfer of *šuwaye-* to the *ḫatrai-* class, leading to possible conflation of both stems in NS documents. Nevertheless, the differences are generally clear. If plene writing of the first syllable occurs, *šu*(*wa*)- "to fill" (s.v.) will show *u*, except in two NH instances, whereas *šuwaye-* will have *ú*.

Friedrich, ZA 36 (1925) 45f.; Götze, ZA 36 (1925) 16f., 263-266; Petschow, ZA 55 (1962) 246f.; Josephson, Heth.u.Idg. (1979) 97-98; Oettinger, Stammbildung (1979) 293f. ("stoßen, verbannen"); Hoffmann, THeth 11 (1984) 133-143; Tischler, HEG S/2 (2006) 1220f.; Kloekhorst, EDHIL (2008) 797f.

Cf. *šuwai-* A.

[*šuyant-*], see *šū-* B, *šuwa-*.

**[...](-)šu-u-ia-aš(-pát)** (mng. unkn. or acephalic); OH/NS.†

[...]x *nakk*[*i-*... ]x(-)*šu-u-ia-aš-pát nu=ššan* [...]x-*aḫḫi* "[...] (is) import[ant(?)] and [...] as well (*=pat*). I do (something with it) [...]" KBo 10.37 i 5-6 (rit. against curse, OH/NS).

It is not clear if the word is acephalic. Haroutunian, FsHoffner 150, 158 reads [... *pa*?-*a*]*š*?-*šu*?-*u*?-*ia-aš-pát* "[ped]estal?"; Christiansen, StBoT 48:182f. (n. 730 "Lesung unsicher"), 229 reads [... $^{\text{N}}$]$^{\text{A}_4\text{?}}$ŠU.U-*i̯a-aš-pát* "Basalt?".

**šuwiye-**, see *šuwe-*.

$^{\text{(SÍG/GADA)}}$**šuil-/šuel-** n. neut.; thread, rope; from OH/NS and MH/MS.

**sg. nom.-acc.** $^{\text{SÍG}}$*šu-ú-il* KBo 15.10 i 7 (MH/MS), KBo 32.15 iii 1 (MH/MS), *šu-ú-il* KBo 39.8 i 31, ii (5), (10) (MH/MS), KBo 44.17 i 31 (MH/MS), KBo 2.3 + KBo 45.191:(24) (MH/NS), KUB 15.39 i (23) (MH/NS), KUB 17.25 i (8), 9 (MH/NS), KUB 17.26:(9) (MH/NS), *šu-i-*⸢*el*⸣ KUB 41.1 iii 13 (MH/NS), ⸢*šu*⸣-*ú-el* JCS 24:37 (no. 62) iii 5 (MH/NS), $^{\text{SÍG}}$*šu-i-el* KUB 47.35 i 12 (NS), KUB 58.107 iv 9 (MH/NS), IBoT 2.126:6 (MH/NS), VS 28.57 iv 16 (MH/NS), *šu-ú-i-el* KUB 45.24 i 10 (2×) (NS), IBoT 2.48 obv. (4) (NS), *šu-ú-i-il* KUB 12.51 i? 8 (NS), $^{\text{SÍG}}$*šu-ú-i-il* KUB 7.3:7, 13 (NS), $^{\text{SÍG}}$*šu-ú-i-*⸢*el*⸣ KBo 31.117:9 (NS), [*šu-ú*]-*i-il* KBo 10.37 i 51 (OH?/NS).

**gen.** *ŠA* $^{\text{[SÍ]G}}$*šu-ú-i-il* KBo 10.37 i 44 (OH/NS), *ŠA* $^{\text{GADA}}$*šu-*⸢*ú*⸣*-i*[*l*] KBo 48.43:21 (OH/NS).

**dat.-loc.** [$^{\text{SÍG}}$*šu*(?)]-⸢*ú*⸣-*i-li* KUB 9.28 iv 3 (MH/NS), $^{\text{⸢SÍG⸣}}$*šu-ú-i-li* KUB 60.36:4 (NS).

**inst.** [*š*]*u-ú-i-li-i*[*t*] KBo 10.37 i 50 (OH?/NS), $^{\text{SÍG}}$*šu-ú-i-li-it* KBo 11.5 vi 9 (NS).

**pl. nom.-acc.** *šu-ú-e-el* KUB 9.32 obv. (7) (MH/NS), HT 1 iii 9 (MH/NS), [*šu*]-⸢*ú*⸣-*il* KUB 9.31 iii 20 (MH/NS).

**dat.-loc.** *šu-ú-i-la-aš* KUB 41.4 ii 21 (NH), *šu-i-la-aš* KUB 51.83 obv.? 4 (LNS).

**reading uncertain:** *šu-*⸢*il*⸣? KBo 11.14 iii 11 (MH/NS), [*š*]*u*?-*ú-i-il* KUB 48.16:3 (if text is not Hattic, cf. Otten apud Kühne, ZA 70:104) (NS).

(Hurr.) *pil=aḫ=i šil=iḫ=a pidari=we šab=ar*(*i*)*=uš šerḫ*(*i*)*=uš* "A thread (*pil=aḫ=i*) is dense(?) like the hair of an ox" KBo 32.15 iv 1 = (Hitt.) *malkianzi=ma kuit* $^{\text{SÍG}}$*šu-ú-i*[*l* ... ] *šukšukkiš maḫḫan* [...] "The thread they spin is [...] like the hair [of an ox]" KBo 32.15 iii 1-2 (Hurr.-Hitt. bil., MH/MS), ed. StBoT 32:294f., comm. 341-343.

**a.** material: the determinative SÍG indicates that the main material of *šuel-/šuil-* is wool. However, linen (GADA) is also attested: *ŠA* $^{\text{GADA}}$*šu-*⸢*ú*⸣*-i*[(*l*)] KBo 48.43:21 (OH/NS), w. dupl. KBo 10.37 i 44 (OH/NS), ed. StBoT 48:188f., 211; GADA-*aš* ⸢*šu*⸣-*ú-el* JCS 24:37 iii 5 (MH/NS) (see c 3′, below).

**b.** color — **1′** red ($\text{SA}_5$): SÍG $\text{SA}_5$ *šu-ú-i-el* KUB 45.24 i 9-10 (NS), ed. Görke, Aštu 112, 115, ChS 1/5:326; $^{\text{SÍG}}$*šu-i-el* S[$\text{A}_5$] KUB 47.35 i 12 (NS), ed. Görke, Aštu 157f., translit. ChS 1/5:481 (both reading *ka*[*t-ta*] for $\text{SA}_5$).

**2′** mixed colors of threads which are braided together — **a′** red and white ($SA_5$ and *ḫarki-*/BABBAR): 1 SÍG*šu-ú-i-il* $SA_5$ *ḫarki⸗ya anda taruppan* "One thread braided together of red and white" KUB 7.3:(7), 13-14 (NS), ed. Velhartická, AoF 36:328f.

**b′** blue and red (ZA.GÌN, $SA_5$): *tueggaš⸗a⸗šm*[(*a*)*š⸗*(*ka*)]*n* SÍG ZA.GÌN SÍG $SA_5$ *šu-ú-il anda iyazzi n⸗*[(*at⸗ša*)]*maš⸗kan dāi* "For thei[r] bodies she braids (lit. makes) together blue wool (and) red wool into a thread and places it on them" KBo 39.8 i 31-32 (Mašt., MH/MS), w. dupl. KBo 44.17 i 31-32 (MH/MS), ed. StBoT 46:65; see KBo 39.8 ii 5, below c 2′.

**c′** white, red and yellow-green (BABBAR, $SA_5$, $SIG_7$.$SIG_7$): ("As to all army commanders, each one lines up a sheep for himself — whether they are white or black is not important —") *nu šu-ú-e-el* (var. [*šu-ú*]*-e-il*) SÍG BABBAR SÍG $SA_5$ SÍG $SIG_7$.$SIG_7$ *anda tarnaḫḫi n⸗at* 1*-an anda taruppaizzi* "I add threads (of) white wool, red wool, (and) green wool and he (i.e., each army commander) braids them together into one" HT 1 iii 9-10 (Ašḫella's rit., MH/NS), w. dupl. KUB 9.31 iii 20-21 (MH/NS), ed. Dinçol, Belleten 49/193:12, 23, tr. Kümmel, TUAT 2.2:286, translit. Chrzanowska (ed.), hethiter.net/:CTH 394 (INTR 2016-07-13).

**c.** use of thread in rituals — **1′** tied to body parts of animals or to figures — **a′** to the horn of a sheep: [(*nu* UDU)] *ūnniyanzi nu⸗šši⸗ššan šu-ú-i*[*l*...? (*INA* SI⸗*ŠU*)] ⸢*ḫa*⸣*manki šu-ú-il⸗ma⸗kan ŠA* ⸢SÍG⸣ x x[...(*alpuemar*)] ⸢EGIR⸣*-pa ḫapušzi* "They drive a sheep here and he/she ties a threa[d of... color] to its horn. A thread of [...-colored(?)] wool replaces (i.e., blunts?) the point (and the curses and oaths are stuck to/on the wool(?))" KUB 17.25 i 7-10 (rit. to expiate murder, MH/NS), w. dupls. KUB 17.26 i 8-10 (MH/NS), KBo 55.33:1-3, ed. StBoT 46:134, Güterbock, RHA XXII/74:100, HW² Ḫ 259b (differently).

**b′** to the mouth of a deer figurine: [*nu t*]*aknaš* ᵈUTU*-un* ᵈ*Išḫarann⸗a* ŠÀ GIŠKIRI₆*⸗kan* ZAG*-za* [GIŠ*a*]*lkištanaš ašaši* PA₅*⸗ma⸗kan* ⸢GÙB⸣*-laza aliyanan* [(*ŠA*)] IM *dāi nu⸗šši⸗ššan* SÍG*šu-i-el kuit ANA* KA×U⸗*Š*[(*U*)] / [(*ḫam*)]*ankan n⸗at taknaš* ᵈUTU*-uš keššarta ḫarz*[(*i*)] "She seats the Sungoddess of the [E]arth and Išḫara in the garden on the right of [br]anches, while she places a deer of clay on the left of the (irrigation) canal. The Sungoddess of the Netherworld holds in her hand the rope, which is tied to its mouth" KUB 58.107 iv 7-10 (Allaituraḫi's rit., MH/NS), w. dupls. VS 28.57 iv 14-17 (MH/NS), IBoT 2.126:4-7 (MH/NS), ed. Haas, FsOtten² 129f., ChS I/5-1:81, 87f., 94.

**c′** to a *šakuš*(*š*)*a-* of "life" (figurine): *ZI-TUM* KÙ.BABBAR*⸗ya⸗kan anda kittari nu⸗šši⸗ššan šakuiššai⸗šši kuit ŠA* SÍ[G S]A₅ *šu-ú-i-el ḫaman*ᵍᵃ*kan nu* MUNUS ŠU.GI ⸢*šu-ú-i*⸣-[*el* ...] "The silver (symbol of) life also lies in (the pitcher). The Old Woman [takes?] the thread of [re]d wool that is tied to his/its *šaku*(*i*)*šša-*" KUB 45.24 i 8-10 (frag. of Hurrian rit., NS), w. dupls. IBoT 2.47 rt. col. 3-5 (NS), IBoT 2.48 obv. 2-4 + KBo 33.37 rev.? 2-3 (NS), ed. *šakuiššai-*, Görke, Aštu 112, 115, ChS I/5:326; cf. Wegner, SCNNH 2:325.

**2′** attached to a human body and then cut off/removed from it: *nu⸗kan ANA* 2 *BĒL* SÍSKUR *kuit* SÍ[G ZA.GÌ]N SÍG SA₅ *šu-ú-*⸢*il*⸣ *tueggaš kitta*... § *n⸗at⸗šamaš⸗kan* MUNUS ŠU.GI *arḫa dāi nu⸗šmaš⸗kan* [*š*]*u-ú-il arḫa tuḫ*ᵘʰ*šari* "The threa[d] of [blu]e (and) red wool that is placed on the bodies of two ritual patrons, ... § The Old Woman takes them (i.e., the thread and other things) away from them and cuts off the [t]hread from them" KBo 39.8 ii 5-6, 9-10 (2Mašt., MH/MS), w. par. KBo 2.3 + KBo 45.191 i 20-21, 24-25 (1Mašt., MH/NS), KUB 15.39 i 19-20, 22-23 (MH/NS), ed. StBoT 45:69f., 115; see also b 2′ b′.

**3′** cut and placed on top of figurines: ⸢*m*⸣*ān lukkatta⸗ma nu* (vars. A & B add DUGDÍLIM.GAL MUŠEN) ALAM.ḪI.A *ka*[(*ttan a*)]*rḫa dāi* GADA*-aš* ⸢*šu*⸣*-ú-el* (var. B: GADA*-ašš⸗a šu-i-*⸢*el*⸣) *tuḫ*ᵘʰ[(*ša n⸗a*)]*t⸗šan ANA* [AL]AM.ḪI.A *šer dā*[(*i*)] "When it becomes morning, she removes the (vars. add: bird-shaped bowl and) figurines from under (the bed); (var. adds and) she cuts the linen thread(s) and lays it/them (i.e., the thread(s)) on top of the [fig]urines" JCS 24:37 (no. 62) rev.! 4-6 (Alli's rit., MH/NS), w. dupls. A: KUB 24.10 ii 29-31 (MH/NS) and B: KUB 41.1 iii 12-14 (MH/NS), ed. Jakob-Rost, THeth

2:42f., Hoffner, JCS 24:84, 86, Mouton, hethiter.net/: CTH 402 (INTR 2016-03-23) ☐ since DÍLIM.GAL always seems to be determined by DUG or GIŠ, we follow Hoffner, JCS 24:84 in reading *ka*[*t*- after ALAM.ḪI.A instead of DÍLIM.[GAL as Jakob-Rost and Mouton do.

**4′** twisted and braided together: see b 2′ a′ and c′.

**5′** other: [$^{\text{SÍG}}$*šu*(?)]-⌈*ú*⌉-*i-li* 6 SÍG SA$_5$ *ḫaminkan* "To a [th]read(?) six (pieces of) red wool are tied" KUB 9.28 iv 3 (rit. for the Heptad, MH/NS); [*kin*(*un*(-)x) *š*]*u-ú-i-li-it* [*d*]*ān irḫ*[*āi*]*zzi* [*n*(*u=šš*)*an šu-ú*]-*i-il* ⌈*kat*⌉*t*[*a*] SIG$_5$-*ui* $^{\text{GIŠ}}$*paddu*[*n*]*i* [(*zik*)*kizzi*] "([No]w (the ritual patron) ma[ke]s the rounds wit[h] a [t]hread for the [se]cond time, [a]nd pl[aces the thr]ead dow[n] in/on the good mortar(?) [...]" KBo 10.37 i 50-51 (rit. against curse, OH?/NS), ed. StBoT 48:188f., see also $^{\text{GIŠ}}$*paddur*; $^{\text{SÍG}}$*šu-ú-i-li-it araḫzanda* x[...] "[... encircles(?) it] round about with a thread" KBo 11.5 vi 9 (Muwalanni's rit., NS), ed. Wegner, ChS 1/3-2:213f.

Friedrich, ZA 37 (1927) 185, 202; idem, HW (1952) 196 ("Faden(?)"); Hoffner, JCS 24 (1972) 86 w. n. 4 ("thread?, ribbon?"; different from *kapina-* "yarn" and *ašara-/ešara-* "string"); Oettinger, "Indo-Hittite" Hypothese (1986) 16, 17; Rieken, StBoT 44 (1999) 478-480; Melchert, Anat&Indog. (2001) 263-272; Tischler, HEG S/2 (2006) 1138-1139 ("Faden, Band, Strick"), Kloekhorst, EDHIL (2008) 777.

**$^{\text{GIŠ}}$šūinila-, $^{\text{GIŠ}}$šūnila-** n. com.; Turkish/Calabrian pine(?) or Stone Pine(?); from OH/NS and MH/MS.†

**sg. nom.** $^{\text{GIŠ}}$*šu-i-ni-la-aš* RS 25.421 obv. 38 (NS).

**gen.** $^{\text{GIŠ}}$*šu-ú-ni-la-aš* VBoT 58 iv 18 (OH/NS), KBo 17.105 iv 23 (MH/MS), $^{\text{GIŠ}}$*šu-ú-i-*[*ni-la-aš*(?)] KUB 9.1 ii 24 (pre-NH/NS).

(Sum.) [$^{\text{giš}}$ù.suḫ$_5$ a.dé.a $^{\text{giš}}$še.ù.suḫ$_5$ šu tag.ga] (for restoration see Civil, JNES 23:2) = (syll. Sum.) a-šu-uḫ ši-da-a še-nu a-šu-uḫ ši-táq-qa = (Akk.) $^{\text{GIŠ}}$Ù.SUḪ$_5$ *ši-iq-qa-ti ša te-re-en-na-a-ti zu-* ʾ*-na-at* "She (sc. the mother) is (like) a pine tree from an irrigated plot (Sum.: an irrigated pine tree), adorned with pine cones" = (Hitt.) $^{\text{GIŠ}}$*šu-i-ni-la-aš=ma=aš* GIM-*an šeššuraš n=aš āššuīt* ⌈*š*⌉[*arā*?] *šūwanza* "She (sc. the mother) is like a irrigated *šuinila*-tree (lit. of irrigation)— she is filled-u[p(?)] with possessions/good things" RS 25.421 obv. 38-40 (signalement lyrique), ed. Laroche, Ugar. 5:774, 775 ("Elle est comme le pin d'irrigation, plein de bonnes choses"), Cohen, Wisdom 70. The Sumerian $^{\text{giš}}$še-ù-suḫ$_5$ and Akkadian *terinnatu* "pine cones" have a free translation in the Hittite version which is given as *āššu-* "goods, possessions."

Wood used as a material: 1 $^{\text{GIŠ}}$*alkištaš ip*⌈*pi*⌉*aš* $^{\text{GIŠ}}$*alkištaš* [...] 1 $^{\text{GIŠ}}$*šu-ú-ni-la-aš* $^{\text{GIŠ}}$⌈*laḫ*⌉*ḫuraš* TUR "One branch of *ippiya*-plant, (one) branch [of ...], one small offering table/stand (made) of *š.*-wood" VBoT 58 iv 17-18 (missing Sun-God, OH/NS), translit. Myth 26; (The king says: "It (i.e., the wheel) will just now come and bring the destruction of the (enemy) land") *nu* 1 $^{\text{GIŠ}}$UMBIN $^{\text{GIŠ}}$*šu-ú-i-*[*ni-la-aš*(?)] *ŠA* 12 *tauilaš* KI.LÁ.BI 12 GÍN [...] "[He takes?] a wheel (made) of *š.*-wood (which) is (the size of ?) twelve *tauila-*, its weight is twelve shekels" (Then the king grasps the wheel and sets it in motion asking the gods to roll it against the enemy Hurrian land) KUB 9.1 ii 22-25 (rit. analog to soldier oath, pre-NH/NS), cf. Beal, Ancient Magic 74; in unclear context: [*k*]*inuna=ššan* $^{\text{GIŠ}}$*šu-ú-ni-la-aš* [... *anda*]*n*(?) *tiya n=at=ta=kan merdu* "Now, step [i]n [...] of a *š.*-tree. And let it vanish for you" KBo 17.105 iv 23-24 (incant. for $^{\text{d}}$LAMMA and the $^{\text{d}}$IMIN.IMIN.BI, MH/MS); cf. HEG S 1139 (reading *natta=kan*).

In previous paragraphs of RS 25.421 the mother is compared with the first rain at the time of sowing, a bountiful harvest providing grain, a desirable garden filled with luxuriant growth (obv. 32-37). Therefore, the *šuinila*-tree and its possessions (sc. cones) should be of the same useful character. According to the texts above this tree is also cultivated, thus one thinks primarily of the nut pine (*Pinus pinea*) and its fruits pine-nuts. These trees grow today in the Levant and a few coastal places in Turkey. On the other hand, if the *šuinila-* is the same tree as the $^{\text{GIŠ}}$ù.suḫ$_5$/*ašūḫu*, this tree was in antiquity cultivated in southern Mesopotamia, and, as Stol, On Trees 16 n. 58 argues, the only pine so cultivated today is *Pinus brutia* (also known as *Pinus halepensis brutia*), "Turkish/Calabrian pine." This tree makes fine timber and produces "honey dew" from which honey bees produce a particularly tasty honey. The translation "fir"/"Tanne"/*Abies* for $^{\text{GIŠ}}$ù.suḫ$_5$/*ašūḫu* can be ruled out as these will not grow in Mesopotamia (Stol, On Trees 16 n. 58). In two further exempla in the Signalement Lyrique the Sumerian word

$^{giš}$še.ù.suḫ$_5$ is replaced by $^{(giš)}$li (Civil, JNES 23:11), which is probably "juniper."

Laroche apud Friedrich, HW 3.Erg. (1966) 29 ("Kiefer, Föhre"); Hoffner, EHGl (1967) 91 ("fir tree"); Laroche, Ugar. 5 (1968) 775, 778 ("nom d'une espèce de 'pin'"); Ertem, Flora (1974) 165 ("an object like $^{GIŠ}$*laḫḫura-*"); Stol, On Trees (1979) 5 n. 15, 18 n. 68 (*ašūḫu* cannot be "fir," rather "Calabrian Pine"); Tischler, HEG S/2 (2006) 1139-1140 ("ein Baum, dessen Holz als Bauholz verwendet wird, 'Kiefer, Föhre, Tanne'?"); Borger, MZL[2] (2010) no. 731 (Ù.SUḪ$_5$ = *ašūḫu* "Tanne").

**šueri-** n. or adj.; (mng. unkn.); MH?/NS.†

**pl. nom.-acc. neut. or sg. dat.-loc. (?)** *šu-u-e-ri-ia* IBoT 3.148 iii 21 (MH?/NS).

*namma apēdani=pat* GE$_6$-*ti* 6 *PA*. ZÍD.DA ZÍZ *A*⸢*NA*⸣ DINGIR.MEŠ ⸢*ḫūmantaš*⸣ *šu-u-e-ri-ia* NINDA *ṢIDĪTI INA* ⸢É.NINDA.DÙ.DÙ⸣ *šu*⸢*nni*⸣*anzi UL=an ANA PĀNI* DINGIR.MEŠ *ape*⸢*da šun*⸣*ni*⸢*anzi*⸣ "Then, in that same night, they pour out six *PARĪSU*-measures of wheat flour for all of the gods (as?) *š.* (and?) travel provision bread (or: in a *š.* as travel provision bread) in the bakery. (But) they do not pour it (i.e., the wheat) there in front of the gods" IBoT 3.148 iii 20-22 (rit. of drawing paths, MH?/NS), ed. ChS 1/9:119 ("Das *šueri-* und *ziti*-Gebäck füllt man in der Bäckerei"), Haas/Wilhelm, AOATS 3:222f., HEG S/2: 1129.

If *š.* and the following NINDA *ṢIDĪTI* describe the purpose of the wheat, *š.* can either be a noun asyndetically joined with the travel provision bread or an adj. In both cases *š.* is most likely pl. nom.-acc. neut. with NINDA as a collective. Alternatively, *š.* could denote the container in which the wheat is poured.

Haas/Wilhelm, AOATS 3 (1974) 284 ("ungedeutetes Nomen"); Haas, ChS 1/9 (1998) 291 (nom.-akk. sg. mit *-ya*); Tischler, HEG S/2 (2006) 1129 ("Nomen u.B., eine Örtlichkeit?," "Dat.-Lok."); Kloekhorst, EDHIL (2008) 772.

**šuitara-(?)** n.? com.; (mng. unkn.); LNS.†

**sg.** *šu-i-ta-ra-an* KUB 36.95 iii 4 (NS).

[...*-z*]*i*?*-ir šu-i-ta-ra-an* [...]x *n=aš=kan* ÚR*=ši anda* [...] KUB 36.95 iii 4-5 (Ḫedammu-myth, NS).

*š.*, in broken context, can be a noun or adj. In case *n=aš*(*=*) in the next line contains the sg. nom. com. subject clitic one could consider a com. gender noun.

**šu-ú-⸢ga/e⸣[(-)...]** KBo 3.7 ii 11 (myth of Illuyanka, OH/NS), unclear in frag. context, ed. Beckman, JANES 14:14 (reading *-ga-*), Rieken et al., hethiter.net/: CTH 321 (TR 2012-06-08) (reading *-e-* after photo collation).

**šukkalli** n., Hurr.; vizier; wr. syll. and $^{LÚ}$SUKKAL; NH.†

**stem form** ⸢*šu*⸣*-uk-*⸢*kal*⸣*-li* KUB 27.1 ii 18 (NS).

(Among thin bread offerings to Hurrian deities and divine beings:) ⸢1⸣ NINDA.SIG $^{d}$*Tenu* $^{d}$U*-ubbi* ⸢*šu*⸣*-uk-*⸢*kal*⸣*-li* TUŠ*-aš* K[I.MIN] "One thin bread to Tenu, the vizier of Teššub, sitting ditto (i.e., he breaks)" KUB 27.1 ii 18 (fest. of *IŠTAR* of Šamuha, NH), ed. Lebrun, Samuha, 78, 89, Wegner, ChS I.3-1:39, 43; see also $^{d}$*Tēnu* $^{d}$*Teššubbi* $^{LÚ}$SUKKAL KUB 34.102 ii 14 (MS).

*š.*, epithet of the god Tenu, is a loanword in Hurrian borrowed from Sumerian $^{lú}$sukkal and Akkadian *sukkallu*.

von Brandenstein, AfO 13 (1939-41) 58 w. n. 11 ("Dienstgott"); Friedrich, HW (1952) 325 ("Verwalter"); Laroche, GLH (1978-79) 241 ("vizir"); Richter, BibGlHurr (2012) 408.

**šukri** n. or adj., Hurr.; (something receiving offerings); NS.†

**sg. dat.-loc. or Hurr. essive** *šu-uk-ri* KBo 33.198 ii 6 (NS?), KUB 40.102 ii 9 (NS), VBoT 116:4 (NS).

1 MÁŠ.GAL 1 NINDA.[GUR$_4$.RA *UPNI šurzi*] *šu-uk-ri* ⸢*tiya*⸣[*ri manuzuḫi šipanti*] § 1 MÁŠ.GAL 1 NINDA.GUR$_4$[.R]A *UPNI* $^{d}$*Kušurni tiyāri m*[*a*]*nuzuḫi šipanti* § 1 MÁŠ.GAL 1 NINDA.GUR$_4$[.R]A *UPNI šurinni* ⸢*ti*⸣*yāri m*[*anuz*]*uḫi šipanti* "[He/she sacrifices] one billy goat (and) one [thick-]bread [weighing a handful to/for *šurzi*] *š.* (and?) Manuzian *tiyāri*. § He/She sacrifices one billy goat (and) one thick bread weighing a handful to/for the divine *kušurni* (and?) Manuzian *tiyāri* § He/She sacrifices one billy goat (and) one thick bread weighing a handful to/for

the divine standard (and?) Manuzian *tiyāri*" KBo 33.198 + KBo 64.43 ii 5-10 (*ḫišuwa* fest., NS), rest. from KUB 12.12 i 21-34, translit. ChS 1/4:162 and KUB 32.54:12-18, translit. ChS 1/4:170; 1 GAL KÙ.GI *ANA* ᵈ*Šurzi šu-uk-ri* [...] 1 GAL KÙ.BABBAR *ANA kušurni* [...] 1 GAL KÙ.BABBAR *ANA šurinni* [...] "One gold cup to the divine *šurzi šukri* [...] one silver cup to *kušurni* [...], one silver cup to the divine-standard [...] KUB 40.102 ii 9-11 (fest., NS); cf. [... ᵈ*Šurz*]*i* ᵈ*Šu-uk-ri* [...] KBo 33.215 vi 20 (NS); [...*š*]*urzi šu-uk-ri* ᵈ[...] VBoT 116:4 (NS).

*š*. is one of a series of items receiving offerings, each of which can also be divinized; for ⁽ᵈ⁾*š*. see van Gessel, OHP s.v. For *š*. in Hurr. personal names see GLH 241. Whether there is a relation with Akk. *šukru* (CAD Š/3:226), attested only in Middle Assyrian, which appears to be part of the eye, is unclear.

Laroche, GLH (1977-79) 241; Haas, Gesch.Relig. (1994) 863 w. n. 70 ("Eine Embleme(?) *šurzi šukri*"); van Gessel, OHP 1 (1998) 409-410; Tischler, HEG S/2 (2006) 1140 ("hurr. Benennung eines Emblems, vielleicht ein Metallgegenstand am Zaumzeug des Pferdes"); Richter, BibGlHurr (2012) 409 ("Segen, Wunsch," "auch deifiziert," "(ein Emblem?)").

**šukšuk(k)a-/šukšukki-** n. com.; (hair or type of hair of oxen and horses); from OH/MS.†

**sg. nom.** *šu-uk-šu-uk-ki-iš* KBo 32.15 iii 2 (MH/MS).

**acc.** *šu-*[*uk-š*]*u-ga-an* KUB 17.10 iv 1 (OH/MS), [*šu-u*]*k-šu-uq-qa-an* KUB 33.54 ii 15 (OH/NS), *šu-uk-šu*[*-uq-qa-an*] KUB 34.76 i 7 (OH/NS), [*šu-ug*]*-šu-ug-ga-an* KBo 54.35:3 (MS?), *šu-uq-šu-qa-an* KUB 7.53 iii 4 (NS), *šu-uk-šu-u*[*q-qa-an*?] KBo 60.56:2 (NS).

**dat.-loc.?** *šu-uk-šu-uk-ki-i*[*a*?] KUB 29.52 i 2 (MH/MS).

[Akk. *ab-bu-tù* = Hitt. *šu-uk-š*[*u-ka-aš*(?)] KBo 1.42 iv 50 (Izi Boğ.), thus read by Goetze, Tunn. 95, but *ṭub-bu-tù* = *la-az-z*[*i*(?)-...] q.v. by Otten, AfO 16:70 n. 6, after coll. and partly followed by MSL 13:142 l. 277, who read *ab-bu-du* = *la-az-z*[*i*(?)-.]

(Hurr.) *pil=aḫ=i šil=iḫ=a pidari=we šab=ar(i)=uš šerḫ(i)=uš* "A thread is dense(?) like the hair (*šerḫi-*?) of an ox" KBo 32.15 iv 1 = (Hitt.) *malkianzi=ma kuit* ˢᴵᴳ*šūi*[*l* ... ] *šu-uk-šu-uk-ki-iš maḫḫan* [...] "The thread they spin is [...] like the hair [of an ox]" KBo 32.15 iii 1-2 (Hurr.-Hitt. bil., MS), ed. StBoT 32:294f., comm. 341-343.

**a.** of an ox: (The patient passes beneath a hawthorn gate while the exorcist incants:) [UD]U-*uš= ta=kkan kattan arḫa paizzi nu=š‹ši›=kan* ˢᴵᴳ*puttar ḫuit‹ti›yaši* GUD-*u*[*š=ta=kkan*] *kattan arḫa paizzi nu=šši=kan šu-uq-šu-qa-an ḫuittiyaš*[*i*] "The sheep passes beneath you and you pull out its hair. The ox passes beneath [you] and you pull out its *š*.-hair. (In the same way let it pull out evil, impurity, sorcery, *āštayaratar*, divine anger, curse, slander and an early death for the patient)" KUB 7.53 iii 1-4 (Tunnawi's rit., NS), ed. Beal/Collins, AoF 23:313 n. 31, Otten, AfO 16:70, Tunn. 18f. (lines 35-38, but misjoined) □ for a reading of MUNSUB$_X$ instead of ˢᴵᴳ*puttar* see Beal/Collins, AoF 23:313 n. 31; for the reading *pu-ut-* (and not *pu-u-ut-*) see Neu, EHS 2:238 and photo coll.; *zig=a=z* ᴳᴵŠ*ḫatalkišnaš ḫamiešḫi=ya=z* BABBAR-*TIM wašša*[*ši*] BURU$_{14}$=*ma=az išḫarwand*[*a w*]*aššaši* GUD-*uš=ta=kkan katti*[*=ti*] *arḫa paizzi nu=šš*[*e=šta šu-u*]*k-šu-uq-qa-an ḫuēz*[*ta*] UDU-*u*[*š=m*]*a=ta=kkan katti=ti* [(*arḫa pa*)*izzi nu=šše*]*=šta ēšri* [*ḫuēz*]*ta* "You are a hawthorn, and you clothe yourself in white in the spring, but in summer you clothe yourself in blood-red. The ox passes beneath you and you pull out it⌈s *š*.-⌉hair. The sheep passes beneath you and you pull out [its] wool" KUB 33.54 ii 13-17 + KUB 33.47:1-5 (rit. and myth, OH/NS), ed. Beal/Collins, AoF 23:312f.; cf. KUB 17.10 iv 1-3 (OH/MS), translit. Myth. 36, tr. Hittite Myths² 17; cf. UDU*=ši=kan kattan a*[*rḫa paizzi*] *nu=šši=kan* ˢᴵᴳ*ēšša*[*rri ḫuittiyazzi*] GUD*=ši=kan kattan ar*[*ḫa paizzi*] *nu=šši=kan šu-uk-šu*[*-uq-qa-an*] *ḫuittiyazz*[*i*] KUB 34.76 i 4-8 (OH/NS); cf. KBo 60.56:2-3 (NS).

**b.** unclear, said of horses: *n=uš=kan šu-uk-šu-uk-ki-*⌈*ia*? *uite*⌉*nit* [...] *namma=aš PĀNÊ=ŠUNU arranz*[*i nu=uš IŠTU* Ì.UDU] *iškanzi* "[They...] them with water on the(ir) *š*. Then they wash their faces [and] rub [them with sheep fat]. ([They put] down for them bedding and install them in the stable)" KUB 29.52 i 2-4 (hipp., MH/MS), ed. Hipp.heth. 196f. □ if correctly read *š*. can be dat.-loc. ("on (their) *š*."?) or (thus Melchert pers. comm.) the neut. pl./collec. nom.-acc. of a derived and substantivized *=iya*-adj. w. a mng. virtually equivalent to the base noun *š*.: "They [...] their *š*. (parts) with water." Neu, StBoT 32:341, suggests reading sg. nom. *šu-uk-šu-uk-ki-i*[*š* but that seems difficult to reconcile with the pl. acc. pron. *=uš*.

Goetze, Tunn. (1938) 95 ("shackle" = Akk. *abbuttu*); Otten, AfO 16 (1952-53) 70 n. 6 ("behaarter Körperteil"); Friedrich, HW (1953) 196 ("Stirnhaar(?) (des Rindes), Mähne (des Pferdes)"); Kammenhuber, Hipp.heth (1961) 196 n. 2; Beal/ Collins, AoF 23 (1996) 314 w. n. 39 ("hair or a type of hair of horses and oxen"); Neu, StBoT 32 (1996) 341-343; Tischler, HEG S/2 (2006) 1140-1141; Kloekhorst, EDHIL (2008) 778 ("hide (of cow or horse)").

**šuku$^{?}$ant-** part.?; (mng. unkn.); MS.†

**pl. nom. com.** *šu-ku?-an-te-eš* KBo 31.143 rev.? 14 (MS).

[...*m*]*inuanteš ēšten* DINGIR.MEŠ *ŠA* $^{d}$*Abi uttar* [...] / [...-]*ieš patalḫeš=meš šu-ku*(?)*-an-te-eš ašan*[*du*?] "[...] you, O gods, be [pl]easing! The word(s) of Abi [...],...[let?] your(?) soles(?) [be] *š*." KBo 31.143 rev.? 13-14, translit. Haas, AoF 34:32 (reading *ḫu*]*inuanteš* and *šu-ma-an-te-eš*) □ since the text shows a consistent difference between the signs KU and MA (compare, for instance, rev.? 15 *ḫūman*, 17 EGIR-*anda=ma*, 18 *parkunum*[*a-*) reading *šu-ku-* seems preferable. For not-writing a glide cf. among other exx. *m*]*inuanteš* in line 13.

**šukkupugullu(?)** n., Hurr.; (probably a river name); NS.†

[1 NINDA.GUR$_{4}$.RA *paršiya n*]*=an PĀNI* DINGIR-*LIM dāi* [EGIR-*ŠU=ma šī*]⌈*u*⌉(?) *šu?-uk-ku*⌉*-pu-gul-lu* BAL-⌈*ti*⌉ "[He breaks a thick-bread and] places it in front of the deity. [Thereafter,] he libates (to) the [riv]er(?) *šukkupugullu*" KUB 27.48 v 14-15 (*Ḫišuwa* fest., NS).

The readings in line 15 are not quite assured. The word [*šī*]⌈*u*⌉ can be restored after line 17. If this restoration is correct, this would be the Hurr. word *šiya-*/*šiu-* "river," and the following *Šukkupugullu* would be the name of a specific river, as listed in Del Monte/Tischler, RGTC 6:550.

Von Brandenstein, ZA 46 (1952) 91; Otten, ZA 59 (1969) 255; del Monte & Tischler, RGTC 6 (1978) 550.

**šukuduti** (mng. unkn.); LNS.†

**unclear:** *šu-ku-du-ti* KUB 10.92 vi 7 (LNS).

List of offerings to deities: [... Í]D.MEŠ *dapiaš* GUB-*aš* 1-*ŠU* KI.MIN [...$^{MUNUS}$SU]ḪUR.LÁL $^{d}$*Ḫe-pát šu-ku-du-ti* [...] GUB-*aš* 1-*ŠU* KI.MIN "ditto (i.e., he/she offers), standing, once to all of the rivers. [...] ditto (i.e., he/she offers), standing, once [... to the l]ady's maid of Ḫebat *š*." KUB 10.92 vi 6-8 (fest. for Teššub, LNS).

Whereas Laroche, GLH 239, includes *š*. as Hurrian, Wegner, ChS I/3-2:231, transliterates it as Akk. (*ŠU-KU-DU-TI*) listing it in her glossary (ChS I/3-3:210) under Akk. *šukuttu* "Ausstattung," cf. CAD s.v. *šukuttu* A "jewelry."

Laroche, GLH (1979) 239; Wegner, ChS I/3-3 (2004) 210.

**šukziy[a(-)...]** (mng. unkn.); OS.†

**unclear:** *šu-uk-zi-i*[*a*?(-)-...] KBo 17.36 ii 9 (OS).

1 $^{LÚ}$*ašušalaš* x[...] *tūni*⌈*k*⌉ *šalakzi* 1 $^{LÚ}$SA[NGA ...] *tīēzzi nu* 3-*ŠU šu-uk-zi-i*[*a*?(-)...] 3-*ŠU ḫalzāi* "An *ašušala*-man [...] kneads (dough for) *tunik*-bread. One pri[est...] steps (in), and three times *šukziy*[*a*...] he calls out three times" KBo 17.36 ii 7-10 (fest., OS), translit. StBoT 30:287 ii 16-19, StBoT 25:122 □ the last sign in *šu-uk-zi-i*[*a*] can also be read "*i*"; see Neu, StBoT 25:122 n. 408. Theoretically, the word could also be read *šu-az-zi-i*[*a*?(-)...].

Neu, StBoT 25:122 n. 408 and StBoT 26:173, suggests that *š*. might be a Luwian LW. It is not listed in CLL however.

**šulla- A/šulli-** (usually preceded by LÚ or DUMU(.MUNUS)) n. com.; hostage (either adult male, child, boy or girl); from MH/MS.

**sg. nom.** LÚ *šu-ul-la-aš* KUB 40.76 obv. 9 (MH/MS), LÚ *šu-ul-li-iš* KBo 14.12 iv 11 (NH).

**acc.** DUMU *šu-ul-la-an* KBo 16.27 iv 25 (MH/MS), DUMU-*an šu-ul-la-*[*an*] KUB 19.49 i 68 (Murš. II), DUMU.MEŠ *šu-ul-la-an* KBo 16.27 + KBo 40.330 i 8, 9 (MH/MS), DUMU.MUNUS *šu-ul-li-in* HKM 102 rev. 16 (MS?), DUMU.MEŠ *šu-ul*‹*-li*›*-in* KBo 43.1 obv.? 7 (MH/NS), DUMU.MEŠ *šu-ul-*⌈*li*⌉*-in* KUB 19.49 i 69 (NH).

**gen.** *ŠA* DUMU!-*ŠU šu-ul-la-aš* KUB 19.39 iii 9 (Murš. II).

**pl. nom.** DUMU.MEŠ *šu-ul-le-e-eš* KBo 16.27 i 12 (MH/MS), DUMU.MEŠ *šu-ul-la-aš* HKM 102 rev. 21 (MS?), DUMU.MUNUS.MEŠ *šu-ul-la-aš* HKM 102 obv. (9), rev. 21 (MS?), DUMU.MEŠ *šu-ul-li-iš* HKM 102 obv. 3 (MS?).

**acc.** DUMU.MEŠ *šu-ul-lu-uš* KBo 16.27 + KBo 40.330 i 10 (MH/MS), KUB 13.27 obv.! 12 (MH/MS), [...] *šu-ul-lu-uš* KBo 16.27 i 14 (MH/MS), [... *š*]*u-ul-le-eš* HKM 89:19 (MH/MS), DUMU.MEŠ *šu-ul-li-uš* KBo 16.34:4 (MS), [...]⌈*š*⌉*u-ul-*

*lu-u*[*š*(-)...] KBo 16.44:3, [...*š*]*u-ul-lu-uš* KUB 26.29 obv. 15 (MH/NS), LÚ.MEŠ *šu-ú-ul-lu-š*(*a*) KBo 8.35 i 17 (MH/MS), [...*š*]*u-ul-lu-š*(*a*) KUB 40.76 obv. 7 (MH/MS).

**dat.** DUMU.MEŠ *šu-ul-la-*[*aš*] KBo 16.27 i 13 (MH/MS).

**broken:** DUMU *šu-u*[*l-*...] KBo 16.27 iv 20 (MH/MS), [DU]MU.MEŠ *šu-ul-l*[*i-*...] KUB 6.50 ii? 3, DUMU.MEŠ *šu-*[*ul-*...] KBo 16.27 i 7 (MH/MS), DUMU.MEŠ *š*[*u-ul-*...] KUB 23.77 obv. 57 (MH/MS), LÚ *šu-u*[*l-*...] KUB 40.76 obv. 11 (MH/MS).

**a.** taken or seized, w. *epp-/app-*: ("I do not know if Luparrui seized the people")...§ [*k*]*inun=a apē ant*⌈*uḫš*⌉*eš arḫa tarn*[*er nu=k*]*an* ᵐ*Luparrūiš peran lē* [*kuie*]*nki ēpzi ammuk=wa* [...(?)] *piš*⌈*k*⌉*iškemi apē=ma=wa* [DUMU.MEŠ(?) *š*]*u-ul-le-eš appiškanzi* "But [n]ow they have release[d] those people. Don't let Liparrui take [anybo]dy in advance (saying): 'I will start [s]urrendering(?) (them), while they that are seizing those [h]ostages!'" HKM 89:15-19 (letter, MH/MS), ed. Letters 251, Alp, HBM 290f. □ Alp and Hoffner both read the traces in between lines 18-19 as [*pa*?-*r*]*a*?-*a*? and take them to immediately precede *š.* in l. 19. Since there seems to be no other ex. of *š.* without LÚ or DUMU(.MUNUS) this is what one expects in the break before *š.* filling the space at the beginning of the line.

**b.** given, w. *pai-* B: [...*ap*]⌈*ē*⌉*l*(?)*=ma* ⌈*šum*⌉*ēš=a* [*d*]*amāuš* DUMU.MEŠ *šu-*[*ul-*...] / [...DUMU.MEŠ *šu*]-⌈*ul*⌉*-la-aš* EGIR-*anda=ya* 5 DUMU.MEŠ *šu-ul-la-a*[*n*...] / [EGIR-*and*]*a=ya* 10 DUMU.MEŠ *šu-ul-la-an pišten n*[*u*...] § [ o o ] LÚ.MEŠ ᵁᴿᵁ*Kammama* DUMU.MEŠ *šu-ul-lu-uš ku*[*iuš*(?)...] / [...]x-*teni uēš* LÚ.MEŠ ᵁᴿᵁ*Kammama nam-*x[...] / [*k*]*ā=ma kuiēš* DUMU.MEŠ *šu-ul-le-e-eš* [ o?]x-*i* [...] / [*nu m*]*ān apēdaš* DUMU.MEŠ *šu-ul-la-*[*aš*...]x[...] / [DUMU.MEŠ] *šu-ul-lu-uš pī*⌈*u*⌉*eni mān* [...] / [*p*]*īueni n=uš=kan* EGIR-*pa* [...] "But, [if they are(?) h]is(?) then you (pl.) [must...] other ho[stages...] for [... h]ostages and later [you must give(?)] five more hostage[s] and [late]r you must give an additional ten hostages an[d...]. § Concerning the hostages th[at] you, the people of Kammama will [...] we [will...] the people of Kamm[ama] but the hostages [h]ere that [...], for those hostag[es...] we will either give [Ø?] hostage[s] or we will [g]ive [...] and them back/again [...]" KBo 16.27 + KBo 40.330 i 7-15 (treaty w. Kaškaeans, MH/MS), ed. Fuscagni, hethiter.net/: CTH 137.1 (INTR 2011-08-24), Kitchen/Lawrence, TreatyLawCovenant 1:356f. (without KBo 40.330), translit. Kaškäer 135 (without KBo 40.330) □ for the agreement of a sg. acc. (twice DUMU.MEŠ *šullan*) following a number larger than 1 see GrHL §9.21-22; *ziqq=a* ⌈*tuē*⌉*l* DUMU-*an šu-ul-la-a*[*n*? *U ŠA B*]*ĒLŪ*ᴹᴱŠ GAL*=ya* DUMU.MEŠ *šu-ul-*⌈*li*⌉*-in pāi nu ANA* ᵈ[UTU-*ŠI* ...] ⌈x x(?)⌉ [*kuwapi*?]⌈*kki* ZI-*anza*⌉ *n=aš apiya* [*t*]*eḫḫi* "Also, you must give both your own son as hostag[e and] also a hostage each(?) [of] the high [l]ords. [Whe]rever [I, My Majesty] desire, there I will [p]lace them" KUB 19.49 i 68-70 (treaty w. Manapa-Tarḫunta, Murš. II), ed. Friedrich, SV 2:10f., Kaškäer 114, Wilhelm, hethiter.net/:CTH 69 (INTR 2012-08-09), Kitchen/Lawrence, TreatyLawCovenant 1:530f. □ the addition of "each" in the translation tries to account for the sg. acc. *šullin* after the pl. DUMU.MEŠ as distributive: each "high lord" had to give one son as a hostage.

**c.** becoming, w. *kiš-*: (Šupp. I responds to the request of the Egyptian envoy to send a son to marry the recently widowed Egyptian queen:) *nu=wa naḫšarriyatten* [*kuwa*]*tqa nu=wa=mu* DUMU*=YA* 〈*a*〉*padda uekišketteni* [*nu=war=a*]*š=za* ᴸᵁ*šu-ul-li-iš kuwapikki kišari* (last two words over eras.) [LUGAL-*u*]*n=ma=war=an=z=an UL* (eras.) *iyatteni* "[Perha]ps you became afraid and for that reason you keep asking me for a son of mine, (but) [h]e will at some point become a hostage and you will not make him your [kin]g" KBo 14.12 iv 9-12 (DŠ frag. 28), ed. Güterbock, JCS 10:97, GestaSupp 122f. ("ostaggio").

**d.** mentioned with captives: [...*lin*]*kiya kattan* [*ki*]*ššan daiš* ᴸᵁ*appanza* 1 DUMU *šu-ul-la-an* x[...] GUD.ḪI.A *ūnnai* "[He] put (it) under [oa]th [as f]ollows: a captive (subj.) one hostage (obj.) ... [...] cattle he will drive" KBo 16.27 iv 24-25, (treaty w. Kaškaeans, MH/MS), ed. Fuscagni, hethiter.net/: CTH 137.1 (INTR 2011-08-24), Del Monte, OAM 2:105, Kitchen/Lawrence, TreatyLawCovenant 1:362f., translit. Kaškäer 138 □ because of the frag. state of the text it is not clear whether the verb *ūnnai* "he drives" has both *š.* and the oxen as its obj. or whether the sign trace following it should be restored to a form of *pai-* B "to give" (thus Kitchen/Lawrence, TreatyLawCovenant 1:362f., Tischler, HEG S/2:1141, and possibly also von Schuler, Kaškäer 138); Del Monte OAM 2:105 restores to *p*[*a-ra-a pa-a-i nu* x] GUD etc. For a similar but even more frag. context compare KBo 16.27 iv 19-20.

**e.** in a tariff list for hostages exchanged between Hittites and Kaškaeans: *ŠA* ᵐ*Tamitiš* LÚ ᵁᴿᵁ*Taggašta* (inserted above the line: IGI.ḪI.A *uškanzi*) ŠÁM 2 DUMU.MEŠ *šu-ul-li-iš* 1 LÚ § (...) § ᵐ*Ḫimu*-DINGIR-*LIM* LÚ ᵁᴿᵁ*Gamamma* IGI.ḪI.A *uškanzi* 2 DUMU.MUNUS.MEŠ ⸢*šu*⸣-*ul-la-aš* 1 LÚ ŠÁM § (...) § ᵐ*Gašaluwāš* LÚ ᵁᴿᵁ*Malaziya* ⸢IGI NU.GÁL⸣ ᵐ*Gapiyaš* EGIR *paitta* 1 DUMU.MUNUS *šu-ul-li-in* ⸢1? LÚ?⸣ *tatta* "Tamiti, man of Taggašta (above the line: sighted, lit. the eyes see): (his) price is two boy hostages (and) one man. § ( ... ) § Ḫimuili, the man of Gamamma, sighted: two girls as hostage (and) one man (is his) price. § (...) Gašaluwāš, man of Malaziya, blind: Gapiya has given (him) back (and) has taken one girl as a hostage (and) one(?) man(?)" HKM 102:2-3, 8-9, 15-17 (MS?), ed. Del Monte, OAM 2:103f., Arıkan, AoF 33:146f. □ for Tamitiš as a probably mistaken nom. after the Akk. preposition *ŠA* compare *ŠA* ᵐ*Kururri* in l. 13 and correctly used nom. (cf. GrHL §16.9) without *ŠA* in ll. 6, 10, 11, 15. For the Kaškaeans mentioned by name as important tribal leaders see Siegelová, Mem.Imparati 735-737.

For the double *a/i*-stem with the *i*-stem as secondary due to Luwian influence from the MH period onwards (cf. the attestations from Maşat Höyük and KBo 16.34:4) see Rieken, HS 107:42-53. The status of Sum. LÚ or DUMU(.MUNUS) that almost always precede *š.* is difficult to establish: *tuēl* DUMU-*an* preceding *šulla*[*n*] KUB 19.49 i 68 is clearly appositional: "your own son as a hostage" with clear word space in between. In most other cases, however, the Sum. and *š.* are written more closely together even when the Sum. is marked as plural. The interchange between LÚ, DUMU, and DUMU.MUNUS (note the absence thus far of *MUNUS *š.*) is an apparently deliberate choice as opposed to the often generic use of determinatives (cf. ᴸᵁ́ in MUNUS ᴸᵁ́IGI.NU.GÁL ᴸᵁ́Ú.ḪÚB "a blind (and) deaf woman" Bo 2731 iii 5 apud StBoT 22:12f.). To what extent there was a spoken Hittite reality behind the Sum. is impossible to say.

Friedrich, SV 2 (1930) 28f. (incorrectly connects with a nonexisting noun **šullai-* "Zank; Ungnade"); Götze, AM (1933) 167 and 310 ("(seines Sohnes) Streit(?)"); Güterbock, IF 60 (1952) 204 with n. 2 ("Geisel(?)"); idem, JCS 10 (1956) 97 ("hostage"); von Schuler, Kaškäer (1965) 113-114 ("Geisel"); Rieken, HS 107 (1994) 45; Tischler, HEG S/2 (2006) 1141-1142.

Cf. *šullai-* B, **šullatar* B.

## šulla- B/šulle-, šullai- C, šulliya/e- v.; 1.

to become arrogant, presumptuous, rebellious, disrespectful, aggressive (abs., no sentence particle), **2.** to be(come) presumptuous toward, disrespectful to, to disrespect (w. dat.-loc. object and w. or without particles *-kan, -šan*); from OH/NS (and MH/MS).

**pres. sg. 2** *šu-ul-le-ši* KUB 36.114 rt. col. 6 (MH/MS), *šu-ul-li-ia-ši* KBo 19.70:11 (Murš. II), KBo 12.70 obv.! 8 (NS).

**sg. 3** *šu-ul-le-ez-zi* KUB 36.114 rt. col. 14 (MH/MS), *šu-ul-le-e-ez-zi* KUB 28.1 iv 36 (OH/NS), *šu-ul-la-iz-zi* KUB 13.32 rev. 7 (NH), *šu-ul-li-ia-zi* KUB 14.3 iv 39 (NH), [*š*]*u*?-*ul-la-a-iz-zi* KBo 25.169 left col. 4 (NS).

**pl. 3** [...(-)]*šu-ul-la-a-an-zi* KBo 43.77:7 (NS) (thus Oettinger, Stammbildung 291 as 38/g), here? [*š*]*u-ul-la-an*[-...] KBo 14.4 i (14) (Murš. II).

**pret. sg. 2** [*šu-u*]⸢*l-le*⸣-*e*-⸢*et*⸣ KUB 14.17 iii 17 (coll. W., Murš. II), *šu-ul-li-ia-at* KUB 1.4 iii (36) (Ḫatt. III), KUB 19.67 + 1102/v (StBoT 24, Plate V) ii 19 (Ḫatt. III).

**sg. 3** *šu-u-ul-le-et* KBo 32.14 ii 19, iii 16, rev. 31 (MH/MS), *šu-u-ul-le-e-et* KBo 32.14 ii 4 (MH/MS), *šu-ul-li-ia-at* KUB 12.60 i 3 (OH/NS), *šu-ul-la-a-it* KBo 5.13 i 4 (Murš. II), KUB 6.41 i 47 (Murš. II), *šu-ul-le-et* KUB 6.41 i 32 (Murš. II), *šu-ul-le-e-et* KBo 16.17 iii 28 (Murš. II), KUB 24.3 ii 28 (Murš. II), KUB 1.4 + 674/v (StBoT 24 pl. III) iii 42, 44 (Ḫatt. III), KUB 19.67 + 1102/v (StBoT 24 pl. V) ii (30) + KUB 1.10 ii! (12) (Ḫatt. III), KUB 26.58 obv. 5a (Ḫatt. III), *šu-ul-li-ia-at-ta* KUB 1.10 ii! 14 (Ḫatt. III).

**pl. 2** *šu-ul-le-et-te-en* KUB 4.1 ii 11 (MH/NS), [*šu*]-*ul-la-at-te-*[*en*] KBo 64.277:2.

**pl. 3** *šu-ul-le-er* KUB 4.1 i 17, ii 15 (MH/NS), *šu-ul-li-i-e-er* KBo 5.8 iv 4 (2×), 9 (Murš. II), *šu-ul-le-e-er* KUB 31.40 obv. 10 (NS).

**pl. nom. neut.** *šu-ul-la-an-da* KUB 24.3 ii 34, KUB 24.4 obv. 23 (both Murš. II), *šu-ul-la-an-ta* KUB 24.1 iii 18 (Murš. II), here? KUB 43.37 iii 3 (NS).

**here?:** [*š*]*u-ul-la-an*[?] KBo 14.4 i 14 (Murš. II).

*šu-ul-la-an-ta* KUB 43.37 iii 3 (thus Tischler, HEG S/2: 1146) is to be read and restored [*a-a*]*š-šu-ul-la-an-ta*; for *aššulant-* as a derivation of *aššul* "wellbeing, welfare" see Groddek, AoF 26:40f.

(Hurr.) *wu*ᵤ́/*pu-ú-ru te-e-lu tap-šu-ú* KBo 32.14 i 3-4, 20, iv 16-17, rev. 26 = (Hitt.) *n=aš* (*mekki*) *šu-u-ul-le*(*-e*)*-et* "and he became (very) arrogant" ibid. ii 4, 19, iii 16, rev. 31 (Hurr. bil., MH/MS), ed. StBoT 32:103, cf. Giorgieri, FsHaas 132f.

(Hattic) [...]-*ki*(-)*ta-ap*? KUB 28.1 iv 35 = (Hitt.) *n=aš šu-ul-le-e-ez-zi* "and he becomes arrogant" ibid. iv 36 (bil. incantation), cf. Ivanov, Kavkazsko-Blizhnevostochnyj Sbornik 7:82f., 169.

**1.** to become arrogant, presumptuous, rebellious, disrespectful, aggressive (abs., no sentence particle) — **a.** in Hurrian wisdom literature: (A deer is driven away from his home mountain and he moves to another one. There he grows fat) *n=aš šu-u-ul-le-e-et nu āppa* ḪUR.SAG-*an ḫurzakiuan daiš* "He became arrogant and began to curse the mountain in return" KBo 32.14 ii 4-5 (MH/MS), ed. StBoT 32:74f. ("er suchte Streit"), Melchert, FsHerzenberg 91, tr. Hittite Myths² 69 ("became discontented"), Ünal, TUAT 3.4:862 ("wurde er streitsüchtig"); (Similarly, a man who ran away from his home town and arrived in another one) *man=aš šu-u-ul-le-et nu=ššan* EGIR-*pa* URU-*ri idālu takkiškiuan daiš* "When he became arrogant, he began to do the city harm in return" KBo 32.14 ii 19-20, ed. StBoT 32:76f., tr. Hittite Myths² 69, TUAT 3/4:862, cf. Melchert, FsHerzenberg 91; (a governor considerably increased his income from a city) *n=aš mekki šu-u-ul-le-et n=ašta namma* URU-*an anda UL aušzi* "He became very arrogant and no longer had regard for (lit. looked at) the city." (Complaints arose and he lost everything) KBo 32.14 iii 16-17, ed. StBoT 32:84f. ("Er suchte großen Streit"), Melchert, FsHerzenberg 91, tr. Hittite Myths² 71, Ünal, TUAT 3.4:863 ("er wurde sehr dünkelhaft"), cf. ibid. rev. 31-32.

**b.** in historical-administrative contexts: (The subjects of the king are required to be loyal to the dynasty:) *mān šu-ul-le-ši=ma nu=kka*[*n*...] *ANA* DUMU.MEŠ ᴸᵁ́.ᴹᴱŠGAL.GAL *idalu k*[*uitki*(?) ...] *nu=tta parḫantaru*...§...*kuiš šu-ul-le-ez-zi=ma ištarn*[*a*...] *takkešzi*..."But if you become rebellious and [...] / [inflict] s[omething] harmful on the children of the grandees, let them chase you (away) [...]...§...But whoever becomes rebellious (and) inflicts [harm(?)...] among [...] (may this oath pursue him)" KUB 36.114 rt. col. 6-7, 14-15 (protocol of dynastic succession, MH/MS), ed. Carruba, SMEA 18:190f., Giorgieri, AoF 32:333; ("I made him (i.e., Aparru of Kalašma) a lord and gave him Kalašma to govern. And I further made him swear") *n=aš šu-ul-le-e-et* [*nu=m*]*u kūrurriaḫta* "But he became disrespectful [and] became hostile to [m]e" KBo 16.17 iii 26-29 (detailed annals, Murš. II), ed. Otten, MIO 3:173f. ("begann er Streit"), Melchert, FsHerzenberg 92.

**c.** in religious contexts (prayers and rituals) — **1′** finite verb forms: *nu kuriwan*[(*aš* KUR.KUR-*TIM k*)*u*(*e*)] *araḫza*˺*nda* KUR ᵁᴿᵁ*Mittanni* (var. ᵁᴿᵁ*Ḫurri*) KUR ᵁᴿᵁ[(*Arzauwa*)] *nu ḫūmanza šu-ul-le-e-et* "And the protectorate countries which are adjacent — Mittanni (var. Hurri), Arzawa — each one has become disrespectful" KUB 24.3 ii 26-28 (prayer Murš. II to Sungoddess of Arinna, pre-NH/NS), w. dupls. KUB 30.12 obv. 16-17, KBo 7.63 rev.? 5-6, ed. Lebrun, Hymnes 161, 169 ("se sont insurgés"), Melchert, FsHerzenberg 93, tr. Hittite Prayers 52 ("are in conflict") □ for *kuriwana-* "territorial, protectorate" see HED K s.v., Melchert, FsHerzenberg 93 n. 8, Beckman, DeuteroGesch. 287; *kinun=at=za* LÚ.MEŠ ᵁᴿᵁ*Gašga dāer nu* LÚ.MEŠ ᵁᴿᵁ*Gašga šu-ul-le-er nu=za apenzan* GÉŠPU *ḫaštai walliškanzi šumaš=a=za* DINGIR.MEŠ *tepnuer* "Now the Kaškaeans have taken possession of them (i.e., the lands) and the Kaškaeans have become presumptious. They are boasting of their own force (and) strength while belittling you, O Gods" KUB 4.1 i 16-18 (rit. before a campaign, MH/NS), ed. Kaškäer 168f. ("haben Streit begonnen"), García Trabazo, TextosRel. 512f., tr. Akal Oriente 13:240; *šumeš=a* DINGIR.MEŠ *ŠA* KUR ᵁᴿᵁ*Gašga šu-ul-le-et-te-en n=ašta ŠA* KUR ᵁᴿᵁ*Ḫatti* DINGIR.MEŠ KUR-*az arḫa šuwatten šumeš=a=za* KUR=*SUNU datten* § ᴸᵁ́.ᴹᴱŠ*Gašga=ya šu-ul-le-er n=ašta ANA* LÚ.MEŠ ᵁᴿᵁ*Ḫatti* URU.DIDLI.ḪI.A=*ŠUNU arḫa dātten* ᴬ.ŠÀ*kuerazz=*(*i*)*ya=aš IŠTU* ᴳᴵŠKIRI$_6$.GEŠTIN.ḪI.A=*ŠUNU arḫa šuwatte*˹*n*˺ "But you, O Gods of Kaška Land, became rebellious and expelled the gods of Ḫatti from (their) land, while you took possession of their land. § The Kaškaeans also became rebellious. You took away from the people of Ḫatti their towns, and you also expelle[d] them from (their) fields (and) their vineyards" KUB 4.1 ii 11-18 (rit. before a campaign, MH/NS), ed. Kaškäer 170f., García Trabazo, TextosRel. 516f., tr. Akal Oriente 13:241.

**2′** part.: *nu* KUR.KUR.ḪI.A LÚ.KÚR *kue šu-ul-la-an-ta ḫaršallanta kuēš=kan tuk ANA* ᵈ*Teli*˹*pi*˺*nu U ANA* DINGIR.MEŠ ᵁᴿᵁ*Ḫatti UL naḫḫanteš* "And the enemy countries which are disrespectful (and) angry, who are not respectful to you Telipinu and to the gods of Ḫatti" KUB 24.1 iii 18-20 (prayer of Murš. II to Telipinu), ed. Lebrun, Hymnes 183, 186 ("agités"), Gurney, AAA 27:32f. ("quarrelling"), Melchert, FsHerzenberg 93 ("disrespectful"), Kassian/Yakubovich, FsKošak 431, 434 ("arrogant"), tr. Hittite Prayers 55 ("are quarrelling"); *waršanda šu-ul-la-an-da* KUR.KUR.ḪI.A «*ANA*» KUR ^URU^KÙ.BABBAR-*ti*=*ma tariyan* KUR-*e nu tariyandan lātten waršiyandan*=*ma tūriyatten* "Rested are the aggressive lands while Ḫatti-Land is a tired land; now unhitch the tired one, but hitch up the rested one" KUB 24.3 ii 34-37 (prayer of Murš. II to Sungoddess of Arinna), w. dupl. KUB 24.4 + KUB 30.12 obv. 23-24, ed. Lebrun, Hymnes 161, 169f. ("querelleurs"), Gurney, AAA 27:28f. ("quarrelsome"), tr. Hittite Prayers 52 ("belligerent").

**2.** to be(come) presumptuous toward, disrespectful to, to disrespect (w. dat.-loc. object and w. or without particles *-kan, -šan*) — **a.** in historical-administrative contexts: ^m^PÍŠ.TUR-*waš*=*ma*=*mu*=*ššan šu-ul-le-et nu*=*mu* KUR ^URU^*Pitaš*[(*ša* LÚ.MEŠ ^URU^*Ḫat)ti*] ÌR.MEŠ=*YA kattan ḫarnamniyat* "But Mašḫuiluwa became presumptuous toward me and stirred up the land of Pitašša, Hittites, my (own) subjects, (against) me" KUB 6.41 i 32-33 (treaty with Kupanta-^d^LAMMA, Murš. II), w. dupl. KUB 6.42:9-10, ed. SV 1:110f., tr. DiplTexts[2] 75 ("quarreled with me"); cf. also *nu*=*war*=*aš*=*mu*=*kan šu-ul-la-a-it nu*=*wa*=*mu* ÌR.MEŠ=*YA kattan ḫarnamniē*[(*t*)] KUB 6.41 i 47 (Kup.), w. dupls. KBo 4.7 i 51 and KBo 5.13 i 4; (They used to give troops to my ancestors and to myself) ⸢*n*⸣=*at*=*mu*=*ššan šu-ul-li-i-e-er nu*=*mu namma* ÉRIN.MEŠ *UL pešker* "They became presumptuous toward me and they no longer gave troops to me" KBo 5.8 iv 9-10 (extensive annals, Murš. II), w. dupl. KBo 16.8 iv 2, 7, ed. AM 160f., tr. del Monte, L'annalistica 112; LÚ-*nili*=⸢*š*⸣*ši watarnaḫḫun šu-ul-li-ia-at*=*wa*=*mu*=*kan* ... *mān*=*war*=*aš*=*mu*=*kan šu-u*⸢*l-li*⸣-[(*ia-a*)]*t ku*⸢*wa*⸣*pi UL m*[(*ān ḫand*)]*ān* LUGAL.GAL *ANA* LUGAL *ṢEḪḪI*⸢*R*⸣ [(*katterraḫḫe*)]*r kinun*=*aš*=*mu*=*kan šu-ul-li-ia-at-ta* (var. A: Ø *-ta*) *k*[(*uit*)] / [(*n*=*an*=*mu* DINGIR.MEŠ) *ḫa*]*nnešnaz katterraḫḫer* "I challenged him in a manly way (thus): 'You disrespected me!' (... and if somebody were to ask me about this I would say:) 'If he had never been disrespectful to me, would they (i.e., the gods) have subjected a great king to a petty king? Because he now disrespected me, the gods have subjected him to me by means of a lawsuit" KUB 19.67 + 1102/v (StBoT 24 pl. V) ii 18-19, 29-33 + KUB 1.10 ii! 11-15 (Apol., Ḫatt. III), w. dupl. KUB 1.4 + 674/v iii 35-36, 42-45, ed. StBoT 24:22f., tr. Hoffner, ANEHST 268.

**b.** in cult inv.: *nu ANA* ^LÚ^SANGA[...] *kuiš šu-ul-la-iz-zi nu*[...] 3 GÍN *pāi* "Who is disrespectful to a priest(?) and(?) [...] he shall pay three shekels (of silver)" KUB 13.32 rev. 6-8 (inv. of sanctuaries, Tudḫ. IV), ed. Hazenbos, Organization 47f. ☐ because it is unclear how extensive the break is it is uncertain if *š.* is the verb of the sentence starting w. *nu ANA* ^LÚ^SANGA [...].

**c.** in Babylonian wisdom literature translated in Hittite: *atti*(*n*)=*tten*=*ta pe*[*ra*]*n l*[*ē kuiški*] *ḫur*⸢*da*⸣*i* AMA-*aš*=*ma*=*ta* x x[...] *nu*=*šši*=*kan* ⸢*l*⸣*ē šu-ul-li-*⸢*ya*⸣*-ši* "Let n[o one] curse your father in fr[on]t of you. But your mother (subj.) [...] and you must not be disrespectful to her" KBo 12.70 obv.! 6-8 (Akkado-Hittite proverbs, NS), ed. Laroche, Ugar. 5:780, Keydana, UF 23:69.

Contrary to HAB 41 (see also Garrett, JCS 42:239) there is no firm evidence for a construction of *š.* w. dir. obj. "to disrespect someone"; for KBo 5.8 ii 2 (extensive annals, Murš. II) see *šullai-* B "to use as hostage." In KUB 19.49 i 68 (Murš. II) we restore *šu-ul-la*[*-an*] acc. sg. of *šulla/i-* "hostage" q.v. instead of *šu-ul-la*[*-i*] (thus SV 2:10). KUB 14.3 iv 39 is too fragmentary to be of use.

Sommer, Heth 2 (1922) 42f. ("hadern," "Streit anfangen," "auszanken"); idem, HAB (1938) 41 (= Akk. *šelû*); Gurney, AAA 27 (1941) 29, 96 ("scold, revile(?)"); Friedrich, HW (1952) 196 ("streiten, zanken; — jem.en auszanken, zornig behandeln"); Kronasser, EHS 1 (1962) 505 ("schelten"); Oettinger, Stammbildung (1979) 291-293 ("sich aggressiv verhalten, Streit suchen, schelten"); Neu, Hurritische (1988) 8-9; Garrett, JCS 42 (1990) 239; Wilhelm, Or NS 61 (1992) 129; Ünal, TUAT 3.4 (1994) 862 ("streitsüchtig werden"), 863, 864 ("dünkelhaft werden"); Melchert, FsHerzenberg (2005) 90-98; Tischler, HEG S/2 (2006) 1144-1147 ("streiten, zanken, jemanden auszanken, zornig behandeln"); Kassian/Yakubovich, FsKošak (2007) 434 (*šullant-* "rebellious(?)"); 448f. (*šullant-* "upstart and impious"); Kloekhorst, EDHIL (2008) 778f. ("to become arrogant").

Cf. *šullatar* A, *šullešš-*.

**šulai- A** n. com.; lead; wr. syll. and A.GAR$_5$; from OS.

**sg. nom.** *šu-la-a-iš* KUB 3.103 rev. 11 (NS).

**acc.** *šu-la-in* KUB 41.7 vi 1 (OH or pre-NH/LNS), *šu-la-a-*⸢*i*⸣-[*in*?] KUB 17.34 iv 4 (NS).

**gen.** *šu-li-i-aš* KBo 17.3 iv 32 (OS), KBo 17.1 iv (37) (OS), *šu-ú-li-ia-aš* IBoT 3.98:9 + KUB 28.82 i 23 (OH?/NS), A.GAR$_5$-*aš* KUB 17.10 iv 16 (OH/MS), KUB 33.3:7 (OH/MS), KUB 33.66 ii 10 (OH/MS?), KUB 33.8 iii 8 (OH/NS), KBo 12.87 rev. (1) (NS), Bo 7615:4 (JCS 4:131), *ŠA* A.GAR$_5$ KUB 9.31 iii 23 (MH/NS), KUB 9.32 obv. 9 (MH/NS), KBo 49.194:7 (NS).

**abl./inst.** *IŠTU* A.GAR$_5$ KUB 44.61 rev. 27 (NH).

**fragmentary** ⸢*šu-li-ia*⸣-[...] KBo 18.155:12 (NH).

**pure logographic uses:** A.GAR$_5$ KBo 17.95 iii 8 (2×) (MS?), KUB 43.60 iv 13 (OH/NS), KBo 15.24 ii 17 (MH/NS), KUB 39.57 i 4, 5 (2×) (NH), KBo 7.22 i 7 (NS), KBo 24.47 iii? 20 (NS), KBo 31.55:11 (NS) (cf. Güterbock, FsOtten 73), KBo 45.241:1 (NS), KBo 47.266 obv. (11) (NS), KUB 58.100 ii? 5 (NS), KUB 12.26 ii 4 (NH), KUB 24.5 obv. 25 (NH), KUB 39.41 i 4 (NH), KUB 12.24 i 12 (NS), KUB 42.38 obv. 18 (NS), KUB 42.97:10 (NS), KUB 59.67 ii 7 (NS), HT 73:3 (NS), IBoT 4.45 obv. (1), (2 coll.) (LNS), A!.GAR$_5$ KUB 41.18 ii 10 (NH), A.GAR$_5$! KUB 46.42 iv 10 (NH/NS).

*šu-ú-*⸢*li-ia*⸣*-aš* IBoT 3.98:9 + KUB 28.82 i 23 (OH?/NS) alternates with ⸢A.GAR$_5$⸣-*aš* KBo 12.87 rev. (1) (NS) (cf. Laroche, RA 59:85).

(Sum.) [A.GAR$_5$] = (Akk.) [*a-ba-ru*] = (Hitt.) *šu-la-a-iš* "lead" KUB 3.103 rev.11 (Diri vocab.), ed. Laroche, RHA XXIV/79:162f., MSL 15:94 (tr. incorrectly aligned). The Sumerian word for lead seems to have been A.GAR$_5$ (PSD A/1 s.v. A.GAR$_5$), but some later scribes may have confused GAR$_5$ with the similarly shaped BÁR, perhaps influenced by the Akk. reading of A.GAR$_5$ as *abāru* A (CAD s.v.). Hittite scribes used a number of similar sign shapes more or less interchangeably for GAR$_5$, GÚG, BÁR, LÙ and TÙN. See Güterbock, JCS 15:71 w. n. 23, FsOtten 71-73 and Rüster/Neu, HZL no. 220. The vocab. entry confirms *š.* as an *ai*-stem (as opposed to an *i*-stem, cf. HW 197, StBoT 26:173).

**a.** as ingots or as pig lead: ⸢34 EME⸣ A.GAR$_5$ 14 $^{URUDU}$GAG ⸢x x⸣ [...] "thirty-four ingots of lead, fourteen copper pegs, ..." KUB 42.97:10 (rit. frag., NS); cf. also [A]N.BAR? 7 EME A.⸢GAR$_5$ x⸣ KBo 9.117 iv? 1 (Kizz. rit. frag., NS); [*š*]*err*⸗*a*⸗*ššan šu-la-in* ⸢*dan*⸣*nantan dāi* "He places the 'empty' (i.e., pure, unmixed?) lead [o]n it" KUB 41.7 vi 1-2 (Ḫutuši's rit., OH or pre-NH/LNS) □ Tischler, HEG T/D 100 understands *šulain dannantan* as "lead free (from impurities)"; ⸢*šē*⸣*r*⸗*a*⸗*ššan* 1 GÍN KÙ.BABBAR [...] 1 GÍN NAGGA 1 GÍN *šu-la-a-*⸢*i*⸣-[*in*?] "[He puts(?)] one shekel of silver, [...], one shekel of tin, one shekel of lead on it" KUB 17.34 iv 3-4 (Ḫutuši's rit, NS).

**b.** used as weights: ("The exorcist takes scales and approaches the king") *nu ANA* LUGAL A.GAR$_5$ *pāi* (eras.) *nu*⸗*ššan* LUGAL-*uš* A.GAR$_5$ *ANA* GIŠ.RÍN ZI.BA.NA *dāi* "He gives the king (a piece of) lead. The king puts the lead on the scales" KBo 17.95 iii 8-9 (rit. naming infernal deities, MS?), ed. ChS 1/5:359.

**c.** used as inlay: 2 $^{GIŠ!}$*allūššaš* A.GAR$_5$ GAR.RA "two (wooden) *allūšša*, inlaid with lead" KUB 58.100 ii? 5 (inv. frag., NS), ed. THeth 10:181; possibly here: 2 *TAPAL* ḪUB.BI.ḪI.A KÙ.BABBAR ŠÀ.BA 1-*NUTUM annutaim*[*a*(?)] 1-*NŪTUM*⸗*ma* A.GAR$_5$ [GAR.RA(?)] "two pairs of silver earrings of which one fitted with *annuta* and one [inlaid with(?)] lead" KUB 42.38 obv. 17-18 (inv. of jewels, NH), ed. THeth 10:147f., Siegelová, Verw 498f.

**d.** made into models of body parts: ZI.ḪI.A A.GAR$_5$ *anda uišurianteš* [...]⸢x x⸣ $^{UZU}$GABA A.GAR$_5$ $^{UZU}$UBUR *ginuwa* A.GAR$_5$ IGI.ḪI.A A.GAR$_5$ ŠU.MEŠ A.GAR$_5$ [GUD.]MAḪ 1 *šēnaš* "Souls of lead are pressed in(to a figurine). There are [a head of l]ead(?), a breast (and) knees of lead, eyes of lead, hands of lead, a [bu]ll (and) one (human) figurine" KUB 39.57 i 4-6 (rit., NH), ed. Torri, Lelwani 47f., for *wišuriya-* see Melchert, FsSiegelová 217; G[I]M-*an*⸗*ma*⸗*kan ḫantezziyaš ḫūprušḫiyaš* 1 EME [A.GAR$_5$] 1 *lingainn*⸗*a* URUD[U] *ḫašši*⸗*kan anda peššiēzzi kēdaš*⸗*kan anda QĀTAMMA peššiyanneškezzi* EGIR-*ŠU*⸗*ma* DINGIR.MEŠ *ABI* DINGIR.MEŠ KUR-⸢*TIM* 1 *ḫ*⸣*ūprušḫin dāi nu*⸗*kan* EME A.GAR$_5$ 1 *lin*[*gainn*⸗*a a*]⸢*nda*⸣ *QĀTAMMA peššiya*[*nneškezzi*] "Just as he throws one tongue of lead and one (model of an) oath of copper into the first *ḫūprušhi*-vessels in the hearth/brazier, in the same way he throws in for each of these (gods mentioned above). Thereafter he takes one *ḫuprušḫi*-vessel (for) the paternal gods (and) country gods. And similarly he throws a tongue of lead [and] one (model of an) oath in [for each]" KBo 24.47 iii ? 16-20 (lists of Hurrian gods, NS); cf. KUB 39.41 i 3-4 (funerary rit., NH), ed. Kassian et al., Funerary 642.

**e.** made into a ring: *nu⸗kan* 1-*EN* $^{NA_4}$NUNUZ 1 *KAMKAMMATUM* AN.BAR *ŠA* A.GAR$_5$⸗*ya* (var. B substitutes *ŠA* $^{NA_4}$NÍR) *anda ne*⸢*ḫ*⸣[(*ḫi*)] *n⸗at⸗kan ANA* UDU.ŠIR.ḪI.A $^{UZU}$GÚ⸗*ŠUNU* SI⸗*ŠUNU*⸗*ya anda ḫamang*[(*ami*)] "I string together one bead (and) one ring of iron and of lead (var. B: of NÍR-stone) and I tie them on to the neck(s) and horn(s) of the rams" KUB 9.32 obv. 9-10 (Ašḫella's rit., MH/NS), w. dupls. KUB 9.31 iii 22-24 (A), HT 1 iii 11-14 (B), KUB 41.18 ii 10-12 (C), ed. Dinçol, Belleten 49/193:12f., 23, cf. *nai-* 5 a 2′.

**f.** made into a comb: (The Sungod and Kamrušipa began to argue with each other while they were combing sheep. Kamrušipa placed a throne of iron) *nu⸗wa⸗ššan* A.GAR$_5$ $^{GIŠ}$GA.ZUM SÍG *dāiš nu⸗wa⸗kan šuppin* ÁŠ.MUNUS.GÀR-*an kiššer* "and she put a lead comb for wool on (it). They combed the ritually pure female lamb (with it)" KUB 12.26 ii 4-6 (myth, NH), ed. Benedetti, SR 1:16, Archi, Or NS 62:406f., Watkins, FsMelchert 358.

**g.** made into lids: *kattan dankui taknī* ZABAR *palḫi arta ištappulli⸗šmet* A.GAR$_5$-*aš zakki*(*š*)⸗*šmiš* AN.BAR-*aš kuit andan paizzi n⸗ašta namma šarā UL uizzi anda⸗ad⸗an ḫarakzi* "Down in the dark earth (i.e., netherworld) stand *palḫi*-vessels of bronze. Their lids are of lead, their latches(?) are of iron. What goes into (them) can not come up again, it perishes therein" KUB 17.10 iv 15-17 (Tel. myth first vers., OH/MS), w. dupl. KUB 33.3:6-9 (OH/MS), ed. DBH 41:20, 28, Rieken et al., hethiter.net/: CTH 324.1 (INTR 2012-05-10), translit. Myth 37, tr. Hittite Myths² 17, Beckman, CoS 1:153; *aruni⸗ma* ⸢URUDU⸣-*aš palḫaeš kianda*[*ri*] *ištappulli⸗šmit* A.GAR$_5$-*aš* "In the sea lie *palḫi*-vessels of copper; their lids are of lead (they contain the following evils)" KUB 33.66 ii 9-10 (myth of Stormgod of Liḫzina, OH/MS?), ed. Hoffner, JNES 27:65, Groddek, ZA 89:37, 39, translit. Myth 130; *ukt*[(*ūri*)]*ya⸗ššan* AN.BAR *palḫi*⸢*š*⸣ *kitta ištappu*⸢*l*⸣*li⸗ššit šu-ú-*⸢*li-ia*⸣*-aš n⸗at⸗kan ištāpu* AN.BAR-*aš⸗šan tarmuš walḫa*⸢*nd*⸣*u* "A *palḫi*-vessel (made) of iron lies on the pyre; its lid is of lead. Let him close it. Let them pound iron nails into it" KUB 9.11 i 2-4 + IBoT 3.98:8-10 + KUB 28.82 i 22-24 (Ḫutuši's rit., OH?/NS), w. dupl. KBo 13.106 i 22-25 (OH/NS) and parallels KBo 12.87 rev.1-2, KBo 13.107:5-8; *ḫalīnaš zēri ḫarmi ta⸗an anda* 3-*iš* LUGAL-*uš* MUNUS.LUGAL-*š⸗a zēriya allapaḫḫanzi ištappulli⸗šet⸗a šu-li-i-aš* ⸢*ta iš*⸣*tāp*⸢*ḫe*⸣ "I hold a cup of clay and into the cup the king and queen spit three times. Its lid is of lead, and I close (it)" KBo 17.3 iv 31-33 (rit. for the royal couple, OS), ed. StBoT 8:38f., translit. StBoT 25:18.

**h.** ingredient in medicine: (Describing the treatment of a penis ailment: "[If] he is not circumcised(?), he pulls his foreskin(?) back. He applies an ointment [...]") *namma⸗an ḫapurin parā ḫuittiy*[*azi* ...] / [... SIG]$_5$-*ri n⸗an* [*IŠT*]*U* A.GAR$_5$⸗*pat iškeškizzi* "Then he pull[s] his foreskin(?) forward. [Until(?) he get]s [wel]l, he continues to apply the ointment [wit]h lead only" KUB 44.61 rev. 26-27 (med., NH), ed. StBoT 19:20f. □ the lead which is used for salving should be contained in the ointment.

**i.** listed with other metals, minerals or stones — **1′** in ritual, festival and oracle texts: with NAGGA(?) KBo 15.24 ii 17 (foundation rit., MH/NS), HT 73:3 (NS); with URUDU KBo 47.266 obv. 11 (Ištanuwian fest., NS), ed. Mouton, ZA 98:255, 258; with AN.BAR(?), NAGGA KBo 45.241:1 (rit. frag., NS), translit. DBH 16:295; with NA$_4$, KÙ.GI IBoT 4.45 obv. 1, 2 (oracle question frag., LNS); with KÙ.BABBAR, URUDU, NAGGA KUB 59.67 ii 5-7 (rit., NS); with KÙ.BABBAR, KÙ.GI, NAGGA, AN.BAR, URUDU, *lulluri* KUB 43.60 iv 12-13 (incantation and myth, OH/NS); with KÙ.BABBAR, KÙ.GI, AN.BAR, NAGGA, *lulluri*, $^{NA_4}$ZA.GÌN, $^{NA_4}$GUG, $^{NA_4}$DUḪ.ŠÚ.A, $^{NA_4}$KÁ.DINGIR.RA, $^{NA_4}$*parušḫa-* VS 28.57 i 7-8 (Allaituraḫi's rit.), ed. ChS 1/5-1:76; with KÙ.BABBAR, KÙ.GI, URUDU, NAGGA, AN.BAR KUB 24.5 obv. 24-25 + KUB 9.13:12 (substitute king rit., NH), ed. StBoT 3:10f.; with KÙ.BABBAR, AN.BAR GE$_6$, NAGGA, AN.BAR, URUDU, $^{NA_4}$ZA.GÌN, TI-*anza* NA$_4$-*aš*, *ša-mu-*⸢x⸣ [...] KUB 12.24 i 8-12 (rit. for Išḫara?, NS), ed. Eothen 3:162 □ could the last word be read as Akkadian *SA*$_x$ *-MU* and identified with NA$_4$ *SĀMU* "red stone, carnelian"?

**2′** in inventory texts: [ ... GÍ]N.GÍN A.GAR$_5$ 10 $^{NA_4}$*kirnuzi* "[...] minas of lead, ten *kirnuzi*-stones/minerals" KBo 31.55 rev.? 11 (glass text, NS); [1]8(?) PAD KÙ.BABBAR 38 M[A.NA KI.LÁ.BI(?)] / [...]-x ⸢*šu-li-ia*⸣-[...] "eight[een(?)] silver bar(s), [weighing] thirty-eight m[inas] / [...] lead [...]" KBo 18.155:11-12 (inv., NH), ed. Siegelová, Verw. 188f. (reading $^{URU}$Š]a$^{?}$šuliya[...] despite apparent word space before the *šu*), translit. THeth 10:245 (*š.* not listed in index).

**j.** uncertain: *urakil ŠA* A.GAR$_5$ KBo 49.194:7 (frag. of unknown nature) □ the first word is alternatively to be read *Ú-RA-KI* (to Akkadian *urāku* "ingot," cf. HZL pp. 186 and 369). However, the following sign "il" would remain unexplained.

Laroche, RHA XI/53 (1951) 71 n.17; Neumann, FsFriedrich (1959) 347-349 (etymology); Laroche, RA 59 (1965) 85; Laroche, RHA XXIV/79 (1966) 162-163, 181, 184 ("plomb"); Burde, StBoT 19 (1974) 25; Haas/Wäfler, UF 9 (1977) 88 n. 9 (Hattian DN Šulinkatte probably does not contain *š.* because it may have an IE etymology); Tischler, HEG S/2 (2006) 1142-44; Savaş, Madencilik (2006) 283-287.

**šullai- B** v.; to use as a hostage(?); NH.†

**pret. sg. 1** *šu-ul-la-a-nu-un* KBo 5.8 ii 2 (Murš. II).
**here? part. sg. nom. com.** *šu-ul-la-an-˹za˺* KBo 16.44:4 (MS).

*n=aš u˹it˺ n=aš=˹mu* GÌR˺.MEŠ-*aš kattan ḫali˹yat˺* [o o(?)] *n=aš=za* ÌR-*anni ˹daḫ˺ḫun n=aš šu-ul-la-a-nu-un namma=šmaš=kan* ERÍN.MEŠ *išḫiaḫḫun nu=mu* ˹ERÍN.MEŠ˺ *piškeuan dāer n=at=mu laḫḫi kattan paišgauwan tīēr* "He (i.e., the leader) came and knelt down at my feet. I took them (i.e., the people) in subjection and used them as hostages(?). Further, I imposed troops on them. So they began to give troops to me and to go with me on campaign" KBo 5.8 ii 1-5 (Extensive Annals of Murš. II.), ed. AM 152f. ("schalt"), cf. Tischler, HEG S 1144 ("beschimpfte"), tr. del Monte, Annalistica 109 ("ne feci ostaggi(?)") □ against Götze, it is not necessary to restore the predicate as *ḫaliyat*[*tat*] since the form *ḫaliyat* does exist.

Due to the above context and the fact that *šullai-* A/*šulliya-* "to be(come) presumptuous toward, disrespectful to" takes a dat.-loc. object, the verb *š.* is best kept separate. With Del Monte, Annalistica 109, it is most likely related to (DUMU(.MUNUS)/LÚ) *šulla/i-* "hostage."

Götze, AM (1933) 152f. ("schelten"); Oettinger, Stammbildung (1979) 292 ("zur Stellung von Geiseln verpflichten"); Tischler, HEG S/2 (2006) 1144 ("beschimpfen" > *šullai-/šulliya-* "streiten").

Cf. (DUMU(.MUNUS)/LÚ) *šulla/i-* A, **šullatar* B.

**šullai- C** v. see *šulla-* B/*šulle-*.

**šullatar A** n. neut.; malice, malicious act, maliciousness, (in dat.-loc. or abl.:) maliciously; from OS.

**sg. nom.-acc.** *šu-ul-la-a-tar* KUB 29.30 iii (14) (OS), KBo 26.19 rt. col. 12 (NS), *šu-ul-la-tar* KBo 6.13 i 9 (OH/NS), KBo 6.26 i 29 (OH/NS), KBo 10.45 i 48, ii (6) (MH/NS), KUB 41.8 i 33, 36 (MH/NS), here? [*š*]*u*?-*ul-la-a-ta* KBo 58.258:3 (NS).
**dat.-loc.** *šu-ul-la-an-ni* KBo 10.45 i 47 (MH/NS), KUB 41.8 i 28 (MH/NS), KUB 12.50:6 (pre-NH/NS), KUB 4.4 obv. rt. col. 6 (NH), here? *šu-la-an-ni* KUB 5.1 iv 40 (NH).
**abl.** *šu-ul-la-an-na-az* KBo 6.3 i (1), 4, KBo 6.10 ii 17 (both OH/NS), KUB 43.37 ii (5) (NS), *šu-ul-la-an-na-za* KBo 6.4 i 6, 14, 16 (NH); possibly KBo 4.14 iii 26 (late NH).

(Sum.) [KI.LÚ×NE](?) = (Akk.) [...]x-*du* KBo 26.19 left col.12 = (Hitt.) [*š*]*u-˹ul-la-a˺-t*[*ar*?] ibid. rt. col. 12 (vocab. frag., Diri(?)), ed. MSL 15:97 □ the restoration in MSL 15 to [*za-a*]*l*!-*du* (Akk. *ṣaltu* "quarrel") and the alleged Sum. equivalent are highly uncertain and probably inspired by *š.* in the Hitt. column.

(Akk.) [*ku*]*ṣṣ*[*u*] *ana arê* /... / *ana ˹ša-ba-ši˺ šiknat* / *napišti ˹ḫarpu*!˺ / *ana murtam libbi ayar kī˹ni˺* / *tabannî attā* "You create the winter for becoming pregnant, summer for the gathering in of living beings, spring for the lovers of the heart" KUB 4.4 obv. middle col. 3, 5-9 = (Hitt.) *kimmantan armaḫḫanni ḫamešḫantan šu-ul-la-an-ni ḫamišḫandaš=ma alel āššiyanni ḫandaš ēšša*[*tti*] "[You] make the winter for pregnancy, springtime for *š.*, but the flower of springtime for love" ibid. rt. col. 3-9 (trilingual hymn to Stormgod, NH), ed. Laroche, RA 58:73, 75, Klinger, AoF 37:321f. □ in both the Akk. and Hitt. versions it is difficult to understand the mng. of Akk. *šabāšu* "gathering in" and its intended Hitt. rendering with *š.* Laroche, RA 58:78 wanted to see here the cycle of procreation and following him Melchert, FsHerzenberg 96, proposes to take *š.* here in its literal mng. "being/becoming swollen (with child)." This lit. mng. is, however, not otherwise attested for the verb *šulla-* B/*šulle-*, *šullai-* A, *šulliye/a-* (q.v.) "to become arrogant, presumptious, rebellious, disrespectful, aggressive" or its derivate *š.* Also, the "becoming with child" is already expressed in the preceding *armaḫanni* "pregnancy." Was the Hittite scribe confusing *šabāšu* "to collect" with *šabāsu* "to be(come) angry"? Or was the Hitt. translator in rendering "the gathering in of living beings" perhaps thinking of *šullatar* B (q.v.) "hostage-ship"? The value of the last sign (*tan*$_x$, i.e., *tén*/*tin*) in both *kimmantan* and *ḫamešḫantan* follows HZL no. 330.

**a.** maliciousness, a malicious act: ("If anyone buys a field and violates the boundary, he shall take a thick loaf and break it to the Sungod (saying):...") $^{d}$UTU-*uš* $^{d}$U-*aš* *UL šu-ul-la-tar* (var.: [*šu-ul-la*]-⌜*a*⌝-*tar*) "O Sungod, O Stormgod! It was not maliciousness" KBo 6.13 i 9 (Laws §169, OH/NS), w. dupl. KUB 29.30 iii 14 (OS), VS 28.127:9 (NS), ed. Melchert, FsHerzenberg 95f., LH 135f. ("No quarrel (was intended)"), HG 76f. ("(Ob) Sonnengott (oder) Wettergott, (ist) kein Streitfall"); *takku āppatriwanzi kuišk*[(*i p*)]*aizzi ta šu-ul-la-tar* (eras. *-an-na-az*) *iēzzi* ⌜*n*⌝*aššu* $^{NINDA}$*ḫaršin našma* $^{GIŠ}$GEŠTIN *išpanduzi k*[*in*]*uzi* "If anyone goes (to someone's house) to commandeer (something), and commits a malicious act (erased: maliciously) (and) b[re]aks open either a thick loaf or a libation vessel of wine (...)" KBo 6.26 i 28-30 (Laws §164, OH/NS), w. dupls. KBo 6.18 + KBo 31.66 iv 7-9 (OH/NS), KBo 25.5:1-2 (OS), ed. Melchert, FsHerzenberg 95, LH 131f., HG 74f.; [(*UL*=*m*)]*a*=*aš šu-ul-la-an-ni ḫalziyau*⌜*en*⌝[*i*] "But w[e] do not call them (i.e., the gods) in malice" KUB 12.50:6 (frag. naming infernal deities, pre-NH/NS), w. dupl. KUB 58.74 obv. 5, ed. Haas, AoF 34:15, 25 ("im Streit"), translit. Popko, AoF 16:84; [*takku* LÚ-*an n*]⌜*ašma* MUNUS-*an šu-ul-la-an-na-az ku*⌝*iški kuen*⌜*zi*⌝ [*apūn arnuz*]*i U* 4 ⌜SAG.DU⌝ *pāi* ⌜LÚ-*n*⌝=*aku* MUNUS-*n*=*aku* [*parna*=*šše*=(*y*)*a*] *š*⌜*uw*⌝*āizzi* § [*takku* ÌR-*an n*]⌜*ašma*⌝ GÉME-*an šu-ul-la-an-na-az kuiški kuenzi apūn arnuzi* [*U* 2 SAG.D]U *pā*⌜*i*⌝ LÚ-*n*=*aku* MUNUS-*n*=*aku parna*=*ššē*=*a šuwāizzi* "[If] anyone kills [a (free) man o]r a woman out of malice (i.e., with malice-aforethought), [he shall brin]g [him/her (to his/her relatives)] and shall give four persons, either male or female and he shall look [to (his) house for it.] § [If] anyone kills [a male o]r female slave out of malice (i.e., with malice-aforethought), he shall bring him/her (to his/her relatives) [and shall] give [two perso]ns, either male or female and he shall look to (his) house for it" KBo 6.3 i 1-5 (Laws §§1-2, OH/NS), ed. LH 17 ("in a quarrel"), Imparati, Leggi 34f. ("per una disputa"), Friedrich, HG 16f. ("infolge eines Streites"), tr. Hoffner, CoS 2:107 ("in a quarrel"), von Schuler, TUAT 1/1:97 ("infolge eines Streites"), cf. Güterbock, JCS 15:66f.=AS 26:237 ("intentional killing for motives other than robbery"); *takku* $^{GIŠ}$IG *šu-ul-la-an-na-az* (var. cc [*šu-ul-la-a*] *n-na-za*) *kui*[(*ški*)] *taiēzzi kuit kuit ḫarakzi ta*=*at šar*⌜*n*⌝*ikzi U* 1 MA.NA KÙ.BABBAR *pāi parna*=*šše*=(*y*)*a šuwāizzi* "If any[one] steals a door out of maliciousness, he shall replace everything that gets lost in the house, he shall pay forty shekels of silver and he shall look to (his) house for it" KBo 6.10 ii 17-19 (Laws §127, OH/NS), w. dupl. Bo "2111" ii 5" (var. cc, sic, Hrozný, CH 114f. nn. 4-8), ed. LH 116 ("as a result of a quarrel"), HG 68f.; DUMU.LÚ.U$_{19}$.LU *UL* ⌜*i*⌝*nnarā uwanun UL*=*ma šu-ul-la-an-ni uwanun* É-*ri*=*kan anda* ⌜*ē*⌝*šḫar išḫaḫru NĒŠ* DINGIR-*LIM šu-ul-la-tar* ⌜*w*⌝*aštauš kišat* "I, a human being, came (to the river) neither of my own accord nor maliciously. (I came because) in (this) house bloodshed, tears, perjury, malice (and/or) misdeed have occurred" KBo 10.45 i 45-49 (rit. for Underworld Deities, MH/NS), w. dupl. KUB 41.8 i 28-30, ed. Melchert, FsHerzenberg 95 ("in anger/wantonness"), Otten, ZA 54:120f. ("im Zorn ... Streit"), tr. Collins, CoS 1:169a ("in quarrel ... quarrel"), Miller, TUAT NF 4:210 ("im Zorn ... Zorn").

**b.** uncertain or unclear (see also *šullatar* B b): ("Given the fact that in the past I confronted you with the following words and that you yourself had said to them: 'May even the smallest thing become difficult for him'") *ŠA* MUNUS=*ya*=*mu*=*kan kuit* GIG *parā appiškit šu-ul-la-an-na-za*=*war*=*a*⟨*t*⟩=*tu*=*za* KAR-*at* "And since the illness of a woman affected(?) me (you are saying thus:) 'You found it upon yourself (-*za*) because of your (-*tu*) maliciousness'" KBo 4.14 iii 25-27 (Treaty of Tudḫ. IV or Šupp. II, late NH), ed. Stefanini, AANL (Serie 8) 20:45 ("la lotta *waratuza* trovasti"), van den Hout, Diss. 294f. ("Mit/im(?) Streit hat es dich angetroffen") □ *šu-ul-la-an-na-za-wa-ra-tu-za* is irregular. If interpreted as *šullannaza*(abl.)=*war*⟨=*at*(neut. for GIG = *inan*)⟩=*t*/*du*(2 sg.)=*za* w. tr. "It found you through maliciousness(?)," the use of an enclitic pronoun as subject of a transitive verb is contrary to Watkins' rule but the alternative analysis *šullannaza*(erg.)=*war*=*a*("and"?)=*tu*(2 sg.)=*za* would have an -*a* "and(?)" out of place after -*wa*(*r*). The only grammatically correct solution is to take KAR-*at* as pret. 2 sg. and -*at* as neut. obj.

Hrozný, CH (1922) 3 w. n. 10 (*šullannaz* "d'intention" or "d'inimitié"); Zimmern/Friedrich, HGes (1922) 5 (*šullannaz* "vorsätzlich"); Friedrich, AO 23/2 (1922) 1* ("aus Zorn");

Sommer, Heth. 2 (1922) 42 n. 1 ("Hader, Zorn"); Götze, Ḫatt (1925) 92 ("Streit"); Gurney, AAA 27 (1941) 96 w. n. 2 ("scold, revile"); Alp, JCS 6 (1952) 95 w. n. 14 (*šullannaz* "aus Feindseligkeit"); Friedrich, HW (1952) 197 ("Zank, Streit; Streitfall"); Imparati, PdP 66 (1959) 188f.; Laroche, RHA XVIII/67 (1960) 83f. ("une manifestation de mécontentement ou d'impatience"); Friedrich, HW 2. Erg. (1961) 23 ("Aufregung, Grund zur Aufregung"); Güterbock, JCS 15 (1961) 66 (*šullannaz* "because of a quarrel," i.e., intentional (killing)); Otten, ZA 54 (1961) 121 ("Streit," *šullanni* "im Zorn"), 147 (*šullannaz* "vorsätzlich"); Imparati, Leggi (1964) 184f.; Haase, FsVolterra, Bd. 6 (1971) 476 n. 29 (against "intention" for *šullanaz*); Hoffner, LH (1997) 166 ("quarrel," *šullanaz* "an intentional but unpremeditated and impulsive action"); Melchert, FsHerzenberg (2005) 90-98; Tischler, HEG S/2 (2006) 1146f. ("Zank, Streit, Streitfall," "Aufregung, Besorgtheit"); Kloekhorst, EDHIL (2008) 778 ("swollen state > reckless act").

Cf. *šulla-* B/*šule-*/*šulliya-*, *šullešš-*.

***šullatar B** n. neut.; hostage-ship(?); MS.†

**sg. dat.** *šu-ul-la-an-ni* ABoT 1.60 obv. 9 (MS), KUB 19.39 iii 10 (Murš. II).

For *šu-ul-la-an-ni* KUB 4.4 rt. col. 3-9 (trilingual hymn to Stormgod, NH) possibly belonging here see *šullatar* A bil. section.

**a.** (The Hittite king had assigned Mašḫuiluwa a place to live) *n=at=ši ŠA* DUMU!*=ŠU šullaš iy[anun(?)* ... ] / [DUMU*=K*]*A*?*=wa kuin šu-ul-la-an-ni uekun nu=w[a=*... ] "[I(?)] ma[de] it into a (place of) hostage for his son. [... (saying:)] 'Y[our father] whom I demanded as a hostage (lit. for hostage-ship), [...]'" KUB 19.39 iii 9-10 (Extensive Annals, Murš. II), ed. AM 166f. ("den ich zum Streit forderte"), Houwink ten Cate, FsMeriggi 273f., 279f., Del Monte, L'annalistica 106f.; ("Early in the morning Neriqqailiš, man of Tapḫalu, approached me, with (the following) message") ⌈*ku*⌉*it=wa šu-ul-la-an-ni ḫarmi* LÚ.KÚR*=wa ku*⌈*iš*⌉ *INA* URU*Tarittara karū anda āraš nu=war=aš* 7 *LIM* "What do I have in the way of hostages (lit. for hostage-ship)? The enemy that has already invaded the town of Tarittara is seven thousand (men) strong!" ABoT 1.60 obv. 9-12 (letter, MH/MS), ed. Letters 177, THeth 16:76f. ("Was das betrifft, daß ich im Streit liege (wörtlich: im Streit halte)"), Laroche, RHA XVIII/67:82f. ("qui me mette en émoi"), cf. 84 (lit. "Que tiens-je pour objet de mon excitation").

**b.** uncertain whether here or under *šullatar* A: dUTU-*ŠI=kan* ḪUR.SAG*Ḫaḫ[arwa* ...]x-*aš*(?)(-) *šu-la-an-ni* EGIR-*an paizzi* "Will His Majesty go behind (or: later to/up?) Mt. Ḫaḫ[arwa...] ...to be held hostage (lit. in hostageship)(?)?" KUB 5.1 iv 40 (oracle on the campaigns, NH), ed. Ünal, THeth 4:84f., tr. Beal, Ktèma 24:52 □ the writing is dense with little word space but the length of the extended AŠ sign preceding *š*. pleads against Ünal's reading ([...] x *aš-šu-la-an-ni* "in Güte"). The spelling with single *-l-*, however, makes the word suspect.

Götze, AM (1933) 167 ("zum Streit"); Gurney, AAA 27 (1941) 96 n.1 ("for reproof(?)"); del Monte, RGTC 6 (1978) 264 ("Geiselhaft"); Tischler, HEG S/2 (2006) 1147 (= *šullatar* A; rejects "Geiselhaft").

Cf. *šulla* A, *šullai-* B

[*šuli-*] n., see *šulai-* A.

**šulli-** n., see *šulla-* A.

**šulle-/šulliya/e-** v., see *šulla-* B.

**šullešš-** v.; to become overbearing, arrogant; NH.

**pres. sg. 3** *šu-ul-le-eš-zi* KUB 57.2:10 (NH), *šu-ul-le-e-eš-zi* KUB 9.15 ii 14 (NH), *šu-ul-li-iš-zi* KUB 9.15 ii 21 (NH).
**pret. sg. 3** *šu-ul-le-eš*!-⌈*ta*⌉ KBo 9.85 l.e. 1 (NH).

*n=an=kan maliyašḫaz* KASKAL-*ši tiyandu adanna=ma=šši akuwanna* SIG$_5$-*in piyandu šu-ul-le-e-eš-zi=ma=aš lē kuitki walaḫzi ḫurdai* (eras.) *lē kuinki* ... *mān=aš šu-ul-li-iš-zi=ma n=an zankilāndu* LUGAL-*uš=ma waštulli kattan arḫa artaru* "Let them set him (i.e., a visitor from the capital) on the road with approval. Let them give to him to eat (and) to drink well. But let him not become overbearing in any way. Let him not hit anything (or) curse anyone (or: do not let him in any way hit (or) curse anyone)." (He may stay in the city over night, but must leave by dawn) "But if he does become overbearing, let them fine him. Let the king not concern himself with (this) misdeed" KUB 9.15 ii 12-15, 21-23 (instr., NH), ed. Melchert, FsHerzenberg 90.

Friedrich, SV 2 (1930) 28 n. 4; idem, HW (1952) 197 ("in Streit geraten"); Oettinger, Stammbildung (1979) 293 ("streitlustig sein/werden"); Melchert, FsHerzenberg (2005) 90-98 ("to become overbearing"); Tischler, HEG S/2 (2006) 147 ("in Streit geraten, zornig werden"); Kloekhorst, EDHIL (2008) 778.

Cf. *šulle/a-* B/*šulliya-*, *šullatar* A.

[*šulešhi*] Tischler, HHwb 154 is Hurr. in Hurr. context, see GLH 242.

**šullittinniš**$^{SAR}$ n. neut.(?); (a vegetable, used for medicinal purposes); NH.†

**sg. nom.-acc.** *šu-ul-li-it-ti-in-ni-iš*$^{SAR}$ KUB 44.61 i 12, (23) (NH).

(In describing the treatment of an illness:) *mān=ma=aš apez UL* ⌜SIG$_5$⌝*-ri nu=šši* x[...] *pāi* SUM$^{SAR}$ *gapanu* GA.RAŠ$^{SAR}$ *gapanu š*[*u-* ...] *šu-ul-li-it-ti-in-ni-iš*$^{SAR}$ *gapanu* [...] *dāi n=at anda tarnai* "If he does not get cured by that, he gives him ... [...]. He/she takes an onion bulb(?), leek bulb(?), a *š*[*u-* ...] bulb(?) [...], *šullittinniš* bulb(?) and he puts them in (i.e., a brew of some kind)" KUB 44.61 obv. 10-13 (med., NH), ed. StBoT 19:18f.; see *šu-ul-li-*⌜x⌝*-*[...] ibid. obv. 23.

Since *š*. is mentioned among bulbous vegetables like onion and leek, it could be of the same character. Burde, StBoT 19:22, assumes that *GAPĀNU* is Akk. (see CAD s.v. *gapnu/gupnu*: "(fruit) tree, vine," AHw: *gapnu* "Strauch"; *gupnu* "Baum(stamm)") and indicates the bulb ("Knolle") of a plant, although this is not easily reconcilable with the Akkadian word. If Hitt. *gapanušši* KUB 43.62 iii 6 is related (cf. *laḫḫurnuzzi-* b and Weitenberg, U-Stämme 256f.) the lower part of a plant ("bulb(?), root(?)") may be meant.

The noun is probably a neuter *š*-stem (cf. other plant/vegetable names *ankiš*, *ḫazzuwaniš*, *zinakkiš*).

Burde, StBoT 19 (1974) 22, 73 ("ein Heilkraut"); Ertem, Flora (1974) 51 ("sap" (= stalk)); Tischler, HEG S/2 (2006) 1147.

[*šulki*[-...]]

Tischler, HHwb 154 and HED 1147 suggests that *šu-ul-ki-*x[...] KUB 12.51 ii 8 is a byform of *zulki-* (a term in extispicy), q.v. However, the text is a ritual, not extispicy, the term is in Hurrian context, and is written with a *š* not a *z*, therefore it is unlikely to be the same word. GLH lists *šulki-* and *zulki-* separately.

**šulupašši-** adj.; of (the town of) Šulupašši, Šulupaššiyan?; NH.†

**stem form?** ⌜*šu-lu*⌝*-pa-aš-ši* KUB 42.48 obv.? 12 (NH).

**sg. gen.** (*ŠA* É.GAL) *šu-lu-pa-aš-ši-ia-aš* KUB 16.27 obv. 6 (NH), here? *šu-lu-pa-aš-ši-i*[*a*(-)...] KBo 38.266 iii 3 (NS).

(In an inventory of tax revenue at the end of the paragraph the origin of goods is stated each time.) É.GAL ⌜*šu-lu*⌝*-pa-aš-ši* "The palace of Šulupašši" KUB 42.48 obv.? 12 (inv., NH), ed. Siegelová, Verw. 244f., translit. THeth. 10:126; ("We questioned the men of the Stone House of the God a[nd they said: ... ") *ŠA* É.GAL *šu-lu-pa-aš-ši-ia-aš U Š*[*A*...] NINDA KAŠ *pē ḫarkanzi* "[...] of the palace of Šulupašši and o[f...] they keep/provide the bread (and) beer" KUB 16.27 obv. 6-7 (NH); frag. [...]x *šu-lu-pa-aš-ši-i*[*a*(-)...] KBo 38.266 iii 3 (frag. Kizz. rit., NS).

In spite of the absence of any determinative, w. Starke, StBoT 31:179, 656, *š*. is in all likelihood a derived adj. of the GN $^{URU}$Šulupašši/a, which is frequently mentioned in the Boğazköy and Kuşaklı texts along with its "palace" or storehouse; see RGTC 6:364-366, RGTC 6/2:148, and Wilhelm, KuSa 1/1:34. According to Tischler, HEG S/2:1147 s.v. *šulupi-*, the place name is a genitival adj. from the bird name *šulupi-* q.v.

**šulupi-** n. com.; (an oracle bird); NH.

**sg. nom.** *šu-lu-pí-iš* KBo 2.6 iii 57 (NH), KUB 5.25 iv 28 (NH), KUB 49.18 i 4 (NH), KUB 52.21 i (5) (NH), IBoT 1.32 obv. 25 (NH), *šu-lu-pé-eš* KBo 16.98 ii 26 (NH), KUB 18.56 iii 25 (NH), KUB 22.51 obv. 6, 9 (NH), KUB 49.58:3 (NH).

**acc.** *šu-lu-pí-in* KBo 2.6 iv 11 (NH), KBo 18.138:(11) (NH), KUB 16.63 rev. 9 (NH), KUB 40.90:10 (NH), KUB 50.100:9 (NH), IBoT 1.32 obv. 25 (NH), *šu-lu-pé-en* KUB 16.59 obv.? 3 (NH), KUB 22.17 i? 2 (NH), KUB 49.28 rt. col. 18 (NH).

**pl. nom.** *šu-lu-pí-uš* IBoT 1.32 obv. 4 (NH).

**a.** observed in bird oracles — **1′** coming (*uwa-*) or going (*pai-*) — **a′** singly: KBo 2.6 iii 57-58 (NH), ed. van den Hout, Purity 210f.; KUB 49.18 i 4 -5 (NH).

**b′** in groups: 2 *šu-lu-pí-uš pe.-an* S[IG$_5$-*za uēr*] *n=at* 2-*an arḫa pāer* "Two *š.*-birds [flew in] in front on the good side and they flew off though the center" IBoT 1.32 obv. 4-5 (NH), ed. Sakuma, Diss. 2:516f.

**c′** flight described as EGIR UGU SIG$_5$-*za uwa-*/UGU EGIR-*pa* SIG$_5$-*za uwa-*: KUB 5.25 iv 28 (NH); KUB 18.56 iii 21-22, 25-26 (NH).

**d′** flight described as EGIR GAM *kuš*(*tayati*) *uwa-*: KBo 2.6 iii 57-58 (NH), ed. van den Hout, Purity 210f.; KUB 49.18 i 4-5 (NH); KUB 49.54 rev. (13) (NH).

**e′** flight described as *pe*(*r*)*an* SIG$_5$-*za uwa-*: KUB 22.51 obv. 5 (NH), ed. Imparati, Eothen 12:763, 765; IBoT 1.32 obv. (4?) (NH).

**f′** flight described as *gun.-li*$_{12}$ *zilawan uwa-*: KUB 22.51 obv. 5 (NH), ed. Imparati, Eothen 12:763, 765; IBoT 1.32 obv. (4?) (NH) ☐ for the hypothesis that *gun.-li* should be read as abbreviated Hittite rather than Sumerian see Sakuma, Diss. 1:106.

**g′** flight described as *pe*(*r*)*an arḫa pai-*: KBo 2.6 iv 11 (NH), ed. van den Hout, Purity 212f.; KUB 49.28 rt. col. (19) (NH); KUB 49.58:3-4 (NH).

**h′** flight described as *takšan*/2-*an arḫa pai-*: KUB 18.56 iii 22, 26-27 (NH); KUB 49.18 i 5 (NH); KUB 50.100:(9) (NH); IBoT 1.32 obv. 5, 25 (NH).

**2′** sitting facing(?) west(?): [...EGIR. KASKAL(?)]-*NI šu-lu-pé-en* [... *n=aš=za*(?)] *ipatarma* TUŠ-*at* "[Behind the road(?)] a *š.*-bird (obj.) [...and] it alighted (lit. sat down) towards(?) the west(?)" KUB 22.17 i? 2-3 (NH), ed. Sakuma, Diss. 2:214 (reading -*e*]*r* rather than EGIR.KASKAL]-*ni*) ☐ *ipatarma* is translated by Puhvel, HED 2:375-377, Melchert, CLL 91, Sakuma, Diss. 1:229-48 (esp. 230), as "west," differently Güterbock, JNES 20:93 w. n. 42 ("astray") and Starke, StBoT 31:504-509.

**3′** sitting and calling, its beak facing away in front: *šu-lu-pé-eš=ma=kan* EGIR [...] *n=aš=za* TUŠ-*at* KA×U=*ŠU=ma=za=kan pe.-an arḫa nāiš* "the *šulupi*-bird [...] back, alighted (lit. sat down) while turning its beak in front" KUB 22.51 obv. 6-7 (NH), ed. Sakuma, Diss. 2:237 (reading *na-*⌈*a*⌉*-a-iš* although the first -*a*- is the remains of a previously written but then only partially erased word).

**4′** being in a specific position: *šu-lu-pé-eš=ma kuiš gu*⟨*n*⟩*.-li*$_{12}$ KUB 22.51 obv. 9 (NH), ed. Sakuma, Diss. 2:237.

**5′** observed (*ĪMUR, NĪMUR*) — **a′** singly: *tar*(*wiya*)*liyan*: KBo 2.6 iv 11; KUB 16.59 obv.? 3; KUB 16.63 rev. (9); KUB 16.72:(18); *gun.-li* KUB 49.28 rt. col. 18; KUB 50.100:9 (all NH).

**b′** in association with a *maršanašši*-bird: KUB 18.56 iii 21, 25 (NH), ed. Sakuma, Diss. 2:34-36; *šu-lu-pí-in=ma maršanaššinn=a gun.-li ĪMUR šu-lu-pí-iš* 2-*an arḫa pait* "He saw a *š.*-bird and a *maršanašši*-bird *gun.-li*. The *š.*-bird flew off through the center" IBoT 1.32 obv. 25-26 (NH), ed. Sakuma, Diss. 2:520f.

**b.** in a court protocol: *UMMA* $^{m.d}$*IŠTAR*-ZA INIM [...] *karaššūni anda=ma=w*[*a* ...] *šu-lu-pí-in=ma=wa kuwapi*(-)x[...] "Thus (speaks) Šauškazidi: 'The matter [of ...] we ceased doing (lit. cut). Furthermore, [...] But where/when [they saw(?)] a *š.*-bird (obj.)'" KUB 40.90:8-10, ed. Werner, StBoT 4:67f.; each of the following two lines mentions INIM ANŠE.GÌR. NUN.NA=*ya* "and the matter of the mule" ibid. 12 and 13.

For an understanding of the actions of the *š.* in bird oracles see Sakuma, Diss. *š.* is also the final element of the composite proper name $^{m}$Ḫalpa-šulupi (NH no. 256).

Ertem, Fauna (1965) 219; Tischler, HEG S/2 (2006) 1147-1149; Sakuma, Diss. (2009) 1:402f.

$^{NINDA}$**šum-x?[ -... ]** n.; (kind of bread or pastry); NS.†

**frag.** $^{NINDA}$*šum*-x?[-o]-x-*aš* KBo 13.167 i 6 (*ḫišuwa*-fest., NS).

Another possible reading would be $^{NINDA}$DÌ[M. ... ] (cf. Akk. NINDA.DÌM.ME, AlHeth. 206), but no such bread is otherwise attested in Hitt.

**-šum(m)a- A** and **B** see -*šma/i-* A and B.

**-šum(m)a- C, -šum(m)i- C** enclitic poss. pron.; our; from OS; wr. syll., and Akkadographically -*NI*.

**sg. nom. com.** *-šum-mi-iš* KBo 22.6 i 5 (OH/NS).

**voc.** *-šum-mi* KBo 40.333 iii (8) (OH/MS?), Bo 6740:3 (apud Starke, StBoT 31:80).

**acc. com.** *-šum-ma-an* KUB 43.53 i 17 (OH/MS), KUB 58.111 obv. 8 (OH/NS), *-šum-mi-in* KBo 3.22 obv. (39) (OS), KBo 17.88 + KBo 24.116 iii (11), 24 (OH/MS), KBo 20.67 iv (11), 17, 25 (OH/MS), KUB 40.31 rev.? 6 (MH?/MS), VS 28.30 iv 15 (OH/NS), KBo 11.33 rev.! 3 (OH/NS?), KUB 60.44:59 (NS).

**nom.-acc. neut.** *-šum-me-e[t]* KUB 36.110 rev. 8 (OS), *-šu-me-et* KUB 40.28:2 (MH/MS) (here or pl.?), *-šum-mi-it* KUB 24.3 ii 18 (Murš. II) (here or under *-šma/i-* "your"?).

**gen.** *-šum-ma-aš* KBo 22.201 iii 7, iv 10 (OH/NS), *-šum-mi-iš* (sic) (mistaken nom. for gen.) KUB 26.71 i 6 (OH/NS).

**dat.-loc.** *-šum-mi* KBo 17.88 iii (8), 21 (OH/MS?), VS 28.30 iv 9, 26 (OH/NS), KBo 14.12 iv 31, 32, 36, (37), 39 (NH).

**all.** *-šum-ma* KBo 47.7 obv. 16 (MS).

**pl. nom. com.** here or 3rd pers. pl.? *-šum-mi-iš* KBo 22.6 iv 18 (OH/NS).

**acc. com.** *-šum-mu-uš* KBo 22.2 obv. 19 (OS).

a. in OH — **1′** in OS — **a′** sg. nom. com.: (no exx.).

**b′** voc.: (no exx.).

**c′** acc. com. — **1″** *-šummin*: *karū* $^{\text{m}}$*Ūḫnaš* LUGAL $^{\text{URU}}$*Zālpuwa* $^{\text{d}}$*Šiu≈šum-m*⸢*i*⸣*-[in]* [$^{\text{UR}}$]$^{\text{U}}$*Nēšaz* $^{\text{URU}}$*Zālpuwa pēda[š app]ezziyan≈a* $^{\text{m}}$*Anittaš* LUGAL.GAL $^{\text{d}}$*Šiu≈šu[m-(*⸢*mi-in* $^{\text{URU}}$⸣*)Z]ālpuwaz āppa* $^{\text{URU}}$*Nē*⸢*ša*⸣ *pē[taḫḫun]* "Previously Uḫna, king of Zalpuwa, [had] carrie[d] off 'Ou[r] Deity' from Neša to Zalpuwa. [L]ater, however, [I,] Anitta, Great King, bro[ught] 'Our Deity' from [Z]alpuwa back to Neša" KBo 3.22 obv. 39-42 (Anitta Proclamation, OS), w. dupl. KUB 36.98a obv. 9-10 (OH/NS), ed. StMed. 13:34f. ("euren") w. n. 6 ("auch 'unser' ... ist ... möglich"), StBoT 18:12f. ("unseres"), see also GrHL §6.4 n. 9.

**2″** *-NI*: *kuin≈wa šanḫiškeweni UM*⸢*MA*⸣*≈NI š≈an wemiyawen* "Whom have we been seeking? Our mother! And thus/so we have found her!" KBo 22.2 obv. 14 (Zalpa tale, OS), ed. *š(u)-* b 1′ b′ 1′ (see there for discussion), StMed 19:30, 39, StBoT 17:6f.

**d′** nom.-acc. neut. *-šummet*: *[L]abarnaš* LUGAL $^{\text{URU}}$*Ḫatti šaḫeššar≈šum-me-e[t]* ⸢*ē*⸣*štu* "Let the [L]abarna, King of Ḫatti, be ou[r] fortification/stronghold(?)" KUB 36.110 rev. 8-9 (Benediction for Labarna, OS), ed. Forrer, MAOG 4:31, Starke, ZA 69:82, *šaḫeššar*.

**e′** gen.: (no exx.).

**f′** dat.-loc.: (no exx.).

**g′** all.: (no exx.).

**h′** abl./inst.: (no exx.)

**i′** pl. nom. com.: (no exx.).

**j′** acc. com. *-šummuš*: *[k]ūš(?)≈za nēku(š)≈šum-mu-uš daškēwen*⸢*i*⸣ "Shall we take [th]ese our own sisters (in marriage)?" KBo 22.2 obv. 19 (Zalpa Story, OS), ed. StMed 19:31, 39, StBoT 17:6f.

**k′** dat.-loc.: (no exx.).

**l′** abl./inst.: (no exx.).

**2′** in OH/MS — **a′** sg. nom. com.: (no exx.).

**b′** voc. *-šummi*: $^{\text{d}}$IM-*t[a a]tta≈šu[m-mi] kuwapi ēšta* "O Stormgod, o[ur f]ather, where have you been?" KUB 33.66 + KBo 40.333 iii 8-9 (Stormgod in Liḫzina, OH/MS?), ed. Groddek, ZA 89:38, 40.

**c′** acc. com. *≈šumma/in*: DINGIR.MEŠ-*nan* $^{\text{d}}$UTU-*i k[(ā)]ša* DINGIR.MEŠ-*aš aši peškemi* ⸢$^{\text{d}}$UTU*≈šum*⸣*-ma-an Labar[(nan)]* DINGIR.MEŠ-*aš aši piškemi* "O Sungod of the gods, hereby I give that one to the gods, Our Sun Labarna. I will give that one to the gods" KUB 43.53 i 16-18 (rit., OH/MS), w. dupls. KBo 17.17 iv? 6-7 (OS), KUB 58.111 obv. 7-8 (OH/NS), ed. Goedegebuure, JANER 2:62, Giorgieri, SMEA 29:64, 68 (*š.* = gen. sg. ("nostro/vostro"); *aši* = acc. sg. neut.), tr. GrHL 145 n. 5 (*š.* = acc. sg. "our"); *aši* = free standing sg. gen.); *āššuš≈aš ḫalugaš wemiškeddu mayantan* $^{\text{d}}$UTU*≈šum-mi-in* $^{\text{f}}$*Tawanannan* AN.BAR-*aš* $^{\text{GIŠ}}$DAG-*ti* "Let the good message find them, (namely) the vigorous one, (that is,) Our Sun (i.e., Our Majesty) (and) the Tawananna on the throne of iron" KBo 17.88 + KBo 24.116 iii 23-25 (monthly fest., OH/MS?), ed. StBoT 37:320f.; cf. also ibid. iii (11), KBo 20.67 iv (11), 17, 25 (OH/MS).

**d′** nom.-acc. neut.: (no exx.).

**e′** gen.: (no exx.).

**f′** dat.-loc. *-šummi*: *karappiya zig≠a warkantaš* GUD.MAḪ.ḪI.A-*aš* UDU.NÍTA.MEŠ-*aš* EGIR-*pa mayantaš* ᵈUTU≠*šum-mi* ᶠ*Tawanannai auriyalaš piddāi* "Arise, (Mount Šariššа)! Run back to the fat bulls (and) rams, to the vigorous ones, (namely) to Our Sun (i.e., Our Majesty) (and) to the Tawananna, the sentinels" KBo 17.88 + KBo 24.116 iii 19-21 (monthly fest., OH/MS?), ed. StBoT 37:320f.; see also ibid. iii (7).

**g′** all.: (no exx.).

**h′** abl./inst.: (no exx.).

**i′–j′** pl. nom. and acc.: (no exx.).

**3′** in OH/NS — **a′** sg. nom. com. *-šummiš*: [... *tuz*]*zi*(*š*)≠*šum-mi-iš* GÌR.MEŠ-*uš* IM-*az lē ē*[*šz*]*i* "Let our troops, (that is) their feet not be muddy" KBo 22.6 i 5 (*Šar Tamḫari*, OH/NS), ed. Rieken, ICH 4 = StBoT 45:478 w. n. 12; for *-šummiš* as a mistaken gen. see below e′.

**b′** voc.: (no exx.).

**c′** sg. acc. com. *-šumma/in*: for *-šumman* KUB 58.111 obv. 8 see a 2′ c′; *āššuš≠aš* [*ḫalugaš*] ⌈*wemeškeddu*⌉ [*mayanta*]*n* ᵈUTU≠*šum-mi-in* [(*taw*)]*annannan ewalin* [(AN.BAR-*a*)]*š* ᴳᴵŠDAG-*ti* "Let the good [tiding] find them, our youthful Majesty (and) the *ewali* Tawananna on the iron throne" VS 28.30 iv 13-17 (monthly fest., OH/NS), w. dupl. IBoT 4.51 + KUB 1.15 ii 1-2 (NS), ed. StBoT 37:366-69; [(É ᵈ*Šiu*)*na*(*š*)≠*š*]⌈*um-mi-in*⌉ *ABNI* "I built the house of our deity" KUB 26.71 i 5 (Anitta Proclamation, OH/NS), w. dupl. KBo 3.22 rev. 56 (OS), ed. StMed 13:40f., StBoT 18:14f. □ this form is a mistake for genitive **-šummaš*, see Neu, StBoT 18:124f.; see also immediately below under e′ for the same phrase with a gen.(?) *Šiunašummiš*.

**d′** nom.-acc. neut.: *n≠ašt*[(*a ANA* DUMU.LÚ.U$_{19}$.LU)] *ḫattatar≠šum-mi-it ḫarak*[(*t*)*a*] "To mankind, our wisdom has been lost" KUB 24.3 ii 17-18 (prayer to Sungoddess of Arinna, Murš. II), w. dupls. KUB 24.4 obv. 8, KUB 30.13 obv. 10, ed. Lebrun, 160, 169 ("votre intelligence"), Rieken et al., hethiter.net/: CTH 376.1 (INTR 2016-01-19) ("unsere Weisheit"), tr. Hittite Prayers 52 ("our wisdom"), 68 (comm. w. lit.) both "our" and "your" (see *-šma/i-* 1 a) seem possible here.

**e′** gen. *-šummaš*: EGIR≠*ma piddāi* ᴸᵁ*ma*[*yantaš*] ᵈUTU≠*šum-ma-aš* ᶠ*Tawann*[*annašš≠a*] AN.BAR-*aš* ᴳᴵŠDAG-*ti* "Run back to the throne of iron of our you[thful] Sun (i.e., Majesty) and of the Tawann[anna]" KBo 22.201 iv 9-11 (monthly fest., OH/NS), translit. StBoT 37:355; cf. also ibid. iii 7 □ Klinger, StBoT 37:357 and 795 tries to explain the form ᵈUTU-*šummaš* as pl. dat.-loc. which would not fit this context factually since a plural use for the concept of "Majesty" is hard to imagine; É ᵈ*Šiuna≠šum-mi-iš ABNI* "I built the house of our deity" KUB 26.71 i 6 (Anitta Proclamation, OH/NS) □ this form either was considered by the NS scribe to be an undeclined divine name, or is a mistake for genitive **-šummaš*, see Neu, StBoT 18:124f.; see also immediately above under c′ for the same phrase with an acc. *Šiunašummin*.

**f′** dat.-loc. *-šummi*: ⌈*maya*⌉*nti* ᵈUTU≠*šum-mi tawannani ewali dalugauš* MU.KAM.ḪI.A-*uš šamniyataru* AN.BAR-*aš* ᴳᴵŠDAG-*ti* "Let long years be created for our youthful Majesty and the *ewali* Tawannana on the throne of iron" VS 28.30 iv 26-29 (monthly fest., OH/NS), ed. StBoT 37:368f., *šamnāi-* b 3′; cf. also ibid. iv 9.

**g′** all.: (no exx.).

**h′** abl./inst.: (no exx.).

**i′** pl. nom.(?)/acc.(?) — **1″** *-šummiš*: *ta≠aš≠za≠kan* ᴸᵁ̇.ᴹᴱŠUR.SAG≠*šum-mi-iš azzikkandu* "May our heroes eat them(?)" KBo 22.6 iv 18-19 (*šar tamḫāri*, OH/NS), ed. Güterbock, MDOG 101:21, 23 (ᴸᵁ̇.ᴹᴱŠUR.SAG≠*šummiš* "eure(?) Krieger"), translit. Rieken, ICH 4 = StBoT 45:578, cf. ibid. 579, and StBoT 17:35 n. 65 ("unsere Helden (= wir Helden)").

**2″** *-NI*: *š≠uš≠ka*[*n* ...] / [LÚ(?)].MEŠ ᵁᴿᵁ*Ḫatti*ᴷᴵ ŠEŠ.MEŠ≠*NI* x[...] "and them [... the people(?)] of Ḫatti, our brothers [...]" KBo 3.45 obv. 2-3 (hist., Ḫantili I/NS), ed. Soysal, Diss. 54, 101; [DINGIR.MEŠ(?)] GUD.ḪI.A≠*NI* UDU.ḪI.A≠*NI* [(*āppan šan*)*ḫer*] "[The gods(?)] looked after our cattle and sheep" KBo 22.7 obv.? 3-4 (hist., Ḫantili I/NS), w. dupl. KBo 3.45 obv. 6, ed. Soysal, Diss. 54f., 101.

**j′–k′** dat.-loc., abl./inst.: (no exx.).

**b.** in MH/MS and MH/NS — **1′** sg. nom.: (no exx).

**2′** voc. *-NI*: ᵈUTU-*ŠI BĒLI*⸗*NI* "O, Your Majesty, our lord, (reply to us soon)" HKM 48:21-22 (letter, MH/MS), ed. HBM 208f., Letters 183.

**3′** acc. com. *-šummin*: ⸢ᵈ⸣UTU⸗*šum-mi-inn*⸗*a paḫḫa*⸢*š*⸣*ḫa* "and I will protect Our Sun (i.e., Our Majesty)" KUB 40.31 rev.? 6 (frag. of treaty, MH?/MS).

**4′** nom.-acc. neut. *-šumet*: *kir*⸗*šu-me-et katkatti*[*š*...] "our(?) heart palpitat[es(?) ...]" KUB 40.28:2 (Kuruštama treaty, MH/MS?), ed. Francia, SMEA 35:94 □ the interpretation of *-šumet* as "our" is based on the predicate *umēni* in pl. 1st person in line 4 of the same fragment; see also StBoT 18:66 n. 97.

**5′** gen. *ŠA* ...⸗*NI*: ᴸᵁ́.ᴹᴱŠ*ṬĒMI UL ŠA BĒLI*⸗*NI* KUR⸗*ya ŠA BĒLI*⸗*NI* "(Are) the messengers not of our lord? The land (is) of our lord too" HKM 55:31-33 (letter, MH/MS), ed. HBM 224f., Letters 201.

**6′** dat.-loc. *ANA* ...⸗*NI*: ⸢*AN*⸣*A* ᵈUTU-*ŠI BĒLI*⸗*NI QIBÎ*⸗*MA* "to His Majesty, our lord, speak" HKM 48 obv. 1-2 (letter, MH/MS), ed. HBM 206f., Letters 183; see also HKM 49:1, 20-21 (letter, MH/MS), HKM 57 obv. 3-5 (letter, MH/MS), KUB 13.4 iv 50-51 (instr. for temple personnel, MH/NS).

**7′** all. *-šumma*: [...] *karūiliya* ᴬ.ŠÀ*kuera*⸗*šumma* [ ... ᵁᴿᵁ]*Adaniya paiwani* "[...]to our old/former field [ ... in/to(?)]Adaniya we go" KBo 47.7 obv. 16-17 (frag. of conjuration rit., MS), ed. Fuscagni, hethiter.net/: CTH 458.89 (INTR 2017-01-12), translit. DBH 33:6 w. n. 18, see also Groddek, HS 126:118.

**8′** abl./inst. *IŠTU* ...⸗*NI*: *IŠTU* ZI⸗*NI* "by our (own) intention" KUB 40.15 ii 1 + KBo 50.266b ii 3 (MH), ed. HittInstr 200f. ("of our own volition"), Giorgieri, Diss. 222, 224 ("dalla nostra anima").

**9′-10′** pl. nom. and acc.: (no exx.).

**11′** inst. *QADU* ...⸗*NI*: *nu*⸗*wa*⸗*nnaš zik* DINGIR-*LUM tuel* ZI-*aš* ⸢*z*⸣*ūwa*⟨*š*⟩ *šer QADU* DAM.MEŠ⸗*NI* DUMU.MEŠ⸗*NI parḫeške* "May you, O god, chase us along with our wives and our children on account of the foods of your desire" KUB 13.4 iv 76-77 (instr. for temple personnel, MH/NS), ed. THeth 26:69, 85, Süel, Direktif Metni 88f.

**c.** in NH; syll. *-šummi* only in *ištarni*⸗*šummi* "mutually, with each other"; otherwise all exx. Akk. *-NI* — **1′** sg. nom.: *anzāš*⸗*wa* EN⸗*NI* [*k*]*uiš* ᵐ*Nipḫururiyaš ēšta nu*⸗*war*⸗*aš* BA.ÚŠ "Our lord, [w]ho was Nipḫururiya, died" KBo 14.12 iv 17-18 (DŠ, Murš. II), ed. Güterbock, JCS 10:98, GestaSupp 122f.

**2′** voc.: *nu*⸗*wa*⸗*nnaš BĒLI*⸗*NI* DUMU⸗*KA pāi* "O our lord, give us a son of yours" KBo 14.12 iv 24-25 (DŠ, Murš. II), ed. Güterbock, JCS 10:98, GestaSupp 122f.

**3′** acc.: *īt*⸗*wa* ᵈ*Telipinun anzel* EN⸗*NI* DINGIR-*LAM ŠA* SAG.DU⸗*NI mugāi* "Go, invoke Telipinu, our lord, our personal deity" KUB 24.2 obv. 5-6 (prayer, Murš. II), ed. Kassian/Yakubovich, FsKošak 428, 432, Lebrun, Hymnes 181, 184, tr. HittitePrayers 54 □ note the additional *anzel* "of us, our."

**4′** nom.-acc. neut.: (not recognizable).

**5′** gen.: DAM *BĒLI*⸗*NI*⸗*ma*⸗*wa*⸗*nnaš* [*w*]*annummiyaš* "The wife of our lord is a widow (now)" KBo 14.12 iv 19-20 (DŠ, Murš. II), ed. Güterbock, JCS 10:98, GestaSupp 122f.

**6′** dat.-loc. *-šummi*: [*k*]*arūiliyaza*⸗*wa* ᵁᴿᵁ*Ḫattušaš* ⁽ᵁᴿ⁾ᵁ*Mizrašš*⸗*a ištarni*⸗*šum-mi āššiyanteš* [*e*]*šer kinun*⸗*a*⸗*wa*⸗*nnaš*⸗*kan kī*⸗*ya ištarni*⸗*šu*[*m-mi*] / [*kiš*]*at nu*⸗*wa*⸗*kan* KUR ᵁᴿᵁ*Ḫatti* KUR ᵁᴿᵁ*Mizr*[*i*⸗*ya*] / [*ukt*]*ūri namma ištarni*⸗*šum-mi aššiy*[*anteš*] "In the past Ḫattuša and Egypt were on good terms with each other. But now this, too, has happened between us! The land of Ḫatti [and] the land of Egypt [will] again be [fore]ver on good terms with each other" KBo 14.12 iv 35-39 (DŠ, Murš. II), ed. DŠ 98, Francia, SMEA 35:95f., GestaSupp 95, 125 □ in this NH composition, when enclitic possessives were no longer part of speakers' own grammar, the correct sense of *istarni*⸗*summi* (probably taken from the earlier MH treaty) was misunderstood to mean simply 'mutually' (Francia, SMEA 35:96: 'tra noi, voi, loro'), applicable to all plural persons. For the NH composer, it is the enclitic ⸗*naš* that marks '(between) us,' not the *ištarni*⸗*summi* 'mutually'; *ANA* ...-*NI*:

*ANA* MUNUS-*TI BĒLTI=NI=ma=war=an AŠŠUM* ⌜LÚ⌝*MUTI=ŠU wekiškeweni* "We request him (i.e., the son of the Hittite king) for our lady as her husband" KBo 14.12 iv 21-22 (DŠ, Murš. II), ed. Güterbock, JCS 10:98, GestaSupp 122f.

**7′** abl./inst.: (no exx.).

**8′–11′** pl.: (no exx.).

**d.** problematic/uncertain — sg. nom. com. *-šummiš*: DINGIR-*LIM=šum-mi-iš* "our deity" KUB 50.78:1 (NH), or to be read rather as DN d*Ši-šum-mi-iš* with van Gessel, OHP 1:406.

Due to the nature of Hitt. texts where the first person pl. is less used than the sg. or the third person (either sg. or pl.), as well as the chronological development of the poss. pron. in general, the attestation of *-š.* is sparing but otherwise fully parallel to, for instance, *-mi-/-ma-* "mine" and *-ši-*B/*-ša-* q.vv. The Hittites often preferred the gen. of the independent personal pron. *anzel*, as the following lexical list shows: (Sum.) á-mu-me-en = (Akk.) *a-na i-ti-ni* = (Hitt.) *anzel kuššan* "(for) our wage" KBo 1.42 i 28 (Izi Bogh. A, NS), ed. MSL 13.133 as line 38. In the paradigm of possessives found in KBo 1.42 i 23-28 the three singular forms "my," "your" and "his/her" are expressed by the enclitic possessives *-mi-*, *-ti-*, *-ši-*, while the plural forms "our," "your," and "their" are expressed by the genitive of the independent personal pronouns (*anzel, šumenzan, apenzan*). For a discussion of why the scribes did not use the enclitics throughout see (s.v. *-mi-*, *-ma-*. While it is possible that the Akk. suffix *-NI* stood for *-š.* in older Hitt., it is also possible that the suffixed *-NI,* particularly in NH, stood for the preposed *anzel.*

Otten, ZA 53 (1959) 180; Friedrich, HE I² (1960) 65 ("Ein enklitisches Possessivpronomen der 1. Person Plur. ist bisher nicht belegt"); Werner, OLZ 57 (1962) 382; Kammenhuber, HbOr (1969) 211 ("*-šmi-* fraglich"); Otten, StBoT 17 (1973) 35 w. nn. 64-65; Neu, StBoT 18 (1974) 65f., 119f., 128-131; Starke, StBoT 31 (1990) 79-82; Giorgieri, SMEA 29 (1992) 54 w. n. 25; Francia, SMEA 35 (1995) 93-99; Tischler, HEG S/2 (2006) 1159 (*šummi-* "gelegentliche (wohl nur graphische) Realisierung von *-smi-/-sma-*); Hoffner/Melchert, GrHL (2008) 138-141 w. nn. 3, 8-9; Kloekhorst, EDHIL (2008) 782f.; Groddek, HS 126 (2013) 118.

**EZEN₄/EZEN₄šumma[...] D** n.; (a festival); NH.†

**frag.** EZEN₄*šu-um-*⌜*ma*⌝[- ...] KUB 25.26 iii 5 (NS).

§ 2 ⌜UDU⌝ x[...] 4 *ŠĀTU* x[...] 1 DUG*ḫaniš*[*šaš* ...] *ANA* EZEN₄/EZEN₄*šu-um-m*⌜*a*⌝[- ...] *zēnandaš takn*[*aš* dUTU-*i*] "Two sheep, [...] four *SŪTU*s [of flour(?)], one *ḫanišša*-container [of beer(?)] for the *š.*-festival of autumn (celebrated) [for the Sungoddess of] the Earth" (followed by similar paragraphs for EZEN₄*dašḫapuna, ḫaršialli-, ḫašš*[*umaš*(?)] etc.) KUB 25.26 iii 1-5 (cult inv., NS).

**šum?maizza** (mng. unkn.); from MS?.†

**unclear** ⌜*šum*⌝?*-ma-iz-*⌜*za*⌝ KBo 13.119 iii 21 (NS), [*šu*]*m?-ma-iz-za* KBo 13.120:5 (MS?).

In an obscure context in connection with a wagon: ... GIŠMAR.GÍD.DA *kī-*⌜x x⌝[...]x-*atnaš* [GIŠM(AR.GÍD).DA] ⌜*šum*⌝?*-ma-iz-*⌜*za*⌝ *peškanzi* KBo 13.119 iii 20-21 (purification rit., MS?), w. dupl. KBo 13.120:5 (ENS?).

[*šummani*] Tischler, HHwb 154 is Hurr. in Hurr. context.

[*šum-ma-an-ma-aš*] KUB 33.108 ii 21 (frag. mentioning *IŠTAR*, NS), ed. Friedrich JKF 2:148f. (without tr.) read Akkadographically as *ŠUM-ma-an=ma=*(*šm*)*aš*(?) "mit Namen" by Rieken et al., hethiter.net/: CTH 350.3 (TX 2009-08-31, TRde 2009-08-31).

[*šumant-*] see *šuku?ant-*.

**(Ú)šum(m)anza(n)-, šum(m)anza-, šum(m)anzana-** n. com., neut.; (bul)rush; from OS.†

**sg. nom. com.** *šu-ma-an-za* KBo 1.45 rev.! 2 (NH), *šu-um-ma-an-za* KUB 12.58 i 21 (NS), *šu-um-ma-an-za-a-aš* KBo 10.45 ii 29 (MH/NS).

**acc. com.** *šu-ma-an-za-n*[*a-an*] HKM 116 ii? 23 (OH?/MS), *šu-um-ma-an-za-na-an* KUB 7.53 ii 4 (NS).

**nom.-acc. neut.** *šu-ma-an-za-an* KBo 20.73 i 3 (OH or MH/MS), KBo 24.3 i 1, 4 (MH/MS), KBo 24.2 i (3), 6 (MH/NS), HT 6 rev. (8), (11) (MH/NS), *šu-ma-an-za-an-n*(*a*) KUB 7.23:9 (pre-NH/NS), KUB 59.54 obv. (6) (pre-NH/NS), *šum-*

*ma-a*[*n-za-na-an*] KUB 39.8 iv 6 (MH?/NS), [*šum-*]⌜*ma-an-za*⌝*-na-an* KUB 39.8 iv 2 (MH?/NS).

**gen.** *šu-ma-a-an-za-na-aš* KBo 20.26 obv. (11) (OS), KBo 30.26 rev. 1 (MS).

**dat.-loc.** *šu-ma-an-za-ni* KBo 20.8 rev.? 14 (OS), *šu-um-ma-an-za-ni* KBo 58.32:3 (NS).

**abl.** *šu-ma-an-za-na-az* KBo 24.3 + KBo 47.130 i 15, 22 (MH/MS), KBo 24.2 i (14) (MH/NS), HT 6 rev. (18) (MH/NS).

**collec. com. and pl. nom.-acc. neut.** *šu-ma-an-za* KUB 35.54 i 15 (MS), KBo 3.8 iii 6, 24 (MH/NS), KBo 11.11 i 9 (NS), KUB 59.43 i 9 (NS), *šum-ma-an-za* KBo 20.111:10 (NS), Ú*šum-ma-an-za* KBo 21.20 i 17 (NH).

**pl. dat.-loc.** *šu-ma-an-za-na-aš* KBo 11.11 i 2 (MH/NS), KBo 55.44 i 2 (MH/NS).

(Sum. pronunciation) [e-eš] = (Sum.) [KU] = (Akk.) *aš-lum* "cord" = (Hitt.) *šu-ma-an-za* "rush (used as a cord")" KBo 1.45 rev.! 2 (S[a] vocab., NS), ed. MSL 3:59 ("rope").

For a toponym URU*Šummanzana* see RGTC 6:366.

**a.** in general as a plant — **1′** listed with other plants growing wild: dIM-*aš ue*⌜*l*⌝[*lu*] ⌜*ḫ*⌝*amikta n*=*ašta anda* [*šuppi*] *šu-ma-an-za ḫami*⌜*k*⌝*ta*…dIM-*aš uellu lāntat* [*n*=*ašt*]*a anda šuppi šu-ma-an-za lāttat* "He (i.e., the great river) bound the meadows of the Stormgod; therein he bound the [sacred] rushes. … The meadows of the Stormgod have been released; in it the sacred rushes have been released" (in analogy, the afflicted (lit. bound) body parts of a child are to be healed (lit. released)) KBo 3.8 iii 5-6, 23-24 (fourth ritual on the tablet, called "spell of binding," MH/NS), ed. Fuscagni, hethiter.net/: CTH 390 (TX 20.03.2017, TRde 20.03.2017), Oettinger, Offizielle Religion 348f., 350, Kronasser, Die Sprache 7:157-159, translit. Myth 169f. □ for the interchange of sg. and pl. in *lāttat* and *lāntat* see Oettinger, Offizielle Religion 350 n. 12; in broken context with an apple (or apple tree: [GIŠ]ḪAŠḪUR) KUB 35.54 i 14-15.

**2′** grows in the meadow: [(*nu*) *šum-*]⌜*ma-an-za*⌝*-na-an udanzi n*=*at IŠTU* ⌜Ì⌝.[(DÙG.GA)] *iškiyazi n*=*at*=*šan ḫaššī anda peššiyazi* ZÍD.DA=*ya*=*kan anda šunneška*[*nzi*] MUNUS.MEŠ(sic)*taptarašš*=*a kišša*⟨(*n*)⟩ *alalamnešk*[*ezzi*] *mān*=*wa*=*kan* Ú.SAL-*un pāiši n*=*ašta šum-ma-a*[*n-za-na-an*] ⌜*l*⌝*ē ḫūittiyaši* "They bring [bul]rush. He anoints it with fine oil and throws it into the brazier. They also pour flour in and a mourning woman lament[s] thus: 'When you go to the meadow, don't pull (up) the bulru[sh]!'" KUB 39.8 iv 2-7 (funerary rit., MH?/NS), w. dupl. KUB 30.19 iv 4-9, ed. Kassian et al., Funerary 588-591, Otten, HTR 44-47.

**3′** produces a fragrance when burned: (The goddess Ḫapantali has brought wood and pebbles and thrown them into a brazier) [*uda*=*w*]*a*=*šši*=*aš* (par. *uda*=*wa*=*šši*=(*y*)*at*) MUNUS.LUGAL-*aš* […] GIŠ*alanzanan* (par. GIŠ*alanzanaš*) [(GIŠ*ḫat*)*alkiš*]*naš* ⌜x⌝? GIŠ*ša*!*maliyaš* [(GIŠ*laḫḫu*)*wa*]*rnuzzi* [(*kalu*)*išna*]*n tuḫḫueššar šu-ma-an-za-n*[*a-an*] (par. *šu-ma-an-za-an-n*=*a*) [*n*=*uš*=*šan*] NA4*paššuelaš šer šu*[*ḫḫa*]*i* "'Bring them to him (i.e., the angry god), O Queen, [namely…], *alanzana*-wood, [foli]age of [hawtho]rn (and) of *šamaliya*-, [*kalwišna*-], *tuḫḫueššar* [and] bulrush […].' She po[ur]s [them] on top of the (hot) pebbles" (The "holy" water is poured over them, which sends a scent to the god to soothe him) HKM 116 ii? 19-24 (rit. in myth, NS), w. par. KUB 7.23:7-9, KUB 59.54 obv. 4-6, ed. hethiter.net/: CTH 335.4 (TX 2009-08-28, TRde 2009-08-28) ("Binse") w. n. 4, 6, Güterbock, JKF 10:207f. ("string"), Haas, FsPopko 144-145; cf. also mention of brazier in KUB 39.8 iv 1-7 above in 1 a 2′ □ *uda*=*wa*=*šši*=(*y*)*at* MUNUS.LUGAL-*aš* in par. KUB 59.54 obv. 4 makes Güterbock's (JKF 10:208) reading *waššiyaš* MUNUS.LUGAL-*aš* "Queen of the Remedies" in HKM 116 ii? 19 less likely.

**4′** standing in sea water and rustling (in the wind?): [EGIR-*a*]*nda*=*ma*=*z šu-ma-an-za-an dāi n*=*a*[(*t*=*ši*)]=*ka*[(*n*)] *š*[(*er*)] *arḫa waḫnuzi ḫukkiškizz*[(⌜*i*=*ma*⌝ *k*)]*i*[(*ššan*)] ⌜*aru*⌝*naš āḫriyatta aruni*=*ma*=*kan* ⌜*an*⌝*da šu-ma-an-za-an daškupāit arunaz*=*kan šu-ma-an-za-a*[(*n*)] *ḫuittiyami* "[Afterw]ards she takes bulrush and waves it over him/her while conjuring as follows: 'The sea is *āḫriya*-ing (i.e., wailing(?)), and in the sea the rush rustled(?). I will pull the bulrush out of the sea'" KBo 24.3 i 1-5 (rit., MS), w. dupl. KBo 24.2 i 3-6 (pre-NH/NS), HT 6 + KBo 9.125 iv 8-11 (NS), ed. Beckman, Or NS 59:43, 49 ("rope"), Haas, Materia 668 ("Strick") □ the rustling of the rushes or reeds as they stand in the shallow sea water may allude to the sound made when wind blows through reeds; if these are reeds, they would have to be of a species that grows in salty water, as in salt marshes.

**5′** wrapped in wool in a ritual: 1 *šīnaš* 3 *QĀTU* 3 EME *išnaš* 4 *šu-ma-an-za n=at* SÍG *antarit anda ḫūlaliyan* "one figure, three hands, three tongues of dough, four (bundles of) bulrush; they are wrapped with blue wool" KUB 59.43 i 9-10 (rit., NS), translit. DBH 14:76.

**6′** can be cut (*kuer-*) in a ritual: § *nu=ššan ANA* NINDA.GUR$_4$.RA.ḪI.⌈A⌉[...] EME.ḪI.A *šum-ma-an-za kuer*[*zi*(?) ...] "On the thick breads [ ... he/she] cut[s] tongues (and?) bulrush" KBo 20.111:9-10 (Kizz. rit., NS), ed. StBoT 46:142f., for cutting see also KBo 24.3 i 7.

**b.** used as a rope or cord in ritual/cultic context: *n=an=kan* GÌR.MEŠ=*ŠU šu-ma-*[*a*]*n-*⌈*za-na-az*⌉ *aršāmi* "I immobilize(?) his feet with bulrush" KBo 24.3 + KBo 47.130 i 15 (Tunnawi's rit., MH/MS), w. dupls. KBo 24.2 i 14 (pre-NH/NS) and par. HT 6 rev. 18 (NS) ☐ we follow Beckman, Or NS 59:49, 55 and CHD L-N 305a, in rendering *aršāmi* w. "immobilize"; note also *n=at=kan išḫimanit ārašmi* "and I immobilize(?) it/them with a cord" in KBo 17.60 obv. 3 (MH/MS); *mān* UN-*an* $^{d}$DÌM.NUN.ME *appiškizzi nu kišan* DÙ[-*mi*?] *ŠA* ŠAḪ.BABBAR $^{Ú}$*šum-ma-an-za* MUNUS-*aš šaknumar* ⌈*ki*⌉*nanduš ḫ*[*a*?-...*daḫḫi*(?)] "If the Lamaštu demon keeps seizing a person, [I(?)] do as follows: [I take(?)] the bulrush of a white pig, defilement/defecation(?) of a woman, assorted [ ...-s]" KBo 21.20 i 16-17 (medical rit., NH), ed. Burde, StBoT 19:42f., Haas, Materia 668 ☐ the exact mng. of "bulrush of a white pig" is unclear (see also Burde, StBoT 19:46): could it refer to the bristles of a pig? For medical and ritual use of the Akkadian $^{(Ú)}$*ašlu*(*m*) "rope" and "a rush" twined and as a medico-magical substance see CAD A/2:447-449 s.v. *ašlu* A and B, and AHw 81 "Binse, Seil"; here?: ("Thus speaks $^{f}$Uruwandā":) *mān lalāš aniyami ta* $^{UZU}$SA *šu-ma-an-za-na-aš=*(*š*)*ta* (var. *šu-ma-an-za-na-aš-ša*) *anda tarupiyami n=at kiššarta ḫarmi n=ašta* $^{UZU}$SA *ANA* GI *anda ḫuittaḫḫari nu=uš=šan ḫamenkeškemi namma=an arḫa kuwakuwarkimi* (var. *kurašk*[*emi*]) *n=an=šan ḫappini peššieškemi šēr=a=ššan kiššan memieškemi* § *kāša=šta katta ḫuittaḫhat idalawaš lalān alwanzinaš* EME-*an šu-ma-an-za* GIM-*an ta*[!]*rupišta* "Whenever I treat (someone for ill effects) of slander/blasphemy, I combine a sinew with bulrushes. I hold them in (my) hand, I pull the sinew to a reed and I start tying them. Then I cut it off (var. cut each off) and throw it into the flame. Over it I start saying thus: 'See, I have pulled down the tongue of the evil one, the tongue of the sorcerer. Just as the bulrushes have been combined, (let [likewise] ... be [...])'" KBo 11.11 i 1-9 (Uruwanda's rit., MH/NS), w. dupl. KBo 55.44:2-6 (MH/NS), ed. Görke, hethiter.net/: CTH 411 (TX 02.05.2012, TRde 20.10.2011), Haas, Materia 667f. ☐ for *šumanzanaš=šta* in KBo 11.11 i 2 as pl. dat.-loc. w. an added -(*a*)*šta* in mid-sentence see Neu, Linguistica 33:144f.; Neu apud Tischler, HEG T/D 240 interpreted *tarupišta* as mid. pres.(!) sg. 3; (in a list of ritual ingredients:)...[SÍG *andaraš t*]*epu* SÍG *mītiš tepu nu šu-um-ma-an-za* ⌈SÍG⌉ *mītišš=a* [*anda tarupp*]*anza* ... EGIR-*ŠU=ma šu-um-ma-an-za-na-an* EGIR-*ŠU=ma pattar dāi n=at=kan šer arḫa waḫnuzi* "..., [blue wool (in) s]mall quantity, red wool (in) small quantity. Bulrush and red wool are (lit. is) [combi]ned. ...Afterwards she takes the bulrush, then the feather (of an eagle) and waves them over (the patient)" KUB 12.58 i 21-22 (Tunnawi's rit., NS), continued by join KUB 7.53 ii 4-5, ed. Tunn. 8-11, cf. also Haas, Materia 585, 668.

**c.** used to make a wreath for the head: (In a description of a statuette of *IŠTAR*) *keššarta* DUG *dannarantan* ⌈*ḫar*⌉*zi INA* SAG.DU=*ŠU=ma šu-um-ma-an-za-a-aš purušiya*[*laš ki*]*ttat* "In (her) hand she holds an empty vessel while on her head was [pl]aced bulrush as a wrea[th(?)]" KBo 10.45 ii 28-29 (rit. for netherworld deities, MH/NS), ed. Otten, ZA 54:122f., Haas, AoF 17:185, Materia 609, *purušiyala-* c; in a description of dressed-up participants in a cult festival: [ ... *šēr*]*ḫ*[*a*]*nn=a ḫarzi šu-ma-a-an-*⌈*za*⌉-[(*na-aš BA*?*NU*-x) ... *ḫa*(*rzi* $^{L}$)$^{Ú}$P(ÌRIG.TUR *uizzi šapraš*)] / [...]x-*in uēšta šērḫ*[(*an*) ...-*t*(*a*? *ḫa*)]⌈*rzi*⌉ "he also holds a/the *šerḫa-*. [...] holds a crow[n(?)] of bulrush. The leopard-man comes (in). He wears a [...]-garment of *šapra*-cloth. He holds the *šerḫa-* [...]" KBo 20.26 + KBo 25.34 obv. 10-12 (KI.LAM, OS), w. dupl. KBo 30.26 rev. 1-4 (MS), ed. Neu, StBoT 25:89, *šerḫa-*, cf. StBoT 26:364.

There are three stems, com. gender *šum*(*m*)*anza*(*n*)-, neut. gender *šum*(*m*)*anza-* and neut. gender *šum*(*m*)*anzan-*. Originally *š.* was a com. gender *n*-stem noun, with sg. nom. *šumanza*, a secondary oblique stem *šumanzan-* (e.g., sg. nom. *šumanza* in KUB 12.58 i 21, followed by sg. acc. *šumanzanan* in KUB 7.53 ii 4) and a collec. *šum(m)anza*. The collec. formed the basis for a sg. neut. backformation *šum(m)anzan*, thus leading to a neut. stem *šum(m)anza-* (see Melchert, IdgNomen 129-133, GrHL § 4.79, p. 113f.). The OS and MS examples show that this word had a single *-m-* and that the NS spellings are not probative for a geminate (GrHL §1.24). As the determinative Ú in KBo 21.21 i 17 indicates, *š.* was originally a kind of grass, most likely (bul)rush (see Melchert, IdgNomen 129-131). It almost exclusively appears in ritual contexts either as raw material for making cords (cf. also bil.section KBo 1.45 rev.! 2) or as materia magica by itself.

Weidner, Studien (1917) 130 ("Strick"); Friedrich, HW (1952) 197 ("Strick"); Otten, ZA 54 (1961) 151 w. n. 307 ("Strick"); Hawkins/Morpurgo-Davies/Neumann, HHL (1973) 33 n. 121; Burde, StBoT 19 (1974) 46, 73 ("Binse(?)"); Oettinger, KZ 94 (1980) 49; Melchert, Die Sprache 29 (1983) 9-10; Neu, StBoT 26 (1983) 173 w. n. 521 ("Band"); Archi, FsPugliese Carratelli (1988) 36-37 n. 45; Beckman, Or NS 59 (1990) 55 ("rope"); Carruba, StMed 7 (1992); Weitenberg, FsHouwink ten Cate (1995) 333-344; Melchert, Toch&IESt 9 (2000) 64 w. n. 34 ("(bul)rush"); Haas, OLZ 97 (2002) 509 ("Hanf," cf. Akk. *qû* "flax, thread" and *qunnabu* "hemp flower, seed"); Haas, Materia (2003) 314f., 667-669; Melchert, IdgNomen (2003) 129-133 ("(bul)rush"); Katz, FsMorpurgo Davies (2004) 202f.; Oettinger, Offizielle Religion (2004) 348 n. 4 ("Binse"; *šumanza* is often collec. (neut. pl.) from a com. sg. *šumanza*); Tischler, HEG T/D (2006) 1149-1152; Kloekhorst, EDHIL (2008) 780f. (rejects com. gender); Soysal, JAOS 133 (2013) 698.

**šummara[(-)...]**; (mng. unkn.); from MS.†

**frag.** *šum-ma-r[a-...]* KBo 24.9 obv.? 11 (MS).

§ ḪUR.SAG-*azza=kan ištu*-x[...] / *pēdaz šum-ma-r[a-...]* / *[d]andukišnan* [...] § "From the mountain ... [...] from the place ... [...] [m]ortal [...]" KBo 24.9:10-12 (MS), ed. Fuscagni, hethiter.net/: CTH 458.19 (INTR 2013-02-06) ☐ due to the lack of word space after *ištu-* we, with Fuscagni, have tentatively analyzed *ištu-* as Hitt. rather than Akk.

Cf. *šummarant-*?

**šummarant-** (mng. unkn.); NS.†

**frag.** *šu-um-ma-ra-an-t[e?-...]* KBo 22.6 iii 10 (NS).

§ $^{m}$*Nurdaḫiš* LUGA[L...] / EN-*i=mi tuzz[i-...]* / *šu-um-ma-ra-an-t[e-...]* / *kišat* "Nurdahi, the kin[g ...] to/for my lord the troo[ps ... ] *š.* [...] became/happened" KBo 22.6 iii 8-11 (Sargon Legend, NS), ed. Güterbock, MDOG 101:20, 22.

Cf. *šummara[(-)...]*

**šum(m)aš** see *šum(m)eš*.

**šumāšila** see *šumešila*.

**šūmātani** n.?, Hurr.; (epithet of the netherworld god $^{d}$U.GUR); MH.†

EGIR-*anda=ma šapši ḫišammi* ALAM $^{d}$NIN.É.GAL $^{d}$U.GUR *šu-u-ma-a-ta-*⌜*ni*⌝ (dupl. *šu-ma-ta-a-n[i]* (or *-r[i]*), *zušši tūēni* $^{d}$*Teššuppina* KI.MIN (dupl. $^{d}$U-*uppina*) KBo 23.67 ii 13-15 (MH/MS), w. dupl. KUB 45.50 ii 5-7 (MH/NS), KBo 43.207:10-12 (NS), translit. ChS 1/3-2:76, 84, cf. von Brandenstein, ZDMG 91:565 n. 2 (reading *-r[i]*).

Von Brandenstein, ZDMG 91 (1937) 565 n. 2 (equivalent to *šaumatar*); Laroche, GLH (1977-79) 219; (following von Brandenstein); Tischler, HEG S/2 (2006) 1154; Richter, BibGlHurr (2012) 412.

Cf. *šaummatar*.

[*šumatar[i(-)...]* von Brandenstein, ZDMG 91:565 n. 2 and Tischler, HHwb 154, see *šūmātani* and *šaummatar,* cf. BibGlHurr. 412.

**-šum(m)i-** see *-šma/i-* A and B and *šum(m)a-* C.

**šummiyara-** adj.; (located) on top; MS.†

**pl. nom.?** *šum-mi-ia-ra[-a-e-eš]* KBo 12.101:9 (MS); **here?** *šum-mi-ia-[ra(?)-...* ] KBo 17.56 rev. 7 (MS).

§ [...]⌜$^{d}$⌝UTU-*waš kunkumāti da*⌜*nku*?-x⌝[...] / [ ... *ḫ]antiyarāēš šum-mi-ia-ra[-a-e-eš]* / [...-]*za kūš dātten kišš[an(?)...]* / [...*ku]kkumāti ḫarmi* § "§ [...] the Sun(god)'s dar[k?] *kunkumāti*-(plant?) [...] / [...](located) in [f]ront (pl.) (and?) (located) on top [(pl.)...] / [...] take these for yourselves(?)! Thu[s...] 'I hold the [*ku]kkumāti*(-plant?).' §" KBo 12.101:8-11 (rit. frag., MS) ☐ Laroche, OLZ 59:564, restores to *šummiya[raēš]* ☐ for *kunkumati/kukkumati* as possibly a plant see Otten/Souček, StBoT 8:97f., HED K 250f., but compare also Luw. *kunkumā(n)*- in Melchert, CLL s.v. For *ḫantiyara*- see the discussion in Oettinger, FsDinçol 543-547, Hoffner, GsOtten 66-75, and HW² Ḫ s.v. Oettinger, 545 translates [*ḫ*]*antiyarāēš šummiya*[*raēš*] as substantivized adjectives "Vorgebirge und Hauptgebirge." Since [*ḫ*]*antiyarāēš š.* seem to be resumed by "take these for yourselves" it is more likely to take them as adj. to objects that can be picked up. For Ḫantiyar(a) und Šummiyara as proper names of two mountains see RGTC 6:78, 366.

Oettinger, HS 114 (2001) 85, 87 ("Hohe"); idem, FsDinçol (2007) 545 (substantively used adjective "Hauptgebirge").

## šum(m)eš A independent personal pron.; you (pl.); from OS.

**nom.** *šu-me-eš* KBo 6.2 iii 18 (OS), KBo 17.4 ii 7 (OS), KBo 22.1 obv. 3, 5 (OS), KBo 22.62 iii 23 (OS), KUB 12.63 rev. 32 (OH/MS), KUB 33.62 iii 10 (OH/MS), KBo 3.1 ii 47 (OH/NS), KBo 3.43 rev. 5 (OH/NS), KBo 6.3 iii 21, (22) (OH/NS), KBo 6.6 i 29 (OH/NS), KBo 8.35 ii 5 (MH/MS), KBo 15.10 iii 50 (MH/MS), KBo 53.10 ii 22 (Arn. I-Ašm., MS), HKM 17 obv. 13 (MH/MS), KUB 15.34 iii 37 (2×), 51 (MH/MS), KUB 17.21 i 6, iv 13 (MH/MS), KBo 12.127 ii 5 (MH/NS), KUB 13.4 ii 73, iii 35 (MH/NS), KUB 23.68 rev. 7 (MH/NS), KUB 41.8 iii 10 (MH/NS), KBo 5.3 iv 25, 29, 31 (Šupp. I), KBo 3.3 iii 10, 24 (Murš. II), KUB 14.16 iii 26 (Murš. II), KUB 21.1 iii 31 (Muw. II), KBo 45.272 i 58 (here?; Muw. II), KUB 21.29 iv 13 (Ḫatt. III), KUB 21.42 iv 4 (Tudḫ. IV), KUB 26.1 iii 11 (Tudḫ. IV), KUB 26.12 iv 33 (Tudḫ. IV), ABoT 1.56 i 9 (Šupp. II), KUB 16.39 ii 29 (here?; NS), KUB 54.1 i 20 (NS).

*šu-meš* KBo 10.37 iii 43, iv 33 (OH/NS), KUB 26.19 ii 21, (38) (MH/MS), KBo 52.26 ii 13 (MH/NS), KUB 30.33 i 5, 14 (here?; MH/NS), KUB 41.8 iv 26 (MH/NS), KUB 36.91 obv. i? 3, 5 (pre-NH/NS), KUB 43.68 obv.? 9 (pre-NH/NS), KUB 12.55 iv 5 (NS), KBo 45.190:(4) (sic, see ZA 63:80, and cf. dupl. *šu-me-eš* KUB 24.9 ii 42).

*šu-me-e-eš* KUB 23.72 rev. 66 (MH/MS), KUB 34.40:2, 3 (MH/MS), KUB 23.68 obv. 28 (MH/NS), KUB 13.3 ii 20, iii 3, 36 (MH?/NS), KUB 14.4 ii 3, iv 9, 13 (Murš. II), KUB 26.12 ii 12 (Tudḫ. IV).

*šu-um-me-eš* KBo 10.37 iv 34 (OH/NS), KBo 12.6:2 (OH/NS), KUB 13.20 i 30 (MH/NS), KUB 1.15 iii 10 (pre-NH/NS), KUB 17.12 ii 16 (NS), KUB 21.37:4, 40, 42, 43, 44 (Ḫatt. III), KUB 26.1 i 6 (Tudḫ. IV), KUB 26.13 i (4), 7, 8 (Tudḫ. IV), ABoT 1.56 iii 21 (Šupp. II), KUB 19.28 iii 10, KUB 21.37 obv.4 (here?; both NH).

*šu-um-meš* KUB 1.15 iii 6 (pre-NH/NS), KUB 31.96 i 1 (NS), *šu-um-me-e-eš* KUB 23.68 obv. 26 (MH/NS), KUB 21.8 iii (14) (NH), KUB 31.80 rev. 10 (here?; NH), *šu-um-me-iš* KUB 26.1 i 2 (Tudḫ. IV).

*šu-me-š*(*a*(-)) KUB 33.10 ii 7 (OH/MS), KUB 31.103 obv. 16 (pre-NH/MS)?, KUB 31.74 ii 11 (OH/NS), KUB 23.72 rev. 61 (MH/MS), KUB 31.104 rt. col. 8 (MH/MS), KUB 36.114 rt. col. 13 (MH/MS), KUB 7.41 rev. 22 (MS?), KUB 21.41 iv 5 (NH), *šu-me-e-š*(*a*) KUB 23.72 rev. 26, 64 (MH/MS), KUB 36.114 rt. col. 12 (MH/MS), KBo 51.16 ii 4 (here?; MH/MS), KUB 11.1 iv 23 (OH/NS), KUB 26.29 obv. 11, 27 (both MH/NS), KBo 5.3 iv 18 (Šupp. I).

*šu-ma-aš* KBo 3.1 ii 72 (OH/NS), *šu-ma-a-aš* KUB 11.2:5 + IBoT 3:84:5 (OH/NS), here?: KBo 5.4 rev. 17, 18 (Murš. II), *šu-ma-a-š*(*a*-) IBoT 3.84:11 (OH/NS), HKM 75:22 (MH/MS), *šu-um-ma-aš* KUB 26.1 iii 45, 50, 61 (Tudḫ. IV).

**acc.** *šu-me-eš* KUB 26.19 ii 23 (MH/NS), KBo 5.3 iv 13, 26 (Šupp. I), KUB 14.13 i 54, iv 5 (Murš. II), *šu-ma-aš* KUB 13.4 ii 66, 67 (MH/NS), *šu-um-ma-aš* KUB 26.1 iii 32 (Tudḫ. IV).

**dat.-loc.** *šu-ma-aš* HKM 57:(27) (MH/MS), *šu-ma-a-aš* KUB 23.77:50 (MH/MS), KUB 21.47 rev.! 14 + KUB 23.82 rev. 19 (MH/MS), *šu-ma-a-š*(*a*(-)) KUB 23.77:32, 33, 38 (MH/MS), *šu-um-ma-aš* KUB 21.42 i 6 (Tudḫ. IV), KUB 26.13 i 15 (Tudḫ. IV), KUB 26.1 i 7 (Tudḫ. IV), *šu-me-eš* KUB 16.39 ii 38 (here?; NS), *šu-me-e-eš* KUB 14.14 rev. 19 (Murš. II), KUB 26.12 ii 25 (Tudḫ. IV), *šu-um-me-eš* KUB 21.29 iv 14 (NS), ABoT 1.56 i 10 (Šupp. II).

**gen.** *šu-me-en-za-an* KBo 53.10 ii 1 (Arn. I-Ašm., MS), KUB 23.77:21, 23 (MH/MS), *šu-me-en-za-n*(*a*-) KUB 23.77:19 (MH/MS), *šu-me-el* KUB 13.20 i 36 (MH/NS).

**abl.** *šu-me-e-da-za* KBo 12.128 rt. col. 16 (OH?/NS), *šu-me-e-da-az* KUB 23.103 rev. 26 (Tudḫ. IV).

**a.** you (subj.) — **1′** in nominal sentences or sentences w. expressed *eš-/aš-* "to be": ("When citizens of Ḫatti who are *ILKU*-people came, t[hey] bowed to the king and said: 'No one pays us wages. They reject u[s], saying:'") LÚ.MEŠ*ILKI*=*wa šu-me-eš* "'"You are *ILKU*-people!"'" KBo 6.2 iii 18 (Laws §55, OS), ed. LH 67 □ note the absence of the particle *-za* in OS, see GrHL §28.32-41; *nu*=*za kāša šu-me-eš* LÚ.MEŠ KUR URU*Išmirika ḫūmanteš IT*[*TI*] ⌜d⌝[UTU-*ŠI*] ⌜*l*⌝[*in*]*kiyaššaš* "Now, you, people of Išmirika, are all s[w]orn t[o His Majesty] (so in the future protect the king, the queen, the princes, and the land of Ḫatti)" KUB 23.68 + ABoT 1.58 rev. 7 (Išmirika treaty, MH/NS), ed. Kempinski/Košak, WO 5:196f., tr. Dipl.Texts² 16; *anda*=*ma*=*za šu-me-eš kuiēš* LÚ.MEŠ É.DINGIR-*LIM nu*=*za ḫaliy*[*aš*] *uddanī mekki paḫḫaššanuwanteš* "Furthermore, you who are temple personnel, be very careful in the matter of the wat[ch]" KUB 13.4 ii 73 (instr. for temple personnel, MH/NS), ed. HittInstr 256f., THeth 26:54f., 77; *šu-me-eš*=*wa*=*šmaš* ÌR.MEŠ *AB*[*I*=*YA* (*ēšten*)] "You were subjects of [my] fat[her]" KUB 14.16 iii 26 (Extensive ann. of Murš. II), w. dupl. KUB 14.15 iii 56, ed. AM 58f. □ instead of the particle *-za* the clitic pron. *-šmaš* is employed, see GrHL §28.32; *šu-um-ma-aš*=*(š)maš kuiēš* LÚ.MEŠ SAG *ḫūdak kā ēšten* "You, eunuchs, who were here immediately, ..." KUB 26.1 iii 45-46 (instr., Tudḫ. IV), ed. HittInstr 302f., Dienstanw. 14.

**2′** in non-nominal sentences: (The king is blaming the nobles) *šu-me-eš* LÚ.MEŠ GIŠTUKUL *tameškketteni* ⌈*a*⌉*pē*=⌈*ya katta*⌉[*n*] *dameškewan dāer kiššan AWAT* (eras.) *ABI*=*YA paḫšanutten takku šu-me-eš natta šaktēni kāni* LÚ.ŠU.GI-*ešš*=*a* NU.GÁL *nu*=*šmaš memai AWAT ABI*=*YA* "You are oppressing the craftsmen, and they began to oppress (their subordinates). Is this the way you have kept my father's command? If you do not remember (lit. know), are there not also old men here, one (of whom) may tell you the word of my father?" KBo 22.1 obv. 3-6 (instr., OS), ed. HittInstr 74f., Archi, FsLaroche 45f.; ("The father of the king stepped into the assembly and instructed them under his seal":) *ītten māḫḫanda ar*[(*e*(*š*)=*šmeš*)] *šu-me-eš-š*=*a* (var. C Ø *-ša*) *apeniššan īšte*[(*n*)] "Go and act just as your comrades (with regard to *šaḫḫan* and *luzzi*)" KBo 6.2 iii 19-20 + KBo 22.62 iii 22-23 (Laws §55, OS), with dupls. KBo 6.3 iii 22-23 (OH/NS) (var. B) and KBo 6.6 i 29 (OH/NS) (var. C), ed. LH 66-68; *nu*=*mu kāšma šu-me-eš*=*pat kuit ḫa*⌈*tr*⌉*ātten* "Now, concerning the matter that you yourselves have written to me" HKM 17 obv. 13 (letter, MH/MS), ed. Letters 124, HBM 142f.; ("Had I ever concerned myself with those people to be resettled, I, My Majesty would have concerned myself and would have taken those people to be resettled and carried them off to Ḫattuša") *šu-me-eš*=*ma*=*šmaš kuēz memiyanaz* EGIR-*an šanḫeškketteni nu*=*šmaš šumel* ZI-*az arḫa dašketteni* "On what basis do you keep concerning yourselves and taking them for yourselves on your own authority?" KBo 3.3 iii 10-12 (Syrian affairs, Murš. II), ed. Klengel, Or. NS 32:37, 43, Miller, KASKAL 4:126, 129, tr. DiplTexts² 172; [*U*]*MMA* mTutḫaliya ⌈LUGAL⌉.GAL LUGAL-*izziaḫḫat*=*wa* [*nu*]=*wa*? *šu-um-me-iš* LÚ.MEŠSAG *ANA* SAG.DU dUTU-*ŠI* [*š*]*er kišan linik*⟨*ten*⟩ "[T]hus (speaks) Tutḫaliya, the Great King: 'I became king, [and] you, eunuchs, have sworn allegiance to the person of My Majesty as follows'" KUB 26.1 + KUB 23.112 i 1-3 (instr., Tudḫ. IV), ed. Dienstanw. 8.

**3′** interchange between *šumeš* (pl. nom.) and *šumaš* (pl. nom.) in the same text or in duplicates — **a′** in OH/NS: *šu-me-eš-š*(*a*) KBo 3.1 ii 47 (Tel. pr.) but *šu-ma-a-aš* ibid. ii 68, w. dupl. *šu-me-eš* KUB 11.6 ii 16 and *šu-ma-aš-š*(*a*) KBo 3.1 ii 72, w. dupls. ⌈*šu*⌉*-um-me-eš-*⌈*š*(*a*)⌉ KBo 12.6:2, *šu-ma-a-š*(*a*) IBoT 3.84:11 + KBo 19.97:3 and KBo 12.4 iii 5.

**b′** in MH/NS: *šu-me-eš* KUB 41.8 iii 10 (MH/NS), w. dupl. *šu-ma-aš* KBo 10.45 iii 18 (MH/NS) □ KUB 41.8 is a little older than KBo 10.45, see Neu/Rüster, FsOtten 231, 233, 242.

**c′** in pre-NH/NS: *šu-um-meš* KUB 1.15 iii 6, *šu-um-me-eš* ibid. iii 10, dupl. [*šu-u*]*m*?*-ma-aš* KUB 40.105 rev. 8, but *šu-um-ma-aš* KUB 1.15 ii 7, iii 2.

**b.** you (dir. obj.): *šu-me-eš-š*=*a karūiliyaš* DINGIR.MEŠ-*aš* dU-*aš* LÚAZU *taknaza uiyat nu*=*šmaš kī uttar tet* "And the Stormgod (who is) the diviner, sent you, the primordial deities, from the earth and told you these words" KBo 10.45 i 51-52 (rit. for underworld deities, MH/NS), ed. Otten, ZA 54:120f. i 58-59; *nu*=*mu m*[*ā*]*n INA* EGIR UD.KAM *šu-me-eš* LÚ.M[EŠ] ⌈URU⌉*Ḫayaša aš*⌈*šul*⌉[*i*] *paḫḫaš*[*t*]*eni ammug*=*a šu-me-eš* LÚ.MEŠ URU*Ḫayaša* m*Mariya*⌈*n*⌉ LÚ.MEŠ*gaeneš ŠA* KUR URU*Ḫayaša aššuli paḫḫašḫi* KUR URU*Ḫayaša*=*ya aššuli paḫḫašḫi* "I[f] you (nom. pl., see above), the peop[le] of Ḫayaša, in the future benevolentl[y] protect me, then I will benevolently protect you (pl.), the people of Ḫayaša, Mariya (and) the relatives by marriage of Ḫayaša. I will also benevolently protect the land of Ḫayaša" KBo 5.3 iv 25-28 (Ḫuqq., Šupp. I), ed. Friedrich, SV 2:134f., tr. DiplTexts² 33; (As my father did once, I also asked you by oracle) *nu šu-me-eš* DINGIR.MEŠ EN.MEŠ=*YA ariyašešnaz ammuqq*=*a UL uemiya*⌈*n*⌉*un* but even I could not find you, the gods, my lords, by the oracle either" KUB 14.13 i 54-55 (PP 4, Murš. II), ed. Pestgeb. 246f., tr. Hittite Prayers 65; ("Because now my house, land, troops, chariots are dying continually") *nu šu-me-eš* DINGIR.MEŠ *kuēz* EGIR-*pa taninumi* "with what will I set you, the gods, in order again?" ibid iv 5, ed. Pestgeb. 248f., tr. Hittite Prayers 66; ("If you take payment for yourselves") DINGIR.MEŠ=*ma*=*kan šu-ma-aš*

*INA* EGIR.UD-*MI anda šanḫeškanzi* "the gods will pursue you till the end of days" KUB 13.4 ii 67 (instr. for temple personnel, MH/NS), ed. THeth. 26:54, 77, HittInstr 254-56.

**c.** to/for you (indir. obj.): *nu kuiš ammuk* LÚ.KÚR *šu-ma-a-aš-š=a=aš* LÚ.KÚR *ēšdu* "and if someone is an enemy to me (i.e., the king) then he must also be an enemy to you!" KUB 21.47 obv. 14 + KUB 23.82 obv.! 19 (instr., MH/MS), ed. HittInstr 238f., Li Xiwen (= Košak), JAC 5:79; *nu=za kāša ANA* KUR-*TI ḫingani* ⌜*šer*⌝ *šu*-⌜*me*⌝-*e-eš ANA* DINGIR.MEŠ [EN.Ḫ]I.A=*YA maškan peškemi* "Behold, because of the plague I am giving to you gods, my [lord]s, a propitiatory gift for the land" KUB 14.14 rev. 19-20 (PP 1, Murš. II), ed. Pestgeb. 174f., tr. HittitePrayers 63; (If somebody is fleeing from My Majesty and arrives at some border) ⌜*šu*⌝-*me-e-eš-š=aš āššu*⌜*š*⌝ *kuedanikki* "(if) he is someone's favorite among you" KUB 26.12 ii 25 (instr., Tudḫ. IV), ed. Dienstanw. 25, tr. HittInstr 286f.; *mā*[*n*] *šu-me-eš=ma* LÚ.MEŠ(eras.) URU-*LIM mazzallašaduwari ku*[*in/t*?]*ki šu-um-me-eš=kan kuit neyari* "But i[f] you (nom., see above) men of the city tolerate/condone(?) some[one/ someth]ing, what will it turn out to be for you?" KUB 21.29 iv 13-14 (treaty with Tiliura, Ḫatt. III), ed. González Salazar, AuOr 12:165, 168, tr. Kaškäer 148. ☐ because of the sg. 3 predicate *neyari* the subject of the final sentence cannot be *šummeš*, which must therefore be dat. "for you (all)." The different spelling of *šu-um-me-eš* against *šu-me-eš* in the previous line may distinguish the grammatical functions of both words in this passage; *nu šu-um-ma-aš BĒLŪ*ḪI.A *apāt* [*k*]*uwatqa kuiški memai* "Perhaps someone says to you, commanders, those (words): ..." KUB 21.42 i 6-7 (instr., Tudḫ. IV), ed. Dienstanw. 23, tr. HittInstr 284f. i 13-14.

**d.** of you, your (gen.): *šu-me-en-za-n=an=z=*(*š*)*an INA* URU=*KUNU* [ ... *l*]*ē pišteni* "[Do not allow] him (i.e., a spy) into your city, [do n]ot give [him bread]" KUB 23.77:19-20 (treaty w. Gašga, MH/MS), tr. Kaškäer 119, Kitchen/Lawrence, TreatyLawCovenant 1041.

**e.** with/through you (abl.): *n=at=za=kan šu-me-e-da-za* x-[ o ].MEŠ-*za še*[*k*]*ten* "Know them (i.e., the words) with your [ ...-]s!" KBo 12.128 rt. col. 16-17 (wisdom text, NS), ed. Archi, SEL 12:19, Cohen, Wisdom 202f.

Hrozný, MDOG 56 (1915) 26; idem, SH (1917) 114-119; Friedrich, HE $1^2$ (1960) 62; Tischler, HEG S/2 (2006) 1154-1158; Hoffner/Melchert, GrHL (2008) 134; Kloekhorst, EDHIL (2008) 779-780.

Cf. *-šmaš, šum(m)aš, šumāšila, šumešila*.

**šumeš B** n. neut.; (a foodstuff, possibly broad bean); from OS.†

**sg. nom.-acc. neut.** *šu-me-eš(-ku)* KUB 42.107 iii? 11 (NH).

**sg. gen.** *šu-me-eš-na-aš* KBo 17.15 rev.! 14 (OS), KBo 20.125 iii? (6) (MS), *šu-me-eš-na*-x KBo 17.40 iv 8 (MS).

3 *PA.* ZÍD.DA ZÍZ *ḫā*⌜*tant*⌝*aš* 6 *PA.* ŠE *SIQŪQI ḫattar=ku zināil=ku šu-me-eš-ku* 20 ⌜*PA.*⌝ *ŠE*[*ĀM*(?)] *ŠA* ANŠE.KUR.RA "three *PARĪSU* of flour (from) dried wheat, six *PARĪSU* of finely-ground-flour (from) barley, (in addition) either lentils(?) or chick peas(?) or broad beans(?), twenty *PARĪSU* of bar[ley] for horses" KUB 42.107 iii? 9-12 (ration list, NH), ed. Watkins, FsKnobloch 494f., translit. StBoT 25:160; [(*katti=šši=ma*)] LÚ*ḫištā arta šu-me-eš-na-aš mēma*[(*l*)] GIŠ*ērḫuit* [(*ḫarz*)*i*] "Next to her (i.e., the wife of the $GUDU_{12}$-priest) stands the man of the *ḫešta*. He holds the coarsely ground broad bean(?) meal in (lit. with) a basket" KBo 17.15 rev.! 13-14 (fest. for netherworld deities, OS), w. dupl. KBo 17.40 iv 8 (OH/MS?), ed. Haas/Wäfler, UF 8:82f., 88f.

Comparing KBo 17.15 rev.! 13-14 with the similar passage DAM LÚ$GUDU_{12}$ *ŠA* GÚ.GAL.GAL *memal* TA! GIŠMA.SÁ.AB *ḫarzi* "The wife of the anointed one holds the coarsely ground broad bean meal with a basket" IBoT 3.1 obv. 23-24 (OH/NS), Otten, OLZ 50:392, suggested that **šumeššar* could be the Hittite reading of GÚ.GAL.GAL (thus also Hoffner, AlHeth. 98f.). Not referring to Otten, Berman, JCS 28:244, assumed that in the coordinated *-ku* ... *-ku* ...*-ku* "whether ... or ... or ..." construction KUB 42.107 iii? 10-11 the words *ḫattar*, *zinail* and *šumeš* modify the preceding ŠE and therefore are types of barley or barley products. Going back to Otten, Watkins, FsKnobloch, 494f., however, compared them with the series GÚ.TUR, GÚ.GAL, GÚ.GAL.GAL together in some text passages, suggesting to identify them as "lentil," "chick pea" and "broad bean" respectively. If these equations are correct, then *šumeš* is indeed identical with GÚ.GAL.GAL "broad bean." Watkins, FsKnobloch 494 w. n. 13, and Tischler, HEG S 1159, both assume a scribal mistake *šu-me-eš‹-šar›-ku* in KUB 42.107, but this is not necessary. Neuter nouns with a nom.-acc. sg. in *-eš/-iš* and oblique forms in *-ešn-/-išn-* are well attested (type *tunnakiš(n-)*, cf. GrHL §4.90).

Otten, OLZ 50 (`955) 392 (*šumeššar* = GÚ.GAL.GAL); Hoffner, AlHeth (1974) 98f. (following Otten); Berman, JCS 28 (1976) 244-245 ("type of barley or barley product," no apparent connection with *šumešnaš* (genitive) "broadbean"); Josephson, Heth.u.Idg. (1979) 96 (= GÚ.GAL.GAL "broad bean"; compares it with Gr. κύαμος and κύμα); Tischler, HDW (1982) 78 ("eine Getreideart ?"); Watkins, FsKnobloch (1985) 494-495 (= GÚ.GAL.GAL "broad bean"); Rieken, StBoT 44 (1999) 393 n. 1980, 489; Soysal, FsPopko (2002) 335 w. n. 52; Tischler, HEG S/2 (2006) 1159 (a scribal error for *šumeššar*); Kloekhorst, EDHIL (2008) 782 (stem **šumeššar*, only citing the gen.).

**šumišaya-x?[(-)... ]** (mng. unkn.); NS.†

**frag.** *šu-mi-ša-ia*(-)[...] KUB 31.116 iv 2 (NS).

LÚ.MEŠNINDA.GUR$_4$.RA x?[ o ] 1(?) BÁN ZÍD.D[A ... ] *šu-mi-ša-ia*-x?[ o o o ]x ⸢*za*⸣?[- ... ] KUB 31.116 iv 1-2 (NS).

[**šumeššar*] see *šumeš* B.

**šumešila, šumāšila** emphatic personal pron.; you yourselves (pl.); from MH/MS.†

*šu-me-ši-la* HKM 42:5 (MH/MS), *šu-ma-a-ši-la* KBo 5.4 rev. 17 (Murš. II).

*n=an MAḪAR* [dUTU-*ŠI*] *šu-me-ši-la* ⸢*l*⸣*iliwaḫḫ*[*ūanzi*] ⸢*u*⸣*watetten* "You yourselves must bring it (i.e., the army?) quick[ly] before [My Majesty]" HKM 42:4-7 (letter, MH/MS), ed. Alp, HBM 194f.; *nu mān šumāš šu-ma-a-ši-la taraššawala nu šarā tiyatte*[*n nu=kan MA*]*ḪAR* dUTU-*ŠI uwatten* "If you yourselves have a resolvable dispute(?), then step up [and] come [bef]ore My Majesty" (so that I, My Majesty, can set you on the proper path by means of a judgement) KBo 5.4 rev. 17-18 (Targ., Murš. II), ed. Friedrich, SV 1:62f., HEG T/D 151 (w. discussion), Devecchi, NABU 2013/4:136f., tr. Beckman, DiplTexts[2] 72f. ("If you yourselves have a resolvable dispute(?)") □ with Hoffner/Melchert, GrHL 279 (§18.7) followed by Devecchi, NABU 2013/4:136, forms in *-ila* are so far only used for reinforcing subjects. However, such an interpretation forces us to take *taraššawala* as a nominal predicate ("If you yourselves are *taraššawala*"), which seems grammatically unlikely. It is not inconceivable that *š.* next to the dat. *šumāš* occasionally came to be used to add emphasis, here with *taraššawala* as a pl. nom.-acc. neut. ("If there are *taraššawala* things to you"), which is how Friedrich, SV 1:62f., and Beckman, DiplTexts[2] 72, took it.

*š.* shows the same formation as *ukila*, *zikila*, *apašila*, consisting of the independent personal pron. *šumeš* "you (pl.)" and the added suffix *-ila* in order to express emphasis of some kind (GrHL §5.3 (p. 132)). The usage of *šumāš* with *šumāšila* KBo 5.4 rev. 17 would indicate a dative sense.

Sommer, Heth. 2 (1922) 48 n. 1; Sommer/Falkenstein, HAB (1938) 141 n. 3; Friedrich, HE I[2] (1960) 62; Puhvel, HED 1 (1984) 88; Tischler, HEG S/2 (2006) 1152, 1158; Hoffner/Melchert, GrHL (2008) 132 §5.3, 279 §18.7; Devecchi NABU 2013/4:136.

**(GIŠ/URUDU)šum(m)ittant-** n. com.; ax; from OH/MS.†

**sg. nom.** GIŠ*šum-mi-it-ta-an-za* KUB 32.123 ii 10 (OH/NS), *šu-mi-*[*it-ta-an-za*] KUB 59.75 i 13 (NS).

**acc.** *šu-um-mi-it-ta-an-ta-an* KUB 12.63 rev. 20 (OH/MS), [URU]DU*šu-um-mi-it-ta-an-da-an-n*(*a*) KUB 13.35 i 46 (NH), *šum-mi-it-ta-an-ta-an* KUB 8.51 ii 4 (LNS), [...*š*]*u-um-mi-*⸢*it*⸣ *-ta-an-da-*⸢*an*⸣ KBo 19.144 i 5 (NS), *šu-mi-it*[-...] KBo 56.15:3 (NS).

**unclear/frag.** *šum-mi-it-ta-an-it* KBo 39.125:4 (NS) (= **inst.** *šum-mi-it-ta-an‹-ti›-it*? Kloekhorst, EDHIL 783 suggests *šum-mi-it-ta-an-da*![-...]), *šu-mi-it*[-...] KBo 31.108 iv 6 (NS).

**a.** used for cutting down a tree: [*Enkiduš*] *šum-mi-it-ta-an-ta-an* ŠU-*az ēpt*[*a*] / [... dGI]Š.GIM.MAŠ-*aš*(eras.)=*ma* GIM-*an* [*aušt*(*a*(?) *nu*)] ⸢*a*⸣*pušš=a* (sic, var. *apāšš=a*) *ḪAṢINNU* [...] *ēpta* [ ... *apā*(*šš=a* GIŠERIN)] *karašta* "[Enkidu] seize[d] an ax with (his) hand. But when [Gi]lgameš [sa]w, he, too, seized an ax [with (his) hand(?) ...] and [h]e, too, cut (down) the cedar-tree" KUB 8.51 ii 4-8 (Gilgamesh, first tablet, LNS), w. dupl. KBo 10.47d iv 1-3 (NS), ed. Friedrich, ZA 39:6f., translit. Myth. 13, tr. Beckman, apud Foster, Gilg. 161.

**b.** w. other tools — **1′** cutting implements: (Ukkura's testimony: "I took for myself as many of the old ones as I wished") 2 URUDU*PĀŠU* GAL⸗*wa⸗za* [1? URU]DU*šu-um-mi-it-ta-an-da-an-na daḫḫun* "two large copper hatchets and [one? copp]er ax I took for myself" KUB 13.35 + KBo 16.62 i 45-46 (dep., NH), ed. Werner, StBoT 4:6f.; *nu⸗za šu-um-mi-it-ta-an-ta-an* (var. *šu-mi-it*[-...]) *PĀŠU* Z[ABAR *dāš*(?)] "(The deity Andaliya) [took(?)] an ax (and) a hatchet of b[ronze]" KUB 12.63 rev. 20 (Zuwi's rit., OH/MS), w. dupl. KBo 56.15:3 (NS).

**2′** other: 1-*NUTIM ŠAGĀRI*ᴴᴵ·ᴬ *mān* ⌈x⌉ [o]⌈x x x⌉ [...] GAL ZABAR *ULU RABÎ ULU ṢIḪIR* 1 *a-x*[...] ᴳᴵˢ*šum-mi-it-ta-an-za* 1 *kantašuwalli* ZABA[R] GÍR ZABAR *ŠA* ᴸᵁMUḪALDIM KUB 32.123 ii 8-11 (Ištanuwian fest., OH/NS); [*nepe*]*š*(?) URUDU *ERṢETUM* URUDU 1[-*NŪTIM šišiyamma* URUDU] / [o ᴳᴵˢ*ḫa*]*ḫḫar* URUDU 3 *muilaš* Z[ABAR *intaluzziš* URUDU ᴳᴵˢ]*kalamma* URUDU 1 *šu-mi-*[*it-ta-an-za* URUDU ᵁᴿ]ᵁᴰᵁBAL KUB 59.75 i 11-14 (Ašdu's rit., NS), ed. Görke, Ašdu 38, 40, ChS 1/5-1:263, (ᴳᴵˢ)*šišiyam(m)a*.

Axes and related tools were multi-purpose instruments, used functionally and ceremonially. At least four terms are known from the Boğazköy texts: Hitt. *š.* and *ateš(ša)-*, Akk. *ḪAṢ(Ṣ)INNU*, and *PĀŠU*. There is no reason not to equate *š.* with Akk. *ḪAṢ(Ṣ)INNU* in KUB 8.51 ii 4-6 as suggested by Friedrich, ZA 39:41f., who tr. both *š.* and *ḪAṢ(Ṣ)INNU* as "Beil" ("hatchet"). Later, however, Friedrich, HW 307, tr. both as "Axt" ("ax"). The juxtaposition of *š.* together with *PĀŠU* "ax" or "hatchet" in KUB 12.63 and with URUDU*PĀŠU* GAL "large ax/hatchet" in KUB 13.35+KBo 16.62 i 45-46 might point at *PĀŠU/ateš(ša)-* being the smaller of the two. Archaeological finds and iconographical evidence show two types of ax among the Hittites: the shaft hole (socketed) ax and socketless ax. In his discussion on axes in Hittite Anatolia, Beal, Diss. 656-664, proposes to identify *šum(m)ittant-/ḪAṢ(Ṣ)INNU/ulmi-* with the shaft hole ax, and *ateš-/PĀŠU* with the socketless ax.

Friedrich, ZA 39 (1930) 41f. ("Beil(?)"); idem, HW (1952) 197 ("Beil, Axt"), 307 (= Akk. *ḫaṣinnu* "Axt"); Košak, THeth 10 (1982) 19 w. biblio. (Hittite word for the Akkadogram *ḪAṢ(Ṣ)INNU*, and etymologically related to the Germanic word for "smith"); Beal, Diss. (1986) 656-664 ("shaft hole ax"); Rieken, HS 113 (2000) 173 (on the possibility of the *u* in *š.* being either graphic or anaptyctic); Tischler, HEG S/2 (2006) 1162-1164; Kloekhorst, EDHIL (2008) 783 (rejecting *u* as an anaptyctic vowel).

**šumrae-** see *šumreške-*.

**šumreške-** v.; to become pregnant; pre-NH/NS.†

    **supine** *šum-re-eš-ke-wa-an* KUB 24.8 iii 11, KUB 36.60 iii 2, KBo 19.106:(7) (all pre-NH/NS).
    **frag.** *šum-re-*⌈*e*⌉?[-...] KBo 47.150:2 (NS).

[(DA)]M ᵐ*Appu šum-re-eš-ke-wa-an dāiš* ITU.⌈1.KAM ITU.2⌉.[(KAM)] [IT]U.3.KAM ITU.4.KAM ITU.5.KAM ITU.6.KAM ITU.7.KAM ITU.8.KAM ITU.9!.KAM *p*[*ait*] *nu* [(I)]TU.10.KAM *tiyat nu⸗za* DAM ⌈ᵐ⌉*Appu* DUMU.NITA-*an ḫašta* ... § ⌈*tā*⌉[(*n⸗za namm*)]*a* DAM] ⌈ᵐ*Ap*⌉*pu šum-re-eš-ke-wa-an dāiš* I[TU.10.KAM *ti*]⌈*yat*⌉ *nu⸗za* MUNUS-*za* (var. B: DAM ᵐ*App*[*u*]) DUMU.NITA-*an ḫašta* "Appu's wife became pregnant. The first month, the second month, the third [mon]th, the fourth month, the fifth month, the sixth month, the seventh month, the eighth month, the ninth month pa[ssed], and the tenth month arrived. Appu's wife bore a son. ... § Agai[n], a second time Appu's [wife] became pregnant. The [tenth] mo[nth arri]ved, and the woman (var. Appu's wife) bore a son" KUB 36.60 iii 2-4 + KUB 24.8 iii 1-3, 11-12 (Appu story, pre-NH/NS), w. dupls. KBo 19.106:7-11 (A) and KUB 36.59 ii 1-2, 8-9 (B), ed. StBoT 14:10f., tr. Hittite Myths² 84.

The supine of *š.* allows three alternatives for a stem: *\*šumrae-*, *\*šumriya-* (as Friedrich, JCS 1:293, takes it), or *\*šumrešš-*. Although *š.* is attested very poorly, its mng. is clear owing to the context of the Appu story. Since Hitt. has *armaḫḫ-* (with -*za* and derived from ᵈ*arma-* "Moongod" and "month") for "to become pregnant" *š.* has been suggested to emphasize the growing-heavy of the womb of a pregnant woman. Neumann, apud Oettinger, Stammbildung 298 n. 78, suggested a connection with an unattested verb *šu-* "to be full" (different from but related to the adj. *šūu-* "full," s.v.) via *\*šumar* "being full," regular outcome through dissimilation from **šuwar* (also see Kimball, Hittite Historical Phonology 247, 375). Cf. the Turkish expression *yüklü* "the loaded one" = "pregnant." Note also Hittite *šannapili-* A 3 "empty = non-pregnant."

Friedrich, JCS 1 (1947) 293-294; idem, HW (1952) 197 (*šumrai-* "schwanger werden"); Oettinger, Stammbildung (1979) 159, 298 n. 78; Melchert, Phon. (1984) 29f. n. 62; Weitenberg, U-Stämme (1984) 138, 139; Zinko, Sprache&Kultur (1998) 193 n. 53; Kimball, Hittite Historical Phonology (1999) 247, 375; Tischler, HEG S/2 (2006) 1164f.; Kloekhorst, EDHIL (2008) 783f.; Soysal, JAOS 133 (2013) 699.

Cf. *šūu*.

**šumumaḫ-** v.; to combine(?), unite(?); OH/NS.†

**imp. sg. 2** *šu-mu-ma-aḫ* KUB 29.1 ii 43 (OH/NS).

("Go to the funeral pyres and bring a *kinupi*-vessel") *kinupi=ma=ššan anda ŠA* UR.MAḪ *šiešai paršanaš* UZU*šišai šu-mu-ma-aḫ n=at ḫarak* § *n=at tarup n=at* 1-*EN iya* "unite(?) the *šišai*(-body part) of a lion, (and) the *šišai*(-body part) of a panther in the *kenupi*(-vessel) and hold them. § Combine them and make them one" KUB 29.1 ii 42-44 (foundation rit., OH/NS), ed. Kellerman, Diss. 15, 28 (as verb), Marazzi, VO 5:154f. ("prepara(?)"), Carini, Athenaeum 60:494f., Rieken, HS 113:171, (UZU)*šišai-*.

Since Hoffner, EHGl (RHA XXV/80) 25 w. n.19, who suggested a meaning "to braid," a general mng. of "putting things together," has been advocated by most scholars, although individual translations and sometimes etymological analyses differ (cf. Rieken, HS 113:171-175, Kloekhorst, EDHIL 784f., Tischler, HEG S/2:1165f. w. lit.).

Kronasser, EHS 1 (1966) 432; Hoffner, EHGl (1967) 25 (s.v. "to braid"); Oettinger, Stammbildung (1979) 456 n.135 (cites the word as *šumumahh-hhi*(?)); Starke, ZA 69 (1979) 89 w. n. 88; Collins, Diss. (1989) 54 ("braid"); Rieken, HS 113 (2000) 171-175 ("vereinigen, zu Einem machen"); Tischler, HEG S/2 (2006) 1165f. ("(etwas) sorgfältig hinlegen, hinschichten, anbinden, festdrücken"); Kloekhorst, EDHIL (2008) 784f. ("to braid together(?)").

**šun(n)a-, šunni-, šun(n)iya/e- B** v.; to fill, pour; from OS.

**pres. sg. 1** *šu-un-na-aḫ-ḫi* KBo 3.38 rev. 17, KUB 33.70 iii? 10, (11) (OH/NS), KUB 43.59 i 7 (NS), *šu-*⌈*un*⌉*-ni-ia-mi* KUB 59.55 ii 9 (NS).

**sg. 2** *šu-un-na-at-t*[*i*] KUB 15.22:14 (NH).

**sg. 3** *šu-un-na-i* KBo 6.2 iv 50 (OS), KBo 20.37 obv. 2 (*šu-un-na-*‹*i*›?, so Neu, StBoT 26:174) (OS), KUB 25.36 ii 23, v 8 (OH?/MS), KUB 30.41 ii 8, 11 (NS), KUB 41.26 iv 9 (OH/NS), KBo 21.69 iv 2, 5 (MS), KBo 24.29 iii 3, 10 (MS), KBo 32.15 ii 10, 11 (MH/MS), KBo 32.16 ii 24, 25 (MH/MS), KBo 17.65 rev. 49 (MH?/MS?), IBoT 1.7 iv 12 (NS), KBo 5.2 i 55, iii 57, iv 38 (MH/NS), KBo 21.34 i 8, 13, 29, 35 (MH/NS), KUB 34.75:12 (pre-NH/NS), KUB 27.1 iii 14, 15 (Ḫatt. III), KBo 4.13 v 12 (NS), KBo 19.142 ii 15 (NH), *šu-un-na-a-i* KUB 59.23 iii 9 (OH/NS), KBo 10.45 iii 8 (MH/NS), KBo 21.37 rev.! 16 (MH?/NS), KBo 13.217 iv 5, v 3, 13 (NS), KBo 13.245 rev. 22 (NS), KUB 20.1 ii 8 (NS), KUB 41.26 iv 17 (NS), KUB 39.71 ii 60, 61 (NH), KUB 10.91 iii 7 (NH?), [*šu-u*]*n-ni-ez-zi* KBo 25.184 iii 59 (pre-NH/NS).

**pl. 1** *šu-un-nu-me-ni* KBo 32.15 ii 16 (MH/MS), *šu-nu-mi-ni* HKM 109:10, (16) (MH/MS), HKM 110 obv. 5 (MH/MS), *šu-nu-mi*‹*-ni*› HKM 109:11 (MH/MS), here? [*š*]*u*?-*ú-nu-me-e-n*[*i*] KBo 51.23:7 (MS).

**pl. 2** *šu-un-na-at-te-ni* KUB 13.4 iv 18 (pre-NH/NS).

**pl. 3** *šu-un-na-an-zi* KUB 35.165 rev. 21 (OS), KBo 25.109 ii 16, iii 13 (OS? or MS?), KUB 10.21 iv 12 (OH/NS), KUB 15.34 iii 25 (MH/MS?), KUB 12.5 i 18 (MH/NS), KBo 21.37 rev.! 19 (MH?/NS), KBo 15.37 iii 41, 55, v 39 (NS), KBo 11.51 iv 7 (NS), KUB 7.38 obv. 4, 9 (NS), KUB 7.24 obv. 9 (NS), KUB 17.35 i 36, ii 23, iii (6), 31, iv 11, 21 (NS), KBo 26.182 iv 3 (NS), KUB 44.21 ii 6, iii 14 (NS), KUB 44.42 obv. 14, 21, rev. 11 (NS), KUB 21.17 iii (14), (16), (17) (Ḫatt. III), KUB 25.23 iv 55 (Tudḫ. IV), *šu-un-na-*‹*an*›*-zi* KBo 2.13 obv. 20 (NH), *šu-na-an-zi* KUB 55.60 iv? 17 (LNS), KUB 51.58 rev.? (7) (NS), *šu-un-an-zi* KBo 21.1 ii 6 (NS), *šu-un-ni-an-zi* KUB 46.47 obv. 15, 19, rev. 3, 18, 19 (NS), KUB 55.58 obv. 29, 31 (MH/NS), IBoT 3.148 iii 21, (22) (MH?/NS), KUB 51.89:9 (NS), KUB 9.32 obv. 40 (MH/NS), *šu-un-ni-ia-an-zi* KBo 15.24 ii 44 (MH/NS), KUB 44.4 rev. 19 (NH), KBo 15.61 i 15 (NS), KUB 53.41:8 (NS), IBoT 4.30 obv. 4 (NS), [*šu-u*]*n-ni-ia-*‹*an-*›*zi* IBoT 4.30 obv. 5 (NS), *šu-ni-i*[*a-an-zi*] KBo 4.2 ii 30 (pre-NH/NS).

**pret. sg. 1** *šu-un-na-aḫ-ḫu-un* KBo 10.2 i 21, ii (23) (OH/NS).

**sg. 3** *šu-un-na-aš* KBo 22.2 obv. 2 (OS), KBo 3.57 obv. 9, KBo 12.3 iii 15 (OH/NS), KUB 19.67 i 10 (Ḫatt. III), *šu-un-né-eš* KUB 8.80:15 (Šupp. I), *šu-un-ni-iš-ta* KUB 1.1 ii 79 (Ḫatt. III), *šu-un-ni-et* KBo 21.33 iv 31 (MH/MS), KBo 23.44 iv 4 (MH/NS), *šu-ni-et* KBo 27.144 + KBo 71.2 iii 12 (MH/NS).

**pl. 3** *šu-un-né-er* KBo 20.114 v 9 (MH/NS), KUB 18.39 obv.? 5 (NH), *šu-un-*⌈*ner*⌉ KUB 31.65 obv. 3 (NH).

**imp. sg. 2(?)** *šu-un-na* KBo 20.37 obv. 2 (OS, or *šu-un-na*‹*-i*› w. Neu, StBoT 26:174?), *šu-un-ni* KUB 6.45 iii 37, 43, KUB 6.46 iv 6, 12 (Muw. II).

**sg. 3** *šu-un-ni-ed-du* KUB 12.58 iv 13 (NS).

**pl. 2** *šu-u-ni-iš-tén* KUB 13.3 ii 27 (pre-NH/NS).

**pl. 3** *šu-un-na-an-du* KUB 41.32 obv. (13) (NS), KUB 41.33 obv. 13 (NS).

**inf.** *šu-un-ni-u-wa-an-zi* KBo 24.68 obv. 4 (MS), *šu-un-nu-ma-an-zi* IBoT 1.7 iv 15 (MH/NS), KUB 58.39 i 5 (NS), KUB 21.17 iii 10 (Ḫatt. III).

**verbal subst. nom.** *šu-nu-*⌈*mar*⌉ KBo 15.33 ii 7, 12 (MH/MS), *šu*(coll.)*-un-nu-mar* KBo 1.42 iii 51 (NH), ⌈*š*⌉*u-un-nu-mar* KUB 59.67 ii 19 (NS).

**gen.** *šu-un-nu-ma-aš* KUB 59.29 iii 17 (NS).

**part. sg. nom. com.** *šu-un-na-an-za* KUB 56.48 ii 15, 18, 36, (39), iii 13 (NS), KUB 42.98 i 21 (NH), *šu-un-ni-an-za* KBo 2.4 iii 25 (NH), *šu-un-ni-ia-an-za* KBo 2.4 ii 15, 21, iii 19, iv (3) (NH).

**nom.-acc. neut.** *šu-un-na-an* KBo 10.24 iii 3 (OH/NS).

**pl. acc. com.** [*šu*]*-un-na-an-tu-*[*uš*] KBo 25.34 ii 12 (OS?).

**imperf. pres. sg. 2** *šu-un-né-eš-ke-ši* KUB 36.12 ii 11 (NS).

**sg. 3** *šu-un-né-eš-ke-ez-zi* Bo 3752 obv.? ii 5 (StBoT 25:179, OS or MS), KUB 12.58 iv 10 (NS), *šu-un-né-eš-ke-zi* KBo 11.32 obv. 7 (OH/NS), [*šu-*]*un-ni-iš-*⌈*ke-ez-zi*⌉ KUB 58.14 rev.? left col. 19 (OH/NS), KBo 24.68 obv. (2) (MS), KUB 27.65 i 22 (NH), *šu-né-eš-ke-ez-zi* KUB 58.35 ii? 8 (NS).

**pl. 3** *šu-un-né-eš-kán-zi* KUB 25.22 iii 11 (LNS), KUB 39.8 iv (4) (NS).

**pret. sg. 2** *šu-un-né-eš-*⌈*git*⌉ KBo 12.70 rev.! iii 14 (NH).

**sg. 3** *šu-un-ni-iš-ke-et* KUB 14.4 iv 19 (Murš. II).

**pl. 3** *šu-un-né-eš-ke-er* KUB 16.16 obv. 20 (NH).

**Luw.? pret. pl. 3.** *šu-ni-iš-kán-ta* HKM 109 obv. 2 (MH/MS).

**imp. sg. 2(?)** *šu-*⌈*un-ni-iš*⌉*-k*[*i*(-)...] KUB 55.31 rev. 3 (if not to be restored otherwise).

(Sum.) ⌈SI⌉ = (Akk.) *ma-lu-ú* = (Hitt.) *šu*(coll.)*-un-nu-mar* "to fill/the filling" KBo 1.42 iii 51 (Izi Bogh.), ed. MSL 13:139 (l. 191).

(Akk.) *ù* É $SIG_5$ (eras.) *um-ta-al-li* "and I filled the house (with) valuables" KBo 10.1 obv. 10 = (Hitt.) *nu* É*-ir=mit āššawīt šarā šu-un-na-aḫ-ḫu-un* "and I filled up my house with good(s)" KBo 10.2 i 20-21 (bil. ann. of Ḫatt. I, OH/NS), ed. (Akk.) StMed 16:36f., Saporetti, SCO 14:77, 80 ( "e la casa con tesor[i](?) ho riempito"), (Hitt.) StMed 12:36f., Imparati, SCO 14:44f. (Hitt., "e la mia casa con (quei) beni empii fino all'orlo"), tr. Houwink ten Cate, Anatolica 11:48.

(Akk.) [... *t*]*u-um-ma-*⌈*al*⌉⟨*-li?*⟩ ⌈*ù*⌉ *kanini=šu* [...] "[...y]ou have constantly filled, and his store-rooms [...]" KBo 12.70 rev.! iv 13 = (Hitt.) *ḫarištaniuš* ⸗*tarpīušš=a kuiēš ḫalkit šu-un-né-eš-*⌈*git*⌉ "(in regard to) the upper stories and store-rooms(?) which you have constantly filled with grain" ibid. iii 13-14 (bil. wisdom, NH), ed. Laroche, Ugar. 5:782, Dietrich, UF 23:62f. (Akk.) (differently), Keydana, ibid. 73f. (Hitt.).

(Hurr.) *zu-wa-ta-at-te i-zu-u-zi ka-ap-p*[*í-li-wa*$_a$*-aš* ...] KBo 32.15 i 10 = (Hitt.) ZÍZ*-tar*[*=ši kui*]*šša* ½ *PARĪSI šu-un-na-i* "each one will pour [for him] one half *PARĪSU* of wheat" KBo 32.15 ii 10 (Hurro-Hitt. bil. wisdom and myth, MH/MS), ed. StBoT 32:290f.; tr. Hittite Myths[2] 75.

**a.** to pour/fill (absol., no particle): [LÚ.MEŠ]⌈SIMUG⌉.A 2 SAG.DU GUD KÙ.BABBAR *udanzi* LÚ.MEŠZABAR.DAB [GAL.ḪI.]A KAŠ.GEŠTIN *udanzi* LUGAL*-aš peran šu-un-na-an-zi* "The smith[s] bring two ox-head(-shaped vessels) of silver. The cellar masters bring wine-beer [cup]s. They pour/fill (them) in front of the king" KBo 11.51 iv 6-7 (*ANDAḪŠUM*-fest., OH/NS), ed. Badalì, SEL 2:71f.; ("[They] bring [...]") *t=aš* LUGAL*-i per*[*an*] *šu-un-na-an-zi* "They pour them in front of the king" KUB 20.83 iii 3-4 (*ANDAḪŠUM*-fest, NS); cf. VBoT 34 obv. 4 (*ANDAḪŠUM*-fest); ("The cellar masters pour out two cups of wine and carry (them) out") LÚSAGI.A *paizzi ANA* 2 MUNUS.MEŠSANGA 3 LÚ.MEŠSANGA*=ya šu-un-na-a-i* "Thereupon the cup-bearer pours for two priestesses and three priests" KUB 59.23 iii 7-9 (fest. frag., OH/NS), translit. DBH 14:44.

**b.** to pour (something into a container, implied or expressed, in order to fill it, usu. without particle) — **1′** foodstuffs: URU*Gašaša kuwapi arunain*⌈*ta*⌉ *ḫalki*ḪI.⌈A *kuen šu*⌉*-ni-iš-kán-ta* ... § ... *ŠA* 1 MU *ḫalki*ḪI.A *šu-nu-mi-ni* § *INA* 2 MU *ḫalkin kuen šu-nu-mi*⟨*-ni*⟩ ... § *ŠA* 3 MU *ḫalki*ḪI.A *kuin šu-nu-mi-ni* ... "The town of Gašaša where they ...-ed: (these are) the grains they poured: (list of seeds) § (list of seeds: these are) the grains of the first year we pour. § (These are) the grain(s) in the second year we pour: (list of seeds) § (These are) the grains of the third year we pour: (list of seeds)" HKM 109:1-2, 10-11, 16 (harvest inventory, MH/MS), ed. del Monte, OAM 2:122 (tr. in each case a form of *seminare*) □ for the reading *arunainta* see Melchert, Sprachkontakt&Sprachwandel 447. The first person plural form *šu-nu-mi-ni* determines the *š.* forms in this passage as the *ḫi*-verb *š.* and not the *mi*-verb *šun(n)iya/e-* A "to sow, dip," despite the single *-n-*; *našma ḫalkiuš kuwapi šu-un-na-at-te-ni nu takšan šarran mematteni takšan šarran=ma=za=kan anda šannatteni nu=šmaš=an uwatteni* EGIR*-zian arḫa šarratteni* "Or, at the time when you (i.e., the deities' farmers) pour the grains and you declare half while you conceal (the other) half for yourselves and afterwards divide it among yourselves" (that is a sin for you) KUB 13.4 iv 18-20 (instr. for temple personnel, pre-NH/NS), w. dupl. KUB 40.63 iv 11-13, ed. HittInstr 262f. ("store"), THeth 26:65, 82 ("store"), Süel, Direktif Metni 76f. ("teslim ettiğiniz, lit. (ambara) doldurduğunuz"), *šarra-* D 1 c 2′; ZÍZ-*tar*[*=ši kui*]*šša* ½ *PARĪSI šu-un-na-i* Š[E....*=m*]*a=šši kuiš*⌈*ša*⌉ 1 *PARĪSA šu-un-na-i* "[Each] one will pour [for him] one half *PARĪSU* of wheat; each one will pour for him one *PARĪSU* of bar[ley.] (But if [Teššub] is (ever) naked, each of us will clothe him with a fine garment)" KBo 32.15 ii 10-12 (Hurro-Hitt. bil. wisdom and myth, MH/MS), ed. StBoT 32:291 ("schüttet"), tr. Hittite Myths² 75 ("heap up"); *namma apēdani=pat* GE$_6$-*ti* 6 *PA.* ZÍD.DA ZÍZ *A*⌈*NA*⌉ DINGIR.MEŠ ⌈*ḫūmantaš*⌉ *šūeriya* NINDA *ṢIDĪTI INA* ⌈É.NINDA.DÙ.DÙ⌉ *šu-*⌈*un-ni*⌉*-an-zi UL=an ANA PĀNI* DINGIR.MEŠ *ape*⌈*da šu-un*⌉*-ni-*⌈*an-zi*⌉ "Then, in that same night, they pour out six *PARĪSU*-measures of wheat flour for all of the gods (and) for the *šūeri-* as the ration-bread in the bakery, (but) they do not pour it there in front of the gods" IBoT 3.148 iii 20-22 (rit. of drawing paths, MH?/NS), ed. ChS 1/9:119 ("Das *šueri-* und *ziti*-Gebäck füllt man in der Bäckerei"), Haas/Wilhelm, AOATS 3:222f.; *šeliaš šu-un-nu-ma-an-zi nu=kan BIBRU ŠA* ᵈLIŠ ᵁᴿᵁ*Šamuḫi* ᵁᴿᵁ*Ḫattušaza katta udanzi nu* ᴰᵁᴳ*ḫaršiyalli ḫēšanzi šeliuš=ma šu-un-*⌈*na-an*⌉*-*[*zi*] "For the pouring of the harvested goods, they bring down the animal-shaped vessel of Šaušga from Ḫattuša to Šamuḫa. They open the pithos. Then the[y] pour the harvested goods (and fill both the pitho[s] of grain and of wine)" KUB 21.17 iii 10-14 (against Arma-Tarḫunta, Ḫatt. III), ed. Archi, UF 5:16, *šeli-*, *šela-* A b, also cf. c 1′ c′ below; EGIR-*anda=ma* NUMUN.ḪI.A *ḫalkiyaš INBI*ᴴᴵ·ᴬ *ŠA* SAR NUMUN *ḫūman* Ì.DÙG.GA Ì.NUN Ì.GIŠ LÀL MUN MUNU$_8$ BAPPIR KÙ.BABBAR KÙ.GI NA$_4$.ḪI.A *zapzagaya šamānaš ḫūmantaš šu-un-ni-ia-an-zi* "Afterwards they pour on all the foundation stones seeds of grain, fruits, all kinds of seeds of vegetables, fine oil, butter, sesame oil, honey, salt, malt, beer-bread, silver, gold, precious stones and glass/glaze" KBo 15.24 ii 41-44 (foundation rit., MH/NS), ed. Torri, hethiter.net/: CTH 415 (INTR 2012-07-30) §19 no. 99 ("si riempiono"), THeth 12:68f. ("füllt"), Kellerman, Diss. 168, 176 ii 62-65 ("on verse"); cf. Güterbock, in Bittel, Boğazköy 1:40 w. nn. 3-4.

**2′** words to/in front of the gods: ("O, Stormgod *piḫaššašši*") *a*[(*mme*)]*l=ma ŠA* ᵐNIR.GÁL ÌR*=KA A*⌈*WA*⌉*TE*ᴹᴱŠ *ŠA* EME*=YA* [(*dā n*)]*=*⌈*at=kan*⌉ *ANA* (var. Ø) *PĀNI* DINGIR.MEŠ ⌈*šu*⌉*-un-ni* "Take the words of my tongue, (that) of Muwatalli, your servant, and pour them out in front of the gods" KUB 6.45 iii 36-37 (prayer, Muw. II), w. dupl. KUB 6.46 iv 4-6, ed. Singer, Muw.Pr. 21f., 40 ("transmit," lit. "fill"), García Trabazo, TextosRel. 346f. ("viértelas"), Lebrun, Hymnes 267, 281 ("précipite-les"), tr. Hittite Prayers 91; *nu=za ANA* DINGIR.MEŠ *kuit arkuwa*⌈*r*⌉ *iyami nu=kan AWATE*ᴹᴱŠ *ANA* DINGIR.MEŠ *anda šu-un-ni n*[(*u=m*)]*u* ⌈*iš*⌉*tamaššandu nu apiya=ya* ᵈU *piḫaššaššin šarliškemi* "The plea which I make to the gods, pour (those) words into the gods, and let them listen to me. Then I shall constantly praise (you), the Stormgod *piḫaššašši*, too" KUB 6.45 iii 42-44 (prayer, Muw. II), w. dupl. KUB 6.46 iv 11-14, ed. Singer, Muw.Pr. 22, 41 ("emit"), García Trabazo, TextosRel. 346f. ("viértelas"), Lebrun, Hymnes 267, 281 ("imbibe"), tr. Singer, Hittite Prayers 92 ("transmit") □ Singer, ibid. 66, discusses alternative interpretations of *šunni* in the two passages above, whether it belongs with *š.* "to fill" (Goetze, ANET 398) or *šun(n)iya/e-* A (s.v.) "to dip, plunge" (Lebrun, Hymnes 287). He decides for the first lexeme, but with a more general meaning "to emit."

**c.** to fill (a container, dir. obj., often w. particle *-(a)šta*, *-kan*) — **1′** cups, and other vessels — **a′** *ḫalwani-* (a drinking vessel): *n=ašta* 1 *ḫalwanin ŠA* KÙ.GI *šu-un-na-i* "He/she fills one golden *ḫalwani-*" KBo 23.67 ii 20 (Hurr. rit., MH/NS).

**b′** ᴰᵁᴳ*ḫanišša-* (a container for liquids): KBo 25.190 obv. 29-30 (MS) (in broken context).

**c′** ᴰᵁᴳ*ḫaršialli-* "storage jar": *nu m*⌈*ā*⌉*n* EN.SÍSKUR *ḫappinanza n=ašta* ᴰᵁᴳ*ḫaršialli*[(ᴴᴵ·ᴬ)] *kuedani* UD-*ti šu-un-na-a-i* EZEN$_4$*=ya=z apēda*⌈*ni*⌉ UD⌉-[(*ti*)] *iyauwanzi ēpzi=pat* "[I]f the ritual patron is wealthy, on the day on which he fills the storage jars, on that day he begins to celebrate the festival as well" KUB 27.59 + KBo 45.168 i 26-28 (*witaššiyaš* fest., NS), w. dupls. A: KBo 29.68:6-7 (NS), B:

KUB 54.24 i 11-12 (NS); *šeliaš šu-un-nu-ma-an-zi nu*=*kan BIBRU ŠA* $^{d}$LIŠ $^{URU}$*Šamuḫi* $^{URU}$*Ḫattušaza katta udanzi nu* $^{DUG}$*ḫaršiyalli ḫēšanzi šeliuš*=*ma šu-un-*˹*na-an*˺*-*[*zi*] *nu*=*kan* $^{DUG}$*ḫaršiyall*[*i*] *ḫalkiyašš*=*a šu-un-na-a*[*n-zi*] *ŠA* GEŠTIN=*ya*=*kan šu-un-n*[*a-an-zi*] "For the pouring of the harvested goods, they bring down the animal-shaped vessel of Šaušga from Ḫattuša to Šamuḫa. They open the pithos. Then the[y] pour the harvested goods and fill both the pitho[s] of grain and of wine" KUB 21.17 iii 10-17 (against Arma-Tarḫunta, Ḫatt. III), ed. Archi, UF 5:16, *šeli-*, *šela-* A b □ note that the clause *šeliuš* ... *š.* with only the obj. poured has no particle, see b 1′.

**d′** $^{DUG}$*ḫuppar* "bowl": in broken context, w. -(*a*)*šta* KUB 33.67 i 7 (NS), ed. StBoT 29:72f.

**e′** *išpantuzzi-* "libation vessel": 2 *išpantuzi* ŠÀ 1-*EN ŠA* GEŠTIN 1-*EN ŠA* KAŠ *ŠA* $^{d}$U $^{URU}$*Ḫaštūwa* É.ŠÀ-*ni šu-un-na-an-zi* "Two libation vessels, one for wine, one for beer, they fill in the inner chamber of the Stormgod of Ḫaštūwa" KUB 60.147 iv? 1-3 (fest. frag., NS), translit. DBH 20:146f.

**f′** *itmari-* (a cultic vessel): *n*=*ašta itmariuš šu-un-na-*˹*i*˺ "and she fills the *itmari*-containers" KBo 19.142 ii 15 (NS), ed. Wegner, ChS I/3-1:202f.

**g′** $^{DUG}$*talaimi-* (a vessel): ("But at night time the *ḫazqara*-women carry the deities' (statues) away, they put them on the altar") NINDA.GUR$_4$.RA.MEŠ *tarnaš*=(*š*)*maš paršiyanzi* $^{DUG}$*talaimiuš*=*kan šu-un-na-*⟨*an-*⟩*zi* "they break the thick breads of a *tarna*-measure for them, they fill the *talaimi*-vessels" KBo 2.13 obv. 20 (cult inv., NH), ed. Carter, Diss. 106, 112; ("Afterwards he breaks seven thick breads of cheese for the spring and crumbles the thick breads of cheese into the spring. He libates sweet milk into the spring") *nu*=*kan* 3 $^{DUG}$*dalaimiuš* KAŠ TÚL-*i šu-un-na-a-i* "and he fills three *dalaimi*-vessels for beer at the spring" KUB 10.91 iii 7 (fest., NH?), ed. Elicker, FsTischler 64, 66 ("füllt").

**h′** *tapišana-* (a vessel): cf. f 7′ b′ (no particle).

**i′** *zuppa-* (a vessel): *namma*=*kan* 2 *zuppan* [KÙ.BABBAR GEŠTIN-*it*] *šu-un-na-i* 2-*at*=*kan wal*[*ḫit*] 2-*e*=*ma*=*kan tawalit šu-un-na-an-zi* EGIR-*pa*=*ma*=*kan* 4 *zūppan* KÙ.BABBAR *šu-un-na-i* "Then (s)he fills two [silver] *zuppa*-containers [with wine]. Two they fill with *wal*[*ḫi*-drink], two with *tawal*-drink. Next (s)he fills four silver *zuppa*-containers" KUB 30.41 ii 7-11 (fest. frag., OH/NS), ed. Poitz, DBH 35:88, 95.

**j′** $^{(DUG)}$GAL "cup": *namma*=*kan* $^{DUG}$GAL.ḪI.A DINGIR-*LIM ḫantezzi*˹*ya*˺ UD-*at maḫḫan šu-un-ni-et kinunn*=*a*=*aš*=*kan* ˹*QĀTAMMA šu-un*˺*-na-i* "Furthermore, just as he filled the cups of the god on the first day, now also he fills them in the same way" KBo 21.33 iv 30-31 (fest., MH/MS), w. dupl. KBo 23.44 iv 3-4 (MH/NS), ed. Salvini/Wegner, ChS I/2:68f. (lines 66-67); cf. par. KBo 27.144 iii 3-6 + KBo 71.2 iii 14-17 (MH/NS) □ note the rare *-mi* conjugation form *šunniet*. For the other *-mi* forms see KUB 12.58 iv 13 (c 5′), KUB 59.55 ii 9 (f 4′), KBo 25.184 iii 59 (see discussion at the end of the lemma); (Wine is poured into a GÌR.KIŠ-vessel out of a storage jar. "Thereupon the anointed priest takes an earthen cup") LÚ GÍR DINGIR-*LIM IŠTU NAMMAN*˹*TI*˺ GEŠTIN *INA* $^{DUG}$GÌR.KIŠ *ḫāni* GAL-*AM INA* ŠU $^{LÚ}$GUDU$_{12}$=*pat šu-un-na-i* "The sword swallower of the god scoops up the wine in the GÌR.KIŠ-vessel with a *NAMMANTU*-vessel and he fills the cup in the hand of that same anointed priest" KUB 53.13 iv 12-14 (fest. performed by a prince, NS); ("They bring from the city Aštuyara one *NAMMANTUM*-vessel of wine ...") *namma*=*kan apēz IŠTU NAMMA*⟨*N*⟩*TUM* GEŠTIN GAL *šu-un-na-i* "Then he fills the cup with that *NAMMANTUM*-vessel of wine" KBo 21.34 i 12-13 (fest. for Teššub and Ḫebat of Lawazantiya, MH/NS), ed. Lebrun, Hethitica 2:117, 125; *nu*=*ššan* ˹*A*˺*NA* GAL.ḪI.A *šu-un-nu-ma-an-zi* 1 DUG *ḫūppa*[*r* G]EŠTIN *anda ḫantaittari* "one *ḫuppar*-vessel of wine for filling cups has been arranged on (it)" IBoT 1.7 iv 15-16 + KBo 21.34 iv 37-38 (MH/NS), ed. Lebrun, Hethitica 2:125, HW$^{2}$ Ḫ 165a; cf. also GAL KÙ.BABBAR "silver cup": ("He takes a *wakšur*-vase of wine") *nu* 1 GAL KÙ.BABBAR *ANA* $^{d}$*Nupatik*(-)*pipitḫi* 1 GAL KÙ.BABBAR=*ma ANA* $^{d}$*Adamma* $^{d}$*Kupapa šu-*[*un*]*-na-an-zi* "They fill a silver cup for Nupatik of *p.*, a silver cup for Adamma (and) Kupapa" KBo 20.114 i 17-19 (*ḫišuwa* fest., MH/NS); cf. (w. *-kan*) KBo 15.49 iv 4, 5 (MH/NS); GAL.ZABAR "bronze cup"

(w. -(*a*)*šta*): KBo 15.37 iii 40 (MH/NS); (DUG)GAL.GIR$_4$ "earthen cup" (no particle): KBo 5.2 iv 38 (MH/NS), (w. *=kan*?): IBoT 1.7 iv 12 (MH/NS); GAL.KAŠ "beer cup": KUB 27.50:3 (frag., NS), KUB 27.65 i 22 (frag., NS).

**k′** *BIBRU* "animal shaped vessel": *namma=kan* EGIR-*anda* DINGIR.MEŠ-*aš ḫūmandaš BIBRI*ḪI.A*=*⌜*ŠU*⌝*NU*! *šu-un-na-an-zi* "Then afterwards, they fill the animal shaped vessels of all of the gods" KUB 10.21 iv 10-12 (fest. frag., OH/NS), ed. Jestin, RA 34:49, 53; cf. also *BIBRU* KÙ.GI "golden animal shaped vessel" KBo 7.46 i 11 (frag., NS), *BIBRU* KÙ.GI TUR "golden small animal shaped vessel" Bo 6575 obv. 15-16 (KBo 21 p. V n. 11; frag.).

**l′** DUG*KUKŪBU* "pitcher": *namma* GEŠTIN LÀL*=ya anda īm*[*mianzi*] *n=ašta* DUG*KUKŪB* KÙ.BABBAR *šu-un-na-an-zi* "Furthermore, [they] mi[x] in wine and honey. They fill a silver pitcher" KUB 12.5 i 17-18 (rit. for *IŠTAR* of Tamininga, MH/NS), ed. Danmanville, RHA XX/70:51, 53.

**2′** leather bags — **a′** (KUŠ)*kaluḫa/it-*: KBo 30.148:12, 15 (frag., MS), KBo 34.155 ii? 17 (MS) (no particle), KBo 34.159 obv. 5 (frag., MS), KBo 30.54 i 5, 7 (*ANDAḪŠUM*-fest., NS), w. dupl. ABoT 1.13 vi 11, 13 (NS), cf. f 7′ b′ (no particle).

**b′** KUŠ*laggašdu-*: (list of different kinds of flour) *nu kī ḫūman anda arnuwanzi n=ašta* KUŠ*laggašduš šu-un-na-an-z*[*i*] "They bring all these (types of flour) in and they fill leather *laggašdu*-s" KBo 13.248 i 20-21 (rit. frag. NS); cf. [...KUŠ*lagg*]*ašdušun*(sic) *šu-un-n*[*a-i*] / [... KUŠ*la*]*ggašdun šanna*[*pilaḫzi*] "[(s)he] fill[s] a [*lagg*]*ašdu*, and emp[ties] a [*la*]*ggašdu*" KUB 43.37 iii 6-7 (NS).

**3′** GIŠ*ḫuḫupal-* (a drum?): ⌜*n*⌝*=ašta maḫḫan* GIŠ*ḫuḫupal* LÚ⌜SAG⌝[I.A *arḫa ekuzi*(?)] / [*na*]*m*[*m*]⌜*a*?*=a*⌝*t šu-un-na-i=pat šanḫazi=ma=at=k*[*an arḫa*? *UL*?] / [*nu Š*]*A* LÚ.MEŠ URU*Lallupiya kuiš* LÚ.GAL*=ŠU*[*NU*] / [*n=at*] ⌜*a*⌝*pēdani pāi nu=šši* GIM-*an* LÚ[...] / [GIŠ*ḫuḫup*]*al šūw*[*a*]⌜*n*⌝[*d*]*a menaḫḫanda ē*[*pzi*] "When the cupbear[er drinks up(?)] the *ḫuḫupal*(-s), he just fills them [aga]i[n], and [does not(?)] wipe them [out(?)]. He gives them to the one who is the leader of the men of Lallupiya. And when the [...]-man holds out to him the filled [*ḫuḫup*]*al*(-s), (he, i.e., the leader of the men of Lallupiya(?), s[ings] opposite [him] likewise, like a woman)" KUB 25.37 i 46-47 + KUB 35.131 i 6-10 (rit. of Lallupiya, NS), ed. Güterbock, FsHouwink ten Cate 66 (differently) ☐ the size of the sign NA in Güterbock's restoration [*n*]*a-at* (*šu-un-na-i-pát*) is not sufficiently large to fill the space preceding the break. The sign remnants in KUB 25.37 i 47 (coll. ph.) do not contradict a restoration [*na*]*m*[*m*]*a*.

**4′** bread: LÚ.MEŠ GIŠBANŠUR *adanna udanzi* NINDA.ḪI.A-*uš* [*š*]⌜*u*-⌝*un-na-an-tu*[*-uš*] SAR.ḪI.A *ḫūnišaš* MUN-*an tiy*[*anzi*] "The tablemen bring to eat. [They] place drenched/stuffed (lit. filled) breads, vegetables (and) salt of the *ḫuniša-* (or: vegetables of the *ḫuniša-* (and) salt)" KBo 25.34 + KBo 25.72 + KBo 38.21 ii 22-23 (/31-32) (KI.LAM fest., OH/OS?), w. dupl. KBo 30.177:1-3 (NS), ed. Groddek, KI.LAM 18f., 37; for NINDA.GUR$_4$.RA BA.BA.ZA KBo 2.4 ii 14 and passim, see d 1′ b′.

**5′** the moon: *mān* ITU GIBIL *mān=aš šu-u*[*n-n*(*a-an-za mān=aš zinnanza*)] LÚ.MEŠ URU*Lalupiya=ma=za aniy*[(*au*)*w*(*anzi=pat appanzi*)] "Whether the moon is new, whether it is full (lit. filled), (or) whether it is finished, the men of Lallupiya just begin to work" KUB 55.65 iii 14-15 (NS), w. dupls. KUB 32.132 iii 17-20 (MS), KBo 8.107:2-3 (NS), ed. Tischler, HEG S/2:1171, translit. DBH 4:121, StBoT 30:309.

**d.** to fill (a container or something with a substance, inst., usually no particle) — **1′** w. liquids — **a′** with *watar*/A "water": DUGGIR$_4$-*aš* GAL-*in uwitenit šu-u-ni-iš-tén n=an=kan* dUTU-*i menaḫḫanda arḫa laḫḫu*⌜*ten*⌝ "You shall fill an earthen cup with water, and empty it out before the Sun(god)" KUB 13.3 ii 26-28 (instr. for palace servants, pre-NH/NS), ed. HittInstr. 80f., Pecchioli Daddi, Or NS 73:460, 466, tr. Goetze, ANET 207 ☐ note the unique spelling *šu-u-ni-* w. *u* instead of *šu-un-ni-* or occasionally *šu-ni-*; *namma=kan* DUGKU.KU A-*nit šu-un-na-an-zi namma apedani pedi apē kinuwanzi* "Furthermore, they fill pitcher(s) with water, then they open ritual pits in that place" KBo 2.9 iv 10-11 (rit. for Ištar of Nineveh, MH/NS), ed. Fuscagni, hethiter.net/: CTH 716.1 (INTR 2012-03-05), tr. Collins, CoS 1:164 □ for the reading $^{DUG}$KU.KU as a phonetic rendering of Sum. $^{DUG}$GUR$_4$.GUR$_4$ instead of restoring $^{DUG}$*KU-KU*‹*-UB*›, see Weeden, StBoT 54:241, 532; 1 NINDA.GUR$_4$.RA BA.BA.ZA *IŠTU* A *šu-un-ni-ia-an-za tarnaš* "One porridge-bread loaf of a *tarna*-measure drenched (lit. filled) with water" KBo 2.4 ii 20-21 (fest. of the month, NH), ed. KN 282f., translit. Součková, GsNeu 295.

**b′** w. GEŠTIN "wine": EGIR-*anda*=*ma*=*kan* 2 SI GUD *ŠA* $^{d}$[LAMMA $^{KUŠ}$*kuršaš*(?)] GEŠTIN-*it šu-un-na-an-zi n*=*at* [...] $^{d}$LAMMA $^{KUŠ}$*kuršaš dāi* 1 GAL K[Ù.GI/BABBAR(?) ...] *ANA* EN-*aš* MUNUS-*ni šu-un-na-i* "Afterwards, they fill the two ox-horns belonging to the [Tutelary Deity of the Hunting Bag(?)] with wine, and he/she places them [in front of (?)] the Tutelary Deity of the Hunting Bag. He/she fills a gol[den/sil[ver(?)] cup [...] for the woman of the lord (i.e., of the Tutelary Deity)" KUB 7.38 obv. 8-11 (rit. for Tutelary Deity of the Hunting Bag, MH/NS); DUMU.É.GAL *namma BIBRU* UDU.ŠIR GEŠTIN-*it šu-un-na-a-i n*=*an* LUGAL-*i pāi* "The palace attendant again fills a ram-shaped rhyton with wine, and gives it to the king" KBo 13.217 v 12-13 (fest. for Ziparwa, pre-NH/NS); *namma* $^{LÚ}$SANGA LUGAL-*i* 1 $^{DUG}$GAL *pāi n*=*an IŠTU* GEŠTIN *šu-un-na-i* "Furthermore, the priest gives to the king one cup, and he fills it with wine" KUB 12.12 v 17-18 (*ḫišuwa* fest., MH/NS), w. dupl. KBo 30.159 + KBo 33.194 v 8-9 (MH/NS), translit. ChS 1/4:165; [*IŠT*]*U* GEŠTIN=*ya* 2 *tapiš*[*anuš*] / [*kattak*]*urandušš*=*a šu-un-n*[*a-i*] "He also fill[s] the two *tapiš*[*ana*-vessels] and the [fla]t-footed(?) vessels with wine" KUB 58.16 ii 20-21 (fest. performed by a prince, NS), translit. DBH 18:43f.; NINDA.GUR$_4$.RA BA.BA.ZA *IŠTU* GEŠTIN.KU$_7$ *šu-un-ni-ia-an-za* (var. *šu-un-na-an-za*) "porridge-bread loaf drenched (lit. filled) with sweet wine" KBo 2.4 ii 14-15 (NH), w. dupl. KUB 56.48 iii 13 (NH), translit. Součková, GsNeu 295; cf. KBo 2.4 iii 18-19 (NH), KUB 56.48 ii 15, 36, iii 18-19 (NS).

**c′** w. *šieššar*/KAŠ "beer": 2 $^{DU}$[$^{G}$*QU*]*LLŪ šiēšnit šu-un-na-an-zi* "They fill two [*QU*]*LLU*-vessels with beer" KBo 25.109 ii 16 (rit. frag., OS? or MS?), ed. Bawanypeck/Görke, FsHaas 36, 45, cf. ibid, iii 13; [$^{MUNUS.(⌜MEŠ⌝}$*ḫ*)*uwašš*]*analleš* 1 GAL.GIR$_4$ KAŠ-*it šu-un-na-i* "The *ḫ*[*uwašš*]*analla*-[wome]n fills(!) an earthen cup with beer" KUB 20.75 ii 7 (fest. for Ḫuwaššanna, NS), w. dupl. KBo 29.88 iii 9 (MS); (We asked them again, and they said:) GEŠTIN=*ya*=*wa* LÚ.MEŠ É.GAL.ḪI.A *UL pišker* ⌜*nu*⌝=*kan* UDU.ḪI.A ⌜*IŠTU*⌝ KAŠ ⌜BAL?⌝-*ker BIBRI*$^{ḪI.A}$=*ya*=*wa*=*kan IŠTU* KAŠ *šu-un-né-eš-ke-er* "Also, the palace servants have not been giving wine, (therefore) they have been consecrating(?) the sheep with beer, and they have been filling the animal-shaped rhytons with beer" KUB 16.16 obv. 18-20 (oracle question, NH), ed. van den Hout, Purity 138f. (suggesting *iš-ki-ir* "anointed" instead of BAL-*ke-er*); *na*[(*mma IŠTU* KAŠ GA)]L.ḪI.A $^{DUG}$GÌ[(R.GÁN)] *šu-un-ni-an-zi* "Then they fill the cups (and) GÌR.GÁN-pitchers with beer" KUB 9.32 + CHDS 2.94 obv. 39-40 (Ašḫella's rit., MH?/NS), w. dupls. KUB 41.17 iii 13 (NS), FHL 95:4 (NS), ed. Dinçol, Belleten 49/193:17, 24 (without join), Chrzanowska (ed.), hethiter.net/: CTH 394 (TX 13.07.2016, TRde 23.03.2016).

**d′** w. oil, honey: EGIR-*an*⌜*da*=*ma* 7⌝ $^{DUG}$*ḫupuwai dāi n*=*at*=*kan* GEŠTIN-*it* Ì *SERDUM pittalwanit* LÀL *šu-un-na-i* "Afterwards, she takes the seven *ḫupuwai*-vessels, and fills them with wine, virgin olive oil (and) honey" KBo 39.8 iii 29-30 (MH/MS), ed. StBoT 46:88f.; (A lead head, lead chest, lead breasts, and lead throat are filled with water. They suck out the water and pour it over the bull(-statuette) and (human-form-)statuette ...) GUD.MAḪ *šēnann*=*a arḫa* [*n*]*eanzi apē*=*ma*=*kan* EGIR-*pa IŠTU* Ì LÀL *šu-un-na-an-zi* [*n*]=*at ANA* $^{d}$UTU AN-*E* EGIR-*pa maniyaḫḫanzi* "They [t]urn the bull(-statuette) and the (human-form-)statuette over, they fill them (i.e., the body parts) with oil (and) honey again, [and] they deliver them back to the Sungod of Heaven" KUB 39.57 i 11-13 (rit., NH), ed. Torri, Lelwani 47f. ("cospargono").

**e′** w. other (and mixed) beverages: (a list of cups and vessels) *IŠTU* KAŠ [Ø?] GEŠTIN *tawalaz walaḫḫiyaz šu-un-*‹*na-*›*an-zi* "They fill (them) with beer, [Ø?,] wine, *tawal*- (and) *walḫi*-" KBo 21.1 ii 5-6 (Tunnawiya's rit., NS), ed. Hutter, Behexung 18f.; w. *walḫi*- and w. *tawal*- see above c 1′ i′ and KUB 44.50 i? 21 (NS); w. KAŠ.GEŠTIN "beer-wine" KBo 14.142 ii 10 (NS).

**f′** w. blood: [*Š*]*AMĀḪU*=*ma IŠTU* ÚŠ *šu-un-n*[*a-*...] / [*n*]=*at*=*kan ANA* $^{LÚ}$˹ŠU.DIB˺ GÚ-*ši an*[*da* ...] "[...] fil[l(s)] an intestine with blood [and hang(s)/place(s)] it on the neck of the captive" KBo 15.18:2-3 (rit. frag., LNS), ed. Kümmel, StBoT 3:27 □ for Akk. *šammāḫu* see CAD S/1:314 ("large intestine"), AHw 1156, Borger, ABZ 359 ("Dickdarm").

**2′** with solids — **a′** w. grain: KBo 12.70 iii 13-14, see lex. sec. above; ˹*takku* LÚ˺-*aš ELLUM ḫalkiaš* ÉSAG-*an t*[(*āīzzi* ÉSAG-*š*)=*a ḫalki*]*n wemizzi* [É]SAG-*an ḫalkit šu-un-na-i* "If a free man burglarizes a grain storage pit, [and] finds [the grai]n of the storage pit, (as punishment) he shall fill the [s]torage pit with grain" KBo 6.2 iv 49-50 (Laws §96, OS), w. dupl. KBo 6.3 iv 48-49 (OH/NS), ed. Hoffner, LH 94f.

**b′** w. flour: [*namm*]*a*(?) $^{MUNUS}$*ḫuwaššannalaš ištananan* [EG]IR-*p*[*a*] *šu*⟨*p*⟩*piyaḫḫi* (eras.) *nu* 2 GAL.GIR$_4$ *IŠTU* ZÍD.DA ZÍZ *šu-un-*˹*na*˺*-i n*=*aš*=*kan* EGIR-*pa ištanani tittanuzi* "[The]n, the *ḫuwaššannala*-woman consecrates the altar [ag]ain. She fills two earthen cups with wheat flour and places them back on the altar" KBo 24.29 iii 1-3 (cult of Ḫuwaššanna, MS).

**c′** w. salt: [1 *šapiyan* Ì.]UDU *šu-un-na-aḫ-ḫi U* 1 *šapiyan* MUN[... *š*]*u-un-na-aḫ-ḫi* "I fill [one *šapiya*-vessel (with)] sheep [fat], and I [f]ill one *šapiya*-vessel (with) salt" KUB 33.70 iii 10-11 (Mallidunna's rit., OH/NS), w. dupl. KBo 41.6 i 5-6 (OH/NS), Bo 5085 obv. 4, ed. Görke, hethiter.net/: CTH 403.2 (INTR 2015-06-08), del Monte, FsPopko 72f., translit. Groddek, AoF 28:108f., cf. s.v. *šēr* 1 c 5′ a′ 2″, $^{(DUG)}$*šapiya-* without dupls.

**d′** w. other foodstuffs (bread, cheese, fruit, meat etc.): 1 $^{DUG}$BUR.ZI-*TUM IŠTU* NINDA.Ì.E.DÉ.A *šu-un-na-an-z*[*a*] "One sacrificial bowl is filled with oil cake" KUB 42.98 i 21 (rit. frag., NH); *nu* 2 $^{GI}$*gurdali IŠTU* NINDA.ḪI.A GA.KIN.AG *par*˹*šiante*˺[*t* (*šu-un*)]-*na-an-zi* "They fill two reed baskets(?) with crumbled breads (and) cheese" KUB 39.7 ii 15 (funerary rit., MH?/NS), w. dupl. KUB 39.8 i 9-10 (NS), ed. Kassian et al., Funerary 492f., Otten, HTR 36f.; ("They butcher the entire sheep") $^{UZU}$*wallin*=*a karša IŠTU* $^{GIŠ}$NU.˹ÚR.MA˺ *karšantit*=*a* UZU-*it šu-un-na-an-zi* "and they fill the shank completely(?) with pomegranate and with cut meat" KBo 19.142 ii 23-24 (fest. for *IŠTAR* of Mt. Amana, NS), ed. Wegner, ChS I/3-1:202f. □ for *karša* see Wegner, ChS I/3-1:203 n. 460 and HED K 108 (*karša* = "outright"); *nu*=*šmaš*=*kan ḫūešawaz kuiēš* GAL.ḪI.A *šu-un-né-er nu*=*šmaš*=*kan zeyantaz*=*iya šu-un-na-an-zi* "They fill the cups, which they filled with raw (meat) for them (i.e., the gods), also with cooked (meat) for them" KBo 20.114 v 8-11 (*ḫišuwa* fest., MH/NS).

**e′** w. aromatic (plants): ("When they celebrate the monthly festival for the Stormgod of Nerik, they slaughter at the left wall") *IŠTU* ŠEM.ḪI.A=*ya* 2 $^{DUG}$GÌR *šu-un-na-an-zi n*=*at*=*kan* ŠÀ É.ŠÀ *natḫiyaš šaminuwanzi* "and they fill two footed-vessels with aromatics. They burn them (i.e., the aromatics) in the bedroom" KBo 2.4 iv 24-26 (fest. of the month, NH), w. dupl. KUB 56.48 iv 9-11 (NS), ed. KN 288f.

**f′** w. ashes: *nu* ALAM.ḪI.A KA×U EME.ḪI.A DÙ-*mi n*=˹*an*˺ KA×U-*iš ḫaššit šu-un-na-aḫ-ḫi n*=*at* IM-*nit* ˹*iš*˺*tappi n*=*at šiyami* "I make figurines (having?) a mouth (and) tongues. I fill their (lit. his) mouth with ashes, I plug them with clay and seal them" KUB 43.59 + KUB 9.39 i 6-8 (Šeḫuzzi's rit., NS), ed. Fuscagni, hethiter.net/: CTH 453.2 (INTR 2012-12-19).

**3′** w. fat (in order to plaster or stuff a container): ("The Queen of Kaniš bore thirty sons in a single year" ... ) *tuppuš šakanda šu-un-na-aš nu* DUMU.MEŠ=*ŠU andan zikēt* ˹*š*˺=*uš* ÍD-*a tarnaš* "She filled (the interstices of) baskets with oil/fat, placed her sons in (them), and launched them into the river" KBo 22.2 obv. 2-3 (Zalpa text, OS), ed. StMed 19:30, 39, Otten, StBoT 17:6f. w. comm. 16-18, cf. Hoffner, HS 107:222-230, BA 58:108-114; cf. frag. KUB 33.70 iii 10 (OH/NS), see d 2′ c″.

**4′** w. mud: (A *kurtali-* container is shaped) *n*=*at puruttit šu-un-na-i* (var. *šu-un-na-a-i*) *n*=*at ēšḫana*⟨*š*⟩ DINGIR-*LIM-ni* GAM-*an dāi* "and he (i.e., the conjuration priest) fills it with mud, and he puts it with the god of the blood" KUB 41.8 ii 42-

43 (rit. for netherworld deities, MH/NS), w. dupl. KBo 10.45 (MH/NS) iii 8-9, ed. Otten, ZA 54:128f.

**5′** w. living beings (in analogy): ("She (i.e., the Old Woman) says: 'Sungod, my lord, as this cow is fertile and she is in a fertile pen'") *nu=za=kan ḫāli«t»* GUD.NÍTA-*it* GUDÁB-*it* ˹*šu-un*˺-*né-eš-ke-ez-zi* ˹*k*˺*āša* EN.SISKUR *QĀTAMMA u*˹*ša*˺*ndariš ēšta*(sic) *nu=za=*˹*kan*˺ É-*er IŠTU* DUMU.NITA.MEŠ DUMU.MUNUS.MEŠ *ḫaššet ḫanzaššit* [*ḫartu*]˹*wati*˺(?) *ḫartūwa*‹*š*› *ḫ*˹*artu*˺*wati QĀTAMMA šu-un-ni-ed-du* "and as she will fill the pen with bulls (and) cows, now let the ritual patron here likewise be fertile; let her likewise fill the house with sons (and) daughters, with grandchildren (and) great-grandchildren, with [descenda]nts (and) successive generations of descendants" KUB 12.58 iv 9-13 (Tunnawi's rit., NS), ed. Tunn. 20-23 □ note the rare *-mi* conjugation form, for the other ones see KBo 21.33 iv 31 (b 1′ j′), KUB 59.55 ii 9 (f 4′), KBo 25.184 iii 59 (see discussion at the end of the lemma).

**6′** to fill with intangibles (in metaphoric expressions) — **a′** wind: (Šaušga is told) *kuedani=wa=za menaḫḫanda išḫamiškeši kuedani=ma=wa=za menaḫḫanda* KA×U-*iš IŠTU* I[M.MEŠ(?)] *šu-un-né-eš-ke-ši* "Before whom are you singing? Before whom are you filling (your) mouth with wi[nds(?)]? (The man (i.e., Ullikummi) is deaf; he cannot hear. He is blind; he cannot see)" KUB 36.12 ii 9-11 (Song of Ullik., NS), ed. García Trabazo, TextosRel 218f. ii 17-19, Güterbock, JCS 6:14f., tr. Hoffner, Hittite Myths² 61.

**b′** sorcery: *nu* URU DINGIR-*LIM=YA* URU*Šamuḫan alwanzešnaza šu-un-na-aš* "He (i.e., Arma-Tarḫunta) filled Šamuḫa, the city of my goddess, with sorcery" KUB 19.67 i 9-10 (Apology of Ḫatt. III), ed. StBoT 24:18f. (iii 19).

**e.** to fill (a container)/pour (using a vessel, inst. or abl.): [*u*]*g=a=šmaš* GIŠ*intaluzzit šu-un-na-aḫ-ḫi* "I will fill/pour for you (pl.) using a shovel" KBo 3.38 rev. 16-17 (in broken context in Zalpa story, OH/NS), w. dupl. KUB 48.79 rev. 3, ed. StMed 19:34, 42, StBoT 17:10f., Soysal, Diss. 48, 99; *namma=kan apēz IŠTU NAMMA*‹*N*›*TUM* GEŠTIN GAL *šu-un-na-i* KBo 21.34 i 12-13, see c 1′ j′; LÚGUDU$_{12}$ *ANA* dZA.BA$_4$.BA$_4$ *šipanduwa*[*nzi*] 3-*ŠU QĀTAMMA irḫāizzi* LÚ dIM-*aš išpanduzziyaššari*˹*t*˺ *šarā* 3-*ŠU QĀTAMMA šu-un-na-i* "The anointed priest makes the rounds to make offerin[gs] to the god ZA.BA$_4$.BA$_4$ three times in the same way. The man of the Stormgod fills (i.e., the *tapišana*-vessel) up using a libation vessel three times in the same way" KUB 25.36 v 5-8 (Nerik fest., OH?/MS), ed. KN 206f., THeth 26:244; UGULA LÚ.MEŠ GIŠBANŠUR [...]-*an* DUG*kattakurantit* [*ša*]*rā šu-un-na-i* "The chief of the table-men fills [u]p a [ ... (cup)?] using a flat-bottomed(?)-vessel" KUB 58.55:9-11 (fest. frag., NS), translit. DBH 18:146.

**f.** associated local adverbs — **1′** *anda*: ZÍD.DA*=ya=kan anda šu-un-né-eš-ká*[(*n-zi*)] "And they are pouring in flour" KUB 39.8 iv 4 (funerary rit., pre-NH/NS), w. dupl. KBo 29.290 obv. 3, ed. Kassian et al., Funerary 590f.; *nu=šši=kan* GAL GIR$_4$ *kiššarī* GEŠTIN-*it anda šu-un-na-i* "He fills a baked clay cup in his hand with wine for him" KUB 12.11 iv 3-4 (*ḫišuwa*-fest., MH/NS), ed. ChS 1/2:307f. iii 3-4; cf. KBo 22.134 iv 14-15 (rit., NH).

**2′** *āppa*: *namma=at=kan* EGIR-*pa*! *ANA* ŠEN ZABAR *anda laḫūwāi nu* ŠEN ZABAR EGIR-*pa šu-un-na-i* "Then (s)he pours it back into the bronze kettle so that (s)he refills the bronze kettle" KUB 44.63 ii 16-17 (medical rit., NH), ed. StBoT 19:38-40, translit. Klinger, TUAT 5:180; see also (w. *-kan*) KUB 39.57 i 12 (rit. frag., NH), see d 1′ d″ above; KUB 46.18 obv.? 20-21 *witaššiyaš*-fest., NS).

**3′** *arḫa*: *nu=kan* NUMUN.ḪI.A *kue šānḫūwanta* NINDA.GUR$_4$.RA.ḪI.A NUMUN.ḪI.[A] *pūrpūriyaš ašaran n=at arḫa šu-ni-y*[*a-an-zi*] GI*paddani=ma arḫa peššiyanzi* "The seeds which are roasted, the bread loaves, the (unroasted) seed[s], a string of balls, they pour them out and they throw (them) into a reed basket" KBo 4.2 ii 29-31 (Ḫuwarlu's incant. rit., pre-NH/NS), ed. THeth 25:30f. ("schü[ttet(?) man] weg"), Kronasser, Sprache 8:93, 97 (no tr.).

**4′** *menaḫḫanda*: [... *warp*]*iškan*˹*z*˺*i ammuk=ma kī* [...]x-*i=kan anda* GA*šimallu* [...] *menaḫḫanda=ma* BA.BA.ZA *šu-*˹*un*˺*-ni-ia-mi* "[While?] they are [bath]ing, I [do?] this: in [... I pour(?)] *šimallu* (a dairy product), while together (with it) I pour porridge" KUB 59.55 ii 7-9 (rit., NS), ed. $^{(GA)}$*šim(m)al(l)u*, translit. DBH 14:94.

**5'** *parā*: [*m*]*ān=aš ḫarg*[!]*anza=ma* $^{d}$IM-*aš nu=šši kuišša* ⌈Ì⌉.DÙG.GA 1 *kūpin pīweni nu=šši išḫueššar parā šu-un-nu-me-ni n=an=kan pallantiyaz āppa tarnumeni* "But [i]f Teššub is hurt, each of us will give him one little flask of fine oil. We will pour out a large quantity for him, and we will bring him back from dire need" KBo 32.15 ii 14-17 (Hurro-Hitt. bil. wisdom and myth, MH/MS), ed. StBoT 32:291, tr. Hittite Myths[2] 75, CHD P 62a ("pour a grain heap for him").

**6'** *šarā* — **a'** (a city): (Muršili I was an eminent king) [*mān=aš*] KUR.KUR.MEŠ-*aš* (eras.) $^{LÚ}$KÚR [*ḫarnink*]*išket nu* KUR.KUR.MEŠ-*aš ḫūmandaš* [*āššu* $^{URU}$*Ḫa*]*ttuši piddāit* [*nu āššuwit* $^{UR]U}$*Ḫattušan šarā š*[(*u-u*)]*n-na-aš* "[When he destroy]ed (all of) the enemy countries, he carried off [the goods] of all of the countries to [Ḫa]ttuša and filled Ḫattuša up [with goods]" KBo 3.57 obv. 6-9 (Muršili I. against Aleppo, OH/NS), w. dupl. KUB 26.72:2-4 (OH/NS), ed. StMed 12:194f. (differs), Soysal, Diss., 57, 101f.; also KBo 10.2 i 20-21 (see lexical section), KUB 8.80:14-15 (Šattiwaza Treaty, Šupp. I).

**b'** (a container): $^{LÚ}$G[UDU$_{12}$ ] / [*t*]*apišan*[*i*]*n* KÙ.BABBAR LUGAL-*i parā ēp*[*zi*] LUGAL-*uš* [*Q*]*ĀTAM* ⌈*dāi*⌉ $^{LÚ}$GUDU$_{12}$ *tapišana*[*n*] *šarā šu-un-na-a-i* "The an[ointed priest] present[s] a silver [*t*]*apišan*[*i*]-vessel to the king. The king lays (his) [h]and (on it). The anointed priest fills up the *tapišana*-vessel" KUB 58.41 rev.? 4-7 (fest. celebrated by prince, NS); UGULA LÚ.MEŠ $^{GIŠ}$BANŠUR *kaluḫit šarā šu-un-na-i* (var. *šu-un-na-a-i*) $^{LÚ}$GUDU$_{12}$ *QĀTAMMA šipanti* LÚ $^{GIŠ}$BANŠUR *kaluḫat šarā šu-un-na-i* (var. *šu-un-na-a-i*) $^{LÚ}$GUDU$_{12}$ *QĀTAMMA šipanti* "The overseer of the table-men fills up the *kaluḫit*(-leather bottle); the anointed priest libates in the same way. A table-man fills up the *kaluḫat*(-leather bottle); the anointed priest libates in the same way" KBo 30.54 i 5-8 (*ANDAḪŠUM*-fest., NS), w. dupl. ABoT 1.13 vi 11-15 (NS).

**7'** *šer*: "to fill up": ("When Arma-Tarḫunta, son of Zida, saw the benevolence of Šaušga, my Lady, and of my brother to me, and when he was in no way successful") *nu=mu=za alwanzaḫḫūwanzi namma QADU* DAM=*ŠU* DUMU=*ŠU ēpper* $^{URU}$*Šamuḫann=a* URU-*LUM* DINGIR-*LIM alwanzešnaza šer šu-un-ni-iš-ta* "then he began to practice witchcraft on me together with his wife and son, and he filled up Šamuḫa, the city of the goddess, with sorcery" KUB 1.1 + 1304/u ii 77-79 (Apology of Ḫatt. III), ed. Otten, StBoT 24:16f., tr. van den Hout, CoS 1:202.

"Filling" and "pouring" are two sides of the same activity: one pours a substance in a container, or one fills a container with a substance. *š.* (w. its relatively rare NH variant *šunniya-*, cf. Melchert, FsBeckman 162f. n. 17) is used as a synonym to *šūwa-* "to fill" (see Friedrich, HW 200 (s.v. *šuwai-*), Tischler, HEG S/2:1166); compare NINDA.GUR$_{4}$.RA.MEŠ *tarnaš=(š)maš paršiyanzi* $^{DUG}$*talaimiuš=kan šu-un-na-*‹*an-*›*zi* "They break the thick breads of (a) *tarna*-measure for them, (and) they fill the *talaimi*-vessels" KBo 2.13 obv. 20 (cult inv., NH) and 1 NINDA *tarna*[*š parš*]*iyanzi* (eras.) $^{DUG}$*tala*[!]*imiuš=kan šūwan*[*zi*] "They [brea]k one bread of (a) *tarna*-measure, (and) they fil[l] the *talaimi*-vessels" KUB 42.91 ii 18-19 (cult inv., NH). *š.* and *šuwa-* may also alternate in the same text, e.g., [...]-*za* LÚ-*LUM* $^{GIŠ}$*intaluzzi* KÙ.BABBAR [... *šu-u*]*n-ni-ez-zi nu kiššan* [....] EGIR-*pa šūwan ēšdu* "[...] a man [takes(?)] a silver shovel for himself, [and f]ills [...], and [says] thus: ['...] may be filled again'" KBo 25.184 iii 58-60 (funeral rit., pre-NH/NS), ed. Kassian et al., Funerary 110-113.

With Laroche, RHA XXXI 92 vs. Friedrich, HW 198, Rosenkranz, JEOL 19:502 ("eine *i̯a*-Erweiterung des gleichbedeutenden *šunna-*"), *š.* is to be kept separate from *šun*(*n*)*iya-* A "to sow; to dip" because of its almost consistent *ḫi*-conjugation inflection, and lack of plene writing of the first syllable.

The forms in -*um*- show that this verb originally belonged to the *tarna-* class. But like *tarna-*, it came to be influenced by the -*a*-/-*i*- class of *unni/a-* "to drive (here)," hence NH pret. 3 sg. *šunnieš* and *šunništa* and imp. 2nd pl. *šunništen*. These forms do not belong to the innovative *šunniya/e-* B, which is a *mi*-verb. The very few instances of *mi*-conjugation forms are NS copies, but there is one instance already in a MH/MS copy (KBo 21.33 iv 31). *šun(n)iya-* A, a *mi*-verb, is consistently spelled with plene *ú* and single *-ni-* in OS and usually in MS, but in NH original documents and NS copies of older compositions we also find spellings with double *-n-* and without *ú*. In some of those cases *šun(n)iya-* A and *š.* can only be distinguished based on context.

Hrozný, SH (1917) 211; Sommer/Ehelolf, Pap. (1924) 24 n. 1; Friedrich, AfO 2 (1924-25) 122; Götze, Ḫatt (1925) 130; idem, NBr (1930) 20; Friedrich, HW (1952) 197-198 ("füllen"; w. *anda* "hineinfüllen," "(Worte ins Ohr) legen"; w. *šarā* "bis zum Rande füllen"; w. *šēr* "(bis) oben (hin) füllen"); Laroche, RHA XXXI (1973) 91-93 (on distinction of *šunna-* "to fill" and *šuniya-* "plonger"); Neu, StBoT 18 (1974) 91; Oettinger, StBoT 22 (1976) 39 n. 76; idem, Stammbildung (1979) 158f.; Georgiev, BalkE 26/3 (1983) 10; Weitenberg, U-Stämme (1984) 137, 138f., 428 nn. 295-298; Neu, AAWLM (1988.3) 16 n. 40; idem, StBoT 32 (1996) 308f., 310, 312, 320-22; Tischler, HEG S/2 (2006) 1166-1172 ("füllen, schütten," "verfüllen (von Fügen), abdichten, kalfateren"); Kloekhorst, EDHIL (2008) 785-786 ("to fill").

Cf. *šū-* B/*šuwa-, šun(n)az(z)iya-/šunizziya-, šunnummeššar, šūu*.

**šunai-** see *šun(n)iya/e-* A.

[*šunalli-*] *šu-na-al-li-iš* and *šu!-na-al-li-in* IBoT 3.148 iv 42 and 45 (so Haas/Wilhelm, AOAT 3:230 and 284) should be read with preceding signs as LÚ.KÚR ⸢*kat-ta-wa-at*⸣*-na-al-li-iš*/-⸢*in*⸣ (thus Haas, ChS I/9:126).

**šunašḫanti-** n. com.; (a kind of personnel?); NS.†

**sg. acc.** [$^{LÚ/MUNUS}$*šu-*]*ú-na-aš-ḫa-an-*⸢*ti*⸣*-in* VS 28.6 ii/v? 14 (NS).

**pl. nom.** [$^{LÚ/MUNUS.}$]$^{MEŠ}$*šu-ú-na-aš-ḫa-an-ti-iš* VS 28.6 ii/v? 17 (NS).

§ [ ...$^{LÚ/MUNUS}$*šu-*]*ú-na-aš-ḫa-an-*⸢*ti*⸣*-in* [...*-z*]*i nu=za ḫūdak* [...] *adanna akuwanna* [... $^{LÚ/MUNUS.}$]$^{MEŠ}$*šu-ú-na-aš-ḫa-an-ti-iš* [...]x *adanna akuwanna* [...] "[He/she/they(?)...] the *š.*[-person (= dir. obj.)] and immediately to eat (and) drink [...] The *š.*-persons [...]...to eat (and) drink [...]" VS 28.6 ii/v? 15-18a (fest. frag., NS), translit. DBH 6:11 □ the copyist Jakob-Rost did not allow in her line numbering for the possibility of another line before the paragraph stroke between her lines 18 and 19. The original width of the column and therefore the space for restorations is unknown.

***šunnatar** n. neut.; filling(?); NS.†

**abl.** *šu-un-na-an-*‹*na-*›*az* KBo 49.194:4 (NS).

[... *ḫa*]*r*$^?$*gayaz šu-un-na-an-*‹*na-*›*az* x[...] "with/from white(?) filling(?)" KBo 49.194:4 (frag. of unkn. nature, NS), translit. DBH 40:121. The preceding acephalic word would appear to be an adjective modifying *šunnannaz*.

**šun(n)az(z)iya-, šunnezziya-** v.; to fill to overflowing, (mid.) become overfull; from MH/MS?.†

**imp. sg. 2** *šu-na-az-zi-ia* KBo 20.107 + KBo 23.50 iii 23 (MH/MS?).

**mid. pret. sg. 3** *šu-un-né-ez-z*⸢*i-ia*⸣*-*[*at-t*]*a* KBo 15.7 obv. 7 (NH).

**part. sg. nom. com.** *šu-na-az-zi-ia-an-za* KBo 20.107 + KBo 23.50 iii 22 (MH/MS?).

**pl. acc. com.** ⸢*šu*⸣*-un-na-zi-an-te-*[*eš*] KBo 11.1 rev. 19 (Muw. II).

**frag.** here? *šu-ni-zi-*[...] KBo 49.49:4 (LNS).

**a.** act. to fill to overflowing (i.e., satisfy): ("O my lord, Tutelary Deity of the Hunting Bag! Spend the night with the pleasant, oily *ḫurta*-stew and fat cake, but cut these toasted (grains)") *nu* EGIR-*pa parna* ⸢*ne*⸣*yanza* EGIR-*pa ne*⸢*ya*⸣ *ḫāšiyamiš ḫāšiya šu-na-az-zi-ia-an-za* EGIR-*pa šu-na-az-zi-ia ANA* LUGAL *tuel* ARAD*=KA U ANA* MUNUS.LUGAL *tuel* GÉME*=KA ANA* KUR $^{URU}$*ḪATTI tuel* KUR*=KA* É.LUGAL *tuel* É*=KA* "As one who has turned back home, turn back. As one satiated, satiate (them, i.e., the royal couple?). As one who has been filled to overflowing (with the offered foods), fill (them) again to overflowing, (all) for the king, your servant, and the queen, your servant, the land of Ḫatti, your land, the palace, your house" KBo 20.107 + KBo 23.50 iii 21-25 (rit. for Tutelary Deity of the Hunting Bag, MH/MS?), ed. HW$^2$ Ḫ 412a, THeth 25:112f., 119 (comm.) □ *pace* HW$^2$ Ḫ 412a, Luw. *ḫāšiya-* "to satiate" w. partic. *ḫāšiyamiš* is not derived from Luw. *ḫaš-* "bone" but is the cuneiform equivalent of Hieroglyphic Luw. (LINGERE)*hasi*(*ya*)-, denominative to (LINGERE)*hasa-* "satiety, abundance" (Melchert, FsMorpurgo Davies 376).

This noun is cognate with Palaic *ḫaš-* "to be satiated" and Hittite *ḫaššikk-* q.v.; dU-*naš aššuli annaš* UZUUBUR *maḫḫan* ⌈*šu*⌉*-un-na-zi-an-te-*[*eš*] ⌈*išpiya*⌉*nteš*=*ma*=*nnaš ANA MÊ KAṢÎ maḫḫan nu* dU EN=*YA* A[...] *n*=⌈*at* DUMU.LÚ.U$_{19}$⌉.LU *išpiyanumar ēšdu* "Just as the breast(s) of a mother are filled to overflowing through the grace of the Stormgod, just as we are saturated with cool water, so [may] the Stormgod, my lord, ...[...] water(?), and may it be saturation (for) mankind (while for the Stormgod, my lord, [may] it [be] a matter of pra[ise])" KBo 11.1 rev. 19-21 (prayer of Muw. II), ed. Houwink ten Cate/Josephson, RHA XXV/81:110, 119, Lebrun, Hymnes 298, Rieken et al., hethiter.net/: CTH 382 (TX 2016-01-05, TRde 2016-01-05) ("Wie der Wettergott uns zum Guten die Brüste der Mutter gefüllt [ ... , ... ]"), tr. Hittite Prayers 85 ("Just as the Stormgod fills the mother's breast for our benefit") □ the reading ⌈*šu*⌉*-un-na-zi-an-te-*[*eš*] follows Kümmel, StBoT 3:40 (also Neu, StBoT 5:157 n. 1, Tischler, HEG S/2:1174, Rieken et al., hethiter.net/: CTH 382 (Expl. A, 05.01.2016) and is preferred to Houwink ten Cate/Josephson's *šu-un-na-zi* d*Te-*[*li-bi-*...] RHA XXV/81:110 (so also, e.g., HW² A 533b, Puhvel, HED A 55, Tischler, HEG S/2:1167). With the Stormgod as subject the plural participle *š.* cannot belong to the predicate (as part of the periphrastic perfect it should have been nom.-acc. neut. sg.), thus one must reject "the Stormgod [has] filled." Either the Stormgod is not the subject, or *š.* is not part of the predicate. The first option requires a plural subject and dU-*naš* as gen.sg. (or as unmarked gen. if *-naš* is 1st pl. pron.): "Just as the breast(s) of a mother (or: our mother) are filled to overflowing through the grace of the Stormgod" (or similar). The second option requires a finite verb, perhaps *ḫar(k)-* "hold" to form the expression *aššuli ḫar*(*k*)- "hold in grace/benevolence," with *š.* in apposition to *-naš* "us," and with UZUUBUR as an unmarked dative, parallel to *ANA MÊ KAṢÎ*: "Just as [you], Stormgod, [kept (?)] us in benevolence, filled to the brim (at) (our) mother's breast(s)."

**b.** mid. to be(come) overfull (i.e., a burden) for the soul: ("The king [...] a bull, [and speaks (thus)]") [*m*]*ān*=*wa MĀMĪTUM* EN=⌈*YA*⌉ [...-*t*]*i našm*[*a*=*wa*=*tta*(?)] ⌈*A*⌉*NA* ⌈ZI⌉ *šu-un-né-ez-z*⌈*i-ia*⌉*-*[*at-t*]*a nu*=*wa*=*za kāša* GU[D.MAḪ-*an*(?)] ⌈LÚ⌉*tar*⌈*pal*⌉*lin teḫḫun* "[I]f (you), the oath deity, my lord, [...] o[r (it)] has be[come] overfull for [your (?)] soul, I have just placed a bul[l] as a substitute" KBo 15.7:6-8 (royal subst. rit., NH), ed. Kümmel, StBoT 3:36f.

Kümmel's suggestion (StBoT 3:39f.) to relate the forms *šunnezziya-* and *šunnaziya-* with *šun*(*n*)*a-* "to fill, pour" (s.v.) also fits the forms with single *-n-* KBo 20.107 + KBo 23.50 iii 22, 23. The formation of *š.* may perhaps be compared with *išḫezziya-* "to dominate" (from *išḫa-* "lord"), and LUGAL-*ezziya-* (**ḫaššuezziya-*) (mid.) "to become king" (from *ḫaššu-* "king"), both derived from substantives on *-zzi-* (Kümmel, StBoT 3:39, Oettinger, Stammbildung 29, Tischler, HEG S/2:1174). *šun*(*n*)*az*(*z*)*iya-* would be based on **šunazzi-*, the expected missing stem in *-zzi-* from *šun(na)-*, s.v., whereas *šunnezziya-* would either be based on **šunnezzi-* (from the NH stem *šunni-*, s.v. *šun*(*n*)*a-*) or be modeled after *ḫaššuezziya-*.

Kümmel, StBoT 3 (1967) 39 ("übervoll werden"), 221 ("übervoll machen(?)"); Neu, StBoT 5 (1968) 157 n. 1 (on mid. *šunnizziyatta*); Oettinger, Stammbildung (1979) 29 ("übervoll sein"); Weitenberg, U-Stämme (1984) 429 n. 298; Tischler, HEG S/2 (2006) 1174-1175 ("übervoll werden"); Kloekhorst, EDHIL (2008) 786 (on *šunnaziyant-* "brim-full").

Cf. *šun*(*n*)*a-*.

**šun(n)iya/e- A, šunai-** v.; **1.** to sow (seed), to seed (a field) (without prev. or particle), **2.** to dip (in), immerse (usu. w. *anda*/ŠÀ and particle), **3.** unclear; from OH/MS?.

**pres. sg. 1.** *šu-ú-ni-e-mi* KBo 32.176 obv. 15 (MH/MS), *šu-ú-ni-ia-mi* KUB 7.30 rt. col. 9 (pre-NH/NS).

**sg. 3.** *šu-ú-ni-i-e-zi* KBo 7.36 i 8 (OH/MS), *šu-ú-ni-e-ez-zi* KBo 15.36 + KBo 21.61 ii (11), 17 (OH/MS?), KBo 17.105 ii 3 (MH/MS), *šu-ú-ni-ez-zi* KBo 15.36 ii 6 (OH/MS?), KBo 3.38 obv. 29 (OH/NS), KBo 6.26 i 34 (OH/NS), KBo 23.12 iv 21 (MH/MS), IBoT 2.45:4 (MS?), KUB 11.31 i 9 (Tudḫ. III), KBo 19.142 ii 29 (NH), KBo 23.1 i 16 + ABoT 1.29 i 15 (NH), KBo 27.141 rev. 5 (NS), KUB 32.42 i 10 (NS), *šu-ni-e-ez-zi* KBo 24.66 iii 18 (MH/MS), *šu-ni-ez-zi* KBo 15.47 iv? 8 (MH/NS), KBo 27.156:3 (NS), KBo 27.196 iii 16 (MH/NS), KBo 20.115:10 (NH), KBo 23.46 rev. 8, 10 (LNS), KBo 23.78 i 4 (NS), KBo 24.78 iii? 7 (NS), *šu-un-ni-ez-zi* KBo 15.48 iv! 38 (MH/NS), KBo 35.82:11 (NS), KBo 40.67 iii 6, iv (5) (MH/NS), KUB 51.85 rev.? 7 (NS), IBoT 4.217 obv. (2), 6, (9), (12) (NS), KUB 58.3 iii 23 (NS), *š*[*u*]-⌈*un*?⌉*-ni-e-ez-zi* IBoT 4.14 rev. 12 + KBo 24.4 rev.! 17 (NS), *šu-ú-ni-ia-zi* KUB 11.22 ii 5 (OH/NS), KUB 20.86 ii 4 (NS), *šu-ú-ni-ia-az-zi* KUB 45.47 i (49), 53, ii 14 (MH/MS), *šu-ni-ia-zi* KBo 19.129 obv. 19 (NS),

KBo 15.48 iv! 31 (MH/NS), *šu-ni-ia-az-zi* KUB 44.61 rev. 24 (NH), *šu-un-*⌈*ni*⌉*-zi* KBo 11.32 obv. 21 (OH/NS), *šu-un-ni-ia-zi* KUB 6.45 iv (5), 9, 14, 19, 24 (Muw. II), KUB 6.46 i 41, 46, 50, 54, 58, 62 (Muw. II), KUB 46.44 rev. (7), KUB 57.110 ii 14 (NS), KBo 19.129 obv. 24 (NS), KBo 40.67 iii (15) (NS), [*šu*]*-un-ni-ia-az-zi* KUB 58.45 iii? 23 (NS), *šu-na-a-iz-zi* KBo 27.143:9 (MH/MS?), KBo 31.143 + KBo 20.49 obv. 23 (MH/MS).

**pl. 3.** *šu-ú-ni-ia-an-zi* VBoT 24 iii 7 (MH/NS), *šu-ni-ia-an-zi* KBo 5.1 ii 4 (MH/NS), *šu-un-ni-ia-an-zi* KUB 6.45 iv 29 (Muw. II).

**pret. sg. 1.** *šu-un-ni-ia-nu-un* KBo 10.2 i 37 (NS).

**sg. 3.** *šu-ú-ni-et* KBo 6.26 i 39 (OH/NS), *šu-ú-ni-e-et* KBo 6.26 i 44 (OH/NS), *šu-ú-ni-at* KBo 32.14 iii 11, 12, rev. 29 (2×) (MH/MS), *šu-ni-et* HKM 111:14, 18 (MH/MS), *šu-un-ni-ia-at* KBo 19.111:4 (NS).

**part. pl. nom. com.** *šu-ú-ni-ia-an-t*[*e-eš?*] KBo 12.101:13 (MS).

**imperf. pres. sg. 3.** *šu-ú-ni-iš-ke-ez-zi* KBo 21.33 iv 13 (MH/MS); **pl. 3.** *šu-ni-iš-kán-zi* HKM 111:23, 27 (MH/MS).

(Akk.) *ina qaqqari=šu ul itārraš=šu* "one never sowed (Gtn pret.) it (i.e., seed) in its (i.e., the town of Ulma's) soil (again)" KBo 10.1 obv. 17 = (Hitt.) *nu=šši=kán pedi=šši* [ZÀ.AḪ.L]I$^{\mathrm{SAR}}$ *šu-un-ni-ia-nu-un* "I seeded [wee]ds on its site" KBo 10.2 i 36-37 (bil. ann. of Ḫatt. I, NS), ed. StMed 16:40f. (Akk.: "e sul suo suolo non si è più seminato") w. n. 100 (Hitt.: "sul suo territorio seminai erbaccia") w. comm. pp. 63-65 and 133, Saporetti, SCO 14:77, 80 (differently), StMed. 12:40-43, Melchert, JNES 37:9f. (differently), cf. Hutter-Braunsar, Der orientalische Mensch und seine Beziehung zur Umwelt 217 n. 33.

(Hurr.) *ḫa-a-šar-ri pu-ú-zi-ḫu-um* ` *pu-ú-zi-ḫu-um ḫa-a-šar-ri* KBo 32.14 iv 11-12 = (Hitt.) *n=an=kan* Ì*-i anda šu-ú-ni-at šakni=an=kan anda šu-ú-ni-at* "He dipped it in oil. In oil he dipped it" KBo 32.14 iii 10-12 (Hurro-Hitt. bil. wisdom and myth, MH/MS), ed. StBoT 32:84f., tr. Hittite Myths[2] 71; cf. also KBo 32.14 rev. 23-24 (Hurr.) = 29 (Hitt.).

**1.** to sow (seed), to seed (a field) (without prev. or particle) — **a.** in the Hittite Laws: *takku* NUMUN*-ni šer* NUMUN*-an kuišk*[*i*] *šu-ú-ni-ez-zi* ... *U* A.ŠÀ*-LAM karū=pat kuiš šu-ú-ni-et ta=z apāš dāi* "If anyon[e] sows seed on top of (another person's) seed, ... (The person) who first seeded the field shall reap it for himself" KBo 6.26 i 34, 39-40 (Laws §166, OH/NS), ed. LH 133; cf. *U* A.ŠÀ*-LAM karū=pat kuiš šu-ú-ni-e-et* ibid. 44, ed. Hoffner, LH 134.

**b.** in agricultural texts from Maşat: *šepit=a* $^{\mathrm{m}}$*Pallana*[*š*] $^{\mathrm{m}}$*Nanataš šu-ni-et* ŠE.ḪI.A $^{\mathrm{m}}$*Pizuinaš* $^{\mathrm{m}}$*Ḫimu*-DINGIR*-LIM* $^{\mathrm{LÚ}}$EN *MAD*⌈*GALTI*⌉ $^{\mathrm{m}}$*Pippapaš* $^{\mathrm{m}}$*Nanataš* $^{\mathrm{m}}$*Uzzū šu-ni-et* § 65 *PA.* ZÍZ.ḪI.A *INA* $^{\mathrm{URU}}$*Tapigta*(sic) $^{\mathrm{m}}$*Ḫalpa*-DINGIR*-LIM*! $^{\mathrm{m}}$*Patiyaš* $^{\mathrm{m}}$*Nunnuš* $^{\mathrm{m}}$*Kililiš* $^{\mathrm{m}}$*Kukuliš šu-ni-*⌈*iš-kán*⌉*-zi* § 28 *PA.* ZÍZ.ḪI.A *INA* $^{\mathrm{URU}}$*Ḫariya* $^{\mathrm{m}}$*Ḫimu*-DINGIR*-LIM* ‹$^{\mathrm{m}}$›*Maruwaš* $^{\mathrm{m}}$*Tiwa*-LÚ $^{\mathrm{LÚ}}$KUŠ$_{7}$.KÙ[.GI] *šu-ni-iš-kán-zi* "The *šepit*-cereal Pallana (and) Nanata sowed. Pizuina, Ḫimuili, the provincial governor, Pippapa, Nanata (and) Uzzū sowed barley. § Sixty-five *parīsu* of wheat in (the town of) Tapigga Ḫalpaili, Patiya, Nunnu, Kilili (and) Kukuli will sow. Twenty-eight *parīsu* of wheat in (the town of) Ḫariya Ḫimuili, Maruwa (and) Tiwaziti, the gol[den] chariot fighter will sow" HKM 111:13-27 (harvest inventory, MH/MS), ed. del Monte, OAM 2:124.

**2.** to dip (in), immerse (almost always w. *anda*/ŠÀ and -(*a*)*šta*, *-kan* or *-šan*) — **a.** pieces from sacrificial animals and from their body-parts: ("[The exorcist] takes cedar wood from the incense vessel and places it on the *ḫuprušḫi* vessel at the hearth ... The ritual patron puts (his) hand on the sheep") *nu=šši=kan* $^{\mathrm{LÚ}}$AZU GÍR*-it AN*[*A* S]AG.DU*=ŠU anāḫi dāi* $^{\mathrm{GIŠ}}$ERIN*=ya=z=*(*š*)*an anda ēpzi* [*n=a*]*t?=šan* $^{\mathrm{DUG}}$*āḫrūšḫi* Ì.GIŠ *anda šu-ni-e-ez-zi* "The excorcist takes a sample from its (i.e., of the sheeps) head with a knife, holds the cedarwood close, [and] he dips [i]t in the incense vessel, in the vegetable oil" KBo 24.66 iii 16-18 (throne of Ḫebat offerings, MH/MS), ed. ChS 1/2:50f. ii 43-45; *n=ašta* $^{\mathrm{LÚ}}$AZU *ANA* MUŠEN.ḪI.A *anāḫi dāi n=at=šan* Ì*-i anda šu-ú-ni-ia-az-zi n=at=šan ḫaššī dāi* $^{\mathrm{UZU}}$ŠÀ*=*[*ŠU*]*NU=ya=šmaš=kan šarā dai n=at=šan ḫaššī* ⌈*p*⌉*eššiyazi* "The exorcist takes a sample from the birds, he dips it in oil and places it on the hearth. He picks up their hearts too, and he throws them into the hearth" KUB 45.47 ii 13-16 (fest. for NIN.GAL, MH/MS), ed. Wegner, ChS I/3-2:182f., Görke, hethiter.net/: CTH 494 (INTR 2012-05-09); [(*nu*)]*=ššan* EN.SÍSKUR *ANA* MUŠEN *QĀTAM d*[(*āi nu=šši=ka*)]⌈*n* $^{\mathrm{LÚ}}$AZU⌉ [(*AN*)]*A* $^{\mathrm{UZU}}$GABA*=ŠU anāḫi dāi n=a*[*t=šan?* ($^{\mathrm{DUG}}$*āḫrušḫiy*)]*a* [(*AN*)]*A* Ì.GIŠ *anda šu-ú-ni-ez-zi* "The ritual patron puts (his) hand on the bird. The exorcist takes a sample from its (i.e., the bird's) breast, and he dips i[t] in an incense vessel, in the vegetable oil" KUB 32.42 i 8-10 + KUB 32.43 i 13-14 (throne of Ḫebat offerings, NS), w. dupls. KBo 27.120 rt. col.

10-12 (NS), KBo 27.162 + KBo 35.85 ii? 4-6 (MS?), translit. ChS I/2:234.

**b.** breads or pieces of bread — **1′** in oil: ("The priest breaks five thin-breads, he recites in Hurrian ...") *nu=kan ANA* NINDA.SIG.MEŠ *anāḫi dāi n=at=kan ANA* Ì.GIŠ *anda šu-un-ni-ez-zi* (var. *šu-ni-ez-zi*) *n=an=šan ḫūprušḫi ḫaššī peššiezzi* "He takes a sample from the thin-breads and he dips it in the vegetable oil. He throws it(?) into the *ḫuprušḫi*-vessel on the brazier" KBo 15.48 iv! 36-40 (*ḫišuwa* fest., MH/NS), w. dupl. KBo 27.156:2-5, ed. ChS I/4:35, 37, translit. Dinçol, Belleten 53/206:17 □ the referent of the encl. pers. pron. *-an* is unclear. Since *anaḫi* is neut. it is not likely to be the referent. This would leave either the oil or the piece of bread that was taken as a sample; ("Afterwards, the exorcist crumbles one thin-bread etc.") *anāḫi=ma=kan peran arḫa daškezzi n=at=šan* (var. *=kan*) *anda ANA* $^{DUG}$*āḫrūšḫi* Ì.GIŠ *šu-ú-ni-iš-ke-ez-zi* "He (i.e., the exorcist) takes a sample away from in front and he dips it in an incense vessel, in the vegetable oil" KBo 21.33 iv 12-13 (throne of Ḫebat offerings, MH/MS), w. dupl. KUB 45.5 iii 19-21 (NS), ed. ChS I/2:66f.; $^{NINDA}$*kugullan* UR.GI$_7$*-aš* UDUN*-niya peran arḫa pittenut parā=an=kan ḫuittiat* UDUN*-niyaz n=an=kan* Ì*-i anda šu-ú-ni-at šakni=an=kan anda šu-ú-ni-at n=aš=za ešat n=an adānna daiš* "A dog ran off with a *kugulla*-bread from in front of an oven. He pulled it out of the oven and dipped it in oil. In oil he dipped it and sitting down he began to eat it" KBo 32.14 iii 9-12 (Hurro-Hitt. bil. wisdom and myth, MH/MS), ed. StBoT 32:85 ("tauchte"), tr. Hittite Myths² 71 ("dropped"), see also bil. section; cf. a *giluši*-animal dipping *kugulla*-bread in oil KBo 32.14 rev. 28-29.

**2′** in honey, or honey and (fine) oil: *nu* 3 NINDA ⌈x-x⌉*-an li*-x[...] *paršiyami n=at=kan ANA* Ì LÀL *anda šu-ú-ni-e-mi n=at [IN]A* $^{DUG}$DÍLIM.GAL IZI *katta teḫḫi* Ì*=ya* LÀL EGIR*-anda lāḫumi* "I break three [...] breads and dip them in the oil (and) honey. I put them down into the bowl for embers. Also, I pour oil (and) honey afterward" KBo 32.176 obv. 14-16 (Walkui's rit., MH/MS), ed. Mouton, Rêves 166, 168 ("Je ... remplis"), Chrzanowska, hethiter.net/: CTH 496.1 (TX 04.03.2014, TRde 04.03.2014) ("ich fülle"); EGIR*-ŠU=ma ANA* $^{d}$*Ḫepat* 3 NINDA.GUR$_4$.RA BABBAR ŠÀ.BA 1 SA$_5$ *paršiya n=aš=kan* ŠÀ*-BI* LÀL Ì.DÙG.GA *šu-un-ni-ia-zi n=aš=kan* $^{GIŠ}$BANŠUR $^{d}$*Ḫepat dāi* "Thereafter, for Ḫebat he breaks three white bread loaves, among (them) one red. He dips them in the honey (and) fine oil, and puts them on the table of Ḫebat" KUB 6.45 iv 13-15 (prayer, Muw. II), w. dupl. KUB 6.46 i 49-50, ed. Singer, Muw. Pr. 26, 43, tr. Hittite Prayers 93; see also KUB 6.45 iv 4-5, 8-10, 18-20, 23-25, 28-31; $^{LÚ}$SANGA 1 NINDA.GUR$_4$.RA GA.KIN.AG *paršiya n=an=kan ANA* LÀ[L *a*]*nda šu-un-ni-ez-zi* [*n*]*=an PĀNI* DINGIR*-LIM dāi* "The priest breaks one thick chees[e]-bread and dips it in the hone[y]. He places it in front of the god" KUB 58.3 iii 21-24 (NS), translit. DBH 18:7.

**3′** in *marḫa*-stew: ("He breaks [one th]ick [bread] for the Stormgod of [Ku]liwišna, *IŠTAR*, [the protective deity, and for] all of the gods") *n=ašta awan arḫa* [*tepu* 3*-ŠU*] *paršiyazzi n=ašta marḫi anda šu-ú-ni-ez!-zi* [*šer=a=ša*]*n* SAR.ḪI.A 3 *AŠRA dāi* "[Three times] he breaks [little (pieces of it).] He dips (them) in the *marḫa*-stew while putting vegetables [on to]p in three places" KBo 15.36 + KBo 21.61 ii 5-7 (Stormgod of Kuliwišna, MH/MS?) and cf. ibid. 10-12, 16-17, ed. Eothen 6:100f. ("taucht (es) in").

**4′** in kneading troughs: 1 NINDA.ÉRIN.MEŠ 1 $^{NINDA}$*wageššar* 7 NINDA.GUR$_4$.RA TUR $^{DUG}$*išnuraš=a=kan šu-ú-ni-ia-an-zi n=ašta šarliya šer arḫa daḫḫi n=an* NINDA*-an iyami* "One soldier-bread, one snack-bread, seven small bread loaves. They dip (them) into kneading troughs. I take away from on top the upper (pieces) and make it into bread" VBoT 24 iii 6-9 (Anniwiyani's rit., MH/NS), ed. *šarli-* ("they put"), THeth 25:60f. ("Teigschüsseln aber füllt man"), Laroche, RHA XXXI 93 ("on les plonge"), Chrest. 112f. ("fill"), Tischler, HEG S/2 ("drückt man") □ note the absence of *anda*.

**5′** in fire: *nu* NINDA.GUR$_4$.RA.ḪI.A SIG *arḫ*[*a* ...] *nu=ššan paḫḫueni* [*anda*(?)] *šu-ú-ni-i-e-zi* "He [breaks(?)] thin bread loaves, and toasts (lit. dips) (them) [in] the fire" KBo 7.36 i 6-8 (fest. frag., OH/MS), cf. HEG S/2:1173 ("taucht er"), Laroche, RHA XXXI 93 ("il (les) plonge [dans] le feu").

**6′** without liquid mentioned: *nekuz meḫur≈ma* NINDA.GUR$_4$.RA *šu-ni-ia-an-zi* DUMU*≈ya šuppiyaḫḫanzi* "At night they dunk (lit. dip) the thick bread and consecrate the child" KBo 5.1 ii 4-5 (Papanikri's rit., NH), ed. Strauß, Reinigung 289, 297 ("tunkt man ... ein") □ note the absence of *anda*.

**c.** cedar in vegetable oil: (The priest pours water with a piece of cedar-wood onto the hands of the king reciting in Hurrian) *n≈ašta* $^{GIŠ}$ERIN *ANA* Ì.GIŠ *anda šu-ni-*⌜*ez*⌝*-zi n≈at≈šan ḫūprušḫi ḫaššī peššiyazi* "He dips the cedar-wood in the vegetable oil, and he throws it into the *ḫuprušḫi*-vessel on the hearth" KBo 15.47 rev.? 7-9 (*ḫišuwa* fest., MH/NS), translit. Dinçol, Belleten 53/206:20; cf. also KBo 15.48 iv! 30-32 (*ḫišuwa* fest., MH/NS).

**d.** a fruit cluster in fine oil: DUMU.É.GAL*≈kan* $^{GIŠ}$*tepaza* $^{GIŠ}$*ippiaš murin* ŠÀ Ì.DÙG.GA *šu-un-*⌜*ni*⌝*-zi* "The palace attendant dips a cluster of (the fruit of) the *ippiya*-tree with a ladle(?) into the fine oil" KBo 11.32 obv. 21 (fest. for infernal deities, OH/NS), cf. also par. KUB 57.110 ii 14 (NS).

**e.** wool in fine oil: *n≈ašta* SÍG.SA$_5$ *ANA* Ì.DÙG.GA *anda šu-ú-ni-ez-zi* "He dips the red wool in the fine oil" KBo 23.1 i 16 + ABoT 1.29 i 15 (Ammiḫatna, Tulbī & Mātī's rit., NH), ed. Strauß, Reinigung 259, 266 w. n. 145., Lebrun, Hethitica 3:141, 149.

**f.** an *ākkuwal*-implement (?) in wine and fine oil: (A priest(ess) takes an *ākkuwal* implement, the ritual patron blows into an offering pit) EGIR-⌜*ŠU≈ma* $^{GIŠ}$*ākk*⌝[*uwal*?] / [*pattešn*]*i*? *anda INA* GEŠTIN Ì.[DÙG].GA *šu-na-a-iz-zi* "After that, she immerses the *ākk*[*uwal*-tool(?)] in the o[ffering pit(?)] in wine (and) f[i]ne oil" KBo 31.143 + KBo 20.49 obv. 23 (precursor of Allaiturahi's ritual series, MH/MS), for join see Groddek, IJDL 2:19, cf. Haas, AoF 34:30f. (w. translit. of pieces separately).

**g.** aromatics into water: *nu≈kan* ⌜*āššiya*⌝[(*tar* $^{GIŠ}$*šaḫin* $^{GI}$)$^{Š}$*parnull*(*inn≈a daššauaš* A.ḪI.A-*naš*) *anda*?] *šu-un-ni-ia-at nu≈kan* A.ḪI.A-*aš a*[(*nda āššiyatar* $^{GIŠ}$*š*)*aḫiš* $^{GI}$($^{Š}$*parnulli wa*)]*ršīet* "(*IŠTAR*) dipped aphrodisiac(?), *šaḫi*-wood and [*parnull*]*i*-wood [in]to the mighty waters and the aphrodisiac(?), *š*[*aḫi*]-wood and *parnulli*-wood released their essential oils (lit. made *waršula*-) in the waters. (When Ḫedammu savored a drop of the brew, a [sweet] dream gripped the soul of the powerful Ḫedammu)" KBo 19.111:3-5 (Ḫedammu, NS), w. dupl. KUB 33.84:4-5 + KBo 19.109:6-7 (NS), ed. StBoT 14:58f. ("schüttete sie"), Kloekhorst, EDHIL 973f. ("strewed"), differently *parnulli*-, $^{(GIŠ)}$*šaḫi(š)*-, tr. Hittite Myths[2] 55 ("filled") □ with Kloekhorst, EDHIL 974, we abandon the translation "to smell" for the verb *waršiya/e*- (so s.v. *parnulli*-, $^{(GIŠ)}$*šaḫi*(*š*)-, Hittite Myths[2] 55), and translate it as "to release, produce *waršula*-." *waršula*- "drop" (Rieken, StBoT 44:470; Tischler, HEG W 370) is a substance that can be seen and tasted, but also a vapor that can be smelled. It is produced by plants as an aroma, and by animals as sweat. As both a highly volatile substance (i.e., something that vaporizes at room temperature or below) and the defining sensory aspect of the releasing entity, *waršula*- should no longer be translated as "smell" (Güterbock, JKF 10:212), nor just "fume, haze, vapor" (Kloekhorst, EDHIL 975) but as "aromatic drop," or "(drop of) essential oil" in the case of vegetation.

**h.** into a (heap of?) dried cress(?): [...] *ANA* ZÀ.AḪ.LI ḪÁD.DU.A$^{SAR}$ *anda šu-ni-ez-zi* KBo 23.46 rev. 8 (Hurr. rit., NS), ed. ChS 1/2:160f. ("streut er") □ the object of the sentence is not preserved; it may be a kind of bread, since in the previous lines various breads are mentioned ($^{NINDA}$*iduri* rev. 6, $^{NINDA}$*šalākar* rev. 7). If so, the object of the dipping may have been to get the spice to adhere to the outside of the bread, enhancing its taste.

**i.** in describing the treatment of a penis ailment: [*mān*] ⌜*a*⌝*pez UL* SIG$_5$-*ri n≈an* EGIR-*ŠU kēz waššiy*⌜*a*⌝[*z*...] / [...*a*]*nda* ⌜*šu*⌝*-ni-ia-az-zi* "[If] he does not get cured by that, [he] afterwards [treats(?)] him with this medicine: [...] / He dips [...] in [...]" (If he is circumcised(?), he [...-s] him etc.) KUB 44.61 rev. 23-24 (med., NH), ed. StBoT 19:20f. (füllt er hinein" > *šunna*-).

**3.** unclear: ("When Ḫakkarpili went to Zalpa [...], he said to them (i.e., the inhabitants of Zalpa)": "The king gave me this. He holds evil [against you]. You must start hostility!") *nu≈za* x[...] *šu-ú-ni-ez-zi nu katta ḫašša ḫanzašš*[*a*...] GÍR-*anza karašdu* "And [he who(?)] sows/dips [...] for himself, may the knife cut [...] (or: may he cut with a knife [...]) down the generations" KBo 3.38 obv. 28-30 (Zalpa story, OH/NS), w. dupl. KUB 48.79 obv. 4-7 (NS), ed. StBoT 17:8f., cf. 41 ("er füllt" > *šunna-*), StMed 19:33, 42 ("fills") ☐ it is tempting to understand these two clauses as the Hitt. equivalent of "you reap what you sow"; [...] 9 *ḫ*⌈*uwalli*⌉*ššin* ⌈9⌉? [...] / [...] ŠU.GI LÚ.M[EŠMU]ŠEN.DÙ ‹LÚ›SANGA*=ya āška parā* [...] / [...]⌈MUNUSŠU⌉.GI *arḫa QĀTAMMA šu-ú-ni-e-ez-zi* "[...] nine pine cones, nine(?) [...] / [... the] old [...], the augurs and the priest forth to the gate [...] The Old Woman completely sows/dips [them] in the same way" KBo 34.47 + KBo 17.105 ii 1-3 (rit. for the Tutelary Deity of the Hunting Bag, MH/MS), ed. THeth 25:86f. ("schüttet ... weg") ☐ in both cases the spelling with *ú* prevents the assignment to *šun(n)a-* "to fill, pour" (s.v.).

*š.* is consistently spelled with plene *ú* and single *-n-* in OS and usually in MS, but in NH compositions and NS copies of older compositions we also find spellings with double *-n-* and without *ú*. For the distinction between *š.* and *šun(n)a-*, *šunni-*, *šun(n)iya/e-* B "to fill, pour" see the latter. *š.* "to dip" (mng. 2) is almost always (exceptions KBo 5.1 ii 4-5 (2 b 6') and VBoT 24 iii 7 (2 b 4')) preceded by *anda*/ŠÀ(*-BI*) "in" w. particles *-ašta, -kan*, and *-šan* (from OH, e.g. KBo 7.36 i 7-8 (2 b 5')).

Hrozný, CH (1922) 129 ("säen"); Friedrich, HW (1952) 198 ("füllen (?); streuen(?); sprengen(?); säen; (Feld) besäen," w. *anda* "hineinfüllen(?)"); Rosenkranz, JEOL 19 (1965-66) 502; Laroche, RHA XXXI (1973) 91-93 (on distinction of *šunna-* "to fill" and *šuniya-* "plonger"); Otten, StBoT 17 (1973) 41; Lebrun, Hethitica 3 (1979) 156; Oettinger, Stammbildung (1979) 159 (on distinction of *šunna-* "füllen" and *šuniya-* "eintauchen, säen"); Lebrun, Hymnes (1980) 287; Weitenberg, U-Stämme (1984) 137; del Monte, OAM 2 (1995) 125; Neu, StBoT 32 (1996) 169 nn. 143-144; Singer, Muw.Pr. (1996) 65, 66; Tischler, HEG S/2 (2006) 1172-1174 ("eintauchen, untertunken, besäen"), Kloekhorst, EDHIL (2008) 786-787 ("to dip").

**šun(n)iya/e- B** see *šun(n)a-*.

**šu-n[i?-...y]a** n.; (an object made of stone (?)); NH.†

Listed in an inventory: 1-*EN šu-n*[*i*?-o-*y*]*a* N[$A_4$ ...] "1 *š.* (of) sto[ne(?)]" KUB 12.1 iii 21 (inv. of Manninni, NS), ed. Košak, Linguistica 18:100, 104; Siegelová, Verw. 444f.

**GIŠšunila-** see GIŠ*šu*(*i*)*nila-*.

**šunnezziya-** see *šun*(*n*)*az*(*z*)*iya-*.

**šunt-**; filled, part. of *šū-* B, *šūwa-*, s.v.

**šunti-** n., Hurr.; (something sacred which receives offerings); from MH/MS.†

**Hurr. pl. abs.** *šu-un-ti-in-na* KUB 29.8 i 57 (MH/MS).

**Luw. pl. acc.** *šu-u-un-ti-in-na-a-an-zi* KBo 5.2 iii 29 (MH/NS), KBo 27.131 iii 17 (MH/NS).

GÙB-*laz=ma kuiš* GUNNI *n=an* d*IŠTAR-gapina šarrēna šu-un-ti-in-na IŠTU* MUŠEN.GAL *šipanti* "He offers the hearth that is on the left with a 'big-bird' (for) the kings (and) the *šunti-* (pl.) of Šaušga" KUB 29.8 i 56-57 (mouth-washing rit., MH/MS), ed. Haas, ChS I/1:89 ("An der Herdstelle ... bringt sie ein Blutopfer für die Könige (und) die šunti ..."), cf. also Friedrich, AfO 14:332 w. n. 19, Wegner, AOAT 36:89; (After making a gate of two reeds, the ritual practitioner attaches two birds to the left and right reed, and places two *ḫupruš ḫi*-vessels of wood to the left and right of the gate) *nu* ZAG-*aš kuiš ḫupruš ḫiš n=an=kan ŠA* dUTU *iniyannāḫi šipanti* § GÙB-*laz=ma kuiš ḫupruš ḫiš n=an=kan ŠA* d*IŠTAR nišḫinzi šu-u-un-ti-in-na-a-an-zi šipanti* "He consecrates the *ḫupruš ḫi*-vessel that is on the right for the *iniyannāḫit* of the Sungod(dess). § He consecrates the *ḫupruš ḫi*-vessel that is on the left for the *nišḫi-* (pl.) and the *šunti-* (pl.) of Šaušga" (presumably by means of the two birds) KBo 5.2 iii 28-29 (Ammiḫatna's rit., MH/NS), ed. Strauß, Reinigung 228, 241 ("den *ḫubrušḫi*-Räucherständer ... opfert er als/für die *nešḫi* (und) *šunti-*"), Friedrich, AfO 14:332 ("Den Altar(?) aber, der links (steht) bespendet er (für) die *nišḫi* (und) die *šuntinna*"), Haas/Wilhelm, AOATS 3:92 w. n. 2 ("das beopfert er für die nešḫi (und) šunti"), Wegner, AOAT 36:89 ("Welches Räuchergefäß aber links (ist), da libiert man die nešhi (und) šunti der Šawuška") ☐ the beneficiary of *šipant-* can occur in the acc. when the acc.-object is not offered but consecrated by means of a liquid, in this case blood (compare *nu=kan* dUTU *kaurī kā=ma* GIŠBANŠUR BAL-*aḫḫi* "Or should I consecrate a table to the Sungod(dess) *kaurī* here?" KUB 5.24 ii 8 (oracle question, NH), see *šip(p)a(n)d(a)-* 2 d).

The Hurrian cultic term *š.* occurs in both passages in the plural. The first form is probably a Hurrian plural in *-na*, although the *-nn-* is difficult to explain. The last one is a hybrid formation having in addition a Luwian pl. ending *-nzi*, which was produced under local "Empire Luwian" dialectal influence in Ḫattuša. For discussion of this particular passage see Friedrich, AfO 14:332f.; for the phenomenon in general see Yakubovich, Sociolinguistics 26-38.

The references show that *š.* belongs along with *nišḫi-* (pl. *nišḫinzi*) and *šarri-* (pl. *šarrena*) to the goddess Šaušga and receives offerings. One of them, *šarri-* "king," is thought to be a kind of cultic figure (see Wegner, AOAT 36:88f.), so that one may consider a *š.* to be something similar.

Friedrich, AfO 14 (1941-44) 332; Laroche, DLL (1959) 87f.; Haas/Wilhelm, AOATS 3 (1974) 92; Laroche, GLH (1976-79) 243; Wegner, AOAT 36 (1981) 89; Melchert, CLL (1993) 197; Strauß, Reinigung (2006) 249f.; Richter, BibGlHurr (2012) 414.

**šunnumar** see *šun(n)a-*.

**šunnummeššar** n.; filling(?); MH/NS.†

**nom.-acc.** ⌈*šu*⌉?-*un-nu-um-me-eš-šar* KUB 13.4 i 7 (MH/NS).

**broken:** *šu-un-nu-um-mi-eš-n*[*a-*...] KBo 49.194:6 (NS) (perhaps to be restored as gen. *-n*[*a-aš*] or abl. *-n*[*a-az*]).

[(NINDA.GUR$_4$.RA UD-*MI*)] / [...] *mān ŠA* 1 *ŠĀTI mā*[*n* ...] / [*Š*]*A* 2 *UPNI* 1 *UPNI* ½ *UPNI* x[ ...] / [*š*]*u-un-nu-um-me-eš-šar tiy*[(*an*) ...] "daily thick loaves [...] either of one *SŪTU* or [...] of two handfuls, one handful, half a handful [...] the filling (is) placed [...]" KUB 13.4 i 4-7 (instr. for temple personnel, MH/NS), w. dupl. KUB 13.6 i 4-6, ed. THeth 26:40, 70.

Since Sturtevant, Gl. 144, *šunnummeššar* is understood as derived from *šunna-* "to fill." Kronasser, EHS 1:291, considers the initial *šu* uncertain and rejects a derivation of this word from *šuniyami* "ich fülle," from which he expects **šuneššar*. However, *š.* is a well-formed *-eššar* formation from the verbal substantive *šunnumar* (*šunna-*, q.v.) compare *weta-/wete-* "to build" with verbal substantive *wetummar* "(the act of) building" and *wetummeššar* "(a) building" derived from the latter. Thus, *š.* should mean "filling (of a pie, cake or bread)." Though fragmentary, the context of KUB 13.4 i 7 supports this with the presence of daily bread and dry measures (*SŪTU, UPNU*). For filled/stuffed breads, see *šun(n)a-* c 4′. Note also that in KBo 49.194:6 two lines before *šunnummiešn*[*a*...] another deverbal noun from *šunna-* appears, *šunnan*⟨*n*⟩*az* from **šunnatar*, q.v.

Sturtevant, Gl. (1936) 144 ("a filling??"); Friedrich, HW (1952) 198 ("Füllung(??)"); Kronasser, EHS 1 (1966) 291; Weitenberg, U-Stämme (1984) 429 n. 298; Tischler, HEG S/2 (2006) 1175; Kloekhorst, EDHIL (2008) 785.

Cf. *šun(n)a-*.

**šup(p)-, šuppiye-, šuppa- C** v.; to (go to) sleep, fall asleep; from OH/MS.†

**act. pres. sg. 3** ⌈*šu*⌉-*up-pí-ez-zi* KUB 12.63 rev. 4 (MS).
**imp. pl. 2** *šu-up-tén* KUB 39.31:3 (NS).
**mid. pres. sg. 3** *šu-up-pa-at-ta* KUB 43.60 i 1 (OH/NS), *šu-up-pa-«at-»at-ta* KUB 43.60 i 2 (OH/NS), *šu-up-ta-a-ri* KUB 4.47 i 3 (NS), *šu-up-ta!-ri* KBo 5.4 rev. 38 (Murš. II), *šu-up-pa-ri* KUB 37.190 obv. 6.
**verbal subst.** *šu-up-pu-u-wa-ar* KBo 13.2 obv. 14 (NS).
**part. pl. com. acc.** *šu-pa-an-du-uš* KBo 12.88:19 (NS) (this word despite single p?).
**sg./pl. gen. or pl. dat.-loc.** *šu-up-pa-an-da-aš* KBo 43.27:3 (NS).
[**inf.** *šu-pu-an-zi* KUB 18.10 iv 33, read ŠU.GÍD-*an-zi*, see s.v. [*šu-pu*]]

(Sum.) [máš-mu] = (Akk.) [*šutt*]*i* = (Hitt.) *tešḫaš=miš* "my dream" / (Sum.) [...] = (Akk.) [...] = (Hitt.) *šu-up-pu-u-wa-ar* KBo 13.2 obv. 13-14, ed. Cohen, JNES 71:6 (lex., NS).

Neu, StBoT 5:157 n. 3 lists two other fragmentary exx. of *šuptari*: KUB 20.68 i 7 (winter fest., NS) is more likely [*ta-r*]*u-up-ta-ri* (see Soysal, JAOS 136:420), while *šu-up-*[...] in IBoT 2.15 i 5 (winter fest., NS) probably belongs to a more common word (*šuppa, šuppi-, šuppiyaḫḫ-*).

**a.** (act.) to (go to) sleep: ("[They say] to the temple of the Stormgod":) *laḫḫiyalaš=wa nu=war=at=ši=kan dāuwani* [...] ⌈*šu*⌉-*up-pí-ez-zi* "'He is a traveler(?)/warrior(?) and we will take it (i.e., the *tarpatarpa*-plant) from him [while/when] he sleeps" KUB 12.63 rev. 2-4 (Zuwi's rit., MS), ed.

(LÚ)*laḫḫiyala-*, Haas, Materia 90 w. n. 421; ("(S)he calls out":) *šu-up-tén=wa* "'Go to sleep!' ([...] Afterwards (s)he calls out: 'Get up!')" KUB 39.31:3-4 (funerary rit., NS), ed. Kassian et al., Funerary 676f.

**b.** (mid., without *-za*) to (fall a)sleep: ("If a god or goddess is [angry(?)] with a person ...") *nu=šši ḫūman* [UD-*ti/az*(?)] KALA.GA *n=aš* $GE_6$-*andaz UL šu-up-ta-a-ri* "and [by day(?)] everything is hard for him and at night he does not (fall a)sleep" KUB 4.47 i 2-3 (rit. against depression, NS), ed. Beckman, FsKošak 69, 74, Mouton, Rêves 144, 146; [...] *REŠ* ŠÀ=*ŠU ITTANANPAḪ* [*U UŠANŠA* ⁝?]*UL šu-up-pa-ri* [...] "If the top of his belly becomes repeatedly swollen/bloated [and he does not sleep, (Hitt.:)] he does not (fall a)sleep" KUB 37.190 obv. 5-6 (Akk. medical text; for the ductus see Wilhelm, StBoT 36:6-9), ed. StBoT 36:41f. □ tr. of *napāḫu*'s Ntn stem follows CAD; for Neu's suggestion (StBoT 5:157) that *UL šupari* "kommt nicht zur Ruhe" is a gloss for *ITTANANPAḪ* "wird immer wieder entfacht" see Wilhelm, StBoT 36:46, who rather suggests that it is a gloss for *UŠANŠA* "he spends the night sleepless" (see CAD *šumšû* "to spend the night awake"); [...]x GUD-*uš* ⸢*šu-up-pa*⸣-*at-ta* UDU-*uš* [*šu-up-pa-a*]*t*?-*ta nepiš šu-up-pa-*«*at-*»*at-t*[*a* KI? *šu-up-pa-a*]*t-ta* "[...]...the ox sleeps, the sheep [sleep]s(?), heaven sleeps, [earth sleep]s" KUB 43.60 i 1-3 (OH/NS), ed. Archi, JANER 7:172f., Katz, IBS 100:206, Polvani ICH 5:615f., Fuscagni, hethiter.net/: CTH 457.7 (INTR 2016-10-17).

**c.** (mid.) to fall asleep (w. *-za*): ("If troops and horse-troops go through [your land]") *nu=za šu-up*⸢*-ta*!*-ri*⸣ *kuiški* "and someone falls asleep (or someone gets sick, or ..., tell a high-ranking officer)" KBo 5.4 rev. 38 (treaty, Murš. II), ed. SV 66f. (reading *šú-up-šá-ri* "und einer marode wird(??)"), StBoT 5:157, tr. THeth. 20:418 ("falls asleep"), DiplTexts[2] 72 □ for soldiers falling down asleep from a column on the march and getting left behind see Beal, THeth. 20:418 n. 1566 w. lit.

The passages under a. and b. are all compatible with either "to sleep" or "to fall asleep/go to sleep," whereas the presence of *-za* (c) seems to only allow the change-of-state reading. The difference between the act. (a) and mid. (b and c) is one of volitionality and/or control, with lack of the latter associated with the mid. The subjects either are unable to sleep when they should (b; KUB 43.60 is unclear due to missing context), or they fall asleep when they should not (c).

Sturtevant, JAOS 56 (1936) 282-84 ("grow weary"); Friedrich, JCS 1 (1947) 294 ("schlafen"); HW (1954) 198; Kronasser, EHS 1 (1966) 508; Neu, StBoT 5 (1968) 157; Oettinger, MSS 34 (1976) 132; idem, Stammbildung (1979) 514; Tischler, HEG S/2 (2006) 1175f.; Kloekhorst, EDHIL (2008) 787f.

**šuppa A, šuppi A** adv., see *šuppi-* A e.

**(UZU)šuppa- B** n. collec. pl. tantum; meat; from OS.

**pl. nom.-acc.** *šu-up-pa* KBo 17.11 iv 5, 10 (OS), KBo 9.140 ii 16, iii 4 (OH/MS), KBo 17.74 iv 31, (36) (OH/MS), KUB 43.61 i? 7, 8 (OH/NS?), KBo 11.45 iv 4, 5 (OH/NS), KUB 10.21 iv 6 (OH/NS), IBoT 3.1 rev. 55, 58, 60 (OH/NS), KBo 15.10 iii 69 (MH/MS), KBo 24.19 ii 14 (MS), KBo 20.72 iii! 18 (MS?), IBoT 1.29 obv. 44, rev. 20, 21, 23, 28 (MH?/MS?), KBo 11.72 ii 41 (MH/NS), KUB 17.28 iii 4 (MH/NS), KUB 7.1 i 10, 17 (pre-NH/NS), KUB 56.39 ii 19, 28, iv 23 (NS), KBo 2.8 iii 7, iv 12 (NH), KBo 2.13 obv. 14, rev. 6 (NH), KUB 27.1 i 15 (Ḫatt. III), KUB 7.24 obv. 7 (Tudḫ. IV), KUB 25.23 i 17, 25, 27, 43, iv 53, l.e. a 4 (Tudḫ. IV), *šu-up-pa(-e-a)* KBo 20.24 iii! 6 (OS), UZU*šu-up-pa*! KUB 35.165 rev. 11 (OS), UZU*šu-up-pa* KBo 21.82 iii 23 (OH/MS), KBo 11.45 iv 8 (OH/NS), KUB 25.32 iii 4, 18 (OH/NS), KUB 20.88 iv 8 (MS), KUB 32.49b ii 16 (MH/MS), KBo 12.96 iv 16 (MH/NS), KUB 9.28 ii 19 (MH/NS), KBo 13.167 iii 2, 7 (MH?/NS), KBo 22.116 rev. 5, 8, 9 (NS), KBo 4.13 iv 30 (NH), KBo 23.42 i 5 (NH), KUB 46.38 ii 22 (NH/LNS), KUB 25.25 i? 11 (Tudḫ. IV), UZU*šu-*‹*up-*› *pa* KUB 25.32 iii 29, 30 (OH/NS).

**dat.-loc.** *šu-up-pa-aš* KUB 41.10 rev. 7, 9 (OH/MS?), KBo 4.9 i 17 (OH?/NS), KUB 7.1 i 13 (pre-NH/NS), *šu-up-pa-ia-aš* KBo 29.213 obv. 18 (NS), KUB 60.27 obv. 10, rev. 8 (NS), UZU*šu-up-pa-aš* KUB 32.1 iii? 11, 14 (NS), KBo 20.43 obv. 10 (NS), UZU*šu-up-pa-ia-aš* KUB 20.88 iv 15 (MS), KBo 24.66 i 29 (MH/MS), KBo 24.59 iv? 5 (MS?), KUB 39.71 iv 6 (NS).

**gen.** *šu-up-pa-aš* KUB 20.13 iv 12 (MH?/NS), *šu-up-pa-aš*! KBo 19.132 obv.? 6 (MH/NS), *šu-up-pa-ia-aš* KBo 10.20 iii 7, 36 (OH/NS), UZU*šu-*⸢*up*⸣*-pa-ia-aš* KUB 21.11 rev. 4 (NS).

**pluralized** UZU*šu-up-pa-ia* KUB 39.71 iii 49 (NS), KUB 39.74 ii 4 (NS), UZU*šu-up-pa*ḪI.A KUB 53.14 ii 3, 29 (OH/NS?), KUB 53.4 rev. 11 (NS).

**a.** in historical, administrative contexts: [...-(x-*na*)] / [(*ku*)]*enta ta ēšḫar=šet šu-up-pa=*[*šet*(?) ...] / [*d*]*āiuen ta pāiuen ta* LÍL-[*ra=šumma*(?)] (var. *kuera=šumm*[*a*(?)]) / [*š*]*ālikuwaštati* "He killed [...] and its blood, [its(?)] meat [...] we [p]ut and went. Thei[r] field we entered (unlawfully(?))" KBo 3.45 obv. 7-9 (Murš. I and Babylon, OH/NS), w. dupl. KBo 22.7 obv.? 4-5 (OH/NS), ed. Soysal, Diss. 54f., 100f., Hoffner, Unity & Diversity 56f.; ("He mistreats the poor man ..." ) ⸢*nu=š*⸣*ši=šta šu-up-pa arḫa danzi* / [... *IŠT*]*U*(?) ⸢LÚ.MEŠx-x⸣ *arḫa šuwanzi* "They take his meat away, they drive [him alongside wi]th [...]-men out (of the land?)" KUB 13.7 i 6-7 (instr., Tudḫ. II/NS), ed. HittInstr 140f.

**b.** in cultic contexts — **1′** raw and cooked meat: *kuitman=ma* LUGAL-*u*[*š* ...] EGIR-*az=ma* LÚ.MEŠAZU *ANA* DINGIR.MEŠ *šu-up-pa ḫuišawaz ziyandazzi=a tianzi* "While the king [...-s,] the diviners place at the rear meat, raw and cooked, for the gods" KUB 10.21 iv 4-9 (fest. frag., OH/NS), ed. Jestin, RA 34:48f., 53; 2 UDU dU 1 UDU ḪUR.SAG*Kilin*⸢*una*⸣ (eras.) BAL-*anti* NA4*ḫūwaši=aš ḫūkanzi* ⸢*šu*⸣-*up-pa ḫuešauwaza* ⸢*ze*⸣*antaza tiyanzi* "He offers two sheep for the Stormgod (and) one sheep for Mount Kilinuna. At the *ḫuwaši*-stone they slaughter them (and) they place the meat, raw and cooked" KBo 2.13 obv. 14-15 (cult inv., NH), ed. Carter, Diss. 106, 111; 1 UDU.GE$_6$ LÚ.MEŠ URUDU$_6$ LÚÚ.ḪUB *piyanzi n=an=kan* LÚ dU BAL-*anti* NA4ZI.KIN-*ši ḫūkanzi* ⸢*šu*⸣-*up-pa ḫuešauwaz zēantaz tiyanzi* "The men of the town of "Deaf Man's Tell" give one black sheep, and the man of the Stormgod consecrates it. They slaughter (it) at the *ḫuwaši*-stone. They place the meat, raw and cooked" KUB 25.23 l. e. a3-a5 (inv. of sanctuaries, Tudḫ. IV), ed. Hazenbos, Organization 35, 40, Carter, Diss. 163, 173f.; the following example gives an unusual sequence of "cooked (and) raw": *šu-up-pa zeyandaza ḫuešawaza tianzi* "they place the meat, cooked (and) raw" KUB 36.89 obv. 7 (prayer to Stormgod of Nerik, OH?/NS), ed. Haas, KN 142f.

**2′** (raw) meat of (or taken from) slaughtered ovine and bovine animals — **a′** UDU "sheep": *nu* EZEN$_4$ *ḫa*⸢*ta*⸣*uri iyazi nu* UDU.ḪI.A *ḫūkanzi nu=kan* [*š*]*u-up-pa danzi n=at zanuwanzi n=at PĀNI* DINGIR-*LIM tianzi* "He (i.e., the prince) performs the *ḫatauri*-festival. They slaughter sheep, take the [m]eat and cook it and place it before the god" KBo 10.20 ii 42-45 (outline of *ANDAḪŠUM*-fest., NS), ed. Güterbock, JNES 19:82, 86; [*nu=ka*]*n ANA* 3 UDU.ḪI.A *šu-up-pa danzi* UZUNÍG.GIG U[ZUŠÀ UZ]UÉLLAG.GÙN.A [*ḫa*]*ppinit zanuwanzi* "[And] they take meat from three sheep. They roast liver, [heart (and)] "multi-colored" kidney by the [open] flame" KBo 11.72 ii 41-42 (rit. for netherworld deities, MH/NS); cf. also [*ap*]*el=pat ŠA* UDU *šu-up-pa ḫ*[*ūešu* ...] "the r[aw] meat of [th]at very same sheep" IBoT 2.66 obv. 7 (fest. frag., NS).

**b′** UDU.NÍTA "wether": *nu* L[Ú.MEŠMU~ ḪALDIM (var. + [*ANA*] SÍSKUR=*ŠUNU*) UZ]U*šu-up-pa* (var. UZU Ì) *ḫu*[*ešu*] *ŠA* 8 UDU.NÍTA *U* [*ŠA* (⸢1 GUD⸣)]ÁB.NIGA ZAG-*an* [UZUZA]G.UDU-*an* UZUGABA.M[EŠ SA]G.DU.MEŠ GÌR.ME[Š] *ištanani peran* GAM *ANA* d*Aa tianzi* "([For] their ritual) t[he cooks] place ra[w] meat of eight wethers and [one] fatted [co]w — the right shoulder, the breasts, heads and feet — down before the altar of Ea" KUB 20.59 iii 9-13 (*ANDAḪŠUM*-fest., OH/MS), w. par. KBo 9.140 ii 16-19 (OH/MS), translit. DBH 13:104.

**c′** SILA$_4$ "lamb": [*Š*]*A* SILA$_4$*=ma=ššan* UZU*šu-up-pa* [...] FHG 12 ii? 21 (*šarra*-ritual, MH/NS),, ed. ChS I/2:156f.; cf. also ibid. ii 11; EGIR-*ŠU=ma=ššan* SILA$_4$-*an šipanti n=an=kan arkanzi nu=šmaš=kan* UZU*šu-up-pa* [*d*]*anzi* "Thereafter he sacrifices a lamb. They divide it up and [t]ake the meat for themselves" KUB 9.28 ii 17-19 (rit. for the Heptad, MH/NS).

**d′** MÁŠ.TUR "kid": [M]ÁŠ.TUR-*aš* UZU*šu-up-pa ANA* [(G)IŠBANŠUR AD.KID *tiyanzi*] FHG 12 ii? 15 (*šarra*-ritual, MH/NS), w. dupl. KBo 14.130 ii! 13 (MH/NS), ed. ChS I/2:154f.; cf. also ibid. ii 8.

**e′** MÁŠ.GAL "billy goat": *nu=kan* MÁŠ.GAL *arkanzi nu šu-up-pa ḫū*⸢*e*⸣[*šu*] [S]AG.DU GÌR.MEŠ UZUGAB UZUZAG.UDU *pattešni šer k*[*uranzi*(?)] "They butcher a billy goat, and [cut off(?)] the ra[w] meat, the [h]ead, feet, breast (and) shoulder over the pit" KBo 13.101 i 8-9 (rit., NS); also see under i′.

**f′** GUDÁB "cow": *nu ŠA* GUDÁB UZU*šu-up-pa-aš katta*[*n*] 1 NINDA*idurin ŠA* 2 *UPNI par*[*šiyanzi*(?)] "beneath cow meat [they] br[eak] an *iduri*-bread of two handfuls" KBo 20.43 obv. 10-11 (list of Hurrian gods, NS), translit. ChS I/3-2:198; also see under i′.

**g′** GUDÁB.NIGA "fatted cow": see under b′.

**h′** GUD "ox": *ŠA* GUD *U ŠA* UDU $^{UZU}$*šu-up-pa ḫūišu* $^{U[Z]U}$GABA.ḪI.A $^{UZU}$ZAG.UDU.ḪI.A SAG.DU.MEŠ GÌR.MEŠ.ḪI.A *PĀNI* DINGIR-*LIM* ⌜*tianzi*⌝ "They place the raw meat of ox and sheep, the breasts, shoulders, heads, feet, in front of the god" KUB 27.59 iv 16-17 + KUB 54.2 iv 17-18 (*witaššiyaš* fest, NS); [*Š*]*A* 10 GUD.ḪI.A *ŠA* 38 UDU.ḪI.A [*š*]*u-up-pa-aš-mi-it* $^{UZU}$SAG!.DU.ME[Š] [$^{UZ}$]$^{U}$GÌR.MEŠ $^{UZU}$GABA.ḪI.A≠*ŠUNU* $^{UZU}$ZAG.⌜UDU⌝.ḪI.A≠*ŠUNU* [$^{UZ}$]$^{U}$*muḫḫarauš≠*(*š*)*muš* [$^{U}$]$^{ZU}$ŠÀ≠*ŠUNU* $^{UZU}$ÉLLAG.GÙN.MEŠ≠*ŠUNU* [$^{UZU}$]x.ḪI.A≠*ŠUNU U* $^{UZU}$Ì.UDU≠*ŠUNU* "the (text: their) meat of ten oxen and thirty-eight sheep, (namely) heads, feet, their breasts, their shoulders, their *muḫḫarai*-parts, their hearts, their multi-colored kidneys, their [...-]s, and their (mutton) tallow" KBo 10.31 iii 30-35 (KI.LAM fest., OH/NS), translit. StBoT 28:103f.

**i′** GUD.MAḪ "bull": [E]GIR-*anda≠ma≠kan* É $^{d}$ZA.BA$_4$.BA$_4$ ⌜*š*⌝*anḫanzi šu-up-pa ḫūešu ŠA* GUD.MAḪ *ŠA* $^{GUD}$ÁB.ḪI.A *ŠA* UDU.ḪI.A *U ŠA* MÁŠ.GAL.ḪI.A *ištanani peran PĀNI* DINGIR-*LIM šanī pedi tianzi* "But [a]fterward they clean the temple of Zababa. They place the raw meat of a bull, cows, sheep, and goats before the offering table, before the god, in the same place" KBo 4.9 i 11-15 (*ANDAḪŠUM*-fest., OH?/NS).

**3′** meat of specific bodyparts: $^{(UZU)}$*šuppa-* seems to be a generic term, which refers to a large number of meaty parts of sacrificial animals. In the lists of meat offerings, first $^{(UZU)}$*šuppa-* is mentioned; there follow the names of specific bodyparts, e.g. UDU-*aš≠kan arkanzi nu šu-up-pa* $^{UZU}$NÍG.GIG $^{UZU}$GABA SAG.DU≠[*S*]*U* GÌR.MEŠ *PĀNI* $^{GIŠ}$BANŠUR *dāi* "They cut up the sheep. The meat —liver, breast, its head and feet—he places before the table" KUB 17.28 iii 4-5 (MH/NS), cf. KBo 10.31 iii 31-35 (OH/NS), KBo 11.72 ii 41 (MH/NS), KBo 13.101 i 9-10 (NS), KBo 22.180 i 9-11 (NS), KUB 9.28 ii 18-20 (MH/NS), KUB 27.1 i 15-16 (NH), KUB 28.102 iii! 22-25 (pre-NH/NS), KUB 32.49b ii 16-18 (MH/MS), KUB 35.133 ii 31-32 (LNS), KUB 45.3 i 8-9 (pre-NH/MS), KUB 45.47 iv 1-2 (MH/MS), KUB 53.20 rev.? 20-22 (OH/MS), FHG 12 ii 8-10 (NS), VBoT 58 iv 46-47 (OH/NS). The most common bodyparts are: $^{UZU}$GABA "breast," $^{UZU}$*kuttar* and $^{UZU}$ZAG.UDU "shoulder," SAG.DU "head," $^{UZU}$*kiššira-* "hand > front hoof," GÌR.MEŠ "feet > legs(?)," $^{UZU}$*walla-* "leg(?)," $^{UZU}$*wallaš ḫaštai-* "thigh," $^{UZU}$*KURĪTU* "shin," $^{UZU}$NÍG.GIG "liver," $^{UZU}$ŠÀ "heart," $^{UZU}$ÉLLAG.GÙN.A "multi-colored kidney," $^{UZU}$TI "rib"; occurring only rarely: $^{UZU}$*auli-* "?" KUB 35.133 ii 32 (LNS), $^{UZU}$[*iku*]*na-* "cold meat(?)" KUB 9.28 ii 20 (MH/NS), $^{UZU}$*muḫḫarai-* KBo 10.31 iii 33 (OH/NS), *parku⟨i⟩ ḫaštāi-* "pure-bone" KUB 35.133 ii 32 (LNS), $^{UZU}$Ì.UDU "(mutton) tallow" KBo 10.31 iii 35 (OH/NS), $^{UZU}$MAŠ.GIM "haunch(?)" KBo 22.180 i 10 (NS), $^{UZU}$ÚR "loin(?)" KBo 22.180 i 10 (NS) and $^{UZU}$*ḪĀŠĪ* "lungs" KUB 35.133 ii 32 (LNS).

**4′** acts pertaining to meat use and preparation in the cultic sphere — **a′** meat is direct object — **1″** *epp-* (w. *anda*) "to hold against," (w. *parā*) "to present": *nu≠kan* $^{LÚ}$*šankunniš* $^{UZU}$*šu-up-*[*pa*] *apēdani ANA* ZA.ḪUM KÙ.BABBAR *an*[*da*] *ēpzi n≠at ANA* DINGIR-*LIM par*[*ā*] [*ē*]*pzi* "The priest holds the mea[t] ag[ainst] that pitcher of silver (which the ritual client is holding) and prese[nt]s it to the deity" KUB 39.70 vi 1-4 (rit. for Ištar-Pirinkir, NS), ed. Beckman, Babilili 29, 40 ("dunks the meat in the silver beaker").

**2″** (*arḫa*) *ed-/ad-* "to eat up": [*l*]*ukkatta* DUMU.É.GAL *PĀNI* $^{GIŠ}$NÁ *šipanti* $^{[UZU]}$*šu-up-pa* GAL GEŠTIN 7 NINDA.GUR$_4$.RA *šarā dāi* [*nu*? $^{L}$]$^{Ú.MEŠ}$*ḫilammiēš kuiēš kuiēš warpanteš* [$^{UZU}$*š*]*u-up-pa arḫa adanzi* GAL.GEŠTIN≠*ya≠kan arḫa* [*akuw*]*anzi* "[The] following morning the palace servant makes an offering in front of the bed. He takes up [the m]eat, wine cup and seven thick breads. Whatever (court)yard-attendants(?) have bathed, they eat up [the m]eat and [drin]k up (i.e., empty) the wine cup" KBo 20.51 i 14-18 (cult of Ḫuwaššanna, MS).

**3″** *iya-* "to make (into stew)": *lukatti≠ma* UD.KAM $^{UZU}$NÍG.GIG *šu-up-pa* $^{UZU}$TU$_7$ *šiyami* DÙ-*zi PĀNI* DINGIR-*LIM tianzi* "The next day is the day of the liver. They make meat into a *šiyami*-meat stew (and) place (it) in front of the deity" KUB 17.35 ii 30-31 (inv. of sanctuaries, Tudḫ. IV), ed. HLC 172f., Carter, Diss. 128, 141, $^{TU_7}$*šiyam*(*m*)*i-*.

**4″** *karp-* (w. or without *šarā*) "to lift (up)": *namma* $^{\text{LÚ}}$*šakunniš* $^{\text{UZU}}$*šu-up-pa-ia ḫūišuwa zeyantā=ya IŠTU* $^{\text{DUG}}$DÍLIM.GAL *šarā karapzi* "Then the priest lifts up the raw and cooked meat with a bowl" KUB 39.71 + KBo 40.93 iii 49-51 (rit. for Ištar-Pirinkir, NS), ed. Beckman, Babilili 20f., 38; *nu šu-up-pa šarā dan*⸢*zi*⸣ § *šu-up-pa karpan ḫarkanzi* "They lift up the meat and hold the meat raised" (and they circle around the hearth) IBoT 1.29 rev. 20-21 (*ḫaššumaš* fest., MH?/MS?).

**5″** *maniyaḫḫ-* (w. *āppa*) "to hand over, deliver": *šu-u*[(*p-p*)]*a ḫūišawaza zeyandaza* EGIR-*pa maniyaḫḫan*⸢*zi*⸣ "They hand over meat, raw and cooked" KUB 24.5 rev. 8-9 (royal subst. rit., NH), w. dupl. KUB 36.94 rev. 5-6 (NH), ed. StBoT 3:12f.; cf. ibid. rev. 18-19.

**6″** *nininк-* "to move, transfer": *šu-up-pa apēdani* UD-*ti* [o-o] *nininkanzi* "That day they move the meat [into ...]" KUB 20.84 obv. 3-4 (fest. frag., NS), translit. DBH 13:145.

**7″** *peššiya-* "to throw": *n=ašta ANA* ⸢UDU $^{\text{UZU}}$⸣*šu-up-pa* $^{\text{UZU}}$GABA $^{\text{UZU}}$ZAG.UDU $^{\text{UZU}}$*auli par*⸢*ku*⸣⟨*i*⟩ *ḫaštāi* $^{\text{UZU}}$*ḪĀŠĪ* $^{\text{UZU}}$NÍG.GIG *n=at=kan ANA* $^{\text{DUG}}$ÚTUL *piššiyazzi* "He (takes) from the sheep meat (to be used in a stew) breast, shoulder, *auli-*, 'pure-bone,' lungs, and liver. He throws them into a pot" KUB 35.133 ii 31-33 (Ištanuwian rit., NS), translit. StBoT 30:280, LTU 110.

**8″** *peda-* "to carry" — **a″** (without prev. or adv.): KUB 25.32 iii 13-14, 29-30 (OH/NS), for ex. see under *šarā dā-* 10″ d″, below.

**b″** w. *anda*: *ta parā pānzi nu=kan šu-up-pa INA* É.DU$_{10}$.ÚS.SA É.ŠÀ-*na anda pēdanzi* "They go out and carry the meat to the washing house, into the inner chamber" IBoT 1.29 rev. 23-24 (*ḫaššumaš*-fest., MH?/MS?).

**c″** *parā*: KBo 29.213 rev. 2 (NS) (broken context).

**9″** *šarra-* (with *arḫa*) "to divide up": *maḫḫa*[*n=ma išnan*(?)] *pāpūwanzi zinnanzi nu=za ŠA* $^{\text{DUG}}$*išnū*[*ri išnan*(?)] GA.KIN.AG $^{\text{LÚ.MEŠ}}$NAR $^{\text{LÚ.MEŠ}}$É.DINGIR-*LIM=ya danzi* $^{\text{UZU}}$*šu-up-pa-az ḫūišu arḫa šarranzi* "But when the [...-s] finish shaping(?) [the dough(?)], the singers and the temple personnel take for themselves [the dough(?)] of the kneading tro[ugh] (and) the cheese and divide up the uncooked meat for themselves" KUB 17.24 ii 4-7 (cult of Ḫuwaššanna, NH?).

**10″** *dā-* "to take" — **a″** (without prev. or adverbs): *maḫḫan=ma lukkatta* $^{\text{UZU}}$*šu-up-pa* $^{\text{LÚ.MEŠ}}$MUḪALDIM *danzi* "When on the following day the cooks take the meat" KUB 60.121 rev. 13 (rit. frag., MS), ed. Popko, AoF 18:241f.

**b″** w. *arḫa*: [$^{\text{UZ}}$]$^{\text{U}}$*šu-up-pa arḫa d*⸢*ā*⸣*i* "He takes away the meat" KUB 36.44 i 13 (OH/MS?).

**c″** w. *peran arḫa*: *nu* $^{\text{LÚ}}$AZU-*TIM* [(*ANA*)] DINGIR.MEŠ $^{\text{UZU}}$*šu-up-pa* NINDA.GUR$_4$.RA=*ya paršiyanduš* [(*per*)]*an arḫa danzi* "The diviners take away the meat and the broken thick breads from before the deities" KBo 24.57 i 4-6 (Hurr.-Hitt. rit., NH), w. dupl. KBo 23.42 i 5-6 (NH), ed. ChS I/2:149, 130.

**d″** w. *šarā*: [GIM-*an=m*]*a INA* UD.2.KAM *lukkatta nu* $^{\text{LÚ}}$GUDU$_{12}$ [*šu-up-p*]*a-ia-aš pēran šipanti nu šu-up-pa šarā dānzi n=at zanuwanzi* TU$_7$ *MÊ* UZU *iyanzi* "In the second day, [when] it dawns, the anointed priest makes a libation in front of the [mea]t. They take up the meat and cook it, they make a meat broth" KUB 20.84 obv. 5-7 (fest. frag., NS), translit. DBH 13:145; DINGIR-*LUM* UGU ME-*anz*[*i*] $^{\text{UZU}}$*šu-*⟨*up-*⟩*pa-ia* UGU ME-*anzi n=at INA* É $^{\text{LÚ}}$MUḪALDIM ⸢*p*⸣*ēdanzi* $^{\text{UZU}}$*šu-*⟨*up-*⟩*pa=kan* $^{\text{GIŠ}}$ZAG.GAR.RA GIN-*zi* "They take up the (statue of the) deity, they also take up the meat. They carry them to the house of the cook. They place the meat (on) the altar" KUB 25.32 iii 29-30 (fest. of Karaḫna, OH/NS), ed. McMahon, AS 25:70f.; cf. also ibid. iii 13-14.

**11″** *dāi-/tiya-* "to put, place" — **a″** (without prev.): ("When they finish sacrificing the *keldi*") *nu šu-up-pa ḫūišawaza* $^{\text{UZU}}$GABA $^{\text{UZU}}$ZAG.UDU $^{\text{UZU}}$SAG.DU $^{\text{UZU}}$GÌR.MEŠ *PĀNI* DINGIR-*LIM tianzi* "they place before the deity meat, raw: breast, shoulder, head and feet" KUB 27.1 i 15-16 (rit., NH), ed. Lebrun, Samuha 75, 86; UDU=*kan ar*⸢*kan*⸣*zi nu* *šu-up-pa* UZUNÍG.GIG UZUGABA SAG.DU*=*⌈*SU*⌉ GÌR.MEŠ *PĀNI* GIŠBANŠUR *dāi* "They divide up the sheep. He places the meat, (namely) liver, breast, its head (and) the feet in front of the table" KUB 17.28 iii 4-5 (incant., NS), ed. Torri, JANER 4:133f.; cf. also: [*t*]*a namma šu-up-pa tiyanniyauwan dāi* "[a]nd then he starts to place the meat" KUB 43.61 i? 7 (incant. frag., OH/NS?); *šu-up-pa* GIN-*anzi* (i.e., *tiyanzi*) KUB 39.54 obv.? 16 (LNS); KUB 25.32 iii 30 (OH/LNS), see *šarā da-* 10″ d″, above.

**b″** w. *āppa*: UZU*šu-*⌈*up*⌉*-pa*ḪI.A *kue* ZAG.GAR.RA-*aš pēran kittat n=e=z* ⌈*l*⌉*ukkatta* LÚ.MEŠSANGA *danzi INA* É.DINGIR-*LIM zanuwanzi nu=ššan ANA* DINGIR-*LIM* EGIR-*pa tianzi adanzi akuwanzi* "On the morrow the priests take the cuts of meat which were deposited before the offering table (and) cook them in the temple. They place them again for the deity (and) eat (and) drink" KUB 53.14 ii 3-5 (fest. for Telipinu, OH/NS?), ed. Haas/Jakob-Rost, AoF 11:41, 45; cf. also [*n*]*u=šša*[(*n AN*)*A* d*Ḫebat*(?)] UZU*šu-up-pa āppa* ⌈*ti*⌉*an*[*zi*] KBo 20.43 obv. 8-9 (NS), w. dupl. KUB 27.33:3-4 (NS), translit. ChS I/3-2:197; *immakku=š*[*ša*]*n* U[Z]U*šu-up-pa* ⌈EGIR⌉-*pa dai*⌈*u*⌉*en nu=kan* $TI_8$MUŠEN *peran* [...] "We just placed back the meat and the eagle [(appeared) ...] in front" KBo 32.123 obv. 8-9 (bird oracle, ENS), ed. Sakuma, Diss. 2:611f. (reading DUG*šuppa*, "*šuppa*-Gefäß") □ in obscure context, but it seems that the meat is used to attract the eagle (and set it in motion in a particular way?).

**c″** w. *pēran*: UDU.ḪI.A *arkanzi* UZU*šu-up-pa ḫuišu* UZUGABA.ḪI.A UZUZAG.UDU.ḪI.A SAG.DU.ḪI.A GÌR.MEŠ GIŠ*ḫalpūtili pēran tīyanzi* "They divide up the sheep. The raw meat, (namely) breasts, shoulders, heads (and) feet they place in front of the *ḫalputili*-object" KUB 20.88 iv 8-10 (fest. celebrated by prince, MS), translit. DBH 13:153, cf. StBoT 61:34 n. 51.

**12″** *uda-* (with or without *anda*) "to bring (in)": *nu* LÚMUḪALDIM UZU*šu-up-pa* (eras.) *ḫūišawaz zeyandaz IŠTU* DUGDÍLIM.GAL *udai n=at=kan* GIŠ*kurši katta* ⌈*d*⌉*āi* "The cook brings meat, raw and cooked, with a bowl and puts it under the hunting-box" KUB 39.71 iii 36-37 (rit. for Ištar-Pirinkir, NS), translit. Laroche, RA 45:135; EGIR-*ŠU ŠA* 7 UDU *šu-up-pa* GIŠ*daḫuppaziyaza anda udanzi* "Thereafter they bring in meat of seven sheep with a *daḫuppazi*-tool/container" IBoT 3.1 rev. 58-59 (*ANDAḪŠUM*-fest. 11th day, OH/NS), ed. Haas/Wäfler, UF 8:92f.; cf. also ibid. rev. 55, KUB 27.69 v 16-17.

**13″** *warnu-* (w. *arḫa*) "to burn up": *maḫḫan=ma nekuza* ⌈*meḫur*⌉ *tiyazi nu=kan* LÚ.MEŠSANGA LÚḪAL *katta pānzi nu INA* $^{NA_4}$*daḫanga am.-šin ḫarpanzi šu-up-pa arḫa warnuwanzi* "In the evening the priests and the diviner go down and pile up the *ambašši* in the *daḫanga*-structure. They burn up the meat" (But what *ambašši* they brought from the palace, let them burn it upon it. But let them not approach the stone of the *daḫanga*-) KUB 56.49 obv. 6-9 (monthly fest., NH), w. dupls. KUB 56.48 ii 3-6 (NS) and KBo 2.4 iii 1-3 (NH), ed. KN 292f. (as Bo 3481).

**14″** *zanu-* "to cook": *lukatti=ma šu-up-pa zanuwanzi* "The following morning they cook the meat" KBo 2.8 iv 12 (cult inv., NH), ed. Hazenbos, Organization 136, 141; ⌈*ŠA* $SILA_4$⌉*=ya=kan* 10 UZU*šu-up-pa QĀTAMM*[(*A da*)*nzi*] *n=at=kan* [*a*]*nda ANA* 2 DUGÚTUL *zanuwanzi* ... § [*ma*]*ḫḫa*[*n=ma=kan*(?) *INA*] ⌈DUG⌉ÚTUL UZU*šu-up-pa zeiyari na=at* [...] "They ta[ke] in the same way also ten (chunks) of lamb meat and they cook it [i]n two pots. ... § [W]he[n] the meat is cooked [in] the pot, it [...]" FHG 12 ii? 11-12, 14 (throne of Ḫebat fest., NS), w. dupl. KBo 14.130 iii? 9-12 (NS), ed. ChS 1/2:134f.

**15″** *zinna-* "to finish": *maḫ*⌈*ḫ*⌉*an=ma ŠA* dU *šu-up-pa ḫu*⌈*ešawa*⌉*z nu* ⌈*ŠA*⌉ dZA.$BA_4$.$BA_4$ *šu-up-pa QĀTAMMA tianzi šer arḫa=ma=kan* UZUÌ.UDU *ḫūittiyanzi* § *maḫḫan=ma* UZU*šu-up-pa ḫuešawaz zinnanzi* "As (they place) the meat of the Stormgod, raw, they likewise place the meat of the god Zababa. They pull off the fat from on (them). § When they finish (preparing) the meat, raw" (they pull off some meat stuck (on) the staff and place them on top of a *paršulli*-bread for the Stormgod) KBo 11.45 iv 4-9 (fest. celebrated by prince, OH/NS).

**b′** meat is the object of a postposition — **1″** UZU*šuppayaš kattan* "beneath the meat," w. *paršiya-* "to break": *nu* LÚAZU UZU*šu-up-pa-ia-aš kattan* 2 NINDA*iduriuš paršiya šer=a=šša*[*n*] UZU*šu-*

*up-pa dāi n=at=šan PĀNI* DINGIR-*LIM* EGIR-*pa dāi* "The diviner breaks two *iduri*-breads beneath the meat. He puts the meat on top of it and places them again in front of the deity" KBo 24.59 i! 5-8 (fest., MS?), ed. ChS I/3-2:192f.; cf. also KBo 20.43 obv. 10-11 (NS), translit. ChS I/3-2:198.

**2″** *šuppayaš pēran/PĀNI šuppa* "in front of meat," w. *šipant-*/BAL "to sacrifice": [GIM-*an=m*]*a INA* UD.2.KAM *lukkatta nu* $^{LÚ}$GUDU$_{12}$ [*šu-up-p*]*a-ia-aš pēran šipanti* "On the second day, [when] it dawned, the anointed-priest makes a libation in front of the [mea]t" KUB 20.84 obv. 5-6 (fest. frag., NS), translit. DBH 13:145; cf. *lukatti PĀNI šu-up-pa* BAL-*anzi* KUB 56.39 ii 28 (cult inv., NS).

**3″** $^{UZU}$*šuppa(y)aš šer* "on the top of meat" — **a″** w. *išḫuwai-* "to scatter": ("They break thick-breads and cheeses") *nu=kan* ⸢NINDA⸣.Ì.E.DÉ.A *memal šu-up-pa-ia-aš* [*šer išḫ*]*ūwai* "He scatters the oil cake (and) the coarsely ground meal on top of the meat" HFAC 54 + KBo 29.213 obv. 18-19 (cult of Išḫara, NS), ed. Prechel, Išḫara 235, 240 ("an reinen Stätten").

**b″** w. *paršiya-* "to break": NINDA.GUR$_4$.RA *ḫauiyaššin=ma dāi n=an=kan* $^{UZU}$*šu-up-pa-aš ḫūišuaš šer paršiyazi nu=kan* $^{LÚ}$SANGA-*niš ANA* EN.SISKUR ZA.ḪUM KÙ.BABBAR *ŠA* KAŠ *arḫa dāi* ⸢*nu=kan*⸣ $^{UZU}$*šu-up-pa-aš* (var. $^{UZU}$*šu-up-pa-ia-aš*) *šer šipanti* "He takes the 'sheep-shaped' thick-bread and breaks it on top of the raw meat. The priest takes away the silver ZA.ḪUM-pitcher of beer from the client, and pours a libation on top of the meat" KUB 32.1 iii? 10-14 (rit. for Ištar-Pirinkir, NS), w. dupl. KUB 39.71 iv 3-6 (NS).

**c″** w. *šipant-* "to sacrifice, pour a libation": KUB 32.1 iii? 14, for ex. see under 3″ b″, above (*paršiya-*).

**d″** w. *dai-* "to place": ("They cook the liver(s) and heart(s) over an open flame. The anointed priest of Telipinu gives three sweet thick breads of a half handful measure to the prince. He breaks them") *šēr=a=ššan* $^{UZU}$NÍG.GIG *ŠALMŪTIM dāi n=at* $^{GIŠ}$*ḫalpūtili peran katta ḫuišuwaš=šan* $^{UZU}$*šu-up-pa-ia-aš šer dāi* "and he puts the intact liver(s) on (them). He places them down in front of the *ḫalputili*-object on top of the raw meat" KUB 20.88 iv 13-15 (fest. celebrated by prince, MS), ed. Taracha, StBoT 61:26f.

**4″** *šuppaš* ZAG-*naz* GÙB-*laz* "on the right and left (side) of meat": 2 *ḫuppar* KÙ.BABBAR *išpantuzziaš* GEŠTIN-*it šūwanteš šu-up-pa-aš* ZAG-*naz* GÙB-*lazz(i)=ya tianzi* "Two silver bowls are filled with the libation wine. They place (them) on the right and left (side) of the meat" KBo 4.9 i 16-19 (*ANDAḪŠUM*-fest., OH?/NS).

**c′** meat is subject — **1″** *ā-* "to be(come) warm": ("They cut up a billy goat, roast the liver, and cook $^{UZU}$*kudur* with a pot") *kuitman=ma* MÁŠ.GAL TU$_7$ *pittalwan* Ì $^{UZU}$*šu-up-pa zeandaz ari* "Until the billy goat, the plain stew, the oil (and) the meat, cooked, heat up (the king goes outside)" KUB 56.45 ii 13-14 (monthly fest., NS), ed. StBoT 37:596f.; cf. KBo 19.132 obv.? 6 (NS), KBo 33.120 i 28 (MS), translit. ChS 1/2:289 obv. 40.

**2″** (*peran*) *ki-* "to lay, to be deposited (before)": KUB 53.14 ii 3, 29 (fest. for Telipinu, OH/MS); for ex. see b 4′ a′ 11″ a″ (EGIR-*pa tiya-*).

**3″** *šeš-* "to sleep (i.e., spend the night)": *nu šu-up-pa PĀNI* DINGIR-*LIM šešzi* "The meat spends the night in front of the deity" (In the morning they pick it up and eat it) KUB 7.1 i 17 (Ayatarša's rit., pre-NH/NS), ed. Kronasser, Die Sprache 7:143f., Fuscagni, hethiter.net/CTH 390 (TX 20.03.2017).

**4″** *zeya-* "to be cooked": FHG 12 ii? 14 (NS), ed. ChS 1/2:154f., see 4′ a′ 14″ (*zanu-*).

**5′** meat counted by portion: ("Thereafter they bring in meat of seven sheep with a *taḫuppazi*-tool/container") *nu* 1-*NŪTI šu-up-pa PĀNI* $^{d}$*Lelwani* 1-*NŪTUM PĀNI* $^{d}$UD.⸢SIG$_5$⸣ 1-*NŪTUM ANA PĀNI* $^{d}$UTU 1-*NŪTUM ANA* $^{d}$*Papaya* $^{d}$*Ištuš*⟨*taya*⟩ 1-*NŪTUM ANA* $^{d}$*Ḫašamili* 1-*NŪTUM ANA* $^{d}$U.GUR "(They place) one portion of meat in front of Lelwani, one portion in front of the 'propitious day', one portion in front of the Sungod, one portion for Papaya and Ištuštaya, one portion for Ḫašamili, one portion for Nergal" (Thereafter the chief cook visits the places with liver for worshiping) IBoT 3.1 rev. 60-62 (*ANDAḪŠUM*-fest. 11th day, OH/NS), ed. Haas/Wäfler, UF 8:92f.

**6′** cultic term "the day of the meat (offering)": [*lu*]*kkatti*=*ma* UZU*šuppaš* UD-*za* [LÚ]SANGA=⸢*kan*⸣ ŠÀ É.DINGIR-*LIM paizzi* [LÚSA]NGA ⸢*A*⸣*NA* DINGIR-*LIM UŠKÊN* [*nu* 1 UDU B]AL-*i* "The [n]ext day (is) the day of the meat (offering). [The] priest goes inside the temple, bows to the god, [and sac]rifices [one sheep]" KUB 58.62 v 11-14 (fest., NS), ed. Popko, AoF 14:255, 258; cf. ibid. ii 6 + IBoT 3.8 obv. 12, ed. Popko, AoF 14:254, 257 ii 19-20; cf. also KBo 10.20 iii 7, 36 (OH/NS), KUB 20.13 iv 12 (MH?/NS) and KUB 21.11 rev. 4 (NS).

The noun UZU*šuppa-* is considered to be a *pl. tantum*. The plural form UZU*šuppa*ḪI.A is to be understood as "the cuts of meat." It is taken from the slaughtered sacrificial animals which are exclusively ovine and bovine animals (see b 2′). It can be external body parts but also can include some of the viscera (see b 3′) □ on meat consumption among the Hittites in general, see Ünal, Or NS 54:419-438.

Laroche, RHA XI/52:43, followed by Friedrich, HW 198, incorrectly equated *šuppa-* KUB 17.35 ii 30, iii 18 with logographic UZUGIG "taboo" KUB 17.35 i 35. The latter is rather UZUGIG.ḪI.A "cut pieces" (Akk. UZU*ḫerṣu*), see HZL no. 269, AHw 341.

The gender of UZU*šuppa-* is neuter. The only problematic case is [...]x DUGÚTUL *šu-up-pa-aš ari* KBo 19.132 obv.? 6. However, this can be translated as "the meat-pot heats up" so that *šuppaš* is rather in the genitive case here.

Sommer/Ehelolf, Pap. (1924) 20 ("Fleisch(?)"); Götze/Pedersen, MSpr. (1934) 19f. ("Fleisch"); Sommer/Falkenstein, HAB (1938) 111; Laroche, RHA XI/52 (1950) 43; Friedrich, HW (1952) 198 ("(kultisch reines) Fleisch (< *šuppaịa* "Reines"?); Goetze, Kl² (1957) 164 n. 12; Haas, KN (1970) 159f.; Tischler, HEG S/2 (2006) 1176-1179; Kloekhorst, EDHIL (2008) 789.

Cf. *šuppi-* A

**šuppa- C** v., see *šup*(*p*)-.

**šuppaḫḫ-** see *šuppiyaḫḫ-*.

**šuppal(a-), šupalla-, šupla-** n. (com./neut.); livestock; from OH/MS.

**sg. neut. nom.-acc.** *šu-up-pa-al* KUB 36.55 ii 30 (MH/MS), *šu-up-pa-la-an* KUB 8.1 iii 13 (NS), KBo 13.16:8 (NS).
**erg.** *šu-up-pa-la-an-za* KUB 36.32:5, 8 (MH/MS).
**com. nom.** *šu-up-pa-la-aš* KBo 3.60 ii 1 (OH/NS).
**dat.-loc.** *šu-up-le*(-) KBo 6.34 iv 15 (MH/NS).
**pl. neut. nom.-acc.** *šu-up-pa-la-a*(*š-še-et*) KBo 6.26 i 22, 26 (OH/NS).
**gen.** *šu-up-pa-la-an* KUB 30.11 obv. 4 (OH/MS), KUB 31.127 i 43 (OH/NS), *šu-pa-al-la-aš* KBo 21.95 i 18 (OH/NS).
**dat.-loc.** *šu-up-pa-la-aš* KBo 13.34 iii 10 (pre-NH/NS).
**unclear** *šu-up-pa-la-an* KUB 59.18 obv.? 12 (pre-NH/NS), *šu-up-pa-la-aš* KBo 12.3 iv 15 (OH/NS).

For *šu-up-pa-le-e-eš* VBoT 124 rev! 6 (OS) (thus Laroche, JCS 1:192, HW 198, and EHS 1:342 §177 II 5) see *šuppaleššar*.

*nu*=*šši*=*ššan wēlluš ḫāli*=*šši ašauni*=*šši šu-up-le-e*=*šši lē luluwaitta* "Let his meadow not survive for his cattle pen, for his sheep pen, (that is,) for his livestock" KBo 6.34 iv 13-15 (soldier's oath, MH/NS), ed. StBoT 22:14f., cf. also ibid. 50, Archi, FsPugliese Carratelli 28 ("que pour lui (qui a violé le serment) le fourrage pour ses (boeufs de l')enclos ne prospère pas, pour son (troupeau du) parc, pour son bétail (vivant en liberté)"), tr. Collins, CoS 1:167; [...]x-*a*=*tta* (or: *n*]*atta*?) *ammuk šu-up-pa-la-an-za kī uttar* x[... *memiš*]*kinun kūn kuin* DINGIR-*LIM-in memaḫḫu*[*n* ...(-)]*ḫūmada* DUMU.NAM.U$_{19}$.LU-*li kuiš* LUGAL-*uš* [...]x=*an ammuk šu-up-pa-la-an-za šā*[*ggaḫḫun*?] "It was me, the livestock, that ... [spo]ke these words to you (or: Was it [n]ot me that spoke these words?). This god whom I mentione[d ...]... whatever king [...] everything(?) to mankind(?) [...] I, the livestock, k[new(?)] it/him" KUB 36.32:5-8 (myth, MH/MS), ed. Archi, FsPopko 5, 9 ("the Beast"), cf. HEG S/2:1180 ("ich, das wilde Tier"), Kronasser EHS 1:261 ("Deutlich auch personifiziert ... 'ich das Vieh'"); *nu* dÉ.A-*aš šu-up-pa-al* EGIR-*pa kiššan punušta* [*kuiš*=*wa*(?) DIN]GIR-*LUM* DINGIR.MES-*aš ištarna* (eras.) *tarḫuile*⸢*š*⸣*zi* "In return Ea asked the livestock the following: ['What g]od among the gods is strong(est)?'" KUB 36.55 ii 30-31 (myth, MH/MS), ed. Archi, FsPopko 5, 8 ("Ea asked again the Beast"), cf. HEG S/2:1179 ("Erneut fragte sie das Tier"); [*mā*]*n lukkatta*=*ma n*=*apa* NIN.DINGIR-*aš arāi* [...]x-*zi* DUMU.NITA-*aš šu-*

*pa-al-la-aš* KÁ.GAL-*aš šar*[*ā* ...] "But when it is morning, the priestess arises and she [...-]s. The/A boy [goes(?)] up to the gate of the livestock" KBo 21.95 i 17-19 (OH/NS, fest. for Tetešḫapi), ed. Nakamura, FsDinçol 536, 538; *takku* MUNUS-*za ḫāši nu*=*šši*=*k*[*an*(?)] SAG.DU=*SU ŠA* ŠAḪ *kiša šu-up-pa-la-aš UL* $SIG_5$-*in* "If a woman gives birth, and its head happens to be that of a pig, the livestock will not prosper" KBo 13.34 iii 8-10 (omen, pre-NH/NS), ed. StBoT 9:26f. □ in omina (*UL*) $SIG_5$-*in* is combined with a dat. (in)commodi, cf. KUR-*eanti UL* $SIG_5$-*in* KUB 8.12:9, *nu*=*šši* $SIG_5$-*in* KUB 43.8 iii 2b. We therefore take *š.* here as plur. dat.-loc. contra HEG S/2:1179f.; [*mān INA* ITU.x.KAM] $^{d}$*SÎN-aš aki* $BURU_7$ *kišan*[*tari*] / [ ...-*t*]*a*$^{?}$*ri šu-up-pa-la-an ḫara*[*kzi*(?)] "[If] the moon dies [in the xth month], the harvest will take place, [but(?) ...] ... (and?) the livestock will perish" KBo 13.16:7-8 (lunar omen, NS), ed. DBH 12:34 ("das Vieh"), cf. HEG S/2:1180 (as plur. gen.: "(die Gesamtheit?) des Viehs"); similarly [*mān*] *INA* UD.15.KAM $^{d}$*SÎN-aš aki arunaš āššu ḫarakzi* [(*naš*)*ma*? *š*]*u-up-pa-la-an tepauēšzi* "[If] on the fifteenth day the moon dies, the bounty of the sea will perish, o[r] the livestock will diminish" KUB 8.1 iii 12-13 (lunar omen, NS), w. dupl. KBo 13.18:2, ed. DBH 12:66, 68 ("Das Vieh"), HEG S/2:1180 ("(Der Reichtum) des Viehs"); *nu ŠA* $UR.GI_7$ [*Š*]*A* ŠAḪ *ḫanneššar zik*[=*pat*? *ḫa*]*nnatta* § *šu-up-pa-la-an-n*=*a ḫannešša iššit kui*[*ē*]*š UL memiškanz*[*i*] *apatt*=*a ḫannattari* "[Only(?)] you, (O Sungod,) arbitrate the case of the dog and the pig. § Also, the case of the livestock, who do not speak with the mouth, that too you decide" KBo 34.22 + KUB 30.11 + KUB 31.135 obv. 11-14 (prayer, OH/MS), w. par. KUB 31.127 + KUB 36.79 i 42-44 (OH/NS), ed. Rieken et al., hethiter.net/: CTH 374 (TX 2018-04-12, TRde 2017-11-24), Güterbock, JAOS 78:240 ("animals"), Lebrun, Hymnes 95, 102 ("animaux"), tr. Hittite Prayers 37 ("animals"); *takku šu-up-pa-la-a*=*ššet kuēlqa šieuniaḫta ta*=*at parkunuzi na*=*at arḫa pennāi išuwanalli*=*ma*=*kan išuwan dāi ari*=*šši*=*ma*=*at UL tezzi* $^{LÚ}$*arašš*=*a UL šakki šu-up-pa-la-a*=*ššet pennāi n*=*at aki šarnikzil* "If someone's livestock go crazy, and he (i.e., the owner) performs a purification ritual on them, and he drives them back home, but he puts the remnants used in the ritual into the refuse pile, but doesn't tell his colleague, so that the colleague—not knowing—drives his own animals there and they die, there will be compensation" KBo 6.26 i 22-27 (Laws §163, OH/NS), ed. LH 130f. ("animals"), cf. 299 ("cattle"), *šiuniyaḫḫ-* ("cattle"); [...] *šu-up-pa-la-a*(*š*)(?)=*šmiš apāš*=*kan*(?)[...] *kuiš ištarni*=*šmi antuwaḫḫ*[*i*]*š a*[*r*]*i* (or: *a*[*k*]*i*) *š*=*an*=*ap azzikanzi* "[...] their livestock. That one [...]. What person arrives (or: dies) in their midst, they devour him" KBo 3.60 ii 1-3 (Cannibal text, OH/NS), ed. Güterbock, ZA 44:104f., Kempinski, ÄAT 4:42 (omitting line 1), cf. Soysal, Hethitica 14:139 □ if *šu-up-pa-la-aš-mi-iš* is not a mistake for *šu-up-pa-la-aš-mi-it*, this is the only unequivocal com. form for *š.* All other, and older, attestations and esp. the erg. point to original neut. gender.

Because he took *šuppala-* in the first example as parallel with *ḫala-* and *ašawar*, which are enclosures for large and small domestic animals, and because of the supposed relation to *šuppi-* "holy, sacred," Archi, FsPugliese Carratelli 28 ("les animaux qui vivent dans un milieu qui leur est propre, c'est-à-dire en liberté," thus also Lebrun, L'animal 95), uses this text as evidence that *š.* refers to wild animals, in contrast to those that live in pens. In addition, Archi (FsPugliese Carratelli 28) believes that the dog and pig in the Sun Hymn represent the domestic animals and that *š.*, in contrast, must refer to wild animals. However, since the *š.* are clearly owned by the individual, they are domestic and not wild. In the hymn to the Sungod the contrast is with the dog and pig, not with domestic animals in general. Dogs and pigs are never included among the rest of the domesticated animals in Hittite texts and it is unlikely they would be used as representatives of domestic animals. Collins, Diss. 14 and Animal World 238, likewise rejects the connection with *šuppi-*, claiming that it does not hold up to scrutiny in either the iconographical or the textual evidence.

Friedrich, ZA 35 (1924) 189f.; Carruthers, Language 9 (1933) 156 ("Schweinestall, Schweineherde"); Güterbock, ZA 44 (1938) 108 ("Schweineherde"); Otten, KUB 31 (1939) vi; Laroche, JCS 1 (1947) 192 ("(domesticated) animals"); Friedrich, HW (1953) 198 ("Vieh"); Goetze, Lg 30 (1954) 404; Laroche, OLZ 51 (1956) 422; Güterbock, Oriens 10 (1957) 357 ("domesticated animals"); Friedrich, 1.Erg. (1957) 19 ("Tier, Stück Vieh"); Ertem, Fauna (1965) 109-111; Rosenkranz, JEOL 19 (1965-66) 506 (etym.); Kronasser, EHS 1 (1966) 261 ("ein

Stück Kleinvieh"), 324, 331, 342 ("ein Stück Vieh"); Goetze, JCS 20 (1966) 128f. ("animals freely roaming in the pasture"); Goetze, JCS 22 (1968-69) 21 ("(herd of) animals"; not animals of the *ḫali* "corral" or *ašawar* "sheep cote," i.e., "not cattle or bétail"); Lebrun, L'Animal (1984) 95; Archi, FsPugliese Carratelli (1988) 28 ("les animaux des champs;" "*š.* sont la personnification sacrée, *šuppi*, des manifestations de la divinité"); Collins, Diss. (1989) 13-19 ("livestock"); Prinz, NeutSg. (1997) 98-100; Tischler, HEG S/2 (2006) 1179-1182 ("Tier, Vieh"); Kloekhorst, EDHIL (2008) 788 ("cattle").

Cf. *šuppaleššar*.

[*šuppala-*] v. KUB 43.60 i 1-3 read as *šup(p)-*, q.v.

[*šu-up-pa-la-ia-an-ta*] IBoT 2.23:7 (fest. frag., NH), thus read by Tischler, HEG S/2:1180 (s.v. *suppal-*, "Unklar"); instead read *šu-up-pa zé-ia-an-ta* "cooked meat" with a faint trace of a small vertical wedge in the alleged *-la-*.

**šuppaleššar** n. neut.; animal kingdom (?), cattle pen (?) or GN?; from OS.†

**sg. dat.-loc.** *šu-up-pa-le-e-eš-ni* VBoT 124 rev! 6 (OS) (not *šu-up-pa-le-e-eš*, thus Laroche, JCS 1:192, HW 198, and EHS 1:342 §177 II 5), KUB 60.20 rev.? (6) (OH/NS).

("The singer recites thus") [*tandukišni* ᵈUT]U?-*uš zi*[*k* DINGIR.MEŠ-(*nan*=*a ištarna*)...] / [...M]UNUS.LUGAL-*aš* ᵁᴿᵁ*Ḫa*[(*škaḫaškiwa*-x) ...] / [...*an*?(*da*)] *lē šuwa*[(*ieši taknaš*=*ta* ᵈUTU-*uš* ⌈*aušzi*⌉ § [...] *šu-up-pa-le-e-eš*[(*-ni lē šuwaieši*)] "[To mankind] yo[u] are the S[ungoddess(?)]. But among [the god]s [you are...], [q]ueen. [At(?)] the town of Ḫaškaḫaškiwa(-)[...] do not look at [...], the Sungoddess of the Earth will see you." § [...] Do not look at the animal kingdom/cattle pen (?)" VBoT 124 iii! 3-6 (invoc. to Hattic deities, OS), w. dupl. KUB 60.20 rev.? 3-6 (OH/NS), translit. StBoT 25:189, DBH 20:18, cf. THeth 11:135, HEG S/2:1179 ("treibe [...] nicht in den Viehpferch!") □ Neu, StBoT 26:358 w. n. 5 takes *š.* as a GN.

Tischler, HEG S/2 (2006) 1179 ("Viehbestand," "Viehpferch"); Kloekhorst, EDHIL (2008) 788.

**šupan(a?)-** (mng. unkn.); NS.†

**sg. gen.** *šu-pa-na-aš* KBo 13.260 ii 35 (NS).

§ [o-o]-x=*kan šu-pa-na-aš* GAL-*in parā* [*pēd*]*anzi n*=*an pera*⌈*n*⌉ [...]-x-*li kuitman ti*[*anz*]*i* "[...] they [br]ing forth a cup of *š.*, and meanwhile they place it at first(?) into the [...]" KBo 13.260 ii 35-37 (Luwian incantations against illness, NS), ed. Carruba, FsWatkins 79 ("un bicchiere di *s.* ..."), translit. StBoT 30:261, cf. Tischler, HEG S/2:1182 ("'Becher des Schlafes' (einen Schlaftrunk?)") □ there is no evidence that KBo 29.27 iv 2-3 is a dupl. of KBo 13.260 ii 35-37 (thus Starke, StBoT 30:258f., Carruba, FsWatkins 79).

Carruba, FsWatkins 79, suggests *š.* is gen. of a *r/n*-stem **šupar*, **šupn-* "sleep" followed by Tischler, HEG S/2:1182, with a denominal verb *šuppariya-*. Tischler emends the alleged variant (KBo 29.27 iv 2 [...-]*pí-aš*) to [*šu*]-*pí*-⟨*na*-⟩*aš*. However, neither the Hitt. nor the immediately preceding Luw. context contain any hint of sleep and *šuppariya-* "to sleep, doze" (q.v.) makes one expect *-pp-* instead of *-p-*. According to the context *š.* qualifies a cup probably indicating the material, the contents, or its owner.

Carruba, FsWatkins (1998) 79 ("sonno"); Tischler, HEG S/2 (2006) 1182 (< **šupar-*); Soysal, FsWilhelm (2010) 340 ("unklar").

**šupanni-** n.?; (a dance movement); NS.†

**unclear** *šu-pa-an-ni* KUB 4.1 iv rt. col. 34 (NS).

The section of the Sammeltafel KUB 4.1 iv 32-42 rt. and left cols. contains descriptions of dance movements (see s. v. *lapat*(*a*/*i*)-): ("The dancers danced: ... § Thereafter *lapatiš* once from afar. § Thereafter *lapatiš šalkupareš* §") EGIR-*ŠU*=*ma tū*⌈*wa*⌉*z SARTŪ šu-pa-an-ni* § "Thereafter dancing(?) *šupanni* from afar. §" KUB 4.1 iv rt. col. 34 (NS), ed. de Martino, Eothen 2:37f. □ it is not clear whether the word is a noun, and if it is, what its stem and case would be; for *SARTŪ* as a n. derived from Akk. *SÂRU* "to dance," see de Martino, Eothen 2:38.

De Martino, Eothen 2 (1989) 38; Tischler, HEG S/2 (2006) 1182 ("Art Tanz oder Art Musik").

**šupar** see *šuparša*.

**šuppariya-** v.; to (fall a)sleep, doze; NH.†

**act. pres. sg.? 3** *šu-up-pa-ri-i[a-zi*(?)] KUB 20.86 v 10 (NS).

**pret. sg. 1** *šu-up-pa-ri-ia-nu-un* KUB 52.91 iii 1 (NH).

**mid. pret. pl. 1** [*šu*]-*up*(coll. photo)-*pa-ri-ia-u-wa-aš-ta-ti* KUB 8.48 i 1 (NH).

**part. sg. nom. com.** *šu-up-pa-ri-ia-an-za* KUB 36.89 rev. 57 (NH), *šu-up-pa-ri-an-za* KBo 19.109:9 (NS), KBo 19.111:7 (NS).

**a.** in general: [*šu*]-*up*(coll. photo)-*pa-ri-ia-u-wa-aš-ta-ti nu lukkešta* "[While?] we were sleeping, it became light" (Enkidu then goes on to describe his dreams) KUB 8.48 i 1 (Gilg., NH), ed. Mouton, Rêves 111 ("'] nous allons dormir.' Ce fut le petit matin"), tr. Beckman, apud Foster, Gilg. 163, cf. Neu, StBoT 5:157 ("[während w]ir schliefen, wurde es hell"), reading following Laroche, RA 59:85, confirmed by coll. of photo by Neu, StBoT 5:157 bottom n. 1 □ for different readings see Stefanini, JNES 28:40, 45 (reading [....?*k*]*a-ri-ia-u-wa-aš-ta-ti* "We shall /can rest (for the night)"), and Friedrich, ZA 39:16f. (reading *pa*?-*ri-ia-u-wa-aš-ta-ti*); (When Ḫedammu had tasted the beer) *nu≠kan* [(*ANA* $^{M}$)]$^{UŠ}$*Ḫedammu tarḫūili* [(ZI.ḪI.A≠*Š*)*U šanezziš*] *tešḫaš ēpta n≠aš* GUD-*aš* A[(NŠ)]E[(-*aš̆š̆*)]≠*a iwar šu-up-pa-ri-an-za* "Sweet sleep seized the soul of the mighty Ḫedammu and, dozing like an ox or (lit. and) ass, (he recognizes [no]thing and gobbles frogs and salamanders(?))" KUB 33.84:6-7 + KBo 19.109:8-9 (Ḫedammu, NS), w. dupl. KBo 19.111:5-7 (NS), ed. StBoT 14:58f. ("wie Rind und Esel dösig"), tr. Hittite Myths² 55 ("he was dozing like an ox (or) ass"), Mitologia 142 ("sonnacchioso come un bue (e) un asino"); [...] EGIR-[*p*]*a šu-up-pa-ri-ia-nu-un* "I fell asleep again, (I saw [...])" KUB 52.91 iii 1 (introducing a dream in an oracle question, NH); *apēdani išp*[*anti* ...] *našma≠aš šu-up-pa-ri-i*[*a-zi*(?)] "In that night [he will...] or he will sleep" KUB 20.86 v 19-10 (rit., NS); see in broken context [...] *šu-up-pa-ri-*[...] KBo 12.74:13 (myth, NS).

**b.** with dir. object a dream: $^{d}$*Tešimi≠wa≠kan āššiyanti genuwa*‹*š*› *šanizziuš tešḫuš šu-up-pa-ri-ia-an-za ēšta arāi* $^{URU}$*Nerigaš* $^{d}$U-*aš* "You were dreaming (lit. sleeping) sweet dreams in the lap of beloved(?) Tešemi, (now) get up, O Stormgod of Nerik" KUB 36.89 rev. 56-58 (cult of the Stormgod of Nerik, NH), ed. KN 156f. ("schliefst du süße Träume"), Mouton, Rêves 304 ("Tu étais en train de voir de doux rêves").

Ehelolf, OLZ 36 (1933) 3-5 ((in dreams) "eingehüllt sein" or "schlafen"); Sturtevant, JAOS 56 (1936) 282-84 ("to sleep" > **šuppar* "sleep"); Friedrich, HW (1952) 198 ("schlafen"); idem, HW 3.Erg. (1966) 29; Kronasser, EHS 1 (1966) 197 ("träumen"), 274 ("schlafen"), 496, 508; Neu, StBoT 5 (1968) 157 ("schlafen"); Oettinger, Stammbildung (1979) 351 ("schlafen"), 529 ("träumen"); Tischler, HEG S/2 (2006) 1182-1183; Kloekhorst, EDHIL (2008) 788f.

Cf. *šup*(*p*)-, *šeš*-.

**šuparša(?)**; n. neut.?; (mng. unkn.); from MH/MS.†

**Luw.(?) sg. nom.-acc. neut.** *šu-pár-ša* KBo 24.26 ii 6 (MH/MS), *šu-ú-pár-ša* KBo 29.216:2 (NS).

[...] ⸢*n*⸣≠*at*≠*za šu-ú-pár-ša* [...] KBo 29.216:2 (cult of Ḫuwaššanna, NS), cf. KBo 24.26 ii 6 (MH/MS) □ in spite of the nearly identical sequence of the two words in both fragments the remaining text does not suggest their being dupls.

Since both frags. belong to the Ḫuwaššanna cult that stems from a Luw. milieu we tentatively analyze *š.* as containing a Luw. neut. sg. nom.-acc. with the particle *-ša/-za*.

Cf. *šupan*(*a*)-.

**šupparwant-** adj.; asleep(?); from MH/MS.†

**sg. nom. com.** *šu-up-pár-wa-an-za* KBo 40.219 rev.? 7 (NS), KUB 60.134:1 (LNS).

**pl. nom.** *šu-up-pár-wa-an-te-eš* KBo 24.56 A ii? 6 (NS).

**broken:** ⸢*šu*⸣-*up-pár-wa-a*[*n*(-)...] HKM 91 obv. 4 (MH/MS).

[*takku/mān*] ⸢UN⸣-*aš šu-up-pár-wa-an-za nu* $^{UZU}$KA×[U-...] / [*ārš*]*akezzi apāš* UN[-*aš*...] / [...]x-*a ašiwandā*[-...]"[If] a person is asleep(?) and [spittle? fl]ows [from his] mou[th], that person [...] ... poverty(?)" KBo 40.219 rev.? 7-8 (omen?, NS) □ this passage is reminiscent of *takku≠kan antuwaḫḫaš* $^{GIŠ}$NÁ-*aš šešzi nu≠šši≠kan iššalli parā* ZAG-*ni meni āršiyazzi* "If a person sleeps in a bed and spittle flows out onto the right (side of his) face" KUB 29.9 i 9-11 (Hitt. excerpt of Akk. *šumma ālu* omens, NS), ed. Güterbock, AfO 18:79; ⸢*ku*⸣*itman* MUNUS.LUGAL *šu-up-pár-wa-an-za* $^{GIŠ}$PISAN NÍG.B[A...] 2 *TA*‹*PAL*›(?) ⸢$^{TÚG}$⸣NÍG.LÁM.MEŠ *anda* DIB-*anta ANA* LUGAL [...] "While the queen is asleep(?), a storage chest as a gif[t ...] two sets(?) of fine garments packed together for the king [...]" KUB 60.134:1-2 (dep.?, NS), translit. Ünal, AoF 22:275 (reading $^{GIŠ}$PISAN NINDA B[A.BA.ZA]). In broken context: *šumeš*⸢*š*≠*a*?⸣ [...] ⸢*šu*⸣*-up-pár-wa-a*[*n*(-)...] *ŠA* KUR-*TI*≠*ka*[*n* ...] KUR-*ya* (or -*YA*) *and*[*a* ...] *UL and*[*a* ...] *apūn* $^{LÚ}$[KÚR(?) ...]§ HKM 91 obv. 3-8 (letter, MH/MS), ed. Alp, HBM 292f. ("schlafen[d](?)").

In Luw. context: § *ḫatēri*-x(-)*wara ša*-x?[...] *šu-up-pár-wa-an-te-eš* [...] § KBo 24.56 A ii? 5-6 (rit. containing Luwian, NS), translit. StBoT 30:376, HW² Ḫ 503a.

If the interpretation of KBo 40.219 rev.? 7-8 as an omen on the basis of KUB 29.9 i 9-11 is correct, *š.* ties in well with *šuppariya-* "to (fall a)sleep, doze" (q.v.). Unfortunately, the other occurrences provide no clear support although they do not contradict it either.

Alp, HBM (1991) 344 ("'schlafend' oder 'schläfrig'"); Tischler, HEG S/2 (2006) 1183; Kloekhorst, EDHIL (2008) 789 ("sleepy(?)").

Cf. *šup*(*p*)-, *šuppariya-*.

**šuppa(-)wašḫanall[i(-)...]** see under *šuppiwašḫanalli-*.

**šuppi- A** adj.; sacred, consecrated, holy, ritually pure (opp. *marša-*, *šaknuwant-*); wr. syll. and KÙ.GA; from OS.

**com. nom.** *šu-up-pí-iš* KUB 60.41 obv. 7 (OS), KBo 23.48 obv. 8 (NS), KUB 58.2 v 10 (NS), Bo 6223 iii 7 (LNS), here? KUB 42.100 iii 7 (NH), *šu-up-pí-iš* KBo 9.137 ii 20 (MS), KBo 39.79 rev.? 4 (MS), KBo 47.217:3 (MS), KUB 41.29 iii 8 (OH/NS), KUB 58.50 iii 11, 18 (OH/NS), KUB 9.4 ii 6 (MH/NS), KUB 41.8 ii 14 (MH/NS), VBoT 120 ii 5 (MH/NS), KBo 3.8 iii 32 (NH), KUB 29.4 iv 27 (NH), KBo 14.70 i 17 (NS), KUB 42.103 iii? 7 (LNS), *šu-up-iš* KBo 5.2 iv 64 (MH/NS), *šu-pí-iš* VS 28.15 ii 15 (NS), *šu-up-pí*‹*-iš*› KBo 5.2 i 3 (MH/NS), here? KBo 5.1 i 6 (NS), *šu*!?(sign GIŠ/ḪAB)*-pí-iš* IBoT 3.1:40 (OH/NS).

**acc.** *šu-up-pí-in* KBo 21.85 iv 22 (OH/MS), KBo 12.89 ii 13 (MS), KBo 29.189:(1) (MS), KBo 10.23 iv 16, v 8 (OH/NS), KBo 32.7 obv. 13 (pre-NH/NS), KUB 32.133 i 18 (Murš. II), KUB 12.26 ii 5 (NH), KUB 16.9 ii (5) (NH).

**nom.-acc. neut.** *šu-up-pí* KBo 17.1 i 14 (OS), KBo 17.3 i 9 (OS), KUB 30.10 obv. 13 (OH/MS), KBo 33.118:80 (MH/MS), KBo 34.38 i 3 (MS), KBo 4.9 iv 26 (OH/NS), KUB 32.123 iii 49 (OH/NS), KUB 35.148 ii 10 (OH/NS), KBo 5.1 i 6 (NH), KUB 24.1 i 22, ii (15) (Murš. II), KBo 3.8 iii 24 (NH), KUB 54.31 obv.? 8 (LNS), KUB 42.100 i 8 (Tudḫ. IV), KÙ.GA KBo 4.11 rev. 42 (NS), *šu-up-pa* KUB 27.29 iii 5 (MH/NS; to be emended to *-pí*?), KBo 11.1 obv. 32, 40 (Muw. II).

**gen.** *šu-up-pa-ia-aš* KBo 10.26 i 29 (OH/NS), KUB 13.4 i 42 (pre-NH/NS), *šu-up-pa-aš* KBo 27.42 i 16 (OH/NS).

**dat.-loc.** *šu-up-pa-i* KBo 25.94:6 (OS), KBo 17.74 iii 36, ii 18 (OH/MS), KBo 20.67 i 14, 27 (OH/MS), KBo 12.3 iv (7), 8 (OH/NS), KBo 11.43 vi 7 (OH/NS), KBo 3.21 iv 11 (MH/NS), KUB 25.1 ii (54) (NS), KUB 26.12 iv 34 (NH), KBo 23.1 ii 20, 26 (= ABoT 1.29 ii 20, 26 + ABoT 1.28 obv. 3, 9) (NH), *šu-up-pa-a-i* KUB 57.63 i 5 (NS), KUB 59.43 i 2 (NS), KUB 46.61 rev.? 4 (LNS), *šu-up-pí* KBo 5.2 ii 59 (MH/NS), KUB 24.13 i 19 (MH/NS), KBo 4.11 obv. 4 (NS), KBo 22.6 i 16 (NS), KBo 7.74:6 (NH), KUB 2.5 i 24 (LNS), KUB 20.50 rev. 7 (Tudḫ. IV), *šu-up-pa*‹*-i*› KUB 30.42 iv 22 (NH), *ANA* ... KÙ.GA KBo 4.9 v 25 (OH?/NS), KUB 34.69 obv. 7 (NS).

**abl.** *šu-up-pa-az* KBo 17.88 + KBo 24.116 ii 10 (OH/MS), KBo 21.22:22 (OH/MS), KBo 17.74 ii (35), (43), iii 17, 23 (OH/MS), KBo 17.52 iii 8 (MS), KUB 56.46 i 5 (OH/NS), VBoT 127 v? 11 (NS), *šu-up-pa-za* KUB 10.52 vi 14 (NS), *šu-up-pa-ia-az* KBo 21.22:23 (OH/MS), KUB 10.19 i 11 (MS?), KBo 27.42 iii 63, iv 20 (OH/NS), KBo 34.164 iv 6 (OH/NS), KUB 25.3 iv 13 (NS), KUB 2.5 i 21 (LNS), *šu-up-pa-ia-za* KBo 13.122:2 (OH/NS), KUB 17.9 i 21 (NS), KUB 5.6 iii 20 (NH), KUB 25.5 ii 15 (NH), KUB 2.5 ii 13 (LNS), *šu-up-pa-ia-az-z*(*i-ia*)(-)[...] KUB 4.47 obv. 17 (NH).

**inst.** *šu-up-pí-it* Bo 3686 iv? 8 (Otten/Rüster, ZA 64:248f.) (LNS), VBoT 126 ii? (1) (NS).

**pl. com. nom.** *šu-up-pa-e-š*(*a*) KBo 25.109 ii (10) (OS or MS), KUB 17.21 iii 4 (Arn. I/MS), *šu-up-pa-e-eš* KUB 17.21 ii 10 (Arn. I/MS), KBo 8.86 obv. 14 (MS?), KBo 10.26 i 37 (OH/NS), KBo 27.42 ii 38 (OH/NS), KUB 23.115:(3) (Arn. I/NS), KBo 23.1 iii 26 (NH), KUB 45.49 iv 8 (NH), KUB 59.60 iii 6 (LNS), KBo 61.219:4 (NS?), *šu-up-pa-eš* KUB 11.34 v 47 (pre-NH/MS?), *šu-up-pa-a-eš* KUB 33.62 ii 2 (OH/MS), ABoT 2.243 rev. 5 (MH/MS), *šu-up-pé-eš* KUB 25.20 iv? (3) + KUB 46.23 rev. (7) (LNS).

**acc.** *šu-up-pa-uš* KBo 30.61 obv.? 3 (MH/MS), KBo 38.45 ii 7 + KBo 21.47 ii 5 (MH/MS), KBo 12.89 iii 13 (MS), KBo 45.82a rt. col. 6 (MS), KBo 9.109 i 13 (OH/NS), KBo 27.42 ii 49 (OH/NS), KUB 7.1 iii 12, 20 (pre-NH/NS), *šu-up-pí-ú-uš* KUB 33.41 ii 10 (OH/NS).

**neut. nom.-acc.** *šu-up-pa* ABoT 1.35 obv. 5 (OS), KBo 17.65 rev. 25 (OH/NS), KBo 3.25:4 (OH/NS), KUB 9.16 i 6 (OH/NS), IBoT 1.29 rev. 28 (MH?/MS?), KBo 11.1 obv. 32 (Muw. II), KUB 33.106 iii 22, 37 (NH), KBo 26.65 iv 27 (NH), KBo 4.11 obv. 16, 18, 23 (NS).

**gen.** *šu-up-pa-ia-aš* KBo 12.70 obv.! rt. col. 10 (NH).

**dat.-loc.** *šu-up-pa-ia-aš* KBo 25.94:(6) (OS), KBo 20.123 i 7 (MH/MS), KUB 56.52 obv.? 5 (MS?), KUB 2.13 ii 51 (OH/NS), KUB 10.21 iii 13 (OH/NS), KUB 25.1 i 23 (OH?/NS), KBo 13.131 rev. 12 (MH/NS), KUB 41.8 ii 20 (MH/NS), *šu-up-pa-aš* KBo 17.74 iv (24) (OH/MS), KBo 30.122 iii (12) (NS).

For possibly š. = Sum. SIKIL see below d 11′ b′; for the various equivalences in Luwian, Hurrian, Akk., Hebrew, and Ugaritic, see Hutter, Purity 161-164, and Feder, JANER 14:87-113.

**a.** deities: 2 NINDA.GUR$_4$.RA.ḪI.A*=ma Š*[(*A* 1 *UPNI*)] *šu-up-pa-ia-aš* DINGIR.MEŠ-*aš* "Two thick breads weighing one handful for the holy gods" KBo 20.123 i 6-7 (rit., MH/MS), w. dupl. KBo 22.106 obv. 11 (MH/NS); *šu-up-pa-ia-aš-š=a=ta=kkan* DINGIR.MEŠ MUNUS-*aš ḫurdāiš lē* ⸢*ari*⸣ "Also, may the curse of the holy goddesses not come upon you" KBo 12.70 obv.! rt. col. 10-11 (wisdom text, NH), ed. Keydana, UF 23:69 ("der Fluch der reinen Göttinnen"); 2-*ann=a* KI.MIN *ŠA* ᵈIM ŠEŠ-*ni šu-up-pí šipan*⸢*ti*⸣ "and he offers the second ditto (= *ḫubrušḫi-*) to the holy brother of Teššub" KBo 5.2 ii 59 (Ammiḫatna's rit., MH/NS), ed. Strauß, Reinigung 226, 239; *šu-up-pí* ᵈUTU-*aš* ZI-*anza* "A holy thing is the Sungoddess (of the Earth)'s soul" KUB 43.60 i 31 (myth, OH/NS), ed. Archi, JANER 7:72f.

**b.** humans and their bodyparts — **1′** the body of the king: [*našm*]*a=šmaš šumeš kuiēš* ᴸᵁ́.ᴹᴱŠSAG *ANA* LUGAL*=kan* [NÍ.TE*=Š*]*U*?-*i šu-up-pa-i šali*⸢*kiš*⸣*ketteni nu=šmaš šuppiešni* [*ḫan*]*da tišḫanteš ēšten mānn=a=kan ANA* ᴸᵁ́SAG [*kue*]*danikki* ḪUL-*luš maršaštarriš* [*ap*]*āšš=a ANA* LUGAL NÍ.TE.MEŠ*=ŠU šaligai* GAM *MĀMĪTI* "[O]r, you who as eunuchs are always in contact with the king's sacred [bod]y, be mindful(?) of your ritually pure state (or: (the king's) ritual purity); also if some eunuch has an evil profane condition and he too comes into contact with the king's body, (it is placed) under the oath" KUB 26.12 iv 33-37 (instr. for eunuchs, NH), ed. HittInstr. 290f., Dienstanw. 28f., Wilhelm, Levitikus 202, Mouton, HR 55:47f. w. n. 21, cf. also *šalik*(*i*)-, *šalink-* 1 b 1′ and *šuppieššar* 1 a.

**2′** cult personnel (see Theth. 26:148-152); in lists of cult personnel "consecrated" individuals are distinguished from ordinary priests: ᴸᵁ́.ᴹᴱŠSANGA ᴹᵁᴺᵁˢ.ᴹᴱŠAMA.DINGIR-*LIM šu-up-pa-e-eš* ᴸᵁ́.ᴹᴱŠSANGA ᴸᵁ́.ᴹᴱŠGUDU$_{12}$ ᴸᵁ́.ᴹᴱŠNAR KUB 17.21 ii 10-11 (prayer of Arn. I and Ašm., MS), ed. Lebrun, Hymnes 136, 144 ("sacrés"), tr. Hittite Prayers 41 ("holy"); cf. also ibid. iii 4-6; *šu-up-pí-iš* ᴸᵁ́SANGA "consecrated priest" in a list of cult officials among whom such religious functionaries as the *tazzelli-* and the GUDU$_{12}$-priests KUB 41.29 iii 8 (OH/NS), ed. THeth. 21:216f. ("der heilige Priester"), tr. THeth. 26:152 ("sacred"); frag. *šu-up-pí-ìš* ᴸᵁ́SANGA-*ìš natt*[*a*? ...] KUB 60.41 obv. 7 (fest., OS), translit. DBH 20:41, StBoT 25:109 (reading ᴸᵁ́SANGAᴹᴱŠ) □ Neu, StBoT 26:175 n. 525 emends ᴸᵁ́SANGA.MEŠ to sg. ᴸᵁ́SANGA-*eš* (ᴸᵁ́SANGA-*iš*), but the handcopy and photo show a clear *eš*; ᴸᵁ́SANGA*=ši šu-up-pí-ìš* "His (i.e., the deity's) priest is consecrated" KUB 42.100 iii 7 (inventory of sanctuaries, NH), ed. Hazenbos, Organization 18, 22 ("pure"); EZEN$_4$.MEŠ *šu-up-pa-ia-aš* ᴸᵁ́SANGA-*aš* KUB 13.4 i 42 (instructions for temple personnel, pre-NH/NS), ed. HittInstr 250f. (reading ᴸ[ᵁ́.ᴹᴱŠ?]SANGA-*aš*), THeth 26:43, 72 ("sacred"), Süel, Direktif Metni 28f. ("kutsal"), tr. McMahon, CoS 1:218 ("holy"); cf. also *šu-up-pa-e-š*[*=a=*]*z* DUMU.MEŠ SANGA *AŠAR=ŠUNU=pat ḫarkanzi* "the consecrated junior priests occupy their places" KBo 25.109 ii 20 (fest, frag, OS?), ed. Bawanypeck/Görke, FsHaas 36, 45 ("Die reinen Söhne des Priesters"), THeth. 26:152 ("low-ranking sacred SANGA-priests"), *šankun*(*n*)*i-* 1 a 6′; ("The scepter bearer then goes out") *n=aš ANA* ᴸᵁ́SANGA KÙ.GA EN ᵁᴿᵁ*Ḫatti* ᴹᵁᴺᵁˢAMA.DINGIR-*LIM* ᵈ*Ḫalkiaš peran ḫūwai* "He runs in front of the consecrated priest, the lord of Ḫatti (and) the *šiwanzanna*-priestess of Ḫalki" KBo 4.9 v 25-26 (*ANDAḪŠUM*-fest. for ZABABA, OH/NS), ed. Badalì/Zinko, Scientia 20:50f. ("dem 'reinen Priester'"); GIM-*an=ma=at* ᴱ́*ḫilamni šarā aranzi nu=kan šu-up-pí-iš* ᴸᵁ́SANGA *ŠA* ᴱ́*ḫeštā U* 3 LÚ.MEŠ ᴱ́*ḫeštā šarāzziya* ᴱ́*ḫilamni ištarni pedi anda tianzi* "But when they arrive up at the portico, the consecrated priest of the *ḫešta*-house and three men of the *ḫešta*-house step into the center of the upper portico" VS 28.5 i 10-14 (*ANDAḪŠUM*-fest., OH/LNS), ed. Alp, Tempel 284f. (as VAT 7470), translit. DBH 6:8, cf. Otten, OLZ 50:390 n. 2 (as VAT 7470); UGULA ᴸᵁ́.ᴹᴱŠMUḪALDIM LUGAL-*i ḫarnaišar pāi* LUGAL-*uš ḫappēni peššiēzzi* ⸢ᴸᵁ́*ḫ*⸣*eš*⸢*tūm*⸣*ašš=a šu-up-pa-i* ᴸᵁ́SANGA *ḫarnāišar pāi šu-up-pí-iš* ᴸᵁ́SANGA *ḫappēni peššiēzzi* "The overseer of the cooks gives *ḫarnaišar* to the king, the king throws (it) into the flame and the man of the *ḫešta*-house gives *ḫarnaišar* to the consecrated priest; the consecrated priest throws it into the flame" KUB 58.50 iii 8-12 (fest., NS), translit. DBH 18:133, cf. ibid. 13-19; GAL

*MEŠEDI zāu* KÙ.BABBAR *ŠA* $^{LÚ}$SANGA *šu-up-pa-ia-aš ŠA* $^{URU}$*Zippalanda udai* "The chief of the guards brings the silver *zau* of the consecrated priest of the city of Zippalanda" KBo 10.26 i 28-31 (KI.LAM-fest., OH/NS), translit. StBoT 28:42, tr. THeth. 26:149; (Several cult officials have been hurling cheeses at each other) *nu* GA.KIN.AG *EMṢU šu-up-pa-e-e[š]* / *[az]zikanzi šaknuwanteš=ma* ⌈*U*⌉*L adanzi UL āra* "The consecrated ones eat the sour cheese, but the defiled ones do not eat; it is forbidden" KUB 45.49 iv 8-10 (rit., NH), ed. THeth 24:57f., translit. ChS 1/8:107; for the immediately preceding context see *šai-* B, *šiye-* 5 b 2′ b′ □ one wonders whether those hit by cheeses became ritually impure and were no longer considered sacred or holy and thus unfit to eat while the unsoiled ones got to eat the cheeses; *[šu-up-p]a-e-eš* $^{LÚ.MEŠ}$*ḫapiēš* KBo 21.95 i 22 (OH/NS), ed. Nakamura, FsDinçol 536, 538 ("rein"); EGIR-*anda=ma* $^{MUNUS.MEŠ}$*katrēš šu-up-pa-e-eš* $^{LÚ}$AZU=*ya* ÍD-*i pānzi* "Afterwards the consecrated *katra*-women and the exorcist go to the river, (and wash with natron two animal figurines belonging to the god)" KBo 23.1 iii 25-27 (Ammiḫatna's rit., NH), ed. Strauß, Reinigung 260, 266 ("rein"), cf. also Miller, CRRAI 47:423.

**3′** humans unspecified: *[m]ān* UN-*aš UL šu-up-pí-iš* "If a person is not consecrated/not ritually pure" HSM 3644 ii 8 (shelf list, NH), ed. Dardano, StBoT 47:130f. ("rein"); 3 UDU *šu-up-pí-iš* MUNUS-*za pāi* "A consecrated woman gives three sheep" KUB 42.103 iii? 7 (cult of Teššub, LNS); *mān antuwaḫḫaš šu-up-pí‹-iš› nu=šši* NINDA-*an maršan kuiški adanna pāi našma=šši* UZU.Ì *maršan adanna pāi našma=šši* NINDA-*an* UZU.Ì *alwanzaḫḫan kuiški adanna pāi* § *našma=šši ŠA* É.NA$_4$ NINDA-*an* UZU.Ì *kuiški adanna pāi našma=šši ŠA* MUNUS *tuēkki=šši ēšḫar akuwanna pāi nu kī* SÍSKUR *šipandaḫḫi* "If a person is consecrated, and someone gives him ritually impure bread to eat, or he gives him ritually impure fat to eat, or someone gives him bewitched bread (and/or) fat to eat, § or someone gives him bread (and/or) fat from a mausoleum to eat, or he gives him blood from (lit. on/in) the body of a woman to drink, I offer this ritual" KBo 5.2 i 3-9 (Ammiḫatna's rit., MH/NS), ed. Strauß, Reinigung 220, 233 ("(kultisch) rein"), Mouton, HR 55:50 w. n. 29; cf. in the colophon of this rit. referring to all the above: *mān* UN-*aš šu-up-iš nu=šši marša kuiški kuitki pāi* "If a person is consecrated and someone gives something ritually impure to him" ibid. iv 64-65, ed. Strauß, Reinigung 233, 245, cf. GrHL §1.12; *[m]ān* DUMU.MUNUS=*ma šu-up-pí-iš* "But if the girl is consecrated/ritually pure" KBo 47.217:3 (omen frag., MS); [...]*šu-up-pí-iš* MUNUS-*za* URU.DU$_6$[...] Bo 6223 iii 7 (fest. frag., LNS).

**4′** eyes: (The Aranzaḫ River says to Gurparanzaḫu:) *kuwat=wa weškiši nu=wa=ta=kkan šu-up-pa-ia-za [šaku]waza išḫaḫru parā ārš[zi]* "Why are you crying? Why do tears flow from your holy eyes?" KUB 17.9 i 20-22 (Gurparanzaḫu story, NS), ed. Pecchioli Daddi, FsFronzaroli 484f. ("pure").

**5′** hair: ("As to the newborn child") *n=aš šu-up-pí-iš tētanuš [ḫ]amiktat* "He, namely (his) ritually pure hair, was bound" KBo 3.8 iii 32 (incantation, NH), ed. Oettinger, Official Religion 350f. ("die reinen Haare"), Kronasser, Die Sprache 7:157, 159 ("die (kultisch) reinen Haare"); in the join piece this is later resumed by *n=an šu-up-pa-uš tetanuš ḫuekdu* "she (i.e., the midwife) shall utter a spell over it (i.e., the child), namely (his) ritually pure hair" KUB 7.1 iii 12 (NH), and *n=an šu-up-pa-uš tetanuš lāūn* "I released him, namely (his) ritually pure hair" KUB 7.1 iii 20-21 (NH), ed. Oettinger, Official Religion 351f. ("die reinen Haare"), Kronasser, Die Sprache 7:158f. ("die reinen Haare") □ confusing *š.* here with $^{UZU}$*šuppa* "meat" q.v. the dupl. (KUB 60.17 rev. 3-4 +) KUB 43.52 iii 14(-15) mistakenly adds the det. UZU: $^{UZU}$*šu-up-pa-u[š]* / [(*tetanuš* KI.MIN)].

**c.** animals: ("The Sungod made a party, and he [su]mmoned up the great [gods]; [he summoned up] the minor gods") *[nu=w]a=z šu-up-pa-uš* TI$_8$$^{MUŠEN.ḪI.A}$ *kallešta* "and he summoned up the sacred eagles" KBo 12.89 iii 13 (incantation, MS), ed. Torri, FsWilhelm 388f. ("the pure eagles"), translit. StBoT 30:243, cf. also ibid. iii 1-2; GÚ.ŠEŠ-*aš* UR.MAḪ-*aš* GIM-*an šu-up-pí-iš* $^{GUD}$*še[rin]* $^{GUD}$*ḫurrin arḫa āriškezzi* "Like a holy lion the bitter vetch washes off the bulls Še[ri] (and) Ḫurri" VBoT 120 ii 5-6 (Allaituraḫi's rit., MH/NS), ed. Haas/Thiel, AOAT 31:140f., ChS 1/5:133 ii 19 ("rein/gelb?"), *pašiḫai-* 1 (w. unnecessary emendation); *nu kē* MUŠEN.⌈ḪI⌉.A ⌈SILA$_4$⌉.ḪI.A 1 AMAR=*y[a]* ⌈*šu*⌉-*up-pa-e-eš UL=aš kuiški ēzzazi*

"And these birds, lambs, and one calf are sacred; no one will eat them" KBo 8.86 obv. 13-14 (rit. for Mt. Ḫazzi, MS?), translit. ChS 1/9:172.

**d.** things — **1′** bed: *īt šuppiyaḫḫut* [*šu-up*]*-pí-ia-aš* GIŠNÁ*-aš šeškiyaḫḫut* "Go, make yourself ritually pure and sleep on a [ho]ly bed" KBo 3.16 iii 8-9 (Naram-Sîn, OH/NS), ed. Güterbock, ZA 44:54-57; [... *š*]*u-up-pa-ia-aš* GIŠNÁ*-aš* ALAM *iwar iyan*[*du*] "Let them make [...] like an image on the [h]oly bed" KUB 39.23 obv. 6 (rit. for Ḫamrišḫara, NS), ed. HTR 94f. ("rein"); LUGAL*-uš* É.ŠÀ*-na paizzi šu-up-pa-ia-aš* «*nu*»? GIŠNÁ!*-aš nu* (over eras.) GIŠBANŠUR *peran tianzi* "The king goes into the inner chamber and to the holy beds; and they place a table in front" (and the king sacrifices a sheep to two deities) KUB 2.13 ii 51-52 (monthly festival, OH/NS), ed. StBoT 37:554f. w. comments 579, translit. DBH 30:90 □ although not noted in the handcopy or ed. there is a partially erased *nu* preceding *šuppayaš* with a second *nu* right after GIŠNÁ*-aš*, which is written over erasure; cf. KUB 10.89 v 5-7, 11-12 (OH/NS), KUB 11.17 v 7-9 (OH/NS), KBo 10.28 iii 7-8 (KI.LAM fest., OH/NS); LUGAL*-u*[*š šu-u*]*p-pa-aš* GIŠNÁ*-aš* GAL*-AM ek*[*uz*]*i* "The king drinks a cup on the holy bed" KBo 17.74 iv 24-25 + KBo 48.128 rev. 5-6 (thunder fest., OH/MS); LUGAL*-uš šu-up-pa-aš* GIŠN[Á*-aš* ...] *šeškezz*[*i*] "The king sleeps on the holy be[d]" KBo 20.88 i 11-12 (fest. frag., MS?); cf. *šašta-*.

**2′** bed(roll): [*l*]*ukkatti kuin* [...] *INA* É.DINGIR*-LIM šar*[*ā* ...] *pēdai nu ap*⸢*ē*⸣[()...] *išpanti* MUNUS*taniti*[(-) ...] *INA* É*ZARATI*-x[...] *šu-up-pa-i* É.ŠÀ*-ni* [...] *šu-up-pa-i šašt*[*i* ...] DUG*šašanuš⸗kan* [*tianzi* ...] "Which (acc.) [...] at dawn, [...] up into the temple [...] s/he carries [...], and [(with/in(to)/of)] that/those [...]. At night the temple-slave [...]. In the tent [...] in the holy inner chamber [...] on the holy bedroll [...]. [They set up] the lamps" KBo 48.86:2-9 (NS), translit. DBH 38:61.

**3′** birthstool: ("If a woman is (seated) upon the birth stool, and the dish (DUGLIŠ.GAL) of the birth stool is damaged, or a peg is broken, and if the woman is not yet giving birth, she will (remain) seated right there, and they open up the windows") *nu namma UL šu-up-pí* "but it (i.e., the birth stool) is no longer (in a state of being) consecrated (i.e., ritually pure)" KBo 5.1 i 6 (Papanikri's rit., MH/NS), ed. Mouton, Naissance 95, 102 ("Elle [= la chaise à accoucher] n'est plus consacrée"), eadem, HR 55:46 w. n. 15, Strauß, Reinigung 286, 295 ("und (sie) ist nicht mehr (kultisch) rein"), StBoT 29:116 w. nn. 306-7 ("it (the birth stool) is no longer pure"), Pap. 2*f. ("Sie ist nun nicht mehr (kultisch) rein"), tr. ChS I/9:69 ("doch ist (der Ort) nun nicht mehr rein") □ the sg. nom.-acc. neut. of *š.* cannot refer to the woman (unless one emends to *šu-up-pí*‹*-iš*›, see KBo 5.2 i 3). The only other relevant item is the birthstool itself (mainly neut. in this text, cf. i 7, 12, 26, 31, 39, com. only in i 44) with the dish and pegs, which has become ritually impure because it has suffered damage.

**4′** bread, meal: *n⸗ašta šu-up-pa-uš* NINDA.GUR$_4$.RA.ḪI.A *anda* É.ŠÀ*-ni pēda*[*nzi*] "[They] carry consecrated breads into the inner chamber" KBo 20.53 ii 4 (cult of Ḫuwaššanna, MS), ed. Lombardi, SMEA 41:236, 239 ("pure"); *nu šu-up-pí-iš* 7 NINDA.GUR$_4$.RA SIG (var. [... NINDA.GUR$_4$.R]A.ḪI.A SIG ⸢*šu*!*-up*⸣*-pí-in*) KBo 29.188 iv 9 (cult of Ḫuwaššanna, MS), w. dupl. KBo 29.189:1 (MS), ed. Lombardi, SMEA 41:238, 241 ("ritualmente pure"); *šu-up-pa* NINDA.ḪI.A MUNUS.MEŠ NA4ARA$_5$ *dānzi* "The women of the mill take consecrated loaves of bread" IBoT 1.29 rev. 28 (*ḫaššumaš*-fest., MH?/MS?), ed. Mouton, JANER 11:10, 16 (differs); (see also below 8′ food and NINDA*šuppi-* B); [*šu-*]*up-pí mema*[*l*] "consecrated meal" KBo 48.74:2 (NS).

**5′** containers — **a′** an animal-shaped vessel (*BIBRU*): [...]*⸗kan šu-up-pa-ia BIBRU wa*[-...] KBo 23.65:4 (NS).

**b′** *nu⸗za* MUNUS*katriš šu-up-pí-in* DUG A KÙ.BABBAR *dāi* "A *katra*-woman takes a consecrated silver water jug" KUB 32.133 i 18 (rit. dividing the Night Goddess, Murš. II), ed. StBoT 46:313f. ("pure").

**6′** festivals and rituals: [*n*]*u⸗tta* EZE[(N$_4$.ḪI.A)] SÍSKUR *INA* KUR URU*Ḫatti* (var. + *⸗pat*) *p*[(*ark*)]*ui šu-up-pí piškanzi* "In Ḫatti-Land (var. only) do they provide festivals (and) ritual(s) for you in a pure (and) holy manner" KUB 24.1 i 21-23 (prayer to Telipinu, Murš. II), w. dupl. KUB 24.2 i 18-19, ed. Kassian/Yakubovich, FsKošak 429, 433 ("festivals and rituals ... in a pure and holy manner"), Lebrun, Hymnes 181, 185 ("propre (et) sacrée"), tr. Hittite Prayers 55 ("pure and holy festivals"), Hutter, Purity 164.

**7′** fire: [...[GIŠ]]AB-*yaš šu-up-pí paḫḫur paraiš* "He kindled/fanned the sacred fire at the windows [...]" KUB 55.37 iii? 8 (rit., NS), ed. *parai-* A 2 a, translit. DBH 4:60.

**8′** food: *šiuni≠mi≠ma≠mu kuit šu-up-pí adanna natta ara n≠at UL kuššanka edun* "At no time did I eat what was sacred to my god and forbidden for me to eat" KUB 30.10 obv. 13 (prayer of Kantuzzili, OH/MS), ed. Lebrun, Hymnes 112, 116 ("sacrée"), THeth 24:46, tr. Hittite Prayers 32 ("holy"); see also KBo 8.86 obv. 13-14 (rit. for Mt. Ḫazzi, MS?); *šuppa tianzi* EGIR-*ŠU šu-up-pa ēšzi* "They place the meat. Thereafter, (it) is sacred" KBo 4.11 obv. 13 (Ištanuwian fest., NS), ed. HEG Wa 344, translit. StBoT 30:339, DLL 163.

**9′** hearth, brazier: ("[Stan]ding, [the king(?)] drinks to" a series of deities and/or divine entities, among which:) [[d]*Izzumi*]*n* [LÚ]SUKKAL! [d]*Kallen* [*mīūn*] MUNUS-*an* ⌈*šu-up-pí* GUNNI⌉ [*kanu*]*ššari*[*y*]*a*[*nta*]*n* [LÚ]SANGA ..."[Izzum]i, (his, i.e., Ea's) vizier, Kalli, [the gentle] woman, [knee]ling at the sacred hearth, the priest ..." KBo 45.25 ii 17-19 (= KBo 13.128 ii 1-5) (LNS), w. dupl. KUB 51.79 rev.? 22 (NS), for further restorations see the pars. KUB 60.40 (= Bo 1303):2-3 (LNS) and KUB 58.43 v 4-5 (NS) (for both see Popko/Taracha, AoF 15:104f.), ed. Popko/Taracha, AoF 15:102, 106f. □ according to Popko/Taracha, AoF 15:104, unpubl. Bo 6925 has an acc. *šuppin* GUNNI-*an*. Unless this is a scribal mistake (thus Popko/Taracha, AoF 15:104 n. 54) the hearth would be one of the divine entities that the king drinks to; [...] *šu-up-pa-ia-aš* GU[NNI.HI.A-*aš*] *warnuwanzi* "They burn [...] on the sacred bra[ziers]" KUB 35.135 rev. 28 (Ištanuwian fest, NS), translit. StBoT 30:323, DLL 166 (w. restoration).

**10′** liver: UDU≠*ma maḫḫan arḫa ḫappišnanzi nu* [UZU]NÍG.GIG *šu-up-pi ḫūišu* [UZU]GABA≠*pat* [UZU]SAG.⌈DU⌉ [UZU]GÌR.MEŠ KUŠ UDU≠*ya* (var. adds [NA4]*ḫ*[*uwašiya*]) *tiyanzi* "But when they dismember the sheep, they place the ritually pure, raw (remainder of the) liver, the breast, the head, the feet and the hide of the sheep (var. adds: at the *ḫ*[*uwaši*]-stone)" (while they roast the shoulder) KUB 32.123 iii 48-50 (Ištanuwian fest., OH/NS), w. dupl. KUB 55.65 iii 36-37 (NS), translit. StBoT 30:311 □ the alternative, taking *šu-up-pi* as a mistake for *šu-up-pa* 'meat', with the raw meat referring to the meaty body parts is unlikely. The slaughter and sacrifice of the sheep takes place in multiple steps. First, part of the liver (and heart in the var.) is roasted, covered by bread crumbs and placed at the *ḫuwaši* stone (KUB 32.123 iii 35-40). When the sheep is further dismembered, the non-meaty body parts are placed at the *ḫuwaši*-stone as well, while only the shoulder is roasted. Only in the final stage, when butchering the torso (UDU≠*ma≠kan ḫūmandan marka*[(*nzi*)] KUB 32.123 iii 54, w. dupl. KUB 55.65 iii 40), the meaty parts are removed and used to prepare a plain stew (KUB 32.123 iii 54-55).

**11′** plants and trees — **a′** *ḫappuriya*-plant: [...]-*zi ḫappuriyan≠ma šu-up-pí-in* [...]x-*ia ezzazzi* "[(s)he ... ]-s, but (s)he eats the sacred *ḫappuriya*-plant [...]" KBo 12.89 ii 13-14 (incantation against diseases, MS), ed. HW[2] Ḫ 257a ("(kultisch) reines Kraut"), translit. StBoT 30:242; *šu-up-pí-iš ḫa*[*ppuriyaš*] KBo 23.48 obv. 8 (rit., NS).

**b′** garlic or onion is called *šuppiwašḫar*, q.v., which may be a calque of Sumerian SUM. SIKIL[SAR]. If so, *šuppi-* = Sum. SIKIL.

**c′** (bul)rush: ("The meadows of the Stormgod were released") [*n≠ašta*] *anda šu-up-pí šumanza lāttat* "In them the sacred rushes have been released" KBo 3.8 iii 24 (rit., NH), ed. Oettinger, Official Religion 350, Melchert, IdgNomen 130.

**d′** trees: [...]x *šu-up-pí* GIŠ.ḪI.A *daḫḫi* "I will take [...] sacred trees [...]" KUB 35.148 ii 10 (Zuwi's rit., OH/NS).

**12′** songs: [ ... *šu-u*]*p-pa-uš* SÌR.ḪI.A S[ÌR-*RU*] "[They] si[ng sa]cred songs" KUB 47.39 obv.? 8 (NS), translit. ChS 1/2:461.

**13′** staff: ("He who is the $GUDU_{12}$-priest of Nerik") *nu≠kan šu-up-pí* [GIŠ]GIDRU *ē*[*pzi*] "[hol]ds a sacred staff" KUB 42.100 i 8 (inventories of sanctuaries, Tudḫ. IV), ed. Hazenbos, Organization 17, 21 ("pure").

**14′** table: *n≠ašta* UGULA LÚ.MEŠ [GIŠ]BANŠUR *šu-up-pí* [GIŠ]BANŠUR *anda udai*

"The overseer of the table-men brings in the holy table" KBo 4.9 iv 26-27 (*ANDAḪŠUM* fest., OH?/NS); LÚ $^{\text{GIŠ}}$BANŠUR=*kan* 2 NINDA.KU$_7$ *šu-up-pa-ia-az* (var. [*šu*]-*up-pa-az*) $^{\text{GIŠ}}$BANŠUR-*za dāi* … *t*=*uš*=*kan* $^{\text{LÚ}}$SAGI.A EGIR-*pa šu-up-pí* (var. [*š*]*u-up-pa-i*) $^{\text{GIŠ}}$BANŠUR-*i dāi* "The table man takes two sweet loaves from the holy table … and the cupbearer puts them back on the holy table" KUB 2.5 i 21-24 (*ANDAḪŠUM* fest., LNS), w. dupl. KUB 25.1 ii 50-54, ed. Badalì/Zinko, Scientia 20:31f., 52 ("reinen"); cf. KBo 30.56 v 5-11 (fest., NS), translit. DBH 2:75; KBo 17.74 ii 36-37 (OH/MS), ed. StBoT 12:22f.; KBo 27.42 iii 63-68 (KI.LAM-fest, OH/NS), translit. StBoT 28:48; KBo 17.88 + KBo 24.116 ii 10 (fest. of the month, OH/MS), ed. StBoT 37:306f., compared w. $^{\text{GIŠ}}$BANŠUR *šuppi* ibid. KBo 20.67 i 12 (same tablet), KUB 10.21 iii 12-14 (fest., OH/NS).

**15′** temples and other holy places incl. features of the physical world — **a′** temple: [(*mā*)*n*] *INA* É DINGIR-*LIM šu-up-pí kuin* [(*imma maršaštarrin*) *wemiy*]*anzi* "If they [find] any sacrilege whatsoever in a holy temple" KBo 7.74 ii 6-7 (shelf list, NH), w. dupl. HSM 3644 ii 4-5 (Güterbock, JCS 19:33) (NH), ed. StBoT 47:152f.; *nu*=*kan nepiš šu-up-pa* É.MEŠ DINGIR.MEŠ $^{\text{d}}$*Ḫebaddunn*=*a anda ištappaš* "It (i.e., the monster) blockaded heaven, the sacred houses of the gods, and Ḫebat" KUB 33.106 iii 37-38 (Ullik. III A, NH), ed. Güterbock, JCS 6:26f., tr. Hittite Myths$^2$ 64; cf. ibid. iv 27-28.

**b′** a place in a temple: *mān*=*kan INA* É DINGIR-*LIM anda šu-up-*[*p*]*a-i* (var. *šu-up-pa*⟨*-i*⟩) *pedi kuin imma kuin maršaštarrin wemiyanzi* "If in a temple in a holy place they find any kind of desecration" ABoT 1.28 obv. 2-5 + ABoT 1.29 ii 19-21 = KBo 23.1 ii 19-21 (colophon of Ammiḫatna,Tulbi&Mātī's rit., NH), ed. Strauß, Reinigung 263, 269, Lebrun, Hethitica 3:144, 151f. for the par. from cat. entry KUB 30.42 iv 22 see ed. StBoT 47:28f., 37; cf. the incipit of the same rit.: *mān*=*kan INA* É DI[(NGIR-*LIM anda šu-up-*)*p*(*a*)]-*i pedi itḫiuš kuiški anda dā*[(*i*)] § *na*⸢*šm*⸣*a*=*kan kuin imma apēdani p*[(*ed*)]*i ma*⸢*rš*⸣*aštarrin andan iyazi* "If in a temple in a holy place someone puts *itḫi*-s (§) or commits any kind of desecration in that place" KBo 23.1 i 3-6 + ABoT 1.29 i 3-5, w. dupl. ABoT 1.28 obv. 8-11 + ABoT 1.29 ii 25-28 = KBo 23.1 ii 25-28, ed. Strauß, Reinigung 258, 264; *šu-up-pa-i pedi* KBo 12.3 iv 7, 8 (Anum-Ḫirbe&Zalpa, OH/NS); (When a person reaches a *šinapši*-building and sits down) *nu*=*šši*=*kan* $^{\text{LÚ}}$*patiliš* SILA$_4$ *arḫa dāi n*=*an*=*kan šu-up-pa-i pedi anda pēdai* "the *patili*-priest takes a lamb away from her and carries it into the holy place" KBo 5.1 iv 24-26 (Papanikri's rit., NH), ed. Strauß, Reinigung 294, 303 ("den reinen/geweihten Platz"), Pap. 12*f.

**c′** an inner room: 1 $^{\text{GUD}}$ÁB … *šu-up-pí* É.⸢ŠÀ-*ni*⸣ BAL-*ti* "He offers one cow (and other items) … in the holy inner room" KBo 4.11 obv. 3-4 (Ištanuwa chant, NS), translit. StBoT 30:339; *šu-up-pa-i* (var. *šu-up-pí*) É.ŠÀ-*ni* KBo 11.43 vi 7 (*nuntarriyašḫaš*-fest., Tudḫ. IV), w. dupl. KUB 20.50 vi 7, ed. Nakamura, Nuntarriyašḫa 181f.; *šu-up-pí* É.ŠÀ-*ni* KBo 45.74 ii 16 (fest. naming the NIN.DINGIR, NS); EGIR-*ŠU* É.ŠÀ KÙ.GA *ekuzi* "After that he drinks (to) the holy inner chamber" KBo 4.11 rev. 42 (NS), translit. StBoT 30:341.

**d′** a place for washing oneself: ("On that day I will instruct my servant":) *šalimani*=*wa šu-up-pa-a-i pāimi nu*=*wa*=*za maḫḫan ḫūdā*⸢*k*⸣ *ārraḫḫi nu*=*wa*=*mu* $^{\text{TÚG}}$NÍG.LÁM=*YA parā ḫūdāk* [*p*]*āi* "I am going to the sacred *šaliman*(*i*)-, and as soon as I bathe, quickly hand me my festive garment" KUB 57.63 i 5-8 (rit. frag., NS), ed. Archi, FsOtten$^2$ 16f., *šaliman*(*i*?)-.

**e′** mountains: *mān*=*ma* ḪUR.SAG=*ma kuiški našma šinapši šu-up-pa AŠRU kuitki* ḪUL-*aḫḫan* "But if some mountain or *šinapši*, holy places, have been offended in any way" KBo 11.1 obv. 32 (prayer, Muw. II), ed. Houwink ten Cate, RHA XXV/81:107, 116, *šinapši-* d, tr. Hittite Prayers 84 ("holy place"); ḪUR.SAG-*i šu-up-pa-i pedi kuwapit* [*w*]*ātar ēšzi* "On the mountain, in a holy place where there is [w]ater (h/she makes a statue of a god)" KUB 9.28 i 10-11 (rit. of Heptad, MH/NS); ("You, O eagle, take them (i.e., these evils) and carry them to heaven, and let them perish there; you, O falcon take them") [*n*=]*at šu-up-pa-ia-aš* ḪUR.SAG.MEŠ *peda n*=*at ar*⸢*ḫa peḫ*⸣*ute* "[a]nd carry them to the holy mountains, and lead them away" KBo 13.131 rev. 11-12 (rit., MH/NS).

**f′** rivers and springs: *nu ANA* ⌈ÍD⌉*Ar*⌈*an*⌉*zaḫi šu-up-pí* ÍD-*i* 1 GUD.MAḪ 7 UDU.ḪI.A=*ya ḫūēkta* "And he slaughtered one bull and seven sheep to the Aranzaḫ, the sacred River" KBo 22.6 i 16-17 (*šar tamḫari*, OH?/NS), ed. Güterbock, MDOG 101:19, 22 ("heiligen"), translit. Rieken, ICH 4 = StBoT 45:578; *mān* GIŠGU.ZA dU NA4ZI.KIN *kuiški katta laknut našma=kan šu-up-pa* TÚL *kuiški šaḫta* "If someone has knocked over the throne of the Stormgod, a stela, or if someone has blocked a sacred spring" KBo 11.1 obv. 40, ed. Houwink ten Cate, RHA XXV/81:108, 117, tr. Hittite Prayers 84 ("sacred spring") □ for *šu-up-pa* as a sg. nom.-acc. neut. see *šu-up-pa ... wātar* KUB 27.29 iii 5 (Allaituraḫi's rit., MH/NS), see at 17′, below; ("Just as the wind disperses chaff and carries it across the sea, may it (i.e., the holy water) also likewise disperse the blood (and) uncleanliness of this house, and may it carry them across the sea §") *n=aš=šan* (var. *n=at=kan*) [(*and*)]*a* ḪUR.SAG-*aš šu-up-pa-ia-aš paiddu* "Let it go into the holy mountains" KUB 41.8 ii 20 (rit. for the netherworld, MH/NS), w. dupl. KBo 10.45 ii 55 (MH/NS), ed. Otten, ZA 54:126f. ii 57 □ the subj. of *paiddu* is either the aforementioned evils (all neut.) or the holy water (*šuppiš* A-*anta*) that will carry them across the sea; the var. *=at* fits the former, the com. gender *=aš* the latter; cf. [1 UDU 1 DUG*P*]*IḪU A*[*NA*] TÚL*šu-up-pa-aš* KBo 49.308 obv. 10 (cult inv., NS); cf. also the river and GN Šuppiluliya, for which see RGTC 6 and 6/2 s.vv.

**g′** uninhabited place: [...]x *dammili šu-up-pa-i pedi* [...] "[...] in an uninhabited holy place [...]" KBo 3.21 iv 11 (hymn to Adad, OH?/NS), ed. Archi, Or NS 52:24, 26 ("reinen Ort"); cf. *peda-* A e 12′.

**h′** holy (place) (abbreviated writing?): *mān=kan* d*Ḫalputiliš šu-up-pa-i šarā paizz*[*i*] "If Ḫalputili goes up to the holy (place)" KUB 12.4 iv 7 (cult inv., NH); *ḫāš nu kuēz uwaši šu-up-pa-az=wa uwami nu=wa kuēz šu-up-pa-ia-az zaḫanittennaz=wa nu=wa kuēz zaḫanittennaz* dUTU-*waš=wa* É-*az nu=wa kuēz* dUTU-*az ēšri=šet=wa* GIBIL-*an* GABA=*ŠU* GIBIL [SAG]=*SU=wa* GIBIL-*an* LÚ-*tar=šet=wa nēwan* "Open (the door)! Where do you come from? I come from the holy (place). From what holy (place)? From the cult room(?). From what cult room(?)? From the Sungod's house. From what Sungod? The one whose form is new, whose chest is new, whose [head] is new, (and) whose penis (lit. manhood) is new!" KBo 21.22:22-26 (blessings for the Labarna, OH/MS), ed. StBoT 62:266, Archi, FsMeriggi[2] 46f. ("un (luogo) puro"), Kellerman, TelAviv 5:200, 202 ("pure") □ on *ḫāš* as imp. sg. 2 see Rieken, StBoT 44:21 n. 75.

**16′** wall: *nu kuttan apē*⌈*z*⌉ [*a*]*rranzi nu kūzza šu-up-pí-iš* "They wash the wall with that (i.e., water, with which they have washed the temple), and the wall (becomes) sacred" KUB 29.4 iv 26-27 (rit., NH), ed. StBoT 46:295f. ("pure"), Schw.Gotth. 30f., tr. Collins, CoS 1:176 ("pure"), see also Beal, Magic and Ritual 207 ("ritually pure").

**17′** water: DUMU É.[(GA)]L *šu-up-pí wātar parā ēpzi* [(LUGAL)]-*i* MUNUS.LUGAL=*ya* LUGAL-*uš* 3-*ŠU aiš=šet ārri* "A palace servant holds out holy water to the king and queen, (and) the king washes his mouth three times" KBo 17.1 i 14-15 (rit., OS), w. dupl. KBo 17.3 i 9-10 (OS), ed. StBoT 8:18f. ("rein"); *parkunuddu šu-up-pí-iš* A-*anza* ḪUL-*lun* EME-*an*... "Let the holy water purify the evil tongue..." KUB 41.8 ii 14 (rit. for the netherworld, MH/NS), ed. Otten, ZA 54:124f. ii 51 ("heilige"); [*udaš=ka*]*n wattarwaš* MUNUS.LUGAL-*aš šu-up-p*[*í w*]*ātar* "The Queen of the Fountain [brought] hol[y w]ater" (which drove evils from Ḫannaḫanna's body) KUB 33.53:16 + FHG 2 iii 18 (missing deity, OH/NS), ed. Haas, Materia 108 w. n. 496, translit. Myth. 81, tr. Hittite Myths[2] 30; [*nu=ššan šu-u*]*p-pí wātar pappariš*[*an*(?)] "[Ho]ly water is sprinkled upon (it)" HKM 116 ii 25 (rit. in myth, OH/MS), ed. Güterbock, JKF 10:207f.; *ḫener=at šu-up-p*[*í wātar*] "They drew/ladled it, the hol[y water]" KUB 33.34 obv.? 6 (myth, OH/NS), translit. Myth 127, tr. Moore, Thesis. 63; *nu=ššan INA* GA[(L.GIR$_4$ *kui*)]*t šu-up-pí* (var. Ø) *wātar* [(*n=at* MUNUS ŠU.G)]I *dāi nu* É-*er* É.Š[À].ḪI.A É*ḫilan ḫūman šuppia*⌈*ḫḫ*⌉*i* "The Old Woman takes the holy (var. Ø) water which is in the earthenware cup and she consecrates the entire house, the inner rooms, and the courtyard structures" KBo 23.23:62-63 + KBo 33.118:80-81 (Allaituraḫi's rit.?, MH/MS), w. dupl. KUB 27.29 i 20-22 (MH/NS), ed. Haas/Thiel, AOAT 31:210f., ChS 1/5:61; *nu šu-up-pí*! *kuit wātar* ZAG.GAR.RA-*ni* [...] *n=at* MUNUSSUḪUR.LÁ *dāi* "The woman attendant takes the holy water, which [is(?)

on] the altar" KUB 27.29 iii 5-6 (Allaiturahi's rit., MH/ NS), ed. Haas/Thiel, AOAT 31:142f., for the emendation see Melchert, FsKošak 516f. n. 13 but compare also *šuppa* TÚL "holy spring" KBo 11.1 obv. 40, a 15' f', above; ⌜*n*⌝⸗*aš⸗kan šu-up-pí-it we*[(*te*)*n*it (*p*)]*apparšzi* "He sprinkles them (i.e., warm seashells) with holy water" Bo 3686 iii 8-9 (fest., LNS), restored after VBoT 126 ii? 1-2 (NS), KUB 28.105 ii? 4-5 (NS), translit. Otten/Rüster, ZA 64:248; *ANA* DINGIR.MEŠ⸗*kan šu-up-pa* A.MEŠ-*a*[*r* ...] "portions of holy water for the gods" KBo 47.45 rt. col. 3 (frag. Kizz. rit., NS), translit. DBH 33:38.

**18'** words (of a ritual): *nu šu-up-pa* INIM. ḪI.A *ŠA* ᴰᵁᴳÚTUL DU₁₁-*zi* § ... *nu⸗kan šu-up-pa uddār anda memanzi* § ...§ *nu⸗šmaš* ᴸᵁ́·ᴹᴱŠ*ašušatalluš šu-up-pa uddār* ᵈU-*ni* IGI-*anda* DU₁₁-*zi* DIB-*zi* "They pronounce the sacred words of the vessel. § ... and at the same time they speak the sacred words. § ... § The *ašušatalla*-men begin to pronounce the sacred words toward the Storm-god" KBo 4.11 obv. 16, 18, 22-24 (Ištanuwian cult, NS), translit. StBoT 30:339f.; cf. [...]x *šu-up-pa uttār* [...] ABoT 1.35 obv. 5 (fest., OS), translit. StBoT 25:121.

**e.** sg. or pl. nom.-acc. neut. *šuppi, šuppa* used as adv. "in a holy way, ritually pure" — **1'** w. *aku-/eku-* "to drink": [*n⸗ašta*(?) *ša*]*nḫanzi nu šuppa* IŠTU GEŠTIN *akuwanzi* "They [cl]ean up (the locality) and drink from the wine in a holy way" KBo 14.94 ii 14 (cult of Ḫuwaššanna, NS) □ for restoration see *n⸗ašta šanḫan*[*zi* ... ] IŠTU GEŠTIN *šu-up-pa* [...] KBo 24.33 iii? 9-10 (MS); [EGIR]-⌜*an*⌝*da⸗ma šu-up-pa* 7-ŠU IŠTU GAL ⌜GEŠTIN⌝ *akuw*[*anzi*] "[Afterwa]rds [they] drink from a wine cup seven times in a holy way" KUB 27.65 i 9 (cult of Ḫuwaššanna, NS); cf. also *šu-up-pa* 7-ŠU 1 GAL *ekuzi* KUB 54.13 ii 5 (NS).

**2'** w. *ašeš-*: *šu-up-pa⸗ma* ᴸᵁ́·ᴹᴱŠSANGA *ašaši* "but he seats the priests in a holy manner" KUB 25.9 ii 7 (fest., NS), ed. Gonnet, Mém.Atatürk 60f. ("les prêtres sacrés").

**3'** w. (-*za*) *šeš-/šaš-* "to sleep in a holy manner, i.e., for incubation" (see *šeš-/šaš-* 3): [*lukka*]*tti⸗ma⸗za* ᴸᵁ́AŠGAB *šu-up-pí šešz*[*i*] "On the following day a leatherworker sleeps in a holy way" KBo 10.16 iv 9 (cult inv.?, NS); *n⸗at⸗š*(*a*)*maš* (dupls. *n⸗at⸗za*)

*šu-up-pa-ia* (var. *šu-up-pa*) *šeš*[(*kanz*i)] "And they sleep in a holy manner" KUB 14.8 rev. 44 (PP 2 §11, Murš. II), w. dupls. KUB 14.11 iv 17, KUB 14.10 iv 13-14, ed. Götze, KlF 1:218f. ("auf reinem (Bette) erschlafen"), Lebrun, Hymnes 209, 215 ("d'une manière sacrée"), tr. Hittite Prayers 60 ("they shall regularly sleep holy").

**4'** w. *warp-* "to bathe in a holy manner > take a ritual ablution, bathe to ritual purity": [...]x *šu-up-pa warpanzi* "They bathe in a holy way (in order to become ritually pure)" KUB 51.32:6 (rit., NS), translit. DBH 15:54; ("A woman goes off to an *arzana*-house") [*nu*] *šu-up-pa wa*⌜*rp*⌝*anza ēšzi ANA* ᴸᵁ́M[U]TI⸗ŠU⸗*ma mān āššu n*[⸗*aš⸗z*]*a katti⸗ šši* [*ezzazi*?] "and she sits there, bathed to ritual purity, but if her husband so wishes he [eats(?)] with her" KBo 17.65 rev. 25-26 (birth rit., OH/NS), ed. StBoT 29:140f. ("she is washed pure"), cf. Wilhelm, Leviti-kus 204 □ for the *arzana*-house see Mouton, Naissance 80; *INA* É.GAL-*LIM⸗ma šu-up-p*[*a*] *warpuwar* "But in the palace (there is) a holy bathing" KUB 9.16 i 6-7 (*nuntarriyašḫaš* fest., OH/NS), ed. Nakamura, Nuntarriyašḫa 17, 19 ("(findet) die 'Rein'-Waschung (statt)"); see also KUB 55.5 iv? 4-7, IBoT 2.8 iv? 4-5; [...] EGIR-*anda šu-up-pa warpzi šu-up-pa-ia-az-z⸗iy*[*a⸗z* ...-*az/ za i*]*škizzi* "Afterwards he bathes to ritual purity and [a]noints [himself] with ritually pure [oil(?)]" KUB 4.47 rev. 16-17 (rit. against insomnia, NH), ed. Mouton, Rêves 145, 147 ("il se lave de manière (con)sacrée"), Beck-man, FsKošak 70, 74 ("takes a purificatory bath").

**f.** unclear: ("From a cup a palace attendant gives water for sprinkling and an aspergillum(?) is in (it); he sprinkles water [with(?)] the asper-gillum(?) once") *tamaiš⸗ma* [DUMU].⌜É⌝.GAL *tuppaz šu-up-pí-in ḫarzi* [...]x LUGAL-*i parā ēpzi* [LUGAL-*u*]*š šu-up-pí-in* 3-ŠU *kuwašzi* "while an-other [p]alace attendant holds a *š.* in (lit. with/ from) a basket/box and he presents (it) to the king. [The ki]ng kisses the *š.* three times" KBo 27.40 obv.? 9-12 (fest., NS), ed. Kühne, Eothen 10:108f. □ According to Kühne *š.* is an inanimate cult object, which has to be kept separate from both *šuppi-* A "holy, sacred" and ᴺᴵᴺᴰᴬ*šuppi-* B "*šuppi*-bread."

Although *š.* can describe deities or divine entities (a, c, and d, "holy, sacred") it is mostly used to describe the perfect condition that renders a person or object fit to be in divine presence (b, c and d, "consecrated"; see Wilhelm, Levitikus 203). As representatives of the gods and intermediaries between the divine and human worlds, the king and certain priests qualify as "holy, sacred." In relation to *parkui-* "pure, clean" (q.v.) *š*. can be seen as hierarchically higher so Mouton, HR 55, Hoffner, ICH 3:324f.; (everything *š*. is also *parkui-*, but not everything *parkui-* is necessarily *š*.) or as a special category or subsystem of purity (so Hutter, Purity 166). Once a person (cf. priests in b 2′ KUB 45.49 iv 8-10) or an object (cf. the birthstool in d 3′) becomes unclean or otherwise defective, it is no longer considered *š*. and therefore unfit for a deity or to be in divine presence. Because humans interact with beings and objects that are *š*., it does not mean "taboo for humans," only that such objects are reserved for sacred use. People have to be in a clean state when interacting with someone/something *š*., but when the *š*. entity is taboo it needs to be explicitly mentioned (see d 8′ KUB 30.10 obv. 13). Note also that the opposite of *parkunumar* "cleansing, purification" (q.v.) is *papratar* "impurity, defilement" (q.v.), forms of which are never used in opposition to *š*. and derivatives. The antonym of *š*. is *marša-* "unholy, unfit for sacred space" (q.v.).

Sommer/Ehelolf, Pap. (1924) 7-8; Götze, AM (1933) 233-34; Friedrich, HW (1952) 199; Moyer, Diss. (1969); Melchert, HS 110 (1997) 50; Hoffner, ICH 3 (1998) 323-325; Wilhelm, Levitikus (1999) 197-217; de Martino, Or NS 73 (2004) 348-362; Tischler, HEG S/2 (2006) 1185-1193; Kloekhorst, EDHIL (2008) 789-790; Christiansen, BN 156 (2013) 131-153; Hutter, Purity (2013) 159-174; Feder, JANER 14 (2014) 87-113 (on general notions of purity in the ancient Near East, for *š*. see 98 n. 44); Mouton, HR 55 (2015) 41-64; Puhvel, AJNES 11 (2017) 116-119.

Cf. ⁽ᵁᶻᵁ⁾*šuppa-* B, ᴺᴵᴺᴰᴬ*šuppi-* B, *šuppiyaḫḫ-*, *šuppiyant-*, *šuppiyatar*, *šuppiyauwar*, *šuppiešš-*, *šuppieššar*, *šuppiššar(a)-*, *šuppiššarant-*.

**ᴺᴵᴺᴰᴬšuppi- B** n. com.; (name of a bread or pastry); MH/NS.†

**sg. nom.** ᴺᴵᴺᴰᴬ*šu-up-pí-iš* KBo 10.34 i (5) (MH/NS), KUB 54.49 obv. 3 (MH?/NS).

("Five or six?) warm breads of half a *SŪTU*, among them") 1 ᴺᴵᴺᴰᴬ*šu-up-pí*[*-iš*] 1 NINDA *EMṢU iduriš ŠA* ½ *ŠĀTI* 1 NINDA *EM*[*ṢU*] *naḫḫitiš ŠA* ½ *ŠĀ*[*TI*] "one *š*.-bread, one *iduri*-bread of sourdough of half a *SŪTU*, one *naḫḫiti*-bread of sourdo[ugh] of half a *SŪ*[*TU*]" KBo 10.34 i 5-7 (enthronement of Tudḫ., MH/NS), translit. AlHeth. 184 □ the clear tendency of the scribe of this tablet to justify the last sign of a line to the right and the evidence of KUB 54.49 supports the restoration to a sg. nom. com.; ("Five warm breads of half a *SŪTU*") 2 ᴺᴵᴺᴰᴬ*šu-up-pí-iš* 20[*-iš*?] "Two *š*.-breads (of) twenty [weight-units(?)]" KUB 54.49 obv. 3 (MH?/NS), ed. DBH 1:128 □ for 20-*iš* see DBH 1:38f.

The absence of word space between NINDA and *š*. in both attestations pleads in favor of *š*. as the name of a dough product instead of NINDA being a Sumerogram standing for a separate noun with a modifying adj. ("sacred bread"). Note also clear instances of *šuppi-* A "holy, sacred" preceding NINDA as an adj. in *šuppi-* A d 4′. Whether *š*. is related to the adj. *šuppi-* A remains an open question.

Hoffner, AlHeth. (1974) 184f., Hagenbuchner, DBH 1 (2002) 127f.

***šuppe- C** v., see *šuppiyauwar.*

**šuppiyaḫḫ-, šuppaḫḫ-** v.; to make holy or sacred, consecrate; to ritually purify, clean (antonym: *maršanu-*); wr. syll. and KÙ; from OS.

**act. pres. sg. 1** *šu-up-pí-ia-aḫ-mi* KUB 14.15 i 7 (Murš. II), HSM 3644:6 (Güterbock, JCS 19:33) (NH), *šu-up-pa-aḫ-*[*mi*] KUB 56.12:7 (NH); **sg. 3** *šu-up-pí-ia-aḫ-ḫi* KUB 29.30 iii (7), 11 (OS), KUB 43.30 ii 3, 10 (OS), KUB 12.5 i 6 (MH/MS), KUB 32.49a ii 12 (MH/MS), KBo 6.26 i 32, 43, 49 (OH/NS), KBo 11.26 obv. 5 (LNS), *šu-up-pí-aḫ-ḫi* KBo 20.10 i 11, ii 8 (OS), KBo 23.23:63 (MH/MS), KUB 20.99 ii 7 (NS), *šu-up-*‹*pí-*›*ia-aḫ-ḫi* KUB 20.24 iii 8 (NS), *šu-up-pí-ia-ḫi* KBo 27.40 rev.? 3 (NS), *šu-up-pí-ia-aḫ-*[*z*]*i* KUB 34.69 obv. 15 + KUB 34.70 i 7 (NS), IBoT 3.115 rev. 7 (MS), *šu-up-pa-aḫ-zi* KUB 49.94 ii 6 (NH), KÙ*-aḫ-ḫi* KUB 28.89 i 11 (courtesy of Ch. Steitler) (LNS), KUB 58.5 i 13 (NS), for KÙ*-ḫi* VS 28.23 obv. 2 (NS) read KÙ.‹G›I. with DBH 6:45 and cf. *laḫanni-*.

**pres. pl. 3** *šu-up-pí-ia-aḫ-ḫa-an-zi* IBoT 1.29 obv. 28 (MH?/MS?), KBo 5.1 ii 5, 6 (NS), KUB 46.47 rev. 8, 10 (NS), KBo 11.1 obv. 34 (Muw. II), KBo 23.1 ii 5 (Tudḫ. IV), *šu-up-pí-aḫ-ḫa-an-zi* IBoT 1.29 rev. 50 (MH?/MS?), KUB 25.42 iii 3 + KBo 15.47 obv.? rt. col. 16 (NS), KUB 25.18 iv 23 (Tudḫ.

IV), VS 28.1 obv. 9 (LNS), *šu-⟨up-⟩pí-aḫ-ḫa-an-zi* KUB 50.36 iv 7 (NH), KÙ-*an-zi* KUB 53.21 rev. 8 (LNS).

**pret. sg. 1** *šu-up-pí-ia-aḫ-ḫu-un* KUB 19.37 ii 17 (Murš. II), KUB 7.60 iii 17 (NS), IBoT 3.98:6 + KUB 28.82 i 20 (OH?/NS), *šu-up-pí-ia-aḫ-ḫu-u-un* VBoT 120 i 12 (MH/NS); **sg. 3** *šu-up-pí-ia-aḫ-ḫa-aš* KUB 12.43:9 (MS).

**pret. pl. 3** *šu-*⌈*up*⌉*-pí-aḫ-*⌈*ḫe-er*⌉ KBo 41.211 left col. 8 (NS).

**imp. sg. 2** *šu-up-⟨pí-⟩ia-aḫ* KUB 33.5 ii 8 (OH/MS).

**mid. pres. sg. 3** *šu-up-pí-ia-aḫ-ta-ri* KBo 17.78 i 4 (MS), KBo 31.144 obv.? 2 (MS).

**pret. sg. 3** *šu-up-pí-a-aḫ-ḫa-ti* KBo 25.112 ii 14 (OS), *šu-up-pí-ia-aḫ-ḫa-ti* KBo 3.16 rev. 11 (OH/NS), KUB 12.43:9 (MS).

**imp. sg. 2** *šu-up-pí-ia-aḫ-ḫu-ut* KBo 3.16 rev. 8 (OH/NS), KUB 33.52 iii 8 (OH/NS), KBo 15.30 iii 5 (NS), KUB 46.13 iv 12 (NS).

**inf.** *šu-up-pí-aḫ-ḫu-u-an*[*-zi*] KBo 14.142 ii 21 (Murš. II), [*šu-up-p*]*í-ia-aḫ-ḫu-u-wa-an-zi* KBo 31.134:4 (NS).

**verbal subst. sg. nom.-acc.** *šu-up-pí-ia-aḫ-ḫu-u-wa-ar* KBo 11.43 i 10 (OH/NS), KUB 30.63 v? (11), (17) (OH/NS), KBo 11.1 obv. 34 (Muw. II), *šu-up-pí-ia-aḫ-ḫu-u-ar* KBo 24.29 iii 4 (MS), KBo 19.140:(6) (pre-NH/MS), *šu-up-pí-ia-aḫ-ḫu-wa-ar* KUB 17.8 iii 9 (pre-NH/NS), *šu-up-pí-aḫ-ḫu-wa-a*[*r*] KBo 19.137 iv? 6 (pre-NH/NS); **gen.** ⌈*šu-up*⌉*-pí-aḫ-ḫu-u-wa-aš* KUB 31.57 i 24 (OH/NS), KBo 27.192:(1) (MS), *šu-up-pí-ia-aḫ-ḫu-wa-aš* KUB 29.8 iv 37 (MH/MS), [*šu-u*]*p-pí-ia-aḫ-ḫu?-aš* FHG 21 iv 35 (MS), *šu-up-pí-ia-aḫ-ḫu-u-wa-aš* KUB 9.38:6 (NS), KUB 36.30:6 (NS), KÙ-*aḫ-ḫu*[*-wa-aš*] KBo 27.41:4 (LNS).

**part. sg. com. acc.** *šu-up-pí-ia-aḫ-ḫa-an-da-an* IBoT 1.29 obv. 38 (MH?/MS?); **neut. nom.-acc.** *šu-up-pí-ia-aḫ-ḫa-an* KUB 46.47 rev. 4 (NS); **pl. com. acc.** *šu-up-pí-ia-aḫ-ḫa-an-d*[*u-uš*] KBo 45.51 ii 2 (NS).

**imperf. pres. sg. 3** *šu-up-pí-ia-aḫ-ḫi-iš-ke-ez-zi* KUB 43.58 i 44 (MH/MS), KUB 55.39 iii 34 (OH/NS), *šu-up-pí-aḫ-ḫi-iš-ke-ez-zi* KBo 2.29 rev. 4 (NS), *šu-up-pí-aḫ-ḫe-eš-ke-e*[*z-zi*] KBo 30.189:5 (NS); **pl. 3** *šu-up-pí-aḫ-ḫi-iš-kán-*[*zi*] KBo 30.54 ii 7 (NS).

For KÙ here, see Laroche, RHA XIX/68:43; HW 3. Erg. 41; Taracha, NABU 2018/106; Steitler, NABU 2019/23.

**a.** consecrating or ritually purifying human beings, their body parts, or gods — **1′** the Hittite Great King: GAL LÚ.MEŠMUḪ[ALDIM *wā*]*tar araḫza udai nu ḫaššāz* [(*ḫul*)]*liš dāi nu and*[*a*] *peššiezzi ta āppa šarā* [(*dāi*)] *nu* LUGAL-*un* ⌈*šu*⌉*-up-pí-ia*[*-aḫ-ḫi*] *tuḫḫuišar* LUGAL-*i parā ēpzi* [(*nu=z=ka*)]*n tuḫša* "The chief of the cooks brings water from outside, and he takes up a cone from the brazier and throws it in (to the water) and takes it back up, and then consecrates the king: he holds out *tuḫḫuišar* to the king, and (the king) *tuḫš*-s himself" KBo 21.25 i 39-42 + KUB 34.123 i 9-12 (Stormfest., OH/MS), w. dupl. KBo 17.11 i 23-24 + KBo 30.29:2-4 (OS), ed. Barsacchi, StAs 12:31f., 41, Alp, Or NS 52 (FsKammenhuber) 17; (The GUDU$_{12}$-priest of Arinna) *wātar išparnu*[*zzi*] / [... LUGAL]-*un šu-up-pí-ia-aḫ-ḫi* "sprinkles water [and] consecrates the [kin]g" KBo 8.102:6-7 (MS); cf. ibid 12-15; (He leads in the Man of the Stormgod, who bows to the king) *ta* LUGAL-*un šu-up-pí-aḫ-ḫi* [*w*]*atar* 3-*ŠU išparnuzi malti* "He consecrates the king, sprinkles water three times, (and) recites" KBo 20.10 i 11-12 (fest. OS), ed. Alp, Tempel 246, translit. StBoT 25:131; cf. ibid. ii 7-9; LUGAL-*uš=za šu-up-pí-a-aḫ-ḫa-ti ANA* [*ḫal*]*pūti mānḫand*[*a*] *māldi kē=a QĀTAMMA* "The king has consecrated himself. As he chants before(?) the *ḫalputi*, so also (he chants) these things in the same way" KBo 25.112 ii 14-15 (invocation of Ḫattian deities, OS), translit. StBoT 25:191.

**2′** other kings: ("Ištar replied to him (i.e., Naram-Sîn): 'Go'"): *šu-up-pí-ia-aḫ-ḫu-ut* [*šup*]*piyaš* GIŠNÁ-*aš šeškiyaḫḫut* ... [(mNar)]*am*-d*SÎN-naš šu-up-pí-ia-aḫ-ḫa-ti šuppayaš* [(GI)]ŠNÁ-*aš* [*šešk*]*iškiuwan dāiš* "'Consecrate yourself and lie down on a consecrated bed ...' Naram-Sîn consecrated himself and lay down on a consecrated bed" KBo 3.16 rev. 8-9, 11-12 (Naram-Sîn legend, OH/NS), w. dupl. KBo 3.18 + KBo 3.19:12-16 (LNS), ed. Güterbock, ZA 44:54-57.

**3′** a person other than a king: [*nu ap*]*ēdani* GE$_6$-*ti* DUMU.LUGAL *QĀTAMMA šu-up-pí-aḫ-ḫa-an-zi* "[Th]at night they consecrate the prince in the same way ([then] they put him to bed)" IBoT 1.29 rev. 50-51 (fest. of begetting, MH?/MS?), ed. Mouton, JANER 11:11, 17, Güterbock, Midwest AOS (1969) 103, 101 = AS 26:112f.; *nu* MUNUSŠU.GI *wātar išnann=a dāi n=a*[*t=*(*šmaš=kan*)] *šarā papparašzi n=aš šu-up-pí-ia-aḫ-ḫi* ... *parkuwaēš=wa=šmaš namma ēšten* KA×U-*it* EME-*it* "The Old Woman takes water and dough and sprinkles i[t] on them (i.e., two ritual patrons) and consecrates them ... (saying:) 'May you be pure again with mouth (and) tongue (i.e., free from slander (and) gossip!(?))'" KBo 39.8 ii 21-22, 24 (Maštigga's rit., MH/MS), w. dupl. KBo 2.3 i 34-35, 36-37 (MH/NS), ed. StBoT 46:73 □ for the relation between *š.*, *šuppi-* and *parkui-* see *šuppi-* A discussion at the end; ("At night they dip a thick-bread") DUMU*=ya šu-up-pí-ia-aḫ-ḫa-an-zi* "And they consecrate the child" KBo 5.1 ii 4-5 (Papanikri's rit., NS), ed. Strauß, Reinigung 289, 297; [...]x *šu-up-pí-ia-aḫ-ḫa-aš apašš=a=z šu-up-pí-ia-aḫ-ḫa-ti* "He consecrated [...] and that person consecrated himself" KUB 12.43:9 (MS); TÚG-*aš mān šu-up-pí-ia-aḫ-ḫu-ut* "Consecrate yourself like a garment" KUB 33.52 iii 8 (conjuration, NS), cf. HEG S/2:1195; *namma=ššan ANA* GÌR.GÁN KÙ.BABBAR *pankun* GEŠTIN *šer tepu šu-up-pí-ia-aḫ-ḫa-an-zi* "Then they consecrate all the wine in small quantities over the silver GÌR.GAN-vessel" KBo 15.37 v 17-19 (*ḫišuwa*-fest., MH/NS), ed. *šer* 1 c 4′ 1′.

**4′** one's hands (w. *=za*): ("When the fourth day dawns, the patient washes himself. The exorcists who are before the patient stand up") *nu=za ḫūmanteš QĀTI=ŠUNU šu-up-pí-*⸢*ia*⸣*-[(a)]ḫ-ḫa-an-zi* "They all consecrate their hands (and they go in before the god)" KBo 23.42 + KBo 35.76 i 3 (fest. for the throne of Ḫebat, NS), w. dupl. KBo 24.57 i 3 (NS), ed. ChS 1-2:130f. (without join); (after an exorcist breaks bread and puts it down before a deity) *nu=za* MUNUS.LUGAL *QĀTI=ŠU šu-up-pí-ia-aḫ-ḫi* $^{LÚ}$AZU*=ya=z QĀTI=ŠU šu-up-pí-ia-aḫ-ḫi* "the queen consecrates her hands, and the exorcist consecrates his hands" KUB 27.16 iv 11-12, 14-15 (fest. for Šaušga of Nineveh, NS), ed. ChS 1/3-1:154f.; ("And in its place they will give a ritual to the deity") *[Q]ĀTI*$^{ḪI.A}$*=ya=za šu-up-pa-aḫ-zi* "and he consecrates his hands" KUB 49.49 ii 6 (oracle question, NH); (An exorcist takes something from the king's hand and puts a thin bread in the ritual pit) *nu=za QĀTI=ŠU* ⸢*šu-up-pí*⸣*-aḫ-ḫi* (var. *[š]u-up-pí-ia-*⸢*aḫ-ḫi*⸣ [LU]GAL*=ya menaḫḫanda šu-up-pí-ia-aḫ-ḫi*) ⸢*t*⸣*=ašta* $^{LÚ}$ḪAL LUGAL-*i* $^{GIŠ}$⸢ERIN⸣ *kiš*⸢*šarī*⸣ *dāi* §... *nu=za QĀTI=ŠU šu-up-pí-aḫ-ḫi* ... *t=ašta* $^{LÚ}$ḪAL LUGAL $^{GIŠ}$⸢ERIN⸣ [ŠU-*az? ar*]*ḫa* ⸢*d*⸣*āi* "he consecrates his hands (var. + and he consecrates facing(?) the king), and the exorcist puts cedar in the king's hand. § ... and he consecrates his hands ... and the exorcist takes cedar out of the [hand] of the king" KUB 27.1 iii 10-11, 13, 16 (fest. for Šaušga of Šamuḫa, NH), w. dupl. KUB 27.3 iv 19 (NH), ed. ChS 1/3-1:45f. 48, Lebrun, Samuha 81, 91f.

**5′** one's mouth: ("Tenth tablet—complete") *ŠA* SÍSKUR *itkalziaš aiš šu-up-pí-ia-aḫ-ḫu-wa-aš* "of the *itkalzi*-ritual, of the mouth consecration" KUB 29.8 iv 37 (rit., MH/MS), ed. ChS 1/1:100 ("Mundwaschung"); ("A *patili*-priest t[akes] *ḫarnai-* from a large bowl (along) with cedar, tamarisk, (and) olive") *nu* MUNUS KA×U*=ŠU šu-up-pí-ia-aḫ-ḫi* "and consecrates the woman's mouth" KUB 9.22 ii 30 (birth rit., NH), ed. StBoT 29:90f., $^{GIŠ}$*pain(n)i-*; *lukatt[a=ma=kan* $^{LÚ}$AZU KA×U*=Š]U parā kiššan šu-up-pí-ia-aḫ-ḫi* ... *nu=za=kan* KA×U*=ŠU parā šu-up-pí-aḫ-ḫi* "In the mornin[g the exorcist] thus ritually cleans out(?) he[r mouth] ... She ritually cleans out her own mouth" KBo 17.65 obv. 10-12 (rit., MH/MS), ed. StBoT 29:132f., see *parā* 1 rr.

**6′** a god: (Ḫannaḫanna tells the bee: "Go search for my son Telipinu. When you find [him] ...") ⸢*n*⸣*=an parkunut n=an šu-up-‹pí-›ia-aḫ* "Purify him and make him holy" KUB 33.5 ii 8 (OH/MS), ed. Otten, Tel. 16, 18, translit. Myths 40, tr. Hittite-Myths² 18; ("An exorcist holds one bird (in his) left (hand) and with his right hand he takes a cup of water with cedar in it; he pours out a little before the deity while he speaks in Hurrian as follows: ditto §") *namma=kan* GAL A *katta* $^{GIŠ}$*laḫḫuri dāi n=ašta* $^{GIŠ}$ERIN *šarā dāi nu* DINGIR-*LAM šu-up-pí-ia-aḫ-ḫi* EGIR-⸢*ŠU*⸣*=ma=aš=za=kan* ZAG-*ni neyari nu* EN.SÍSKUR *šu-up-pí-ia-aḫ[-ḫi]* "then he puts the cup of water down on the *laḫḫura*-table, takes out the cedar and consecrates the deity; then he turns to the right side and consecrates the worshiper" KUB 45.3 i 15-17 (pre-NH/MS), ed. ChS 1/2:266-269; ("Then it(?) goes out to the temple of Ziparwa §") *nu* DINGIR-*LAM kiššan [š]u-up-pí-ia-aḫ-ḫa-an-zi* "and they consecrate the deity thus" IBoT 2.80 rev. 7-8 (fest. for infernal gods, NS).

**b.** consecrating or purifying animals and inanimates — **1′** a temple: *mā[n (INA* É.DINGIR-*LIM šuppi kuin)] imma maršaštarrin [wemi(yanzi nu ki)]ššan šu-up-pí-ia-aḫ-[ḫa-an-zi]* "I[f] they [fi]nd any sacrilege whatsoever in a holy temple, they shall (re)consecrate (it) as follows" HSM 3644:4-6 (Güterbock, JCS 19:33) (cat., NH), w. dupl. KBo 7.74:6-7, ed. StBoT 47:128f.; *kī ŠA* É.DINGIR-*LIM šu-up-pí-ia-aḫ-ḫu-wa-ar* "This is the consecration of the temple" KUB 17.8 iii 9 (conjuration, OH/NS); for a *šinapši*-structure and an altar in a temple see below d.

**2′** a house and its cultic implements, which have been profaned: [(*t*)]*a* É*=SU* EGIR-*pa šu-up-pí-ia-aḫ-ḫi* "he shall consecrate his house again" KBo 6.26 i 31-32 (Laws §165, OH/NS), w. dupl. KBo 25.5 ii 3 (OS), ed. LH 132; (They clean out the tent in which the Old Woman treated the worshipper; they sprinkle it and wave *ḫuppanni* and *ḫušta* in it and discard them at the doorway) *nu=ššan INA* GAL GIR$_4$ *kuit* (var. + *šuppi*) *wātar āšzi n=at* MUNUS ŠU.GI *dāi nu* É-*er* É.ŠÀ.⌈ḪI⌉.A [É]*ḫilann=a* [*š*]*u-up-pí-ia-aḫ-ḫi* (var.. *šu-up-pí-aḫ-ḫi*) "The Old Woman takes the (var. + consecrated) water which remains in the baked clay cup and consecrates the house, the inner chambers and the courtyard (with it)" KUB 27.29 i 20-22 (Allaituraḫi's rit., MH/NS), w. dupl. KBo 23.23:62-63 + KBo 33.118:80-81, ed. ChS 1/5:130 i 49-51, Haas/Thiel, AOAT 31:136f., cf. ChS 1/5:61.

**3′** a town made sacrosanct to a deity: *nu=kan* [URU]*Timmuḫalan* [*ANA* [d]]U EN*=YA šippandaḫḫun n=an šu-up-pí-ia-aḫ-ḫu-un* "I sacrificed the city of Timmuḫala [to] the Storm[god], My Lord, and I consecrated it. (I set its boundaries and no one lived there)" KUB 19.37 ii 16-17 (ann., Murš. II), ed. AM 168f.; [*nu=wa=kan*] [URU]*Palḫuišša ANA* [d]U *šip*⌈*pan*⌉[*daḫḫi nu=war=an* ...] *šu-up-pí-ia-aḫ-mi* KUB 14.15 i 15-17 (ann., Murš. II), ed. AM 34-37 w. comm. 234, see also Melchert, Mem.Güterbock 140.

**4′** a boundary of a field which has been profaned: *ta āppa šu-up-pí-ia-aḫ-ḫi* "and he shall consecrate (it) again" KBo 6.26 i 43 (Laws §167, OH/NS), ed. LH 134; [(*ta* A.ŠÀ-*LA*)]*M āppa šu-up-pí-ia-aḫ-ḫi* "and he shall consecrate the field again" KUB 29.30 iii 11 (Laws §168, OS), w. dupl. KBo 6.26 i 49 (OH/NS), ed. LH 134f.

**5′** other objects and/or animals: UGULA [LÚ.MEŠ]MUḪALDIM [d]*Ḫebat šu-u*[*p-pí-ia-aḫ-ḫi*] GUD*=ya* UDU.ḪI.A *šu-up-p*[*í-ia-aḫ-ḫi*] "The chief of the cooks consecr[ates] (the statue of) Ḫebat and he cons[ecrates] cattle (and) sheep" KUB 25.41 iii 3-4 (fest., LNS), translit. ChS 1/3-2:243 (without restorations); UGULA MUḪALDIM [GIŠ]ZAG.GAR.RA GUD UDU *šu-up-pí-ia-aḫ-ḫi* DINGIR.MEŠ*=kan* [GIŠ]ZAG.GAR.RA-*za* GAM *danzi* ⌈[LÚ.MEŠ]MUḪALDIM⌉ [GIŠ]*šientin tianzi* [GIŠ]ZAG.GAR.RA-*ni ḫūkanz*[*i*] "The overseer of the cooks consecrates the altar, the cattle (and) sheep; they take the gods down from the altar; the cooks put the *šientin* in place and slaughter at the altar" KBo 11.26 obv. 5-7 (fest., LNS), ed. [GIŠ]*šientin-*; ("In the morning they seat the deity") *UNŪTĒ*[MEŠ] *araḫza pēdanzi n=at* [LÚ]AZU *šu-up-pí-ia-aḫ-ḫi* "They carry the implements outside and the exorcist purifies them" KUB 12.5 i 5-6 (rit., MH/MS), ed. ChS 1/3-1:83f.; ("As soon as they bring the implements to Arinna") *nu=šmaš=at* LÚ.MEŠ É.DINGIR-*LIM* GIM-*an šekkanzi n=at QĀTAMMA šu-up-pí-ia-aḫ-ḫa-an-zi* "the temple men consecrate them as they know how" KUB 22.70 rev. 58-59 (oracle question, NH), ed. THeth 6:96f.; [...]x [MUNUS]*ḫuwaššannalaš ištananan* [EGI]R-*p*[*a*] *šu-pí-ia-aḫ-ḫi nu* 2 GAL. GIR$_4$ *IŠTU* ZÍD.DA ZÍZ *šun*⌈*na*⌉*i n=aš=kan* EGIR-*pa ištanani tittanuzi n=at=za šu-up-pí-ia-aḫ-ḫu-u-ar ḫalziššanzi* "A priestess of Ḫuwaššanna reconsecrates the altar: she fills two earthenware cups with wheat flour and stands them back on the altar, and they call this 'consecration'; (she stands one cup on the left and one on the right and puts breads on top of them)" KBo 24.29 iii 1-4 (cult of Ḫuwaššanna, MS); *lukatti=ma=za* [LÚ]SANGA GIBIL [GIŠ]ZAG.GAR. RA *šu-up-pí-ia-aḫ-ḫu-u-wa-aš* EZEN$_4$ DÙ-*zi* "The next day the new priest performs the festival of the altar consecration" KUB 44.21 ii 2-3 (NH); ("The [chief] of the blind men gives the king a cup; the king libates; the chief of the blind men libates into the pipe") *ta* LUGAL-*i šer šu-up*‹-*pí*›-*ia-aḫ-ḫi* "and he consecrates (it) for the sake of the king, (and a scribe calls out)" KUB 20.24 iii 8 (fest. for infernal deities, NS), translit. DBH 13:42, cf. HEG S/2:1194 ("reinigt (es))," cf. par. *šer šu-up-pí-aḫ-ḫi* (var. *šer šu-up-pí-ia-ḫi*) ibid. iii 35, w. dupl. KBo 27.40 rev.? 3; see also KBo 15.37 v 17-19 (above a 3′). For *šer š.* "consecrate on behalf of" see *šer* 5 a; for consecrating a garment see KUB 33.52 iii 8, above, a 3′.

**c.** consecrating or purifying intangibles: MU.KAM-*ann=a šu-up-pí-aḫ-ḫa-an-z*[*i*] "And they consecrate the year" (*ANDAḪŠUM*-fest. outline, LNS), translit. Houwink ten Cate, FsHoffner 208; URU*Neriqqa lilan kuwapi* KÙ-*an-zi* "Nerik: when they consecrate pacification(?)" KUB 53.21 rev. 8 (list of festivals, LNS), ed. HED L 78, translit. KN 310 □ *lila-* in this sentence appears to fall into the same semantic sphere as references s.v. *lila-* A, but the meaning given there, "conciliation, pacification" (also HED 78), is based on a supposed relationship with the v. *lilai-*.

**d.** verbal noun: *nu* EGIR-*pa šu-up-pí-ia-aḫ-ḫu-u-wa-ar maḫḫan n=at QĀTAMMA* EGIR-*pa šu-up-pí-ia-aḫ-ḫa-an-zi mānn=a maršanuwan kuitki n=at šekkanzi maḫḫan n=at QĀTAMMA* EGIR-*pa šu-up-pí-*⌈*ia*⌉[*-aḫ-ḫa-an-zi*] "and just as there is (a rite of) re-consecration, thus they will re-consecrate it (i.e., a *šinapši*-structure q.v.), and if something has been desecrated, just as they know it, thus [they will] re-consecr[ate] it" KBo 11.1 obv. 34-35 (prayer to Stormgod of Kummanni, Muw. II), ed. Houwink ten Cate/Josephson, RHA XXV/81:107, 117; UGULA LÚ.MEŠMUḪALDIM *tuḫḫu⟨eš⟩nit* GIŠZAG.GAR.⟨RA-⟩*an šu-up-pí-aḫ!-ḫi!* GUD.ḪI.A UDU.ḪI.A=*ya šu-up-pí-ia-aḫ-ḫi* UGULA LÚ.MEŠMUḪALDIM *šu-up-pí-i*[*a-ḫ*]*u-wa-aš* INIM.ḪI.A *memai nepiš* [*mā*]*n parkūi* [DINGI]R.M[EŠ-*aš ištananaš*] *aulieš«iš»* [NINDA*ḫaršiš* DUG*išp*]*anduzi* [*apeniššan* ...] *parkū*[*i*]*š*! ⌈*ēšdu*!⌉ "The overseer of the cooks consecrates the altar with *tuḫḫueššar*, he consecrates the cattle and sheep. The overseer of the cooks speaks the (following) words of consecration: 'As heaven is pure (*parkui*), let the [go]ds[' altar], sacrificial victims, [thick bread,] (and) libation be pure [in the same way]'" KUB 25.20 iv? 13-17 + KUB 46.23 rev. 17-23 (*ANDAHŠUM* fest., LNS); probably so also in broken passages KUB 20.59 i 10-15 (*ANDAḪŠUM*-fest., LNS), KBo 49.22:2-5 (*ANDAḪŠUM*-fest., NS) and IBoT 1.2 ii 1-7 (fest. for LAMMA of the River, NS), ed. McMahon, AS 25:192.

**e.** substances used to make holy, sacred or to consecrate — **1′** (holy) water: ("The exorcist washes his hands") *nu ŠA* SÍSKUR GIŠBANŠUR AD.KID *wetenaz šu-up-pí-ia-aḫ-ḫi* "and he consecrates with water the wicker table for (lit. of) the ritual" KUB 32.49a ii 11-12 (MH/MS), ed. ChS 1/2:46f.; (After water for the hands is brought ...) *nu ḪAṢṢINA* TÚG[ŠÀ].GA.DÙ=*ya* EGIR-*pa ANA* LÚAZU *pā*[*i*] *n=at wetenit* [*š*]*u-up-pí-ia-aḫ-ḫi n=at PĀNI* DINGIR-*LIM* [*dāi*] "She (i.e., the Queen) give[s] the ax and the sash(?) back to the exorcist. He consecrates them with the water and [puts] them before the deity" KUB 45.32 iii 9-10 (fest. for *IŠTAR* of Tamininga, NS), ed, ChS 1/3-1:88, 90; cf. ⌈*šu-up*⌉*-pí-aḫ-ḫu-u-wa-aš wātar* KUB 31.57 i 24 (OH/NS); cf. KUB 27.29 i 21-22 (above b 2′). In the act of consecrating (*šuppiyaḫḫ-*) sometimes *šuppi watar* "holy water" is employed KBo 23.23:62-63 + KBo 33.118:80-81 (b 2′, above), sometimes *parkui watar* "pure water" KBo 17.93 obv. 6-7.

**2′** wine and *marnuwant*-beer: *nu=za* DUMU.É.GAL *marnuandaš* DUG*tapišanan dāi* ... § *nu tamaiš* DUMU.É.GAL *ŠA* GEŠTIN DUG*tapišana*[*n*] *ḫarzi nu anda šu-up-pí-ia-aḫ-ḫa-an-z*[*i*] "§ A palace-attendant takes a *tapišana*-vessel of *marnuwant*-beer. ... § Another palace-attendant holds a *tapišana*-vessel of wine. They consecrate together" KUB 2.4 iv 13-14, 21-24 (Ziparwa-fest., NS).

**3′** *tuḫḫueššar*: UGULA LÚ.MEŠMUḪALDIM *dannarandan* DUGGAL *ḫarzi nu=ššan wātar lāḫūwan anda=ma=kan* ⌈*tuḫ*⌉*ḫueššar kitta* § UGULA LÚ.MEŠMUḪALDIM NA4*ḫuwaši* [*šu-u*]*p-pí-ia-aḫ-ḫi* EGIR=*ŠU* UDU.ḪI.A MÁŠ.GAL [SILA$_4$?] MÁŠ.TUR *šu-up-pí-ia-aḫ-ḫi* "The overseer of the cooks holds an empty cup. Water has been poured in and *tuḫḫueššar* lies in (it). § (With it) the overseer of the cooks [con]secrates the *ḫuwaši*-stone; after that he consecrates sheep, goat(s), [lambs(?)] (and) kid(s)" KUB 20.85 i 11-17 (spring fest. at Tapala, LNS), translit. w. summary Kühne, Relig.Bez. 235f.; cf. [...] x=*pat tuḫḫuišnit šu-up-p*[*í-ia-aḫ*]*-ḫi* "The aforementioned [...] he consec[rate]s with *tuḫḫueššar*" KBo 24.36 + KBo 29.190:7 (cult of Ḫuwaššanna, NS), w. dupl. KBo 46.249 obv.? 7.

**4′** cedar: [...] DINGIR-*LAM* ⌈GIŠERIN⌉*-az wetenit* [...] *šu-up-pí-ia-aḫ-ḫi* "he consecrates [...] the deity (i.e., its statue) with cedar (and) water" KUB 27.22 i 13-14 (fest., NS), translit. ChS 1/3-2:245 (but reading GIŠERIN as DUGGÌR.GÁN); ("[Afterwards] the exorcist takes a bronze ax. [Th]en red thread is attached to it. He places it for each of the patrons ...") *namma* ᴳᴵŠERIN-*a*[*z š*]*u-up-pí-ia-aḫ-ḫi* "Then he consecrates with cedar (and places it before the deity)" IBoT 3.115 obv. 7-8 + KUB 47.69 obv. 4-5 (*ANDAḪŠUM*-fest, OH/MS), ed. de Martino, La Danza 58, 60, ChS 1/3-1:113f.; see further KUB 27.1 iii 10-11, 13, 16 (above a 4′), KUB 9.22 ii 30 (above a 5′), KUB 45.3 i 15-17 (above a 6′), see also KBo 22.126 rev. 4-8 (rit., NS).

**f.** w. adverbs — **1′** w. *anda* "to consecrate together": § UGULA ᴸᵁ́.ᴹᴱŠMUḪALDIM UGULA LÚ.MEŠ ᴳᴵŠBANŠUR*=ya anda šu-up-pí-ia-aḫ-ḫa-an-zi* § "§ Together the overseer of the cooks and the overseer of the table-men perform the consecration §" KBo 4.9 iii 4-5 (OH/NS), ed. Badalì/Zinko, Scientia 20:32f. ("reinigen sich gegenseitig"), cf. HEG S/2:1195 ("reinigen sich drinnen") ☐ for *anda* "together" see Francia, StAs 1:132-134; for the means of consecration in this passage, see the wine mentioned in ii 51 and *tuḫḫueššar* in ii 29-32; see also KUB 2.4 iv 13-14, 21-24 (above e 2′); see further KBo 44.139 iv 6 (fest., NS), KBo 45.19:8 (fest., NS), KBo 45.78 rt. col. 11 (fest., NS).

**2′** w. *āppa* "to re-consecrate": [...] EGIR-*pa šu-⟨up-⟩pí-*⌜*aḫ*⌝*-ḫa-an-zi* KUB 50.36 iv 7 (oracle question, NH); see also Laws §§165, 167, 168 (above b 2′, b 4′), KBo 24.29 iii 1-4 (above b 5′), KBo 11.1 obv. 34-35 (above d).

**3′** w. *arḫa* "to de-consecrate(?): *AŠRA=ma arḫa witenaz šu-up-pí-ia-aḫ-ḫa-an-zi* "They de-consecrate(?) the place (of sacrifice) with water" KBo 21.34 iii 2 (fest. frag., NS), ed. Lebrun, Hethitica 2:121, 130; *nu* ᴳᴵŠBAN[Š]UR SISKUR *wetenaz arḫa šu-up-*⌜*pí-a*⌝*ḫ-ḫa-an-zi* "They de-consecrate(?) the table of the sacrifice with water" KUB 25.42 iii 2-3 + KBo 15.47 obv. rt. col. 16-17 (*ḫišuwa*-fest., MH/NS), translit. ChS I/4:82; [...*arḫ*]*a šu-up-pí-ia-aḫ-ḫi* ᴳᴵŠBANŠ[UR...SÍ]SKUR *arḫa šu-up-pí-ia-*[*aḫ-ḫi.../...*]*=kan* É-*ri anda pānz*[*i*...] § [...SÍ]SKUR *ANA* DINGIR-*LIM* [...] ⌜DINGIR-*LIM arḫa*⌝ *š*[*u-up-pí-ia-aḫ-ḫi*] KBo 35.90 rev.? 7-8, 10, 12-13 (throne of Ḫebat fest., MS), see also rev. 4, translit. DBH 19:102; ☐ our interpretation of *arḫa š.* as "de-consecrate" is tentative. The act of de-consecration intends to make a formerly consecrated object ready for regular every-day use again. Note how in KBo 21.34 ii 64-iii 2 they pick up offering materials that were previously used "before the Stormgod" (iii 1) and then *arḫa š.* the area (*AŠRA*) possibly referring to the place where offerings had taken place. Similarly, albeit in very fragmentary context, in KBo 35.90 rev.? 7-8 somebody *arḫa š.*-s twice, then picks up something after which "they leave." For *arḫa* to indicate "to turn something to its opposite," see Zuntz, Ortsadv. 39, HW² A 282.

**4′** w. *parā* — **a′** w. dir. obj. and *-kan* "to ritually clean/wash out(?)": see KBo 17.65 obv. 10-12 (above a 5′), and *parā* 1 rr.

**b′** w. only indir. obj., without *-kan*: [GAL ᴸ]ᵁ́.ᴹᴱŠMUḪALDIM *ištanani parā tuḫḫešnit* [*š*]*u-up-pí-ia-aḫ-ḫi* "Using *tuḫḫeššar* the [Chief] of the Cooks ritually cleanses forward in the direction of the altar" VS 28.10 iv 16-17 (Storm fest., MS), ed. Barsacchi, StAs 12:114, 116 ("purifica in direzione dell'altare"), differently Kloekhorst, EDHIL 892f. (mistaking *parā* for *peran*: "in front of the altar").

**5′** w. *šarā* "to consecrate completely" (only using wine and *marnuwant*-beer; for *šarā š.* see *šarā* B 4 h): ("The king steps up; a cupbearer brings a *kangur* of wine, and an earthenware cup is placed over/upon it; the chief of the cupbearers walks alongside him; the chief of the cupbearers gives the king a cup from (lit. of) the *kangur* § The chief of the cupbearers takes [...] wine and fills a cup in the hand of ...") GAL ᴸᵁ́SAGI *kangurazza šarā* 3-*ŠU šu-up-pí-ia-aḫ-ḫi* LUGAL-*uš ANA* ᵈIM 3-*ŠU lāḫui* "The chief cupbearer consecrates from the *kangur* completely three times; the king pours three times to the Stormgod" KUB 25.36 ii 24-26 (fest., OH/MS); ("The overseer of the cooks holds out a libation vessel of wine to the king. The king places his hand (on it). The overseer of the cooks libates three times at the hearth") [(UGULA LÚ.MEŠ ᴳᴵŠB)ANŠ]UR *šarā šu-up-pí-ia-aḫ-ḫi* "The overseer of the table-men consecrates (it) completely... (§The overseer of the cooks holds out a libation vessel of *marnuwant*-beer to the king. The king places his hand (on it). The overseer of the cooks libates [three times] below the table in front of the hunting bag") UGULA LÚ.MEŠ ᴳᴵŠBANŠUR *šarā šu-up-pí-ia-aḫ-ḫi* The overseer of the table-men consecrates (it) completely" KUB 43.30 ii 3, 10 (fest., OS), w. dupl. KBo 21.88 iii 4 (OH/NS), translit. StBoT 25:77;

cf. KUB 43.30 ii 14; cf. Tischler, HEG S/2:1194 ("segnet nach oben").

For a discussion of the relation to *parkui-* and its derivatives, see s.v. *šuppi-* A end. For *maršanu-* as the antonym of *šuppiyaḫḫ-* compare KBo 11.1 obv. 34-35 (prayer to Stormgod of Kummanni, Muw. II) (above d).

Götze, AM (1933) 233f.; Friedrich, HW (1954) 199; Laroche, RHA XIX/68 (1961) 42-45; Kronasser, EHS 1 (1962) 377, 428, 431; Friedrich, HW 3. Erg. (1966) 41; Tischler, HEG S/2 (2006) 1193-1196; Taracha, NABU 2018/106.

Cf. *šuppi-* A.

**šuppiyant-** adj.; consecrated; from OH/MS?.

**sg. nom. com.** *[š]u-up-pí-ia-an-za* KUB 59.53 i 2 (NS).
**acc. com.** *šu-up-pí-ia-an-ta-an* KUB 45.47 ii 1 (MH/MS), KBo 11.14 iii (21) (MH/NS), *šu-up-pí-ia-an-da-[a]n* KuT 53 (Wilhelm, MDOG 134:346) ii 30 (MH/MS), *šu-up-pí-an-ta-an* KUB 27.68 i 14 (NS), *⸢šu⸣-up-pí-an-da-an* Bo 4929 v 15 (Otten, JCS 4:121), KUB 54.83 rev. (8) (NS).
**nom.-acc. neut.** *šu-up-pí-ia-an* KUB 32.123 iii 38 (OH/NS), *šu-pí-an* KBo 40.155 iii 3 (NS?).
**dat.-loc.** *šu-up-pí-an-ti* KUB 41.15 obv.? 6 + KUB 53.15 i! 16 (NS).
**pl. acc. com.** *šu-up-pí-ia-an-du-uš* KUB 45.47 ii 17 (MH/MS), *šu-up-pa-ia-an-du-uš* KBo 23.9 i 15 (MH/NS).
**gen.** *šu-up-pí-ia-an-t[a-aš]* KUB 2.1 iv 34 (Tudḫ. IV).

**a.** (said of offering materials, i.e., meat, bread): (When they divide up a slaughtered sheep, they cook the liver and heart over an open flame) *nu ANA* LÚ.MEŠ $^{URU}$*Lallupiya kuiš* $^{LÚ}$GAL*=ŠUNU nu* 1 NINDA.ÉRIN.MEŠ *paršiyanzi* (sic) (var. *paršiya*) *šer=ma=ššan* $^{UZU}$NÍG.GIG (var. adds $^{UZU}$ŠÀ) *šu-up-pí-ia-an* (var. *šuppaya*) *dāi nu* $^{NA_4}$*ḫuwašiya ANA* $^{d}$U *⸢ŠA⸣* $^{URU}$*Išdanuwa* $^{d}$UTU-*i dāi* "He who is the leader of the Lallupiya men, breaks(!, text has pl. 3, var. correctly sg.) one soldier-bread, and puts the consecrated liver (var. + and heart) on (it). He places (it) on the stela for the Stormgod of Ištanuwa (and) for the Sungoddess" KUB 32.123 iii 36-40 (Ištanuwian fest., OH/NS), w. dupl. KBo 8.107:18-21 (NS), translit. StBoT 30:311; [2? $^{URUDU}$*š]epikušteš n=aš=šan šu-up-pí-an-ti* NINDA.KAŠ *paš⸢k⸣anteš* $^{GIŠ}$BAN⸢ŠUR⸣-*i [dā]i nu* 1 LÚ *karapzi* "There are [two(?) copper] pins. He [plac]es them, stuck into consecrated beer bread, on the table, and one man lifts (it)" KUB 41.15 obv.? 6-7 + KUB 53.15 i! 16-17 (rit., NS), ed. Beckman, BiOr 42:143, DeMartino, Eothen 2:79f.; ("The Chief of the Palace Attendants takes one sweet thick bread, ..., holds it out to the king and the king puts his hand on it") *n=an=šan* GAL DUMU.MEŠ.É.[GAL] *šu-up-pí-ia-an-da-[a]n=pát PĀNI* $^{GIŠ}$*minuziya [dāi]* "The Chief of the Palace Attendants [puts] it—still consecrated—before the *minuzi-*" KuT 53 ii 29-30 (rit., MH/MS), ed. Wilhelm, MDOG 134:346f.; $^{GIŠ}$*ḫatta⸢lw⸣aš* GIŠ-*ru«i»* *⸢IŠ⸣TU* Ì *išk[iyaizz]i(?) nu=ššan* NINDA.GUR$_4$.RA *šu-⸢up⸣-pí-⸢ia⸣-an-ta-[an* ...]x-⸢t⸣ *an* $^{GIŠ}$*ḫattalwaš* GIŠ-*rui dā⸢i⸣ n[u=ššan] šer* NINDA.Ì.E.DÉ.A *dāi* "He/She ano[int]s the doorbolt with oil, places a consecrated [...] thick bread on(?) the door bolt and puts an oil cake on top" KBo 11.14 iii 20-23 (Ḫantitaššu's rit., MH/NS), ed. Ünal, Ḫantitaššu 23, 30 ☐ for NINDA.GUR$_4$.RA *šu-up-pí-an-da-an* see Bo 4929 v 14-15 (Otten, JCS 4:121).

**b.** (said of birds): MUŠEN*=ma=ššan šu-up-pí-ia-an-ta-an warḫ[uin] A[N]A* NINDA.SIG *par⸢ši⸣yanti šer dāi n=an dagān dāi* "He places the bird, consecrated (and) unplucked, on top of the broken thin-bread, and he lays it on the ground" KUB 45.47 ii 1-3 (fest. for NIN.GAL, MH/MS), ed. ChS I/3-2:182f. ("rein"), Bawanypeck/Görke, hethiter.net/: CTH 494 (TX 19.02.2016, TRde 19.02.2016); ("The exorcist takes a sample from the birds, he dips it in oil and places it on the brazier. He picks up their hearts too, and he throws them into the brazier") MUŠEN.ḪI.A*=ma šu-up-pí-ia-an-du-uš wa⸢r⸣ḫuwauš PĀNI* DINGIR-*LIM t[ag]ān dāi* "He lays the birds, consecrated (and) unplucked, in front of the deity on the g[ro]und" KUB 45.47 ii 17-18 (fest. for NIN.GAL, MH/MS), ed. ChS I/3-2:182f., Bawanypeck/Görke, hethiter.net/: CTH 494 (TX 19.02.2016, TRde 19.02.2016).

**c.** (mentioned in connection with holy geographical environments): [$^{d}$*Āl]aš* ḪUR.SAG.MEŠ-*aš ḫūma‹n›taš* [$^{d}$*Āl]aš* ÍD.MEŠ-*aš ḫūmantaš* [$^{d}$*Āl]aš duwadu⸢na⸣‹š› ḫumantaš* [$^{d}$]*Ālaš šu-up-pí-ia-an-t[a-aš]* (var. *[šupp]eššanaš*) *[ḫ]ūmantaš* "[Āl]a of all the mountains, [Āl]a of all the rivers, [Āl]a of all the *duwaduna-*(?), Āla of [a]ll the consecrated ones (var. "all consecrated places")" KUB 2.1 iv 31-35 (fest. for all ᵈLAMMAs, Tudḫ. IV), w. dupl. Bo 6113:7-11, ed. E. Gordon, JCS 21:82 w. n. 32 ("of the Springs(!!)"), McMahon, AS 25:112f. (tr. following Gordon), Archi, SMEA 16:112 w. n. 66 (tr. following Gordon).

**d.** (said of persons): [... ᴸᵁ́*pur*]*apšiš* ᵁᴿᵁ*Kizzuwatni* [...*š*]*u-up-pí-ia-an-za šipanti* "[...a *pur*]*apši*-priest in Kizzuwatna [...] libates in a consecrated state" KUB 59.53 i 1-2 (rit. frag., NS), translit. DBH 14:91.

We see no support for Gordon's, JCS 21:82 w. n. 32, Archi's, SMEA 16:101 and McMahon's AS 25:113, translation "spring" or "pool." For the *-ant* suffix as a derivation of the base adj. *šuppi-* A (q.v.) see GrHL §2.26. Despite the similarity in meaning with *šuppi-* A, the use of *š.* is far more restricted, both in what nouns it modifies and in number of attestations. *š.* does not occur with nouns that are inherently holy, such as deities, the king, certain cultic personnel, and their bodyparts, or objects like holy beds, the birthstool, etc. Whereas *šuppi-* refers to an almost natural state, a permanent aspect of an entity, *š.* seems to be used when the state of purity is achieved for a specific occasion, although in a few cases *šuppi-* is used in that sense as well, as shown by the alternation ᵁᶻᵁNÍG.GIG *šuppiyan* KUB 32.123 iii 38 versus ᵁᶻᵁNÍG.GIG ᵁᶻᵁŠÀ *šuppaya* KBo 8.107:20 (also cf. d 3′ (bread), 9′ (liver)).

Otten, JCS 4 (1950) 121 w. n. 12 ("kultisch rein," corresponds to Akk. *ŠALMU*); Friedrich, HW (1952) 199 ("(rituell) rein, heilig"); Kronasser, EHS 1 (1960) 266; E. Gordon, JCS 21 (1967) 82 w. n. 32 (takes *šuppiyant-* as an erg. adj. of *šuppi-* and identifies the noun with TÚL-*anza* in the meaning "sacred spring, clear pool"); Archi, SMEA 16 (1975) 101 (*šuppiyantaš ḫūmantaš* "di tutte le fonti(?)"); McMahon, AS 25 (1991) 113 (*šuppiyantaš ḫūmantaš* "of all the springs(?)"); Tischler, HEG S/2 (2006) 1196-1197 ("rein, heilig, geweiht"), Kloekhorst, EDHIL (2008) 789 ("purified, sacred").

Cf. *šuppi-* A, *šuppiyaḫḫ-*.

**šuppiyatar** n. neut.; **1.** consecration(?), **2.** (a specific part or phenomenon of the moon, fullness?); from OH/NS.†

**sg. nom.-acc.** *šu-up-pí-ia-tar* KBo 34.145:10 (NS), KUB 57.66 iii 18 (NS), IBoT 4.35 obv. rt. col. 8 (NS), KBo 26.20 ii (5)? (NS).

**dat.-loc.** *šu-up-pí-ia-an-ni* KUB 8.14 rev. iii! 13 (OH/NS), KUB 8.12:(1), (8), 10 (OH/NS).

(Sum.) [...]-x-x-x-⸢a⸣ = (Akk.) [...] = (Hitt.) [*šu-up-p*]*í*(?)*-ia-tar* KBo 26.20 ii 5 (Erimḫuš Bogh., NS), ed. MSL 17:106. Restoration of the word is proposed ibid., note for l. 5. In the preceding two lines the entries [*parkui*]*š* "clean/pure" and [*me*]*kki parkuiš* "very clean/pure" do appear which are semantically close to [*šupp*]*iyatar* "[consec]ration."

For *šu-up-pí-ia-an*!*-ni* KUB 36.83 i 5 (rit.), as read in THeth 25:266f. see *šuppieššar/šuppiyaššar*.

**1.** consecration(?): [...]-x-*ša* ⸢*ē*⸣*š*⸢*ta*⸣(?)(coll. ph.) *nu*≈*kan šu-up-pí-ia-tar* [...]⸢≈*za*≈*kan* ᵈUTU⸣-*ŠI apadda šer* ⸢*kišan IQRU*⸣[*B*] "[...] was [...], and the consecration(?) [...] for that reason His Majesty mad[e] a vow in the following way" KBo 34.145:10-11 (vow, NH), ed. deRoos, Votive 150; unclear [...](-)*arnu*(-)x-x-*iššiš* MUNUS-*za šu-up-pí-ia-tar ḫašt*[*a*] KUB 57.66 iii 18 (ritual, NS).

**2.** (a specific part or phenomenon of the moon): *takku* ᵈ*SÎN-mi š*[*u-u*]*p-pí-ia-an-ni-i*≈*šši* 2 MUL.ḪI.A [(*katti*)≈*ši*] *aranta* KUR-*eanti UL* $SIG_5$-*in* § *takku* ᵈ*SÎN-mi šu-up-pí-ia-an-ni-i*≈*šši* 3 MUL.ḪI.A *ka*[(*tt*)*i*≈*ši*] *aranta* LÚ.GAL *kuiški aki* "If two stars are stationed by the *š.* of the moon (lit. the moon, its *š.*), it is not favorable for the land. § If three stars are stationed b[y] the *š.* of the moon, some important man shall die" KUB 8.12:8-11 (lunar omens, OH/NS), w. dupls. KUB 8.14 rev.! 2-5 (pre-NH/NS), ed. DBH 12:79 ("in seinem (höchsten) Glanze" = "bei Vollmond"), 262, cf. HW 199 ("heller Teil des jungen Mondes"). If the relationship between ritual purity and perfection (see disc. under *šuppi-* A, and *šuppišarant-*) applies to *š.*, the *š.* of the moon means "fullness of the moon."

Friedrich, HW (1952) 199 ("Reinheit"; "heller Teil des jungen Mondes"); Moyer, Diss. (1969) 33; Riemscheider, DBH 12 (2004) 79-80 w. n. 4 ("(höchster) Glanz des Mondes, Vollmond"), 262 ("Reinheit, Helligkeit"); Tischler, HEG S/2 (2006) 1197 ("zur Bezeichnung des hellen Teils des Neumondes"); Kloekhorst, EDHIL (2008) 789 ("purity").

Cf. *šuppi-* A, *šuppiyaḫḫ-*, *šuppiyant-*, *šuppieššar*.

**šuppiyauwar** n. neut.?; purification?; NH.†

**neut.** *šu-up-pí-ia-u-wa-ar* KBo 1.44:15 (NH).

§ (Sum.) [...] = (Sum. pronunciation) [...] = (Akk.) *ŠU-UK-KU-U* = (Hitt.) *šu-up-pí-*[(*ia-u-wa-ar*)] / (Sum.) [...] = (Sum. pronunciation) [...] = (Akk.) *UṢ-ṢÚ-TÙ* = (Hitt.) *parā* [(*pāuwar*)] / (Sum.) [...] = (Sum. pronunciation) [...] = (Akk.) *ŠU-UP-PU-U* = (Hitt.) *gul-k*[(*u-le-eš-ki-iz-zi*)] § KBo 26.23:4-6, w. dupl. § KA.ZU.KAL.LA = (Sum. pronunciation) qa-zu-gal-la = (Akk.) *ŠU-UP-PU-U* = (Hitt.) *šu-up-pí-ia-u-wa-ar* / (Sum.) PÀ.È.A = (Sum. pronunciation) pa-e = *UṢ-ṢU-TÙ* = *parā pāuwar* ("going forth") / (Sum.) GÚ.GIL.AN.NA = (Sum. pronunciation) da-na = (Akk.) *ŠU-UK-KU-U* = (Hitt.) *gul-ku-le-eš-ki-iz-zi* KBo 13.1 iv 14-16 (NH), ed. Scheucher, Diss. 634-636, translit. StBoT 7:15, cf. 22f.

A Sum.-Akk. par. gives [pa]-è = *šu-pu-u* "splendid" CT 18.48 iv 18. Otten speculates that the Hittite scribes saw the È and "corrected" the text and so equated it with a form of Akk. *waṣû* and then correctly equated the latter with *parā pauwar*. Alternatively, the scribes equated PÀ.È with PA.È = *šu-pu-u* "to cause to appear, to bring forth," and chose *uṣ-ṣu-tù* "exit, emergence" as an unexact equivalent. *Šuppû* could have been understood as the D stem of *šapû* "to quiet, silence, subdue" (CAD *šapû* C & AHw *šapû* III), which fits more or less with the suggested meanings of the *kule-* family (StBoT 7:22-24, Beal, OrNS 57:173f.). KBo 26.23's scribe then mistook Akk. *šukkû* for Akk. *zukkû* "to cleanse" and more or less correctly translated the latter as a form of *šuppi-* (StBoT 7:23, HEG S/2:1197). The scribe of KBo 1.44 took the confusion one step further by thinking that Akk. *šuppû* was cognate with Hittite *šuppi-* and so switched the entries (StBoT 7:23, HEG S/2:1197). The form of *šuppi-, šuppiyawar*, that he used as translation (which may or may not have been the form used by the scribe of KBo 26.23) is a hapax. Perhaps there was a verb **šuppe-* "to be ritually pure," like *nakke-* "to be important, an obstacle," from which *šuppiyawar* was the verbal subst. (cf. StBoT 7:23, HEG S/2:1197). Alternatively, note that EDHIL 786 suggests "*šupp(iye/a)-*$^{zi}$ see *šupp-*$^{(tt)a(ri)}$ "to sleep." Although EDHIL does not mention our *šuppiyawar* under *šupp-* (or *šuppi-*), perhaps the scribe of KBo 1.44 was thinking of Akk. *šapû* "to quiet, silence" and translating it with *šupp-* "to sleep." What, in any case, the scribe of KBo 1.44 was thinking in equating Akk. *šukkû* with *gulkuleškezzi* is problematic, unless this Hittite word is not related to the *kule-* family or we have mistaken the root meaning of *kule-* words.

**šuppiešš-** v.; to become consecrated (opp. of *maršešš-*); from MH/MS.†

**pres. sg. 3** *šu-up-pí-eš-zi* KUB 29.8 ii 23 (MH/MS), KUB 29.4 iv 40 (NH).

**pret. sg. 3** [*š*]*u-up-*⌈*pí-eš*⌉*-ta* KUB 22.69 ii? 16 (NH).

**imp. sg. 3** *šu-up-pí-iš-ke-ed-du* Bo 6565 rt. col. 5 (apud Oettinger, Stammbildung 250, ref. pers. comm. Oettinger; context very fragmentary).

**a.** said of cultic procedure (opp. of *maršešš-*): ("When the patient finishes bathing, they pour that water into an empty wash basin, either of pottery or of bronze, which is not damaged(?). Thereupon it (i.e., the basin) is mixed with the (other) utensils") *UL kuwatqa maršešzi UL=ma=aš kuwatqa šu-up-pí-eš-zi* "By no means does it become profane (i.e., unfit for sacred use) or consecrated (i.e., fit for sacred use)" KUB 29.8 ii 22-23 (mouth washing rit., MH/MS), ed. HED M 84f., cf. also Haas, ChS 1/1-1:91, followed by HEG S/2:1193, who interpret the passage differently taking as subject of the sentence the consecration priest.

**b.** said of a deity and her temple: *nu* DINGIR-*LUM* KÙ.GI *kuttan UNŪTĒ*$^{\text{MEŠ}}$ ⌈*ŠA*⌉ [DINGIR-*L*]*IM* GIBIL *ḫūman ēšḫarnumanzi nu* DINGIR [GIB]IL É.DINGIR-*LIM=ya šu-up-pí-eš-zi* "They apply blood to the goddess(' statue) of gold, the wall, the utensils of the new [goddess], everything, so (that) the [ne]w goddess and the temple become consecrated" KUB 29.4 iv 38-40 (transfer of Goddess of the Night, NH), ed. StBoT 46:296f. ("become pure"), HEG S/2:1193 ("wird ... rein"), Kronasser, Schw.Gotth. 32f., Moyer, Diss. 31 ("are pure"), tr. Collins, CoS 1:176 ("are pure").

**c.** said of a queen(?): *kī kui*[*t* $^{\text{d}}$]⌈U? $^{\text{URU}}$⌉*Nerik* ⌈SI×SÁ⌉*-at* [MUN]US?.LUGAL*=za kuit* ⌈*ANA*⌉ x[...] / [*š*]*u-up-*⌈*pí-eš*⌉*-ta* "Concerning the fact tha[t] the Storm[god] of Nerik was determined (to be the cause): since the [que]en became [c]onsecrated for ... [...]" KUB 22.69 ii? 15-16 (oracle question, NH).

Friedrich, HW (1952) 198 ("rein werden"); Kronasser, EHS 1 (1966) 402; Moyer, Diss. (1969) 31; Oettinger, Stammbildung (1979) 250; Tischler, HEG S/2 (2006) 1193; Kloekhorst, EDHIL (2008) 789.

Cf. *šuppi-* A, *šuppiyaḫḫ-*.

***šuppieššar, šuppiyaššar** n. neut.; **1.** consecration, consecrated state, ritual purity, in the expression *šuppiešni/šuppiyašni ḫanda,* **2.** consecrated place; from MH/MS.†

**sg. dat.-loc.** *šu-up-pí-eš-ni* KUB 26.12 iv 34 (Tudḫ. IV), VS 28.11 ii 1 (NS), *šu-up-pí-ya-aš*(coll.ph.)*-ni* KUB 36.83 i 5 (NS).

**gen. (or pl. dat.?)** *šu-up-pí-eš-na-aš* KBo 16.24 ii 24, (27) (MH/MS).

**pl. nom.** [*šu?-up-p*]*í-eš-šar-ri*$^{\text{ḪI.A}}$ KUB 18.24 iii 5 (NH).

**acc.** [*š*]*u?-up-pí-eš-šar-ri*^HI.A^ KUB 18.24 iii 9 (NH).
**uncertain:** *šu-up-pí-eš-*⌈*šar?*^HI.A^⌉ KUB 5.11 iv 21 (NH).

For the alleged nom.-acc.sg. **šuppeššar* as read by Laroche, CTH p.167, in the catalogue text KBo 31.4 vi 25 (1963/c vi 1 ["10"]), see instead StBoT 47:106 w. n. 25 (reading [*ta-ru-u*]*p-pé-eš-na*). The occurrence *šu-up-pé-e*[(*š-šar*)] in KUB 33.102 iii 20 is a scribal error, and should be emended to «*šu-*»*up-pé-e*[(*š-šar*)] after the dupl. KUB 33.98 iii 10, see Güterbock, JCS 5:154 n. 35.

**1.** consecration, consecrated state, ritual purity, in the expression *šuppiešni/šuppiyašni ḫanda* — **a.** in instructions: [*našm*]*a*=*šmaš šumeš kuiēš* LÚ.MEŠ.SAG *ANA* LUGAL=*kan* [NÍ.TE-*Š*]*U?-i šuppai šal*⌈*ik*⌉*išketteni nu*=*šmaš šu-up-pí-eš-ni* [*ḫan*]*da tišḫan*⌈*t*⌉*eš ēšten mānn*=*a*=*kan ANA* ^LÚ^SAG [*kue*]*danikki* ḪUL-*luš maršaštarriš* [*ap*]*āšš*=*a ANA* LUGAL NÍ.TE.MEŠ=⌈*Š*⌉*U šaligai* GAM *MĀMĪTI* "[O]r, you who as eunuchs are always in contact with the king's sacred [bod]y, be mindful(?) [abo]ut your ritually purity. Also, if [so]me eunuch has an evil profane condition (lit. profanement), and [h]e too comes into contact with the king's body, (this is placed) under the oath" KUB 26.12 iv 33-37 (instr., Tudḫ. IV), ed. Dienstanw. 28f., HittInstr 290f., cf. HEG T, D/3:382.

**b.** in rituals: *nu*=⌈*kan*⌉ ŠAḪ-*an* [o-o]=*ŠU išḫiyanzi n*=*an*=*kan pattešni kattanta* [*tia*]*nzi namma*=*šši šu-up-pí-ya-aš*(coll.ph.)*-ni ḫanda šer* [*a*]*rmizziyanzi* § [*n*]*u*=*ššan* EN.SÍSKUR *ANA* ⌈ŠAḪ⌉ *šer tiyaizzi* "They bind the pig's [...], and [p]ut it down into the pit. Then, in compliance/accordance with its ritual purity they bridge over it (i.e., the pig). § The patient steps on the pig" KUB 36.83 i 3-7 (rit., NS), ed. THeth 25:266f., Fuscagni, hethiter.net/: CTH 456.2.1 (TX 13.10.2014, TRde 28.02.2014).

**2.** consecrated place — **a.** related to pools: [*nu* LÚ.MEŠ(?)] É.DINGIR-*LIM namma punuššūen nu memier INA* ^URU^*Kun*-x[...] / [É.DINGIR]-*LIM ēšta nu*=*wa paiškeuen nu*=*wa* DINGIR-*LUM* BAL-*anzake*⌈*u*⌉[*en*] / [*šu?-up-p*]*í-eš-šar-ri*^HI.A^=*ya*=*wa altanniš kuiēš ēššer* [*nu*=*kan? per*]*an anzāš ēššūen nu*=*wa* É.DINGIR-*LIM arḫa war*-x-x[...] / [...]x=*ya*=*wa arḫa ḫarakta* GIM-*an*=*ma*=*wa* É.DINGIR-*LIM uter* [*anz*]*āš*=*ma*=*wa UL namma tarnanzi nu*=*wa* DINGIR-*LUM* x x[...] / [*š*]*u?-up-pí-eš-šar-ri*^HI.A^=*ya*=*wa altanniuš UL namma* [...] "We asked the temple [personnel] again, and they said: 'In the town of Kun-x[...] there was a [temple.] We used to go (there) and make offerings for the deity. And as to the pools that were [consec]rated places, we were the ones who were [resp]onsible (for them). But the temple [ ... -ed] away, and [the ...] perished. Now, since they built (in text: brought) the temple, they do not let us (in) anymore. [...] the deity, and [they(?)] no longer [take care of/treat(?)] the pools as consecrated places'" KUB 18.24 iii 3-9 (oracle question, NH) □ for uncertain restorations of *šuppiššarri*^HI.A^ in lines 5 and 9 see Kammenhuber, MIO 2:404f. n. 7. HW² A 63, s.v. (^TÚL^)*altanni/a*-, translates line 5 as "welche Geschenke (und) *a.* machten" in which the word is taken as *uppeššar* and *ēššer* as "they made." Alternatively, in view of the next clause with *ēššūen* as pret. 1 pl. of *eš-* "to be," *ēššer* could be attributed to *eš-* as well. (For both as rare variants of *e-šu-u-en* and *e-šer*, see HW² E 93b). This is further supported by *altanniš* "pools" as nom. pl. (for the ending *-iš* instead of *-eš*, see GrHL 88 n. 56) and the subject of the sentence, contrast the acc. pl. *altanniuš* in iii 9.

**b.** other: ("[Āla of the mountains], Āla of the rivers, ..., [Āla] of the [*duwad*]*una*-(?)") [^d^*Āla šu-up-p*]*í-eš-*⌈*ša*⌉*-an-na-aš* (var. *šuppiyant*[*aš*]) *ḫūmandaš* "Āla of all the consecrated places" Bo 6113:11 (fest. for all ^d^LAMMAs, Tudḫ. IV), w. par. KUB 2.1 iv 34-35, ed. McMahon, AS 25:112f. w. n. 144 ("all purity"), Archi, SMEA 16:112 w. n. 66 (translit. [*šu-up-p*]*é-eš-ša-na-aš*) □ for the form see GrHL 128f.; see in a broken context *šu-up-pí-eš-*⌈*šar?*^HI.A^=*ya*⌉ KUB 5.11 iv 21 (oracle question, NH); [...]x=*?ya* GIŠ *šu-u*⌈*p-pí*⌉*-eš!-ni aran*[*ta*] "The [... and] wooden [...] stand in a consecrated place" VS 28.11 ii 1 (fest., NS), translit. DBH 6:21 (differently).

**c.** unclear: *mān*=*at*=*šan* [...] *IŠTU* DINGIR.MEŠ *parku*[*eš?*...] *ḫannari Ū*[*L kuiški*(?)...] *šu-up-pí-eš-na-aš* [...] *mān* DINGIR-*LUM* x[...] *teddu ku*-x[...] *šu-up-pí-eš-n*[*a-aš?*...] "If they [... are found] innoce[nt(?)] through the gods, [...] no [one (else)] will judge. [...] of the consecration/in consecrated places [...] If the god [...] let him say ... [...] o[f] the consecration/in consecrated place[s] [...]" KBo 16.24 ii 21-27 (instr., MH/MS), ed. Rizzi Mellini, FsMeriggi² 528f.

Friedrich, HW (1952) 198 ("Reinheit"); Kammenhuber, MIO 2 (1954) 404-405 n. 7 ("(kultische) Reinheit"); Friedrich, HW 1.Erg. (1957) 19; Moyer, Diss. (1969) 33-34; Rizzi Mellini, FsMeriggi[2] (1979) 549 ("riparazione" or "purificazione"); Oettinger, IF 91 (1986) 123; Tischler, HEG S/2 (2006) 1183-1184 ("Reinheit"); Kloekhorst, EDHIL (2008) 789 ("purity").

Cf. *šuppi-* A.

**šup(p)ina (šubena)** (Hurrian divinity name or epithet); NS.†

**Hurr. absol. pl.** *šu-pí-na* KUB 47.64 iii 5 (NS), *šu-up-pé-e-na* KUB 27.1 ii 56 (NS).

**frag.** *šu-u*[*b-*...] IBoT 2.59:9 (NS).

Among thin bread offerings to Hurrian deities and divine beings: 1 NINDA.SIG ᵈ*turra šu-up-pé-e-na* (var. *šu-pí-na*) KUB 27.1 ii 56 (fest. of *IŠTAR* of Šamuḫa, NH), w. dupl. KUB 47.64 iii 5, ed. Lebrun, Samuha, 80, 90; for IBoT 2.59 see Wegner, ChS I/3-1:77 □ for the combination as possibly meaning "bad men," see Wilhelm, RlA 14:207 ("Böse Männer??").

[*šuppeššar*] Laroche, CTH p. 167 see *šuppieššar*.

**šuppiš(š)ar(a)-, šuppeššar(a)-,** adj.; **1.** consecrated (said of a young girl or woman), **2.** intact (said of food offerings); from MH/MS?.†

**sg. nom.** *šu-up-pí-iš-ša-ra-aš* KUB 33.62 iii (16), 18 (MH/MS), *šu-up-pé-eš-ša-ra-a*[*š*] KUB 54.73:(11) (MS), KBo 41.16 iv 1 (NS), *šu-up-pé-eš-šar-aš* KUB 9.27 i 14 (MH/NS), *šu-up-pé-eš-šar-aš* KBo 22.110 obv. 3 (NS), *šu-up*‹*-pí*›*-šar-aš* KBo 47.42 rev. 6 (MH/MS), *šu-up-pí-šar-aš* KUB 7.5 i 6 (MH/NS), *šu-up-pí-ša-ra-aš* KBo 23.97 i 12 (NS), KUB 7.19 obv. 9 (NS).

**acc.** *šu-up-pé-eš-ša-ra-an* VBoT 24 i 25 (MH/NS), *šu-up-pé-eš-š*[*a-*]⸢*ra*⸣[*-a*]*n* KBo 31.128 iv 8 (MS), ⸢*šu*⸣*-up-pí-iš-ša-ra-a*[*n*] KBo 34.89 iv 6 (NS).

**dat.** *šu-up-pí-iš-ša-ri* VBoT 24 iii 34 (MH/NS), [*š*]*u-up-pé-eš-ša-ri* VS 28.64 obv. 13, here? [*š*]*u-up-pí-ša-*[*r*]*i* KBo 34.49 iii! 21 (NS).

**pl. nom.** *šu-up-pí-iš*‹*-ša?*›*-*⸢*re*⸣*-e-eš* KUB 33.62 iii 19 (MH/MS).

**pl. unclear case** *šu-up-pí-iš-ša-ra-aš* KBo 13.160 i 9 (NS), [*šu-up*]*-pí-iš-ša-ra-aš* KUB 33.32 iii 8 (NS).

**1.** consecrated (said of a young girl or woman) — **a.** DUMU.MUNUS "girl, daughter" — **1′** in rituals assisting a Old Woman: ("When it grows bright, they cut off the blue and red wool from the client and everything (else, i.e., bed, bed posts, chariot, bow and quiver). He puts it down in the basket") *n*=*ašta* ŠÀ É-*TI* DUMU.MUNUS *šu-up-pé-eš-ša-ra-an pēḫudanzi n*=*an*=*kan* KÁ-*aš anda ti*⸢*t*⸣*tanuanzi nu* ŠU-*it iššanaš* MUŠEN *ḫarzi nu* DUMU.MUNUS *ḫalzāi parā*=*wa*=*kan eḫu* ᵈLAMMA *lulimi*⸢*eš*⸣ *anda*=*wa*=*kan* ᵈLAMMA *innarauwanza uizzi* "They lead a consecrated girl into the house and make her stand in the gate. She holds in her hand a bird of dough, and the girl cries out: 'Come out, O Tutelary Deity of Femininity, (so that) the Tutelary Deity of Virility (may) come in'" VBoT 24 i 25-29 (Anniwiyani's rit., MH/NS), ed. THeth. 25:54f. ("Jungfrau"), Chrest. 106-109 ("virgin?"), tr. Hoffner, RlA 12:320; *n*=*an* DUMU.MUNUS *šu-up-pí-iš-ša-ri pāi nu uiēškezzi anda*=*ma*=*kan kiššan memiškezzi* § *anda*=*kan eḫu* ᵈLAMMA ᴷᵁŠ*kuršaš nu*=*nnaš*=*šan anda mīēš nu*=*nnaš*=*šan anda tallīēš karpinn*=*a kartimmiyattan šāuwar arḫa tarna* "She (i.e., the Wise Woman) gives it (i.e., the tied *galaktar* and *parḫuena-*) to a consecrated girl. She starts screaming while saying as follows: 'Come in, Tutelary Deity of the Hunting Bag! Be gentle among us, be quiescent among us and let go of your anger, rage, (and) sullenness'" VBoT 24 iii 34-41 (Anniwiyani's rit., MH/NS), ed. THeth. 25:60-63, Chrest. 114f.; [*n*=*a*]*t* ⸢DUMU⸣.MUNUS *šu-up-pé-eš-šar-aš karpz*⸢*i*⸣ EN.SÍSK[UR=*m*]*a* [*wa*]*rpanza n*=*aš* EGIR-*an iyattari* "A consecrated girl lifts [the]m (i.e., the materials) up; the patient is bathed. He walks behind (them/her)" KUB 9.27 i 14-15 (Paškuwatti's rit. against sexual dysfunction, MH/NS), ed. Hoffner, AuOr 5:272, 277, Mouton, Rêves 130, 136, tr. Goetze, ANET 349; ("The exorcist speaks concurrently ...") [...] *našma*=*wa*=*za* DUMU.MUNUS *šu-up-pí-šar-aš* [*kiš*]*at*(?) *nu*=*wa*=*šši*=*kan andakitti*=*šši kattanta pait* "[...] or you [became(?)] a consecrated girl. He/She went down to her/his loins" KUB 7.5 i 6-8 (Paškuwatti's rit. against sexual dysfunction, MH/NS), ed. Melchert, FsHoffner 283, Hoffner, AuOr 5:272, 277, Mouton, Rêves 131, 136, cf. also Simon, RAI 60:100, tr. Goetze, ANET 349 □ for the male interpretation ("He ... his loins"), see Miller, JANER 10:86f.

**2′** participating in a festival: ("Two wolf-men, the priestess of (the deity) Titiwatti, the overseer of the KAR.KID-women and the KAR.KID-women dance. When they finish dancing §")

*nu* DUMU.MUNUS *šu-up-pí-ša-*[(*r*)]*a-*⌜*aš*⌝ (var. B [*šu-u*]*p-pé-eš-ša-r*[*a-aš*]) *ŠA* ᵈ*Ti*⌜*tiw*⌝*atti* TÚG SA₅ *IŠT*[*U*...] *karappan ḫarzi* ⌜*A*⌝*NA* TÚG SA₅*=ma=ššan šer* MUNUS(?)-*a*-x[...] *kittari nu=šmaš=aš peran ḫūyanza* "a consecrated girl holds the red garment of Titiwatti lifted up wit[h...] while on the red garment [a(n)...of(?)] a [...]-woman is placed. She is marching in front of them. (After her come the priestess of Titiwatti, the overseer of the KAR.KID-women and the KAR.KID-women. The two wolf-men run before them)" KBo 23.97 i 12-14 (fest. for ᵈTitiwatti, NS), w. dupl. KUB 7.19 obv. 9-11 (var. A, NS), KUB 54.73:11-13 (var. B, MS), ed. THeth 26:318f. ("a girl (who is) a sacred companion to the deity Titiwatti"), Pecchioli Daddi, FsAlp 103f. ("vergine").

**3′** mentioned in a broken context of the myth of the missing god of the scribe Pirwa: [...*šu-up*]-*pí-iš-ša-ra-aš* DUMU.MUNUS.MEŠ [...]-x-*ta nu* ZI*=KA* ᴳᴵŠ*allayan*[*i*(?)...] / [... *ki*]⌜*t*⌝*ta*(?) *nu* ZI*=KA* [...] KUB 33.32 iii 8-10 (myth frag., NS), translit. Myth. 66, tr. Moore, Thesis 61 ("virgin girls"), cf. Otten, Tel. 64.

**b.** modifying MUNUS-*za* "woman": (The ritual practitioner (?) throws pebbles in a cup with water, then ties colored threads to the cup, and covers it with a cloth) *n=an* MUNUS-*za šu-up*⟨-*pí*⟩-*šar-aš IŠTU* ᵁᶻᵁZAG.U[DU ...] *karapzi kattan=ma=za* ˢᴵᴳ*kišri*[*n*?] *dāi pūrišiyalaš=aš iyanza* "The consecrated woman lifts it with the shoulder piece (of a slaughtered billy-goat), and beneath it she places a skein of wool, in the shape of a wreath (lit. it is made into a wreath)" KBo 47.42 rev. 6-8 (frag. Kizzuwatnan rit., MH/MS), translit. DBH 33:37.

**c.** in connection with ᴹᵁᴺᵁˢSANGA "priestess": [...-*y*]*aš* ᴹᵁᴺᵁˢSANGA ᵈ*Ḫalkiyaš šu-up-pé-eš-ša-ra-a*[*š*] "[ᶠP]N, the consecrated priestess of Ḫalki" KBo 41.16 iv 1 (colophon of rit., NS), ed. Waal, StBoT 57:340 □ alternatively, taking the gen. as preposed to a non-preserved head in iv 2, translate "the priestess of [Ḫalk]i(?), the consecrated [girl/woman] of Ḫalki."

**d.** unclear: ᵈUTU *BĒLI=Y*[*A kāša*(?)] / [ᴹ]ᵁᴺᵁˢKI.SIKIL *nu kāš* ᴹᵁᴺᵁˢKI.SIKIL *ma*[*ḫḫan* (?)...] ⌜*U*⌝*L=za* LÚ-*n*[*aš* (?)] *antagan*[ ...] / [*n*?]*=aš kē*[*l Š*]*A* ᴹᵁᴺᵁˢKI.[SIKIL...] / [*š*]*u-up-pí-ša-*[*r*]*i* [...] "O Sungod, my Lord, [here is(?)] a young girl. J[ust as (?)] this young girl (is) [...], i.e., she has not [seen(?)] the loins [of(?)] a man, [let(?)] him/her [...] of this young girl [...] for the consecrated [...]" KBo 34.49 iii! 17-21 (rit., NS), ed. Collins, Virginity (forthcoming).

**2.** (modifying food offerings) intact (Akk. *ŠALMU*): § [...] ⌜*I*⌝*NA* UD.1.⌜KAM⌝ 2-*ŠU mugāizzi karū*(-)*a*⌜*ri*⌝-x x? [...] ⌜x x⌝ 1-*ŠU nu* DINGIR.LÚ.MEŠ-*aš kuiš* 1 NINDA.KU₇ ⌜*tar*⌝*naš* [... *šu-up-pí-iš*]-⌜*ša-ra*⌝-*aš ITTI* ᴰᵁᴳGAL GEŠTIN-*it* [...]⌜*k*⌝*ittari PĀNI* ᵈIM ᵁᴿᵁ*Kuliuiš*⌜*na*⌝*=ya=ššan* [...] ⌜x x⌝ *šu-up-pí-iš-ša-ra-aš* [...*ki*]*ttari n=at=šan šu-up-pí-iš-*⟨*ša*?-⟩⌜*re*⌝*-e-eš* [...*kiyanda*]⌜*ri*⌝(?) "On the first day he entreats [the male deities(?)] twice. Early in the morning(?), [...]...once. As for the one sweet loaf of (one) *tarna*-measure of the gods, [and an int]act [...], that [l]ie [in/on...] along with a cup of wine, in front of the Stormgod of Kuliwišna also [a/the...and] a/the intact [...] lie and they, the intact (food offerings) [li]e(?) on [the...]" KUB 33.62 iii 14-20 (Stormgod of Kuliwišna, MH/MS), ed. Glocker, Eothen 6:40f. ("rein"), Moore, Thesis 103f., 106 ("virgin") □ the photo of the end of l. 14 shows more damage than the hand copy suggests and there may be evidence for erasure as well; possibly a form of *karuwariwar* was intended. In the same ritual we also find food offerings with the derived adj. s.v. *šuppišarant-* "intact" (KBo 15.34 ii 31); cf. in similar context: 1 NINDA.GUR₄.RA KU₇ *tarnaš=ma* [...] *n=an=šan ANA PĀNI* [ᵈ...] ⌜*šu*⌝*-up-pí-iš-ša-ra-a*[*n*...] KBo 34.89 iv 4-6 (frag. Kizzuwatna rit., NS); see *šuppiššarant-* with a similar meaning; see discussion there.

Friedrich, HW 198, assumed that this word modifying girl was derived from the adj. *šuppi-* "holy, pure" (q.v.) by the addition of the derivational suffix *-šara-*. However, this suffix forms feminine counterparts to masculine words, and is added only to nouns (*išḫa-/išḫaššara-*, *ḫaššu-/*ḫaššuššara-*, ÌR-*aš*/*GÉME-*aššara-*). The consistent word space between DUMU.MUNUS and *š.*, as well as its use without it, point to an adj. rather than a noun. Oettinger, IF 91:123f., suggests for this word another formation, namely **šuppi-ššar-* (different from **šuppieššar*, q.v.), which is later extended to an *a*-stem *šuppiššara-*; cf. likewise *šakuwaššar(a)-* "complete, entire," *walkiššar(a)-* "skilled, expert." The derived adj. *šuppiššarant-* (q.v.), modifying liver and heart, confirms that the suffix *-ššar(a)-* does not denote females.

DUMU.MUNUS *š.*, is literally "consecrated daughter." There is no positive evidence that it means "virgin," although those designated by *š.* might well be. There is no term for virginity in Hittite: the notion is described as "not having gone to a woman" for males (e.g., DUMU.MEŠ NITA ... MUNUS-*ni≈ššan kuiēš nāui pānzi* "boys ..., who have not yet gone to a woman" KUB 9.31 ii 10 (Zarpiya's rit., MH/MS), further see *pai-* 5 a), while the term KI.SIKIL "adolescent, unmarried girl" likely developed the connotation "virgin," given that unmarried girls might be presumed to be sexually innocent (Collins, Virginity). The expression "not having [seen(?)] the loins of a man" could provide the paraphrase for female virginity KBo 34.49 iii! 17-18, see 1 d above.

In mng. 1, *š.* is a religious designation that does not only apply to girls or daughters, but also to women and perhaps priestesses. The "consecrated daughter, girl" and "consecrated woman" provide assistance during rituals of the MUNUS. ŠU.GI (Old Woman) (Collins, Women in Antiquity 332) by manipulating ritual materials and reciting key incantations. The only other assistant mentioned in Old Woman rituals is the MUNUSSUḪUR.LÁ "temple woman" (s.v.) (for this translation instead of "prostitute, hierodule," see Marcuson, Diss. 409-411), so perhaps MUNUS/DUMU.MUNUS *š.* is the reading behind MUNUSSUḪUR.LÁ.

Goetze, apud Sturtevant/Bechtel, Chrest. (1935) 109, 119-20 ("virgin(?)"); Ehelolf, ZA 43 (1936) 186 ("sexuell feminines Appellativum auf *-šara-*"); Goetze, ANET (1950) 349 ("virgin, girl"); Friedrich, HW (1952) 198 (lists only a noun "die Reine; Jungfrau"); Kronasser, EHS 1 (1966) 109 ("Jungfrau, Reine (Art Priesterin oder jugendliche Funktionärin im Tempel)"); Moyer, Diss. (1969) 31; Oettinger, IF 91 (1986) 123f. (on the word formation); Hoffner, AuOr 5 (1987) 284 ("virgin"); Haas, Materia Magica (2003) 552 (equating *š.* with Akk. *batultu*); Taggar-Cohen, THeth 26 (2006) 318 n. 836 ("sacred companion < *šuppi-* + *ara-*"); Tischler, HEG S/2 (2006) 1184f. (lists only a noun "(eine Kultfunktionärin, wörtlich) 'die Reine', DUMU.MUNUS *suppessaras* 'reine Tochter'"), Hoffner/Melchert, GrHL (2008) 59; Kloekhorst, EDHIL (2008) 789 ("a priestess, 'purified woman' "); Collins, Women in Antiquity (2016) 332 (on *š.* as a religious designation); eadem, Virginity.

Cf. *šuppi-* A, *šuppiššarant-*

**šuppiššarant-** adj.; intact, Akk. *ŠALMU*; MH/MS.†

**pl. acc. neut.** *šu-up-pí-iš-ša-ra-an-ta* KBo 15.34 ii 31 (MH/NS), Bo 6575 ii (7) (cf. Glocker, Eothen 6:203).

**Akk. pl. acc.** [*ŠAL*]*-MU-TIM* KBo 15.33 i (6) (MH/MS).

(They drive in one ram and the lord of the house sacrifices it in the inner chamber to the Stormgod of Kuliwišna. They move it into the kitchen and cut it up. They cook the liver and the heart over a flame) *nu* LÚEN É-*TIM* 1 NINDA. GUR$_4$.RA *ŠA* 1/2 *UPNI anda daminkantān dāi nu≈ššan šer* UZUN[ÍG.G]IG UZUŠÀ *šu-up-pí-iš-ša-ra-an-ta dāi* [*n≈a*]*t*⌈*≈šan*⌉ *PĀNI* ⌈d⌉IM URU*Kuliuišna ANA* NINDA.ÉRIN.MEŠ*≈šan šer dāi* [(*memal≈ya išḫu*)*w*]*āi* "The lord of the house takes one thick bread of one-half measure (which) is pressed in. On it he places the li[ve]r (and) heart, each intact. He places [the]m on the soldier-bread in front of the Stormgod of Kuliwišna and he pou[r]s the coarsely ground meal" KBo 15.34 ii 29-33 (Stormgod of Kuliwišna, MH/NS), w. dupl. Bo 6575 ii 5-9, ed. Glocker, Eothen 6:48-51 ("rein"), Moore, Thesis 94f., 99 ("unstained"); ("They drive in a ram and the lord of the house sacrifices it in the inner chamber to the Stormgod of Kuliwišna. They cook the liver and the heart over a flame") [*nu* LÚ.MEŠNINDA.D]Ù.DÙ [(1 NINDA.GUR$_4$.RA KU$_7$ *anda*)] *taminkanta*[*n*...] x *andan udānzi* § [(*n≈an* LÚ*BĒL* É-*TIM AN*)]*A* dIM URU*Kul*[*iui*]*šna* d*IŠTAR-li* dLAMMA*≈ya* [(*paršiya nu≈*)*ššan še*]*r* UZUNÍG.GIG UZU[ŠÀ *ŠAL-M*]*U-TIM* [(*dāi n≈a*)]*t≈šan* EGIR-*pa* D[UG*ḫar*]*šia*⌈*lli*⌉*ya* [(*ANA* dIM URU*Kuliui*)]*šna* NINDA.ÉRIN.MEŠ-*i≈šš*[*a*]*n šer dāi* "[The bak]ers bring in one sweet, thick bread (which) is pressed in [...]. The lord of the house breaks it for the Stormgod of Kul[iwi]šna, Anzili and the tutelary deity. [On it] he places the liver (and) [heart], (each) [in]tact. He places [the]m on the soldier-bread behind the storage vessel for the Stormgod of Kuliwišna" KBo 15.35

+ KBo 15.33 i 3-8 (Stormgod of Kuliwišna, MH/MS), dupl. KUB 41.10 i 8-11 (MS), ed. Glocker, Eothen 6:60f. ("rein"), 239 ("unverzehrt, ganz, untadelig, (kultisch) rein"); compare ("They cook the liver(s) and heart(s) with an open flame. The anointed priest of Telipinu gives three sweet thick breads of a half handful (measure) to the prince. He breaks them") *šēr=a=ššan* UZUNÍG.GIG *ŠAL-MU-TIM dāi* "and he puts the intact liver(s) on (them)" KUB 20.88 iv 13-14 (fest. celebrated by prince, MS), ed. Taracha, StBoT 61:26f.

The form *šuppiššarant-* is a distributive ("each") *-nt*-derivative from *šuppiššar(a)-* without any meaning differences, as per Melchert, Toch&IESt 9:59f. (cf. GrHL 56 §2.25). KBo 15.34 only mentions one ram, so presumably it is its liver and heart that have been roasted, and then placed intact on the soldier bread, that is, without further treatment such as cutting to pieces. The equivalence of *š.* (and perhaps of *šuppiyant-* (q.v.)) and *ŠALMU* "healthy, sound, in good condition, whole, intact" etc. (CAD Š/1:256-260) further supports the relationship between ritual purity and the perfect condition that renders a person or object fit to be in divine presence (further see *šuppi-* A).

Carruba, StBoT 2 (1966) 17 n. 22 (on formation of *šuppiššarant-*); Friedrich, HW 3. Erg. (1966) 29 ("(jungfräulich) rein, unbefleckt"); Moore, Thesis (1975) 99 ("unstained"); Tischler, HEG S/2 (2006) 1185 ("(kultisch) rein"); Kloekhorst, EDHIL (2008) 789 ("being purified").

Cf. *šuppi-* A, *šuppiššar(a)-*, *ŠALMU*.

[*šupiššešar*] KBo 34.149 ii 10 (fest., LNS) read by Klinger, StBoT 37:408 and 795 as [ ... *š*]*u-pí-iš-še-šar* (without tr.). The reading of the first sign as *šu* is, however, not certain and the alleged *še* is rather *eš* written over(?) another sign. As an alternative [*ḫa-a*]*p*(?)*-pí-«iš-»eš-šar* "limb, body part" might be considered; cf. the frequent attestation of UZUÚR in the same text ii 12, 13, 18 etc.

**šuppe/ištuwara- A** adj.; ornamented, decorated; from OS.

**sg. nom. com.** *šu-up-pí-iš-tu-wa-ra-aš* KBo 20.64 rev. (4) (NS) (here? or noun?), *šu-up-pí-iš-tu-wa-ar-aš* KBo 17.43 i 6 (OS).

**nom.-acc. neut.** *šu-up-pí-iš-tu-wa-ra-an* KBo 20.2 i? (3) (OS), KBo 2.12 ii (11), v 9 (OH/NS), KBo 9.128:(14) (NS) (here? or noun?), [*šu-up-p*]*í-iš-du-wa-ra-*⸢*an*⸣ KBo 17.75 i (61) (OH/NS), *šu-up-pé-eš-du-wa-ra-an* KUB 12.1 iv 15 (NH), KUB 38.11 obv. (6) (NS), *šu-up-*[*p*]*é-eš-du-wa-ra-a-an* KUB 12.1 iv 24 (NH), *šu-up‹-pí›-iš-du-wa-ra-an* KUB 29.4 i 47 (NH), *šu-up-pí-iš-d*[*u-wa-ra-an*(-)...] KUB 7.55 obv. 1 (NS).

**inst.** *šu-up-pí-iš-du-wa-ri-it* KBo 17.74 iii (32), 37, 42, 47, (52) (OH/MS), [*š*]*u-*⸢*up*⸣*-*[*p*]*é-eš-tu-wa-ri-it* KBo 46.159 ii 2 (NS).

**pl. acc. com.** *šu-up-pí-iš-tu-wa-ru-uš* KBo 2.12 v 12 (OH/NS).

**unclear** *šu-up-pé-eš-du-*[*wa-ra-*...] KBo 22.186 iii 7 (NS) (here? or noun?), *šu-up-pé-eš-du-wa-*[*ra-*...] KBo 18.152:(5), 6, (8) (NH).

**a.** describing objects: 1 TÚG 1-*NUTIM* TÚGGÚ.È.A 1-*NUTIM* TÚGGÚ.È.A *Ḫurri* 1 TÚG ŠÀ.GA.AN.DÙ *MAŠLU šu-up‹-pí›-iš-du-wa-ra-an* 1 TÚGE.ÍB *MAŠLU* 1-*NUTIM* TÚGBAR.DUL$_8$.MEŠ ... 1 GIŠBAN 1 KUŠÉ.MÁ.URU$_5$URU 1 *ḪAṢṢINNU* 1 GÍR *kī=ma ŠA* LÚ-*LIM* "One garment, one set of dress garments, one set of Hurrian dress garments, one trimmed cloth belt ornamented, one trimmed tunic, one set of robes, ... one bow, one quiver, one axe (and) one knife—these are (the garments) of a man" KUB 29.4 i 46-50 (NH), ed. StBoT 46:277f. ("decorated"), Schw.Gotth. 10f. ("verziert"), tr. Collins, CoS 1:174 ("ornamented"); (In a list of cult objects) 1 GIŠ*tuppaš* 1-*EN* dU$_4$.SAKAR-*za* KÙ.GI NA$_4$ *šu-up-pé-eš-du-wa-ra-an* "One box, ornamented with one gold (and) jeweled crescent" KUB 12.1 iv 15 (inv., NH), ed. Košak, Linguistica 18:102, 105, Siegelová, Verw. 448f. ("plattiert") □ the divine det. is because the crescent is divinized, compare GIŠ/dDAG; [1 DUG]*ḪAPANNATUM šu-up-*[*p*]*é-eš-du-wa-ra-a-an tattapalān* "[One] *ḪABANNATU*-container ornamented and *tattapala*-ed" KUB 12.1 iv 24 (inv., NH), ed. Košak, Linguistica 18:102, 105, Siegelová, Verw. 448f.; [...] 1 ALAM KÙ.BABBAR TUR 1 ŠU-*aš*(?)[... *šu-up-pé*]*-eš-du-wa-ra-an IṢṢU* GIŠESI [...] "One small silver statue; one hand(?)[...orn]amented, logs/pieces(?) of ebony [...]" KUB 38.11 obv.? 5-6 (cult inv., NH), ed. (Jakob-)Rost, MIO 8:198f.; [ALAM(?) m]*Uḫḫamūwan* AN.BAR *šu-up-pí-iš-d*[*u-wa-ra-an*(-)...]x DÙ-*zi* ŠU-*i=ma=ššī=kan anda* [*dāi*] "He makes an iron [statuette?] (of) Uḫḫamūwa, ornamen[ted ...] and [places(?)...] in his hand" KUB 7.55 obv. 1-2 (rit., NS), ed. Beal/Collins, AoF 23:311 ("ornamented"); [UGULA LÚ].MEŠMUḪALDIM *išpanduwan* ˹KÙ˺.BABBAR GEŠTIN *udai* ˹*nu*˺ $^{\mathrm{GIŠ}}$BANŠUR-*i* [*pera*]*n* 3-*ŠU šipanti* ˹*n*˺*=ašta* $^{\mathrm{LÚ}}$˹SAGI˺ *BI*[*B*]*RA* GUD KÙ.GI [*šu-up-p*]*í-iš-du-wa-ra*-˹*an*˺ ˹GEŠTIN(?)˺-*it šun*˹*nai*˺ "[The overseer] of cooks brings a silver libation vessel of wine and libates three times [in front of] the table. Then the cupbearer fills with wine(?) an [orn]amented gold ox-rhyton" KBo 17.75 i 59-61 (thunder fest., OH/NS), ed. StBoT 12:68; LUGAL *U* MUNUS. LUGAL ˹*ašandaš*˺ *aruwanzi* GAL $^{\mathrm{d}}$IM *šu-up-pí-iš-du-wa-ri-it akuanzi* LUGAL-[*uš*] *ḫūppari šipanti* "The king and queen bow while seated. They drink from the ornamented cup of the Stormgod. The king libates into a basin" KBo 17.74 iii 47-48 (fest., OH/MS), ed. StBoT 12:28f. ("aus dem glänzenden? Becher"), cf. KBo 17.74 iii 12-13, 19-20 + KBo 30.66:2-3, 9-10, and KBo 17.74 iii 25-26, w. dupl. KUB 43.26 iii 6-7 (OS), KBo 17.74 iii 32-33, 52-53; [... Z]U$_9$.AM.SI ŠÀ.BA 2 *šu-up-pé-e*[*š-du-wa-ra*-...] "[...of iv]ory, among them two are orna[mented]" KBo 18.152:5 (inv., NH), ed. Siegelová, Verw. 467f. ("(in der) *š*.(-Weise) plattiert"), translit. THeth 10:163.

**b.** describing animals: [1 GUD.MAḪ *šu-up-pí-i*]*š-tu-wa-ra-an* [*n*]*atta arkandan* [*dāi*] "[He takes] one [bull, deco]rated, not butchered" KBo 25.15:3 + KBo 20.2 i? 4 (*MELQĒTU*, OS), translit. StBoT 25:47; cf. 1 GUD.MAḪ *šu-up-pí-i*[*š-tu-wa-ra-an*] *natta arkanta*[*n*] 1 UDU *natta arkan*[*tan*] *dāi* KBo 2.12 ii 11-13 (KI.LAM, OH/NS), ed. THeth 21:100f. ("hellschimmernden"); $^{\mathrm{LÚ.MEŠ}}$*ḫāpēš* $^{\mathrm{LÚ.MEŠ}}$UR.BAR.RA $^{\mathrm{URU}}$*Kartapaḫumnieš* 1 $^{\mathrm{UZU}}$ÚR ŠA[Ḫ] *ANA* $^{\mathrm{LÚ}}$SAGI DINGIR-*LIM pianzi kuršan kuiš karpēzzi* 1 UDU *šu-up-pí-iš-tu-wa-ra-an natta arkantan* $^{\mathrm{MUNUS}}$*išpunnalaš dāi* 10 UDU.ḪI.A *šu-up-pí-iš-tu-wa-ru-uš natta arkanteš* LÚ.MEŠ $^{\mathrm{URU}}$*Zipalanda danzi* "The *ḫapiya*-men (and) the wolf-men (of the town) of Kartapaḫ give one body part of a boar to the cupbearer of the god, who lifts the hunting-bag; the *išpunnala*-woman takes one decorated sheep, not butchered; the men of Zipalanda take ten decorated sheep, not butchered" KBo 2.12 v 5-14 (KI.LAM, OH/NS), ed. THeth 21:106f. ("hellschimmernde"), HED A 142 ("clean"); 1 UDU *šu-up-pí-iš-tu-wa-ar-aš INA* $^{\mathrm{DUG}}$UTÚL *marritt*[(*a*)] "One decorated sheep is stewed in a pot" KBo 17.43 i 6 (Hattian fest., OS), w. dupl. KBo 17.18 ii 7 (OS), ed. HED M 62 ("visibly unblemished"), 67 ("unblemished") (w. "visibly" HED M probably follows Neu, StBoT 12:69, cf. the cross reference to *š*. in HED E/I 485 s.v. *istuwa-*), translit. StBoT 25:104, cf. StBoT 26:176 ("'hellschimmernd, glänzend, rein'?").

*š*., both noun and adj., is commonly thought to be a compound containing *šuppi-* "ritually pure." However, the variant *iš-piš-du-wa-ra-a-aš* (KUB 42.64 rev. 2, see *šuppe/ištuwara/i-* B) excludes the connection with *šuppi-*, since it shows that the *-u-* in the principal variant is anaptyctic (Melchert, JLR 14/3:188). Goetze's, Cor.Ling. 48 n. 2, neutral "ornamented" for the adj. works in most cases. In the case of the adj. used for animals (*š*. b) that have been killed and are *š. natta arkantan* "ornamented, not butchered," one could think of animals that had been decorated with colorful woolen strands that the cultic personnel apparently had left on while the animals were killed. In the KI.LAM passage (KBo 22.224 obv. 1-3 + KBo 22.195 ii! 12-14, *šuppe/ištuwara/i-* B 1 a) where *šuppištuwarieš* (as noun) are part of a procession, they may be ornaments of some kinds that were to be used later to decorate unnamed objects. The passages where the noun *š*. is mentioned as a drinking vessel (KBo 17.74 i 19-20, KBo 46.159 ii 2-3, see *š*. B 2) may show a specialized mng. "ornamented cup" through ellipsis of an original noun e.g. KBo 17.75 i 61 (*BIBRA*), or KBo 17.74 iii 47 (GAL).

Laroche, RHA IX/49 (1948-49) 23 n. 6 (a zoomorphic vessel); Friedrich, HW (1952) 199 ("geweiht(??)"); Goetze, Cor.Ling. (1955) 48 n. 2 ("opposite of *dannara-* 'empty', i.e., 'unornamented'"); Neu, StBoT 12 (1970) 67-69 (as adj. "hellschimmernd, glänzend"; as n. "ein hellschimmernder Becher"); Kammenhuber, SMEA 14 (1971) 151 ("..."); Watkins, IESt 2 (1975) 536 n. 4 ("declared and recognised as reserved for sacred use, as tabu"); Košak, Linguistica 18 (1978) 110 ("ornamented"); idem, THeth 10 (1982) 53 ("sparkling?"), 150 (on *išpišduwara-*); Singer, StBoT 27 (1983) 96 (adj. "something covered/mounted/sheathed in (ornamented) metal," n. "vessel made of (ornamented) metal plate"); Siegelová, Verw. (1986) 618 (*šuppešduu̯ara-* "Auflage," *šuppešduu̯ant-* "(in einer bestimmten Technik) plattiert, überzogen"); Neu, Hurritische (1988) 28-32 ("(glänzende) Applikationen"); Archi, Eothen 1 (1988) 30 n. 30; Rieken, FsNeumann² (2002) 408; Miller, StBoT 46 (2004) 335 ("decorated"); Tischler, HEG (2006) 1193, 1197-1200 ("geschmückt (Attribut von Opfertieren), verziert (Attribut von Gefäßen und Kleidungsstücken)");

Kloekhorst, EDHIL (2008) 790f.; Siegelová, RlA 12 (2009) 239 ("Applikation"); Melchert, JLR 14/3 (2016) 188.

Cf. *šuppe/ištuwara-* B n.

**šuppe/ištuwara/i- B, išpeštuwara-(?)** n. com.; **1.** ornament(ation), **2.** ornamented cup(?); from OS.

**sg. nom.** *iš-piš-du-wa-ra-a-aš* KUB 42.64 rev. 2 (NH).
**acc.** [*š*]*u-up-pí-iš-tu-wa-ra-an* KBo 17.74 i 19 (OH/MS).
**inst.** *šu-up-pí-iš-du-wa-ri-it* KBo 32.14 i 43 (MH/MS), [*š*]*u-u*[*p-p*]*é-eš-tu-wa-ri-it* KBo 46.159 ii 2 (NS).
**pl. nom.** *šu-up-pí-iš-tu-wa-a-re-eš* KBo 25.12 ii 15 + KBo 20.5 ii! 3 (OS), *šu-up-pí-iš-tu-wa-re-eš* KBo 22.195 ii! 12 (OH/MS), *šu-up-pí-iš-du-wa-ri-i-e-eš* KBo 32.14 ii 59 (MH/MS), *šu-up-pí-iš-du-wa-ri-iš* KBo 35.246 obv. 13 (MS), KUB 42.69 obv. (3), (5) (NH), *šu-up-pí-iš-du-wa-re-eš* KUB 42.69 obv. 18 (NH).
**pl. acc.** *šu-up-pí-iš-du-wa-ri-uš* KBo 32.14 ii 56 (MH/MS).
**unclear** *šu-up-pé-eš-du-wa-ra*[-...] KUB 42.26 obv. 3 (NH), *šu-up-pé-eš-*⌈*tu*⌉*-wa*[-...] KBo 25.171 ii? 6 (OH?/NS).

(Hurr. *elki:*) (Hurr.) ka-a-zi ta-bal-li-iš ḫe-e-lu-u-wa$_a$ ta-wa$_a$-aš-tu-u-um ↖ ta-wa$_a$-aš-tu-u-um mu-šu-u-lu-u-um e-él-ga-a-e tu-nu-u-uš-tu-um ↖ a-ku-ú-úr-na a-ku-lu-ú-wa ši-i-ir-na-am-ma ta-šu-lu-ú-wa § ... § i-te-i-e ka-a-zi te-eš-šu-u-pa-aš e-el-ki za-am-ma-la-aš-du-uš ↖ ku-ú-du ka-a-zi bé-el-le-e-ni e-él-ki-il-la ši-i-e-ni KBo 32.14 i 42-45, 56-59 = (Hitt.) *teššummin* [LÚ]SIMUG *walliyanni lāḫuš lāḫuš=an tiššāit n=an šu-up-pí-iš-du-wa-ri-it daiš n=an gulšta nu=šši=šta maišti anda lālukkišnut* § ... § *walḫdu=ya=an* [d]IM*-aš teššummin nu=šši šu-up-pí-iš-du-wa-ri-uš arḫa šakkuriēd‹du› teššummiš=kan anda amiyari maušdu šu-up-pí-iš-du-wa-ri-i-e-eš=ma=kán anda* ÍD*-i muwāntaru* "A coppersmith cast a cup for (his own) glory. He cast it (and) finished it. He provided it with ornamentation and engraved it. He made (them) gleam on it with brilliance. § ... § Let the Stormgod strike it, the cup. Let him knock off its ornamentation. Let the cup fall into a ditch, and let the ornamentation fall into a river" KBo 32.14 ii 42-45, 55-60 (Hurro-Hitt. bil. wisdom and myth, MH/MS), ed. Neu, Hurritische 28, 32, StBoT 32:80-83 ("glänzenden Applikationen"), cf. 157f., tr. Hittite Myths[2] 70.

**1.** ornament(ation) — **a.** in festivals: [*IŠTU* É [d]]*In*[(*ar*)] *šu-up-pí-iš-tu-wa-re-eš* (var. *šu-up-pí-iš-tu-wa-a-re-eš*) *uenzi ḫ*[*uit*]*ār ša*[(*menzi*)] *pēreš uizzi INA* UD.2.KAM *p*[*ēr*]*iš ḫuidā*[(*rr=a*)] NU.GÁL "[From the temple of] Inar the ornaments come, the (images of) wild animals pass by. The *peri-* comes. On the second day, there are no *peri-* and no wild animals" KBo 22.224 obv. 1-3 + KBo 22.195 ii! 12-14 (KI.LAM, OH/MS), w. dupl. KBo 20.5 ii! 3-5 + KBo 25.12 ii 15-17 (OS), translit. StBoT 28:34, tr. StBoT 27:96 ("a vessel made of (ornamented) metal plate"), cf. *ša(m)men-* ("attachments"), HEG 1198 ("die Geschmückten").

**b.** in lists and inventories: [... *š*]*u-up-pí-iš-du-wa-ri-iš* KÙ.GI $NA_4$ *anda* § KUB 42.69 obv. 3 (inv., NH), cf. ibid. obv. 5, ed. Siegelová, Verw. 456f.; [... *per*]*an piddunaš* KÙ.GI 34 *šu-up-pí-iš-du-wa-re-eš* KÙ.GI "[...] carriers-forth of gold, thirty-four gold ornaments" KUB 42.69 obv. 18 (inv., NH), ed. Siegelová, Verw. 456f., translit. StBoT 12:67, *peran pēdumaš* d; [o o o] ⌈*šu-up*⌉*-pé-eš-du-wa-ra*[-...] 4 $SA_5$ *šu-up-pé-eš-du-wa-ra*[-...] KUB 42.26 obv.? 2-3 (inv., NH), ed. Siegelová, Verw. 466; [... *š*]*u-up-pí-iš-du-wa-ri-iš* x[ o o K]Ù.⌈BABBAR⌉ x[...] KBo 35.246 obv. 13 (list of offerings, MS); here? § 1 [ o o o o o o o o ]x 22 *iš-piš-du-wa-ra-a-aš* KÙ.GI $NA_4$ KUB 42.64 rev. 2 (inv., NH), ed. Siegelová, Verw. 426f., translit. THeth 10:148 □ for *išp-* as a variant writing of *šupp-*, see Košak, THeth 10:150, and Rieken, FsNeumann[2] 407f. w. lit.

**c.** ornament(ation) on a cup: see bil. sec.

**2.** ornamented cup(?): [(⌈LÚS⌉)AGI *š*]*u-up-pí-iš-tu-wa-ra-an udai* LUGAL*-uš* MUNUS.LUGAL*-ašš=a šarā tienzi* [(*aruwa*)*nzi* [LÚ]*kī*]*taš ḫalzāi* GAL [d]IM *akuanzi* "The cu[pbearer] brings the ornamented cup(?). The king and queen step up (and) bow. [The *ki*]*ta-*man cries out. They drink the cup (of) the Storm God" KBo 17.74 i 19-20 (thunder fest., OH/MS), w. dupl. KBo 25.95 i 1-2 + KBo 17.11 i 4-5 + KBo 34.11 + KBo 30.25 i 20-21 (OS), ed. Alp, Tempel 210f. (= l. 20-21), StBoT 12:12f. ("glänzenden? Becher des Wettergottes"), dupl. translit. StBoT 25.64 □ Neu, StBoT 12:12 and StBoT 25:64, restored GAL [d]IM in the break before *š.* but there is not enough room to accommodate this; [...] ⌈GÙB⌉*-aš* [d]UD*-AM*[? (or *n*[*e-*?]) / [*š*]*u-u*[*p-p*]*é-eš-tu-wa-ri-it kurup*[*šini* ...] *akuwanzi* "Standing, [the king and queen(?)] drink to the Divine Day from/with(?) a *kurup*[*šini-*...] ornamented cup(?)[...]" KBo 46.159 ii 2-3 (fest, NS), ed. StBoT 12:68 (as 99/r) □ for a comparable passage w. *BIBRU* in place of *š.*, see LUGAL MUNUS.LUGAL GUB*-aš* [d]UD*-AM IŠTU BIBRI kurupšini akuwanzi* KUB 10.89 i 38-39 (monthly fest., OH/NS), see also HED K 279.

For discussion and bibliography, see *šuppe/ištuwara-* A.

Cf. *šuppe/ištuwara-* A adj., *šuppešduwarant-*.

**šuppešduwarant-** adj.; ornamented; NH.†

**sg. nom.** *ʳšuʾ-up-pé-eš-du-‹wa-ra-›an-za* KUB 42.26 obv.? 6 (NH); **pl. nom.** *[š]u-up-pí-iš-du-wa-ra-an-te-eš* KUB 42.69 rev. 17, (26) (NH).

[... *šu-up-p*]*í-iš-du-wa-ra-an-te-eš lammamenzi* [...] "[...-s, orna]mented (and) *lammā*-ed" KUB 42.69 rev. 26 (inv., NS), ed. Siegelová, Verw. 460f., cf. *lammami-*, see also ibid. 17 □ for *lammamenzi* as possibly "soldered," see Starke, StBoT 31:423 w. n. 1524; cf. 6 *peran pedum*[*aš*...] *ʳšuʾ-up-pé-eš-du‹-wa-ra›-an-za* [...] 1 *peran peduma*[*š*...] KUB 42.26 obv.? 5-7 (inv., NH), ed. Siegelová, Verw. 466f., translit. THeth. 10:53.

Cf. *šuppe/ištuwara-* A & B.

**šuppiwašḫanalli-** n.; (a cultic utensil, kind of table, or container?); from OS.†

**sg. dat.-loc.** *šu-up-pí-wa-aš-ḫa-n*[*a-al-li*]*-ia* KBo 20.61 i 10 (+) KBo 31.183 i 4 (OH/NS).

**pl. dat.-loc.** *šu-*[*up-pí-wa-aš-ḫa-na-al-li-ia-a*]*š* KBo 20.12 i 11 (OS), [*šu-up-p*]*í-*[*w*]*a-aš-ḫa-na-al-li-i*[*a-aš*] KBo 17.74 i 10 (OH/MS), *šu-up-pí-wa-aš-ḫa-n*[*a-al-li-ia-aš*] KUB 34.120:5 (OH/NS), [*šu-up-pí-w*]*a-aš-ḫa-n*[*a-al-li-ia-aš*] HFAC 50:4 (NS).

**broken:** *šu-up-pí-wa-aš-ḫ*[*a-na-al-li-*...] KBo 13.227 i 21 (NS).

For *šu-up-pa wa-aš-ḫa-na-al-l*[*i*(-)...?] KUB 11.8 + 9 iii 20 (NH), see s.v. *wašḫanalli-*.

An object upon which the royal napkin (lit. knee-cloth) is placed: [(DUMU.É.GAL) *Š*]*A* LUGAL DUMU.É.ʳGALʾ MUNUS.LUGAL *pānzi ʳta* LUGAL-*ašʾ* MUNUS.LUGAL-*ašš=a* [(*ginuw*)]*aš* GADA.ḪI.A *patānn=a* $^{GIŠ}$GÌR.GUB *danzi g*[(*inuw*)]*aš* GADA.ḪI.A [(*šu*)-*up-p*]*í-*[*w*]*a-aš-ḫa-na-al-li-i*[*a-a*(*š t*)]*ianzi* $^{GIŠ}$GÌR.GU[B *t*]*agān* [(*t*)*ia*]*nzi* DUMU.MEŠ É.GAL *āppa* [*tienz*]*i ta=z pēʳda=šmeʾt appanzi* "The attendant of the king (and) the attendant (of) the queen go. They take the king's and queen's napkins (lit. knee-cloths) and footstool(s). They place the napkins (lit. knee-cloths) in/on *š.*-s, they put the footstool(s) on the ground. The palace attendants step back and take their places" ABoT 1.9 i 9-12 + KBo 17.74 i 8-11 (Storm-fest., OH/MS), w. dupl. KBo 20.12 i 9-11 (OS), ed. Neu, StBoT 12:10f.; [...LU]GAL-*waš* MUNUS.[LUGAL-*ašš=a*] / [*ginuwaš* G]ADA.ḪI.A *da*[*nzi*] / [*ta*? *šu-up-pí-w*]*a-aš-ḫa-n*[*a-al-li-ia-aš*] / [*tiyanzi p*]*atann*[*=a* $^{GIŠ}$GÌR.GUB] / [*danzi*] *n=e dag*[*ān tiyanzi*] "[They] take the [ki]ng's [and] que[en's knee-c]loths [and place (in/on)] *š.*-s. [They take the f]oot[stool(s)] and [put] them on the gro[und]" HFAC 50:2-6 (Storm-fest., NS), restored from par. KUB 34.120:3-7 (OH/NS); cf. KBo 13.227 i 21 (fest., NS); [*n=ašta*] *ʳAʾN*[*A*] LUGAL MUNUS.LUGAL DUMU.MEŠ É.GAL *ginuwaš* G[ADA.ḪI.A *da*]*nzi n=at=šan šu-up-pí-wa-aš-ḫa-n*[*a-al-li-*]*ia tianzi* § GÌR.ḪI.A-*n=a* $^{GIŠ}$GÌR.GUB.MEŠ [*šar*?]*ʳāʾ danzi n=at dagan tianzi* "The palace attendants take the knee-c[loths] away from the king and queen, and place them on the *š.* § They also pick [u]p(?) the footstools (from the throne dais) and place them on the floor" KBo 20.61 i 8-12 (+) KBo 31.183 i 2-6 (Storm-fest., OH/NS), ed. Goedegebuure, NABU 2017:105f.

In the description of a cultic ceremony, e.g., ABoT 1.9 i 9-12 + KBo 17.74 i 8-11, it is said that the footstools of the royal couple are put down on the ground, but their napkins(?) (lit. knee cloths) are placed in/on the *š.* The most conceivable candidate for placing the royal napkins(?) would be a table, a stand, or a container of some kind. Neu, StBoT 12:36, suggested *šuppiwašḫanalli-* is an *-alli-* formation from *šuppiwašḫar*$^{(SAR)}$ (q.v.) "Zwiebel." This would require an oblique on *-n-*, which is unlikely since *šuppiwašḫar* is a com. gender noun that thus inflects like *keššar*, *keššaraš* (gen.) "hand." More probably, *š.* is a compound of *šuppi* A "pure, sacred" and Luw. **wašḫanalli-* "(thing) for consecrated objects."

Goetze, JCS 1 (1947) 320 (takes *šuppa*(-)*wašḫanalli-* as the name of a profession); Friedrich, HW 198 (1952) 198 (*šuppa*(-) *wašḫanalli-*: "Zwiebelhändler(?)"); van Brock, RHA XX/71 (1962) 106f. ("frotté d'oignon"); Neu, StBoT 12 (1970) 36f. ("eine Art von Tischen ( ... ) oder auch Tische mit Zwiebeln ( ... ) oder gar irgendwelche Zwiebelbehälter ... Zwiebelbündel, ... wie man sie noch heute (nicht nur in der Türkei) an die Decke bzw. in das Deckengebälk hängt"); Oettinger, Stammbildung (1979) 34 (cites an unattested form *šuppiwašḫanae-* "mit Zwiebel würzen(?)"); Tischler, HDW (1982) 79 ("Zwiebelbund" o.ä.); Neu, StBoT 26 (1983) 176 ("Zwiebelbündel"); Rieken, StBoT 44 (1999) 311-314 (eine substantivische Zugehörigkeitsbildung); Tischler, HEG S/2 (2006) 1200f. (adj. "zwiebelförmig, mit Zwiebeln versehen;" n. "Zwiebelbehälter,

Zwiebelbündel"); Kloekhorst, EDHIL (2008) 791f. ("having onions (?)").

Cf. *šuppi-* A, *šuppiwašḫar*$^{(SAR)}$.

**šuppiwašḫar$^{(SAR)}$** n. com.; garlic; wr. syll. and SUM.SIKIL$^{(SAR)}$ from MH/MS, OH/NS.†

**sg. nom. com.** *šu-up-pí-wa-aš-ḫar*$^{SAR}$ KUB 29.7 rev. 28 (MH/MS).

**acc.** *šu-u[p-pí-w]a-aš-ḫar*$^{SAR}$ KUB 29.7 rev. (27), 30 (MH/MS).

**gen.** *šu-up-pí-[wa-aš-ḫa-ra-a]š* KUB 29.7 rev. 30 (MH/MS).

**Sum.** SUM.SIKIL$^{SAR}$ KBo 9.93:7 (MS?), KBo 6.12 i 4 (OH/NS), SUM.SIKIL KBo 8.78 rev. 9 (NS), KBo 46.186:(4) (NS), KUB 60.57:(10).

**a.** laws concerning theft of garlic: [*takku* $^{GIŠ}$GEŠTIN-*an našma*] $^{GIŠ}$*maḫlan našma* $^{GIŠ}$*karpinan* [*našma* SUM.SIKIL$^{SAR}$ *kui*]*ški tāiēzzi karū* [*ANA* 1 $^{GIŠ}$GEŠTIN 1 G]ÍN.GÍN KÙ.BABBAR *ANA* 1 $^{GIŠ}$*maḫli* 1 GÍN.GÍN KÙ.BABBAR [1 $^{GIŠ}$*karpini* 1 GÍN.GÍ]N KÙ.BABBAR *ANA* 1 ZU$_9$ SUM.SIKIL$^{SAR}$ 1 GÍN.GÍN KÙ.BABBAR [*pešker*] "[If any]one steals [a vine,] a vine branch, a *karpina-*, [or garlic,] formerly [they paid one s]hekel of silver [for one vine,] one shekel of silver for one vine branch, [one sheke]l of silver [for one *karpina-*,] one shekel of silver for one clove of garlic" KBo 6.12 i 1-5 (Law §101, OH/NS), ed. Hoffner, LH 99 ("garlic").

**b.** in cultic context — **1′** used analogically both for the curse and for the remedy: EGIR-*anda*=*ma*=*šši š*[*u-up-pí-wa-aš-ḫ*]*ar*$^{SAR}$ *pianzi anda*=*ma*=*kan kiššan memai mān*=*wa ANA PĀNI* DINGIR-*LIM kuiški kiššan me*[*miškez*]*zi kāš*=*wa māḫḫan šu-up-pí-wa-aš-ḫar*$^{SAR}$ *ḫurpaštaz anda ḫūlaliyanza nu araš aran ar*[*ḫa U*]*L tarnai idālauwanzi*=*ya NĪŠ* DINGIR-*LIM*=*ya ḫurtaiš papranna*[*nz*]*aš*=*a* ⌜*e*⌝*ni* É.DINGIR-*LIM šu-up-pí-*[*wa-aš-ḫa-ra-a*]*š iwar anda ḫūlaliyan ḫardu kinun*=*a kāša kūn šu-u*[*p-pí-w*]*a-aš-ḫar*$^{SAR}$ *arḫa šippanun* [*kinun*]=*an katta* 1 *kākin dawanin kurkun idālu*=*ya uttar NĪŠ* DINGIR-[*LIM ḫu*]*rtaiš paprātar ANA* DINGIR-*L*[*IM* É=*Š*]*U arḫa QĀTAMMA šippaiddu* "Next they give to him (i.e., the ritual patron) a (clove of) g[arli]c. In doing so she speaks as follows: 'If before a god anyone s[peak]s as follows: "Just as this garlic is enveloped in skins (lit. leaves), and one does [n]ot let go o[f] the other, let the evil ⟨word?⟩, perjury, curse and unclean[ne]ss envelop that temple like a gar[lic.]" So now, right here I have stripped this ga[rl]ic. [No]w I have one clove (lit. tooth) (and) a stem(?) left. In the same way let him (i.e., the ritual patron) strip the evil, perjur[y, c]urse, (and) uncleanness [awa]y from the god's [house]'" KUB 29.7 rev. 27-32 (Šamuḫa rit., MH/MS), ed. Lebrun, Samuha 123f., 131 ("un oignon"), Hoffner, AlHeth 108 ("onion"), Torri, StAs. 2:142 ("cipolla"), Marquardt, FsKošak 503f. ("Zwiebel"), Görke/Melzer, hethiter.net/: CTH 480.1 (TX 15.02.2016, TRde 10.02.2016) ("Zwiebel"), translit. Goetze, JCS 1:318, Haas, Materia 339f., cf. HED K 19 ("onion") □ for Luw. *dawani-* "stalk, stem(?)," see CLL 225 s.v. The *i*-stem form of *kakin* (vs. Hitt. *gaga-* "tooth") is likely to be due to Luw. influence as well (differently HED K 17f. s.v. *kaki-*).

**2′** listed among materials, sometimes with specific measurement: [...]⌜x⌝-*ya*=*ma kuiš* $^{LÚ}$SANG[A...] / [...*ḫ*]⌜*ū*⌝*man* ⌜SUM⌝$^{SAR}$ SUM.SIKI[L$^{SAR}$ ...] / [... U]ZU.ÙZ UZU.UR.G[I$_7$ ...] "but which pries[t (or: (if) some priest) ... a]ll (this) onion, garli[c, ...] goat [m]eat, do[g] meat [...]" KUB 60.57:9-11 (purification rit., NS), cf. Marquardt, FsKošak 503; [...]x 1/2 *ŠĀTI* SUM.SIKIL$^{SAR}$ 1/2 *Š*⌜*Ā*⌝[*TI* ...] / [...] ⌜1?⌝ *wakšur* Ì.UDU 1 *wakšur* L[ÀL? ...] "a half *SŪTU*-measure of garlic, a half *SŪ*[*TU* of ...], one(?) *wakšur* of sheep fat, one *wakšur* of ho[ney ...]" KBo 9.93:7-8 (Ištanuwian fest., MS?), translit. Starke, StBoT 30:320.

**3′** others: mixed in bread (i.e., garlic bread?): § *našma* NINDA-*i kuedani*⌜*k*⌝[*ki*...] SUM.SIKIL *imiyanza* (var. *immiyanza*) *apāš*[...] *našma*=*kan ANA* $^{DUG}$ÚTUL UZ[U...] *nu*=*kan apēzza IŠTU* U[ZU? ...] ⌜*i*⌝*yanzi n*=*at ē*⌜*z*⌝*zaz*[*zi*] "§ or, wha[t] bread [...] the garlic is mixed in, that one [...] or (in)to the pot the mea[t ...] From that m[eat(?)...] they make [a cooked dish/stew(?)], and he eat[s] it" KBo 8.78 rev. 8-12 (fest. frag., NS), w. dupl. KBo 46.186:3-7 (NS).

According to Goetze, JCS 1:320, *šuppiwašḫar* is a loan translation of the Sumerian sum.sikil$^{sar}$, which he interpreted as "holy garlic" i.e., "onion." However, Gelb, FsLandsberger 57-58, advocated a very opposite interpretation for this word as "pure onion" i.e., "garlic." On the discussion of whether *šuppiwašḫar* (SUM.SIKIL)^SAR is "onion" or "garlic," see Hoffner, AlHeth 108f. and more recently idem., LH 198f. He prefers the meaning "garlic" because of the unit $ZU_9$ "tooth" KBo 6.12 i 4 is more appropriate for a clove of garlic, which looks like a canine tooth (thus also Marquardt, FsKošak 505). Compare for example the Turkish expression *bir diş sarımsak* "a clove of garlic" (*diş* "tooth"). For onion there is another expression, namely *bir baş soğan* "a knob of onion" (*baş* "head, top").

It is generally assumed that *šuppiwašḫar* is a composite noun consisting of *šuppi-* "holy, sacred" and *wašḫar* "bulb" or "onion/garlic." The second element *wašḫar* is attested without *šuppi* KUB 60.57:7 (see Marquardt, FsKošak), but the broken context gives no clue as to its meaning. Note that the same fragment (line 10) also has [S]UM^SAR SUM.SIKI[L^SAR] see above b 2′. In view of the consistent com. gender agreement (see the passages in b 1′ and 3′) we give the word as such.

Goetze, JCS 1 (1947) 318-20 ("onion"); Friedrich, HW (1952) 199 ("Zwiebel"); Kammenhuber, MSS 14 (1959) 81-82 n. 15 (on word formation of *š.*); eadem, Or NS 31 (1962) 370 (on word formation); Kronasser, EHS 1 (1966) 126, 285 (on word formation); Hoffner, Or NS 35 (1966) 380 (on word formation); idem., AlHeth (1974) 108-9 ("onion or garlic"), 198 ("garlic"); Ertem, Flora (1974) 32f. ("soğan"); Stol, BSAg 3 (1987) 59-61 (SUM.SIKIL = "onion"); CAD Š/1 (1989) 298-301 (an alliaceous plant, "shallot"?); Košak, ZA 84 (1994) 289; van den Hout, BiOr 51 (1994) 123; Hoffner, HL (1997) 99, 198-99, 326 ("garlic"); Zinko, StBoT 45 (2001) 754-757; Bachvarova, Diss. (2002) 19 ("onion"); Tischler, HEG S/2 (2006) 1201-1203; Marquardt, FsKošak (2007) 503-506; Kloekhorst, EDHIL (2008) 791.

Cf. *šuppi-* A, *wašḫar, šuppiwašḫanalli-*.

**šupla-** see *šuppal(a-)*.

**šubri- A** n. Hurr.; (mng. unkn., epithet of gods); from MH.†

**Hurr. gen.** *šu-ub-ri-bi* KBo 21.37 obv.? 9, (10) (MH/MS).

**Hurr. definite article + gen.** *šu-bur-ri-bi* SBo 1.39 B inner ring (Muw. II), *šu-bur-ri-bi-ia* Bo 6030 right col. 12, translit. SBo 2 p. 53.

**a.** without article: [# NINDA.GU]$R_4$.RA *ANA* ^dU *eḫlibi šu-ub-ri-bi paršiyanzi še⸢r⸗ma⸗ššan* ^UZU⸣GAB ⸢^UZU ZAG⸣.[UDU o o ]x? [*dāi*(?) *n*]*⸗at⸗šan ištanāni* EGIR-*pa dāi* EGIR*⸗ŠU⸗ma* 2 NINDA.$GUR_4$.[R]A *at⸢t⸣aš* DINGIR.[MEŠ-*aš eḫlibi šu-u*]*b-ri-bi* ‹*paršiyanzi*› ⸢*šer*⸣*⸗*[*ma⸗š*]*šan* 2 ^UZU MAS.SÌLA 2 ^UZU *muḫrainn⸗a dāi* "They break [# thi]ck-[bread(s)] to the Stormgod of Salvation and *š.* On top of them [(s)he puts(?)] breast- and shoulder-meat [...a]nd (s)he places them back on the altar. Thereafter, ‹they break› two thick breads for the paternal god[s of salvation and] of ⸢*š.*⸣ On top of them (s)he places two shoulder blades and two *muḫrai*-s" KBo 38.260 obv.? 10-12 + KBo 21.37 obv.? 9-11 + KBo 8.91 obv. 1 (fest. of Šulupašši and Šapinuwa, MH/MS), translit. Trémouille, GsImparati 846f. □ for the Stormgod of Salvation, see Wilhelm, Kaskal 10:155f., and Giorgieri/Murat/Süel, Kaskal 10:175 w. n. 20.

**b.** with article: ^dUT[U] ^U[^RU... ^dU *š*]*u-bur-ri-bi* SBo 1.39 g 2 and B inner ring (Muw. II), cf. SBo 1 p. 20 w. n. 62 and SBo 2 p. 53; cf. also *ANA* ^dU *šu-bur-ri-bi-ia QĀTAMMA* Bo 6030 right col. 12, translit. SBo 2 p. 53 (quoted as "ii?"), ChS I/9:176 (quoted as "Rs. III?") □ this word is *šubri-* (q.v.) + *ne* (article) + *bi* (gen.).

The context above suggests that the word *š.* (with Hurr. gen. ending *-bi* ‹ *-we*, i.e., *šubriwe*) is an epithet of the paternal gods. A Hurrian word *šub/pri* is known from other Hurr. texts; see Laroche, GLH 238 and Haas, ChS I/1:423f., listed with oblique forms; for Hurr. words in the seal legends of Muw. II see BoHa 23:74. In some Hurr. contexts (IBoT 2.39 rev. 2, 43) *šupri⸗bi* occurs alongside *eḫli⸗bi,* both Hurr. genitives, as epithets of Teššub.

It is unclear if this word is related to the GN Šubriya of the Neo-Assyrian inscriptions. This place was located in the mountains between the upper Tigris and the Murad Su and probably, at least in part, Hurrian speaking. This GN, is in turn, related to the GN Subartu (Kessler, RlA 13:239), attested in Mesopotamia from early Urukian to Neo-Babylonian texts referring to "northern Mesopotamia" (not a specific political entity), large portions of which would have been inhabited by Hurrians.

Already in the OA texts "Šubiriatam" refers to the Hurrian language (Michel, RlA 13:226).

There is also a Hittite (or loan) word *šupri(ya)-* (q.v.), which appears in the gen. *šupriyaš* KBo 26.100 iv 9 as an epithet(?) of the Stormgod. A direct relationship between the Hurr. gen. *šubribi* and Hitt. gen. *šupriyaš* "of the *š.*" cannot be claimed yet.

Güterbock, SBo 1 (1940) 52; idem, SBo 2 (1942) 53 (related to *šuḫurribi*?); Laroche, GLH (1977-9) 238 s.v.; Trémouille, GsImparati (2002) 852; Bawanypeck, BoHa 23 (2011) 74; Richter, BibGlHurr (2012) 417.

**šupri- B/šupriya-** n.; (mng. unkn.); pre-NH/MS.†

**sg.(?) gen.** *šu-up-ri-ia-aš* KBo 26.100 iv 9 (pre-NH/MS).

(said of the Stormgod:) *nu≠za na*⸢*kk*⸣*iš* ⸢d⸣U-*aš* x[...] / [...-*y*]*aš šu-up-ri-ia-aš tagn*⸢*ā*⸣*š nep*[*iš*]*aš* [...] / [...]x *ḫūmandāš* DUMU.N[AM.LÚ.U]$_{19}$.LU-*aš* LU⸢GAL⸣-*uš* [...] "and the mighty Stormgod [...] / [...the lord(?)] of [...], of *š.*, of earth (and) sky [...] / [...] the king of all man[ki]nd" KBo 26.100 iv 8-10 (myth, pre-NH/MS).

According to the passage above *š.* might be something the Stormgod rules over, parallel to *tekan/takn-* "earth" and *nepiš* "sky." Whether *š.* is related to (Hurr.) *šubri-* A (q.v.) is unclear.

Cf. *šubri-* A.

**šuprumi(y)a?-** n. com. (or **šupru-** n. neut.); (an anomaly(?) on the human body); NS.†

**sg. nom.** *šu-up-ru-mi-aš* (or: *šu-up-ru*) KUB 43.8 iii 11a (NS).

[BE-*an≠ka*]*n*? UN-*ši šu-up-ru-mi-aš*? (or: *šu-up-ru* DUGUD?) *anda*? (or: DINGIR-*it*/«DINGIR-*it*»?)DINGIR.MEŠ-*it UL kanišan*⸢*za*⸣ "[If] there is *š.* (or: a heavy *š.*) inside of/on a person, he/she is repudiated by the gods" KUB 43.8 iii 11a-b (physiognomic omens, NS), ed. DBH 12:150, 152 □ Riemschneider, DBH 12:262, interprets the form *šuprumiaš* as pl. dat.-loc. ("[Wenn] einem Menschen in den ..."). In his translit. (but not in his hand copy) he assumes an extra line 12a-b, but the photo does not support this. In comparison with previous apodoses the absence of a clear "antecedent" either through the dem. pron. *apa-* (l. 7b)/BI-*aš* (ll. 8b, 10b, see Goedegebuure, StBoT 55:494) or the repetition of UN (l. 9b) makes the text suspect. Is the alleged *-mi-aš*/DUGUD to be read as ⸌BI?-*aš* with the Glossenkeil marking the start of the apodosis since only here does it starts in the left column?

The possibility that *š.* indicates a physical anomaly is based on other cases of deformities of the human body listed in previous lines of the same text iii 8a, 9a, 10a (long legs, turned tongue, lion-shaped head, etc.).

Riemschneider, DBH 12 (2004) 262 ("unklar"); Tischler, HEG S/2 (2006) 1203 (mng. unkn.).

[*šupš-* v.] *šu-up-ša-ri* KBo 5.4 rev. 38 (Targ.), ed. SV 1:66f. read *šu-up-ta*!*-ri*, for which see *šupp-*.

[*šu-pu*] KUB 6.2 obv. 10, 14, 16, 17, 18, [*šu-pu-an-zi*] KUB 18.10 + KUB 6.12 iv 33 read ŠU.GÍD and ŠU.GÍD-*an-zi*, respectively. ŠU.GÍD means "to observe, investigate, check (in haruspicy)."

[*šu-pu-an-zi*], see [*šu-pu*].

**šuburribi** see *šubri-* A.

**(NA4)šur** n. neut.; (a natural stone or object made of stone where sacrifices are made); from OH?/NS.†

**sg. nom.-acc.** *šu-u-ur* KBo 27.51 obv.? 6 (fest., NS).
**dat.-loc.** *šu-u-ri* KBo 34.155 ii? 14 (OH?/NS).
**pl. dat.-loc.** *šu-u-ra-aš* KUB 34.124 ii? 6, 7, 9, 12, 15 (OH?/MS), ABoT 1.13 vi (7), 9 (NS), KBo 23.89:13 (NS), here? KBo 17.9 i 12 (OS), KBo 47.95 obv.? 5 (preceded by $NA_4$-*aš*) (NS), [*š*]*u-ra-aš* or [*šu*]-⸢*ú*⸣-*ra-aš* KBo 30.54 i (3) (NS), NA4*šu-u-ra-aš* IBoT 4.75 obv. rt. col. (8) (NS), VBoT 95 i 9 (NS).
**broken:** NA4*šu-u-r*[*a-*...] VBoT 95 i 13 (NS).

⸢GAL?⸣ LÚ.MEŠ*tarš*[*pala-*...] ⸢Ù⸣?/⸢NA4⸣?*šu-u-ur* [...] *kuiēš a-*x[...] *tuppaš* É-*a*[*z*...] § LUGAL-*uš laḫḫa*[*z*...] URU*Arinna* [...] KBo 27.51 obv.? 5-10 (fest., NS); [(LUGAL-*uš≠kan paizz*)]*i*(?) *šu-u-ra-aš katta UŠKĒN t≠aš tīēz*[*zi*] § [(LÚGUD)]$U_{12}$ ⸢*pa*⸣*izzi* NINDA.$GUR_4$.RA $SA_5$ *paršiya šu-u-ra-aš* (var. NA4*šu-u-r*[*a-aš*]) *katta* 3 *paršu*⸢*l*⸣*li* $NA_4$-*ašš≠a katta tagān* 3 *paršull*[*i*] *dāi* LÚ$GUDU_{12}$ *paizzi* NINDA.$GUR_4$.RA BABBAR *paršiya šu-*

*u-ra-aš katta* 3 *paršulli* $NA_4$-*ašš=a katta tagān* 3 *paršulli dāi* § $^{LÚ}$GUDU$_{12}$ *paizzi* NINDA.GUR$_4$.RA BABBAR *paršiya šu-u-ra-aš katta dāi namma* NINDA.GUR$_4$.RA *paršiya ta* $NA_4$-*aš katta d*[*āi*] § $^{LÚ.MEŠ}$MUḪALDIM 4 UDU.ḪI.A *šu-u-ri ḫ*⸢*ūkanzi*⸣ $^{LÚ}$GUDU$_{12}$ *paizzi išpantuziaššar* KÙ.BABBAR GEŠTI[N *d*]*āi šu-u-ra-aš katta* 3-*ŠU* $NA_4$-*ašš=a katta* 3-⸢*ŠU*⸣ [*šip*]⸢*an*⸣*ti* "The king goes (and) bows next to/down at the *š*.-s (Then) he take[s his place.] § The GUDU$_{12}$-priest goes, crumbles a red thick loaf (and) places three crumbs next to/ down at the *š*.-s and three crumbs on the ground next to/down at the stones. The GUDU$_{12}$-priest goes, crumbles a white thick loaf (and) places three crumbs next to/down at the *š*.-s and three crumbs on the ground next to/down at the stones. § The GUDU$_{12}$-priest goes, crumbles a(nother) white thick loaf (and) places (it) next to/down at the *š*.-s. Again he breaks a thick loaf and pl[aces] (it) under the stones. § The cooks slaughter four sheep at the *š*. The GUDU$_{12}$-priest goes, [t]akes a silver libation vessel of/for win[e] (and) [li]bates three times next to/down at the *š*.-s and three times next to/down at the stones" KUB 34.124 + KBo 34.155 obv.? ii 6-16 (*ANDAḪŠUM* fest., OH?/MS), with par. IBoT 4.75 obv. rt. col. 6-13 (NS), ed. Popko, Kultobjekte 132f., and AoF 13:178 □ because of the possible OH date of this composition, a sg. gen. w. *katta* cannot be excluded; $^{LÚ}$GUDU$_{12}$ $^{UZU}$NÍG.GIG [*šu-u-r*]*a-aš dāi* $NA_4$-*ašš=a dāi* § [$^{DUG?}$*iš*]*pantuzziaššar* KÙ.BABBAR x (eras.) [GEŠTIN? *d*]*āi* ⸢*šu*⸣*-u-ra-aš* (var. [*š*]*u-ra-aš*) *pe*[(*r*)]*an* 3-*ŠU* [($NA_4$-*ašš*)]*=a peran* 3-*ŠU* ⸢*ši*⸣*panti* "The GUDU$_{12}$-priest puts the liver on/ at the *š*.-s and on the stones. § He [t]akes a silver [li]bation vessel of/for [wine(?)]. He libates three times in front of *š*.-s and three times in front of the stones" ABoT 1.13 vi 6-10 (*ANDAḪŠUM* fest., NS), w. dupl. KBo 30.54 i 1-4 (NS), ed. THeth. 22:90f.; LUGAL-*uš šu-u-ra-aš a*⸢*ri*⸣ "The king arrives at the *š*.-s" KBo 23.89:13 (NS); *t=aš INA* $^{URU}$*Arinna a*[*ndan* ...] § *mān* LUGAL-*uš* $^{NA_4}$*šu-u-ra-aš* ⸢*a*⸣[*ri*(?)...] "He (i.e., the king) [enters(?)] Arinna. When the king a[rrives(?)] at the *š*.-s [...]" VBoT 95 i 8-9 (NS); *ištanani=aš* $^{NA_4}$*šu-u-r*[*a-*...] "He [...-s] to/on the altar [to?] the *š*.-stone(s)" ibid. i 13; perhaps here: [...]x-*aš*(-)*šu-u-ra-aš katta* 1 *ekuzi* KBo 17.9 i 12 (KI.LAM fest., OS), for suggestions see Singer, StBoT 27:99 n. 33, 100 n. 35 (connected to $^{d}$Šura (sic)), and Neu, StBoT 26:176, 310 n. 2 with further bibliography.

$^{(NA_4)}$*š*. is mostly attested in texts dealing with the 7-8th days of the *ANDAḪŠUM* festival. *š*.-stones seem to constitute a sacral unit down at (*katta*) or before (*pēran*) which offerings are placed or libations are performed and animals are sacrificed. They also have some connection with an altar. In no text, however, do they directly receive offerings. They may have been a particular location at which the king arrives in the course of the *ANDAḪŠUM*-festival. Tischler, HEG S/2:1203, suggests a connection with the place name $^{URU}$*Šu-ra-aš* Bronze Tablet i 51, but contra Laroche, Rech. 77, there is no connection between $^{NA_4}$*šūr* and the divine name Šurra.

Popko, Kultobjekte (1978) 132-133; Tischler, HDW (1982) 79 ("verehrungswürdiges Kultobjekt, aus Stein?"); idem, HEG S/2 (2006) 1203-1204.

Cf. $^{LÚ}$*šūr*(*r*)*ala-*.

$^{LÚ}$**šūr(r)ala-** n. com.; (a functionary in the palace kitchen); MH?/NS.†

**sg. nom.** $^{LÚ}$*šur-ra-la-aš* KUB 13.3 ii 24, $^{LÚ}$*šu-u-ra-la-aš* KUB 13.3 iv 21 (MH?/NS).

Listed among the personnel of the palace kitchen: *anda=ma šumēš BĒLŪ*$^{MEŠ}$ TU$_7$ *ḫūmanteš* $^{LÚ}$SAGI.A LÚ $^{GIŠ}$BANŠUR $^{LÚ}$MUḪALDIM $^{LÚ}$NINDA.DÙ.DÙ $^{LÚ}$*dāwalalaš* $^{LÚ}$*walaḫḫiyalaš* $^{LÚ}$ZABAR.DAB $^{LÚ}$*pašandalaš* $^{LÚ}$*EPĪŠ* GA $^{LÚ}$*kipliyalaš* $^{LÚ}$*šur-ra-la-aš* $^{LÚ}$*tappālaš* $^{LÚ}$*ḫaršiyalaš* $^{LÚ}$*zuppālaš* LUGAL-*waš* ZI-*ni šer* ITU-*mi* ITU-*mi linkišketen* "Further, all you kitchen personnel—the cupbearer, the table-attendant, the cook, the baker, the *tawal*-maker, the *walḫi*-maker, the cellarmaster, the food-taster(?), the dairy-man, the *kipliyala*-man, the *š*.-man, the *tappala*-man, the keeper of *ḫarši*-breads, (and) the keeper of the *zuppa*-—swear on the king's soul month by month" KUB 13.3 ii 20-26 (instr. for palace servants, MH?/NS), ed. HittInstr 80f. ("*surra*-maker"), Pecchioli Daddi, Or NS 73:460, 465f. ("preparer of the *šurra*"), KN 36 n. 4, Friedrich, MAOG 4:47, 49 (no tr.), tr. Goetze, ANET 207; cf. also ibid. iv 19-22.

A connection between the *š.* and the stone *šūr*, s.v., is possible. There is no clear connection with the divine name Šurra as Laroche, Rech. 77, Alp, JKF 1:131-132 n. 99, and Tischler, HEG S/2:1204, with reservations, suggest.

Laroche, Rech. (1947) 77 ("cuisinier?"); Alp, JKF 1 (1950-51) 131-132 n. 99 ("Priester(?) der Gottheit Sura"); Friedrich, HW (1952) 199 ("Angestellter in der Palastküche"); van Brock, RHA XX/71 (1962) 100; Kronasser, EHS 1 (1966) 173 ("Küchenangestellter"); Haas, KN (1970) 36 n. 4 ("Bereiter des *šurra*"); Pecchioli Daddi, Mestieri (1982) 59 ("preparatore del *surra*"); Puhvel, HED K (1997) 187 (relates "probably to solid victuals"); Tischler, HEG S/2 (2006) 1204.

Cf. NA4*šūr*.

**(NA4)šūraš** Tischler, HHwb 156 see NA4*šūr*.

**(˂)šūraš(š)ūra-(MUŠEN), šurašūwa-MUŠEN, āššuraššura-** n. com.; (a kind of bird, crow (?)); from MH/MS.

**sg. nom.** *šu-u-ra-šu-u-ra-aš* KuT 49 obv. 25 (apud Wilhelm, MDOG 130:179) (MH/MS), KUB 30.34 iv 27 (MH/NS), KUB 39.104 iv (5) (MH/NS), *šu-u-ra-šu-u-ra-aš*MUŠEN KuT 49 obv. 30 (apud Wilhelm, MDOG 130:179) (MH/MS), *šu-u-ra-šu-u-wa-aš*MUŠEN KUB 30.34 iv 6 (MH/NS), ˂*šu-ra-šu-ra-aš* KUB 18.9 ii 8 (NH), MUŠEN*šu-ra-aš-šu-ra-aš* KUB 36.89 obv. 24, rev. 6, 53 (NH), *šu-u-ra-aš-šu-u-ra-aš* HKM 47 obv. 23, 27 (MH/MS), KBo 63.59:(8) (MH/MS), KBo 47.226:(9) (MH/MS), KBo 12.91 iv (4) (MH/NS), KUB 44.53 rev. 7 (NS), *šu-u-ra-aš-šu-u-ra-aš*MUŠEN KUB 50.1 ii 16, 22, iii 12 (NH), *a-aš-šu-ra-aš-šu-ra-aš* KUB 16.77 iii 50 (NH).

**acc.** *šu-ra-šu-ra-a*[*n*] KBo 13.131 iii 5 (MH?/NS), *šu-ra-šu-ra-an*MUŠEN KBo 9.119 iv 10 (MH/NS), *šu-u-ra-šu-u-ra-an* KUB 30.34 iv 19, 25 (MH/NS), *šu-u-ra-aš-šu-u-ra-an-ma*(sic)MUŠEN KBo 12.91 iv 3 (MH/NS).

**gen.** [*šu-ra-š*]⸢*u-ra-aš*⸣ KBo 13.131 iii 13 (MH?/NS).

**stem form (for voc.?)** *šu-u-ra-šu-u-wa*MUŠEN KBo 54.14 iii 9 (MH/LNS).

**pl. nom.** *šu-u-ra-šu-re-eš* KuT 50 obv. 22 (apud Wilhelm, MDOG 130:184) (MH/MS), [*šu-*]*ra-aš-šu-u-re-e-eš* KBo 53.106:4 (NS), here? [MUŠEN?]*šu-u-ra-šu-u-ra-*[*aš*] KUB 39.103 rev. (3) (MH/NS).

**pl. gen.(?)** *šu-ra-aš-šu-ra-aš* KBo 10.45 ii 26 (MH/NS).

**a.** in prayers: *kāša=wa=ta ḫalzeššai ḫalziyau*[*waš* dU *uid*]*du=aš* MUŠEN*šu-ra-aš-šu-ra-aš nu=war=an iš*[*da*]*mmaš* "It is just now invoking you, [O Stormgod [of] Invoking: let it, (namely) the *š.*-bird, [come] and listen to it" KUB 36.89 obv. 24-25 (prayer to the Stormgod of Nerik, NH), ed. Haas, KN 144f., tr. Hittite Myths² 23, Mazoyer in Freu/Mazoyer, Débuts 347 □ Haas's, KN 144f., restoration *ḫalziyau*[*wanzi uid*]*du=aš* "um [zu] rufen soll er, der *šuraššura*-Vogel [kom]men!" is problematic because of the position of the clitic *=aš*; for DN *ḫalziya(u)waš* see HW² Ḫ 110b; *mieš* (eras. MUŠEN*šu-ra-aš-*) MUŠEN*šu-ra-aš-šu-ra-aš ḫalziyauwanzi* ‹*uiddu*?› ZI DINGIR-*LIM apāš uwateddu* "Be mild, ‹let› the *š.*-bird ‹come(?)› to call, let him bring the divine will (saying): ('Let the Stormgod (and) the Sungoddess of Arinna release from heaven the mild rains')" KUB 36.89 rev. 52-53, ed. KN 156f.

**b.** in rituals: *n=aš=za naššu* É*ḫalinduwaš šuḫḫi ēštat našma=zzan* (for **=z=šan*) *INA* É.DINGIR.MEŠ *šuḫḫi ēštat kinun=a* É*ḫalinduwa*«*š*» (var. B É*ḫalituwa*) É.DINGIR.MEŠ*=ya parkunut nu kī* ‹(*i*)›*nan ēšḫar NĪŠ* DINGIR-*LIM kuwapi* ⸢*pa*⸣*izzi zik šu-u-ra-šu-u-wa-aš*MUŠEN (var. A [MUŠEN?]*šu-u-ra-šu-u-ra-*[*aš*], var. B *šu-u-ra-šu-u-wa*MUŠEN) *apadda ītten* ⸢*nu*⸣ *ēšḫananza linkiyaz* É*ḫalinduwa* É.DINGIR.MEŠ *lē ēpzi* "It (i.e., the *š.*-bird) settled either on the roof of the palace complex or on the roof on the temple. Now it has purified (thereby) the palace complex and the temple. Where(ever) this illness, blood (and) perjury go, you, O *š.*-bird, go (pl.!) to right there. Let not bloodshed (and) perjury seize the palace complex (and) temple" KUB 30.34 iv 2-8 (rit. for purification of a town, MH/NS), w. dupls. (A) KUB 39.103 rev. 1-5 (MH/NS), (B) KBo 54.14 iii 5-11 (LNS), ed. Haas/Wäfler, OA 16:229f., Alp, Tempel 112f.; [*n*]*u=kan* MÁŠ.GAL-*an šu-u-ra-šu*(eras.)*-u-ra-an-n=a* URU-*ri* ⸢*iš*⸣*tarna arḫa pēdai n=ašta antuḫšuš* ⸢*kuēz*⸣*za* KÁ.GAL.ḪI.A-*za katta kunanna* ⸢*pē*⸣*ḫudanzi apūš=a=kan apēz katta* ⸢*peda*⸣*tti nu antuḫšeš apiya kuedani pedi* ⸢*e*?⸣*ker n=uš apē*‹*da*›*ni pedi pēdatti* § [*n*]*u* MÁŠ.GAL-*an warnuwanzi šu-u-ra-šu-u-ra-an-n=a* [*ḫ*]*a*⸢*ri*⸣*yanzi nu tezzi ki=ašta maḫḫan* M[ÁŠ].GAL *šu-u-ra-šu-u-ra-aš-š=a kattan taknaza pāer* ⸢*k*⸣*ī=kan ŠA* URU*Ḫatti inan ēšḫar NĪŠ* DINGIR-*LIM pangauwaš* EME-*aš QĀTAMMA* GAM-*anda taknaza paidd*[*u*] "He/she carries a goat and a *š.*-bird through the town. You bring them (i.e., the two animals) down through that gate, through which one brings down people to be killed. You bring them to that place where people died. § They burn the goat and [b]ury the *š.*-bird and he/she says: 'As these, the g[o]at and the *š.*-bird, have gone down to/through the earth, so may these, (namely) the illness, bloodshed, perjury (and) all slander of Ḫatti, likewise go down to/through the earth'" KUB 30.34 iv 19-29 (MH/NS), ed. (partial) StBoT 3:158, cf. similarly KBo 12.91 iv 2-8 (MH/NS) and KUB 39.104 iv 1-7 (MH/NS); (Someone takes an eagle, a falcon, and a *š.*-bird and encourages the eagle and falcon to take away evils) § [...*šu-ra-š*]*u-*⌈*ra-aš*⌉ *naššu* UN-*aš* UZUÌ *ez*(eras.)*zāš* [... *naš*]*ma*(?) KA×U*=ŠU išḫanuwanza* x[...] "[The *š.*]-bird ate either human fat [or ... o]r(?) its bill is bloody ... [...]" KBo 13:131 iii 5-6, 13-14 (purification rit., MH?/NS); *namma ANA* dU [É]*ka*⌈*r*⌉*immeya*[ o ](eras.) GUD *ḫuršalamin* [ o ]x 1 MÁŠ.TUR 1 T[U$_8$MUŠEN] 1 SUR$_{14}$.DÙ.AMUŠEN 1 *IRIBU*MUŠEN [1 *ḫa*]*pupin* 1 x[...]x 1 *šu-ra-šu-ra-an*MUŠEN [1 *ki*]*priti*⌈*n*⌉M[UŠEN? *pēd*]*anzi*(?) *nu* dU-*an* ⌈É⌉*kari*⌈*m*⌉[*meya a*]*rḫa waḫnuwanzi* "Then they [br]ing(?) to the Stormgod's temple [...] a *ḫuršalami*-ox, [one ...], one kid, one ea[gle], one falcon, one raven, one owl(?), one [...], one *š.*-bird, [one *ki*]*priti*-b[ird(?)] to the temple and they make the Stormgod circle round the temp[le]" KBo 9.119 iv 7-12 (Palliya's ritual, MH/NS), ed. Ertem, Fauna 189f., Haas/Wilhelm, AOATS 3:44 w. n. 1; *išdammane=šši(y)=an ašušeš šu-ra-aš-šu-ra-aš I*[*NA* G]ÙB? *ašiškanzi* "They set in her ear rings(?) (in the form) of *š.*-bird(s) o[n the l]eft" KBo 10.45 ii 26-27 (rit. for Netherworld Deities, MH/NS), ed. Otten, ZA 54:122f., Haas, AoF 17:185.

**c.** in oracle texts — **1′** sitting and calling: *šu-u-ra-aš-šu-u-ra-aš*MUŠEN *ašanza*/*ašānza ḫalz*[*iyanza*] KUB 50.1 ii 16, 22, iii 12 (MH/MS); cf. *šu-u-ra-šu-u-ra-aš ḫalzianza* GUN KuT 49 obv. 25-26 (MH/MS), ed. Wilhelm, MDOG 130:179f.

**2′** in *tarwiyali*-position calling with a message: *šu-u-ra-aš-šu-u-ra-aš taru. ḫalugaz ḫalzaīš* "The *š.*-bird called *tarwiyali* with a message" HKM 47 obv. 23 (MH/MS), ed. HBM 204f.; *šu-u-ra-aš-šu-u-ra-aš taru. ašanza ḫalukit ḫalziyanza* HKM 47 obv. 27-28 (MH/MS), ed. HBM 204f.

**3′** other movements or positions in broken contexts: ꜛ*šu-ra-šu-ra-aš-ma* ⌈*tar.*⌉*l*[*iš*(?)...] KUB 18.9 ii 8 (NH); [*šu-u-ra-aš-š*]*u-u-ra-aš* EGIR-*an pí*?[-...] KBo 47.226:9 (MH/MS); EGIR KASKAL-*NI a-aš-šu-ra-aš-šu-ra-aš* KUB 16.77 iii 50 (NH), ed. van den Hout, Purity 252f., cf. HW² A 537 (cross reference of *āššuraššura-* to *š.*); [*šu*]-*ra-šu-ra-aš gun.-liš* KUB 22.17 i? 1 (NS); ("An eagle (flew) down behind *maštayati*") *šu-u-ra-šu-re-eš gun.-eš nu kē* MUŠEN.ḪI.A *laḫla*⌈*ḫim*⌉*aš* § "*š.*-birds (flew) *gun.-liš*. These (were) the birds of agitation" KuT 50 obv. 21-23 (bird oracle, MH/MS), ed. Wilhelm, MDOG 130:184, 186, Hoffner, Letters 264; compare *laḫlaḫ*(*ḫ*)*ima-* c; *šu-u-ra-šu-u-ra-aš*MUŠEN GUN KuT 49 obv. 15 (bird oracle, MH/MS), ed. Wilhelm, MDOG 130:178f.

Listed alongside eagle, falcon, raven, and owl (KBo 9.119 iv 7-12, above b) the *š.*-bird may well have been a raptor; note also the reference to its having eaten human flesh (KBo 13:131 iii 5-6, 13-14, above b). These characteristics, combined with the bird's use in ornithomancy point at the crow. The Glossenkeil (KUB 18.9 ii 8) and the spelling with plene initial *ā-* (KUB 16.77 iii 50) point to a Luwian origin.

Laroche, RHA X/51 (1949-1950) 19 (a bird name of Hattian origin); Friedrich, HW (1952) 199-200 ("ein Vogel"); Otten, ZA 54 (1961) 150, 151f. n. 308; Ertem, Fauna (1965) 210-212; Hoffner, RHA XXIII/76 (1965) 12f. n. 41 ("dove(?)" equalling Akk. *summatu*); Haas, KN (1970) 173-74 (a rain announcing bird; rejects "dove"); Zinko, Grazer Beiträge 14 (1987) 17, 18-19; Sakuma, Diss. (2009) 1:137, 381, 469 ("Krähe, Rabe oder Dohle (?)").

**šuri- A** n. com. or adj.; (a feature of the exta); from MH/MS.

**sg. nom.** *šu!-ú-ri-i-iš* KBo 16.97 rev. 10 (MH/MS), *šu-re-eš* KUB 6.2 obv. 2, 12 (LNH), KUB 22.52 obv. 16, 18 (NH), KUB 22.54:16 (NH), KUB 22.55 obv. 12 (NH), KUB 46.37 obv. 3, 19, rev. (26), 32, 35 (LNH), KUB 52.34 obv. 14 (NH), HFAC 73:3 (NH), ⌈*šu-ri*⌉*-i-eš* KUB 5.1 iv 43 (NH), *šu-ri-iš* KUB 5.3 i 53 (NH), KUB 5.24 i 62, 64 (LNH), KUB 22.40 iii 33 (NH), KUB 22.70 obv. 3, 44, 50, rev. 32, 68 (NH), KUB 49.90:11 (NH), KUB 50.44 i 7 (LNH), KUB 50.114 rev.? 6 (NH), KUB 52.73 obv. 9 (NH), *šu-ri-i-iš* KUB 5.1 iv 50 (NH), KUB 5.24 i 20 (LNH), KUB 16.29 obv. 26, 31, 36 (NH), KUB 50.90 obv. 7, rev. 24 (NH), KUB 16.54:6 (NH), KUB 16.71:10 (NH).

**a.** *zi*(*zaḫi*)*=ma šuriš* (reverses the outcome): IGI-*zi* SU.MEŠ SIG$_5$ *zi.=ma šu-ri-iš* NU.SIG$_5$ EGIR-*z*[*i* SU.MEŠ ...] ⌈NU.SIG$_5$⌉ "The first exta are favorable. But there is a *š.* on the *zizaḫi* (or:

the *zizaḫi-* is *š.*) — unfavorable. The secon[d exta: ...] unfavorable" KUB 22.70 obv. 2-3 (oracles on cult of Arušna, NH), ed. Ünal, THeth 6:54f. (differently); see also KUB 22.70 obv. 44, 50, 67-68 (oracles on cult of Arušna, NH) and Beal, Magic and Divination 63 w. n. 54.

**b.** EGIR-*ŠU šuriš* (see HW² Ḫ 594f.) — **1′** (reverses the outcome): IGI-*zi TE.*$^{MEŠ}$ *ni.-ešškan* ZAG-*na pe*⌈*š*⌉*šiyat* EGIR-*ŠU šu-ri-iš* S[IG$_5$] EGIR *TE.*$^{MEŠ}$ SAG.ME NU.SIG$_5$ ... IGI-*zi TE.*$^{MEŠ}$ NU.SIG$_5$ ⌈EGIR-*ŠU*⌉ *šu-ri-*⌈*iš* SIG$_5$⌉ EGIR *TE.*$^{MEŠ}$ *tautiš* NU.SIG$_5$ "The first exta: the *nipašuri-* threw to the right. After that, there is a *š.* (or: it is *š.*) — fav[orable]. The second exta: The SAG.ME — unfavorable. (...) The first exta are unfavorable. After that, there is a *š.* (or: it is *š.*) — favorable. The second exta: the *tauti-* — unfavorable" KUB 5.24 i 62-63, 64-65 (LNH), translit. StBoT 38:254; IGI-*zi* SU.MEŠ *ni. ši. ki.* KASKAL NÍG/4(?)-*aššza andan* ME-*aš* 10 ŠÀ *DIR.* SIG$_5$ EGIR SU.MEŠ SIG$_5$ EGIR-*ŠU šu-ri-iš* NU.SIG$_5$ "The first exta: the *nipašuri-*, the *šintaḫi-*, the *keldi-*, the road. The ... (?) took them inside itself(?). Ten turns of the intestines — favorable. The second exta: favorable. After that there is a *š.* (or: it is *š.*) — unfavorable" KUB 5.3 i 51-53 (oracle on the king's wintering, NH), tr. Beal, CoS 1:210; cf. KUB 5.24 i 20; see Beal, Magic and Divination 63 w. n. 54 since NÍG is not known as a feature of the exta one can also consider reading 4-*aš* "the 4th"(?), i.e., KASKAL.

**2′** outcome not specifically given or broken: (After a "bed" oracle): $^{GIŠ}$ŠÚ.A-*ḫi* GÙB-*an* EGIR-*ŠU šu-ri-i-iš* "The throne is on the left. After that there is a *š.* (or: it is *š.*)" KUB 16.29 obv. 26 ("bed" and flesh oracle, NH), cf. Hoffner, FsHallo 118; cf. ibid. + KUB 16.81 obv. 30-31; ibid. obv. 35-36; KUB 5.1 iv 42-43; ibid. 49-50, KUB 49.90:11-12, KUB 50.90 obv. 6-9; cf. also KUB 50.90 rev. 23-24 (broken).

**3′** not reversing the outcome: *TE.*$^{MEŠ}$ NU.SIG$_5$ EGIR-*ŠU šu-ri-i-iš* NU.SIG$_5$ "The exta are unfavorable. After that there is a *š.* (or: it is a *š.*) — unfavorable" KUB 16.54:6 (NH).

**4′** not in final position: [...E]GIR-*ŠU šu-ri-i-iš* 10 $^{ŠÀ}$*DIR.* SIG$_5$ KUB 16.71:10 (NH); [...E]GIR-*ŠU šu-ri-iš* 12 $^{ŠÀ}$*DIR.* SIG$_5$ KUB 50.114 rev.? 6 (NH).

**c.** placement on the gall bladder described: *nipāšūriš* ZAG-*aš* GAL GÙB-*lašsma* TUR *šintaḫiš* 2 *tanāniš nsašta* GÙB-*laš iššī anda šu*!-*ú-ri-i-iš ANA* ⌈UZU⌉ZÉ *ataniti kittari* KASKAL *ANA urnirnismasššan* ZAG-*aš lattiš* GÙB-*lazzsi*⌈*ya*⌉ *walḫan* "The *nipašuri-*: (its) right (side) is large while (its) left (side) is small. The *šintaḫi-*. There are two *tanani-*: the left one is in the mouth. The *š.* is lying on the gall-bladder (and?) the *atanit-* (or: The left one is *š.* in the mouth. It is located on the gall bladder on/at an *atanit-*). The road: toward the finger there is the righthand *latti-* and it is beaten on the left (side)" KBo 16.97 rev. 8-11 (extispicy, MH/MS), ed. Schuol, AoF 21:104, 109 ("*šuri-* liegt am *atanita-* der Gallenblase"), cf. HW² A 569 ("auf der Gallenblase liegt *a.*"); here? [...] *ši.* $^{GIŠ}$TUKUL GAR GÙB-*aš šu-re-eš* [...] "[The *nipašuri* ...], the *šintaḫi*, the 'weapon' is placed. The *š.* of the left [...]" KBo 41.131 rev.? 6 (NH).

**d.** other: [...] ZAG-*za* RA-*IṢ šu-re-eš* § "[...] is beaten on the right. *š.*" KBo 41.135 obv.8 (NH); cf. ibid. 2.

*š.* cannot be the singular of *šurit*(*a*)- (thus Tischler, HEG S/2:1207f.) q.v. "coil/skein(?) of yarn." Schuol, AoF 21:288, suggests an equation with Akk. *qû* "string, filament," but, unlike the usage of Akk. *qû*, Hitt. *š.* does not occur with verbs such as "seize, attach, hold, constrict."

Laroche, RHA XII/54 (1952) 30, 37; Friedrich, HW (1952) 200 ("Geflecht(??), Matte(??)" (auch von einem Teile der Orakelleber)); Laroche, RA 64 (1970) 137 (Hurrian; "marque de diverses parties omineuses"); idem, GLH (1979) 244f. ("en hépatoscopie hitt., marque omineuse"); Starke, StBoT 31 (1990) 209 (no link w. *š.*); de Martino, ChS I/7 (1992) 154; Schuol, AoF 21 (1994) 287-288 (= Akk. *qû*); Beal, Magic and Divination (2002) 63 w. n. 54 (reversing the oracular meaning of the other signs; an adj.); Tischler, HEG S/2 (2006) 1207-1208 (sg. of *šurita*; "Geflecht, Knäuel, Matte," same word as *šuri-* B); Richter, BibGlHurr (2012) 419.

Cf. *šurita-*.

**šūri- B, (d)šurinni/a** n., Hurr.; (an item receiving offerings); NS.†

**Hurr. essive or Hitt. dat.-loc.** *šu-ú-ri-ia* KBo 8.89 obv. 7 (NS).

**Hurr. sg.** *šu-ri-in-ni* KUB 40.102 ii 11 (MH/NS), *dšu-ri-in-ni* KBo 9.133 obv. 13 (NS).

**Hurr. pl.** *šu-ri-in-na* KUB 12.12 i 32 (MH/NS).

*šu-u-ri-ia* KBo 19.139 iii 14 (NS) in Hurr. context and written w. *-u-* may not belong here.

**a.** *šūri*: [1 MUŠEN ...]-⌜*ya*⌝ 1 MUŠEN *šu-ú-ri-ia* 1 MUŠEN x-*maitḫiya* "[(They sacrifice) one bird] for [...], one bird for *šūri*, one bird for [...]-*maitḫi*" KBo 8.89 obv. 7 (frag. of Kizzuwatnan rit., NS), translit. ChS I/9:178, Haas/Wilhelm, AOATS 3:264.

**b.** *(d)šurinni/a*, listed among consecrated things of Hurrian provenance: 1 GAL KÙ.GI *ANA dšu⌜r⌝zi šu⌜k⌝ri* ⌜1 GAL⌝ KÙ.BABBAR *ANA kušurni* ⌜1 GAL⌝ KÙ.⌜BABBAR⌝ *ANA šu-ri-in-ni* "One golden cup for (the deity) *Šurzi* (of ?) *šukri*, one silver cup for *kušurni*, one silver cup for *šurinni*" KUB 40.102 ii 9-11 (*ḫišuwaš* fest. 8th tablet, MH/NS); in a Hurrian recitation: *nu* LÚSANGA *namma* 1 NINDA.GUR$_4$.RA KU$_7$ *paršiya šu-ri-in-na tiyari manuzuḫi* "The priest once more breaks one sweet thick-bread (saying): '*šurinna, tiyari, manuzuḫi*!'" KUB 12.12 i 31-32 (*ḫišuwaš* fest., MH/NS), ed. ChS I/4:144f. 162.

*šurinni* and *šurinna* probably belong with *šūri-* B, extended with the Hurrian article *-ni* and *-na* (plural), respectively. In the offering lists KBo 8.89 obv. 3-7 and KUB 40.102 ii 9-11, *š.* receives offerings alongside other sacred items (*aḫrušḫi-, kušurni, dŠurzi, tapri-, tūni-, tūmapirni-, ḫiššammi-, ḫarni-*), so that one may consider *š.* to be of similar character. There is no obvious connection to *šuri-* A.

Haas/Wilhelm, AOATS 3 (1974) 123 (a Hurrian offering term); Laroche, GLH (1979) 244f.; Tischler, HEG S/2 (2006) 1206-1208 (same word as *šuri-* A and *šurita*).

**(SÍG)šurit(a)-** n. neut.; coil(?), skein(?) of yarn; from MH/NS.†

**pl. nom.-acc. neut.(?)** *šu-ri-ta* KBo 5.1 iv 2 (MH/NS), SÍG*šu-ri-ta* ABoT 1.17 ii 7 (NS), KUB 5.10 i 10 (NS), KUB 9.22 ii (10) (NS), SÍG*šu-ú-ri-ta* KBo 5.1 iv 7 (MH/NS).

**gen.?** [SÍG?*š*]*u-ú-ri-ta?-aš* KBo 31.108 i 9 (NS).

**Luwian pl. nom.(?)-com.** [SÍ]G?*šu-ri-ta-an-zi* KUB 58.10:5 (NS).

**here?, broken:** *šu-ri-i*[*t*(-) ... ] KUB 34.125 rt. col. 9 (NS).

**a.** In rituals — **1′** prepared along with red wool and wrapped around the sacrifice's head: *nu* MUNUS.MEŠ*katrēš* TÚG-*an šarānzi* § *maḫḫan=ma* TÚG-*an šarāuanzi zinnanzi nu* SÍG.SA$_5$ *anda taruppanzi n=at=šan ANA* TÚG *šer tianzi šu-ri-ta=ya iyanzi* "The *katra*-women unravel(?)/embroider(?) (a piece of) cloth. When they finish unraveling(?)/embroidering(?) the cloth, they collect red wool and place it on the cloth and they make a *š.* (coil or ball of yarn?). (The *patili*-priest takes water (and) fine oil and brings it out. They wipe down a lamb with the water. He (i.e., the *patili*-priest) washes its mouth (and) its foot, then anoints it with the fine oil) *nu=ššan* SÍG.SA$_5$ *ANA* GÌR.MEŠ=*ŠU ḫamanki* SÍG*šu-ú-ri-ta=ma=šši=ššan ANA* SAG.DU=*ŠU anda ḫūlaliyanzi* "He ties the red wool onto its feet, but the *š.* (coil of yarn?) they wrap around its head" KBo 5.1 iii 52-iv 8 (Papanikri's rit., MH/NS), ed. Strauß, Reinigungs 293, 301f. ("Knäuel"), Pap. 10*-13*, StBoT 29:118f. ("ball of yarn") □ for *šarai-* "unravel," see CHD s.v., for "embroider," see Kloekhorst, BiOr 64:429

**2′** unclear: [...]-*zi* SÍG*mitieškanzi* [...SÍG?*š*]*u-ú-ri-ta?-aš* dLAMMA-*aš memieške*⌜*zz*⌝[*i*] "[...] they tie with red wool(?). [...] the Tutelary Deity of(?) [C]oils(?) of Yarn start[s] speaking (thus)" KBo 31.108 i 8-9 (rit., NS), translit. StBoT 29:100; comparing the other *ša* and *ta* signs on the photo makes deciding on a reading difficult; for lines 4-8 and for a tentative interpretation of context, see SÍG*mitai-*, cf. also Melchert, Kadmos 37:37f.; [...SÍ]G?*šu-ri-ta-an-zi-ia*(-)x [...] KUB 58.10:5 (Kizzuwatnan rit., NS) □ this is perhaps to be analyzed as *=ia* "and" added to a Luwian pl. nom. in *-nzi*; alternatively, it might be a denominative pres. pl. 3 verb "they coil?" from (SÍG)*šurita-* (cf. SÍG*mitai-* "to tie with red wool(?)") or even a rare abl. (see GrHL 77 §3.33) in *=anza* plus *=ia* "and."

**b.** As one of the symbols of female life employed in the Festival of Womanhood for the goddess d*IŠTAR* of Nineveh: (As they celebrated the Festival of Womanhood, from the palace they used to give to the goddess (dIŠTAR) one shekel of silver, red-brown wool and blue wool, and leather curtains) *kinun≈a≈wa* EZEN$_4$ *ašraḫitaššin iēr* KÙ.BABBAR≈*ma≈wa* SÍG SA$_5$ SÍG ZA.GÌN KUŠNÍG.BÀR≈*ya UL pīēr* SÍG*šu-ri-ta-wa wēzzapanta ŠA* LÚ*kireštena*!≈*ya≈wa* EZEN$_4$ *ḫalziyawaš UL iyanza* "But now they have celebrated the Festival of Womanhood without, however, giving the silver, the red wool, the blue wool and the leather curtains. The coils(?) of yarn are old (i.e., long in need of replacement), and the Festival of Invocation of the *kireštena*-man has not been performed. (... Is the goddess angry for these reasons?)" KUB 5.10 i 9-11 (oracle questions on the cult of *IŠTAR* of Nineveh, NH), tr. Friedrich, AO 25-2:26 ("Beutel(??)"), cf. Sommer, Pap. 71, Wegner, AOAT 36:133f. w. nn. 419-422.

**c.** other: [(DUG*KUKUB* I)M?...] NINDA*muriyališ* (var. [*muriya*]*liuš* sic) *katt*⌈*a gang*⌉[*anteš*] SÍG*šu-ri-ta≈ya≈kan peran arḫa d*[(*ā*?*nzi*)] "A jug of cla[y(?), ... ], grape-cluster(-shaped) breads are han[ging] down and they take the coil(s) of yarn(?) away from in front (of them)" ABoT 1.17 ii 5-7 (birth rit., NS), w. dupl. KUB 9.22 ii 9-11 (NH), ed. Beckman, StBoT 29:88f. (reading the verb equally plausibly as *kuranzi* "they cut").

It remains uncertain whether *š.* is related to Akk. *šur'ītu*, occurring only in a lexical text = Sum. siki.šab, and which von Soden, AHw 1284a, defines as "eine Art v. Wolle." CAD Š/3:367-68 considers this Akk. word a sg. fem. adj. from *šūru*, an adj. of uncertain meaning and attested at Boğazköy, but which occurs in lexical texts among types of *naḫlaptu*-garments. If the broken *šu-ri-i*[*t*(-) ... ] KUB 34.125 rt. col. 9 (*ḫišuwa*-fest., NS), ed. Groddek, RANT 8:116, 120 ("Wollknäuel[-"), indeed belongs here, there can be no relation with *šuri-* A q.v.

Sommer/Ehelolf, Pap. (1924) 13*, 71, 90 ("etwa ein Ballen, Knäuel?"); Friedrich, HW (1952) 200 ("Knäuel?; Binde?"; Hurr. pl. to *šuri-*?); Laroche, RHA XII/54 (1952) 37; Tischler, HDW (1982) 79 ("Geflecht, Knäuel?"); Beckman, StBoT 29 (1983) 100, 119, 297 ("ball of yarn?"); Starke, StBoT 31 (1990) 209; Tischler, HEG S/2 (2006) 1207-1208 ("Geflecht, Knäuel, Matte"; pl. nom.-acc. neut. of *šuri-* A&B, and reminds one of the masculine PN *šuritanu* on seal E8.573 from Troy, for which see Hawkins/Easton, Studia Troica 6:112); Kloekhorst, EDHIL (2008) 792 ("braid(??)"); Richter, BibGlHurr (2012) 419.

Cf. *šuri-* A, B.

**šurita- B** v.; "to coil(?)"; see (SÍG)*šurit*(*a*)- a 2′.

**šurki/a-** n. com.; root; from OS.†

**sg. acc.** *šur-ki-in* KBo 8.130 ii 6 (MS).
**gen.** *šur-ki-ia-aš* KUB 33.117 i 13 (NH).
**pl. nom.** *šu-ur-ki-iš* KBo 17.22 iii 10 (OS).
**acc.** *šur-ku-uš* KUB 29.1 iv 16 (OH/NS), HT 38:(8) (OH/NS, coll. by Gadd apud Ehelolf, KUB 29 p. III n. 4), Gießen frag. (ZA 71:123):4, *šu-u-ur-ku-uš* KUB 29.1 iv 14 (OH/NS), Bo 5621 iv (9) (apud Marazzi, VO 5:144, 160), *šu-úr-ku-*[*uš*] KUB 60.113:(5), (6) (OS?).

(Hatt.) [*ta-ba-a*]*r-*⌈*na*⌉*-an le-eš-tu-up ḫa-a-an-wa$_a$ ḫa-š*[(*a-a-aḫ-ḫu*)] KBo 37.49 rev. 18, w. dupl. KUB 28.8 obv.! left col. 7 = (Hitt.) *Labarnas šu-ur-ki-iš-š*[*e?-eš* ...] *tēga(n)≈ššet uemiya*[*nzi*] KBo 17.22 iii 10-11, w. dupl. KBo 37.48 (+) KUB 28.8 obv.! rt. col. 9-10; for Hitt. passage see below a.

**a.** roots contrasted with leafy branches: *Labarnas šu-ur-ki-iš-š*[*e?-eš* (*arunaš*)] *tēga*(*n*)≈ *ššet uemiya*[*nzi Labarnaš*] *laḫhurnuzziyant*[(*eš≈a nepiš*) *uemiya*(*nzi*)] "Labarna's roots [shall] find (i.e., reach) the bottom of the sea while the branches [of Labarna] shall [reach] the sky" KBo 17.22 iii 10-12 (Hatt.-Hitt. praise for Labarna, OS), w. dupl. KBo 37.48 (+) KUB 28.8 obv.! rt. col. 7-9 (OH/NS), ed. Klinger, MemCarter 158-160, Kloekhorst, EDHIL 793 (differently), translit. StBoT 25:208 w. n. 694 (prefers reading *šu-ur-ki-uš*MEŠ(-)) but cf. StBoT 26:177, Tischler, HEG S/2:1209; *nu* GIŠGEŠTIN-*aš* GIŠ*maḫlan tianzi* KI.MIN (= *nu kiššan memiyanzi*) GIŠGEŠTIN≈*wa maḫḫan katta šu-u-ur-ku-uš* (var. A [*šu-ú*]*r-ku-uš*, B and C *šur-k*[*u-uš*]) *šarā≈ma≈wa* GIŠ*maḫluš šīyaizzi* LUGAL-*š≈a* MUNUS.LUGAL-*š≈a katta šur-ku-uš* (var. A *šu-úr-ku-*[*uš*]) *katta≈ma* (var. B *šarā≈ma≈wa*) GIŠ*maḫluš šīyandu* "They place a branch of a grapevine, ditto (= and speak as follows): 'Just as the grapevine pushes down roots and branches up, let both the king and queen push down roots and branches up (so text B, main text erroneously: down)'" KUB 29.1 iv 13-16 (rit. for foundation of a palace, OH/NS), w. dupl. A: KUB 60.113:4-6 (OH/NS) and pars. B: HT 38 obv. 7-9 (OH/NS) and C: Gießen frag. (Otten/Rüster, ZA 71:123):3-5, ed. Kellerman, Diss. 19, 31, Marazzi, VO 5:160f., Carini, Athenaeum NS 60:502f.

**b.** mentioned during therapeutic treatment (preparing a drug?): [...]x-*kannališa šur-ki-in kuwaškuzi* "He (i.e., the physician) ... crushes the root [...]" KBo 8.130 ii 6 (frag. containing Luw., MS), ed. HED K 312, translit. StBoT 30:224, Haas, Materia 362 □ *š.* was added above the line.

**c.** unclear: [...]x-*naš šur-ki-ia-aš* KUR-*e ḫūwanduš* [...]x *pāi* "shall give the land, the winds and(?) [...] to the roots of ... [...]" KUB 33.117 i 13-14 (frag. naming Kumarbi, NH), ed. hethiter.net /: CTH 346.1 (INTR 2009-08-21).

Ehelolf, KUB 29 (1938) Inhaltsübersicht p. III ("*šurkuš* Akk. Pl. = 'die Wurzeln'?"); Friedrich, HW (1952) 200 ("Wurzel"); idem, HW 1.Erg. (1957) 19 (prefers the *i*-stem); Haas, Materia (2003) 362f.; Tischler, HEG S/2 (2006) 1209f.; Kloekhorst, EDHIL (2008) 792f.

**[(-)]šu-ur-ni** KBo 34.99:3, see GIŠ*šurunni-*.

**(GIŠ)šuruḫḫa-** n.; (a tree(?) and its wood); from OH?/NS and MS.†

**sg. acc.** *šu-u-ru-uḫ-ḫa-an* KBo 15.46 rev.? 8 (MS), GIŠ*šu-ru-uḫ-ḫa-an* KBo 2.8 iii 9, iv 13 (NH).

**gen.** GIŠ*šu-ru-uḫ-ḫa-aš* KBo 4.9 iii 38, iv 30 (OH?/NS), KBo 27.42 ii (9) (OH/NS), KUB 9.31 ii 19 (MH/NS), KBo 31.200 ii 3 (NS), KUB 34.125 rt. col. (13) (NS), KUB 58.2 ii! 4 (NS), KUB 51.13:4 (LNS), KBo 58.128 iii (3) (LNS), *šu-ru-uḫ-ḫa-aš* KUB 20.80 iii? 16 (LNS), KBo 2.8 iii 17 (NH), KUB 42.29 v? 12 (NH) (or nom.?), KBo 53.95 obv.? 2 (LNS).

**broken:** GIŠ*šu-ru!-uḫ-ḫa-*[...] IBoT 4.284 obv. 7 (NS), *šu-ru-*˹*uḫ-ḫa*˺-[...] ABoT 1.54 left col. 2 (NH).

**a.** material a staff is made of — **1′** in festivals: LUGAL-*uš šu-ru-u*[*ḫ-ḫa-aš* G(IŠ˹GIDRU˺ *ḫarzi*)] "The king holds a/the staff [of] *š.*-wood" KUB 34.125 ii 13 (*ḫišuwa*-fest., NS), w. dupl. KBo 43.200:19 (MS?), ed. Groddek, RANT 8:116, 120; *n=ašta* GAL *MEŠEDI anda uizzi nu* GIŠŠUKUR KÙ.GI *ḫarzi anda=ya=za=kan* GIŠ*šu-ru-uḫ-ḫa-aš* GIŠGIDRU-*an ḫarzi n=aš=kan* LUGAL-*i menaḫḫanda tiyazi* "The Chief of the Royal Bodyguards comes in and he holds a golden spear. Furthermore, he also holds a staff of *š.*-wood. He steps opposite the king" KBo 4.9 iii 36-40 (*ANDAḪŠUM*-fest., OH?/NS), ed. Badali/Zinko, Scientia 20:20, 49; see [...GI]Š*šu-ru-uḫ-ḫ*[*a-aš* GIŠGIDRU-*an*] *ḫarzi* KUB 58.66 "v" 1-2 (OH?/NS); 3 LÚ.MEŠ *MEŠEDI* GIŠBANŠUR-*i* ZAG-*naz iyantari* GIŠŠUKUR KÙ.GI *U* 3 GIŠGIDRU GIŠ*šu-ru-uḫ-ḫa-aš ḫar*˹*kanzi*˺ "Three royal bodyguards walk to the right (side) of the table. They hold a golden spear and three staffs of *š.*-wood" KBo 4.9 iv 28-30 (*ANDAḪŠUM*-fest., OH?/NS), ed. Badali/Zinko, Scientia 20:22, 50; *IŠTU QĀTI=ŠUNU=ma* [*ku*(˹*e*˺)] 3 (var. 2 GIŠ)ŠUKUR KÙ.GI 3 G[(IŠGIDRU.ḪI.A)] GIŠ*šu-ru-uḫ-ḫa-aš ḫark*[(*anzi*)] *n=at ANA* 1 L[Ú(*MEŠEDI* x) ... (x)] *pianzi* "The three (var. two) golden spears and three staffs of *š.*-wood, [whi]ch they hold in (lit. with) their hands, they give to one royal bodyguard" KBo 31.200 ii 1-5 (KI.LAM fest., OH/NS), w. dupl. KBo 27.42 ii 8-10, translit. StBoT 28:56; LÚSANGA dLAMMA=*za* KUŠ*guršan ŠA* dLAMMA URU*Kaštamma karapzi* LÚ*kantikkipiš=ma=za* [GI]ŠGIDRU.ḪI.A *šu-ru-uḫ-ḫa-aš ŠA* dZA.BA$_4$.BA$_4$ *dāi* [L]ÚGUDU$_{12}$=*ma=za* GIŠGIDRU.ḪI.A d*Zaliyanu dāi* "The priest of the Tutelary Deity lifts the hunting bag of the Tutelary Deity of Kaštamma for himself. The *kantikkipi*-man takes the staffs of *š.*-wood of the god ZABABA for himself. The GUDU$_{12}$-priest takes the staffs of the god Zaliyanu for himself" KUB 20.80 iii? 14-17 (fest. celebrated by a prince, LNS), ed. Haas, ZA 78:294f. ("Stäbe der Lanzen"), translit. DBH 13:139f., tr. RGTC 6:194; [(LÚGUDU$_{12}$ *pe*)]˹*r*˺*an ḫūiyanza* [GI]Š˹GIDRU DINGIR˺-*LIM=ya* GIŠ*šu-ru-uḫ-ḫa-aš ḫarkanz*[*i*] LÚ*kandikipiš=*˹*ma*˺ LÚSANGA dLAMMA=*ya* GIŠGIDRU.ḪI.A *anda pēda*(eras.)[⟨*nz*(*i*)⟩] "The GUDU$_{12}$-priest is running in front and they hol[d] the staff of the god (made) of *š.*-wood, while the *kandikipi*-man and the priest of the Tutelary Deity carry the staffs in" KUB 58.2 ii! 3-7 (fest. celebrated by a prince, NS), w. dupl. KBo 58.128 iii 2-5 (fest. frag., LNS), translit. DBH 18:2; cf. also KUB 51.13:4 (fest. frag., LNS) and IBoT 4.284 obv. 7 (fest. frag., NS), translit. DBH 23:198.

**2′** in rituals: *nu=za BĒL* É-*TIM* GIŠ*šu-ru-uḫ-ḫa-aš* GIŠGIDRU-*an n=aš=kan ANA* KÁ *anda tiyazi nu lūi*˹*li*˺ *kiššan ḫukkiškezzi* "The lord of the house ⟨takes?⟩ the staff of *š.*-wood for himself. He steps into the gateway and he recites spells as follows in Luwian" KUB 9.31 ii 19-21 (rit. of Zarpiya, MH/NS), translit. LTU 15, StBoT 30:52f., tr. Collins, CoS 1:163 (§ 16).

**b.** in cult inventories: *šuppa ḫu*!*ešawaza ze*˹*ya*⟨*n*⟩*t*˺*a*⟨*za*⟩ *tiyanzi* MUNUS*palwatallaš*

$^{\text{GIŠ}}$*šu-*⸢*ru*⸣*-uḫ-ḫa-an* 1 $^{\text{UZU}}$*ḫapeššar* (sign *šar*$_x$ = *šir*) 3 NINDA.GUR$_4$.RA 1 $^{\text{DUG}}$*ḫuppar* KAŠ $^{\text{LÚ.MEŠ}}$*ḫazziwiyaš peran iya⟨t⟩tari* "They place the meat, raw and cooked. A female-crier ⟨takes⟩ *š.*-wood, one loin, three thick-breads, (and) one *ḫuppar*-vase of beer and goes before the cultic performers" KBo 2.8 iii 7-11 (cult inv., NH), ed. Hazenbos, Organization 135, 139f.; $^{\text{MUNUS!}}$*palwatallaš* 3-*ŠU palwaizzi* $^{\text{GIŠ}}$*šu-ru-uḫ-ḫa-aš PĀNI* $^{\text{NA}_4}$ZI.KIN *tiyazi* $^{\text{MUNUS}}$*palwatallaš* 3 NINDA.GUR$_4$.RA 1 $^{\text{UZU}}$*ḫapeš*⸢*šar*!⸣ $^{\text{GIŠ}}$*marinn=a dāi* "The female crier cries out three times. She takes her place before the stela of *š.*-wood. A(nother?) female crier takes/places three thick breads, one loin, and a spear(?)" KBo 2.8 iii 16-19 (cult inv., NH), ed. Hazenbos, Organization 135, 140, Badalì, Or NS 59:134 ☐ Tischler's HEG S/2:1210, translation: "das *suruhha*-Holz steht vor dem Kultmal" is unlikely since it is extremely rare and idiomatic for *tiya-* "to take a position" to have an inanimate subject. iii 9 and iv 13 show that only one *š.* is involved, so *šuruḫḫan*, not **šuruḫḫuš* (pl. acc.), would be expected if Hazenbos', Organization 140, solution: "They(!) put pieces of *šuruḫḫa*(-wood) in front of the *ḫuwaši*(-stone)," emending *tiyazi* to *tiyanzi* "they place," were to be accepted; Badalì's, OrNS 59:134, solution "la recitatrice ... si sistema con lo scettro di fronte alla stele" makes one expect an abl. or instr. for *š.*, which it is not; *lukatti=ma šuppa zanuwanzi* $^{\text{MUNUS}}$*palwatalla*[*š*] / [$^{\text{G}}$]$^{\text{IŠ}}$*šu-ru-uḫ-ḫa-an dānzi* "The following morning they cook the meat. They take the *š.*-wood [of] the female crier" KBo 2.8 iv 12-13 (cult inv., NH), ed. Hazenbos, Organization 136, 141.

**c.** in broken contexts: [...]x-*RI-A-AM šu-ru-*⸢*uḫ-ḫa*⸣-[...] ABoT 1.54 left. col. 2 (inv. list, NH), ed. Siegelová, Verw.132f.; *šu-u-ru-uḫ-ḫa-an* ⸢*ḫāriya*⸣[...] KBo 15.46 rev.? 8 (divine mountains list, MS).

Badalì's statement Or NS 59:134 n. 12 referring to Popko, Kultobjekte 98f., that *š.* is the, or a, Hittite reading of $^{\text{GIŠ}}$GIDRU is unlikely (thus also Popko), because according to the occurrences given under usage a, *š.* (always as gen. materiae) indicates a kind of wood, of which the staffs are made. These staffs are used in festivals with ceremonial purposes; they are carried by the king and royal bodyguards together with golden spears. They can belong to a specific deity, e.g., Zababa. Therefore, *š.* probably was a valuable kind of wood and may at times have been used elliptically for a staff made of *š.*-wood (usage b). There is no reason to assume with Carter, Diss. 195, that *š.* could be a musical instrument.

The deities $^{\text{d}}$Šuruḫe, $^{\text{d}}$Šuruḫ(ḫ)i (see OHP 1 s.v.) and the epithet(?) $^{\text{d}}$U-*up šuruḫḫa* (Haas, SMEA 14:136; Popko, Kultobjekte 98f.) are of Hurrian origin and any relation to *š.* is hypothetical. The derivation of *š.* through Hurr. *šurri-* "lance" with a *-ḫḫi*-suffix by Haas, ZA 78:295 n. 49, is formally possible but must remain speculative as well.

Sturtevant, Suppl. (1939) 40 (gen., "a kind of wood"); Friedrich, HW (1952) 200 ("ein Baum und sein Holz"); Carter, Diss. (1962) 195 ("conceivably a musical instrument, possibly a drum"); Haas, SMEA 14 (1971) 136 (the tree and the Hurr. word); Ertem, Flora (1974) 142-143; Popko, Kultobjekte (1978) 98f. (possible reading of $^{\text{GIŠ}}$PA); Košak, THeth 10 (1982) 238 ("kind of wood"); Tischler, HDW (1982) 79 ("ein Baum und sein Holz; aus diesem Holz werden auch Lanzen gefertigt"); Haas, ZA 78 (1988) 295 n. 49; Badalì, Or NS 59 (1990) 134 with n. 12 ("scettro," "lettura ittita di $^{\text{GIŠ}}$PA"); Tischler, HEG S/2 (2006) 1210-11.

$^{\text{GIŠ}}$**šurunni-** n. com.?; (a wooden object); NS.†

**sg. acc.** $^{\text{GIŠ}}$*šu-ru-un-ni-in* KBo 63.112:14 (NS), $^{\text{GIŠ}}$*šu-r*[*u-*...] KBo 58.159 rt. col. (3) (NS).

EGIR-*ŠU=ma ŠA* $^{\text{d}}$*Tašmi* $^{\text{GIŠ}}$ŠUKUR [...]x ZABAR *pē ḫarkanzi* [(EGIR-*Š*)*U=ma*...] $^{\text{GIŠ}}$*šu-ru-un-ni-in pē ḫarkanzi* [(EGIR-*ŠU=ma*) ... ($^{\text{GIŠ}}$*z*)]*uppari pē ḫarkanzi* [(EGIR-*ŠU=ma Š*)*A*?... ($^{\text{GIŠ}}$*ḫattall*)*an*] *pē ḫarkanzi* "Afterwards [they hold ready(?)] the spear of Tašmi. They have ready the bronze [... of ...]. They have ready the *š.* [of ...]. They have ready the torch [of ...]. Afterwards they have ready the mace of [...]" KBo 63.112:12-16 (rit. frag., NS), w. dupl. KBo 58.159 rt. col. 1-7 (NS).

If Hurr. in origin the base could be *šurni-* (cf. (-)]*šu-ur-ni* KBo 34.99:3, and in Hurr. context *šu?-ú-úr-ni-i*(-) KUB 47.1 i 6, translit. ChS I/6:56) followed by the article *-ne/na*.

$^{\text{(URUDU/ZABAR)}}$**šurzi- A** n. neut.; snaffle bit; from MH/MS.†

**sg. nom.-acc.** $^{\mathrm{URUDU}}$*šu-ur-zi* KUB 30.32 i 4 (MS?), $^{\mathrm{URUDU}}$*šur-zi* KUB 42.28 obv. 6, 7 (NH), KUB 42.29 ii? 17 (NH), $^{\mathrm{ZABAR}}$*šu-u-ur-*⌜*zi*⌝ IBoT 1.36 iii 57 (MH/MS).

**pl(?). nom.-acc.** $^{\mathrm{URUDU}}$*šur-zi-ia* KUB 42.28 obv. 5 (NH), *šur-zi-ia* KBo 18.170a rev. 8 (NH).

**broken:** [$^{\mathrm{URUD}}$]$^{\mathrm{U?}}$*šur-z*[*i* ...] KUB 40.95 iii 5 (NS).

**a.** worn by a horse: ("The king mounts (lit. seizes) the chariot") *karšuwaš=a kuiš* $^{\mathrm{LÚ}}$*MEŠ*⌜*EDI*⌝ *nu* $^{\mathrm{GIŠ}}$GIDRU *ḫarzi nu* ZAG-*an* ANŠE.KUR.RA ZAG-*az kiššaraz* $^{\mathrm{ZABAR}}$*šu-u-ur-*⌜*zi*⌝ *ēpzi* GÙB-*laz=ma* $^{\mathrm{GIŠ}}$*kāpur ḫarzi* $^{\mathrm{GIŠ}}$GIDRU*=z=(š)an anda ḫarzi nu* $^{\mathrm{GIŠ}}$GIGIR *menaḫḫanda tameššan ḫarzi n=*⌜*at*⌝ *UL akkurriya*⌜*i*⌝ "while the guard who is (in charge) of closing holds a staff and grasps the right horse with right hand by the bit, but with the left (hand) he holds the *kāpur* (while) holding the staff. He keeps the chariot counterbalanced (so that) it does not tilt(?)" IBoT 1.36 iii 56-59 (instr. for royal guards, MH/MS), ed. AS 24:28f., Jakob-Rost, MIO 11:196f. □ Jakob-Rost, MIO 11:218, takes the form *šūrzi* here as the dat.-loc. of an *a*-stem *šurza-*.

**b.** in inventories, counted w. *TAPAL* as collec. nouns in sets (cf. GrHL 159f.): 4 *TAPAL* $^{\mathrm{URUDU}}$*šur-zi-ia* ⌜*MAN*⌝*DATI* 8 MA.NA URUDU IGI.DU$_8$.A 9 *TAPAL* $^{\mathrm{URUDU}}$*šur-zi MANDATI=ma=kan ANA* $^{\mathrm{KUŠ}}$KIR$_4$.TAB.ANŠE *anda* 2 *TAPAL* $^{\mathrm{URUDU}}$*šur-zi* IGI.DU$_8$.A 8 MA.NA URUDU *ŠALMU* "Four snaffle bits as tribute, (made of) eight minas of copper of excellent quality; nine snaffle bits — included among the bridles as tribute are two snaffle bits of excellent quality — (made of) eight minas of good copper" KUB 42.28 obv. 5-8 (inv., NH), ed. Siegelová, Verw. 150f.; ⌜5?⌝ *TAPAL* $^{\mathrm{KUŠ}}$KIR$_4$.TAB.ANŠE *QADU šur-zi-ia* ZABAR "Five(?) bridles including snaffle bits of bronze" KBo 18.170a rev. 8 (inv., NH), ed. THeth 10:110f., Siegelová, Verw. 486f.

**c.** production: [...] *šālaš a-*⌜x-x⌝[...] GAL $^{\mathrm{LÚ.MEŠ}}$AŠGAB *iy*[*azz*]*i* $^{\mathrm{URUDU}}$*šu-ur-zi* $^{\mathrm{LÚ.MEŠ}}$[SIMUG.A(?) *iyanzi*] URUDU NAGGA *tup*⌜*paš=pat*⌝ É-*az pian*[*zi*] "The chief of the leatherworkers ma[ke]s a [...] of *šāla-* (a leather strap or "of leather"?). The [metal workers make(?)] a snaffle bit. They giv[e] copper and tin only from the storehouse (to make it)" KUB 30.32 i 3-5 (inv., MS?), ed. Haas/Wäfler, UF 8:96f., $^{\mathrm{(KUŠ)}}$*šāla-*, Hoffmann, GsForrer 382f.

Jakob-Rost, MIO 11 (1966) 218 ("etwa 'Trense' oder ein Teil derselben, vielleicht die Wangenplatten, jedenfalls ein Metallgegenstand am Zaumzeug des Pferdes"); Košak, THeth 10 (1982) 64 ("snaffle, bridoon"), 238 ("horse-brass"); Tischler, HDW (1982) 156 ("Metallgegenstand am Zaumzeug des Pferdes, etwa 'Trense' oder dgl."); Siegelová, Verw. (1986) 619 ("Pferdegebiss, Zaumgebiss"); Güterbock/van den Hout, AS 24 (1991) 56, 83 ("bit"); van den Hout, RlA 10 (2004) 487f.; Tischler, HEG S/2 (2006) 1211f.; Trémouille, RlA 13 (2012) 347.

$^{\mathrm{(d)}}$**šurzi- B** n., Hurr.; (something consecrated, also name of a sacred location); from MH/NS.†

**sg. dat.** (*ANA*) $^{\mathrm{d}}$*šu-*⌜*ur*⌝*-zi* KUB 40.102 ii 9 (MH/NS), [$^{\mathrm{d?}}$*šu-u*]*r-zi* VBoT 116:4.

**gen.** *šur-zi-ia-aš* KBo 15.37 i 2 (MH/NS), KBo 9.133 obv. 10 (NS), KBo 35.254 obv.? (8) (NS).

**Hurrian context:** *šu-ur-zi* KUB 12.12 i 24 (MH/NS), KUB 32.54:(13) (NS).

**a.** receives offerings: 1 GAL KÙ.GI *ANA* $^{\mathrm{d}}$*šu-*⌜*ur*⌝*-zi šu*⌜*k*⌝*ri* ⌜1 GAL⌝ KÙ.BABBAR *ANA kušurni* ⌜1 GAL⌝ KÙ.⌜BABBAR⌝ *ANA šurinni* "One golden cup for (the divine) *š.* (and?) *šukri*, one silver cup for *kušurni*, one silver cup for *šurinni*" KUB 40.102 ii 9-11 (8th tablet of *ḫišuwaš* fest., MH/NS), cf. *šuri-* B b.

**b.** invoked(?): *nu* $^{\mathrm{LÚ}}$SANGA *namma* 1 [NINDA.GUR$_4$.RA KU$_7$ *paršiya*] *nu memai šu-ur-zi* [*šukri tiyari*] *manuzuḫi nu anāḫi* N[INDA.GUR$_4$.RA...] "The priest [breaks] one more [sweet thick bread] and says: '*š.* [*šukri tiyari*] *manuzuḫi*!' A morsel of [thick] b[read...]" KUB 12.12 i 23-25 (*ḫišuwaš* fest.; MH/NS), ed. ChS I/4:144f. 162; see also VBoT 116:4.

**c.** the place of the *š.*, a type of emplacement for divine statues: *namma* $^{\mathrm{d}}$IM *manuzi* DINGIR.MEŠ*=ya šur-zi-ia-aš pēdaš kattan arḫa udanzi n=aš=šan* EGIR-*pa tapriti daninuwanzi* "Then they carry out the (statue of the) Stormgod of Manuzi and the (other) gods down through the place of the *š.* and arrange them again on the chair" KBo 15.37 i 1-4 (last tablet of *ḫišuwa*-fest., MH/NS), w. dupl. KBo 35.260 + SZM 51.2401 vi! 16-19, ed. Tremouille, Eothen 4:83, Groddek, RANT 8:135, 139, translit. Everling/Földi, NABU 2015/69, Groddek, Muséon 117:4; *n=ašta* $^{\mathrm{d}}$IM *manuz*[*i*...] *katta* *danzi n=*[*aš*(?)...] *taninuwanzi* $^{d}$*L*[*elluri*...] *šuppin* DINGIR-*LIM-in* $^{d?}$[...] *tapriyaza katta* [...] *n=aš šur-zi-ia-aš pedi* [...] GÙB-*laza daninuwan*[*zi*...] ZAG-*za=ma=šši* $^{d}$*kušurn*[*i*...] $^{d}$*šurinni manuzuḫi* x[...] ⌜*tani*⌝*nuwan*[*zi*] "and the Stormgod of Manuz[i...] they take down and [them(?)...] they arrange. The god L[elluri...] the sacred god (acc.) [they(?)...] down from the chair [...] and them at the place of the *šurzi-* [...] they arran[ge] on the left [...] while on its right side they arran[ge] the (divine) *kušurn*[*i*...], the (divine) *šurinni* of Manuzi [...]" KBo 9.133 obv. 5-14 (frag. of *ḫišuwaš* fest., NS), translit. Groddek, Muséon 117:3; compare similarly w. *AŠAR* instead of *peda-* KBo 35.254 obv.? 8-9 (frag. of *ḫišuwa-* fest., NS), translit. DBH 19:317.

*š.* is likely Hurrian in origin and occurs so far solely in the texts belonging to the *ḫišuwaš* festival. It indicates something consecrated, or even deified, since it sometimes bears the divine determinative. *šurziyaš pedan* appears to be the name of a sacred location where the divine statues can be placed, arranged or removed. Whether the GN $^{HUR.SAG}$Šuwarziya and $^{URU}$Šuwarzapa (see RGTC 6 and 6/2 s.vv.) belong here remains unclear.

Laroche, GLH (1977-79) 156 (s.v. *kurzi*, corrected by Haas, BiOr 39 (1982) 605), 245 (on the offering term); Dinçol, Belleten LIII/206 (1989) 23; Trémouille, Eothen 4 (1991) 83 n. 26; Tischler, HEG S/2 (2006) 1211f. (same word as $^{URUDU/ZABAR}$*šurzi-*); Richter, BibGlHurr (2012) 421; Trémouille, RlA 13 (2014) 347.

[*šušarāuwar*] KUB 32.117 obv.! 3 according to EHS 1:284, 307, read with HEG S/2:1212; see *šarawar*.

[$^{NINDA}$*šuši-*] see [*šušiš*].

$^{(GIŠ)}$**šušiyaz(za)kel** n. neut.; (part of a wheeled vehicle, perhaps "linch pin"), from OH/NS.†

**sg. nom.-acc.** $^{GIŠ}$*šu-ši-ia-az-za-ke-el* KUB 11.23 vi 5 (OH/NS), $^{GIŠ}$*šu-ši-az-ke-el* KUB 11.23 vi 7 (OH/NS), [ ...-*ke*]-*el* KUB 25.18 ii 29 (Tudḫ. IV), [ ...-*a*]*z-ki-il* KBo 34.25:3 (NS), $^{GIŠ}$*šu-ši-az*!-*k*[*e-el*?] KBo 17.90 ii 8 (NS).

**erg.** *šu-ši*!-*ia-az-ki-la-an-za* KBo 17.90 ii 12 (NS).

**inst.** [$^{GIŠ}$*šušiyaz-k*]*i-li-it* (eras.) KUB 46.23 rev. 27 (NS).

**broken** $^{GIŠ}$*šu-ši-ia-az-*[...] KBo 41.3:3, 10 (MS).

(In a recitation in the course of a festival expressing good wishes for the king and the land:) *labarnaš=ma* LUGAL-*uš* AN.BAR-*aš* $^{GIŠ}$*šu-ši-ia-az-za-ke-el ēšdu nu* $^{URU}$*Ḫad*⌜*du*⌝*šan ḫurki*‹*š*?› (var. A: $^{GIŠ}$MAR.GÍD.DA) *mān* $^{GIŠ}$*šu-ši-az-ke-el* (var. A: [...-*k*]*i-li-it* (erasure)) ⌜*w*⌝*edau nu kezza arunaš* [*i*]*rḫan wemiškeddu* [(*k*)]*ezzi=*[(*y*)]*a arunaš* [*i*]*rḫa*[*n*] *wemiškeddu* "May Labarna, the king, be a *š.* of iron. Like wheels(?) (var. a wagon) with a *š.* may he carry (the land of) Ḫattuša. Let him reach (lit. find) the border of the sea on this side and let him reach (lit. find) the border of the sea on the other side" KUB 11.23 vi 4-11 (*ANDAḪŠUM* fest., OH/NS), w. dupls. KUB 46.23 rev. 24-31 (var. A) (NS), KUB 25.18 ii 28-31 (var. B, Tudḫ. IV), ed. Archi, FsMeriggi² 48, translit. Klinger, MemCarter 167 □ based on an incorrect analysis $^{GIŠ}$*šušiyazza kel* in KUB 11.23 vi 5 Jasink-Ticchioni, SCO 27:160, states "il *šušiyaz* era un simbolo della dignità regale"; for correction see Hoffner, apud Košak, FsGüterbock² 132; [...] ŠÀ.BA 9 $^{GIŠ}$GAG *ŠA* $^{GIŠ}$MA.NU 9 $^{GIŠ}$[GAG *ŠA* ...] § *nu araḫzanda tarmāizzi* [...] *ŠA* $^{GIŠ}$MAR.GÍD.DA $^{GIŠ}$*šu-ši-az*!(tablet has *uk*)-*k*[*e-el*? ...] *šer arḫa=ma=kan* MUN-*an* [*waḫnuzi*(?)] *n=ašta anda kiššan me*[*mai* ...] *idālušš=a šagaiš* GAM-*an* [...] § *šu-ši*!(tablet has *wa*)-*ia-az-ki-la-an-za=ma=ššan* [GIM-*an*] $^{GIŠ}$MAR.GÍD.DA.MEŠ *pedi* [*ēpzi*(?)] § *idālu=ya=kan uddār id*[*āl-*...*=ya*?] *pēdi QĀTAMMA appāru n*[*=at* ...] EGIR-*pa idālauwanni* x[...] "[...], among which are nine pegs of cornel wood (and) nine [pegs of ...]. § He nails (them) down all around [...] the wagon's *š.* [...]. He [ ...-s] salt over (it), while spe[aking] as follows: ['Just as ...], [... likewise] also the evil sign [...] beneath [...] § [Just as] the *š.* [holds(?)] a wagon(s) in place, § may likewise also the evil words [and] the evi[l ...] perish(?) in place, and [may ... ] back to evil" KBo 17.90 ii 6-16 (rit. frag., NS), ed. Groddek, IJDL 3:112, 116, Fuscagni, hethiter.net CTH 458.29.1 (INTR 2013-10-23) □ Otten, KBo 17 p. VI (Inhaltsübersicht) reads $^{GIŠ}$*ŠU-ŠI-UK-K*[*I*] and refers to $^{GIŠ}$*ŠA-AŠ-ŠU-KU* in the field cadasters from Boğazköy. For $^{giš}$mes-gam = *šaššugu*/*šuššuku*, see Salonen, Die Landfahrzeuge des alten Mesopotamien (AASF B 72, 3) 143f.: "fliessender Zürgelbaum," d.h. "Bitterkornbaum, Eberesche(?)." If our emendation here is correct, the resulting ergative would support the neut. gender of *š.*; for the sg. 3 imp. med.-pass. *appāru*, see Neu, StBoT 5:24 n. 10, HW² A 163 ("soll umkommen, vernichtet sein"), and Groddek, IJDL 3:115; a similar listing of GIŠGAG.ḪI.A with *š.* among them KBo 41.3:1-11 (rit. frag., MS), translit. Groddek, IJDL 3:120; uncertain because partly restored in a list of objects: KBo 34.25:3 (myth frag., NS), translit. Groddek, IJDL 3:120f. □ the sign in line 3 read as *-a]z-* could also be *-u]k-*, but no word ending in *-ukkil* fits the context here. The restoration [GIŠ*šu-ši-a*]*z-ki-il*, therefore, is provisional.

*š.* is part of a wagon's (GIŠMAR.GÍD.DA) wheel according to both KBo 17.90 ii 8 and KUB 11.23 vi 4-11 (w. dupls.). With Groddek, IJDL 3:111-123, *š.* might well be the "linchpin," i.e., a "toggle pin passing through the axle end to prevent the wheel from slipping off the axle" (thus Littauer/Crouwel, Wheeled Vehicles 6). Since the determinative GIŠ indicates that *š.* is made of wood, the iron character of this object emphasized in the recitation KUB 11.23 vi 4 might be interpreted rather in a figurative sense like "firm, lasting etc."

The structure and ending of *š.* (cf. Kronasser, EHS 1:324), as well as the recitation including the king's title Labarna KUB 11.23 vi 1-12 suggest foreign (Hattian?) origin (see Tischler, HEG S/2:1213).

Kronasser, EHS 1 (1966) 324 ("vielleicht ein Fahrzeug; ein Schiff?"); Ertem, Flora (1974) 165; Tischler, HDW (1982) 79 ("ein hölzernes Fahrzeug, Art Schiff?"); Hoffner apud Košak, FsGüterbock² (1986) 132; Rieken, StBoT 44 (1999) 494 ("hölzerner Teil des Wagens"); Klinger, MemCarter (2000) 165f.; Melchert, Anat&Indog. (2001) 268 ("part of a wagon," possibly loanword); Groddek, IJDL 3 (2006) 111-123 ("Achsnagel, Vorstecker"); Tischler, HEG S/2 (2006) 1213 ("ein Teil des Wagens, vielleicht 'Achsnagel'" ... "fremdsprachigen Charakter"); van den Hout, RlA 14 (2016) 622 s.v. Wagen B.

[*šušiš*] in NINDA(-)*šu-ši-iš* e.g., KBo 16.81 i 9, KUB 51.1 i 6, KBo 25.140:7, thus read by Haas, KN 308, and Tischler, HDW 79, but corrected as Akk. *ŠU-ŠI-IŠ* "sixty times" in Tischler, HEG S/2:1212. A full Akk. reading is not necessary and *ŠU-ŠI-iš* w. Hitt. phon. compl. *-iš* can be read w. Neu, IF 89:302, Eichner, Numerals (1992) 89, and Hagenbuchner-Dresel, DBH 1:69; for such *i*-stem multiplicatives, see GrHL 168f. §§9.54-58.

**šutai-** v.; to seal, plug up(?); MH/NS.†

**pres. sg. 3** *šu-ta-a-i-iz-zi* KBo 5.2 i 61 (MH/NS).

**pl. 3** *šu-ú-da-an-zi* KBo 19.130 i 10 (MH?/NS), *šu-ta-an-z[i]* KBo 31.164:4 (NS).

("[The AZU-priest] takes up from the river [two times] seven pebbles. He throws seven pebbles into [one ju]g of water, and seven pebbles [he throws] into another jug of water") [...GIŠŠIN]IG?*=ya=kan ANA* 1 DUG *MÊ*[*...anda pe*]*ššiyazzi nu* GIŠŠINIG [...]x 2 DUG A *šer šu-ta-a-i-iz-zi* "He also [th]rows [tama]risk(?) into one jug of water [...] and the tamarisk [...and(?)] he plugs up(?) the two jugs of water" KBo 5.2 i 59-61 (Ammiḫatna's rit., MH/NS), ed. Strauß, Reinigung 223, 236 ("füllt er (bis) oben (voll)?"), Polvani, Minerali 89f. (no tr.), Kloekhorst, EDHIL 793f., Witzel, HKU 102f. ("sprengt er"), *šer* 1 c 5′ d′; [...LÚ.MEŠN]AR*=ya* [...(-)*a*]*nda šu-ta-an-zi* [...-*z*]*i* [...-*a*]*z* GIŠ*nataḫḫit*[*a*] [...] LÚ.MEŠSANGA [...] "And [the si]ngers [...] they *š.* [...] they [...] beds [...] priests [...]" KBo 31.164:3-7 (rit., NS); (They fill a silver vessel with something and throw(?) seven pebbles in the silver vessel and in a *taḫašši*-vessel) [*n=aš/t=k*]*an welkuit šu-ú-da-an-z*[*i*] "They seal(?) [them, i.e., the vessels] with grass" KBo 19.130 i 10 (MH?/NS), ed. Eothen 7:120f. ("ils rempliss[nt] (sic) jusqu'au bord"), translit. ChS 3/2:103 i 19.

Most authors follow Oettinger, Stammbildung 377, who tentatively suggests a relation with *šūu*, *šū-* B "full" and translates "vollfüllen(?)." However, the spelling with ⟨ú⟩ precludes Oettinger's connection with *šūu*, which is always spelled with ⟨u⟩ in the first syllable. Also, in the two better preserved contexts where *š.* is attested, the containers have already been filled previously (cf. KBo 5.2 i 55, KBo 19.130 i 6), using the verb *šunna-*. Based upon a similar description where the verb *šaḫ-* "to plug up, stop up, stuff" takes the place of *šutai-* (DUG*KUKUB* KÙ.BABBAR *dāi n=at*[*=kan*] *wetenit šunnai arunaš=a=kan* [...] 7 NA₄*paššiluš anda pešši*[*ya*]*zi namma=kan* Ì.DÙG.GA *tepu anda za*[*ppanuzzi*] *šerr=a=ššan* GIŠ*pain*[*i*] *šāḫi* "(S)he takes a silver pitcher and fills it with water. Into it (s)he throws [...] seven pebbles of the sea. Then (s)he dri[ps] in a little fine oil and on top (s)he stuffs tamarisk (leaves/branches)" KBo 17.103 obv. 13-15 (+) KUB 46.48 obv. 17-19 (cf. also KBo 17.103 obv.

25-26), cf. *šaḫ-* A b 1′; a mng. "to cover" or "to plug up" therefore seems more likely.

Oettinger, Stammbildung (1979) 34, 377 ("voll machen(?), vollfüllen(?)"); Tischler, HDW (1982) 79 ("vollfüllen(?)"); idem., HEG S/2 (2006) 1213f. ("anfüllen, vollfüllen?"); Kloekhorst, EDHIL (2008) 793f. (rejecting the connection with *šūu*).

**šutari-** n. com.; (a part of a lyre); NH.†

**sg. nom.** *šu-u-ta-ri-iš* KUB 42.11 ii 11 (NH).

**acc.** *šu-u-ta-ri-in* KBo 23.42 rev. 25 (NH), KBo 24.79:12 (NH), KUB 47.37:7 (NH).

**a.** part of a lyre: [(*nu* LÚAZU Ì.DÙG.GA *pēda*)]⌈*i*⌉ *nu ŠA* GIŠ dINANNA *šu-u-ta-ri-in pe*[(*r*)*an*] / [(*šiēz tepu iš*⌈*ki*⌉*zzi ḫur*)]*lili=ma kiššan* [(*memai*)] "The AZU-priest brings the fine oil and smears the *š.* of the lyre a little bit in front on one side while speaking in Hurrian as follows" KUB 47.37 + KBo 35.121:7-8 (rit. w. Hurr., NH), w. dupls. KBo 23.42 rev. 24-26 + KBo 38.280 left col. 7-8 (NH), KBo 24.57 iv 5-6 + KBo 27.175:9-10 (NH), ed. ChS 1/2:142f., 186, Schuol, Kultmusik 101, Goedegebuure, FsdeRoos 180f. ☐ contra GLH 239, *š.* in KUB 47.37:7 does not necessarily represent a Hurrian form. Cf. also the further context mentioning a musician/singer: [...](-)x-*aššan ANA* LÚNAR dx[...] / [...]x *šu-u-ta-ri-in peran* [...] KBo 24.79:11-12 (libation to the throne of Ḫebat, MS).

**b.** mentioned among objects from Egypt: 2 GIŠPISAN KUR ⌈*M*⌉*izr*[*i* ... ] ŠÀ=*ŠU* 28 NA₄ZA.GÌ[N ...] 1 SAG.DU *kinuḫi*[*š*? ...] 1 *šu-u-ta-ri-iš* x[...] 16 AŠ.ME ZA.GÌN ŠÀ 1 T[UR?...] 1 *ME* 78 *UN*⌈*QA*⌉ NA₄G[UG *Mizrī*(?)...] *anda išḫūwān*(-)[...] *anda išḫūwān*(-)[...] *kī=kan UNŪTUM ki*[-...] *ANA* 2 GIŠPISAN *Mizri*[...] "Two Egyptia[n] chests, [...] therein twenty-eight lapis lazu[li stones, ...] one head/pommel of a *kinuḫi*-(dagger?), [...] one *š.*, [...] sixteen blue sun-discs, of which one (is) s[mall(?),...] 178 (seal-)rings of [...] car[nelian, ...] filled in, [...] filled in, [...] this gear [...] into two Egyptian chests [...]" KUB 42.11 ii 8-17 (inventory of chests, NH), ed. Cornil/Lebrun, OLP 6/7:101f., 104, Košak, THeth 10:32f., 35, Siegelová, Verw. 400f.

Košak, THeth 10 (1982) 38, 238 ("defines a musical instrument"); Siegelová, Verw. (1986) 619 ("Teil eines Musikinstrumentes?"), Schuol, Kultmusik (2004) 101; Tischler, HEG S/2 (2006) 1214.

**šuturi(ya)-** n. neut.; (a fabric or web of wool); NH.†

**pl. nom.-acc.** *šu-tu-ri-ia* KUB 29.4 i 34 (NS), 36, KUB 29.5 i 18, (20) (NS).

SÍG.SA₅ SÍG.ZA.GÌN SÍG *ḫanzanaš* SÍG.SIG₇.SIG₇ SÍG.BABBAR *danzi n=at* 2 *TAPAL āzzallaya iyanzi nu namma* SÍG.ZA.GÌN SÍG.SA₅ SÍG *ḫanzanaš* SÍG.SIG₇.SIG₇ SÍG.BABBAR=*ya danzi n=at šu-tu-ri-ia iyanzi* 2 GAG ZABAR *n=aš=kan ŠA* É.DINGIR-⌈*LIM*⌉ Éḫ*īlaš* KÁ-*aš anda* (var. Ø) 1-*EN kēz* 1-*EN=ma kēz walaḫḫanzi* (var. *walḫanzi*) *n=ašta šu-tu-ri-ia katta gankan* "They take red wool, blue wool, black wool, yellow wool, (and) white wool, and make them into two *āzzallaya*. Then they take blue wool, red wool, black wool, yellow wool, and white wool, and make them into two *š.* There are two pegs of bronze. They nail them into the courtyard door of the temple, one on this side and one on the other side. The *š.* are hung down (from them)" KUB 29.4 i 31-36 (dividing the Night Goddess, NH), w. dupl. KUB 29.5 i 15-20, ed. StBoT 46:276, Schw.Gotth. 8-11, tr. Collins, CoS 1:173f.

Both *š.* and *āzzallaya* are made (woven?) of colored wools. The passage above does not give sufficient information about their intended use. Unlike *āzzallaya,* the *š.* are hung down (or stretched?) between two pegs on the courtyard door of the temple. On the phonetic level, both words are reminiscent of akkadian *azamillu*/*aza'illu* ("sack, with netlike reinforcement," CAD A/2:525) and *šuturu* (a fine garment, CAD Š/3:415).

Kronasser, Schw.Gotth. (1963) 34, 43 ("ein Gewebe, Schleier oder Netz"); idem, EHS 1 (1966) 169; Friedrich, HW 3.Erg. (1966) 30 ("ein Gewebe"); Miller, StBoT 46 (2004) 335 ("(a type of fabric)"); Tischler, HEG S/2 (2006) 1215 ("ein vielfarbiges Gewebe, Schleier, Netz, o.ä").

**šūu-, šū- A**, adj.; full; from OS.†

**sg. nom. com.** *šu-u-uš* KBo 20.8 rev.? 4, 6 (OS), KBo 10.23 iv y+5 (OH/NS), KBo 41.108 obv. 4 (MS), KBo 46.80:4 (MS), KUB 9.28 i 13, iii 23 (MH/NS), KUB 7.1 i 41 (pre-NH/NS), KBo 18.180 rev. (8)? (NH).

**acc.** *šu-u-ú-un* KBo 25.72 ii 20 (OS?), *šu-u-un* KBo 21.72 i 13 (OH/NS), KBo 31.214:8, (9) (OH/NS), KUB 58.27 vi 10

(OH/NS). Erroneous citation of *šu-u-un* KUB 1.16 ii 58 (OH/NS) for *ku-u-un* in EDHIL 794.

**nom.-acc. neut.** *šu-u-ú* KBo 47.80 obv. 8 (OH/NS), KBo 19.132 rev.? 14 (MH/NS), KUB 11.19 iv 22 (NS), perhaps here *šu-ú* KBo 49.87:4, *šu-u* KBo 12.14 rev. 4 (OH/NS), KUB 39.46:8 (OH/NS), KBo 11.12 i 5 (MH/MS), IBoT 2.123 obv. 5 (MH/NS), KBo 6.34 iii 12 (MH/NS), KBo 55.41:5 (MH/NS), KUB 39.57 i 7 (NH), KUB 41.11 obv. 6 (NS).

**gen.(?)** *šu-u-aš* KBo 10.27 iv 33 (NS) (occurrence is doubtful, cf. Weitenberg, U-Stämme, 140). Perhaps read KÙ.⌈BABBAR⌉-*aš*.

**abl.(?)** *šu-u-az* KBo 20.97 iv? 17 (MS), *šu-u-wa-u-az* KBo 38.78:5 (MS) (both occurrences are doubtful, cf. Weitenberg, U-Stämme, 140).

**pl. nom. com.** *šu-wa-u-e-eš* KBo 38.73 rev. 3 (NS?).

**acc.** *šu-u-wa-mu-uš* KBo 17.1 i 26 (OS), KBo 17.3 i 21 (OS), KBo 17.6 ii 2 (OS).

**a.** full, w. filling substance in inst. (from OS) or occasionally abl. (MH/NS, NH) (StBoT 22:39 n. 77) — **1′** w. water —**a′** (hollow) statuettes: (A warning to the oathbreaker which is illustrated with a graphic analogy of what would happen to him:) *n[u*=*šm]aš*=*kan* ALA[M LÚ Š]À=*ŠU uidan‹da› šu-u* [*INA Q*]*ĀTI*=*ŠUNU d*⌈*ā*⌉[*i n*]*u kišan tezzi* [*k*]⌈*ā*⌉*š*=*wa kuiš U*[*L*=*ma*(?) *l*]*inkiškit* [*nu*] DINGIR.MEŠ-*aš pera*[*n link*]*atta* [*n*]*amma*=*kan NĪŠ* DINGIR-*L*[*IM šarr*]*adda n*=*an linkianteš ēpper n*=*aš*=*ša*[*n*] ŠÀ=*ŠU šuttati nu*=*za šarḫuwandan QĀTI*=*ŠU peran* UGU-*a karpan ḫarzi* "He place[s a male] figur[e] —its [in]side full ‹of› water— [in] their [h]ands [a]nd he says thus: "Who is [t]his? Did he n[ot s]wear? He [sw]ore befo[re] the gods, [t]hen he [transg]ressed the oat[h]. The oaths seized him, and with respect to his inside he is swollen up (with water). His hand has lifted (his) belly up in front" KBo 6.34 iii 12-19 (soldiers' oath, MH/NS), ed. StBoT 22:12f., García Trabazo, TextosRel. 534f., tr. Beal, Ancient Magic and Ritual Power 64 □ the figure whose inside is full of water demonstrates a person suffering from dropsy, see Oettinger, StBoT 22:71-73. For archaeological evidence for such statuettes see Börker-Klähn, FsAlp 70, 72; [GUD].MAḪ.GE$_6$ 1 *šēnaš* SAG.DU=*kan* $^{UZU}$GABA $^{UZU}$UBUR *ginuwa* ZI-*TUM* [A-*a*]*z šu-u ANA* GIDIM IGI-*anda* DIB-*anzi* "(There are) a black [bu]ll (and) one statuette. They hold the head, chest, breasts, knees (and) soul, full o[f water], against the (image of the) deceased" KUB 39.57 i 6-7 (rit., NH), ed. Lorenz/Rieken, HS 124:86, HEG S/2: 1042, differently Kapełuś, BiOr 67:267 (reading [...]x ŠU.U).

**b′** containers: 1 $^{DUG}$⌈*NAMMANDU waḫ*⌉*ešnaš uitenit šu-u-uš* "a measuring vessel full of *waḫeššar*-water" KUB 7.1 i 41 (Ayatarša's rit., pre-NH/NS); $^{[GI]Š}$*GANNU šerr*=*a*=*ššan* $^{DUG}$GUR$_4$.GUR$_4$-*aš uedanda šu-u-uš* "There is a stand. On it there is a jug full of water" KUB 9.28 i 12-13 (rit. for the Heptad, MH/NS).

**c′** frag.: [...*ued*]*anda šu-u dāi* "[...] takes [...] full of [wat]er" KUB 41.11 obv. 6 (rit. frag., NS); [...] *uidanta šu-u-u*[*n*...] KBo 31.214:9 (fest. frag., OH/NS).

**2′** w. *tarlipa*-liquid: *anda*=⌈*kan*⌉ *ḫalīnaš teššummiuš tarl*⌈*ipi*⌉*t šu-u-wa-mu-uš* 2-*TAM p*⌈*ēt*⌉*umini* "Twice we carry inside the cups of clay full of *tarlipa*-liquid" KBo 17.1 i 26-27 (rit. for royal couple, OS), w. dupl. KBo 17.3 i 21 (OS), ed. StBoT 8:20f., Montuori (ed.), hethiter.net/: CTH 416 (TX 03.03.2015, TRit 24.07.2015), translit. StBoT 25:6; [*ḫalī*]⌈*n*⌉*aš* [(*teššummiuš* 4-*uš tarli*)*p*]⌈*it šu-u-wa-mu*⌉-*uš iyami* "I prepare four cups of [...] full of *tarli*[*p*]*a*-liquid" KBo 17.6 ii 1-2 (rit. for royal couple, OS), w. dupls. KBo 17.1 ii 8, KBo 17.4 ii 16 (both OS), ed. Montuori (ed.), hethiter.net/: CTH 416 (TX 03.03.2015, TRit 24.07.2015), translit. StBoT 25:19.

**3′** w. other beverages (wine, wine-beer, *marnuwan*-beer): $^{LÚ}$SANGA $^{d}$LAMMA=*ma tapišanan* KÙ.BABBAR *ḫarz*[*i*] *n*=*aš* GEŠTIN-*it šu-u-uš* "The priest of the Protective Deity hold[s] a silver bowl. It is full of wine" KBo 10.23 iv y+3-5 (KI.LAM fest., OH/NS), translit. StBoT 28:13, tr. Klinger, TUAT NF 4:195; [...K]Ù.GI GEŠTIN-*it šu*⌈*-u-un*⌉ [...] "a golden [...] (acc.) full of wine" KBo 31.214:8 (fest. frag., OH/NS); KÙ.BABBAR-*aš palḫi‹n›* KAŠ.GEŠTIN-*it šu-u-un akuwanzi* "They drink a silver *palḫi*-vessel full of wine-beer" KUB 58.27 vi 10-11 (cult. rit. in Ziplanta, OH/NS), ed. THeth 21:122f. ("Der silberne Kessel (ist) voll Wein, (und) sie trinken"), tr. DBH 18:70; [...]⌈x x⌉ *marnuantet šu-u-un* "[a...] (acc.) full of *marnuwan*-beer" KBo 21.72 i 13 (fest. frag., OH/NS).

**4′** w. coarsely ground meal: $^{\text{[DUG]}}$⌜GAL⌝ (?) *memalit* ⌜*šu*⌝*-u-ú* "[a] cup(?) full of coarsely ground meal" KUB 11.19 iv 22 (fest. frag., NS).

**5′** w. *šemeḫuna-* (a crushed grain): [...] *šemeḫunit šu-u-uš* "[...] is full of *šemeḫuna-*" KBo 20.8 rev.? 6 (fest., OS), translit. StBoT 25:70.

**6′** w. clay tongue models: 1 *kurt*[(*ali* IM)] / [(*n*=*at IŠTU*)] EME.ḪI.A IM *šu-u* "One *kurtali*-container of clay. It (is) full of tongues of clay" IBoT 2.123 obv. 4-5 (Alli's rit., MH/NS), w. dupls. KBo 11.12 i 5 (MS), KBo 12.126 i 4 (var. A), KBo 55.41:5, KUB 41.2 i 1 (var. G), ed. THeth 2:20f., Mouton, hethiter.net/: CTH 402 (TX 10.11.2014, TRfr 27.02.2013).

**7′** frag.: 2 LÚ.MEŠ *ZITT*[*I*] *uenzi* 1 LÚ *ZITTI RIQAM* DUG-*in ḫarz*[*i*] *ta*=*šše*=*šta* $^{\text{LÚ}}$ZABAR.DAB *ēpzi āppa*=*ma*=*šše* 1 DUG KAŠ.GEŠTIN *šā*[-...-*it*] *šu-u-ú-un pāi* "Two participants enter. One participant holds an empty vessel, and the cellar master takes (it) away from him. He gives back to him one vessel (for) wine-beer filled [with] *šā*[-...]" KBo 25.72 + KBo 25.34 ii 18-20 (KI.LAM fest., OS?), ed. Groddek, KI.LAM 18f.; [...-]*it šu-wa-u-e-eš* KBo 38.73 rev. 3 (NS?).

**b.** the material which fills a container or location is in the nom. (or acc.?): 1 *kurtali* IM EME. ḪI.A IM *šu-u* "One *kurtali*-container of clay, full (of) tongues of clay" KBo 11.12 i 5 (Alli's rit., MH/MS), cf. a 6′ above for variants with the inst.; 2 $^{\text{DUG}}$*KUKUB* ŠÀ.BA *INA* 1 $^{\text{DUG}}$GUR$_4$.GUR$_4$-*BI* (var. [*IN*]*A* 1 $^{\text{DUG}}$*KUKUBI*) *akuwannaš paršuil šu-u-uš* 1 GI [(*š*)]*uḫmiliš tarnanza* "Two pitchers: among these, in one pitcher for drinking, full (of) *paršuil*, a rigid drinking straw is inserted" KUB 9.28 iii 22-24 (rit. for Heptad, MH/NS), w. dupl. KBo 19.132 rev.? 10-11 (MH/NS), ed. Catsanicos, BSL 81/1:153 (differs: "dans l'un d'eux (se trouve) de la bière à boire (et) de *paršuil*; (il en est) plein"), HED P 161, Soysal, FsNeumann$^2$ 467 (differs: "In einer davon, einer Bierkanne voll (mit) *paršuil* zum Trinken, ist ein steifes/hartes Rohr (ein)gelassen"), StBoT 54:242 ("two pitchers. In a pitcher among them there is a full *paršuil*. One *rigid* reed (has been) inserted"), HEG S/2:1125 ("Zwei Kannen. In einer Kanne der beiden (befindet sich) Bier zum trinken (und) *parsuil*. (Sie ist) voll"), EDHIL 775 ("Two pitchers: in one pitcher of beer for drinking, a *šuḫmili-* drinking straw full of *paršuil* is inserted"), s.v. *paršuil* ("in one pitcher of beer for drinking, a rigid(?) drinking straw full (of?) *p.* (or: 'a full *p.*'(?)) is inserted") ☐ for the reading $^{\text{DUG}}$GUR$_4$.GUR$_4$-*BI* instead of $^{\text{DUG}}$ḪAB.ḪAB KAŠ, see Weeden, StBoT 54:242; the syntax is unclear. *š.* normally agrees with the head noun, which in this case should be GI "drinking straw;" however, *š.* always follows its head noun, which should then point to $^{\text{DUG}}$GUR$_4$.GUR$_4$-*BI* "pitcher;" in view of KBo 19.132 rev.? 14 (see next) it seems that the latter option is preferable despite the lack of agreement in case between the head and *š.*; [ ... (x x *akuwa*)]*nnaš šīēššar šu-u-*⌜*ú*⌝ *šipanti* "(The exorcist) libates a [jar/vessel(?)] for drinking, full (of) beer" KBo 19.132 rev.? 14 (rit. for the Heptad, MH/NS), w. dupl. KUB 9.28 iii 27-28; cf. also [ ... -*y*]*a* Ì.DÙG. GA *šu-u ḫarz*[*i*] "hold[s] a [...] full (of) fine oil" KUB 39.46:8 (funerary rit. frag., NS).

**c.** without filling substance: *šemēnaš* (or *šemē*⟨*ḫu*⟩*naš*) *ḫūpparaš šu-u-uš* [...] *n*=*aš*=*šan* $^{\text{GIŠ}}$*pūriyaš* BABBAR *k*[*itta*] "A full *ḫuppara*-vessel for *šemē*⟨*ḫu*⟩*na-* [...] It is p[laced] on a white tray(?)" KBo 20.8 rev.? 4-5 (fest., OS), translit. StBoT 25:70, cf. *šemēna-*; perhaps here [...]x-*an šu-u* LUGAL-*uš* $^{\text{URU}}$*Ḫalpa* [...] "[...]... (is) full. The king of Ḫalpa [...]" KBo 12.14 rev. 4 (hist., OH/NS), ed. Soysal, Diss. 75, 108, StMed 12:124f. (*š.* is the conjunction *š*(*u*)- (q.v.). cf. Carruba, Part. 57 n. 41).

*š.* is synonymous with *šuwant-*, part. of *šū-* B, *šūwa-*, s.v., and *šunnant-*, part. of *šun*(*n*)*a-*, s.v. It is mainly attested in OH and MH, giving way to *šuwant-* in MH and NH.

Note that sometimes the signs *šu-u* are to be read ŠU.U "diorite" instead of *šu-u*: [...(-)*l*]*ašš*[*i*]*š* $^{\text{NA}_4}$NÍR ŠU.U KBo 18.176 i 9 (inv., NH), ed. Siegelová, Verw., 46f., differently Polvani, Eothen 3:149 (reads *šu-u*), translit. THeth 10:61f. (reads *šu-u*); [...-*A*]*K-TÙ*(?) ŠU.U 1 $^{\text{GIŠ}}$x[...] / [... *šu*?]-*u-uš* 1 $^{\text{KUŠ}}$A.GÁ.LÁ *ú*-[...] KBo 18.180 rev. 7-8 (inventories, NH), ed. Siegelová, Verw., 88f., translit. THeth 10:62f. (reads ]-*ak-du šu-u*).

Goetze, Lg. 30 (1954) 404 n. 13 (*šuwu-* "full"); Friedrich, HW 1. Erg. (1957) 19 ("voll"); Kronasser, Acta Baltico-Slavica 3 = FsOtrebski (1966) 81; Kümmel, StBoT 3 (1967) 39 w. n. 115; Otten/Souček, StBoT 8 (1969) 100; Berman, Diss. (1972) 188f.; Jakob-Rost, THeth 2 (1972) 59; Weitenberg, Hethitica 1 (1972) 39; Oettinger, StBoT 22 (1976) 39f.; Weitenberg,

U-Stämme (1984) 136-140; Tischler, HEG S/2 (2006) 1125-1128; Kloekhorst, EDHIL (2008) 794 (stem *šūu-*/sóu/, *šūwaw-*/sóau-/).

Cf. *šū-* B, *šunt-*, *šuwant-* (s.v. *šū-* B, *šuwa-*), *šun(n)a-*.

# Addendum

**šekan** n. neut.(?); (a measurement of unknown length); from MH/MS.

**sg. nom.-acc.** *še-e-kán* KBo 18.54 rev. 23, 24 (MH/MS), KUB 12.44 iii 13 (NS), KUB 40.55 + KBo 50.280a i 8, 9, 14, 16 (MH/MS, indirect join w. following), KUB 13.1 iv 21 (MH/MS), KUB 31.87 ii 8 (MH/MS), KBo 26.228 i 7, 10 (NS), KUB 38.32 rev. 19 (NS), *še-kán* KBo 50.80 obv.? (3)?, 13 (MS), KUB 13.2 ii 7 (MH/NS), KUB 31.84 ii 4 (MH/NS), KBo 2.1 i 8, 37, 39 and passim (NS), KUB 7.24 obv. 2 (Tudḫ. IV), KUB 29.4 i 29, KUB 38.23 obv. 8, 9 (NS).

**uncertain** *š[e-* (?) KUB 8.57 i 8 (NS).

**a.** describing statuettes and figurines ("Bildbeschreibungen"): ("Mount Malimaliya: formerly there was no divine statue. His Majesty Tudḫaliya (installed) it:") ALAM LÚ AN.BAR 1 *še-kán* ½ *še-kán-n=a* IGI.ḪI.A KÙ.GI *ANA* UR.MAḪ AN.BAR-*aš=kan artari* "Statuette of a man, iron, one and a half *š.*, golden eyes, he stands on an iron lion" KUB 7.24 obv. 1-3 (cult inv., Tudḫ.IV), ed. Carter, Diss. 116, 119, Hazenbos, Organization 27f.; 1 ALAM MUNUS TUŠ-*aš* KÙ.BABBAR 1 *še-kán* "One statuette (of) a woman, seated, silver, one *š.* (under her two mountain-sheep of iron, under her an iron pedestal ...)" KBo 2.1 iv 4-5 (cult inv., NH), ed. Bildbeschr. 64, Carter, Diss. 58, 68, HLC 202f.; [... *ḫupi*?*t*]*auwanza* 1 *še-kán* 1 *UPNU=y*[*a*...] "[figurine ...] wearing a [vei]l(?), (of) one *š.* an[d] one palm(?) (measure)" KBo 12.56 i 2 (cult inv., NS), ed. Hazenbos, Organization 54f., tr. THeth. 26:359 □ for another ex. of *š.* combined w. *UPNU*, see KBo 50.80 obv. 13 (see below b.); for the restoration, see KUB 38.26 obv. 31; for more attestations from cult inv., see KUB 38.31 obv. 4, 6 (NS) (½ and 3 *š.* resp.), KUB 17.35 ii 36 (NS) (1 *š.*), KUB 38.13 rev.? 8 (NS) (2 *š.*), KUB 38.18 obv. 2, 4 (NS) (2 and 1½ *š.* resp.), KBo 2.16 obv. 11, 13 (NS) (both 2 *š.*), KBo 12.56 i 2, 15 (NS) (1 *š.*), KBo 26.147:10 (NS) ( 1 *š.*), KBo 52.100:4 (NS) (1 *š.*), KBo 64.334 obv. 2 (NS) (1 *š.*).

**b.** various usages: ("And let the lord of the outposts stack fire-wood logs for the fortifications as follows:") *ḫantaz=at=kan* 12 *galulupaš ēštu* GÍD.DA-*ašti=ma=at* 1 *gipeššar* 4 *še-kán-n=a* (var. *še-e-kán=*) *ēštu* "on the cross-cut side they should be twelve fingers, in the length they should be one ell(?) and four *š.*" KUB 13.2 ii 5-7 (*BĒL MADG.*, MH/NS), ed. Dienstanw. 44, w. dupl. KUB 31.87 ii 5-8 (MS); for a further ex. from the Bel Madg. instr., see s.v. [(GIŠ)]*mariyawanna-*; in connection with fields(?): *nu duwan* 1 *gipeššar* 5 *še-e-kán-n=a* [ ... ] "and in one direction one cubit and five *š.*" KUB 13.1 iv 21 (Bel Madg., MH/MS), ed. Pecchioli Daddi, StMed. 14:188f., HittInstr. 234f. □ for *duwan* here as "in one direction," see Melchert, FsHKoch 205 w. n. 12; ("Furthermore, where in the vineyard the Maliyanni-deities are seated") *nu* [d]*Maliyannaš peran tek*[*an*] *paddaḫḫi* 2 *še-e-kán arnum*[*mi*] "before the Maliyanni-deities I will dig up the earth (and) I will remove two *š.* (of earth)" KUB 12.44 iii 10-13 (rit., MS), ed. Haas, FsOtten[2] 138-139 ("zwei Spannen 'schaffe ich fort'"); ("(...) two offering tables(?), two tables, two wooden pot stands") 1-*NŪTIM* [GIŠ]*kišḫita pargašti* 6 *še-kán* "one chair, six š. in height" KUB 29.4 i 28-29 (rit., NS), w. dupl. KUB 29.5 i 13 (NS), ed. Kronasser, Schw.Gotth. 6-7, StBoT 46:275f.; ("But when My Lord speaks as follows: 'Why doesn't it (i.e. the siege) succeed?' (the answer will be:)") *nu=kan* BÀD *kuit ištarna EGĀRU=ma kuiš* 4 (eras.) *še-e-kán kuiš=ma* 3 (eras.) *še-e-kán* "because within the fortification there is a wall of four *š.* and another of 3 *š.*" KBo 18.54 rev. 20-24 (letter, MH/MS), ed. Letters 343, Singer, FsEph'al 259-261, THeth.12:77-78, Pecchioli Daddi, Mesopotamia 13-14:204, 207; a beam or log(?): 1 [GIŠ]ÙR *walli*[š...] 3 *še-kán* 1 *UPNU-wa* ⌈*dā*⌉[-...] KBo 50.80 obv. 12-13 (frag. of letter, MS), tr. DBH 28:70, Jakob-Rost, MIO 9:176 (without the *-wa* after *UPNU*) □ since a quotative particle *-wa* would be out of place here, is the *-wa* a phonetic compl.?

**c.** uncertain: ("The great gods created Gilgameš") ALAM=*ši pa*[*rgašti*] 11 *AMMATUM* GAB=*ma=šši palḫašti* 9 *š*[*e*?-*kán* ] [UZU]*miniuš=ma=šši dalugašti* 3 [...] "His stature was eleven ells in height, his chest in width nine *š.*(?), his face in length three [...]" KUB 8.57 i 6-9 (myth), ed. *palḫašti-* b, Rieken et al., hethiter.net/: CTH 341.III.1 (TX 2009-08-27, TRde 2009-08-27) (reading *w*[*akšur*?]), tr. Beckman apud Foster, Gilg. 158 ("[spans]") □ Otten, IM 8:98, restored *w*[*a-ak-šur*], which, however, is never attested as a measure of length, only of time and capacity. Therefore, the above restoration seems preferable. Rieken et al. and HW² Ḫ, 323 read *ḫarniuš* "?" instead of *miniuš*; (While waving a billy-goat over a ritual patient, the man of the Stormgod narrates a Kataḫzipuri myth: "Kataḫzipuri always purifies the hearth, she always purifies her land, she always purifies her oxen (and) sheep. She took the evil uncleanness from the king's head and it went to the [py]re") *uktūriyaš[*=*šan* ...(-*aš*?)] *pankuš ḫandāit* (par. *kit*[*tat*]) *n*=*aš*=*š*[*a*(*n*) (par. *t*=*aš*=*šan*) ...-*e*(*kta*)] *še-e-kán laḫuttat* GUD-*u*[(*n* UDU-*un* LÚ).U$_{19}$.L(U.DUMU-*an*)] *taruppiyaḫḫaš ut*!*ni*=*y*[*a* EGIR-*p*(*a taruppiaḫḫiš*)] "The entire [...] lined up/arranged(?) [at] the pyre. It/she was.... A *š*. (of it)(?) was poured out. She brought together ox, sheep, man, and she brought together the land again" KBo 13.106 i 13-16 (Ḫutuši's rit., OH/NS), w. dupl. KUB 28.82 + IBoT 3.98 i 13-16, par. KUB 41.7 i? 12-15, cf. Corti, HethLit 54, 56 □ alternatively, *š*. is the conj. *š*(*u*)-, s.v., followed by nom.-acc. pl. neut -*e*- and the particle =*kan* "they (i.e., the impurities) were poured out," resuming sing. ḪUL-*lu papreššan* "evil uncleanness" (KUB 28.82 i 12).

*š*. was part of a system of length measures with *UPNU* and *gipeššar* as its nearest lower and upper units respectively. The lowest number for *š*. is ½, the highest is 6 (KUB 29.4 i 28-29, above b). As a subdivision of a *gipeššar* "cubit" of ca. 48-50 cm (see Müller-Karpe, StBoT 58:148f., Schachner, StBoT 58:193 w. n. 25) with a highest number of 5 (see KUB 13.1 iv 21, above b) in combination w. *gipeššar*, *š*. cannot have been larger than 8-8.5 cm (differently Cammarosano, HLC 59). Moreover, the fact that most figurines of men and women described in the cult inv. measure 1 *š*. and by far the majority of preserved figurines from Anatolia in the Late Bronze Age (see Ekiz, Statuettes 9) measure between 5 and 8 cm points in the same direction. Such a length does, however, create problems vis-à-vis *UPNU*, which is usually taken as "palm, fist" of ca. 7-8 cm; for other problems and the earlier identification of *š*. w. a span (= ½ *gipeššar*, about 22 cm). see van den Hout, RlA 7:518f. Since the largest amount of *UPNU* as a subdivision of *š*. is 1, the difference between the two may not have been large, however.

The equation of *š*. with Akk. *UṬU* "half-cubit" (so HEG S 978, with ref.), describing the height of statuettes in four texts: *ŠA* 1 *UṬU* KUB 38.14 obv. 2; 3 and 1 *UṬI*, resp. KUB 38.29 obv. 5, rev. 8; 1 *UṬU* IBoT 2.102 rev. 9; 4 *UṬ*[*I*] KBo 26.218:2, must remain speculative.

van den Hout, RlA 7 (1990) s.v. Masse und Gewichte 518-520, w. lit.; Tischler, HEG S (2006) 978f.; de Roos, Anatolica 34 (2008) 1 n. 2 ("1 *šekan* is probably ca. 50 cm"); Cammarosano, HLC (2018) 59 ("*šekan* plausibly measures around 15/25 cm").

THE HITTITE DICTIONARY OF THE ORIENTAL INSTITUTE
OF THE UNIVERSITY OF CHICAGO

VOLUMES IN PRINT AND AVAILABLE ONLINE

The Oriental Institute
1155 East 58th Street
Chicago, Illinois 60637-1569

Telephone: (773) 702-9508
Email: oi-publications@uchicago.edu
Website: oi.uchicago.edu
Catalog of Publications: oi.uchicago.edu/research/catalog-publications

**Chicago Hittite Dictionary (CHD)**

| | |
|---|---|
| Volume L–N, fascicle 1 | *la-* to *ma-*. Edited by Hans G. Güterbock and Harry A. Hoffner. 1980. Pp. xxxii + 96 (1–96) |
| Volume L–N, fascicle 2 | *-ma* to *miyahuwant-*. Edited by Hans G. Güterbock and Harry A. Hoffner. 1983. Pp. 128 (97–224) |
| Volume L–N, fascicle 3 | *miyahuwant-* to *nai-*. Edited by Hans G. Güterbock and Harry A. Hoffner. 1986. Pp. 128 (225–352) |
| Volume L–N, fascicle 4 | *nai-* to *nutarnu-*. Edited by Hans G. Güterbock and Harry A. Hoffner. 1989. Pp. xxx + 124 (353–477) |
| Volume L–N, fascicles 1–4 | *la-* to *nutarnu-*. Edited by Hans G. Güterbock and Harry A. Hoffner. 1980–1989. Pp. xxx + 477 (1–477) (Hardcover) |
| Volume P, fascicle 1 | *pa-* to *para*. Edited by Hans G. Güterbock and Harry A. Hoffner. 1994. Pp. xi + 112 (1–112) |
| Volume P, fascicle 2 | *para-* to [(UZU)]*pattar* A. Edited by Hans G. Güterbock and Harry A. Hoffner. 1995. Pp. 128 (113–240) |
| Volume P, fascicle 3 | [(UZU)]*pattar* A. to *putkiya-*. Edited by Hans G. Güterbock and Harry A. Hoffner. 1997. Pp. xxxii + 163 (241–403) |
| Volume P, fascicles 1–3 | *pa-* to *putkiya-*. Edited by Hans G. Güterbock and Harry A. Hoffner. 1994–1997. Pp. xxxii + 403 (1–403) (Hardcover) |
| Volume S, fascicle 1 | *šā-* to *šaptamenzu*. Edited by Hans G. Güterbock, Harry A. Hoffner, and Theo P. J. van den Hout. 2002. Pp. viii + 208 (1–208) |
| Volume S, fascicle 2 | *šaptamenzu* to *-ši*. Edited by Hans G. Güterbock, Harry A. Hoffner, and Theo P. J. van den Hout. 2005. Pp. 124 (209–332) |
| Volume S, fascicle 3 | *še-* to [LÚ]*šizišalla-*. Edited by Hans G. Güterbock, Harry A. Hoffner, and Theo P. J. van den Hout. 2013. Pp. 176 (333–508) |
| Volume S, fascicle 4 | *-šma/i-* A. to *šūu-*. Edited by Hans G. Güterbock, Harry A. Hoffner, Theo P. J. van den Hout, and Petra M. Goedegebuure. Pp. 661 (508–661) |
| Volume S, fascicles 1–4 | *šā-* to *šūu-*. Edited by Hans G. Güterbock, Harry A. Hoffner, Theo P. J. van den Hout, and Petra M. Goedegebuure. Pp. xliii + 661 (Hardcover) |

**Chicago Hittite Dictionary Supplements (CHDS)**

CHDS 1. Ankara Arkeoloji Müzesinde bulanan Bogazköy Tabletleri II - Bogazköy Tablets in the Archaeological Museum of Ankara II. 2011. Rukiye Akdogan and Oğuz Soysal. Pp. xii + 50; 64 plates

CHDS 2. Unpublished Bo-Fragments in Transliteration I (Bo 9536–Bo 9736). 2015. Oğuz Soysal. Pp. xvi + 224; 234 illustrations

CHDS 3. Unpublished Bo-Fragments in Transliteration II (Bo 6151–Bo 9535). 2019. Oğuz Soysal and Başak Yıldız Gülşen. Pp. xvi + 306; 316 illustrations